Praise for *Boone*

"[A] comprehensive and deeply sympathetic biography. . . . Ideally suited to today's reader with its vivid descriptive passages . . . , its persuasive portrait of Boone and its firm sense of his place in American history."
—*The Washington Post Book World*

"[A] long, passionate, and authoritative biography."
—*Entertainment Weekly*

"Stunning, and perhaps determinative in settling the frontiersman's reputation."
—*The Dallas Morning News*

"Highly readable. . . . [Morgan] brings fresh context and depth to this portrait."
—*The Christian Science Monitor*

"[A] revelatory biography. . . . [Morgan] crafts images that carry the reader into that world which Boone saw. . . . What Morgan has done with his *Boone,* is to make the man important as an entry point for today's readers into what has become legend."
—*The Boston Globe*

"Intriguing. . . . Morgan effectively demonstrates the way Boone's life exemplified different ideals later taken up by Romantic writers and artists in America and Europe, from Ralph Waldo Emerson, Henry David Thoreau and Walt Whitman to Lord Byron and the Hudson River School painters."
—*Chicago Tribune*

"By carefully drawing on many different accounts, Morgan works toward as clearly focused a picture of the real man as possible."
—*The New York Review of Books*

"Morgan's skills as a novelist and poet help in making this the most detailed and compelling life of Daniel Boone to date. . . . This is a work of genuine scholarship."
—*Bookforum*

"[Morgan] brings to this new biography his novelist's instinct for drama, an eye for telling details and valuable insight into human nature. . . . The flesh-and-blood Boone who emerges is vivid and rare, a far cry from the enigmatic icon. This is historical biography at its best."
                                                    —*St. Louis Post-Dispatch*

"[A] beautifully written account of a life that was important for itself as well as for the legends that grew from it."
                                                    —*The Commercial Dispatch*

"A model of its genre—both thoroughly researched and powerfully written."
                                                    —*The Louisville Courier-Journal*

"Robert Morgan is a genius. . . . [He] brings his deep understanding of metaphor and his brilliant storytelling to the life of this complicated and fascinating frontiersman."
                                                    —*The Raleigh News & Observer*

"An excellent biography based on a mountain of research. Robert Morgan . . . is exactly the writer to produce this inquisitive study."
                                                    —*The Roanoke (VA) Times*

"Phenomenal."
                                                    —*The State* (SC)

"Admirable. . . . Define[s] the misty edges of the legend."
                                                    —*Winston-Salem Journal*

"Engaging and sympathetic. . . . [Morgan] brings to Boone a novelist's eye for detail and pacing."
                                                    —*The Columbus Dispatch*

"[A] beautifully written study of Boone."
                                                    —*Richmond Times-Dispatch*

"Perfect."   —*The Week*

"A masterwork contribution to the scholarship on America's frontier trailblazing. . . . A fine tribute to the historical figure and to the conflicted realities of the man."   —*The Grand Rapids Press*

"Splendid. . . . A richly textured masterpiece."
—*Rocky Mount (NC) Telegram*

"What emerges from this intelligent, beautifully written and well-researched biography is an American frontiersman who was completely drawn into his time and place, a shrewd, articulate adventurer who has come to symbolize the valiant, resourceful individual as American hero."   —*The Southern Pines (NC) Pilot*

"In addition to rendering a complete portrait of Boone, Morgan lends insight into life on the frontier."   —*The Newark Star-Ledger*

"[An] impressive new biography of the American legend. . . . Meticulously researched and elegantly told. . . . Written with admiration and great care. . . . The narrative teems with fascinating asides."
—*BookPage*

"[An] absorbing and stirring chronicle of the great frontiersman. . . . Outstanding."   —*Booklist*, starred review

"A beautifully written biography. . . . Strongly recommended."
—*Library Journal*, starred review

"Boone comes alive in [these] pages. Morgan's objectivity gives us a completely realized man."   —*Publishers Weekly*

"Wow. *Boone* is a pleasure. I wish more first-rate novelists-poets wrote biography. Robert Morgan has given us the man himself, so much more interesting and impressive than all the myths about him."

—Richard Bausch, author of *Wives and Lovers*

"A narrative tour de force. . . . Informed by serious scholarship and propelled by superb storytelling, Morgan's book captures the heart of an American original."

—Daniel Blake Smith, author of the screenplays *Trail of Tears* and *Black Indians*

"This exquisitely written, meticulously researched biography is as compelling and unputdownable as a great novel."

—Ron Rash, author of *Saints at the River*

"A riveting account of the *real* Boone. . . . Morgan's compelling and richly contextualized narrative reflects the author's intimate knowledge and feel for the terrain that Boone explored."

—Michael Kammen, author of *Mystic Chords of Memory*

Boone

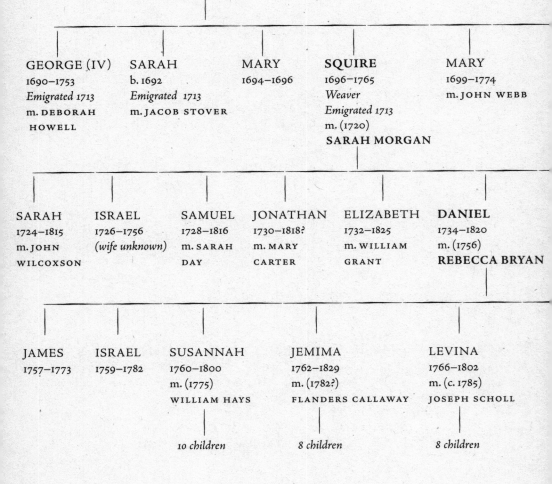

GEORGE BOONE (I)

GEORGE BOONE (II)

GEORGE BOONE (III)
1666–1744
Weaver
Emigrated from England to Pennsylvania 1717
m. **MARY MAUGRIDGE**

GEORGE (IV)	SARAH	MARY	**SQUIRE**	MARY
1690–1753	b. 1692	1694–1696	1696–1765	1699–1774
Emigrated 1713	*Emigrated 1713*		*Weaver*	m. JOHN WEBB
m. DEBORAH	m. JACOB STOVER		*Emigrated 1713*	
HOWELL			m. (1720)	
			SARAH MORGAN	

SARAH	ISRAEL	SAMUEL	JONATHAN	ELIZABETH	**DANIEL**
1724–1815	1726–1756	1728–1816	1730–1818?	1732–1825	1734–1820
m. JOHN	*(wife unknown)*	m. SARAH	m. MARY	m. WILLIAM	m. (1756)
WILCOXSON		DAY	CARTER	GRANT	**REBECCA BRYAN**

JAMES	ISRAEL	SUSANNAH	JEMIMA	LEVINA
1757–1773	1759–1782	1760–1800	1762–1829	1766–1802
		m. (1775)	m. (1782?)	m. (c. 1785)
		WILLIAM HAYS	FLANDERS CALLAWAY	JOSEPH SCHOLL
		10 children	*8 children*	*8 children*

Sources:
Spraker, Hazel Atterbury. *The Boone Family.* 1922.
    Reprint, Salem, MA: Higginson, 2005.
Lofaro, Michael A. *Daniel Boone: An American Life.* Lexington:
    University Press of Kentucky, 2003.

Boone Family Genealogy

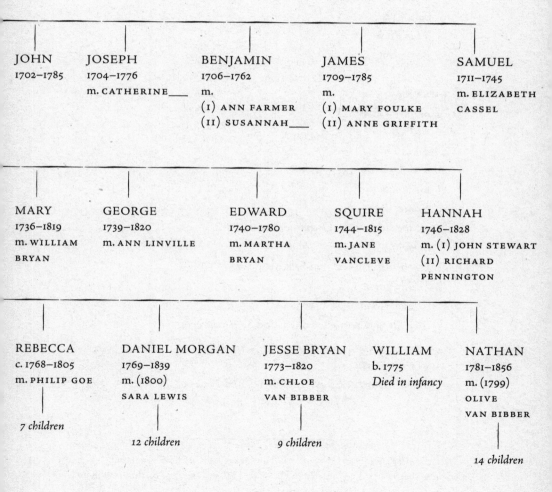

JOHN
1702–1785

JOSEPH
1704–1776
m. CATHERINE____

BENJAMIN
1706–1762
m.
(I) ANN FARMER
(II) SUSANNAH____

JAMES
1709–1785
m.
(I) MARY FOULKE
(II) ANNE GRIFFITH

SAMUEL
1711–1745
m. ELIZABETH
CASSEL

MARY
1736–1819
m. WILLIAM
BRYAN

GEORGE
1739–1820
m. ANN LINVILLE

EDWARD
1740–1780
m. MARTHA
BRYAN

SQUIRE
1744–1815
m. JANE
VANCLEVE

HANNAH
1746–1828
m. (I) JOHN STEWART
(II) RICHARD
PENNINGTON

REBECCA
c. 1768–1805
m. PHILIP GOE

7 children

DANIEL MORGAN
1769–1839
m. (1800)
SARA LEWIS

12 children

JESSE BRYAN
1773–1820
m. CHLOE
VAN BIBBER

9 children

WILLIAM
b. 1775
Died in infancy

NATHAN
1781–1856
m. (1799)
OLIVE
VAN BIBBER

14 children

Also by Robert Morgan

Daniel Boone. Fred G. Walker. Oil on canvas. 24¾" × 29½". Ca. 1914.
Based on a Chester Harding portrait and presented to Berea College by the artist in 1914.
(Courtesy Berea College, Berea, KY.)

Boone

A BIOGRAPHY

BY *Robert Morgan*

A Shannon Ravenel Book

ALGONQUIN BOOKS OF CHAPEL HILL

2008

For my grandson Grayson

ℝ

A Shannon Ravenel Book

Published by
Algonquin Books of Chapel Hill
Post Office Box 2225
Chapel Hill, North Carolina 27515-2225

a division of
Workman Publishing
225 Varick Street
New York, New York 10014

© 2007 by Robert Morgan. All rights reserved.
First paperback edition, Algonquin Books of Chapel Hill, September 2008.
Originally published by Algonquin Books of Chapel Hill in 2007.
Printed in the United States of America.
Published simultaneously in Canada by
Thomas Allen & Son Limited.
Design by Barbara Williams.

Library of Congress
Cataloging-in-Publication Data
Morgan, Robert, 1944–
Boone: a biography / by Robert Morgan.—1st ed.
p. cm.
Includes bibliographical references.
ISBN-13: 978-1-56512-455-4 (HC)
1. Boone, Daniel, 1734–1820. 2. Pioneers—Kentucky—Biography.
3. Explorers—Kentucky—Biography. 4. Frontier and pioneer life—Kentucky.
5. Kentucky—Biography. 6. Kentucky—Discovery and exploration. I. Title.
F454.B66M67 2007
976.9'02092—dc22

[B]   2007014204

ISBN-13: 978-1-56512-615-2 (PB)

20 19 18 17 16 15 14 13 12 11

Contents

LIST OF MAPS

1702   George Boone III and Mary Maugridge Boone in Bradninch, Devonshire, England, join the Cullompton Meeting of the Society of Friends (Quakers).

1717   George Boone III and the rest of his family arrive in Philadelphia, following his sons George IV and Squire and daughter Sarah, who came in 1713.

1720   Squire Boone marries Sarah Morgan at Gwyneth Meeting House, September 23.

1734   Daniel Boone, sixth child of Squire and Sarah, born November 2 (October 22, Old Style).

1747   Daniel is given his first "short rifle gun" and becomes an expert hunter.

1750   Squire Boone sells his property in Pennsylvania and moves his family to Linnville Creek, near Harrisonburg, Virginia. The next year they go on to the Yadkin Valley in North Carolina.

1755   Daniel serves with the North Carolina militia in the French and Indian War and is present at Braddock's Defeat. Meets John Findley, who has been to Kentucky.

1756   Daniel marries Rebecca Bryan August 14.

1757   James Boone, first son, born May 3.

1759   Israel Boone born January 25. Because of Indian attacks Daniel and his family move to Culpeper, Virginia. Boone returns to North Carolina to hunt and serve in the militia.

1760   Susannah Boone born November 2. Boone hunts beyond the Blue Ridge Mountains.

1762   The Boone family returns to the Yadkin after peace is made with the Cherokees. Jemima Boone born October 4.

1765   Squire Boone dies January 2. Daniel and his brother Squire II join party to explore Florida.

1766   Levina Boone born March 23.

1768   Rebecca Boone born May 26. Regulator rebellion builds in North Carolina.

1769   Daniel, John Findley, John Stewart, and three others leave for Kentucky May 1. Regulator activity increases in North Carolina. Daniel Morgan Boone born December 23.

1771   Daniel returns to the Yadkin from Kentucky in May as Regulators surrender to colonial militia.

1773   Jesse Bryan Boone born May 23. Boone and William Russell attempt to settle in Kentucky but are turned back by an Indian attack in which son James is killed.

1774   Boone and Michael Stoner ride into Kentucky to warn surveyors of Indian hostilities. Lord Dunmore's War ends with treaty in October after the Battle of Point Pleasant.

1775   Boone leads a crew to hack a trace through Cumberland Gap for the Transylvania Company, which has purchased much of Kentucky from the Cherokees. Revolutionary War breaks out in April with the battles of Lexington and Concord in Massachusetts. William Boone born in July and dies.

1776   Jemima Boone and two Callaway girls are abducted by Indians on July 14 and later rescued. A copy of the Declaration of Independence reaches Boonesborough in August.

1777   Shawnees attack Boonesborough and Boone is wounded. His mother, Sarah, dies in North Carolina.

1778   Boone is captured by the Shawnees near the Blue Licks and is a
        prisoner at Chillicothe for four months. He escapes in June and
        defends Boonesborough successfully against a Shawnee-British
        raid. Afterward he is charged with treason and exonerated.

1779   On Christmas Day Boone, with family and friends, moves to
        Boone's Station near future Athens, Kentucky.

1780   Boone is robbed of about twenty thousand dollars near
        Williamsburg, Virginia.

1781   Boone serves in the Virginia legislature. Nathan Boone born
        March 2. Cornwallis surrenders at Yorktown, October 17.

1782   As lieutenant colonel of the Fayette County militia Boone
        fights at the Battle of the Blue Licks, where his son Israel is
        killed.

1783–84 Boone moves to Marble Creek and meets John Filson, who
        publishes "The Adventures of Col. Daniel Boon" in 1784.

1785–86 Boone moves his family to Limestone on the Ohio River,
        where he operates a store, tavern, and surveying business and is
        sued by former clients over disputed land claims.

1788   Boone takes a keelboat load of ginseng to Maryland, and on a
        visit to Pennsylvania he decides to leave Kentucky and move to
        Point Pleasant, Virginia, on the Ohio River.

1789   At Point Pleasant Boone keeps a small store and continues to
        hunt and trap.

1791   Boone serves as a lieutenant colonel in the militia and is elected
        to the Virginia legislature. He agrees to supply militia compa-
        nies in western Virginia but fails to fulfill his contract.

1792   Boone moves to remote cabin near present Charleston, West
        Virginia.

1795   Boone returns to Kentucky with Rebecca and lives on Brushy
        Fork of Hinkston Creek in son Daniel Morgan's cabin. He

hunts bears on the Big Sandy and is summoned to court repeatedly in land disputes.

1798 Son Daniel Morgan Boone returns to Kentucky from Missouri with invitation from Lieutenant Governor Trudeau for Boone to settle there in Spanish territory. Boone moves to the Little Sandy River to prepare for immigration to Missouri.

1799 Boone and family leave Kentucky for Femme Osage Creek in Missouri. The next year, Boone is appointed "syndic" for that region.

1800 Susannah Boone Hays dies of fever.

1802 Daughter Levina Boone Scholl dies in Kentucky.

1803 The United States negotiates the Louisiana Purchase. Boone has been given about ten thousand acres of land in Missouri but has not made improvements or completed the paperwork for the deeds.

1805 Daughter Rebecca Boone Goe dies in Kentucky.

1806 Boone learns the American government may not recognize his Missouri land claims. He continues to hunt, trap, and explore the region.

1809 Boone petitions Congress for recovery of his land claims.

1810 Boone joins a hunting expedition to the upper Missouri, going perhaps as far as the Yellowstone.

1813 Rebecca Boone dies March 18 and is buried on Tuque Creek.

1814 Boone is awarded one thousand arpents of land, most of which he has to sell to pay debts.

1820 Boone dies in his son Nathan's large stone house and is buried beside Rebecca.

1845 Daniel's and Rebecca's bodies are brought to Frankfort, Kentucky, for reburial.

Introduction

FORGET the coonskin cap; he never wore one. Daniel Boone thought coonskin caps uncouth, heavy, and uncomfortable. He always wore a beaver felt hat to protect him from sun and rain. The coonskin-topped Boone is the image from Hollywood and television. In fact, much that the public thinks it knows about Boone is fiction. He was neither the discoverer of Kentucky nor the first settler in the Bluegrass region. He did not discover the Cumberland Gap, known to the Indians as Ouasiota, nor was he the first white man to dig ginseng in the North American wilderness. And though he held the rank of lieutenant colonel in the militia more than once, he was for the most part a reluctant soldier and Indian fighter. As one of his first biographers said, "He never delighted in shedding human blood, even that of his enemies in war, and avoided it whenever he could." The real story of Daniel Boone is more complicated than the fiction, stranger, and far more interesting.

It was Emerson who said, "All history resolves itself very easily into the biography of a few stout and earnest persons." Certainly Boone was one of those stout and earnest individuals.

Even in his own time Boone had a number of detractors, debunkers, and critics. He was at different times accused of treason, fraud, and hypocrisy and was once court-martialed, only to be exonerated and given a promotion by the board of presiding officers. He was blamed for dishonest and incompetent land surveying, and sued again and again for debt. Yet surviving records show he was a competent surveyor, though sometimes careless with clerical and legal work. By the end of his life he had paid off all that his accusers said he owed. He was also blamed for siding with Indians, accused of being a "white Indian," yet he fortified and defended Boonesborough against an attack led by his adopted father, the Shawnee chief Blackfish. Boone was also accused of being a Tory, a British sympathizer, during the American Revolution, yet he fought the British-led Indian attacks on Kentucky forts again and again.

"For me, the most striking and surprising result of a closer look at Boone is the way his sterling moral character shines steadily through all the vicissitudes of his remarkable life," the scholar Nelson L. Dawson wrote in 1998.

Known as a scout and hunter, Boone became a patriarch, serving in legislatures and militias and on boards of trustees. A humble person who described himself as "a common man," Boone was famous in both America and Europe. At one time he may have owned upward of thirty thousand acres of land in Kentucky; he ran a tavern, a store, and a warehouse, and he traded furs, hides, ginseng, horses, even slaves, and land. He lost it all. A recognized leader all his life, he moved often as a gypsy. With little formal education and uncertain spelling, he read a number of books and had a flair for language, even eloquence.

Like most great figures in American history, Boone has been both lucky and unlucky in his biographers. The schoolmaster and sometime surveyor and land speculator John Filson (ca. 1747–88) made Boone famous when Boone turned fifty in 1784. Filson's *Discovery, Settlement and Present State of Kentucke* included a long chapter called "The Adventures of Col. Daniel Boon," written in the first person as though it was autobiography. The little book, destined to become a classic, was translated into French and German and pirated and paraphrased by a number of other authors. Reprinted by Gilbert Imlay in *A Topographical Description of the Western Territory of North America*, published in London in 1793, the narrative made Boone famous in Britain and helped inspire such budding Romantic poets as Wordsworth, Coleridge, and Robert Southey.

Only recently have we come to appreciate how much American Romanticism may have influenced British Romanticism. But the impact of Boone's story and legend on William Bartram, Wordsworth, Byron, and other writers of the Romantic era is only the beginning of the story of the Boone legend and biography. Few other Americans have had their lives told so often and in such a wide range of styles, combining truth, insight, myth, hearsay, and outright fabrication. Because he became a figure of American folklore even while alive, Boone has been thought by many to be virtually a fictional character, subject of tall tales like Mike Fink the Keelboatman, or even Paul Bunyan. A professor with a PhD in English and tenure at a major university once said to me, "I never realized Daniel Boone was an actual person; I thought he was a creation of folklore." I told her that even though she was wrong she was also half right, because the Boone most people know about *is* largely the creation of folklore. It is hard to rescue figures like Daniel Boone and Johnny Appleseed from the distortions of television and Walt Disney. The folklore and legends are part of the story too but should be identified and separated from the facts. When viewed in the larger context of the colonial age, the Boone legend is in many ways typical of the way stories and figures of quest and conquest were romanticized, as Europeans conquered lands and peoples. Yet many aspects of Boone's character are atypical, virtually unique.

While Boone more than once told visitors that Filson's account of his life was "true, every word truth," he was not so pleased with Daniel Bryan's would-be epic poem *The Mountain Muse* published in 1813, which portrayed him as a ridiculously heroic figure, a kind of American Moses. "Such productions ought to be left until the person was put in the ground," he is reported to have said. Of the rumor that he still went hunting at the age of eighty, he observed to Rev. John Mason Peck, "I would not believe that tale if I told it myself. I have not watched the deer's lick for ten years. My eyesight is too far gone to hunt."

During Boone's later years many accounts of his exploits and adventures were published in newspapers in America and Britain. Most took their details and rhetoric from Filson, and some contained an element of truth but also included rumors and fancy, often portraying the old woodsman as a fierce Indian killer, wrestling bears and panthers in hand-to-hand combat. More than once he read accounts of his own death in newspapers.

The stories that formed around Boone's name while he was alive were only the seeds of what would come later. The Reverend Timothy Flint, who had visited Boone in 1816, published the first book-length biography, *Biographical Memoir of Daniel Boone*, in 1833. The book was very popular and for its time a best seller. But while it contained some valuable information it was also filled with colorful yarns, such as the improbable story of young Daniel almost shooting his future bride, Rebecca, while fire hunting on the Yadkin. When questioned about some of the exaggerations in his narrative, Flint is supposed to have answered he was not writing a book "for use but to sell." It was Flint who gave to the world the most famous Boone quote about wanting "more elbow room."

Another itinerant minister who wrote about the western frontier, Rev. John Mason Peck, visited Boone in December of 1818, two years before the woodsman's death. Expecting to find a rough backwoodsman, Peck was surprised by Boone's calm good manners, his modesty and cheerfulness. Peck was struck by the affection in which Boone was held by his children and grandchildren and neighbors. When Peck published his *Life of Boone* in 1847, he stressed the image of Boone as peacemaker, diplomat, reluctant Indian fighter, and instrument of Manifest Destiny. Boone's descendants much preferred Peck's account to Flint's. It was Peck who told the story of Boone's journey back to Kentucky to pay his debts after he sold the land Congress had awarded him in Missouri. According to Peck, Boone then returned to Missouri with only fifty cents in his pocket. "No one will say, when I am gone, 'Boone was a dishonest man,'" he quipped.

Boone was most fortunate of all in attracting the scholar and writer Lyman Copeland Draper, who never finished or published his *Life of*

Daniel Boone. A native of upstate New York, Draper (1815–91) worked as a clerk, editor, and journalist but devoted his life to collecting information and documents for the study of the western frontier and the Revolutionary War era. He borrowed, bought, begged, copied — some said stole — thousands of documents and interviewed hundreds of survivors and descendants. He corresponded with hundreds more and seemingly came in contact with everyone who ever lived in the frontier Ohio Valley or was descended from the pioneers there.

Draper interviewed Daniel Boone's youngest son, Nathan, and Nathan's wife, Olive Van Bibber Boone, at length in 1851, at their home in Greene County, Missouri. As secretary of the State Historical Society of Wisconsin in Madison, Draper collected and hoarded documents and transcripts, rather than completing his projected biographies of Boone and George Rogers Clark and other pioneers. At his death he left an ocean of interviews and papers scholars have been struggling through and sifting ever since. Draper was small in stature but a giant of American historical scholarship. "I am a small bit of a fellow," he wrote to one correspondent. "Yet small as I am, and as 'good for nothing' as I often think myself, I yet feel that I have something to do."

One of the assistants Draper trained at the State Historical Society of Wisconsin was Reuben Gold Thwaites (1853–1913). When Draper retired, Thwaites succeeded him as director of the society and became one of the most important editors and writers on frontier history of his time. In 1902 Thwaites published his own biography of Boone, called simply *Daniel Boone*. It was the first published life of Boone to make use of the hoard of documents Draper had collected.

In 1920 a professor of mathematics at the University of North Carolina at Chapel Hill, Archibald Henderson, published *The Conquest of the Old Southwest* to much acclaim. Henderson was a descendant of Judge Richard Henderson, founder of the Transylvania Company and Boone's employer, and he stressed the significance of the Transylvania venture in the founding of Kentucky and Tennessee. Henderson planned to follow that history with a life of Daniel Boone, but a peculiar chemistry began to work on the professor as he proceeded with his project. He decided that his ancestor Richard Henderson was the real hero of the story of Kentucky and that Daniel Boone was little more than a hired hand. He became a debunker of Boone, and at Fourth of July celebrations and memorial ceremonies he made a spectacle of himself attempting to build up the reputation of his ancestor and belittle the scout and hunter who had hacked Boone's Trace and given his name to Boonesborough. In the end Archibald Henderson was unable to write the biography, and his research material was left to the University of North Carolina as the Henderson Papers, a valuable resource in the North Carolina Collection.

Probably the most successful biography of Boone ever published was John Bakeless's 1939 volume, *Master of the Wilderness: Daniel Boone*. Bakeless, a historian and professor of journalism at New York University, drew heavily on modern research of the frontier period and made extensive use of the Draper Collection at Madison. The book went through several editions and is still in print. Many Boone enthusiasts still consider it the best Boone biography ever written. However, Bakeless had little interest in Indians and Indian culture, except to portray them usually as savages, or in the slaves who were present in so much of the activity of the frontier. Implicit in much of Bakeless's narrative is the assumption of the superiority of white culture destined to subdue and transform the wilderness into the ideal of American civilization.

In 1992 John Mack Faragher published *Daniel Boone: The Life and Legend of an American Pioneer* and brought to his study of Boone a formidable knowledge and insight about Indian culture and the impact of Indian culture on white culture. Faragher took Boone studies up to a new level with his sensitivity and erudition concerning Native American history. He also included in his portrait of Boone the rumor that Boone was not the father of one of his children, begotten while Boone was away hunting or in the militia in January 1762. Faragher makes the story exciting and plausible, a significant element in drawing the characters of Boone and his wife, Rebecca. Yet most Boone scholars have considered the story as little more than a composite of contradictory rumors, passed on by elderly informants with vague memories, improbable if not impossible.

A major service to Boone scholarship has been performed in recent years by the scholar Ted Franklin Belue. In 1998 he published a transcribed and annotated edition of Draper's unfinished *Life of Daniel Boone*. Only those who have tried to read Draper's notes and documents on microfilm can appreciate the value and difficulty of Belue's achievement. With this volume Belue put at our fingertips the heart of Draper's work on Boone and, through his notes and chronology, provided an invaluable resource for further study.

In 1999 the Kentucky architect and Boone scholar Neal O. Hammon published *My Father, Daniel Boone*, a compilation of the interviews Draper conducted with Boone's youngest son, Nathan, and Nathan's wife, Olive, in 1851. Gathering the material from several locations in the Draper Collection, Hammon arranged the pieces into a coherent narrative, making easily accessible the words of our most reliable informant about Daniel Boone.

Michael A. Lofaro published *Daniel Boone: An American Life*, a short biography for popular audiences, in 2003. Lofaro's book presents the Boone narrative in thrilling, condensed form, yet also provides one of the most useful bibliographic and scholarly resources we have to date.

Among the younger historians, I have learned the most from Stephen Aron, author of *How the West Was Lost* and *American Confluence*. Aron is especially adept at showing the complexity and flux of events on the American frontier and placing those events in the context of continental and even world history.

It requires a certain bravado to enter a field as crowded as Boone biography. Of major figures in early American history, only Washington and Franklin and Jefferson have had their stories told more often and in greater detail. What recklessness or delusion could tempt a writer to take on a subject so often studied, attacked, dramatized?

My fascination with Boone goes back to boyhood. My father, who was a wonderful storyteller, had a lifelong interest in Daniel Boone and loved to quote the hunter and explorer. Since Daniel's mother was Sarah Morgan, my father thought we were related by blood. Though I have not found more than a distant family connection, I always felt a kinship with the hunter and trapper and scout.

The classic author I struggled with and learned most from as a young writer was Henry David Thoreau. Thoreau's observation, knowledge, wisdom, integrity, artistry, and stubbornness remain unsurpassed in American literature and culture. And more than any other single author Thoreau expresses much that was likely the experience and aspiration and genius of Boone. Thoreau put into sentences the poetry and thought Boone had lived.

Many boys, both old and young, feel a connection with Boone, but growing up in the mountains of western North Carolina in the 1940s and 1950s, hunting and trapping, fishing and wandering the mountain trails, I may have felt the kinship more literally than most. Living on a small farm, without a truck or tractor or car, plowing our fields with a horse, keeping milk and butter in the springhouse, listening to stories about the old days by the fireplace or on the porch in summer, I always felt an intimate contact with the past, with the Indians, with the frontier. Working in the creek bottoms day after day, I turned up arrowheads and pieces of pottery. The Indians seemed to haunt the ground beneath my feet, and the laurel thickets, and the mutter of creek and waterfall. Once after a flood scoured away several feet of alluvial soil in the field by the river, I found the charred remains of a campfire perhaps a thousand years old.

It was writing the novel *Brave Enemies*, set in the American Revolution and culminating at the Battle of Cowpens in South Carolina in 1781, that led me back to Boone. As I did my research on the Revolutionary period in the Carolinas, I grew more and more preoccupied with life on the frontier, where white settlers mingled and fought with and learned from the Native populations. I came to see what an extraordinary story that was, the collision of different worlds right in my own backyard, as British confronted French, Indians fought Indians, white Regulators confronted the colonial government, and finally Americans fought the Crown. And through it all the thread of slavery stretched like a poison filament from earliest colonial times to the nineteenth century and Civil War.

I found Boone a much more complex person than I had noticed before. Why was he remembered, romanticized, revered, and written about when many other figures on the Kentucky frontier were pretty much forgotten? I wanted to find out what it was about Daniel Boone that made him lodge in the memory of all who knew him and made so many want to tell his story. How was a scout and hunter turned into such an icon of American culture?

In the course of my research I discovered that Boone had been a Freemason and that his membership in that society connected him in unexpected ways with leading figures of the American Revolution, such as Benjamin Franklin and Washington, and with the new spirit of brotherhood, liberty, and reason spreading through Europe and North America. No other Boone scholar seemed to have noticed Boone's association with Masonry. I also found that Boone was a great dreamer, and a significant part of his dream was a vision of hunting and living at peace with the Indians, in the wilderness over the mountains. It was a vision and a longing that set him apart from many other hunters of the time.

Boone many times referred to himself as a woodsman. It was the description he seemed to prefer, the identity he chose to claim. When he wrote to Gov. Isaac Shelby in 1796 asking for the contract to rebuild the Wilderness Road, Boone said, "I am no Statesman I am a Woodsman and think My Self . . . Capable of Marking and Cutting that Rode." When young I studied engineering and wanted to build roads also. Many of the narratives I have written concern path blazing and road building. That was another aspect of Boone I felt a deep connection with: Boone the artisan and artificer, Boone the road maker.

Some have said the name Boone comes from the Norman Bohun, from the nobleman Henry de Bohun (1176 – 1220). The Boones had lived in Devonshire for centuries, working as weavers and blacksmiths, before they immigrated to Pennsylvania. Boone's mother was Sarah Morgan, descended from Welsh Quakers from Merionethshire in the mountains of North Wales.

In one of the happiest accidents of punning etymologies known, Americans acquired the word *boondocks* from Tagalog in the Philippines, and from that wonderful word, meaning "mountains," derived the term *boonies*, referring to the hinterlands, the backcountry. Many wrongly assume *boonies* comes to us from the name Boone, explorer of hinterlands and backcountry. And we also have the Old French word *boon* as in "boon companion" from the Latin *bonus*, meaning "good." And from Old Norse we have *boon*, meaning a "blessing or benefit," coming from a word that meant "prayer." *Boon* is also an Old English word for the rough fiber taken out of flax as it is prepared for spinning into thread. The Boones had been weavers for generations in Devonshire. Boone was fortunate in his name, if not in his business enterprises.

"They may say what they please of Daniel Boone, he acted with wisdom in that matter," Simon Kenton remarked about rumors of Boone's dishonesty and treachery once when he surrendered some salt boilers in 1778. Kenton meant that the truth of the man's deeds and character would rise above all the clouds of rumor spread by detractors. And for more than two centuries it has.

Boone

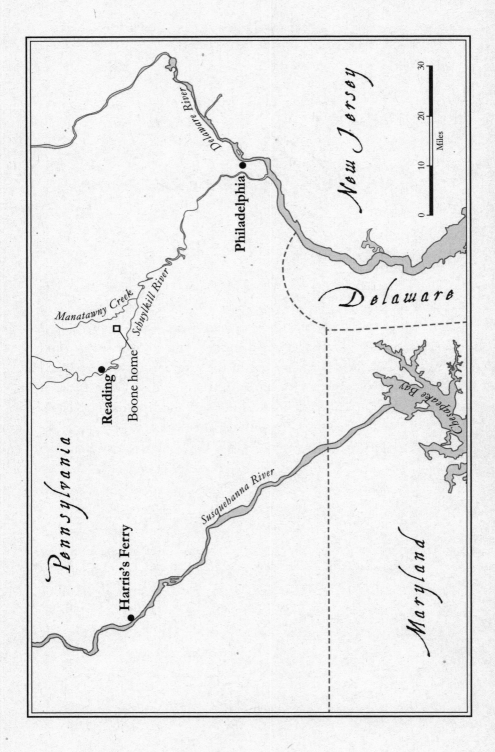

CHAPTER ONE

The Mother World of the Forest

1734 – 1750 ◡

The Quakers of Devonshire lived as farmers and weavers in hamlets and mountain valleys. They had broken away from the official church and been punished by fines and ostracism, sometimes by prison and whippings. As Quakers they could not hold office or vote. As pacifists it was against their faith to serve in the army or navy. They could not attend school or train for the learned professions. As followers of George Fox, they called themselves Friends, and they did not have a hierarchy of clergy or ritualized service. They met in silence and spoke only as the spirit stirred them. The ties of neighbors and among the Friends were very close. Though often persecuted and exploited, they attempted to live lives of calm goodwill and honest work, farming and weaving linen and wool, blacksmithing and helping one another.

The Boones were Quakers from Devonshire in the extreme southwest of England. Devonshire is one of the most beautiful counties of Great Britain, a place of highlands and moors covered with heather and bracken, high rocky hills, long pleasant valleys running down to the sea. The river Exe rises out of a bog in the north and runs through Brampton, Tiverton, Stoke Canon, Exeter. The Boone family had been settled in this area for at least two hundred years, living primarily around Exeter, an ancient town with buildings dating from Roman,

Saxon, Norman, and Tudor times. Exeter's splendid cathedral dated
from the eleventh century and had been rebuilt between 1280 and 1370
as a Gothic masterpiece.

Exeter had long been a center for the weaving and dyeing trades,
producing a woolen cloth of serge weave. But it was also a market center where many goods as well as produce were sold near the cathedral. Smiths made guns, horseshoes, hinges, and tools for the village.
George Boone II completed an apprenticeship as a blacksmith and
married Sarah Uppey around 1660 before settling down to his trade
at Stoke Canon. George II was a member of the Church of England,
prosperous, entitled to a pew at the parish church. He was the father
of George III, born in 1666, who became a Quaker.

The man who founded the Society of Friends, George Fox, was born
in Nottinghamshire in 1624 to a Puritan family and was apprenticed to
a shoemaker. At the age of eighteen he experienced a conversion, a call,
and began to wander from town to town, valley to valley, witnessing
and exhorting, encouraging drunkards and sinners to repent and re-
form. He supported himself by making shoes. In Nottingham Fox was
jailed for intruding on a church service, shouting, "Truth is not in this
meeting." He was arrested in Derbyshire for preaching in the street.
His message of humility and simplicity began to attract followers, and
enemies, and in places he and his listeners were stoned. His flocks
were primarily artisans and farmers. His followers were especially well
received in the West Country, in Devon and Cornwall. But in much of
England Quakers were accused of vagrancy and jailed. Fox himself was
imprisoned for refusing to take off his hat in court. In prison he drew
a large following among the inmates and local people.

Quaker communities became tightly knit. Before a Quaker could
move away he had to get a "certificate of cleanness" from his meeting,
declaring his faith and good character. Quakers were expected to visit
the sick and bereaved, talk with the troubled, and discuss problems
and plans in the family and community. To marry, they had to obtain
approval of the committee of Friends and were forbidden "to keep com-

pany" or marry outside the community of Quakers. They had to avoid all gambling, music, frivolity. But because Quakers were known to be trustworthy in their dealings, they gained the respect of society and their businesses prospered.

George Boone II chose the weaver's trade for his son George III, who was born in the sixth year of the Restoration, 1666. George III established his weaving business in the village of Bradninch, where he had probably served his apprenticeship. In 1687 young George married Mary Maugridge, from an old Bradninch family. Mary, the daughter of John Maugridge, was baptized in Bradninch in 1668. She gave birth to her third child, Squire Boone, in 1696. The other children were George IV, baptized in 1690; Sarah, 1692; Mary, 1694 (d. 1696); Mary, 1699; John, 1702; Joseph, 1704; Benjamin, 1706; James, 1709; and Samuel, 1711. It would seem the Boones always had large families. George III and Mary Maugridge Boone joined the Friends Meeting in nearby Cullompton sometime after 1702.

After the Treaty of Utrecht in 1713, which ended the War of the Spanish Succession, the woolen trade declined. There was widespread unemployment in Devon. Norwich and Yorkshire had begun to produce a less expensive kind of wool cloth. This decline in their business almost certainly influenced the Boones to think of immigrating to the New World. George IV, Sarah, and Squire Boone traveled to Pennsylvania as early as 1713, and George IV and Squire soon joined the Friends Meeting there.

It would seem the younger Boones were sent to Pennsylvania to scout out opportunities for George III, and the rest of his family soon followed. But before he left Devonshire for America, George Boone III wrote out a confession to the local Society of Friends. The handwritten copy still exists in the Devon Hall of Records in Exeter. In the letter he admits a number of failings:

I am constrained to make mention of this my transgression
not without grief but with trouble and sorrow of heart for this my

wickedness — which was keeping of wild company and drinking by which I sometimes became guilty of drunkenness to the dishonour of truth.

And then he goes on to confess another shortcoming:

> I fell into another gross evil which I also confess to my great shame and sorrow that I did so little regard the Lord and the dear mercies of the Lord, but went on in another gross sin by which the honour due unto marriage was lost, for the marriage bed was defiled.
>
> *Bradninch, 29th of the 12th month, 1716*

Many Quakers had already gone to the New World in the 1600s. William Penn, the son of an admiral highly respected by King Charles II, had been inspired by the "inner light" as a youth and was expelled from Oxford University for refusing to attend Anglican services. He became associated with George Fox and preached on the Continent. He served as trustee for Quakers immigrating to the New World. By 1678 there were hundreds of Quakers from Yorkshire living in New Jersey. Some had already crossed the Delaware into what would become Pennsylvania, where Swedish immigrants had earlier built settlements. The headquarters of the Quakers in America was established at Burlington, New Jersey, in 1677. George Fox visited the community there to encourage the members.

On March 4, 1681, Charles II, to settle a debt claim to William Penn's late father, granted Penn a charter to twenty-eight million acres, all lands west of the Delaware River between forty and forty-five degrees and extending five degrees west. The king named the region Pennsylvania in honor of the late admiral. William Penn himself came to the colony in 1682. Penn's proprietary land agent granted tracts of land to immigrants on generous terms. After a parcel was surveyed, the purchaser paid an annual quitrent of a penny an acre. Land could be bought outright, fee simple, at the price of one hundred pounds for five thousand acres. Settlers started to pour into the colony. Between

1682 and 1684, fifty ships arrived in Philadelphia, bringing settlers from London, Bristol, Ireland, Holland, and Germany. A number of Welsh began to arrive.

The Welsh immigrants tended to settle near each other in what was called the Welsh Tract, forty thousand acres with towns named Merion, Radnor, Haverford. The only physicians in the colony at this time were members of the Welsh community.

Edward Morgan of Bala, a Welsh Quaker who had arrived in 1691, settled with his family in the Moyamensing District of Philadelphia County. Nine years later they moved to Towamencin Township near Gwynedd. Here Squire Boone, who would become the father of Daniel Boone, met Edward's daughter Sarah. A Friend's meetinghouse had been established at Gwynedd in 1701. George III and Mary Boone had moved there soon after they arrived in America.

The Morgans of Merionethshire in North Wales had become Quakers soon after George Fox visited there in 1657. Morgan is one of the most common names in Wales, along with Jones. Edward Morgan belonged to the tenth generation descended from Llewelyn Ap Morgan. That part of Wales is renowned for its mountain crags and mists. In the seventeenth century its main businesses were sheep grazing; knitting stockings, gloves, sweaters; and making wigs. Writing in the 1180s the historian and priest Giraldus Cambrensis described Merionethshire as "the roughest and rudest of all the Welsh districts. The mountains are very high, with narrow ridges and a great number of very sharp peaks, all jumbled together in confusion. If the shepherds who shout together and exchange comments from these lofty summits should ever decide to meet, it would take them almost the whole day to climb up and down again."

Quakerism had taken root in that part of Wales following the preaching of Morgan Lloyd and John Ap John. Since the times of the Druids, the Welsh had been a people who loved music and praise. One of their own in the fifth century, named Morgan, had called himself Pelagius, translating Morgan ("of the sea") into Latin, when he rose to high office in Rome and preached a doctrine denying original sin. He gained many followers, until he was denounced as a heretic by Augustine of Hippo. The Welsh had always loved a religion of praise, and independence, preferring to seek peace, liberty, and happiness on their own terms and in their own rugged world.

When George Fox visited Wales, he found a small, though receptive, audience for his "quietism" and pursuit of the "inner light." Fox's best reception was in the mountains of Merionethshire, and there he invited his listeners to come to Pennsylvania to take part in the "holy experiment" with freedom and brotherhood on the banks of the Delaware and Schuylkill. Edward Morgan and his family had answered that call.

WHEN George III and Mary Boone arrived in Pennsylvania in 1717 with their six younger children, Mary, John, Joseph, Benjamin, James, and Samuel, they first lived with their son George IV and his wife, Deborah Howell Boone, in Abingdon. Before winter they moved to the Quaker community of North Wales. George IV had presented the certificate "of his orderly and good conversation" from Cullompton, Devonshire, to the Friends' Abington meeting on "8 mo. 26, 1713."

It was at Gwynedd, near Oley, that Squire Boone and Sarah Morgan were given permission to marry on the thirtieth day of the Sixth Month in 1720. Quakers referred to the months by numbers to avoid using the pagan names such as January and February. Earlier that same year George III had been required to confess to the Gwynedd Monthly Meeting his "forwardship in giving his consent" to the marriage of his daughter Mary to someone "Contrary to the Establish'd order amongst us." This was not the last time a Boone would be asked to confess and apologize to the Friends for the behavior of his children.

Squire Boone has been described as a rather small man, with fair skin, red hair, and gray eyes. Sarah Morgan was taller than most women, with black eyes and black hair, strong and active. The marriage of Squire and Sarah is described in the Gwynedd Friends Meeting Book:

> At a solemn assembly of the said people [Quakers] . . . the said
> Squire Boone took the said Sarah Morgan by the hand (and) did in a
> solemn manner declare that he took her to be his wife, promising to
> be unto her a faithful and loving husband, until death should sepa-
> rate them, and then and there in the said assembly Sarah Morgan did
> likewise declare.

In April 1718 George III moved his family to Oley, in Berks County, where his older daughter, Sarah, and her husband, Jacob Stover, had been living for three years. The new meetinghouse in Oley was named Exeter, after the town back in Devonshire. The stone building still stands and is used as a meetinghouse. George III bought four hundred acres of fine meadowland and forest. By 1728 George III had built a mill at Exeter, and we have the impression of years of prosperity. But after a period of peaceful relations with Indians, the area was sud-denly threatened by Shawnees. George Boone wrote to the governor requesting help: "Our condition at present looks with a bad vizard, for undoubtedly the Indians will fall down upon us very suddenly, and our inhabitants are generally fled, there remains about 20 men with me to guard my mill."

Many settlers were so frightened they left their homesteads. Within days eleven Indians, painted for war and carrying weapons, arrived near Van Bibber's Township, going door to door demanding provisions and drink. A posse of twenty local men gathered to pursue the war-riors. The leader of the Indian band refused to negotiate and fired on the settlers, wounding two before fading into the forest. The settlers took refuge in a mill, possibly George Boone's. The Shawnees were on their way to join a party of Delawares in a campaign against the

"Flatfeet," as the Catawbas were sometimes called. In all they wounded five settlers in what luckily turned out to be the only ever hostile encounter between whites and Native Americans in the Philadelphia area.

BECAUSE OF their cooperation, craftsmanship, division of labor, and hard work, the Quakers were well adapted for frontier life. They were used to being frugal, self-reliant, resourceful. They raised their own sheep and flax, spun their own wool and linen, wove their own cloth. In the Philadelphia area the Quakers were in the majority and became the leaders of the colony.

The Boones were leaders of their community. Squire Boone became a trustee of the Oley Monthly Meeting, and his brother George IV and his wife, Deborah, deeded land for the Quaker burial ground. George III was a justice of the peace. Several Boones served as delegates to the quarterly and annual meetings of the Friends. The strong sense of community and brotherhood among the Quakers helped sustain them through the hardships of the frontier. They provided care and aid to the sick or struggling. At the same time they were strict about the conduct of their members, requiring violators to make a written confession of errors and acknowledgment of justice. The confessions were posted on the door of the meetinghouse.

Squire Boone was a weaver and blacksmith. He also farmed his land and ran a gristmill, and he had a substantial herd of cattle. A man of many parts, hardworking and talented, Squire was neighbor to Mennonites, Swedish Lutherans, Presbyterians, Huguenots, and Moravians as well as Quakers. Though he grew increasingly independent and liberal in his thinking, he was a man of patience and common sense. And like his father before him, he was touched with restlessness, curiosity, an urge to move on.

Among the Boones' neighbors in the area were the extensive Lincoln family. "Boones and Lincolns several times intermarried. Sarah Lincoln sister of John Lincoln who was the gr[eat] grandfather of President Lincoln, married William Boone son of George Boone and Deborah (Howell) Boone by Friends Ceremony 8th mo 27th 1761." Anne Boone, daughter of Squire's brother James, married Abraham Lincoln on July 10, 1760. Because Lincoln was not a Quaker she was condemned by the Friends Meeting. Their daughter Mary later married a James Boone. Both Boones and Lincolns are buried in the yard of the Exeter Meeting House. The Boones and Lincolns would be acquainted later also in Virginia and Kentucky.

Squire and Sarah's sixth child, Daniel, was born November 2, 1734 (October 22, Old Style). From the very beginning the family sensed that Daniel was different from the other children. Lively, apparently tireless, curious, when very young he helped out in the family trades of blacksmithing, milling, and farming. But family lore has it that from the very first Daniel liked to roam in the woods. Oley was mostly forest then, a green world of rolling hills and small streams, and from his childhood Daniel preferred to rove and study the ways of the wild. He seemed born to be an outdoorsman and hunter, the way John Keats was born to be a poet. One early biographer described the infant Daniel playing with his father's powder horn and rifle where they had been laid down after a hunt.

Daniel's closest relationship was with his mother, tall Welsh Sarah, with her black eyes and cheerful disposition. From his birth she seemed to favor Daniel of all her children, tolerating his pranks, his tendency to slip away into the woods for hours, for whole days. The bond between mother and son was intense, affectionate, inspiring. It seems she put her fondest hopes in this independent, sometimes wayward boy driven by enthusiasms for the wild and curiosity about the world beyond the farm, beyond the river. Daniel's uncle John Webb took a particular interest in the boy also, "keeping him and petting him for weeks together" at his house with his own four children.

In October of 1744 Squire Boone bought twenty-five acres of land five miles north of his home in Oley. That was where he pastured his livestock, and from the age of ten Daniel accompanied Sarah there in summer to look after the cattle and sheep. From spring until fall he lived with her in a cabin in the woods. For the rest of his life Daniel would look back on those summers as an idyllic time. He was assigned to keep an eye on the herds and help with the cows, while his mother milked and made butter and cheese. Once a week they carried the milk and milk products on foot back to the homestead. For Daniel the forest was his mother world, a place of shadows and mystery, infinite diversions and pleasure; the settlement and town were the masculine world of trade and business, meetinghouse, authority and strictness. He would always be closer to the mother world than to the father world. His deepest affinity was with the forest and the streams.

Daniel spent much of those summers exploring the nearby and not-so-nearby woods. Though he had little formal schooling, he studied the ways of animals, of deer and bear, foxes and panthers. He learned to read signs, tracks and droppings, broken twigs, bent-down grass, torn moss. As an early biographer, W. H. Bogart, phrased it, "He learned lessons of the snow and the leaves and moss, and to detect, with a quick eye, the tread of foot." From Sarah he seemed to have inherited a Quaker calm and patience, a sense of intimacy with place and weather, with all life, including Indian life and Indian ways. He delighted in solitude. It is likely that most of the milking and work with the dairy was done by his mother, since milking and butter making were considered women's work.

From the beginning, the complexities and contradictions of Daniel's character seemed evident. He loved most to spend time alone in the woods, observing and learning, tracking and trapping and killing game. Indians still lived in the neighborhood when Boone was a boy. One Indian, a close friend of George Boone, built a cabin on Boone's land, lived to an old age, and was buried close by. The local Shawnee Indians liked him because he respected their ways and admired their knowledge of the land and forest. There was almost a Franciscan humility and reverence for life in the young Boone, yet he was a hunter, a killer of the wild animals.

And though he was a Quaker, Daniel was a fighting Quaker. The stories of his youthful pranks and fights, told by Boone's son Nathan to Lyman Draper in 1851, make it clear the young Daniel was no pacifist. Once two sisters, carrying a bucket of fish guts to empty during the shad run, saw Daniel sleeping under a tree. Unable to resist the temptation, they dumped the contents of the bucket on his face. Brushing the slimy entrails out of his hair and eyes, the young Daniel jumped up and bloodied the girls' noses and sent them home howling. Within minutes the girls' mother stormed into Sarah Boone's kitchen and accused Daniel of attacking her daughters. But the peaceable Quakeress would not tolerate the tirade against her son. "If thee has not brought up thy daughters to better behavior," she said, "it is high time they were taught good manners. And if Daniel has given them a lesson, I hope for my part that it will in the end do them no harm. And I have only to add that I bid thee good day."

The young Daniel often demonstrated a tendency to wander off without much concern for the worry his absence might cause others. However much he loved his mother, and however much he later loved his wife, Rebecca, his urge to hunt and wander and explore always came first.

From the time he was a boy Boone had a flair for the dramatic. He seemed to know instinctively how to make himself noticed, remembered. As a young man he began to create for himself the role of Daniel Boone, and he spent much of his life perfecting that role. Despite his later protestation that he was "but a common man," he seemed aware from early in his youth that he was not just playing himself but a type, what Emerson would later call a Representative Man. Boone would embody in his actions and attitude the aspirations and character of a whole era.

At least once, Daniel became so distracted by his own explorations that he forgot the hours of the day, his home, the fact that he was supposed to help his mother. Before it got dark, Sarah had to round up the cattle herself and do the milking, strain the milk, and put it in the springhouse to stay cool. Calm and prayerful, she worked at churning butter from clabbered milk. But when Daniel did not come home by the next morning and still had not returned by noon, she had no choice but to walk the five miles back to town to get help.

A search party was formed and they combed over the Oley Hills all the way to the Neversink mountain range northwest of the Monocacy Valley. They found no sign of Daniel that afternoon. But starting out early the next morning they traveled farther and spotted a column of smoke. Late in the afternoon they reached the source of the smoke and found Daniel sitting on a bearskin and roasting fresh bear meat on the fire. When asked if he was lost, he said no, he had known where he was all along, on the south shoulder of the hill nine miles from the pasture. The search party accused him of scaring his mother and forcing them all to waste time looking for him. But he calmly answered he had started tracking the bear and didn't want to lose it. And besides, here was fresh meat for everybody.

Whether this story is true, or just one of the legends that grew around Boone in later life, it reveals as much about the way he was perceived and remembered as it does about his character. People later recalled that even from his boyhood there was a sense that Daniel had been singled out. The story of the search party echoes the story in Luke 2:49 of the twelve-year-old Jesus lost from Mary and Joseph. The boy is finally found in the temple conversing with the elders. When he is questioned and scolded, he explains that he has been "about his Father's business." The sense of the story is that Boone had already found his calling and his destiny. It is clear he also knew how to make a memorable impression.

For Boone there was something erotic about the woods, a play-ground, a place of sometimes dangerous pleasure. And some would later suggest that with his lifelong passion for hunting, there was a part of Boone that never quite grew up.

Boone's cunning and love of pranks are also recorded in many of the childhood anecdotes Lyman Copeland Draper and others collected later. One tale Boone himself liked to repeat in old age concerned his confinement to the house during an outbreak of smallpox. His mother would not let him or his sister Elizabeth outdoors to play. Sick of the imprisonment, young Daniel and Elizabeth decided to catch the small-pox themselves and get it over with so they could go out to play as usual. That night they slipped away to a neighbor's house and crawled into bed with friends who were infected with smallpox, then returned home before daybreak.

When a few days later the red marks began to appear on him, Sarah grew suspicious. "Now, Daniel," she said to her son, "I want thee to tell thy mother the whole truth." Daniel readily confessed the initiative he had taken. "Thee naughty little gorrel," she cried, "why did thee not tell me before, so I could have had thee better prepared." Sarah called him an Old English word for knave but was too affectionate to punish him. It was the kind of story Boone as an old man liked to recall of his beloved mother.

Squire Boone, however, was not so indulgent with his sons. When he punished them he would swing the strap until they begged for forgiveness. Then he would quit whipping and talk with them calmly. But Daniel was more stubborn than his brothers and endured the punishment in silence. "Canst thou not beg?" the frustrated fa-ther would ask. But Daniel would never answer, leaving Squire to make up his own mind when the punishment was sufficient. Even as a boy Boone showed the stoicism and self-control he was later renowned for.

While he roved the woods and tended his father's cattle, Daniel cut and carved a stick which he used to kill animals — rabbits and squirrels, possums and wild turkeys. Before he owned a gun Boone was already a hunter, with the patience, sharp eye, and deadly aim of the successful hunter who learned something new every day as he went into the woods again. He was proud of his skill at cleaning and dressing a turkey. Often he cooked outdoors for himself and Sarah, hanging the bird on a stick over the flames, turning it to bake on all sides. With a piece of curved bark he caught the drippings, which he used to baste the turkey. When his mother asked how he had learned to do that, he said merely that an Indian had told him how it was done.

When Daniel was almost thirteen he was given his first firearm, a "short rifle gun" with which he roamed the nearby Flying Hills, the Oley Hills, and the Neversink Mountains. The Flying Hills were named for the flocks of turkeys that lived there. The rifle was probably made by Squire Boone, who, besides keeping six looms busy with hired hands, farming, and running his blacksmith shop and mill, was also a gunsmith. His skill at making and repairing guns was passed down to his fourth son. It would be an essential, lifesaving skill in later years, in the wilderness beyond the mountains.

As a blacksmith Squire Boone had taken an apprentice named Henry Miller, two or three years older than Daniel. Henry and Daniel soon got into a fistfight, and then, as often happens with those who begin by fighting, they became lifelong friends. Henry taught Daniel blacksmithing and gunsmithing, as he learned the skills himself. Together they hunted and fished and played pranks on neighbors and on other members of the Boone family. Once they overloaded a rifle that was to be lent to a neighbor named Wilcoxen. Wilcoxen, who knew little about guns, was to pick up the already loaded rifle in the morning for a deer hunt. During the night the boys took out the lead ball, added six times the usual amount of powder, and replaced the bullet.

As soon as the neighbor took the rifle away, the boys realized what they had done. A seriously overloaded rifle might well explode, injuring Wilcoxen, perhaps even killing him. Sick with guilt and dread, they listened as he stalked off into the woods. Later they heard a report like the blast of a cannon and, running toward the sound of the blast, were relieved to see Wilcoxen stumbling out of the woods, his face bruised and bloody from a cut on his forehead. He said the recoil of the gun had thrown him to the ground.

When he heard the story, Squire Boone answered that the load had been so light he could have rested the gun on his nose without hurting it. Daniel and Henry asked Wilcoxen if he had killed the deer, but the poor man was so surprised by the force of the blast he hadn't noticed his target. But Wilcoxen recovered his dry wit and commented that he thought "it was a pretty *dear* shot." The boys ran into the woods and found the deer and brought it to the neighbor, who likely after that learned to load his gun for himself.

BECAUSE OF the family's strict Quaker principles, the Boone children were not allowed to attend parties or dances. But Daniel and Henry heard of a frolic to be held in a distant town, and giving each other courage, or daring themselves, they decided to borrow Squire Boone's horse in the night and ride away to the dance. After an evening of celebration, perhaps after sampling some of the local hard cider, they decided to jump the horse carrying both of them over one of Squire's cows sleeping in the pasture. The cow awakened and started to rise, rear first, just as the horse began its leap. Daniel and Henry slammed to the ground shaken but unhurt, but the horse broke its neck and died. The boys returned the bridle and saddle to the barn and crept back into the house as if nothing had happened. Squire never solved the mystery of how a healthy horse could let itself out of the barn and break its neck in an open pasture.

One of the pranks credited to Boone and Henry Miller was taking apart piece by piece the wagons of neighbors who had scolded

them and placing the wagonwheels on the ridgepoles of the owners'
barns. But these may have been Halloween tricks more than acts of
revenge.

Daniel began to acquire a reputation for prowess, cunning, and will-
power. From an early age he could walk miles without getting tired and
swim any river or pond. He could outrun other boys and he always
seemed to win fights and wrestling matches. With bow and arrow he
always seemed to win shooting matches, and with a rifle he was without peer. If he and his friends played "Hunt the Indian," he always
found the Indian. If it was his turn to be the Indian, he disappeared
and could not be found. Once he and Henry and other boys were carrying their rifles in the woods and surprised a panther sunning on the
riverbank. It screamed and started to charge. The other boys ran, but
Daniel stood his ground, leveling his sights at the bounding cat. Just
as the creature was about to leap at him, he fired and the cat fell dead
at his feet.

THERE HAS been much debate about Boone's education. Late in
life he told his children he had never had one day of schooling. A
nephew later told a story of young Daniel attending a school taught
by an Irishman who was both fond of the bottle and handy with the
cane. The teacher frequently repaired to the woods for a sip from his
hidden jug. One day while squirrel hunting Daniel found the bottle
and laced the liquor with an herbal emetic. Later, as he was wracked
by violent heaves and spasms, the teacher noticed Daniel giggling
and realized he was the culprit. Attempting to whip the boy, the sick
Irishman got knocked to the floor by the independent youth. Sarah
Boone rebuked her son for violence but didn't force him to return to
school.

Whatever the truth about his schooling, the fact is that Daniel
Boone could read and write. As a militia officer, storekeeper, land
agent, surveyor, magistrate, and legislator he wrote thousands of letters

and reports, many of them still in existence. And he enjoyed reading, especially history books, the Bible, and later *Gulliver's Travels*. There is reason to believe he knew *Robinson Crusoe* quite well. But his spelling was erratic, even imaginative. The orthography of his many notes and letters, bills and survey accounts, is part of the legend. Lyman Draper reports that Boone was actually taught to read and write by his brother Samuel's wife, Sarah Day. Draper offered his own description of Boone's writing: "He could at first do little more than write his own name in an uncouth and mechanical way. To these humble beginnings, he added something as he grew up, by his own practical application ... His compositions bear the marks of a strong common sense, yet, as might be expected, exhibiting defects in orthography, grammar and style, by no means infrequent."

Draper applies strict, Victorian standards to Boone's handwriting and spelling. Another story relating to Boone's education, or rather lack thereof, concerns his bachelor uncle John who kept a subscription school nearby and was liberal in applying the rod. Daniel refused to attend, and Sarah took his side, critical of excessive caning. John complained to his brother Squire.

"It's all right, John," Daniel's father answered. "Let the girls do the spelling and Dan will do the shooting, and between you and me that is what we most need." Whether the story is true or not, it implies a very common course of events, as educated immigrants to America found little opportunity or time for education for their children. The second generation of the immigrants often had less education than the first. "They took the powder horn and left the ink horn at home," the biographer W. H. Bogart later wrote. From infancy Daniel had been exposed to daily readings from the Bible, and it is likely its words made a lasting impression on him "in the mighty solitudes of his after years."

There were few schools in the area of Oley at the time. But the fact is all the other Boone sons received a respectable education. As far as we know only Daniel avoided school and the rules of grammar and spelling. It would seem his parents early on recognized his skills as a hunter and woodsman who provided the family with venison and turkey, squirrels and rabbits, as well as hides and furs. It was practical to let him do what he did better than anyone else.

Later in his life, in a moment of great danger, Boone would write sentences such as, "Your company is desired greatly, for the people are very uneasy, but are willing to stay and venture their lives with you, and now is the time to flusterate their [the Indians'] intentions, and keep the country whilst we are in it." This letter, written to Richard Henderson on April 1, 1775, as Boone and his men were hacking out Boone's Trace after being attacked by Indians, shows he had some command of language, as well as a flair for making up words and spelling. We don't know, of course, how much help he had with the letter from his son-in-law Will Hays.

However poor or creative Boone's spelling was, he did know how to spell his name, always with an *e* at the end, proving that the famed inscriptions such as "D. Boon Cilled a bar on tree in the year 1760" were almost certainly made by someone else.

Young Daniel's greatest teachers were the woods themselves and the Indians he watched and questioned and imitated. We talk often of the impact of the white culture on the Native Americans, but the influence of the Indian culture on the white was just as significant. As John Mack Faragher has pointed out, in Europe hunting was the preserve of the nobility. Most of those who came to America learned to hunt from Indian ways. Not only did the settlers and hunters learn much about hunting and trapping and survival from the Indians, they also learned the use of herbs and roots and berries, medicines, the lay of the land and courses of rivers to the west.

The Boone family, like William Penn himself, had always been known to be friendly to the Indians. George III had organized a rescue of two Indian girls who had been kidnapped. Indians passing through the neighborhood were often invited to eat and drink and stay the night at the Boone home. In 1736 a chief called Sassoonan, "King of the Schuylkill Delawares," stayed at the Boone homestead with a party of twenty-five.

Relations between Indians and whites in Pennsylvania were more peaceful than in the other colonies. In the woods along the Schuylkill above Philadelphia, white hunters who lived like Indians were seen frequently along the trails and beside the streams. Indians of many different tribes mingled in the hills and villages north of Oley, Tuscaroras and Tutelas, Conoys and Nanticokes, Shawnees and Susquehannocks and Delawares. One nearby Indian village, called Manangy's Town, was later renamed Reading.

Besides the minor outbreak of fighting in 1728, there were no Indian raids on the southeastern Pennsylvania frontier in the eighteenth century. It was a time when the Indians were learning from the Europeans to use firearms, wear woven cloth, build log cabins, use metal tools, and drink whiskey. And from the Natives the white hunters learned the ways of the American woods, the best techniques for hunting deer and bear and trapping beavers, mink, and otter. From the Indians the hunters learned to prepare bear bacon and jerk from venison. They learned to cure deer hides and buffalo hides and bearskins. And they learned the beauty and value of furs, the glistening pelts of beavers that populated almost every stream in the forest. The pelts of mink and otter, fox and muskrat, raccoon and pine marten, were also useful and beautiful, warm and silky to the touch. Most luxuriant of all was the otter, its fur deep and dark and sparkling, soft as a whisper to the fingertips, shining with mystery. In the Old World fur was reserved for royalty. In the North American forests fur was there for anyone with the skill to take it.

The hide of the deer was used mostly for clothing. Scraped and tanned, softened and smoothed, buckskin was common as khaki is now. Deer hides were such a familiar item of frontier trade that the Spanish dollar, worth about one hide, came to be called a buck. Buckskin served many purposes on the frontier, used for clothes, strings, and pouches. Prepared right, it was soft and pliable. However, when wet, buckskin tended to become very heavy, and it shrank as it dried out.

The American long rifle, developed by German gunsmiths in Pennsylvania, was the weapon of choice for hunters of both races. It was light and sturdy and could be accurate at up to two hundred yards in the hands of a skilled marksman. But both white and Indian hunters used other firearms as well — British muskets, Dutch shotguns, pistols. A man's rifle was his most important companion in the forest. The saying was he should select a rifle as carefully as a wife.

As they interacted more and more with the whites, Indians changed their customs and dress. With the traditional buckskin leggings and breech clout, the Indians often wore the long linen hunting shirts donned by the white woodsmen. The log cabin and stockade were almost impossible to build without metal tools. For centuries the Indians had lived in shelters made of poles and bark, hides and brush. But once the Indians had metal axes and saws, adzes and augers, they too made log dwellings, similar to those the whites built. It is said that Indians preferred to notch their logs on the underside, while whites notched theirs on the top.

It has long been observed that white and Indian communities on the frontier mirrored each other in many ways. From the Indians the whites learned herbal medicines, hunting techniques, crops fitted to the local climate and soil, preparation of hides and furs, geography of the regions farther west. From the whites the Indians acquired firearms, metal tools, whiskey, cloth, small grains, and a number of diseases that killed more Natives than all the wars combined.

It was in this world of mingling Indian and European cultures that Daniel Boone's character and aspirations were formed. He became an expert marksman, tracker, and trapper. He never forgot a trail or place he'd seen. But at the same time he was part of a large close family, loyal and affectionate, good natured and often funny.

He loved to enjoy himself and be with friends before vanishing into the woods again, emerging days later with bear meat, a deer, pelts to trade. These two sides to his character seemed to be there from the first. From childhood he seemed to inhabit a "middle ground" between white and Indian cultures. And he served at times as a kind of double agent, his loyalties complex and divided between his several worlds and kinships.

ALONG TEN THOUSAND SLOPES sap rose in maples, and arbutus bloomed in late February and shad bushes in March and April. On stream banks, buffalo grazed, along with elk and deer. Bears slept through the winter in their dens, bowels sealed with a fecal plug, then crawled out in late winter, awakened by thunder, to eat laurel leaves, which opened them again, and foxes barked in the hills. Beavers, muskrats, mink, and otters busied themselves along creeks, their fur luxuriant.

Blending into this wilderness, Indians lived in villages of bark and logs, skins on poles, brush and thatch; they caught fish in wicker traps, killed game with bows and arrows, fought wars with spears and stone hatchets, prayed to the mountains and the spirits of bears and stars. Their lives were complex and evolving.

By the early 1700s Indians in eastern North America had been dealing with English-speaking settlers for about a century. Welcoming the invaders at first, the Indians shared their knowledge. What the Europeans saw as virgin land was often "widowed land" Indians had abandoned. Because Indians tended to move where hunting was most rewarding, they did not seem to "own" land or "improve" land in ways the whites recognized. Nor did they raise livestock. Colonists were surprised that Indians showed so little interest in accumulating wealth.

The two cultures generally misunderstood each other. Europeans often assumed Indians had no religion because they saw no recognizable ritual or symbols of worship. The Indians had no word for "animal" or "beast" as distinct from human. To them, all living things had spirits or souls. Not only did the animals have spirits, but the guardian spirits of people usually appeared as animals. Owning land in the

Timucua Indian Hunters Observed in Florida Wearing Deer Costumes. Theodor de Bry. Engraving 1590. Based on a painting by Jacques Le Moyne. Reprint, Paris, 1927. The classic images by the Flemish engraver de Bry (1528–98) of Indians in Virginia, Florida, and South America were made from rough sketches by Jacques Le Moyne (1533–83). (Courtesy Cornell University Library.)

white way made no more sense than "owning" a tract of air or sunlight. Indians were rich by "desiring little," William Cronon writes.

Probably the greatest initial difference between Indian and white land use was the keeping of livestock. The English plowed their fields, and plowing changed the ecology. In a few short years the landscape looked drastically different. The settlers' ranging livestock destroyed crops and drove away the game. White settlers meant to stay in one place, exhausted the land by growing mostly corn. The English introduced many pests, including rats and dandelions, and diseases they brought helped thin out the Native populations. In 1709 an English colonist reckoned that in the Carolinas six out of seven Indians had died of disease in the previous fifty years.

Cornstalk, Chief of the Shawnees in the Scioto Valley of Ohio. Artist unknown. Engraving. *American Legion* magazine, February 1975. Cornstalk was the outstanding political leader and diplomat of the Ohio Shawnees during the period of Lord Dunmore's War in 1774. (Courtesy *American Legion* magazine.)

The English passion for accumulating wealth struck the Indians as insanity. For this and other reasons Indian holy men began to describe whites as created for a different purpose. Both Indians and whites suspected each other of witchcraft. Indians were thought to worship the devil, and Indians in turn were convinced the English were in league with evil spirits. All too soon, the Indians concluded the invaders were stupid, and laughed.

But whites who got to know Indians found them more honest and tolerant than most members of their own race. It was said by some that Indians were more "Christian" than the English, showing greater charity toward the land and its inhabitants.

As the Indians were pushed back from their traditional lands, prophets rose among them urging the nations to resist the white encroachments, and teaching a militant pan-Indianism. Indian nations were divided between those who sought accommodation with the whites and those who preached Nativism and urged a return to ancient beliefs and rituals. One difficulty of organizing Indian resistance was that chiefs were not rulers in the European sense. Decisions were made by consensus, and often there was a war chief, a peace chief, and a woman who served as leader of the women.

And yet the story of the meeting of whites and Indians was not always one of misunderstanding and tragedy. In the French-claimed lands of the Middle Ground, as the Ohio and Illinois country was called, whites and Indians lived in close proximity through much of the eighteenth century, learning from each other, trading, intermarrying. But the Americans who moved into the Middle Ground had other ambitions, other visions.

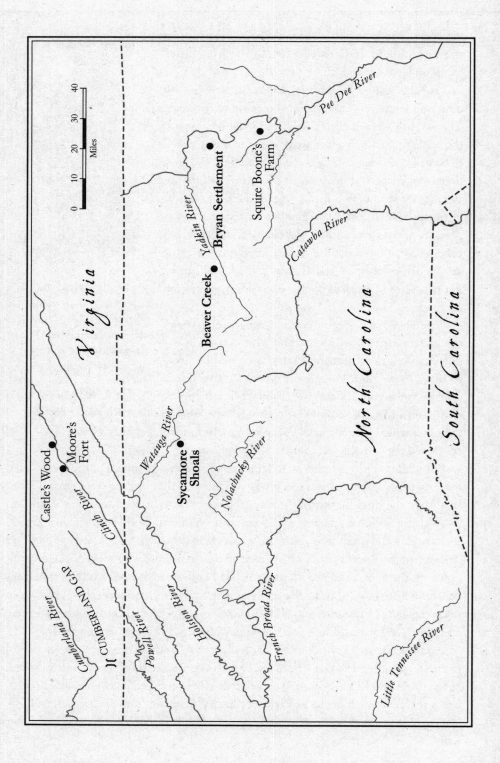

Pee Dee River

40
30
20
10
Miles
0

Virginia

Yadkin River

Bryan Settlement

Squire Boone's Farm

Beaver Creek

Catawba River

North Carolina

South Carolina

Castle's Wood

Moore's Fort

Clinch River

Watauga River

Sycamore Shoals

Nolachucky River

Cumberland River

CUMBERLAND GAP

Powell River

Holston River

French Broad River

Little Tennessee River

CHAPTER TWO

The Hills beyond the Yadkin

1751 – 1755 ↜

There has been much speculation about why Squire and Sarah Boone and their family left the peaceful countryside of Oley, Pennsylvania, for the wilder Shenandoah Valley of Virginia, and then the even wilder Yadkin Valley of North Carolina. Commentators have described the Boones as a restless family, as "fiddle-footed," with the "itching foot." Certainly it was an age of restlessness, when those who had made the great migration from their ancient roots in Britain or the Continent felt little hesitation in picking up again and moving on. The horizon called and curiosity prodded them to go, and then go again.

Most biographers and students of Daniel Boone have pointed out that Squire grew less and less in harmony with the community of Friends at the Exeter Meeting. As early as 1742, when Daniel was only eight, and Sarah, the oldest of his siblings, married a neighbor named John Wilcoxson, who was not a Quaker, both parents were rebuked and confessed their fault. Ironically, the 1730s and 1740s were a time of religious revival in the American colonies, when the movement called the Great Awakening was sweeping over the land. Preachers such as Jonathan Edwards and George Whitefield conducted services in New England where worshipers swooned, had fits, or cringed in terror of hellfire. But it was also a time when parents and churches seemed to be losing control over the young. More and more young women had children out of wedlock. There is a tradition in American humor and folklore that religious revivals also inspire a surge in illegitimate births, as religious fervor seems to stir sexual fever. Such revivals, it was said, "led to more souls being made than saved." After the great revival at Cane Ridge in Kentucky in 1801, it was reported, "Becca Bell 'is with child to one Brown'; Kate Cummins also 'got careless' and 'had a bastard'; Patty McGuire 'has been whoring.'" The Reverend Charles Woodmason, who traveled into the Carolina backcountry at this time, noted that "94 percent of the brides whom he married in the past year were pregnant on their wedding day."

In 1747, the year Daniel was given his first rifle, his older brother Israel also married outside the Quaker community. Again a committee was appointed "to speak with Squire Boone about his son's disorderly marriage." But this time Squire refused to submit to public humiliation and confess his fault. The investigating committee reported "that he could not see that he had transgressed, and therefore was not willing to condemn it." It is possible that the spirit of independence in the new land had made him more resistant to the strictures of the Friends. Perhaps he had begun to drift away from the faith itself.

More likely Squire had learned, as many parents do, then and now, how hard it is to direct the affections of their offspring. And because he also liked the mates chosen by his children, Squire may have felt the unfairness of the Friends' rebuke. His father, George III, had endured the humiliation of public confession. The minutes of the meeting for 1747 show that Squire not only refused to confess his fault but flung arguments back at the Friends, "giving Room to a reflecting Spirit even against his friends." He later sent a heated letter to the committee and in March of 1748 he was expelled from the Exeter Meeting until he would confess his faults and show "his coming to a Godly Sorrow in himself." While Sarah and the children continued to attend the meeting, Squire after that kept the Sabbath by staying at home.

There is reason to believe, based on symbols carved on his tombstone in North Carolina, that Squire, like his son Daniel later, had been initiated into the society of Freemasons. Leaders such as Benjamin Franklin were known to be enthusiastic Masons. Formed in England early in the eighteenth century, the secret society was devoted to fellowship, ceremony, charity, and service to the community. Joining the Freemasons could have made Squire feel even more independent of the Quaker Meeting.

Freemasonry offered a fresh way of looking at society and mankind—liberal, rational, committed to a useful, moral life, not based on revelation, class, monarchy. Jews and even African Americans and Native Americans might be initiated into lodges. It seems likely the Boones' affiliation with Masonry strengthened their sense of belonging to the fraternity of all men, whether white or Indian, American or British, and helps explain Daniel's conduct later in the complex, dangerous time of the American Revolution.

It is likely that his father's resistance and excommunication from the Quaker Meeting made a deep impression on Daniel. Years later he supposedly told his young friend Peter Houston that he had never known anything good to come from religious disputes. All his life Boone avoided religious organizations and sectarian arguments. Though he showed a reverent spirit, treated others with respect and kindness, demonstrated an inner calm, and developed the habit of daily Bible reading, he never belonged to any church nor ever confessed to any established creed.

Like many gifted children, Daniel seems to have inherited the best of both his parents. From his father he appears to have received a boldness and independence, great physical strength and courage, tenacity and leadership, and skill with working metal. Daniel was driven by the same restlessness and curiosity that Squire demonstrated. Both father and son had a way with tools and an ability to lead others. From his mother Daniel may have taken his noted calm and peacefulness, his resistance to panic and anger, his affection for family, forest and countryside, his goodwill and optimism, a trust in others that was sometimes misplaced, and a love of music.

BESIDES HIS disaffection with the Exeter Friends, Squire would have had other reasons to think of leaving Pennsylvania. His sister Sarah Stover and her husband, Jacob, had moved to the south fork of the Shenandoah River in Virginia and sent back letters praising the land and climate of that region. Land there could be gotten very cheaply, and farther south, in the hills of North Carolina, acres could be had for even less. It was the dream of free or cheap land that drove most of the great migrations in eighteenth- and nineteenth-century North America. Religious freedom and political freedom were also important, as was escape from debt and indenture. Servants who had finished their terms of indenture on the eastern seaboard usually headed west and south to the cheaper land of the frontier. Those who had served in prison for debt and other causes sought a new start in the recent settlements and land just vacated by Indians. Already a resentment was beginning to build between the great landowning class of the tidewater and lowlands and the poor who sought their own acres in the hill country. Acquiring new land was a thrilling prospect to those whose ancestors had lived under feudal rule for a thousand years, under an order of aristocracy and gentry, with no hope for advancement.

Most of the sunny uplands and fertile meadows of the South were to be had for just getting there with oxen and horses, a few tools and livestock, and a small down payment. All a man needed was a wife, a gun, and two hands to work. Perhaps a dynasty, a great estate, an empire, waited to be wrought into being. Perhaps even fame could be won in a developing country where the failures of the past could be forgotten and the potential, the future, was opening its doors. And underneath that urge to move west was the ancient myth, common to most European cultures, of an earthly paradise, an Eden, a place of the blessed, somewhere over the ocean and over the mountains, where a golden future whispered. The call of the West was in the blood and bred in the bone of those who began settling the foothills of the Alleghenies and dreamed of crossing the Alleghenies to find a promised land, a new Canaan in the interior.

Around 1750 Squire Boone moved his whole family away from Oley to the south and west, along the path of the great migrations of that time. Besides Daniel there were seven other unmarried children, ranging from Elizabeth, eighteen, to Hannah, who was only four. With them were Sarah and her husband, John Wilcoxson, and Israel and Samuel and their wives. Henry Miller, the apprentice and Daniel's best friend, joined the party, as did one of Squire's nephews.

With the belongings they chose to take — which would have included tools for a blacksmith and gunsmith, weaver and farmer — packed in heavy covered wagons pulled by oxen, they would have gone west on the Allegheny Trail to Harris's Ferry across the Susquehanna, then turned south, following the line of the Appalachian Mountains by what was called either the Virginia Road or the Great Wagon Road. (Interstate 81 now roughly follows this same route.) The road was already so well traveled that some farmers along the way had set up "stations" to sell grain for livestock, with pens for horses and cattle, hogs and sheep, and rough accommodations and supplies for the travelers. Farmers at river crossings made extra money by poling travelers across on ferries. Already stories of bandits and robbers, con men and bushwhackers, were common. It was much safer to travel in a large group. According to a report made to the Board of Trade in London in 1751, it was 435 miles from Philadelphia to the Yadkin Valley.

After crossing the Potomac at Williamsport, Maryland, the route followed the Shenandoah River into the Great Valley of Virginia. There is some disagreement about where the family stopped first in Virginia. Descendants later told Lyman Draper that the entourage settled at Linnville Creek just north of Harrisonburg for at least one and perhaps two years. "William L. Boone told me they tarried two years on Linville Creek in Virginia, and then in 1752 (perhaps summer or early fall) they moved to the Yadkin River valley," Nathan Boone told Draper. It is thought the family arrived in Virginia in time to make a crop in the summer of 1750 and again in 1751 before they continued on to North Carolina. Linville Creek, in Rockingham County, was near the later home of Squire's old friend John Lincoln. In 1779 Daniel would lead John's son, Abraham, grandfather of the president, over the Cumberland Gap into Kentucky.

More important for sixteen-year-old Daniel, the stop in Virginia gave him the opportunity for his first long hunt, inspired by Indian patterns and habits, an extended foray into the wilderness in quest of fur and game and adventure. At some point after the corn was laid by, Daniel and his friend Henry Miller set out on an expedition that took them hundreds of miles into the wilderness. They first explored the mountains near the Shenandoah all the way to Great Lick, later Roanoke, then dropped south through Roanoke Gap and the chain of the Blue Ridge into the Piedmont backcountry of North Carolina, where the game and furs were still more plentiful.

On this trip Daniel first saw the Yadkin Valley, with its wide rich bottomlands and forests of sycamores, poplars, oak, and hickory. Between its wooded banks, hung with wild grape and peavines, the river curved out of the hills, puckered and scarred by rocks and sunken logs. The pools were filled with catfish, bass, and bream in the lower, slower stretches, and flashed with trout in the upper tributaries. Mink and muskrat, otter and marten, had worn slides in the banks.

William Byrd had explored the region twenty some years before and described it in *A History of the Dividing Line* in 1728. "The Soil is exceedingly rich on both sides of the Yadkin, abounding in rank Grass and prodigiously large Trees; and for plenty of Fish, Fowl and Venison, is inferior to No Part of the Northern Continent. There the Traders commonly lie Still for some days to recruit their Horses' Flesh as well as to recover their own Spirits." Twenty years before Byrd, John Lawson, the surveyor-general of North Carolina, had visited the Yadkin Valley, called then the Sapona or Sakona, and described the beauties of the region, mentioning the soil was as rich as any informed person had seen in the Western world.

Some historians think the name Yadkin comes from the family name of Atkins. But others suggest it has an Indian source. The Ca-

tawbas apparently called the river Sakona or Sapona, the name of a
related Indian nation, but which may also have meant elk. Canebrakes
covered long stretches in the flats along the Yadkin, stalks crowded together twelve or fifteen feet high. The American bamboo, *Arundinaria
gigantea*, filled much of the Piedmont and Trans-Appalachian valleys.
Deer and elk, bears and panthers, wolves and wildcats, hid in the tall
shimmering reeds. The buffalo were mostly gone, though a few could
be spotted from time to time. Their trails could still be seen winding
into the hills along the streams into the Cherokee country, the high
hunting ranges that seemed to float in blue mystery on the horizon.

Evidence of hunting parties of Catawbas could be seen in the valleys, but no villages were in sight. Daniel and Henry shot all the game
they wanted and collected as many hides and furs as they could carry.
Pound for pound, beaver skins and mink and otter were worth the
most. A packhorse could carry at least two hundred pounds. It was
on this first long hunt into the southern wilderness that Daniel saw
where his destiny lay. He was at the age when a young man begins to
know the shape and direction of his inclination and future, begins to
see who he is. If he had doubts before about his calling, the hills and
streams of the colony of Carolina (named in 1629 for King Charles I)
probably reassured him.

When Daniel and Henry returned to Virginia (named in the sixteenth century for Elizabeth, the "Virgin Queen") in late fall, they
didn't stay for long with the family at Linnville Creek but continued
back, all the way they had come the previous spring, to Philadelphia,
to sell their furs and deer hides. Years later a grandson of Henry
Miller said that his grandfather and Boone, after a year of hunting
and trapping, carried their furs to Philadelphia and sold them for
thirteen hundred dollars and then went on "a general jamboree or
frolick" until the profits of their hunt were spent. Afterward Miller
was disgusted with himself and vowed to never again waste the earn-
ings of his effort. He told his descendants that "Boone was very profligate," happy to blow whatever he made. It appears that from the

beginning Boone had little interest in accumulating wealth. Young Henry Miller settled down in Augusta County, Virginia, becoming a prosperous blacksmith. He and Daniel remained friends, however, and when Boone served in the Virginia legislature many years later he took his wife and young son Nathan with him on a visit to Miller's considerable estate. The two kept in touch from time to time for the rest of their lives.

While the family stayed in Virginia and Daniel hauled his furs to Philadelphia, Squire Boone traveled on to North Carolina himself and put in a claim for a square mile of land, 640 acres, on Grants Creek, near the Yadkin. The cost was only three shillings, but the claimant had to pay a quitrent to the Earl of Granville, who owned much of the western section of the colony. Records show that Squire served as a chain man for a survey in Anson County on October 4, 1750. Through the quitrent system, charging an annual fee to settlers who had bought parcels of land, the proprietors and administrators of the colonies were able to continue something of the European feudal system in the New World. Settlers throughout the colonies would chafe under the burden of quitrents, and the system of perpetual payments would become an issue in the American Revolution, a quarter of a century in the future.

The Boones arrived on the Yadkin in the fall of 1751. The Yadkin and its feeder creeks moved fast enough to turn gristmills and saw mills. The bottomlands and meadows offered unsurpassed soil for farming, and the higher ground was ideal for grazing. Rumor has suggested that the family lived in a cave by the river, still known as one of many "Boone's Caves," that first winter. Whether they lived temporarily in a cave or not, it is certain that they soon built a cabin on their land. By 1753 it seems Squire Boone had bought more adjoining land. His holdings eventually became substantial enough for him to give generous sections to some of his married children. The extended family of Boones formed a whole settlement by themselves, and the value of their property rose as other families streamed into the beautiful valley and surveyed and cleared acreage.

It is hard for modern readers to visualize the amount of labor necessary to settle a farm on the frontier in the eighteenth century. Once the first rough shelter was made on the claimed land, the work had hardly begun. Pens and huts for livestock had to be built of poles or pickets, split rails, and brush, and then the necessary kitchen garden cleared and fenced to keep out the deer, livestock, raccoons, and ranging hogs. Just to clear a garden patch required days of chopping and sawing, digging out stumps and grubbing up roots. Luckily the North Carolina Yadkin soil was not as rocky as the Pennsylvania fields.

The soil along the river and tributary creeks of the Yadkin Valley was a rainbow of colors and textures. Near the streams, the ground, once cleared of roots and exposed to the sun, was a black alluvial powder, a mixture of silt and sand and rotted vegetation perfect for growing watermelons and corn, crops favored by loose, damp soil. In a rainy season streams sometimes overflowed and left standing pools in the hot sun that scalded the roots of species such as beans.

Farther from the river, on gently rising land that rarely flooded, the topsoil was rich brown, the color of dark roast coffee. Stiffer than the loam along the river, the dirt was still loose when plowed, with glittering bits of quartz and mica among its crumbs and sugary lumps. Among the brown cortex of soil were patches of silver clay drawn up by the plow, and yellow splotches of oxide-rich subsoil exposed by cultivation or erosion, as well as beds and bands of red clay.

And farther back on hillsides the ground was mostly red clay, in shades ranging from light orange to terra-cotta to blood brightness and maroon. But the tilted ground washed quicker, grooved by runoff like gathered cloth. The upland fields washed out and had to be replaced in three or four years by cleared new ground. The higher land was better for pasture than for crops. Worn-out acres good for nothing else were used as sites for churches and schools, hence the term *old field schools.* Higher ground out of reach of floods was chosen for the first graveyards.

John Lawson, who had explored the Carolina foothills in 1700, wrote about the region, "The Land was very good and free from Grubs and Underwood. A man near Sapona [the Yadkin] may more easily clear ten Acres of Ground than in some places he can one . . . That day we passed through a delicious Country (none that I ever saw exceeds it.) We saw fine bladed grass six feet high, along the Banks of these pleasant Rivulets."

The greatest labor was clearing the fields for corn and other crops. The bottomlands along the Yadkin were covered with giant sycamores and tulip poplars, eight, ten, or sometimes fourteen feet in diameter. Wetter ground was called maple swamp, buried beneath huge maple trees and choking vines and standing pools in the rainy season. The only practical solution was to girdle the big trees, hacking rings around the trunks, cutting off the lifeblood of sap in the bark from root to branch tips. Such a deadened tree, sometimes called a belted tree, could not put out leaves to shade the soil beneath. After the first year the twigs and branches would begin to rot and fall in wind and storms. Over the following years the bigger limbs would fall and the deadened field would look like a harbor of weathered, crooked masts. Great shields of bark peeled off the trunks and dropped to the ground, making the field, when covered with rotting watermelons in exposed red clay, look like a Homeric battlefield.

But meanwhile the soil beneath the dead trees was being tilled with hoe and bull-tongue plow pulled by oxen, loosened by heavy grubbing hoes that chopped through roots. Corn could be grown in these rough acres where smaller grains such as rye and wheat could not. Corn grew faster in the powerful soil than the weeds around it, reaching up into the hot southern sun that came through the deadened canopy. Corn, which had been introduced to Europe, was native to this soil and had been grown here by Indians for thousands of years.

Corn was the essential, universal crop for the settlers on the Yadkin. It could be eaten as roasting ears in the milk, when first ripe, or it could be gritted on a grater into bread when a little more mature. When hardened in the fall, corn could be ground into grits or meal and made into mush, pudding, or bread. Corn could be fed to horses, cattle, hogs. The sweet fodder was stripped from the lower stalks in late summer and kept as winter feed for the horses. The tops of the stalks were cut just above the ears and piled in stacks for winter feed for cattle. Corn-shuck-filled ticks were used for mattresses. Corncobs were used for starting fires in the morning, for tobacco pipes, and for a purpose later served by toilet paper.

Without a gristmill nearby, corn had to be crushed by a heavy wooden pestle on a hollowed stump, called a hominy block, as Indians did. But every settlement soon had at least one mill turned by a stream, where carved stones with grooves ground the grains into meal. Skilled masons cut the millstones, carving the grooves precisely with little picks. As millstones got worn, the grooves had to be sharpened again with the little picks.

Of course the favorite use for corn for many was to dampen the grains and let them sprout. The sprouted kernels were then ground up with sprouted barley to make malt. Mixed with water and sugar, the malt was allowed to ferment into a strong beer. When the beer mash was heated, the alcohol boiled off as steam and could be caught in a still and cooled as drops of whiskey. Boiled again, the whiskey was refined into doublings, or potent moonshine. Wherever the settlers went, they had mills and deadened fields and stills. And once they had apple trees they made cider and hard cider and applejack.

THE HARSH conditions and hard work, and relative freedom from oversight by officials and gentry, encouraged a rough, reckless culture on the frontier. Travelers such as the Reverend Charles Woodmason were astonished by the behavior of both men and women in the region. Woodmason noted that the women "expose themselves often quite naked without ceremony — rubbing themselves and their hair with bears' oil and tying it up behind in a bunch like the Indians — being hardly one degree removed from them." Woodmason was only one of many who noticed how white and Indian cultures came to resemble each other in the backcountry.

By 1752 surveyors in the area were using Squire Boone's land as a reference for their callings. And it seems that by the next year Squire had acquired even more acres of land. In the new location there were no Quaker meetinghouses for Sarah to attend with her children. Sometimes Squire organized nondenominational services, and he rose to be an important figure in the developing region, a magistrate and justice of the peace. The closest seat of government and commerce was Salisbury, about twenty miles away. Rowan County's *Minutes, Court of Pleas and Quarter Sessions* for 1755 to 1767 show that Squire served on local juries. Squire helped lay out the town of Salisbury and may have named a street Freemason Street in honor of his affiliation with the order, though there was no official lodge in Rowan County at that time.

FROM THE time he was a boy, Daniel had hated the spirit-numbing work of farming. "He never took any delight in farming or stock raising," Daniel's nephew Daniel Bryan said many years later, "but followed hunting untill he grew to Manhood." Like other farm boys, he longed for rainy days when the fields were too wet to hoe or plow or even harvest. Instead of staying in the house when it rained, as others did, he took his gun and vanished into the dripping forest.

There is a good deal of testimony that Boone never minded falling weather. In fact he seemed to enjoy rain, for damp woods were good for hunting, and he rarely stopped a hunt because of falling snow. He may have been one of those who feel the woods are more alive in the rain, the air more intimate, immediate with sounds and smells, with moisture and falling drops. Every sound, every leaf, is vivid. In wet woods you can step without making a sound. In rain he was alone with the trees and brush, the cane and mosses and the animals and birds that ventured out, feeling safe in the dampness. His hearing was more acute, and his eyesight sharper, without sun dapples and shadows, as the trees dripped and the air ticked and tapped and hummed.

On the Yadkin Daniel began to make a substantial profit with his gun and traps. Deer hides and bearskins were worth several shillings each. Bear bacon was the favorite meat of the place and time. Furs and ginseng could be traded for cash and for more lead and powder, metal traps, a beaver felt hat. Bear Creek in the Yadkin Valley was supposedly so named because one winter Daniel killed ninety-one bears along its banks. And Daniel and an unnamed companion were said to have killed thirty deer in one day. Deer were more important for the hides than the venison, which was often tough and stringy.

Before the white trappers introduced the metal trap, the Indians had depended on snares and dead falls, pits and arrows. Animals could be caught in nets spread under leaves that wrapped the prey up when the trigger was sprung and jerked them up to hang high in the air. Small animals could be caught in nooses. A mink or otter was more likely to be taken in a deadfall, a rock or heavy log fixed to hit its victim when a trigger was tripped. Beaver were usually speared with a barbed gig. The Indians knew how to attract beavers with castoreum, a scent taken from the gland of another beaver. Bigger animals such as foxes and wolves could be taken in pits dug in trails and covered with thin sticks and leaves and a trap door that tipped the animal into the deep hole.

The Indians were adept with their methods, perfected over thousands of years. They used furs for clothing and decoration, ceremonies and talismanic signs, for crafting pouches, quivers, and headdresses, for trading with other tribes. When the Europeans arrived, the Indians discovered furs were their most valuable commodity. Wars were fought and whole villages massacred over the fur trade, once the traders made fur so important. Religious orders established missions in Canada and farther south, partly to save the souls of Indians and partly to serve as forts to protect the lucrative fur trade. Conflicts over the regions of supply, and control of the tribes, contributed to the so-called French and Indian War of the 1750s and 1760s.

With traditional methods Native trappers might gather scores of skins from creek banks and high valleys in a season, but with hand-forged iron traps they could garner thousands in the same time. The action of a metal trap is a powerful spring shaped like tongs. When the tongs are pressed closed, the jaws of the trap fall open as semicircles on hinges. When the trigger is slipped in place, caught in the "dog," the jaws stay open. On the trigger is a pan almost like a coin, and when the pan is pressed the jaws slam shut. Some traps have jaws with sharp teeth. Daniel Boone knew how to make iron traps and repair them. Such traps were crafted in all sizes, then as now, from tiny ones to catch muskrats and weasels, larger ones to catch otter and fox, still larger for beaver, and biggest of all for bear. A bear trap was so powerful it had to be set with clamps, and it could break a man's leg. On dry land, on a trail, a trap was baited with scents or meat, and carefully hidden under leaves or duff to snap on a fox or wolf, panther or bear. Hardest of all to catch was a fox, which seemed able to smell a human touch no matter how many times a trap had been boiled and handled with boiled gloves.

The most valuable animals lived in or near the water, and fur was at its best in late fall and winter when because of the cold weather it was thick and shiny with oil. To catch these animals and prevent them from biting off their clamped feet was delicate work. The trap had to be set in water so the caught animal would drown. But if the water was too deep, the mink, otter, muskrat, or beaver would swim over the trap. Therefore traps were set below slides or runs, or where paths entered the stream, or between rocks where the animal was known to pass. The trap was hidden in the water, but it had to be chained to a rock or root or sapling, or the animal would jerk it away and be carried downstream. Within minutes the prey must drown and its body be mostly concealed by the current. Trappers were very secretive about their methods and about their trails and sequences of sets, called trap-lines, stretched along streams. A thief who stumbled on a trapline could follow it and steal every pelt that had been caught, not to mention the traps themselves. In some places furs were almost the medium of exchange, more than coins, more than blankets, more than anything except whiskey and rifles, and later tobacco.

Once animals were caught, their hides had to be peeled off and scraped carefully, so as not to cut or damage the valuable skin. The mink pelt was turned inside out like a sock, and a beaver pelt cut to stretch flat on a hoop made of grapevine or a hickory shoot, called a withe. Mink and otter hides were stretched inside out on boards or a bent limb. A trapper cached his furs in thickets and caves, usually dividing his hoard among several locations, in case one of them was found by Indians or white thieves. He also made his camp some distance from the trapline. Cured pelts could be tied in bundles and carried on packhorses. A trapper might come out of the woods in March with more wealth than the wages of a blacksmith or miller or weaver for a year's work.

In his late teens Daniel Boone became widely known in the Yadkin area as an expert trapper and hunter, a deadly marksman. When he brought his furs into the county seat at Salisbury to trade for lead and powder, a new gun or new horse, he liked to take part in shooting matches, which were very popular. Boone seemed to always win and was so sure of his prowess he demonstrated trick shots, such as holding out his rifle with one hand only and hitting the target. According to Stephen Aron, "The boldest supposedly outdid William Tell by aiming at targets placed between legs instead of atop heads; probably a tall tale but graphically illustrative of the connection between marksmanship and manhood."

Part of the legend of Boone at this time is the story of a young Catawba warrior named Saucy Jack, who was also proud of his reputation as a marksman. Apparently Boone had beaten him in a shooting match, or perhaps he just resented the reputation Boone had acquired. Inspired by whiskey on one of his visits to Salisbury, probably to sell his furs and hides, Saucy Jack bragged that he would kill this

Daniel Boone to show who was the better marksman. As was often the case, Boone was away hunting at the time, but when Squire Boone was told of the threat he grabbed a hatchet and went looking for Saucy Jack. "Well, if it has come to this, I'll kill first," the old blacksmith and former Quaker said. Luckily someone told Saucy Jack that Squire was looking for him and the brave sobered up enough to disappear to his village to the south along the Catawba River.

This story is significant because it not only illustrates the loyalty of the close-knit Boone family but also how Daniel himself was able to learn from his experience. In later life, when shooting with Indians, he was careful to let them win some too. "I often went hunting with them, and frequently gained their applause for my activity at our shooting matches. I was careful not to exceed many of them in shooting; for no people are more envious than they in this sport," he told John Filson, his first biographer. This bit of wisdom almost certainly saved his life more than once and helped him survive in four months of captivity among the Shawnees in the late winter and spring of 1778. In general, Native Americans admired Boone as though he were one of their own and again and again showed him a particular respect. He returned their respect.

By 1751 the Catawbas, for whom the river west of the Yadkin was named, were mostly living on a tract of land the British government had given them on the river near the South Carolina line. The "People of the River" were a Siouan nation and had been known as fierce warriors earlier, but in the eighteenth century they became peaceful and cooperative with whites and absorbed refugees from many other nations fleeing from white incursions. The Catawbas were admired by all for their basket making and pottery.

Around this time, relations between Indians and whites on the western frontier began to be affected more and more by politics on a larger, even global scale. For almost two hundred years the rivals for dominance of North America had been Britain and France and Spain, countries now waging war on several other fronts as well, in what was called the Seven Years' War. North of Florida and east of the Mississippi it was primarily a struggle between France and Britain. The English had settled most of the eastern seaboard from Maine to Georgia, establishing the thriving port cities of Boston, New York, Baltimore, and Charleston, as well as several cities at the fall lines of rivers where navigation stopped — Richmond, Albany, Philadelphia. The English had cleared land to raise tobacco, rice, cotton, and indigo. They'd built ships and hunted whales.

Instead of clearing land and building cities, the French had developed the fur trade with Indians in Canada and as far west as the lands of the Dakota Sioux, sent missionaries and explorers, married with the Natives. The French claimed all the land west of the Appalachian Mountains and had built forts at Detroit and along the Mississippi River. Their influence spread west into the plains and south to New Orleans, where they encountered the presence of the Spanish.

To strengthen their hold on the territories, both England and France formed alliances with the larger Indian nations. From the earliest times the English had allied themselves with the Iroquois, providing the Five Nations and then the Six Nations — with the addition of the Tuscaroras around 1722 — with firearms, whiskey, trade goods. The Iroquois were a powerful confederation in what would become upstate New York, and they were effective in attacking the French and French allies like the Shawnees and Hurons. Many of the midwestern and Great Lakes Indians, such as the Shawnees, Mingoes, and Delawares, had earlier been driven out of their homelands by the English, and they were happy to side with the French against their old adversaries. The French encouraged their allies to attack the English settlements on the western frontier, and the English did not discourage their own allies, the Cherokees and Iroquois, from attacking the French and the French allies. The sorest point of contention in 1753 was western Pennsylvania, where the Allegheny and Monongahela rivers come together to form the Ohio, which the French called *la belle rivière*. Whoever could control the head of the river might dominate the wide river valley below.

Everyone, including Virginians such as George Washington, had their eye on the meadowlands and rolling hills of the Ohio Valley, called the Middle Ground.

Groups from the English colonies, such as the first Ohio Company and the Loyal Company, had already sent scouts into the region, hoping to claim the land and sell it to future settlers. Benjamin Franklin and others formed the Vandalia Company to claim land in the region. In 1750 Dr. Thomas Walker and a party for the Loyal Company crossed through Ouasiota, or Cumberland Gap, and wandered around the headwaters of the Big Sandy before returning to Virginia. If hunters such as James Patton had tried to keep the wilderness over the mountains a secret for their own enjoyment and exploitation, Walker had no such scruples.

In the same year, the woodsman Christopher Gist, a neighbor of the Boones on the Yadkin, was employed by the Ohio Company to make a probing excursion into the Ohio Valley, almost twenty years before Boone and John Findley would go there. Important political leaders, like Gov. Robert Dinwiddie of Virginia and young George Washington (who was only two years older than Daniel Boone), had these western lands very much on their minds also. Joseph J. Ellis has written, "From 1754 to 1759, Washington spent the bulk of his time west of the Blue Ridge, leading a series of expeditions into the Ohio Country that served as a crash course in the art of soldiering. They also provided him with a truly searing set of personal experiences that shaped his basic outlook on the world." Washington, only twenty-one then but already a surveyor and ranger, with scout Christopher Gist and four others, was sent by Governor Dinwiddie of Virginia to march into the western wilderness in 1753 to warn the French to stay out of territory the English claimed. Though it was the middle of winter, Washington and Gist found the French, who initially treated them with great courtesy and then told them to go to hell.

The next summer, 1754, Washington was sent back into the wilderness with a small army to strengthen British claims there. But they found the French had already built a stockade, Fort Duquesne, at the forks of the Ohio. Washington won an initial skirmish with the French and their Indian allies and built a blockhouse called Fort Necessity about thirty miles from Duquesne, but he was later attacked by the French and forced to surrender and return unharmed to Virginia.

In 1755 the British sent Gen. Edward Braddock to North America to assemble an army of British regulars and militia to drive the French out of Fort Duquesne and the western lands. Braddock had a considerable reputation as a military man, and he was confident he could expel the Indians and French trespassers. While in Philadelphia gathering his forces, he told Benjamin Franklin he was sure he could defeat the enemy in two or three days. Franklin warned him that Indians had their own way of fighting in the American backwoods. But Franklin later reported that Braddock "smil'd at my Ignorance, and reply'd 'These Savages may indeed be a formidable Enemy to your raw American militia; but upon the King's regular and disciplined Troops, Sir, it is impossible they should make any impression.'"

A force of more than two thousand men was "embodied," or brought together, from several colonies in June 1755 at Fort Cumberland in western Maryland. Maj. Edward Dobbs, son of the governor of North Carolina, brought a company from the western part of that colony, including Daniel Boone, who had joined as a teamster and blacksmith. Many people who would become important later were involved in the expedition to drive the French from Fort Duquesne. Daniel Morgan of Winchester, Virginia, who would later distinguish himself in the Revolution at the Battles of Saratoga and Cowpens, was there as a teamster for Washington's militia, which would support Braddock's army of regular soldiers. According to Daniel Boone's son Nathan, his father said Daniel Morgan was a cousin of the Boones', though modern scholars have not confirmed this claim.

It may have been at this time that Boone was initiated as a Freemason. Masonry was popular in Virginia, and Washington and many of the other officers of the militia were devoted Masons. Washington had been initiated November 4, 1752, at the lodge in Fredericksburg, Virginia, and Boone may have joined there also in 1755. During the later Revolutionary period Washington would encourage the establishment of military lodges among his army. Masonry served as a bulwark against monarchy and feudalism, Roman Catholicism, and the emotional extremes of some Protestant sects, and offered a way to put in practice new ideas of fraternity, progress, rational thought.

Thomas Gage, who would later serve as commander in chief of British forces in North America, was with Braddock as a young officer. Horatio Gates, who would later serve as a general with American forces in the Revolution, was also in the brigade. Dr. Thomas Walker, perhaps the first Englishman to find the gap called Ouasiota, which he renamed for the Duke of Cumberland, served as commissary for Braddock's army. Among the men was a young trader named John Findley, who had gone down the Ohio to trade with Shawnees in Kentucky in 1752. He had seen the great meadows and the cane lands there, and he described them to young Boone.

Braddock's campaign seemed to be under a curse from the beginning. Moving clumsily through the forest with artillery and a long baggage train, in terrain fit only for packhorses, not wheeled vehicles, it took the column a week to travel the first thirty miles. Braddock was neither the first nor the last general trained in European warfare to be baffled by the obstacles and cover provided by the American woods. On July 9, 1755, Braddock's army crossed the Monongahela and, marching to fife and drum, followed by many pieces of artillery, proceeded toward Fort Duquesne for a bombardment and siege. Suddenly the path ahead was blocked by French Canadians, and the woods on either side erupted with rifle fire. Bullets tore into the red and blue uniformed soldiers. Hit by fire from both sides and the front, Braddock's force was helpless.

It was an ambush that could have been avoided had Braddock used Indian scouts ahead and on either flank. A Delaware chief named Shingas had offered scouts if Braddock would assure him the Ohio

Valley would not be settled by the English. Braddock had answered, "No savage should inherit the land," and said that, besides, he did not need their help. With no videttes or flanking scouts, Braddock had marched into a death trap.

It was reported later that the militiamen behaved better than the British soldiers once the attack began, perhaps because they were more familiar with woodland fighting. The soldiers panicked and began firing wildly, killing their own men. "Entire companies were wiped out by 'friendly fire' from British muskets. As Washington described it later, 'they [militiamen] behaved like Men and died like Soldiers' while the regulars 'broke & run as sheep before Hounds.'"

Many years later Nathan Boone said his father blamed Braddock for not using spies and guards on his flanks. As a teamster Boone was with the baggage train to the rear. As the surviving soldiers began to retreat, shoving and leaping over each other in a rout, the teamsters were trapped in the melee. The French and Indians rushed to take prisoners, and the teamsters, unarmed and responsible for the heavy baggage wagons, were helpless as wounded and frightened soldiers stumbled back past them. To save himself, young Boone cut his horses loose and rode after the fleeing troops.

CHAPTER THREE

The Yadkin Was the Wild West

1756–1759

After the debacle of the Battle of the Monongahela, Boone walked across Pennsylvania to visit relatives in Exeter. He had witnessed one of the bloodiest defeats the British ever experienced in the colonial period. But he got away unwounded, as the French and Indians turned back to scalp the dead and take the wounded prisoners to be tortured and burned at the stake.

In the mountains of Pennsylvania, as he was crossing a bridge over the Juniata River, he confronted an Indian who drew a knife on him. Bragging that he had killed many a Long Knife — what the Indians of the Ohio Valley called the Virginians, because of their hunting knives and sabers — the brave said he would take one more scalp. Many years later Boone told the sons of Henry Miller that he had killed only three Indians in a long life in the wilderness. The first was on the Juniata. Facing the drunken Indian, who flourished the knife over his head, Boone decided he would not back away. Waiting for his chance, he lowered his head and drove his shoulder into the Indian's gut, knocking him off his feet and off the bridge. The Indian fell on the rocks below. But Boone must not have been certain the Indian was killed, for he later told his son Nathan that the only Indian he was sure he ever killed was at the Battle of the Blue Licks. The confrontation on the bridge was the kind of incident Boone was almost always able to evade.

On the disastrous Braddock expedition, Boone had heard about the gap called the Cumberland, which led to the hunting ground of Kentucky. And by the campfire on the way to Fort Duquesne Boone had heard John Findley tell of the new Eden of cane and clover, buffalo and beaver, the island in the wilderness, where only a few Indians hunted and fewer seemed to live. Findley described a world that contained beaver so numerous a man could take all the pelts he could carry. Best of all was the news that so few Indians lived in this ideal hunting ground. Shawnees, Mingoes, and Delawares hunted there. But there seemed to be only the villages of Lower Shawnee Town, and perhaps Eskippakithiki, south of the Ohio, north of the Cumberland. Some scholars have thought the Indians considered Kentucky taboo for permanent settlements, a sacred hunting ground where none should settle. More think the powerful Iroquois had maintained the meadowland as their buffalo hunting grounds, driving away all other tribes. The bounty was there for the taking, for anyone with the courage and enterprise to go there.

Since the time of the Vikings, perhaps since the days of the Romans, westering had been in the blood of Europeans. The Romans pushed as far toward the sunset as Britain and Ireland, and Irish monks and Erik the Red had sailed all the way to Iceland. Leif Eriksson had reached Greenland and the New World. Columbus and his successors had discovered lands and peoples that changed European ways of thinking about the globe and the future. Driven by greed or piety, lust for power or curiosity, romance, or some combination of all five, Europeans were relentless in exploration, going farther and farther with the sun, the stars, and the moon, always to the west.

For the colonists in North America the West meant free land and independence from feudal rule and quitrents, from debt and debtor's prison, from censures of the church and the class system, from servitude and poverty. The West was the place to rise, to become better, larger. For someone like Boone, the West was a place of mystery and shadow also, a stage on which to act a larger, more dramatic role, to play parts written on a different scale, in meadows and forests, along rivers and canebrakes, with buffalo far as the eye could reach, with flocks of passenger pigeons that filled the sky for days. From the time he returned from Braddock's campaign, Boone began to think more and more about the land beyond the mountains, and he began to reach farther westward with each hunt, into the hills and mountains near the head of the Yadkin.

AFTER HE returned to the Yadkin, Boone initiated another important change in his life. Two years before, he had met fifteen-year-old Rebecca Bryan at a family wedding. Rebecca was the daughter of Joseph and Aylee Bryan, immigrants to Pennsylvania, and then Virginia, where Rebecca was born January 9, 1739, and then the Yadkin. "Morgan Bryan came to Pa about 1700 . . . he there married Mary Strode, whose parents came from France . . . then moved to the Shenandoah Valley near the present site of Winchester." The Bryan family had lived in Ireland, and then in Denmark, before coming to North America. The Bryans had settled a few miles north of the Boones in North Carolina. Like the Boones, the Bryans were a large family that moved and settled close together, presided over by Rebecca's grandfather, Morgan Bryan. In the court records of Rowan County, Morgan Bryan's name appears often as jury member or magistrate. Daniel had hunted and associated with three of Rebecca's brothers.

The meeting of Rebecca Bryan and Daniel Boone is the beginning of one of the great romantic tales of the frontier and eighteenth-century America. Celebrated in film and television, folklore and history, Rebecca has been portrayed as the ideal wife, patient, resourceful, a great beauty, a crack shot with a rifle, moving again and again with Daniel and their family from North Carolina to Virginia, back to North Carolina, to Tennessee, to Kentucky, to Virginia again, and back to Kentucky, then finally to Missouri. According to Annette Kolodny, in her landmark study of women on the frontier, *The Land Before Her*, Timothy Flint first portrayed Rebecca with "the same heroic . . . nature" he attributed to Boone but then toned down his portrait to suit Victorian tastes. Others would suggest that Rebecca loved the wilderness as much as Daniel did, and rumor would ascribe to her the training of her sons in marksmanship while Daniel was away. Kolodny adds, "It is said by some that she was a fair shot, by others that she rivaled her husband in marksmanship; and the rumor persisted that she, not her husband (. . . often away from home), had taught their sons the use of the gun." Rebecca was rumored to have shot six deer in one day.

Daniel was already the champion hunter, trapper, marksman, and wrestler of the Yadkin region. A descendant later referred to Rebecca as "one of the handsomest persons she ever saw." She was also described as mild, pleasant, and kind. Rebecca had fair skin and coal black hair and striking black eyes. She was a good bit taller than average, about Daniel's height; she was called buxom and larger than the average woman of the time. Though no portrait of her has ever been found, we have a vivid sense of her beauty and vitality. She was a woman capable of the hard work and childbearing and dangers, and excitement, of the American frontier.

Rebecca's nephew Daniel Bryan later remarked on her pleasant manner and speech. A granddaughter would recall that Rebecca "was one of the neatest and best of house keepers, proverbial for the tidiness and Quaker-like simplicity and propriety of all her domestic arrangements." When Boone first saw Rebecca he was nineteen and she was only fifteen, and he always called her "my little girl." The folklore of the Yadkin region spawned many tales of the meeting and courtship of Daniel and Rebecca. One of the most popular, first recorded by Timothy Flint, described Boone out fire hunting with a friend. Fire hunters carried a blazing torch into the woods at night, and startled deer would stand frozen, staring at the flame. The glow of the eyes made a perfect target. According to Flint, young Rebecca Bryan is out looking for a stray cow and gets lost in the woods as night falls. She sees a light and walks toward it. Boone aims at the shining eyes but holds his fire, as if warned by instinct. Rebecca sees what is happening finally and runs away. Boone follows her to the Bryan cabin and falls in love. He knows also that he will give up fire hunting. One of Rebecca's nieces later pointed out that the story could not be true, because human eyes do not reflect the way animal eyes do. Rebecca's daughter-in-law Olive Van Bibber Boone quipped that the only shining was in the lovers' eyes when they married. "And if there was any 'shining of the eyes' it must have been there."

There are stories in the folklore of many cultures about the hunter who falls in love with his prey. The fire-hunting story of Daniel and Rebecca may have been adapted from a similar Indian story. The sexual resonance of the story reaches across all cultures, and the renunciation of fire hunting at the end suggests a Victorian twist added by Flint. But Annette Kolodny sees the fire-hunting story as an example of the way Rebecca was marginalized in the accounts of Boone's life, especially in the nineteenth century.

Another tale, which the Boone family never denied, describes Daniel and Rebecca meeting at a cherry picking in the summer of 1756. Just naming the occasion gives the story a nice erotic overtone. The couple sit in the grass of the cherry orchard, Rebecca wearing a fine cambric apron, showing at once her practicality and love of finery. Cambric was hard to get on the frontier. Daniel, perhaps nervous, takes out his hunting knife and begins to flourish it around. The knife rips the fine apron in three places. But Rebecca Bryan does not protest or reproach him and seems to ignore the damage. Boone later explained to his descendants that he had meant "to try her temper" to see if she would get angry. Because she ignored the damage, Boone said he knew she was the woman he must marry. The tale shows Boone's love of a good story, and it also demonstrates how in old age he could turn what must have been embarrassing at the time into a quip that made him look wise even in his youth. It is quite possible that Rebecca saw what Daniel was about and only pretended not to care that her fine apron was ruined.

Another episode in the legend of the courtship has Daniel killing a deer and bringing it to the Bryan house to show Rebecca what a good provider he is. Of course it is impossible not to get bloody, carrying a deer with its throat cut and a bullet hole in its head or heart. Daniel dresses the carcass outside the Bryan house, getting even bloodier, while Rebecca cooks dinner inside. When the suitor is called in to eat, his hunting shirt is filthy, and he hadn't thought to bring a change of clothes. The Bryan girls, from a more prosperous family than the Boones, giggle and snicker at his condition. But Daniel will not be laughed at without retaliating. As he sits down he lifts a cup and looks into it. "You, like my hunting shirt, have missed many a good washing," he says. The quip was repeated often and always got a laugh, showing Daniel had evened the score. One Boone relative said it showed how proud women needed to be brought down a notch or two.

Rebecca and Daniel were married, along with two other couples, August 14, 1756, with Squire Boone in his capacity as justice of the peace officiating. Though the romance and marriage of Rebecca and Daniel were the stuff of legend almost from the time they occurred, Rebecca has figured less in the Boone story than one might expect. Annette Kolodny blames biographers such as Timothy Flint for suppressing the image of Rebecca as courageous and even heroic, in her long life on the frontier, to make her seem the meek and patient wife of the Victorian ideal. "Flint effectively annihilated any possibility that she might achieve mythic status on her own." But in recounting some of the incidents in Rebecca's life, Flint gives at least a partial picture of the active role Rebecca and other women took in sustaining and defending family and community.

Many of the deeds Boone became famous for were done away from home, among Indians or other hunters and soldiers. But it is impossible to imagine Daniel Boone's career without Rebecca. It is true that he loved the wilderness, the solitude of the long hunts, the adventure of the unknown. But he was also a man of intense loyalties, a family man, who came from a big family and raised a big family. Without a woman as strong and resourceful as Rebecca, he could not have gone into the forest again and again for extended periods. Without a woman as steady and independent as Rebecca he could not have even considered the many moves to strange places. Without her his world would have collapsed under debt and uncertainty. The tall, buxom Rebecca inspired him and always drew him back from his great voyages of discovery and business. It is clear she also had what men most truly desired and needed in a wife: she could be relied on to keep the household together and raise the children, whether he was around or not. Later, when Boone was captured by the Shawnees and assumed dead, it was Rebecca who would lead her family back across the mountains to the safety of the Yadkin Valley.

Rebecca Bryan Boone is one of the best examples in American history of the adage "Behind every good man . . ." During the siege of Boonesborough women dressed as men and carrying rifles paraded along the walls of the fort to make the attackers think there were many men inside the stockade. Indeed, some of the women in Kentucky were crack shots and expert hunters. In 1777 Esther Whitley of St. Asaph's Station, at a shooting match, would beat all the men, who kept firing at a target until it got dark, attempting to equal her marksmanship.

REBECCA AND Daniel first lived in a cabin on Squire Boone's property. After Daniel's brother Israel died of consumption, they took in his sons Jesse and Jonathan and raised them as their own. Nine months after their wedding a son named James was born May 3, 1757, and another son named Israel was born January 25, 1759. Rebecca would have eight more children over the next quarter century, and she would later adopt six children of a widowed brother.

Soon after their marriage the young couple moved to a new place in the Bryan settlement, farther up the Yadkin on a creek called Sugartree, which ran into Dutchman's Creek, near present-day Farmington,

North Carolina. The name of the creek suggests the presence of sugar maples. Maples were tapped on the frontier for syrup and sugar, at a time when other sweetening was hard to come by. Bees were not common among the settlements then, and sorghum cane had not yet been introduced to the region. The Boones must have begun their habit of annually collecting and boiling maple sap there, a custom they continued in all the places they lived until the end of Rebecca's life. Boiling maple syrup together seemed to be something that Daniel and Rebecca particularly enjoyed, in the periods he was at home and not roving. When he was away Rebecca made syrup with their children. In the worst of times, later, when he had lost most of his land and was deeply in debt, they fell back on this forest occupation, making hundreds of gallons of syrup. On Hinkston Creek in Kentucky in 1797, while Boone was being sued for debts and land surveys, they would boil down enough sap to make more than five hundred pounds of maple sugar to sell and use.

It is easy to see why sugar making attracted Daniel. He did not much care for farming. Maple syrup was not something that had to be cultivated in the fields, in long days in the hot sun plowing and hoeing and weeding. Maples grew in the forest, like the game, and could be tapped in the cool days of late winter as the sap rose from the deep root systems. Once the trees were tapped and the sap wept into buckets was carried to the boiling furnace, the main work was keeping the fire going. It takes forty gallons of sap to boil down to one gallon of syrup, and ten gallons of syrup to boil down to eight pounds of sugar. But the product was unsurpassed sweetening to use in cooking, sell, or give to friends. Maple sugar was the sweetening the Indians had before the whites arrived. Once made, the syrup could be fermented as a kind of mead or distilled into spirits. The boiling was done in late winter as snow was disappearing, just as arbutus was beginning to bloom. Sugaring came at the end of the trapping season, as the fur was getting thinner, less valuable, before the deer hides were in their prime spring and summer condition. Sugaring was the first sign that spring was on the way, a ritual to welcome the new season. Sugar making gave Daniel and Rebecca an opportunity to work together, a chance they rarely missed.

The house Daniel built on Sugartree Creek, when he was about twenty-two years old, was more substantial than a simple cabin. The logs were hewed flat and fit snugly together. A big fireplace and chimney of soapstone and wood provided heat for cooking and living, and much of the light in the evenings. There was an outside kitchen for cooking in summer, and Daniel later added a puncheon floor fixed with wooden pegs. The house measured eighteen by twenty-four feet and, according to a resident in the area at the time, was still standing a century later.

Settlers on the frontier were accustomed to living in small spaces. There could be little privacy with children of all ages, babies crying, someone breaking wind or coughing. In the eighteenth and nineteenth centuries people slept two and three to a bed, when there was a bed. Four or five children might sleep on the same cot or pallet. Because of lack of space and lack of beds, they slept packed together on ticks stuffed with leaves or straw or corn shucks. In cold weather the several bodies in bed together helped them keep warm in a corner or loft far from the fireplace.

There are many accounts of travelers stopping for the night at cabins or houses along their way. Common courtesy of the time and place required that visitors be invited to dinner and to stay the night. In a cabin where ten people normally slept, the visitor would be invited to unroll his blanket near the fireplace and undress or half undress in the dark or semidark. A kind of privacy was created by everyone ignoring each other. And even if you woke in the night and heard the sounds of lovemaking nearby, you pretended not to notice. That the crowding in the cabins and little houses was no hindrance to lovemaking is proved by the number of children born on the frontier to families such as the Bryans and Boones. Judging by the birthrate, the hardships and crowding seem to have been a spur to fertility, not a restraint.

One of the paradoxes of this frontier living is that settlers did not congregate in villages, as most of their ancestors had in Britain and on the Continent, but moved into the woods and cleared an isolated place. The large families might live close together, clearing land in common, working, eating, sleeping in very intimate proximity. But in general new arrivals moved far out into the valleys on their own claims. This apparent contradiction is related to another paradox of the life of Daniel Boone: though an accomplished and legendary hunter and trapper, scout and explorer, gone for months and sometimes even years at a time, he was also an affectionate, hardworking, loved, and respected family man when home, at once a loner and a beloved father, husband, and son. Virtually all relatives and acquaintances who later left accounts of him spoke with pronounced respect and affection for the man, and many followed him wherever he moved.

In these early years of their marriage, Boone farmed and Rebecca almost certainly grew a large garden. They would have had at least one milk cow, a horse, chickens, and hogs that ran loose in the woods, rooting and feeding on acorns and anything else they could find. Daniel worked at times as a blacksmith and gunsmith, and he hauled produce to Salisbury, the county seat, in his wagon and returned with store-bought goods. He preferred working as a drover to farming. But even then his main business in the summer was not corn growing or tobacco raising but deer hunting. The best practice, Ted Franklin Belue tells us, was to gather "deerskin in the red before the frosts plumped the skin and blued them." A rule of thumb in those days was to trap in the months ending in the letter r, plus January and February, and hunt deer in the other months.

As the deer were hunted out closer to the Yadkin, Daniel had to range farther into the hills for the bucks that provided the core of his summer income. Though he sometimes had companions, it's said he preferred to hunt alone. Deer hunting then and now is done by waiting near a deer trail early in the morning, or late in the evening, for a buck to wander into range. A marksman like Daniel Boone would choose to shoot the deer either in the heart or in the head. A head shot would not damage the hide, but it was riskier at a great distance.

"There is a period in the history of the individual, as of the race, when the hunters are 'the best men,' as the Algonquins called them," Thoreau says in *Walden*. Boone's lifelong obsession with hunting shows that in some important way he never quite shed his youthfulness. As a boy Daniel had learned to approach deer by crawling or easing closer while their heads were down grazing, then freezing while their heads came up. No doubt he sometimes used such an Indian-like technique, especially for hunting with spear or bow at close range. But with his long rifle, Daniel probably more often waited for the buck to wander within range and into the open.

To carry a deer a long way through the woods is hard work, even for someone as strong as Boone. Modern hunters use wheeled carriers and all-terrain vehicles to haul game back to camp. Horses were used in earlier times. It is brutal work to carry for miles through thickets and over rough ground a deer that may weigh 100 or 150 pounds. The method used in Boone's time, when they were hunting without a horse, not far from camp, was "hoppusing," a technique learned from the Indians. The carcass was strapped over the hunter's shoulders by strips of hide called tugs. *Hoppus* was used as a verb, as in "He hoppused the deer home." As Daniel ranged farther into the hills in his hunting, he did not return home at night but instead camped and skinned the carcasses, returning days or weeks later with hides strapped to his packhorse. A deer hide weighed about two and a half pounds and sold for forty cents a pound. A horse of that time, typically fourteen hands high, could carry about two hundred pounds.

A story that illustrates Boone's character, and the extraordinary burden placed on women such as Rebecca, was told after his death by members of his family. One of their neighbors in the Bryan settlement on the Yadkin was Samuel Tate, a frequent hunting companion, older than Daniel. When he returned from a hunt and found his own family out of flour, Daniel went over to Morgan Bryan's place to thresh out and grind some rye. On the way Boone stopped at the Tate house and found their supplies running low because Samuel was away on a hunt, and Mrs. Tate was sick. On his way back home Daniel dropped off some of his own rye flour with the Tates.

A few days later Tate returned from his hunt and angrily confronted Daniel, asking what right Boone had to stick his nose in Tate's business. And Tate accused Boone to others of flirting with the young Mrs. Tate. "Later Boone met with him and gave him a severe flogging," Nathan Boone told Lyman Draper, "and said he would do it again if he ever threw out similar intimations."

There are only a few stories of Boone losing his temper in his long life. This story is one of maybe a half-dozen remembered instances when anger overcame him. Tate's ingratitude and suggestion that he was casting a lustful eye on Mrs. Tate were too much even for Daniel. The story reveals a good deal about the good-natured Daniel, about the willingness of frontier folk to help each other, and about how on occasion Daniel, like his father, could become a fighting Quaker. Because of the dangers and hardships of the frontier, settlers learned to share and share alike. It was a generosity of spirit Boone carried into later times, and his generosity then was to prove a liability. And the story also shows how Daniel rarely held a grudge, because he later hunted again and again with Samuel Tate, in North Carolina and Kentucky.

But the account suggests something else as well, how throughout his life some other men tended to be jealous of Daniel. Saucy Jack, the Catawba, was jealous of his reputation and skill as a marksman and hunter. The older Samuel Tate was jealous of Boone's youth and attractiveness to women, as well as of his considerable hunting skills. Later, men like Richard Callaway would be jealous of Boone's leadership, of the way people just seemed to look up to him and follow him. And still later many would be jealous of his fame, after Filson's biography made him a legend in America and in Europe. The legend of Daniel Boone would be both a blessing and a curse for the rest of his life. Some of his legal and business difficulties in later life had their origin in jealousy of his accomplishments and his reputation for accomplishment.

Samuel Tate must have been a difficult man, for there is another story about Boone's beating him up in a later fight about hunting territory. Tate kept claiming more and more of the hunting range for himself, and Boone kept giving in to him, until it seemed Tate was claiming all the territory for his own hunting and bragging he was the better hunter. He also bragged he could whip Boone any time he chose to. "I believe I could whip you," Boone said to Tate, and beat the older hunter until he was in no shape to hunt anywhere for several weeks.

IN THE LATE 1750s the Yadkin Valley was attacked in a number of Indian raids. Shawnees to the north, from as far away as Ohio, struck settlements along the Carolina frontier, taking lives and scalps as well as supplies. Encouraged by the French, who were still conducting their long war with the British, the Indians surprised the settlements again and again. Several times in the early years of their marriage the Boones had to retreat to forts. This was called forting up, and while settlers were gathered in the forts, their crops were often destroyed and their cabins burned.

In 1756 Fort Dobbs had been constructed a few miles south and east of the South Fork of the Yadkin. The commander of the local militia was Maj. Hugh Waddell, and Boone was an active member of the defense forces in the region. "Fort Dobbs was an oblong space forty-three by fifty-three feet, girt by walls about twelve feet high, consisting of double rows of logs standing on end; earth dug from the ditch which surrounded the fort was piled against the feet of these palisades, inside and out, to steady them."

Cherokees, from the extended federation of towns across the mountains, raided the Yadkin settlements also. Though allied with the English, the Cherokees resented the settlements that encroached farther and farther into their hunting grounds. Even if a war party only burned crops and stole horses, rumors of murder and scalp taking spread through the frontier.

Closer to home on the Yadkin, gangs of white outlaws preyed on the scattered farms, stealing and killing and sometimes kidnapping women and girls. Spreading rumors of an Indian attack, these outlaws plundered farms after the settlers had hurried to forts or hidden in the woods. An especially notorious gang of horse thieves and robbers was active near the Yadkin. Once they kidnapped a young girl, and her father organized a posse of more than forty men to search for her. As the minutemen rode into the woods, they met the girl running out. Her captors had gotten drunk and begun to fight about who would take his pleasure with her first. She led the rescuers back to the camp, where three men as well as women and children were seized. The leader of the outlaws escaped, but three of his cohorts were taken back to Salisbury to be tried and hanged.

The rumor was that these outlaw gangs planned to lead the French and their Indian allies to the settlements in the backcountry. The gangs were hated as much for this suspected treachery as for their stealing. Once, a nearby farmer was discovered with a cache of stolen goods. Persuaded by a little torture, he confessed and led the sheriff and his posse to the outlaw lair in the woods. The leaders were captured and hanged, but the farmer was later murdered for his betrayal. The Yadkin was the lawless West of its time, both literally and figuratively. A missionary traveling in the Yadkin region in this period wrote, "The people about here are wild."

The conflict with the Indians was more often than not started by the whites. Indians were sometimes attacked and killed seemingly at random. A group of Cherokees in May 1758 stole some wandering horses in far southwestern Virginia, not thinking it wrong, as they saw it often done by the whites. The owner of the horses, forming a posse, pursued the Indians and killed twelve or fifteen. The relatives of the dead Indians vowed revenge. In the fall of 1759 Cherokees began attacking the settlements of western North Carolina more consistently.

Enraged because British soldiers had raped several Cherokee women and scalped and murdered braves, the war chief Oconastota, overriding the diplomatic Attakullakulla, the "Little Carpenter," led his warriors against the Yadkin settlements. Major Waddell raised a force of fifty men to march to Fort Dobbs. Boone later told his son Nathan that he had served with Waddell at Fort Dobbs.

In February of 1760 the Cherokees attacked the fort, and Waddell let himself and a small force be decoyed into the open by a seemingly small band of Indians. They walked into an ambush of more than sixty warriors and barely managed to get back into the fort. Fearing that the Indians had attacked their homes, Boone and a number of militiamen slipped out of the stockade to return to the Yadkin. Their fears were confirmed when they found dead, scalped bodies at an outlying farm. The Cherokees had killed more than twelve people on this raid.

Rebecca and Daniel, like others on the Yadkin, decided to retreat to Virginia until the Indian troubles quieted down. Squire and Sarah Boone, and their three unmarried children, Squire, Edward, and Hannah, accompanied Daniel and Rebecca, and Elizabeth Boone Grant and her husband, William. They moved all the way to Culpeper County, Virginia, and stayed with friends.

For several months Daniel worked as a teamster in Virginia, hauling tobacco to market and supplies back to the farm. His first daughter, Susannah, was born November 2, 1760. Though Boone may have been initiated as a Freemason in 1755, his return to Virginia in 1760 also provided an opportunity for joining the brotherhood. An important lodge had already been established in nearby Fredericksburg, and there are rumors that the Boones met George Washington in Fredericksburg also. It is possible his father, Squire, became a Freemason at this time also, or renewed his Masonic connections begun earlier in Pennsylvania.

With mother and daughter doing well, Boone left for North Carolina because it was time for fall hunting and the beginning of trapping season. In all his long life Daniel never missed a hunt if he could help it, even if the Indians were on the warpath and, later, even if he was supposedly sitting for a session of the Virginia legislature. It is likely that Boone also rejoined the Waddell militia the next spring, after the hunt was over and the hides and furs sold. In 1760 Waddell's forces invaded several Cherokee towns on the Little Tennessee River. In a bloody campaign the militia murdered and scalped women as well as men. On November 19, 1761, the Cherokees agreed to peace terms at the Long Island of the Holston, and things were quieter in the Carolina backcountry for a while.

IT IS HARD FOR US in the twenty-first century to imagine a wife's burden on the frontier when her husband was away hunting. Gathering fodder, threshing wheat and rye, carrying grain to mill, and shucking corn, was the heavy work that fell to women. And when there was no heavy work to be done outside, they spun thread from wool or flax, wove cloth, tanned buckskin.

Women on the frontier did all the scrubbing and scouring and washing. There were always dirty diapers and underclothes, night clothes and petticoats. With dirt floors and mud in the yard, smoke and ashes from the fireplace, sweat in the summertime, outer clothes needed laundering also.

A woman had to gather enough wood to heat water in an iron wash pot, water that had to be carried from a spring or stream or well. Once the fire was going and the pot steaming, the woman soaked the clothes and scrubbed them on a washboard or beat them with a stick. The fabric was wrung out by hand and rinsed in cold water and wrung out once more. Washed clothes were draped over bushes, hung from limbs, or strung on cords to dry.

The only soap was what she made herself from fat and lye. To this end she scraped ashes out of the fireplace and piled them in wooden ash hoppers, V-shaped troughs with a crack at the bottom. Straw or grass in the trough acted as a strainer. When the hopper was full she poured water over the ashes, and the liquid that leached through the hopper was lye, or "ley." The lye was boiled in a large kettle until it was thick enough to float an egg. The woman saved fat from her cooking, the drippings of meat and bear bacon. When the fatty oils were mixed with lye, the alkali in the lye acted on the fat to make the metal salts that are soap, with a side product of glycerol. With salt added to the brew, soap in the form of light curds floated to the surface of the alcohol. When the liquid was drained off and the curds washed with a salt solution, the mixture was allowed to settle. The upper layer, as it hardened, was the pure soap, called settled soap which could be chipped or flaked, broken into bars.

For tanning hides, women gathered oak bark in late winter when it was full of sap and cut it up and pounded it so the tannic acid seeped out into a water-filled trough. When the solution was strong enough, hides were soaked for at least a month. Deer hides were softened by drawing them back and forth across a straking board in a process called graining. Indian women often soaked deerskins in dung and urine to make them soft.

We know little about the sanitary facilities of cabins, forts, and stations. Early accounts do not mention such things. The outhouse, as we know it, had not been invented at this time. Most likely, settlers just went out into the woods or used a chamber pot at night, if they had one.

But at a fort where upward of a hundred people were enclosed in palisades, some kind of facility must have been a necessity. Likely it was a hut or shed constructed against the wall of a stockade, a pit in the ground, or a ditch. In hot weather lime could be thrown in a latrine to neutralize the stench. We do know chamber pots were sometimes emptied from the blockhouses onto attacking Indians.

It was a great improvement when a cabin was given a puncheon floor made of logs split in two and laid flat side up. Settlers would sprinkle fine white sand from branches onto the puncheons. When the sand got dirtied with tobacco juice, ashes, mud, or dripped grease, the covering could be swept away and replaced with more clean sand.

With neither metal nor ceramics, the settlers had to rely on wooden spoons and carved bowls. William Clinkenbeard, an early settler in Kentucky, told John Dabney Shane that when he and his wife married at Boonesborough they had no spoons, dishes, or any other utensils. Luckily William Poage, who arrived in Kentucky in 1779, was a fine craftsman in wood. "Noggins hollowed out of knots of trees served as cups. [Poage] also carved piggins (small wooden pails with one stave extended upward as a handle), trenchers (wooden platters for serving food)."

The preferred yard around a cabin was bare ground. Weeds and grass were cut away. Snakes were easier to spot on bare ground, and children were safer. Women tied switches together to make rough brooms called besoms with which to sweep the ground and scoured away chicken piles and other stains with kettles of hot water splashed on the dirt. A swept yard sparkled and when flowers and shrubs were planted at the edges became an island of beauty and order in the threatening wilderness.

Women Carrying Buckets at Bryan's Station. From Elizabeth S. Kinkead, *History of Kentucky*, 1896. Though the story has been questioned by historians, eyewitnesses told of white women, children, and slaves boldly going outside the fort to get water early on the morning of August 16, 1782, as Indians surrounded Bryan's Station. (Courtesy Kentucky Historical Society.)

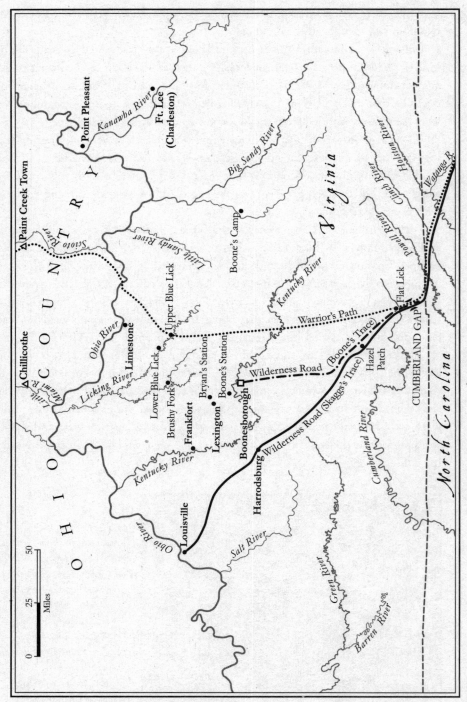

Point Pleasant

Kanawha River

Ft. Lee
(Charleston)

Big Sandy River

Scioto River

Paint Creek Town

O H I O   C O U N T R Y

Chillicothe

Little Miami R.

Ohio River

Limestone

Licking River

Little Sandy River

Boone's Camp

Virginia

Kentucky River

Warrior's Path

Flat Lick

Powell River

Clinch River

Holston River

Cumberland Gap

Watauga R.

Upper Blue Lick

Lower Blue Lick

Brushy Fork

Frankfort

Bryan's Station

Boone's Station

Lexington

Boonesborough

Wilderness Road

(Boone's Trace)

Hazel Patch

North Carolina

Harrodsburg

Wilderness Road (Skagg's Trace)

Kentucky River

Louisville

Ohio River

Salt River

Cumberland River

Green River

Barren River

50

25

Miles

0

CHAPTER FOUR

In Search of the Real West

1760 – 1768 ᷾

Between 1760 and 1769 Daniel Boone, still a young man, was attempting to define himself. It is an odd fact that those who accomplish the most often spend years fumbling and stumbling to find what it is they can achieve. The first half of a life may be given to experiment, trial and error, failure after failure. If Boone had a sense of his destiny at the time, it was frustrated again and again by false starts, dead ends, detours, and digressions. While his fame as a hunter grew, his debts also grew. Though he seemed to have had a sense of his calling from his youth, he must have suffered serious doubts about the exact nature of the call, his purpose, his future. The decade of the 1760s could be called a time of wandering in the wilderness for Boone, in a metaphoric as well as a literal sense. It might be said he was auditioning for parts in the unfolding story of his life and times.

In Rowan County's *Minutes, Court of Pleas and Quarter Sessions* the following entry can be found: "A Deed of Gift from Squire Boone and Sarah his wife to Daniel Boone his son for 640 acres of Land 18th Day of October 1759. Proved by Thomas Banfield." Squire apparently gave two of his married sons each a square mile of land. And while Daniel may have farmed on that property, it appears he and Rebecca continued to live in the cabin on Sugartree Creek. With that much land of his own he may have been expected to give up hunting and settle down to a farming life, but nothing could have been further from his plans.

Around 1760 Boone began to go on longer and longer hunts into the Blue Ridge Mountains to the north and west of the Yadkin and to the valleys beyond the Blue Ridge. It was Cherokee country and hunters had to be discreet, never calling attention to themselves, building small campfires in hidden coves, behind rocks and logs, leaving little evidence that they had been there. The ideal was to slip into the valleys as silent and unseen as an Indian, extract the hides and bear meat, beaver and mink and otter pelts, and withdraw again. The best hunting was always on Indian land, and Boone became an expert at infiltrating, spying, and harvesting the bounty there.

According to one account the Cherokees found Boone's tracks one day in the region that would later be Washington County, Tennessee. Discovering he was being followed, he turned away from his camp and ducked behind a waterfall. Concealed by the curtain of water, he waited as the Indians puzzled over his tracks that disappeared into the creek and never emerged. They decided he had been turned into a ghost that haunted the place and they fled the scene. The creek was later named Boone Creek and the falls Boone Falls.

Beyond the Blue Ridge were the Alleghenies, called the Unakas by the Cherokees, meaning White Mountains, because of the haze over the peaks much of the year. Later they would be called the Smokies. For a hunter in the 1760s who was willing to risk the danger from Cherokees and roving bands of Chickasaws, and Shawnees from north of the Ohio, the mountains offered unlimited opportunities for taking furs and hides, for meat and adventure and sheer beauty.

"I have often heard Father speak of hunting in the Smoky, Brushy and Little Mountains, and also Pilot Mountain," Nathan Boone said. "While hunting in and passing over these mountains he would never consider he had discovered the real west, which was Kentucky."

By then Boone had become a commercial hunter. The idea was to return from these long hunts with a packhorse carrying more than a hundred deer hides or two hundred or three hundred beaver pelts, worth enough to sustain a family for a year and buy a new rifle, powder, lead, steel traps, a horse. A beaver skin was a unit of value, same as a pound sterling or a silver dollar. But for Boone and many of the men he knew, these long hunts were from the beginning much more than business. They were voyages of exploration and discovery. The hunters were driven by a craving and curiosity, a lust for wonder and wandering. The wilderness was like a beautiful woman that must be pursued and loved. And it is likely the danger was part of the attraction. A wilderness without Indians would seem bland, hardly a wilderness at all. And Boone may have sensed, even then, that when the Indians were gone from a region the game would soon be gone also.

Boone sought oneness with the wilderness as a mystic seeks union with the creator or a lover yearns to merge with the beloved. The feminist critic Annette Kolodny has described Boone's passion for the wilderness as a male fantasy of "privatized erotic mastery." "The isolate woodland son, enjoying a presexual — but nonetheless eroticized — intimacy within the embraces of the American forest." Kolodny goes on to distinguish the desire of men for wildness and exploitation of the virgin wild from the desire of women for a home.

One of Boone's companions on these long hunts was his neighbor Nathaniel Gist, son of Christopher Gist, scout for the first Ohio Company and for George Washington's expeditions into the backcountry. Nathaniel Gist would later marry a Cherokee woman and become, according to some, the father of the great Cherokee inventor Sequoya, who developed the Cherokee alphabet. But in December of 1760 Gist was hunting in the Brushy Mountains just west of the Yadkin with Boone. It was at this time that they met a slave named Burrell who served as a cowherd near the head of the Watauga River for one of the settlers. Burrell lived to be over a hundred years old, and around 1845 he told a boy named Thomas Isbell that he had guided Daniel Boone to the cabin built earlier for herders on his first trip across the Blue Ridge.

Burrell had spent years in the mountains looking after cattle and other livestock and, at the same time, exploring the mountains and valleys farther west. He told Boone and Gist of even richer hunting grounds farther on and showed them buffalo traces that led through low gaps to reach there. He took them to a herder's cabin built by Benjamin Howard on a high, sweeping meadow. Water on the east side flowed to the Yadkin, on the north to the New River, and on the west to the Watauga and the Tennessee. Boone and Gist had found what was called then "the backwater," water moving toward the Mississippi, drawn in the direction they were drawn.

The hunters followed another path into southwestern Virginia. It was spectacular country. Boone used the Howard cabin for several years for his long hunts. Stones from the chimney of the hut are now incorporated in a monument to Boone in Boone, North Carolina. From this area Boone began to push farther and farther west on successive hunts. The point of each new season was not just to come home with hides and pelts but to come back having seen new valleys and rivers, while managing to evade the Cherokees. In the early 1760s Boone reached as far west as the Holston River and the Clinch, tributaries of the Tennessee. His reputation as a hunter and scout grew, as he pushed farther and brought in more hides and pelts. He was not by any means the first white man to see these regions. The French, the Spanish, and others had been there long before. But Boone explored the regions more thoroughly and hunted there more profitably than anyone else had. He was known for his precise memory. Once he saw a piece of ground he seemed to never forget it. It was said of him that "he never crossed a route that he had once traversed without at once recognizing the place and knowing that he was crossing one of his former trails."

In late 1761 Boone and Gist were camping in far southwestern Virginia, at a site where Black's Fort would later be built. During the night they were attacked by a pack of ravenous wolves and with great difficulty beat off the animals with rifles and axes. They named the place Wolf Hills, but later settlers changed the name to Abingdon.

Boone's prowess as a hunter and scout became part of the folklore of the region. A century later stories still circulated on the Yadkin about his exploits. A good hunter might be referred to as a "Boone." This was a time when to be called an excellent hunter was about the highest honor a man could aspire to. There was a political dimension to hunting also. Hunting could level the social playing field in a society where the great landowners and leaders were rarely hunters, the reverse of the case in the Old World. While expressing contempt for the rough backwoods hunters, the gentry resented their democratic independence.

It is likely that by this period Boone had also become a digger of ginseng to supplement his income. Called "sang" in the southern Appalachians, ginseng (*Panax quinquefolius*) was reputed to be a general tonic and aphrodisiac. The root could be sold to the Chinese for a substantial profit. In Boone's time the woods were filled with ginseng, if one knew where to look, and what to look for. The herb preferred shady forest slopes and valleys. It had to be found while the leaves were recognizable or the berries bright red. In winter the bare stalks were hard to identify. Once dug, the roots were dried and kept dry to prevent mildew and rot. It's because the root of ginseng can grow roughly in the shape of a man's body that according to the doctrine of signatures, it is a stimulant for the whole body and for sexual potency, nature's own Viagra. When hunting, Boone hid the sang he had dug in caches throughout the mountains. Later he'd come back and collect the roots. It was said he would later return "strait to them all with unerring accuracy."

In those years on the Yadkin, Boone also acquired a reputation as a storyteller and wit. A century later people in the region were still quoting his anecdotes and jokes. He is supposed to have said, "I wouldn't give a tinker's damn for a man who isn't sometimes afraid. Fear's the spice that makes it interesting to go ahead." And he is credited with observing, "Wisdom comes by facing the wind; fools let it carry them." And on another occasion he said, "Hurry? Why don't you know a man will overrun a heap more than he will overtake." There were many other sayings and stories attributed to him: When a man said to a smoker, "Don't you know even a hog don't use tobacco?" the smoker answered, "Well, who does that make more like a hog, me or you?" (Nathan Boone later said his father never used tobacco in any form.) It was said of a man with no socks in very cold weather that his feet would freeze. Boone answered, "Even taters wouldn't freeze with that much dirt on them."

It is a pity that we know so little of the herder and guide named Burrell. Throughout his long career Boone was often accompanied by African Americans on his hunting expeditions. For a slave such as Burrell, the occupation of highland herder must have been a godsend, allowing him to escape the fieldwork and hardships of the plantation for the beauty and adventure of the upland forests. Only one-tenth of the families on the Carolina border at that time owned slaves, and most of the households that did owned only a few. But it is striking how often references to black people appear in accounts of the frontier. Usually they are not named, mentioned only in passing, but we know they were there. Some slaves ran away to join the Indians and became members of the tribes. Others were kidnapped by the Indians and used as interpreters, guides, and marksmen.

Though Boone did go on long hunts with neighbors and friends and his brother Squire, and was known as a good companion around the campfire, expert at roasting turkey and eating it with relish, it was safer to slip through the woods on his own. He liked spending several weeks in the mountains wandering and hunting with only his dog and horse. One early biographer, the Reverend John Mason Peck, said Boone had developed "the habit of contemplation" while alone in the woods. Emerson later said, "If a man would be alone, let him look at the stars." The sage of Concord could well have been putting into words Boone's experience of many nights in the wilderness with only the stars for company.

When Boone camped in the woods he usually built a little hut open on one side to the campfire and the southern sun, called a half-face and made of limbs on poles, pine boughs, bark, and even moss. Within the shelter, warmed by blankets or bearskins or buffalo skins, with his feet to the coals, he could survive the coldest nights, looking out at the stars that seemed to chatter just beyond the treetops. His favorite meal at this period was said to be elk's liver.

According to his son Nathan, Boone learned to watch the direction bears moved in the fall looking for plentiful mast of acorns and hickory nuts, and he followed them. Boone knew that the secret of hunting, as in so many other pursuits, was not just in marksmanship, but in attention, preparation, watching and listening, before one made a move. Bear meat was especially sweet and tender because of all the nuts the bears ate in late summer and autumn.

On later hunts Daniel was known to carry a Bible and other books, including *Gulliver's Travels*. "In middle life, he read considerably in history, which was his favorite reading," Nathan said. Late in his life Boone wrote his widowed sister-in-law that it had always been his habit to read the scriptures. Nathan said he read the Bible more than any other book in his later years. It's possible Boone took the Bible with him on these early hunts to savor by the campfire. He already had a pronounced sense of the sacredness of life, of the forest and Natives who lived in it, probably influenced as much by Indian beliefs as by his Quaker upbringing. "His worship was in secret and he placed his hopes in the Savior," Nathan told Draper.

Daniel told the story of being awakened one winter night in his camp near later Jonesborough, Tennessee, to find himself surrounded by Cherokees, as one lifted the snow-covered blanket off him. "Ah, Wide-Mouth, have I got you now," the brave exclaimed. The Cherokees had given him that name, perhaps because he was prone to laughter and storytelling, and to them that's how Boone was always known. The exclamation shows how elusive they had found Boone, though he was ranging in the heart of their hunting grounds. Not showing surprise, Boone sat up and smiled and shook hands with his captors. Though deeply asleep minutes before, he chatted with the braves and probably passed his flask. He usually traveled with a jug or flask of whiskey or applejack. His aplomb and steadiness, ease and gracefulness, as well as his marksmanship and skill, gave him an extraordinary rapport with the Indians. Of famous white Americans, only Sam Houston appears to have had a comparable knack for fitting in with Native peoples.

The Cherokees did not harm Boone but took all his furs. They could have scalped him, or tomahawked him, or taken him back to their village for a night of torture and burning at the stake. Instead they claimed his precious hoard of pelts and his fine Pennsylvania rifle. This would happen to him again and again in his career in the woods. He would hunt and trap for weeks, even months, only to have his harvest taken from him. Undaunted, Boone would return to the woods as soon as he'd replaced his supplies and traps and rifle, and begin all over again. There is little evidence that he ever expressed bitterness or sought revenge for these losses. He could always trade for a new rifle, forge some more traps. If he had to he could even make a rifle. And it's likely he understood how the Cherokees felt, facing a poacher and spy who could shoot and trap and track as well as they could, on their own land. The Indians may have monitored his activities from a distance, waiting until he had accumulated a hoard of furs, before they robbed him. When Indians stole Boone's furs and rifle, they often did it in the guise of a trade. It was bad manners to steal outright. They offered to trade their musket for his fine rifle, a worn-out knife for his new one, a little wampum for all his furs. Boone understood the protocol and charade and complied. Theft might be considered wrong in tribal ethics, but a "trade" was respectable.

Boone may not have cared as much about possessions and wealth as other hunters did, the ones who got angry, fought back, and were killed. Much as he loved trapping, it was still worth going into the wilderness, even if one did return to the settlements without a fortune in beaver skins and deer hides. And he could always catch more beavers and kill more deer. It would seem, in fact, that Boone sometimes hunted *with* the Cherokees. Wellborn Coffey told Lyman Draper, on September 28, 1884, that Boone was once hunting with a band of Cherokees when they came across what appeared to be buffalo tracks. Buffalo had been gone from that part of the Blue Ridge for some time, as the white settlements encroached on Cherokee lands. But Catawbas would sometimes make what appeared to be buffalo tracks to lure Cherokees into an ambush. "No buffalo," one Cherokee said. "Tawbers." But Boone led them farther down the trail until they came to a huge pile of buffalo droppings. "Tawbers no make so," a Cherokee said, and Boone laughed, and likely the Cherokees laughed with him.

THE FIRST inscriptions on trees with Boone's name in the Watauga area appear to date from this period. Hunters of the time were fond of carving their names on beech and other trees, on boulders, cave walls. Indians also carved pictures and signs on trees and rocks, to mark a path or to record their passing through an area or a victory in war. Hunters' inscriptions have been found in North Carolina, Tennessee, and Kentucky. As Boone's fame spread, so did the number of inscriptions. Boone certainly seemed to get around. Perhaps an authentic one was found on the Clinch River:

> *Daniel Boone*
> *come on boys*
> *here's good water.*

No doubt the urge to write one's name, or make one's sign, inscribe the name of a lover, is enhanced by solitude and distance from others. Indians sometimes left a tomahawk to show where they had been. It appears Boone merely left his name.

WHEN DANIEL returned to Virginia for his family in 1762, legend has it that he'd been gone for twenty-four months. There in Culpeper County he found Rebecca nursing a new baby, Jemima, born October 4. Boone's response to the new daughter, born, some would say, while he had been away two years, is one of the high points of his legend. The story is told in several different variations, but all versions agree about Boone's gracious acceptance of the fact.

An old settler named Josiah Collins told Rev. John Dabney Shane a version of the story in 1841. "When Boone returned home after a two-year absence, there was a new child in the cradle. "'Oh well!' says he, 'whose is it?' 'Why brother Squire's,' replied his wife. 'Well,' says he, 'One of the name is all the same'; and so hushed her up."

Lyman Draper collected different versions of the story, and the one he found most plausible was told by James Norman, who claimed to have returned to North Carolina from Virginia with the Boone family that fall of 1762. According to Norman, Rebecca fell on her knees when Boone returned to Culpeper from his militia service and long hunts in the Blue Ridge. Rebecca explained that he was gone so long she assumed he was dead, and she had given birth to someone else's child. When Daniel asked whose child it was, Rebecca confessed the baby belonged to his brother Ned. Rebecca was reported to have said that Ned "looked so much like Daniel."

As John Mack Faragher points out, such stories color the folklore of the frontier. With men gone on long hunts, on expeditions with militias, prospecting for minerals, or captured by Indians, there were many opportunities for husbands to disappear so long they were assumed to be dead. In some stories the husband or fiancé reappears just as the woman is about to take her vows in a new marriage. In almost all versions, the husband and wife reconcile, and if there is a new baby, the returned husband accepts it as his own.

In all its variations, this has been one of the favorite stories about Boone for the past two centuries and more. For some it has illustrated what a lazy, easygoing man Boone was, staying off in the woods hunting and gallivanting, maybe cohabiting with an Indian wife, while Rebecca did the farmwork and raised the children, not knowing if Daniel was alive or dead, but assuming he was dead. With the desires of any healthy woman, she had sought the comfort of another man.

When Boone returns, he is so shiftless and feckless he doesn't seem to care much one way or another. But others have seen the story as an illustration of Boone's tolerance and large spirit. He understands the trials and temptations Rebecca has known, and when told the child is Ned's or his brother Squire's, he says, "At least it's in the family," his wit and humor intact. In no version does Daniel get angry, accuse his wife, or threaten to leave her. At the very least he accepts the inevitable; at the very best he takes the child as his own and leads his family back to Sugartree Creek on the Yadkin.

It is an interesting fact that Jemima became Boone's favorite child. It was she he rescued in a daring pursuit when she was kidnapped at Boonesborough in 1776. It was Jemima who waited for him to return to Boonesborough after he was captured by the Shawnees in 1778, when the rest of the family, assuming he was dead, returned to North Carolina. It was with Jemima that Boone lived much of the time after the death of Rebecca in Missouri, near the end of his life.

Those who argue against the truth of the story point out that the treaty with the Cherokees was signed at the Long Island of the Holston November 19, 1761, and after that Boone likely left the militia and returned to Virginia and brought his family back to the Yadkin, in plenty of time to father Jemima. They also point out that Ned had recently married Rebecca's sister Martha, and it is unlikely he would have been sleeping with his double sister-in-law, Rebecca. Daniel's brother Squire was serving his apprenticeship as a blacksmith in Maryland at this time. They also note that the witnesses such as James Norman have so many facts wrong that their stories are not to be credited. All versions of the story contradict each other.

It's likely that Boone did return to his family in Virginia during the 1761–62 winter and bring them back to Sugartree. The biographer H. Addington Bruce stated flatly that "he brought his family back to the Yadkin as soon as peace had been made." The genealogist Spraker says that Jemima was born in North Carolina. There is no evidence to suggest otherwise. With Daniel's known distaste for farming, he would have brought Rebecca and the children to help him plant a crop before he went on his summer hunt. Culpeper, Virginia, is about 250 miles from the Yadkin, a week's journey by horseback.

Folklore grows from the pleasure of telling a good story, adding an even better surprise and punch line. In the many versions of this story of the illegitimacy of one of Boone's children we see folklore come to life and grow. If a story is good enough, it takes on a vitality, a kind of truth of its own, with little connection to its source. Whether true or not, the story of Jemima's begetting adds something important to the portrait of Rebecca that has come down to us. Her beauty and strength and grace and kindness are mentioned in every account. But the story of the child conceived with another man while Daniel was away and presumed dead makes her vivid in a special way, giving her a life independent of Daniel. She is not just the patient, handsome wife toiling while her husband is away. She is also human, with fears and desires, insecurities and hopes. Without Daniel, her life would still go on. Assuming that her husband is dead, she is lonely and in need of love, and she turns to a man nearby who looks like her husband, then must live with the scandal of the new pregnancy, and anxiety about her husband's possible return.

Many years after Boone's death, Draper corresponded with an old man named Stephen Hempstead, who claimed to have heard a version of the story from Boone himself when they were neighbors in Missouri. In this clearly apocryphal version Boone said he had been captured by Indians and when he returned home had found his wife with a new baby. "She had supposed him dead etc. etc. he inquired who would be the father of the child when born, she told him a certain Boone he answered, you need not distress yourself about it." He told her not to worry for he had one or two Indian wives while away. "Mrs. Boone was present at the time he told me," the old neighbor related to Draper and "she made her knitting needles fly very fast I assure you."

In the Victorian era the stories of the illegitimate child were suppressed by several Boone biographers who thought they might damage the reputation of the frontier hero. The Reverend John Mason Peck, who interviewed Boone in 1818 but did not publish his biography until 1847, avoided the story altogether and explained that Boone was free to go into the wilderness for long periods because he had large sons who could do the farmwork for Rebecca. Each age wants to see its heroes in its own image, in ways that reflect the pieties and sentiments of its day. As Faragher reminds us, it is important to remember that frontier culture in the eighteenth century was much rougher and more tolerant than that of the nineteenth-century society.

In one version of the tale of the illegitimate child, told by a woman, Rebecca gets the last line. "You had better have staid at home and got it yourself," she says to Boone.

THE BOONES' fifth child, Levina, was not born until March 23, 1766, about four years after the return to Sugartree Creek on the Yadkin. Whether this reflects discord between Daniel and Rebecca we cannot know. But we do know this was a period of increasing economic difficulty for Boone. His family and his responsibilities were growing, and the game on which he depended for his livelihood was receding farther and farther. As more settlers moved in, and the valley was safer from Indian attacks, he had to range farther to the west to find deer and beavers, mink and otter. It was a dilemma he faced after each of his moves. Wherever Boone went others would follow and soon the game was thinned out, the streams empty of fish and fur. He and others like him helped destroy the very thing that drew them to the woods. One cannot kill thirty deer in a day or ninety-plus bears in one season and keep repeating the pattern in the same place for long.

One of the reasons that Boone was attracted to regions that still had Indians was that when the Indians left, the game soon disappeared. Only hunters like himself, willing to risk hunting in Indian country, found the best game. As the settlements moved westward, there was a window of a few years when he could hunt the way he preferred, with the Indians and among the Indians.

This collision between love of hunting and hunting skill, and a sustainable ecology, is at the heart of the contradiction in Boone's life, and the history of modern America. The prowess and persistence of men like Boone made the decline of the game inevitable. There is some evidence that Boone began to understand this later in his life or at least had an inkling of the consequence of settlement and sustained hunting. In the charter of rules voted on at Boonesborough in May 1775 he urged restrictions on the wanton slaughter of game. But there is little evidence that he restrained himself in his commercial hunting for deer hides and furs. He never took part in the mass killing of buffalo for sport and for their tongues, but he was very much a part of the rush to strip the wilderness of its finest yield. In his time, of course, the wilderness and game seemed endless. The very world he sought to flee followed him and planted itself in his tracks.

Much has been written about Daniel Boone as debtor. Many documents showing sums he owed date from the early 1760s. Already, by the time he brought his family back from Culpeper, Virginia, there was an established pattern that would recur throughout much of the rest of his life. He goes on a long hunt and needs supplies, provisions, powder, lead; he needs steel traps, sometimes a new horse, tools for rifle repair. His growing family needs provisions, cloth, tools for farming, shoes, coffee or tea. He buys from merchants in Salisbury, who are happy to extend him credit, for he is an outstanding hunter and popular with his neighbors. When he returns from the hunt in the spring he has furs that bring in money, but the cash never seems to go far enough. He pays some of his debts, but others are left outstanding, and with interest the debts keep growing. And besides, he needs more supplies, not to mention seeds and a new plow for spring planting. And Rebecca and the children need new clothes. Interest accumulates on the debts he can't pay until the harvest is in or until he returns from the next long hunt.

Balzac is supposed to have said that most people cannot appreciate that a debt is an act of imagination. A debt is a gesture of faith, of confidence in the future, a reaching forward to make use of wealth not yet acquired. Debtors, like gamblers, live in an uneasy state of hope and despair but try to dwell on hope. The qualities that made Boone such a legendary man of the frontier also contributed to the mire of debt he never seemed able to struggle out of, for by the time he paid off one debt he had already acquired others. His hopefulness, his curiosity, his forward-looking faith in himself and others, his confidence in his destiny — characteristics that made him a successful hunter and explorer and leader — seemed to cripple him when it came to business. His way of dealing with the troubles in town, the mounting figures in ledgers, and the summonses to court was to plunge into the mountains again, to harvest hides and meat and furs and ginseng to pay the debts, but also to forget the unpleasant consequences of his borrowing.

It has been said that Boone had the temperament of an artist, that he was a poet of the woods, the hunt, the exploration of mysteries beyond the next ridge. Boone was described by the early biographer Timothy Flint as essentially a poet. He was an acute observer, studying the signs and weather and the Natives, and he felt an ancient kinship with the forest. He loved contemplation and solitude, yet was a good companion on the trail, popular with neighbors, fellow hunters, and scouts. The Indians seemed to be in awe of him.

But back in the settlements, in the world of the towns and the legal world of the court, the father world, Boone appeared to be out of his depth. Again and again, throughout his life, instead of registering a deed, doing the paperwork, paying off a debt, reading the fine print of a contract, he ignored business, forgot business, and returned to the hunt, to the storytelling by the fireside, to the trail that went on to the next ridge. Business did not interest him for long. He always convinced himself that he could put the matter off and catch up on the mere details later. This attitude hampered him even in the early years of his marriage. He was known already in the Yadkin Valley as a "slow pay" and as "not thrifty." His taxes often went unpaid. These habits led to disaster later when he was famous and got into the business of surveying and trading land on a big scale. Then his carelessness with details embroiled him in lawsuits and debts that hounded him almost until the end of his long life.

His tranquillity was disturbed by the unpleasant facts. Seventeen sixty-four was a hard year. Daniel had to sell the one tract of land he had been given by his father. The house on Sugartree Creek was on Bryan land. After 1764 he may not have owned one piece of property, in a region where even the poor often had hundreds of acres.

Frustrated by debt and failure as a farmer, Boone sought partners and backers for his expeditions across the mountains. He must have felt he was intended for something greater than just gathering deer hides in the Blue Ridge Mountains. According to Archibald Henderson, Boone was hired by the lawyer Richard Henderson and his associates in Salisbury to spy and explore land over the mountains as early as 1764. Hunters reported encountering Boone and Richard Callaway and Henry Skaggs as far west as the Clinch River in future Tennessee at that time. Boone met a group, known as the Blevens Connection, on their return from a long hunt in Kentucky and told them he was studying the "geography and locography of these woods." The Richard Callaway who accompanied Boone on this expedition was the nephew of Col. Richard Callaway with whom Boone would associate in Kentucky. On one of these early expeditions to the Cumberland Mountains, Boone was reported to have first sighted a large herd of buffalo from a peak and cried out, "I am richer than the man mentioned in Scripture who owned cattle on a thousand hills — I own the wild beasts of more than a thousand valleys."

Nathan Boone would later say that his father was not employed by Henderson and company until around 1774, but it is possible, even likely, that Richard Henderson, on his own account, paid Boone to report on the country he had explored across the mountains years before the Louisa Company was formed in 1774, or at the very least Henderson helped Boone avoid jail for debt, in return for information about the lands across the mountains. Archibald Henderson tended to exaggerate the importance of Richard Henderson to Boone's career. It is more likely Boone's association with Henderson began in 1769 or after, not in 1764.

Boone's father, Squire, died on January 2, 1765, and was buried in Joppa Cemetery in Mocksville, North Carolina. He was sixty-nine years old. The tombstone reads:

> *Squire Boone*
> *Departed*
> *this life in*
> *the sixty ninth year*
> *of his age*
> *in they year of our Lord 1765*
> *Geneiary tha 2.*

The inscription may have been cut by Daniel himself, for the imaginative spelling resembles that in many of the documents in Daniel's handwriting. The symbol of the point within a circle carved in the stone suggests that Squire was indeed a Freemason. In those days the sign was most often intended to show the duty of the individual brother to "God and man by means of the circumference." But it was also a sign often taken to mean "the Divine Spirit indwelling creation and abiding in the nature of man." It is possible that the sign was used to illustrate Tertullian's definition of God as a circle whose center is everywhere and circumference nowhere. According to *A Dictionary of Freemasonry*, it is a symbol of the creation of the world.

There is no more important milestone in a man's life than the death of his father. The death of a father may bring its own cloud of grief or regret, a sense of unfinished business, of questions that will forever go unanswered. A son feels alone in a particular way when his father dies. Suddenly he is on his own, and there may be a new sense of freedom, that whatever has to be done is now up to him. The rest of life opens before the son, and there is no one he has to answer to but himself and the future. And the future is all too short, though it is a sweeping vista of obligation. The death of a father is a time for reaching out, for stretching, moving ahead.

When some friends from Virginia arrived on the Yadkin in late summer of 1765 and announced they were on their way to Florida, Boone decided to go with them. He should have been harvesting his crops, preparing his house for cold weather, and getting ready for the trapping season. But this adventure to the mysterious world of Florida could not be resisted. And it would not hurt to be away from the constant reminders of his debts. Perhaps his future and fortune lay far to the south, in Florida. From the scant records that exist, we can construe that the trip south was something of a frolic of young males. His brother Squire went along, and his brother-in-law — Hannah's husband — John Stewart. Free land had been announced in the Panhandle of Florida after England acquired the region from France and Spain with the Treaty of Paris in 1763, and the eight young men were going down to have a look. Planning to hunt along the way, they traveled south to Fort Ninety-Six in South Carolina, then to Savannah, and on to St. Augustine.

One document from the trip records Boone losing three pounds at dice. His companion, named Slaughter, was apparently an expert gambler. According to Nathan Boone, "Slaughter was fond of gambling and won money going and coming back from Florida. This along with the deer skins of the party, was enough to meet most of their expenses while passing through the settlements." In later years Boone described this journey as if it was an extended holiday, with exotic scenery, birds, and pretty Spanish and Indian girls.

But when the party turned to hunting in the hammock country of the St. Johns River basin, they found the swamps and thickets of Florida rough going. The country was almost impassable and easy to get lost in. Florida seemed to be mostly muddy trails and swamps, with little game other than alligators. John Stewart, who was an excellent woodsman and hunter, got lost and wandered on his own for several days. The others in the group became so lost they were rescued by Seminoles, who took them to their village and fed them. The vine-entangled marshes of Florida were very different from the woodlands of the Appalachians, which ironically De Soto had named for the Apalachee Indians, who lived on the Florida Panhandle.

In Pensacola Boone is supposed to have made a down payment on a house and tract of land, perhaps with money from deer hides harvested along the way. It would seem that he planned to return to Florida with his family to settle in the regional capital. He was a man of enthusiasm and curiosity, and the strange and forbidding country seemed to have worked a spell on him, though he later told Nathan that Florida was devoid of game except for deer and birds.

From the Panhandle the company explored their way back north, taking a route through the Creek country that would be traveled a few years later by William Bartram and described in his classic prose. They reached Augusta and the Savannah River. Near the end of the journey Boone delayed their progress so he could keep his promise to Rebecca to arrive home on Christmas Day.

According to his son Nathan, Boone announced that Christmas Day on the Yadkin, as they celebrated his return, that he had bought land in Florida and planned to move them there. But Rebecca, however happy she was to have her husband home again, flatly refused to go that far south. Florida was too distant from her family and friends. A few months before, she had refused to move into the wilderness to the west and north of the Yadkin. These are the only reported instances in the many years of their marriage when she absolutely put her foot down against Boone's notions and whims and would not budge. None of the stories recounted afterward explain any special circumstances, and a few years later Rebecca was willing to accompany Boone into the very dangerous land of Kentucky. But on their moves they were always accompanied by many friends and kin. Wherever Boone was to find his destiny, it would not be in Florida.

IN THE FALL of 1766 Rebecca agreed to move several miles up the Yadkin to Holman's Ford, near the Brushy Mountains. This area was much less settled than the Sugartree Creek community. The next spring, after Daniel returned from his long hunt, they moved again, farther up the valley to the mouth of Beaver Creek. The next year they moved yet again, to the opposite side of the river, and Boone built a cabin on a hill looking south across the Yadkin.

On this move up the river Rebecca and Boone were accompanied by a number of relatives, including Boone's brother George and his wife, who was a cousin to Rebecca, and his brother Ned, married to Rebecca's sister Martha. Boone's brother Squire moved to the area also, as did his sister Hannah and her husband, John Stewart, one of Boone's favorite hunting companions, an excellent woodsman, and a man who could be depended on, even if he did get lost in Florida.

It was a pattern repeated again and again. A hunter who loved the solitude of the forest, Boone was also a part of an extended, close-knit community of relatives and friends that stayed with him in different combinations throughout his many moves on the Yadkin, across the mountains into Kentucky, and eventually all the way to Missouri. In the late 1760s they were settling the area around the future Wilkesboro, North Carolina, at the edge of the Blue Ridge Mountains.

At the mouth of Beaver Creek, Boone was within a day's ride of his favorite hunting camp high in the Blue Ridge. Many quotes about his urge to stay two steps ahead of civilization date from this period. A story told on the Yadkin many years after he had left has him commenting after someone has cleared a farm twelve miles away from his, "The place is getting entirely too thickly settled when a man can come and cut down trees without permission in your back yard."

In 1767 Benjamin Cutbirth and John Stewart and other young men from the Yadkin set out on an extended hunt into the western wilderness that took them all the way to New Orleans. They had many narrow escapes from snags in the river, whirlpools, tornadoes, and Indian attacks. They were robbed of all the wealth from furs they sold but nevertheless became local heroes for their daring expedition. Cutbirth's story of their journey only whetted Boone's determination to find the way through the mountains "leading to the Mesopotamia of Kentucky."

IN THE FALL and winter of 1767–68 Boone made what was perhaps his most extended hunt yet beyond the Blue Ridge and the Smokies, searching for his fortune. Since meeting the Irish peddler John Findley on the trail to Braddock's Defeat in 1755, he had been thinking about the place called Kanta-ke, about the legendary hunting ground beyond the mountains. With his brother Squire and a neighbor named William Hill he crossed the ridges to the Holston River and then the Clinch River. From there they crossed farther mountains into the headwaters of a river that flowed north, later to be called the Big Sandy. It is possible that Boone mistook the Levisa Fork of the Big Sandy for the headwaters of the Louisa or Kentucky River. His plan was to reach the Ohio River and follow it down to the falls that Findley had described to him in 1755.

Following a buffalo trace that ran roughly where Highway 23, the Country Music Highway, goes now, they came to a salt lick near present day Prestonsburg, Kentucky. Here they were trapped by a deep snow and forced to stay in camp most of the winter. But there was plenty of game around the salt lick, and the party lived on buffalo and bear meat. The place was especially notable for the number of bears nearby. Without knowing it, Boone was within the boundaries of the future state of Kentucky. But the place looked nothing like the cane lands and clover and bluegrass he had heard described by the peddler John Findley. The Kanta-ke Boone had heard praised around the campfires in 1755 was a land of meadows, savannas, with groves of hickory, oaks, and sugar maples. It was a land of wide rivers and buffalo grazing as far as the sight could reach, with bold salt springs where the game animals gathered to lick the salty dirt as though presenting themselves to be taken. Kanta-ke was a land of endless beaver, of fur beyond counting.

Kanta-ke was paradise on earth, an island in the wilderness, the land of heart's desire.

The beaver skins of Kanta-ke were not as valuable as beaver taken farther north or at higher elevations, where, because of colder weather, the fur was thicker, more luxuriant. But the streams of Kanta-ke were also rippling with fur besides beaver — with otter and mink, muskrat. Deer and elk, bears and panthers, foxes and raccoons, haunted the woods and streams there. Incredibly, the bounty was to be taken by whoever could find his way there over the mountains or down *la belle rivière*, the Ohio, and bring the fortune in furs back. The problem in Kanta-ke was not to gather fur and hides and meat but to transport them all the way back to the eastern markets, through hundreds of miles of Indian country. While Boone was exploring the headwaters of the Big Sandy, Findley was just across the mountains trading with the Indians in Kanta-ke.

The Boones and Hill returned to the Yadkin in the spring, with little to show for their winter hunt near the Big Sandy. Boone put in a crop as usual and planned his hunting trip for the next fall. At just this time John Findley reappeared in Boone's life. Apparently they met again by accident, the peddler roving into the upper Yadkin to sell his pins and needles, threads and thimbles, and discovering that Boone was there. The Boone children later recalled the colorful tales the peddler told of the promised land of Kanta-ke. He entertained the folks and charmed them with tall tales to help sell his goods and to find a place to stay for the night.

As Boone and Findley talked, after not having seen each other for thirteen years, Findley admitted he was a peddler and adventurer, not a scout or woodsman. But with a hunter as accomplished as Boone, surely they could follow the Warrior's Path west and find the defile in the mountains that led to the golden plains of Kanta-ke. Cherokee Indians had been going north to fight the Shawnees that way for centuries. And once they reached the Louisa River country, Findley could easily find the lush meadows, the cane lands and clover, the streams crowded with beaver, and the village of Eskippakithiki, where he had traded with the Indians.

It is possible that Boone had not been able to reach Kentucky before because he was too poor to outfit a successful expedition. He felt that his fate and his future lay in Kentucky, but for such an extended exploration he would need packhorses, a large supply of lead and powder, rifles and traps. Cumberland Gap was hundreds of miles away through the mountains, and the meadows of Kentucky more than a hundred miles beyond the gap. Because he was always in debt, Boone's credit was not adequate for outfitting such a venture until Findley came along and offered to throw in his lot, and perhaps Richard Henderson and the Hart brothers underwrote some of the expense in hopes of getting both furs and information about the overmountain region.

CHAPTER FIVE

Visions of Eden

1769–1771 ↪

At the Treaty of Fort Stanwix in 1768 the Iroquois ceded their claim to the hunting ground of Kanta-ke to the British, in return for thirty or forty thousand pounds' worth of trade goods. The Iroquois had attempted to dominate the region for more than a century, keeping the Shawnees and other tribes mostly out of their choice hunting grounds. The Shawnees particularly resented the Iroquois claims to the Ohio Valley, and their fury was fanned by the Treaty of Fort Stanwix because their presence and rights were ignored. The Shawnees were ignored again at the treaties the British made with the Cherokees in South Carolina at Hard Labor in 1768 and at Lochabar in 1770. Considering the Six Nations the slaves of the British, the Shawnees sought to organize a general campaign against the whites west of the mountains and sent a "painted hatchet" to the Cherokees, whom they had fought earlier, inviting them to join an attack on the white incursion into Kanta-ke. Contention over hunting rights there may have been the main reason Kanta-ke was almost empty of Indian villages at this particular window in Native history.

At the Treaty of Hard Labor, South Carolina, in October 1768, the British, somewhat ambiguously and contradictorily, conceded that the Cherokees, who lived to the south and east of the Clinch River, had some legal claim to the Kanta-ke region or at least to the southern portion of it. Hunters and explorers took the Treaty of Fort Stanwix to mean the Great Meadow, the Middle Ground, was open for hunting and possibly even settlement. Entrepreneurs took the Treaty of Hard Labor to mean that Kanta-ke might possibly be bought from the Cherokees. The British government and officials such as the colonial governor of Virginia, as well as speculators like George Washington, saw the Ohio Valley as a place for future development. They had already decided to award tracts of western land to veterans of the French and Indian War. These conflicting treaties and plans set in motion many schemes and designs that would figure in the future of Kanta-ke. Among the many schemers and dreamers were Daniel Boone and John Findley on the upper Yadkin. Boone had failed in his previous expeditions, but he was eager to try again. The historian Daniel Blake Smith would later write, "Kentucky was, first and perhaps foremost, an idea. It was an idea born of need and hope."

On May 1, 1769, Daniel Boone, John Findley, and John Stewart, with three assistants who were to serve as camp workers, left the upper Yadkin with the hope of reaching Kentucky. Their supplies and equipment were loaded on as many as fifteen packhorses. This May Day is one of the important turning points not only in Boone's life but also in the western progress of the frontier just on the eve of the Revolution and birth of the Republic.

It was a good time to get out of North Carolina, especially for a man in debt. But Daniel Boone had taken no part in the local rebellion, the Regulator disturbances. All his life he tended to avoid political disputes and confrontations. His peaceableness cost him dearly later, but he preferred to fight with the elements and with the mostly uncharted wilderness to the west. And by 1769 he and Findley and Stewart were bending all their talents and energy toward the quest for Kentucky. Only if they could reach the Great Meadow, the Middle Ground, the Bluegrass island, would their lives be renewed and their fortunes prosper.

Over the years there has been much discussion about the origins and meaning of the name *Kentucky*. It was once fashionable to say that the word meant, in Cherokee or Shawnee, "the dark and bloody ground." But according to George R. Stewart in *American Place Names*, the word comes from the Iroquois, *Kanta-ke*, "the meadow-land," a combination of *kenta* (level) and *aki* (place). As early as 1753 a traveler referred to the Shawnee Blue Lick town as on the "Cantucky River." The Shawnee name for a town on a tributary of the Red River was *Eskippaki-thiki*. It is easy to see why the early explorers and surveyors preferred the Iroquois word *Kanta-ke* as a name for the region.

But many people have continued to believe that the name *Kentucky* means "dark and bloody ground." One story is that a Cherokee called Dragging Canoe described the region that way to Boone in 1775 at Sycamore Shoals. But Boone was not present at the signing of the Sycamore Shoals treaty. Others have suggested that Kentucky was called the dark and bloody ground because the Ohio had been called by some the "Bloody River." It has even been suggested, as a joke, that *Kaintuck* comes from *canetuck* because of all the canebrakes in the region.

But there are other arguments about the origin of the name *Kentucky*. Some said it was a Wyandotte name meaning "the land of tomorrow." And John Mason Peck, writing in 1847, said, "*Kain-tuck-ee* is a Shawanese [Shawnee] word, and signified 'at the head of the river.'" Still others have argued that the name, in any case, is an invention of the whites. It has been suggested that the name *Kentucke* stuck because it was favored by the Cherokees. Those coming into Kentucky through Cumberland Gap passed through Cherokee lands to get there.

Some words have a resonance, a color, and are memorable even before we know what they mean. We love to say them just to feel them in the air and on our tongue. Some words have a peculiar rightness and catch on like a bit of poetry. *Kanta-ke* is such a term, and people have never tired of saying it since it was first heard by whites in the middle of the eighteenth century. There is a symmetry to the word, to the balance of vowels and consonants, beginning with the *k* sound and ending with the *k* sound. And of course the name was thought to have an etymological and semantic rightness too. Whatever they called it, those who sought Kentucky already saw it as a mythic, Edenic place. Whatever the etymology of the word, Kentucky certainly seemed like the land of the future to Boone and Findley and many other explorers of the time.

It appears that Boone had reasons to leave the Yadkin, perhaps as strong as the lure of Kentucky. He had accumulated more debts than property, and from time to time had been taken to court over unpaid debts, some as large as fifty pounds. And since his father had died in 1765, Boone was free to make bold moves, and take his place in the world. The prominent businessman, lawyer, and later judge Richard Henderson had prosecuted Boone and would secure a warrant for his arrest in 1770, after Daniel had left for Kentucky. Boone was sued at least twice in 1770 while he was away in Kentucky.

In the North Carolina State Archives in Raleigh we find this record of the Salisbury District Superior Court:

WILLIAMS & HENDERSON ESQ. VS DANIEL BOONE
Debt,
4 cont. 56
Conditions performed
    Jury empanelled & sworn find the conditions was performed.
Assess damages to 20.00 sixpence costs

And for the same court in September 1770 we find the following record:

No. 105
HUGH MONTGOMERY VS. DANIEL BOONE
Debt.
    Judgement Con _____ by Avery for sum of 61.13.2 proc. Money & interest from the 20th March
1770 till paid 7 Costs —

Richard Henderson and Nathaniel Hart were among the many entrepreneurs and land speculators in backwoods North Carolina. Like others, including George Washington and Patrick Henry in Virginia, they had their eye on the fortune to be made in western lands bought up cheaply or claimed for nothing and later sold to settlers. With a relatively small investment one might become wealthy and powerful as the territory was developed, with cities and towns and commerce in the future.

As mentioned earlier, there is a good deal of disagreement about the beginning of Boone's relationship with Richard Henderson and his partners Thomas and Nathaniel Hart and John Williams. Thomas Hart was the sheriff who presumably served the warrant for Boone's arrest, which Richard Henderson and his law partner John Williams had issued.

The Kentucky historian Thomas D. Clark, among others, has argued that Boone and his companions may have been working for Henderson as early as 1769 on their first expedition to Trans-Allegheny lands. At the very least Boone was spying out the land for Henderson, perhaps conducting a rough survey. As Thomas D. Clark put it, "He wasn't just bird counting." Archibald Henderson and others have claimed Boone was in the employ of Richard Henderson as scout and spy as early as 1764, when Boone was exploring the Tennessee country. Many agree that Boone must have been serving Henderson in some capacity when he set out for Kentucky in 1769. Henderson was an eloquent and famous lawyer, a rich man, and a visionary. "He was considered the Patrick Henry of North Carolina." John Mason Peck, who interviewed Boone in his last years in Missouri, stated flatly that Boone's 1769 expedition to Kentucky was funded by Richard Henderson. "As confidential agent of the land company, Boone carried with him letters and instructions for his guidance upon this extended tour of exploration."

Because of his great skill at scouting through the wilderness unseen, exploring dangerous and unknown regions, there was often a hint of espionage about Boone's activities. His ability to remain hidden, to observe, to return and report what he had seen, makes him appear a bit of a spy from first to last. And more than that, he was a kind of double agent, moving between Indian and white culture, friendly with either and both, making some wonder where his true loyalty lay. He was exploring in the interests of his own curiosity and plans and for sponsors such as Richard Henderson. Because he could slip in and out of and function between these worlds so easily, he would be seen by some as a kind of secret agent, by others as a traitor. With his acute senses and capacious memory, Boone had the frontier world under surveillance. Sometimes he was working for Richard Henderson, sometimes for William Russell or the government of Virginia. Mostly he was spying in the service of his great curiosity and relish for the unexplored country.

In any case there are no documents proving that Boone was in the employ of Henderson before 1774. In his interviews with Lyman Draper, Nathan said his father was not employed by Henderson's company until 1774 or 1775. But Nathan was not born until 1781, and while he is one of the most reliable informants about Boone's life, even he is sometimes mistaken. And it does seem at least plausible that Henderson agreed to continuances and delays in the debt cases against Boone in exchange for information about the mysterious and alluring land over the mountains. As far as we know, Boone was never actually put in jail for his debts. And it is possible that a lawyer and businessman such as Henderson might be filing a suit for a client on the one hand while negotiating with the defendant on the other. Stranger conflicts of interest have been known in the pursuit of business and the practice of law. Richard Henderson is on record as saying, "[Boone] had the honor of having more suits entered against him for debt than any other man of his day, chiefly small debts of five pounds and under contracted for lead and powder."

Archibald Henderson wrote that Boone was under a pledge of secrecy about his early employment by Richard Henderson and that he never violated that confidence. Whatever his role in the 1769 Kentucky expedition, events intervened in the career of Richard Henderson at just that moment to prevent him from openly pursuing any western land scheme for a few years. He was appointed judge for the North Carolina Superior Court in 1769, and while he served on the bench, he was not free to proceed with such ventures, which had been declared illegal by the colonial governors of North Carolina and Virginia.

A descendant of Nathaniel Hart later said it was Boone's colorful descriptions of Kentucky after he returned in 1771 that inspired the businessmen to form Henderson and Company and plan the purchase of western land. This story is probably true but doesn't preclude an earlier personal interest in Boone's explorations on the part of Henderson and Hart. Many mammoth projects such as the Transylvania Company have their seeds in smaller, tentative enterprises. And significant actions are also taken for mixed and even contradictory motives.

LEAVING HIS debts and obligations, hardscrabble farming, and political unrest behind, Boone was reaching out toward a world of unlimited freedom, where great rivers chased themselves all the way to the horizon, and the land was hardly touched by the surveyor's chain or described in courthouse deed. There are particular events that seem to define a life on the way to becoming a legend. For Washington, it is the winter at Valley Forge, and crossing the Delaware. For Franklin it is the key on the kite string that touches lightning, and negotiating the alliance with the French that guaranteed the survival of the rebellion fumbling its way toward a republic. For Boone, it is the image of a man finding his way through a narrow gap into the Eden of Kentucky and leading others there, guaranteeing that the new nation about to be born would extend over the mountains and encompass the West. Whatever other deeds he did or did not do, this is the image that has stuck.

Of the party of six — Boone, Findley, Stewart, James Mooney, Joseph Holder, and William Cooley — three had been beyond the mountains before: Boone and Findley, of course, and John Stewart, who the previous year had gone on the hunting adventure with Benjamin Cutbirth and a few others all the way into future Tennessee and had carried their furs and hides to market in New Orleans. Nathan many years later said Boone had great confidence in his brother-in-law John Stewart. "My father even said he never had a brother he thought more of than he did of John Stewart. He had all the confidence in him that one man could have in another; he was faithful in the performance of his promises, a most essential requisite, as Father always said, in a hunting companion." Stewart knew how to handle a rifle and he could be depended on to be at the right place at the time he had agreed to.

On May 1, 1769, the party climbed the mountain chain by following Elk Creek in western North Carolina and crossed the Blue Ridge at Cook's Gap into a high mountain meadow. In the following days they crossed a series of mountain chains, Stone Mountain and the Iron Mountain range. Somewhere near Wolf Hills they joined the Great Warrior's Path, an ancient trail that ran across the southwestern part of Virginia, crossing the Clinch and then Powell's River, then turned north through Ouasiota, or Cave Gap, which Dr. Thomas Walker or others had named the Cumberland Gap. *Ouasioto*, according to some, is a Wyandotte word. Others have suggested it is a Shawnee word: *scioto* means "deer," therefore, the gap is Deer Pass. Walker named the gap for the Duke of Cumberland, and he or someone else named the central river in Kentucky the Louisa for the duke's sister.

To the modern eye the Warrior's Path, called Athiamiowee, or "Path of the Armed Ones" by the Indians, might have been hardly discernible in some places. Where it followed a buffalo trace along a stream or through a gap in the mountains, it was a worn track. In places Indian trails were well marked; in others, almost invisible to whites. Indians trails usually ran on high ground in the mountains, out along ridges to avoid thickets and small streams. William E. Myer, in *Indian Trails of the Southeast*, tells us that "some parts of [the trails] had become worn down below the surface of the soil, while other stretches might be almost invisible, save to the practiced eye of the Indian." But to a Native American or a white woodsman such as Boone, the path was legible, running out between trees and skirting large rocks, crossing a creek on stepping stones or at a shallow ford, crossing a meadow at a level place, avoiding marshy places where tracks would be conspicuous. In places, war parties had left signs cut on trees or scratched or painted on rocks, perhaps to brag about who had come this way, who had made a successful raid against the Iroquois in the north, the Cherokees in the south, the Shawnees in the west.

Boone and his party followed the Warrior's Path across Moccasin Gap to the Clinch River. Then they climbed Powell's Mountain and ascended Wallen's Ridge into the valley of Powell's River. At Powell's Valley they met a group led by Joseph Martin, who were clearing land for a settlement. Martin's Fort was the westernmost settlement of the English colonies at that time.

Leaving this last outpost of white civilization, Boone and his companions moved down the river until they could see the cliffs called the White Rocks, set like teeth in the mountain rim. Boone would later describe to Filson the sense of dread and horror that chain of mountains and cliffs could evoke, appearing to be an insurmountable barrier. And then Boone and his party saw the gap, opening a way into the west. Sharp as a gunsight cut into the mountains, this defile was the place where hundreds of hunters and explorers would line up their sights on Kentucky and the West, and hundreds of thousands of settlers would follow over the next half century. Cumberland Gap became the most famous pass in America, a gateway to the future. Many had passed through the gap before. Gabriel Arthur had crossed there in 1674, escaping from captivity, but it was Boone who made it famous and drew so many to its threshold.

As the historian Frederick Jackson Turner famously put it, "Stand at Cumberland Gap and watch the procession of civilization, marching single file — the buffalo following the trail to the salt springs, the Indian, the fur-trader and hunter, the cattle-raiser, the farmer — and the frontier has passed by." The Indian name for the gap, Ouasioto, would be forgotten, and the name of the Duke of Cumberland, Butcher of

Culloden, would stick to the gap and mountain range, river and plateau. History and geography are a tissue of such ironies and paradoxes.

Beyond the gap the Warrior's Path swung to the north. Boone and his companions entered Pine Mountain Gap, a water gap and the final gateway into Kentucky, crossed the Cumberland River near Flat Lick, then the Laurel River, Rockcastle River, beyond Hazel Patch, then stepped through the low Sand Gap, or Boone's Gap, into the watershed of the Louisa or Kentucky River. Here the mountains began to peter out into sharp hills known as the Knob Country. A few miles down the river, in a meadow where the town of Irvine would later be, they pitched their Station Camp. Boone climbed nearby Pilot Knob, and from there he could look into the far distance and the land of rolling forests, meadows, and canebrakes along the river. If Boone had wondered before whether Kentucky was only a fable, he could now see the place was a splendid fact.

Many historians have referred to Boone's Pisgah vision from Pilot Knob. Pisgah was the mountain described in Deuteronomy 34:1, which Moses climbed after wandering in the wilderness, to look over into the Promised Land. A number of painters have portrayed Boone gazing from a height into the new land of Canaan. Like Moses looking over into the Land of Canaan after so many years of wandering in the wilderness, Boone gazes on the goal of his quest, the Great Meadow. But as Draper points out, there was "this important difference, that the Lord's prohibition of Moses ever going thither did not . . . apply in Boone's case." And so this image of Boone's first sighting the bluegrass of central Kentucky became an icon of American history and myth. But what Boone viewed was already colored and enhanced by the expectations he carried with him. In Arthur K. Moore's words, "What Daniel Boone saw from Pilot Knob in June, 1769, was not only a magnificent forest enveloped in a blue haze but also a fabled garden interpenetrated with myth." Boone and others brought the idea of Kentucky with them, and what they actually found sometimes surpassed their expectations.

While Stewart and the others continued to build shelters at Station Camp, Boone and Findley began to explore the country to the north. They followed the Warrior's Path to Findley's old camp on the stream that would be named Lulbegrud Creek, a tributary of the Red River, and found the remains of his stay there. "On the seventh day of June following, we found ourselves on Red-River, where John Finley [*sic*] had formerly been trading with the Indians, and, from the top of an eminence, saw with pleasure the beautiful level of Kentucke." It was the sight of Findley's former camp that proved conclusively that Boone and his party had reached Kanta-ke. Boone and Findley had found the site that the Shawnees had called Blue Lick Town, but the Shawnees were gone and their huts burned. Much of Boone's history, and Kentucky's, would be connected to a place farther north on the Licking River called the Lower Blue Licks.

There was another blue that caught the explorers' attention, the grass that covered so much of the meadowlands of the region, called ever after the bluegrass. Bluegrass would come to be understood as almost synonymous with central Kentucky and Kentucky culture. There has been a good deal of discussion about what is actually meant by the term *bluegrass*. Some have suggested the bluegrass is of European origin and brought by early traders in the hay they packed their trade goods in. Scattered in their camps, the seeds swept over Kentucky, filling an ecological gap, and became a prominent feature of the region. Most botanists agree that bluegrass is *Poa pretensis*, which seems to have originated in Pennsylvania, though it could have been brought there from Europe in the seventeenth century. Some say bluegrass came from England where it was called smooth meadow grass. What seems certain is that the grasslands of Kentucky were covered with this and similar grasses by the time Boone and Findley were gazing on the rolling hills and gentle valleys in 1769. Though we have no proof, it seems likely that such extensive growth had taken much longer than seventeen years, perhaps centuries, to spread so thoroughly. The region's limestone soil, on which the grass thrives, lies on the formation geologists call the Cincinnati Arch, said to be the oldest soil in North America. According to the historian George W. Ranck, the term *bluegrass* is an abbreviation of "blue limestone grass."

Christopher Gist had noted the "blue grass" in that region in 1751. The name and the image of bluegrass had entered the language, and the folklore and imagination of the country, by 1745, and they have stayed vivid to this day. Whatever its origins, the sweeping savannas of lush, shining grass were a sight to behold. It is a wonderful paradox of our language that bluegrass music refers to music of the mountains, the backcountry, whereas the bluegrass region is the aristocratic, race-horse-breeding area of central Kentucky.

Some historians have suggested that fires set by Shawnees and Iroquois in hunting to drive game were the source of the open meadows and savannas of the Bluegrass region. Certainly the Iroquois had cleared the region in more senses than one. A later historian and archaeologist, Nancy O'Malley, would describe the region: "The realized niche of the Inner Bluegrass was an uncommonly rich one, being well wooded but with occasional openings that were amenable to clearing. Its soils were generally rich and deep; and its rolling topography was more erosion resistant than many other areas. Other environmental realities included a sometimes uncertain surface-flowing water supply ameliorated by the presence of numerous permanent springs." Recently ecologists studying the records have decided that the central region of Kentucky had more forests than meadows, though some of the more fertile areas had curiously open woodland or "savannah" with large canebrakes (*Arundinaria gigantea*) on uplands, and stretches of grassland that might be called prairie. The botanist Short in 1828 said that large sections of central Kentucky were covered with orchards of pawpaws.

There has been little disagreement about the fertility of the ground in this section of Kentucky. Every early traveler noted the richness of the limestone soil. Some said there were no leaves under the trees because the ground was so rich the fallen leaves rotted before winter was over. George Croghan, a trader who had seen Kentucky more than once, would report in 1765 that the land was too rich for growing anything but hemp, flax, and Indian corn.

That June, Boone and his companions began an idyll in the wilderness. Game was so plentiful that buffalo and elk, deer and turkeys, practically stationed themselves in front of a rifle sight. Boone and Stewart and Findley hunted while the others stayed in camp and prepared the hides. To be worth a "buck," a buckskin had to be shaved and the rough outer skin scraped away. According to Draper, "[T]he skin was thoroughly rubbed across a staking-board until rendered quite soft and pliant, thus stripping it of all unnecessary weight and fitting it for packing more compactly."

Boone also took the opportunity to go farther afield in his explorations. It was during this summer and fall that Boone began to learn Kentucky. It is likely no other white man ever knew the whole of the pristine Great Meadow so intimately and completely. At this time he ranged as far west as the Falls of the Ohio, where Fort Nelson and then Louisville would later be built. He hunted north of the Blue Licks to the Ohio and followed the river, which the French explorer La Salle had called *la belle rivière*, down to the cane lands near the mouth of the Kentucky River. He found dozens of salt springs and licks, and the oil springs. He found a thousand bold springs where water issued blinking into the light from under the roots of a tulip poplar or dogwood. Boone found the mouths of caves in the limestone where cool air breathed out in summer and cooler air was pulled inside in winter. He saw ebbing and flowing springs that gushed and then slowed to a trickle as the catchment inside the rock filled and then was siphoned empty again. "He was on a mission," William Gilmore Simms wrote of Boone in 1845. "The spiritual sense was strong in him. He felt the union between his inner [self] and the nature of the visible world and yearned for their intimate communion. His thoughts and feelings were those of a great discoverer."

This first exploration of Kentucky caused writers of the nineteenth century such as C. W. Webber to dip their pens into purple ink. "Here the mother that he had worshiped had put on her beautiful garments at last, and revealed herself to him as God had caused her to be. Here he would realize the joy of worship, the soft terror of an over-coming awe, and transported, cry aloud in wonder." In 1852 Webber described Boone's exuberance on this first hunt into Kentucky. "[Boone] only felt yearnings — ungovernably strong — the meaning of which he could not know — but which led him deeper and deeper with yet more restless strength into the cool profounds of the all-nourishing bosom of his primeval mother." Even in the Victorian age, the gender and sexual overtones of Boone's passion for Kentucky were implicitly understood.

As far as we know, Boone did not have a compass with him. He depended on the sun by day and the stars at night to keep his orienta-tion. And of course he could look at moss on the north sides of trees, except in deep woods and hollows where moss grew on all sides of the trunks. Navigation in the wilderness, especially when exploring, is less a matter of quadrant directions than of following land features such as mountain ranges and river systems. Knowing where the watershed of the Rockcastle River ended and that of the Kentucky River began was more important than knowing true north or the degree of latitude. In a deep forest where it was hard to even see the sky, it would be difficult to know which direction to pursue to reach a gap or river gorge. There the best method of finding your way was to choose the tallest tree in sight and climb it. A hunter, careful not to leave his rifle on the ground, laid it on limbs out of the reach of the ground. Once in the top he could part the limbs and look far out over the tops of the other trees to a river sparkling in the distance or a peak he recognized rearing to the left.

Though honeybees had not reached the Kentucky wilderness in 1769, and the most common milk in the region was buffalo milk, the place was in a metaphorical sense a land flowing with milk and honey. The buffalo fed on clover and wild peavines and shoots of young cane, and bears on grubs and acorns and a dozen kinds of berries. Fox grapes ripened on the creek banks after the first frost. Though Boone and his companions were primarily collecting deer hides, they also killed elk and buffalo from time to time. Elk hides were cut up to use as harness and straps, and bear and buffalo skins were used for bedding. It was an extended frolic, every day presenting new vistas, a wonderful summer that stretched into fall and a wonderful Indian summer. Among the wonders was the fact that it was an Indian summer in which they saw no Indians, although called that because it was the season when Indians were most likely to be on the warpath.

For convenience and safety, Boone and his party had made several smaller camps in a large semicircle around their base at Station Camp. That way the hides and furs were cached at different locations. If Indians attacked one camp and took the furs, they might miss the others, and the men could slip away into the forest. However, the bulk of their equipment and supplies, as well as hides and furs, was kept at the Station Camp, hub of their operations.

On December 22, a bright, beautiful day, Boone and Stewart were roaming the woods with their rifles, relishing the bounty around them, when a party of Shawnees appeared out of a canebrake and took the hunters prisoner. In Filson's account of 1784 Boone says, "In the decline of the day, near Kentucke river, as we ascended the brow of a small hill, a number of Indians rushed out of a thick cane-brake upon us, and made us prisoners. The time of our sorrow was now arrived, and the scene fully opened. The Indians plundered us of what we had." Surprised and outnumbered, Boone and Stewart had no choice but to surrender. The Shawnees, returning from a hunt on the Green River to their villages north of the Ohio, probably as surprised by the encounter as Boone and Stewart, ordered the hunters to show them their camp.

Boone tended to display a remarkably cool head in emergencies. As the Shawnees threatened him with their tomahawks, he cheerfully agreed to show them one of the outlying camps. As they approached the camp, Boone took care to make enough noise so that his companions working there would be warned. The men who were in the camp got the warning and slipped away unnoticed by the Shawnees. Boone calculated that the men who had fled would warn the others and that they would quickly hide the accumulated pelts and hides, and the valuable supplies at the base camp, in the woods. To give them time he led the Shawnees to each of the outlying camps one by one. All guns and powder and lead, traps and precious salt, were confiscated along the way. When he finally had no choice but to lead his captors to the main camp, Boone was astonished to find that the other men had simply fled into the woods, leaving the great hoard of furs and hides, supplies and horses, in plain sight. His stalling for time had been wasted.

The Shawnees, led by a chief who called himself Capt. Will Emery (Indian chiefs often took English names and the title of captain), loaded a fortune in hides and furs on the hunters' own packhorses. Shawnees had only a few horses then. Captain Will apparently had no interest in harming Boone and Stewart. The Shawnees took all they had and gave them in return a small supply of powder and lead and a cheap musket. But Captain Will warned Boone, before he left, to go home and not return to Kentucky, "for this is Indians' hunting ground, and all the animals, skins and furs are ours; and if you are so foolish as to venture here again, you may be sure the wasps and yellow-jackets will sting you severely." Captain Will probably thought he was being correct, even generous, to the trespassers and poachers from North Carolina. By his code, he was treating Boone and Stewart with respect. Boone took it all with apparent good cheer and shook hands with his captors.

By the time Boone and Stewart encountered Will Emery and his band of Shawnees that December day in 1769, "[t]he Shawnees . . . were a scattered people, living in small contingents and mingling with other Indian groups in Alabama, Georgia, the Carolinas and Pennsylvania," Stephen Aron tells us. As many as two hundred had lived in the village of Eskippakithiki in 1736, but that village had been abandoned by 1769. Many Shawnees lived in what would become Ohio on the Scioto and Little Miami rivers. War, disease, internal conflicts, displacement, had already diminished the Shawnee population by the time they returned to their old homeland in the Ohio country. Different groups of Indians lived in their villages, making the villages home to an assortment of refugees from other tribes, as well as several adopted whites. At Chillicothe at least three languages were spoken by the residents.

Shawnees and other Indians were relatively tolerant of hunters of either race who were only killing for meat. Everyone had a right to eat. But hunters accumulating furs and deer hides to sell angered them. Indians had fought among themselves over hunting rights so long some had indeed come to call it the "Dark and Bloody Ground." The Reverend David McClure recorded an account of Indian hunters presenting their furs and meat to widows and the elderly. Hunters were honored for providing for their kin and for the aged who could no longer hunt themselves. Indian courtesy required that the first game killed on a hunt be presented to a hunting partner. Indians did not deplete the game at the rate white hunters did, not because they were less interested in demonstrating their mastery as hunters, but because of the ethic of killing only for need. Believing that it angered the spirits of animals to kill wantonly, Indian hunters restrained their killing, while white hunters were known to shoot large animals such as buffalo and elk for diversion, for target practice.

It took several days for the Shawnees to loot and destroy all the group's hunting camps. When they finally left for their towns north of the Ohio River, Findley and the others emerged from the forest. They were devastated by their losses, and deeply shaken by the sudden appearance of and destruction wrought by the Shawnees. Findley, Mooney, Holder, and Cooley said they had had enough of Kentucky. They were going back to North Carolina. But Boone was determined to retrieve some of the wealth that had been taken from them. At the very least they might steal back some of the horses. Otherwise they would have to walk back to North Carolina. With horses they could return to the Yadkin for necessary supplies.

Boone and Stewart started out after the Shawnees and caught up with them in a few days. They watched the Indian camp until the small hours of the night, then crept to the clearing where the horses were hobbled and took four or five of the mounts, among them an Indian pony.

For a day and a night Boone and Stewart rode south toward Station Camp. But on the second day, as they were resting themselves and their horses, they heard a rumbling of hoofbeats, and suddenly the Shawnees rode out of the woods upon them. "Steal horse, ha?" one of the Shawnees said, and they threatened Boone and Stewart with tomahawks. They laughed and mocked the white men for being so clumsy. They took a bell from a horse and put it on Boone and made him dance and prance around the clearing while they laughed at him. And then they took their prisoners and horses and started north again.

This episode shows Boone with his guard down. Since they had not seen any Indians in the first seven months in Kentucky, he was not taking the necessary precautions. And after stealing the horses, he and Stewart made no effort to cover their tracks. They hoped to outrun the Shawnees or assumed the Indians would write off the loss of the horses and continue on to their villages.

As the Shawnees and their captives began the march north again, Boone and Stewart submitted gracefully to their fate. Boone later said he was pretty sure they could escape if they were patient. On their part the Shawnees seemed more amused than angry with their prisoners. Every day they hinted that the next day Boone and Stewart would be freed, but when the next day came they continued their journey toward the Ohio. At night Boone and Stewart were not bound, but each was forced to sleep between two Indians.

On the seventh day, when they were almost within sight of the Ohio River, the band camped beside a thick canebrake, between the Lower Blue Licks and the mouth of Cabin Creek on *la belle rivière*. While the Indians were gathering wood for the cooking fires and hobbling the horses, Daniel signaled to his friend it was time to escape. Each grabbed a gun and powder and lead and plunged into the cane before their captors realized what was happening. It was getting dark, and the Indians secured the horses to prevent them from being stolen. They acted reluctant to enter the cane to search, for the cane was thick and it was already getting dark. Boone and Stewart inched their way through the stalks and then into the forest. Walking all night, guided by the stars, they made it back to their old camp in about twenty-four hours of continuous walking.

But Station Camp had been abandoned, though warm ashes from a campfire indicated someone had only just left. Boone and Stewart, without pausing, followed Findley and the others south and overtook them on the Rockcastle River. After a dash of almost a hundred miles Boone was pleased to find that his brother Squire had arrived with much-needed new supplies and a friend named Alexander Neely. According to Filson's account, Boone was overjoyed at seeing his brother, and exhilarated by his escape from the Shawnees. "Our meeting so fortunately in the wilderness made us reciprocally sensible of the utmost satisfaction."

No one has ever explained why Squire Boone, ten years younger than Daniel, chose to look for his brother at this time, in the middle of winter, or how he was able to find Boone. It is clear that Squire was an accomplished woodsman himself. According to some reports he and Neely had failed to find Boone, and Squire was devastated, heading back to Cumberland Gap and the settlements. It is quite possible that Squire had been sent out by Richard Henderson to find and resupply Boone and his party, and to bring back the furs and hides they had accumulated. Somebody had provided the horses and provisions Squire and Neely brought. Since Squire was usually in debt as much as Daniel, it is unlikely he funded the mission himself. Archibald Henderson would state positively it was Richard Henderson who sent Squire to Kentucky.

Findley and the three others were determined to return to North Carolina, but Boone and Stewart were equally determined, now that Squire had arrived with fresh supplies, to stay and hunt to make up some of the losses to the Shawnees. If Boone was deeply in debt back on the Yadkin, and evidence suggests that he was, then he had an additional incentive to stay through the winter. Beaver skins probably offered his only real hope of paying off his creditors. Much as he may have missed Rebecca and his children, he had other calls to duty to heed. And he had his intelligence on the land of Kentucky to gather and compile. That Squire and Neely agreed to stay and help with the hunt only confirmed his decision. Boone never saw John Findley again, and it is thought Findley was killed by Indians while on another trading trip in 1771.

THE STREAMS of Kentucky were filled with beaver and beaver dams, with otters and mink. Even among such abundance, some skill was required in the preservation of fur. While beaver pelts are cut so they can be stretched out flat on hoops of grape vine or hickory withes, mink and otter skins are peeled off whole so they can be stretched over boards or limbs, inside out, to dry and cure. In the winter of 1770 the Boone brothers, with Stewart and Neely, directed all their hopes and all their efforts toward trapping. They had a substantial supply of jerk and bear meat, dried buffalo tongues, and in the camp they were warmed by buffalo robes and bearskins. At night they slept with bare feet to the fire while moccasins and leggings dried.

It may have been in this period that they read by the campfire a copy of *Gulliver's Travels*, which Neely had brought with him. In a deposition given years later in a land dispute, Boone described their habit of reading. "Saith that in the year 1770 I encamped on the Red River with five other men and we had with us for our amusement the History of Samuel Gulever's Travels where In he gave an account of his young Mistress Glomdelclerk carrying him on a market day for a show to a town called Lulbegrud." (It is not clear whether Boone is referring in this deposition to the five men who came with him to Kentucky in 1769 or to other hunters who may have joined him and Squire, Stewart and Neely, on Lulbegrud Creek.)

As January turned into February, Squire and Neely hunted and walked the traplines together, while Boone and Stewart split up to cover separate territories, being already familiar with the region. They agreed to meet at the camp every two weeks. They had made a small canoe out of bark for crossing the Kentucky River and to reach traps along the river and its branches.

A hard winter rain began and continued for many days, and the river raged in flood. When the appointed day for their meeting came, Stewart did not appear. As the flood subsided, Boone crossed the river and found the remains of a campfire near a tree where Stewart's initials had been carved. There were no other signs of his friend. Boone vowed he would not return to North Carolina until he had found Stewart.

The disappearance of Stewart was an intimidating mystery. He seemed to have vanished into the damp winter air. But five years later, while Boone and his crew were hacking out Boone's Trace, the bones of a man were discovered in a hollow sycamore tree near the area where Stewart disappeared. Boone examined the remains and found a powder horn with John Stewart's initials scratched on the brass band. The left arm had been broken, but the skull was intact. There was no sign of his rifle.

The most likely explanation was that he had been attacked by Indians, was wounded, and lost his rifle. Fleeing into the woods, he found the hollow sycamore and hid, and there he had either frozen to death or bled to death. "My father always thought that Stewart either got killed or sickened and died in the wilderness," Nathan told Draper.

Alexander Neely was so shaken by the disappearance of Stewart that he decided to return to the settlements. After he was gone, the Boone brothers, committing themselves to a longer stay, still hoping to find Stewart, built a better shelter on the banks of the Kentucky River. Having plenty of meat, they again directed their efforts toward gathering furs. Boone told Filson, "We were then in a dangerous, helpless situation, exposed daily to perils and death amongst the savages and wild beasts, not a white man in the country but ourselves . . . Thus situated, many hundred miles from our families in the howling wilderness, I believe few would have equally enjoyed the happiness we experienced."

BY THE TIME spring arrived and the trapping season came to an end, Boone and Squire had caught and cured a valuable stock of furs. They were running low on ammunition and supplies. It would have seemed the natural time to return to the Yadkin, but Boone decided that only Squire would take the packhorse carrying their treasure of furs, sell the harvest, and put in crops in North Carolina. He himself would stay in Kentucky to hunt deer and explore.

There has been a good deal of speculation about Boone's decision to stay a second year in Kentucky. It would have seemed logical for him to have returned to his family in the spring, grow a crop of corn, and return to Kentucky in late fall. A number of motives for his staying in 1770 have been advanced: he was still avoiding creditors, he needed to make further explorations for Henderson, he felt guilty about Stewart and was still trying to find his friend. Others have said that the game was so plentiful that Boone could not tear himself away from the hunt.

Any or all of these motives may have been factors in his decision to stay alone while Squire returned to the Yadkin. Likely there were still regions of Kentucky he needed to explore for his own satisfaction and his report to Henderson. But there may have been other reasons too, some hard to define. Now thirty-five years old, Boone had reached the age when a man of ambition and vision has to define himself. Frustrated by his failures at farming, in debt, unsuccessful previously in reaching Kentucky, he could not give it up now that he was finally there. He may have sensed that this was his moment, his destiny. In his midthirties a man either reaches out toward risk and glory or stays within the routines of the expected and ordinary. It is the age when men leave safe homes and jobs and go on voyages, odysseys, perform transforming sacrifices. It is the age when Whitman wrote *Leaves of Grass* and Columbus started to plan his voyage to the Indies. It is the age at which visionaries become prophets or explorers or inventors, or make fools of themselves trying. Putting behind him his accumulated failures and humiliations, such a man must seize the new prospect and ride with it to greatness or defeat. There is no turning back.

When Boone decided to stay alone in the forests of Kentucky while his brother Squire returned to conduct business, he made a choice that revealed himself to himself. He would not do what most other men would do. He would not be just a commercial trapper. He was that, but he was something else too. There was something he wanted to learn in the wilderness, and he needed to be alone. He had hunted alone before, for days and weeks. But what he needed to learn was here, and he couldn't say exactly what it was, but he sensed the uniqueness of the opportunity. He had been given a role to play, the best role he had ever known, and he meant to make the most of it.

"He now proceeded to make those remarkable solitary explorations of Kentucky which have given him immortality." Boone was a leader and an English-speaking colonial. He had been called a white Indian, and he was an expert marksman, scout, trapper, navigator of the forest. He was a woodsman, but there was more, and he knew he was seeking more. In the name of his people, and perhaps Richard Henderson as well, and his own nature, he was spying on the western wilderness, as if there was a secret he must obtain. It was beyond the next ridge, and it was farther down the river of his days, the intelligence he must gather. Two years may be the time it takes to leave behind one's old self and see the world in a larger, clearer way. It would be the time Thoreau spent in his cabin at Walden, the definitive period of his life. It was the time Goethe spent in Italy in 1786–88, in a visit that transformed his vision of himself and his future.

Some would have said it was fame Boone was seeking in Kentucky, without quite knowing it, and they would not be entirely wrong. For fame was one facet of what he felt immanent inside himself. He wanted to be known across the reaches of geography, across the boundaries of time. But it was more than that, something sacred, almost like religion.

It was something he shared with the Indians more than with white people. It was about his contemplation of the clouds over the grasslands and the wooded ridge, and the sunset over the hurrying river. It was about how time would seem to stop even as the stars came out. He must play his part in the great curve of time. It was about the lay of the new land just waiting for him to see and walk over it.

Boone studied the different kinds of springs in the land, the springs that boiled out of limestone, the cove springs deep in hollows, cave springs that issued out of caverns, salt springs surrounded by licks, sulfur springs. He studied the bones exposed in the raw salt licks. He must know this land as a man knows a beloved woman. He was determined to keep out of sight as he pursued his passion. And somehow he felt he was chosen. It was not just his decision after all. It was as if he had been separated out for this mission of relish and discovery. It was a moment that would never come again, not in his lifetime, not in ten thousand years, and he had been sent there and burdened with the desire to cherish it. There were other hunters and scouts with their eye on Kentucky, and speculators greedy to claim it, but he was not responsible for them. His duty was to this mission. He had been called out, as others are inspired to preach or nurse the sick or lead in battle. He would not tell anyone what it was, not even Richard Henderson, and he would keep his humor and his wit, and modesty, but he knew he had been given a sign and a window, and he must step across that threshold.

"Boone deliberately chose the peace of solitude, rather than mingle in the wild wranglings and disputings of the society around him — from whom it was ever his first thought to be escaping — or he would never have penetrated to those secret places where later his name became talisman," wrote William Carlos Williams.

BOONE TOLD Filson that after Squire left him on May 1, 1770, he was tempted to plunge into a deep melancholy. He was without salt, sugar, bread, companions, even a horse or a dog. "The idea of a beloved wife and family and their anxiety upon the account of my absence . . . made sensible impressions on my heart. A thousand dreadful apprehensions presented themselves to my view, and had undoubtedly disposed me to melancholy, if further indulged."

Philosophers of the sublime have long stressed the combination of delight and fear. The most intense experiences, indeed the sublime itself, is a mingling of terror and joy. The danger of the Kentucky wilderness intensified Boone's relish for its wonders.

As the summer continued, Boone ran so low on powder and lead he had to give up hunting for hides and hunt only for subsistence. This provided him with an excuse to devote more time to exploration. In these weeks and months he appears to have crossed all the land from the Licking River west to the Ohio at the Falls. It was the most beautiful part of Kentucky, and many have considered Kentucky the most beautiful place in North America. Near the end of his life Boone was described as "naturally romantic and fond of the chase" and at no point in his life did he fit that label better than in his first exploration of Kentucky.

Among the many salt and sulfur licks Boone found in the limestone country was the famous Big Bone Lick near the Ohio between future Cincinnati and the mouth of the Kentucky River. He was by no means the first white explorer to see this curiosity of the Middle Ground. French traders had seen it as early as 1735 and reported finding the skeletons of "seven elephants." Christopher Gist had seen the site on his 1750–51 expedition. And many others, including Thomas Ashe, had described the "giant sloths and giant beaver bones at Big Bone Lick." The size of the bones and their number gave the place an air of fantasy. There were tusks five feet long and teeth weighing four pounds. Nearby was a medicinal spring whose waters, Filson would later say, could cure "the itch by once bathing."

The caves of Kentucky are one of the most spectacular features of the region. Indians had taken shelter in them and explored the covert passages for thousands of years, and animals had lived in them long before that. Underneath the surface of much of Kentucky, including some of the Bluegrass area, conditions were perfect for cave formation, beginning with a water-soluble layer of limestone. With plenty of rainfall, runoff picked up carbon dioxide from the air and soil to make carbonic acid that seeped downward through faults and crevices, eating away the rock, to reach a base water level where pools and streams gathered. Rotting vegetation on the surface produced even more acid to cut away at the limestone.

The pools and streams that collected underground made tubes and tunnels, draining toward river basins, creating gutters, a maze of abandoned drains. Because of the many colors of the salts and stone, the underground chambers and corridors lit up like flower gardens, chapels, sculpture salons, when a torch was brought into the whispering, dripping passages, opening into one another like chains of buried memories, half-suppressed dreams. Besides bats, crickets, rats, turtles, and salamanders, animals that came in and left the caves, there were permanent residents of the dark hallways, alcoves, and grottoes: white eyeless fish, crayfish, flatworms, beetles, and spiders.

The water and minerals made their own decorations, stalagmites and stalactites that resembled trees, statues, drapery. Colorful streaks called bacon festooned the walls. Cave pearls were made by the tumbling action of dripping water. Other formations were called snowballs, gypsum flowers, angel hair, cave cotton, cave grass. Some stalagmites were translucent as flesh.

The shadow world of the caves was no less a wonderland than the landscape above. Boone lived in many caves and carved his initials on several, as did other white hunters. Indians before them had left their talismanic signs on the hidden surfaces. The caves were a refuge, a secret world, sanctuary for the wet and cold, the pursued and frightened. It was a land beneath the threshold of hunting and settlement, multiplying the mysteries that Kentucky offered.

Several times during this summer of wandering, Boone saw Indians but hid before they spotted him. Of course they may have been watching him and he never knew it. He built small cooking fires of dry wood that made little smoke, usually hidden by rocks or bark walls he took care to construct to conceal the flames. Often he did without a fire and slept in a canebrake for safety. At the Falls of the Ohio, where Louisville would later be built, he found a recently dead horse at the foot of the falls and saw the ruins of a chimney and cabin. It is possible the camp had been built by his former partner, John Findley, when he traded at the Falls in 1752.

Striking east from the Ohio, Boone traveled to the Kentucky River about where Frankfort would later be. There, he said afterward, he saw an Indian on a log over the river fishing. "While I was looking at him, he tumbled into the river, and I saw no more of him," Boone reportedly told his son Nathan, implying that he had killed the Indian. It is one of the few incidents reported by Nathan that does not ring true. And though Isaac Boone, a cousin of Daniel's, said he heard the same story from Daniel in his later years, the anecdote sounds more like a punch line than a true incident.

Shooting an unsuspecting Indian in cold blood is out of character with everything we know about Boone and his dealings with Indians. Of course people sometimes act out of character, but it is hard to believe the man who never retaliated against the Indians for torturing and killing his son James and killing his brother Ned would shoot an Indian who had not harmed him and then brag about it. "It was understood from the way in which he spoke of it that he had shot and killed the Indian; yet he seemed not to care about alluding more particularly to it," Nathan told Draper.

Beyond the issue of Boone's known character there are the considerations of practicality and safety. A man nearly out of powder and lead, spying an Indian fishing, would almost certainly back away into the forest and save his ammunition until it was needed. And a shot would alert other Indians who might be hunting or fishing nearby. Boone's story makes it sound as though he shot the Indian on a whim. It seems likely it was a joke the old man liked to tell to entertain his visitors. He was also known to tell tales about encountering great hairy monsters like the yahoos in *Gulliver's Travels*. Most likely it never happened. Boone didn't actually state that he killed the Indian fisherman; he let his listeners assume that's what he meant, and was reluctant to say more.

But Draper takes the story as fact and, to excuse the murder by calling it self-defense, says, "and it may have been the means of preserving his life for great future usefulness to his family and country." He ignores the implausibility of the quip and its dry humor in the context.

IT APPEARS that Boone stayed awhile in a cave on Shawanoe Run, a tributary of the Kentucky River, that summer. A tree over the entrance once had "D.B. — 1770" carved on it. Years later the remains of campfires were found on the cave floor. It is still called Boone's Cave.

On the nearby Dix (Dick's) River another of the legendary events of Boone's career supposedly occurred that summer. As he told it, Boone was surprised by Indians on a bluff over Dix River, less than a mile above the junction with the Kentucky River. The bank far below was covered with trees that reached up within a few feet of the bluff. Rather than surrender, Boone said he took a leap into the top of a sugar maple, and the top bent with his weight, cushioning his fall, as he grabbed on to an upper limb. He then dropped from branch to branch until he reached the ground sixty feet below. On the riverbank he ran through the thickets, then swam the stream, leaving the Indians stunned by the speed of his escape. Though Isaiah Boone, Daniel's nephew, and several scholars have expressed skepticism about the anecdote, it could be true. As a boy Boone had probably climbed and learned to ride a bending treetop, drop from limb to limb to the ground. With practice an agile boy could reach the ground in seconds from the top of the tallest trees, breaking his fall by grasping one limb and swinging to the next, all the way to the forest floor.

Boone's solitary wanderings seemed to make him more alert, more vigorous, more certain of his purpose. "To many it would have been the means of weakening the mind, but in Boone it only seems to have renewed his energies," the biographer W. H. Bogart says. "In the three months that no response awaited the word, he learned how much the thought could speak." In the account Filson gives us of this summer, Boone sleeps in canebrakes and thickets, fearing Indians are watching his camps. Wolves howl in the night and circle. Ignoring fear, he luxuriates in the solitude and plenty of the forest. It is his definitive period, when his truest and best self emerges and clarifies its essential nature. "For three months he was alone," William Carlos Williams says. "Surely he must have known that it was the great ecstatic moment of his life's affirmation." Like Alexander Selkirk, the sailor who was the model for Robinson Crusoe, before him, Boone may have "seen deep truths about himself revealed through the cleansing simplicity of the demands of survival."

On July 27, 1770, Squire Boone returned to Kentucky. With the money from the furs, Squire had paid some of Boone's debts and bought new supplies. He had assured Rebecca that Boone was well and thriving and would return after another trapping season. Squire may well have brought Boone a message from Richard Henderson with the additional supplies. Each brother had achieved success in his separate mission. For safety the brothers moved to a cave near the mouth of Marble Creek on the Kentucky River. Here they lived for two months, then moved to another cave farther down the river near the mouth of Hickman Creek. Boone carved his initials on the walls of each of these caves, and a nearby bluff was called Boone's Knob.

But for safety and convenience in their hunting, Boone and Squire kept moving. To avoid detection they stayed in no camp for very long. Once returning from a hunt, they found their camp had been raided and many supplies stolen. Blankets, moccasins, leggings, were missing. Even the kettle had disappeared. Finding wolf tracks, they followed them to a den under a blown-down tree, where wolf cubs slept on the remains of one of their blankets. They killed the mother wolf, recovered the kettle she had stolen, and tried to tame the cubs as pets but without success.

At the end of the deer season the brothers packed up the hides for Squire to take back to the settlements. It had been a good year. Again Boone was alone in the wilderness for many weeks. But heavy rains delayed Squire's return from the Yadkin. Impatient and worried, Boone set out to meet his brother. On the way he encountered an old Indian man left in the woods to die. Boone gave him most of the meat of a deer he had killed. Hurrying ahead, Boone spied what appeared to be a tree on fire. Approaching warily, he discovered to his relief it was the camp of the returning Squire, who had brought with him additional supplies as well as packhorses.

IT HAS BEEN suggested that people of genius do their great work in a decade's time. For mathematicians and physicists the decade is often their twenties; for poets and composers the best years are usually their thirties. For others the glory period may come later. But in each case their lives lead up to the ten years of inspiration and greatness, peak, and then trail away into years of more ordinary achievement. Examples cited are romantic poets such as Wordsworth and Coleridge, who had their years of towering accomplishment from about 1798 to 1808, or Walt Whitman, who wrote most of his best work between 1854 and 1865. Emerson did almost all his greatest writing between about 1835 and 1846. Though Daniel Boone was a frontiersman and explorer, not an artist of words, he embodies and enacts many of the qualities and ideas Romantic writers such as Emerson, Thoreau, and Whitman would later articulate.

It is hard not to think of Boone when we read Emerson on solitude ("But if a man would be alone, let him look at the stars"), or Thoreau on walking and wildness. The self-reliance, the intense curiosity, and relish of experience in Whitman's "Song of Myself," the peaceableness and love of the wild, suggest Boone more than any other single historical person. Whitman also came from a family of Quakers. Boone was a great Romantic artist, but his work of art was his life, his example of attention, exhilaration, and contemplation. "Prayer is the contemplation of the facts of life from the highest point of view," Emerson said, echoing the spirit of the scout and explorer. Fifty years after Boone explored Kentucky and relished its wilderness for two years without returning to the settlements, the Hudson River painters captured something of his transcendental view of the mountains and rivers in their art. Boone saw nature as both fact and fable, and every cloud and sunset, tree and blade of grass, as instance of both the real and the ideal, physical and spiritual. Everyone who ever interviewed him mentioned his calm and his poise. The sense of the spiritual was something he shared with the Indians and likely learned, in part, from them. Every tree and river, rock and cloud, was alive, haunted, significant.

After Boone would come many other great naturalists and artists, but none of them would have the legendary status of Boone, the air of the original. None had so much influence or inspired so many who came after. Like Washington, like Lincoln later, Boone inspired the craving for an ideal self, with Quaker tolerance for others, reliant and integrious, with a large capacity for wonder and reaching out toward the new and mysterious, brave but cautious, sociable, diplomatic, calm in the face of danger. A lover of song and reading, a notoriously erratic speller.

Daniel Boone did most of the things for which he is remembered between about 1770 and 1782. He lived until 1820 and was a legend for the last thirty-six years of his life. But the legend is based almost entirely on the events of those eleven or twelve years.

WHILE DANIEL and Squire were hunting and trapping and exploring Kentucky in 1770–71, evading Indians and accumulating hides and furs, they were not the only white men in the western wilderness. A number of Virginians were also roving and hunting in the region. In 1769–70 a group including Hancock and Richard Taylor, Abraham Hempinstall, and a man named Barbour descended the Ohio River to the Mississippi and explored the Arkansas River. Hancock Taylor and Hempinstall went on to New Orleans and sailed from there back to New York, but Richard Taylor and Barbour turned east and explored the Yazoo and the Creek and Choctaw country, reaching Georgia and Florida.

Another large party from Virginia, which included Casper Mansker, explored Powell's Valley and the Cumberland River in the summer of 1769. They found big herds of buffalo around the salt licks as they worked their way through the Cumberland Valley. A party of Cherokees destroyed their camp. Some of the group returned to the settlements while ten others built canoes and descended the Cumberland to the French Lick, site of future Nashville. Continuing on to the Ohio and Mississippi, they were robbed again by Chickasaws. Descending the river to Natchez, they made their way back home from there.

George Washington, who owned tracts of land west of the Alleghenies, made another expedition down the Ohio River in 1769–70, getting as far as the mouth of the Kanawha in future West Virginia, and the Levisa Fork of the Big Sandy in Kentucky. From journals kept during the journey, it is clear he foresaw trouble between the Indians and settlers who were already making their way from Fort Pitt down into the Ohio Valley. As Joseph J. Ellis phrases it, "[Washington] looked west to the land beyond the Alleghenies as the great prize worth fighting for. And although he did not know it at the time, the rewards he received for his soldiering in the form of land grants in the Ohio Country would become the lifetime foundation of his personal wealth." Washington, like many others, seemed to have an obsession with the West. Ellis points out that this interest even affected the way he remodeled his house. When Washington renovated Mount Vernon, he rebuilt the mansion so its main entrance faced west.

Another group who made a foray into the wilderness at the time was a party called the Long Hunters because they stayed in the woods for long periods. They were about fifty in number and included many from earlier hunts such as Casper Mansker, James Drake, and Isaac

Bledsoe, all from the New River area of Virginia. Equipped with three packhorses each, ammunition, traps, hunting dogs, they made their way into Kentucky in the fall of 1770. This group hunted in the same region where the Boones had been busy the year before. James Dysart discovered the Knob Licks, where they saw more than a thousand buffalo. From the region of Dix River they moved west to the Green River, where they killed many deer and collected more hides. But their camp was found by a group of Indians led by Capt. Will Emery, who had captured Boone and Stewart the December before, and their hides were taken or destroyed. Three of the hunters had disappeared and all their supplies were destroyed. "Upon a large, spreading beech tree beside the camp, they rudely carved in the bark, 'Fifteen hundred skins gone to ruination.'" But the remaining men continued the hunt in smaller groups, using the horses and supplies they had left.

During the 1770–71 winter Casper Mansker and several companions were hunting, away from the larger group, in the region of the Green River, when they heard a very odd sound. It seemed neither animal nor Indian. Mansker told the others to stay hidden while he went to investigate. Moving from tree to bush, the way he might approach a deer or Indian camp, the hunter saw a sight that astonished and then made him laugh. Lying on his back on a deerskin in a little clearing, a bare-headed man was singing to the sky. It was Daniel Boone, alone in the forest, indulging his love of song and craving a human voice, even if it was his own.

This image of Boone, assuming he was alone, singing in the wilderness, has a resonance that early became part of the legend. Many woodsmen were fond of singing, but it is the story of Boone that has come down to us. Though surrounded by forests, where Indians and wolves and panthers might be prowling, not to mention rival hunters, he is so at ease he lies on his back and sings to the clouds and trees and passing birds. He sings for the sheer joy of hearing a voice.

But why would a man trying to avoid detection by Indians lie in the woods singing at the top of his voice? Boone knew his life and his mission depended on his ability to fade through the forest without being seen. It seems likely he had already spotted Caspar Mansker and the Long Hunters, had had them under surveillance, perhaps for days, monitoring their wandering, and as they approached he put on a show for them. Lying on his back and singing as they got close, he created another never-to-be-forgotten image of his legend, which we are still talking about.

The sight of Boone singing in the woods resonates with our image of Audubon playing his flute in the wilderness, and Thoreau playing his flute by Walden, and the great Hudson River painter Thomas Cole carrying his flute, along with his brushes and canvas, into the Catskills and Adirondacks to make music by his campfire. This anecdote of Boone the solitary singer resonates also with Whitman's image of the bird and poet in the Lincoln elegy, "When Lilacs Last in Dooryards Bloomed," and with the Enlightenment sense of harmony in nature and between man and nature. In this vision all creation sounds out in concert if we can just attend to its polyphony.

Casper Mansker's party spent several days hunting with Daniel and Squire Boone. One has the impression of an exuberant expedition along the Green River. They hunted down along the Cumberland River also, and gave their names to Casper's River, Drake's Creek, Skaggs's Creek, Bledsoe's Creek. At the French Lick they discovered a group of French hunters had killed all the buffalo for their tongues and left the bodies rotting. With no buffalo to browse on the cane, the brakes had grown impenetrably thick. "'Bledsoe told me,' says General Hall, that 'one could walk for several hundred yards in and around the lick and on buffellows skuls, & bones.'"

In March of 1771 Daniel and Squire loaded their furs and hides on the packhorses Squire had brought from North Carolina the previous fall and headed back to the Yadkin. It took them several weeks, searching for the best trails around canebrakes and thickets, the best fords across rivers and rain-swollen creeks, to reach Powell's Valley. While camped there and hunting for meat, Squire encountered a startling apparition of a man, gaunt, in torn clothing, dirty, wandering without direction. It was his old friend Alexander Neely.

Neeley had come with a hunting party back to the region around Cumberland Gap and gotten lost. He had fired all his powder, hoping his shots would be heard and he would be rescued. But no one heard him, and he had wandered, helpless without powder, almost starving. One day while he was sitting weak and in despair, a dog appeared and came near him, as if pleased to find a human in the woods. Grabbing the dog by the neck, he cut its throat with his hunting knife and started a fire with the flint of his gun to cook the dog's carcass. Jerking most of the meat, he packed it in a sack made of the dog's skin and started out again to find his way.

Squire told Neely he could join the Boones at their camp, but he must eat sparingly, being semistarved for so long. Neely threw away the residue of his dog meat, which Squire saw was infested with maggots. Daniel and Squire nursed him in their camp until he regained his strength. They also mended his clothing, which had been ripped and torn in his rambling. After several days Neely was strong enough to follow after his party of Long Hunters. It is likely Squire and Daniel gave him detailed directions for reaching the Cumberland Gap. Years later Squire Boone would visit Neely at his home in the New River Valley.

Anxious to get home with the furs, the Boones followed the Warrior's Path east, nearing the westernmost settlements of Virginia. Since they had spent the winter and spring on the Cumberland, they may not have known how much war activity was going on among the Indian tribes that spring. The Iroquois were attacking the Cherokees and Catawbas. Shawnees and Delawares were at war with the Cherokees, and the Chickasaws were attacking the French-speaking outposts in the Illinois country.

While camped in Powell's Valley and roasting some meat for supper, the Boones were accosted by a party of six or eight Indians. At first the exchange was friendly, and then the Indians offered to trade their muskets for the fine rifles Daniel and Squire carried. The brothers refused, and their rifles and all their furs were seized. One brave demanded Squire's shot pouch, and when it was not handed over quickly, he grabbed the strap.

It is not clear why Boone was so reluctant to comply with the Indian demands on this occasion. Perhaps he realized this was his last chance to return to the Yadkin with a hoard of furs, after two years in the wilderness. It is possible Squire became angry and resistant and Daniel was caught between his brother and the Indians. On only one other occasion, years later, would he lose his temper when he was surprised by Indians as he was about to eat after a long fast. Perhaps in Powell's Valley in 1771 he was aggravated by hunger. Both Boones got in scuffles with the Indians, and a large warrior raised his tomahawk and ordered them to flee, which they did. At the end of two years of wandering Boone may have been exhausted, impatient to get home. Hiding in the brush a few hundred yards away, they watched the Indians depart. Then they ran to the nearest settlement, probably a few miles away on the Clinch River, to get help. Having lost their rifles, furs, and horses, they were extremely vulnerable.

A party was formed in the settlement and followed the Indians, but apparently the group was in a bad mood. One member shot a deer that wandered across their path, and the others got angry because he had given away their presence. The ensuing argument caused so much ill feeling that the band gave up the pursuit and decided to return to the settlement. Later Boone learned that the Indians had been waiting for them in an ambush and it was fortunate they all turned back when they did.

As they were returning to their homes, some members of the posse killed two Indians near a remote cabin and divided their belongings among the group. Later they learned some of the war party that had robbed the Boones were drowned crossing a river in flood. It was a week of mindless brutality and loss, and a sad ending to the two most significant years of Boone's life.

THE EVENTS THAT came to be known as the Regulator Movement had a dramatic impact on the region and on Boone. Increased taxes imposed in the 1760s by the colonial government on the people of North Carolina brought on the Regulator actions. When the elegant governor's palace was built around 1768, a new poll tax was introduced to pay for it, which led to increased agitation.

It was a class conflict between the eastern planters, who employed slave labor, and the settlers farther west who worked their own farms. Corruption was rampant at all levels of colonial administration in North Carolina. Fees for the same service, collected two or three times under different names, often never reached the capital in New Bern.

The Regulator Movement organized the growing alienation of the settlers from the Crown. Those in the Piedmont got angry enough to defy the king and his representatives. The movement was the seedbed of the Revolution, though a breakaway from the monarchy was still inconceivable to most in 1769.

The most hated official of the colonial government was Edmund Fanning of Orange County, registrar of deeds, judge of the superior court, colonel of the militia, and member of the North Carolina Assembly. He was arrogant and came to represent everything the Regulators despised.

But the new Governor's Palace tax was the final straw. "Regulators" stated their demands: (1) no more taxes until it was proved the new levies were legal, (2) no fees larger than those required by law, (3) the right to meet as Regulators, (4) the right to collect money for the movement's expenses, and (5) agreement to abide by the decision of the majority.

When the officials of Orange County took a member's horse in lieu of his unpaid taxes, a band of Regulators rode to Hillsborough, fired into Edmund Fanning's mansion, and recovered the horse. Fanning arrested two rebel leaders, William Butler and Herman Husband. The arrests incited so much anger that seven hundred people converged on the jail where Butler and Husband were held and set them free.

Alarmed, Gov. William Tryon warned local officials against taking illegal fees. The Regulators answered by charging Edmund Fanning with corruption. The governor called out a militia of almost fifteen hundred men to occupy Hillsborough and keep the peace while Butler and Husband were tried for rioting. Fanning was tried at the same court session for extortion.

Husband was acquitted. Butler and two others were found guilty but were pardoned by Governor Tryon. Fanning was convicted of corruption and extortion and resigned from the position of registrar, yet no sentence was imposed, more evidence of the unfairness of the courts.

In 1769 four counties elected Regulators to serve in the assembly, whereupon Governor Tryon dissolved the body. In September 1770 Judge Richard Henderson, presiding over the superior court in Hillsborough, was attacked by a force of 150 Regulators and driven from the bench. Rioting spread throughout Hillsborough, innocent citizens were beaten, and Edmund Fanning's fine house wrecked. When the assembly met December 5, 1770, news came that the rebels had gathered at Cross Creek to march toward New Bern.

The assembly quickly passed a bill known as the Bloody Riot Act, which in essence proclaimed martial law. It was the Bloody Riot Act that inspired the greatest number of citizens to join the Regulator Movement and declare Edmund Fanning an outlaw to be executed when caught. Colonial courts would be ignored. Finally, in 1771, the governor ordered a special court to be held at Hillsborough. Again he called out a militia to protect the court and keep peace in the region. Regulators — some two thousand of them — gathered near Alamance Creek and sent a letter to Governor Tryon asking for an audience. The governor agreed only if they laid down their arms. The Regulators rejected the demand. After waiting an hour the governor sent a message that he was ready to fire on them. "Fire and be damned!" was the Regulator retort.

In the battle that followed, the colonial militia was outnumbered, but their superior training and equipment guaranteed victory over the ragtag crowd of Regulators. Tryon offered pardon to any rebel willing to swear allegiance to the Crown and colonial government. Most of those who had taken part in the rebellion conceded defeat and swore the oath.

Some, however, did not take the oath. Instead they crossed the mountains beyond the Yadkin into the valley of the Watauga River, settled at a place called Sycamore Shoals and negotiated an agreement with the Cherokee Nation to lease land. Known as the Watauga Association, it became a model for future American republics.

Governor William Tryon Addresses a Group of Backcountry Farmers at the Time of the Regulator Movement. Felix O. C. Darley. Drawing. Ca. 1876. Engraving by Albert Bobbett for the magazine Our Country, 1877. (Courtesy North Carolina Collection, Wilson Library, University of North Carolina at Chapel Hill.)

CHAPTER SIX

Return to the Bluegrass Island

1772–1774 ↳

The four years from 1771 to 1775 were frustrating for Boone. His overwhelming desire was to settle in Kentucky and bring his family and friends there. His dream was to hunt in Kentucky and live in peace with the Indians on this "Bluegrass island." Almost everything he did was aimed at this overriding goal. But between his desire and its fulfillment lay hundreds of miles of dangerous mountains, the opposition of the governors of North Carolina and Virginia, the land grabbing of large entrepreneurs and political leaders, lack of funds, and outbreaks of fighting between Indians and whites on the frontier. The early 1770s was a time of roadblocks, hurdles, detours, digressions, and disturbances caused by the Regulators in North Carolina. Every step turned into a misstep. It must have seemed at times he would never be able to settle in the land he felt had been promised to him. When Daniel reached his farm on the Yadkin after twenty-four months away, robbed of his furs and even his rifle, he was poorer than when he had started out on May 1, 1769. Some of his debts had been paid by Squire the year before, but more had been incurred for supplies for the second winter in the wilderness, and by his family while he was away. With accumulating interest, the debts had grown and were still growing.

According to Archibald Henderson, "The reports of his extended explorations, which he made to Judge Henderson, were soon communicated to the other partners of the land company; and their letters bristle with glowing and minute descriptions of the country as detailed by their agent." Though the Louisa Company was not formally organized until three years later, subsequent testimony makes it clear Henderson and the others were already thinking of purchasing Kentucky lands from the Cherokees, perhaps as early as 1768. Boone's report was crucial to their planning. Boone's description of the land of Kentucky spurred much discussion and many letters between Henderson and his friends. However, Henderson was still a judge in the colonial court, appointed about the time Boone had left for Kentucky in 1769, and had much on his mind besides real estate in Kentucky, including Regulators and the accelerating acts of defiance and rebellion.

Though his two years in Kentucky were a failure in any accountant's ledger, they could be seen as a triumph when measured in other ways. Though he returned empty-handed, he had found the Bluegrass island. He had *seen* Kentucky and traveled it from one end to the other, and he had survived. He had found the defile to the west and stood on a high peak in the Knob Country. He had seen more deer and bears and buffalo than he could describe, and he had seen the wonders of the caves, the salt licks, the mammoth bones, the sweeping savannas of bluegrass, clover, and cane, and followed the Kentucky River to the wide curving procession of the Ohio. He had found the Falls of the Ohio and the valley of the Green River and followed the Cumberland to the French Lick.

The most valuable thing he had accomplished he probably could not have put into words. At the cost of loneliness, and worry about his family far away over the mountains, he had evaded Indians and endured cold and wind, floods and summer heat, flies and snakes, wolves and capture. He had lost his close friend and brother-in-law, John Stewart. He had been robbed twice of everything. But his victory was something that had happened within him. He was a different man from the one who had set out from the Yadkin in 1769. Alone in the wilderness, he had found something in himself beyond the thrill of hunting, beyond the vision of profit from commerce in hides and furs and ginseng.

Whatever the looks and muttering of his neighbors as he returned again empty-handed from his voyage, and whatever the unpleasant duns and demands from creditors, he felt richer as he resumed his life on the Yadkin. It was time for spring planting. Everyone who knew Boone knew he was in some important way *different*. Some did not approve of that difference, but they recognized it. His peculiar ability to rise above enormous setbacks and keep his thoughts on other things is one example of his difference. Some called it naïveté, others laziness, and still others accused him of indifference to his family. From their perspectives they may have been partly right. The thoughts that occupied Boone were not always intelligible to others. Most intelligent and practical people who had returned from two years in the wilderness broke would have settled down to business the way his friend Henry Miller had years earlier. But Boone was different.

As far as is known, Boone returned to the business of farming and local hunting in 1771. His daughter Rebecca had been born on May 26, 1768, and his son Daniel Morgan on December 23, 1769, almost eight months after he left for Kentucky. It is quite possible that was the birth that gave rise to the legend that one of the Boone children was illegitimate. His next child was Jesse, born in 1773. If Rebecca was angry at him for his long stay in Kentucky, no comment to that effect has come down to us in any of the interviews with descendants and relatives and friends. A Moravian missionary named George Soelle preached along the Yadkin in September 1771 and recorded in his diary meeting the wife of one "Nath. Buhn." He says that "Mrs. Buhn" was the daughter of Joseph Bryant. This likely is Rebecca, and Reverend Soelle mistook "Daniel" for "Nathaniel." "Mrs. Buhn" expressed great fears and uncertainty. "She is by nature a quiet soul, and of few words. She told me of her need, and that her heart was often restless and anxious, though then the feelings would again leave her, xxx She can not read. I heard her gladly and told her of the loving heart of Jesus, open to her, and bade her turn to Him wherever she was by day or night. She seems less earnest in the matter than he, but has more feeling." It is possible that Daniel had to "sleep on the couch" for a while as her resentment cooled and wore itself out, but there is no testimony to that effect. In any case, Daniel's long absence gave her a rest from the almost continuous effort of childbearing.

A better story of Daniel's reunion with Rebecca in 1771 was told to Draper by one John B. Roark. When he reached Beaver Creek on the upper Yadkin, Daniel found that his family had gone to a neighborhood frolic. Arriving at the dance, he realized he was so disheveled and his beard and hair so long no one recognized him. He went up to Rebecca and asked for a dance. When she drew back, he said, "You need not refuse me for you have danced many a time with me." Rebecca recognized his voice, and tears filled her eyes as she hugged him. The neighbors were amazed to see her hug this old, unkempt hunter. Then they too recognized him and he entertained the company all evening with tales of his adventures in Kentucky.

WHILE DANIEL had been away, the region around Beaver Creek had become far more populated than it had been when he left in 1769. Not only was the upper Yadkin becoming too thickly settled for Boone's taste, but his creditors would not leave him alone. In March 1771 a complaint had been filed in court accusing him of hiding from the law and his obligations in the wilderness. A warrant for seizure of his property had been obtained. "We therefore command you that you attach the Estate of the said Daniel Boone (if to be found in your Bailiwick) or so much thereof replivable on Surety given as shall be of value sufficient to Satisfy the said Debt and Costs."

It is not clear exactly when Boone moved his family across the mountains farther west. His youngest son, Nathan, not born until 1781, recalled hearing tales from his siblings of Cherokee Indians visiting their home, apparently near Sycamore Shoals on the Watauga River, in what would become far eastern Tennessee. Nathan told Draper the move was made in 1772 or 1773. Sycamore Shoals was a place that would later figure prominently in Boone's life. It is a wide, beautiful valley where the river chops over rocks in a section the Cherokees called Watauga, or "the broken waters."

The settlement of the Watauga Valley had begun around 1769, just as Boone was leaving for Kentucky. In 1772 the settlers, many of whom had fled North Carolina after the collapse of the Regulator Movement, would organize as the Watauga Association and lease their land from the Cherokees. Though sanctioned by neither the colonial government of North Carolina nor Virginia, they would become the first white community west of the North Carolina Blue Ridge. Lord Dunmore, the governor of Virgina, wrote at this time, "[Watauga] sets a dangerous example to people of America, of forming government distinct from and independent of his Majesty's authority."

Though often neglected by historians, the Watauga experiment set a precedent with far-reaching significance. It was a model for other independent communities such as Transylvania, Cumberland, and the State of Franklin.

Records show Boone buying goods from a trader in the Holston Valley, about thirty miles away, at this time. In the 1771–72 winter he hunted in what would later become the state of Tennessee. In the fall of 1772 Daniel returned to Kentucky with a group of hunters, including his old friends Samuel Tate and Benjamin Cutbirth, and a hot-tempered young man from the Yadkin named Hugh McGary, destined to figure in Boone's life more than once as the years passed. They hunted near Hickman Creek and Boone's Knob. In the next century an inscription was found on a cave wall nearby, "D.B. 1773." Below Boone's initials was Hugh McGary's name. The two hunters also left their names carved on a tree in the Green River country.

While this group was hunting, the fever for land speculation in Kentucky was growing in the colonies to the east. There are reports from this period of revival preachers promising from the pulpit that "heaven is a Kentucky of a place." Surveyors for many companies and speculators were already crawling through the thickets and driving stakes, planting flags, and blazing trees all over the region. It was understood that a fortune and a future were to be made by anyone who could nail down a claim there. Pretending to be hunting, the surveyors hid their compasses, which Indians called land stealers. Among the exploring parties was one that included James Harrod of Pennsylvania. According to some accounts, Boone met Harrod in Kentucky in 1773 and agreed to join him later in establishing a settlement at the Big Spring on the Salt River.

The eyes of the world had turned to the paradise that Boone had seemed to have virtually to himself three years before. It was time for anyone who hoped to make a move and stake a claim to do so. Kentucky was nominally Fincastle County, Virginia, and the governor of Virginia planned to allow veterans of the French and Indian War to stake out claims in the region. Besides Harrod, the McAfee brothers, Robert and James, were locating and marking their own claims. Capt. Thomas Bullitt surveyed tracts around the Falls of the Ohio in 1773, and the next year Col. William Preston, surveyor of Fincastle County, sent his own surveying party under John Floyd to resurvey and claim the region around the Falls again. It was about this time that Richard Henderson, whose term as a judge was coming to an end, began to formally set in motion his scheme, which he had been pondering for years, to buy Kentucky.

He knew the colonial governments of North Carolina and Virginia, following the Royal Proclamation of 1763, forbade the private purchase and settlement of land west of the mountains. Henderson had to be especially careful to conceal his scheme, because he feared on the one hand the anger of citizens who resented his status and wealth, and on the other the wrath of the colonial governors, who had forbidden civilian purchases of western land. He also had to prevent competitors, as well as Indians, from knowing his plans. George Washington had instructed his own agent in the Ohio Valley to survey land there "under the guize of hunting game."

Boone's first attempt to settle in Kentucky was a joint venture, not with Henderson but with a man named William Russell, an important trader, landowner, and captain of militia, who had already settled in the extreme southwestern corner of Virginia, on the Clinch River. Boone appears to have been hired on as a scout and guide. Russell held military warrants primarily intended for use on land east of the mountains. But he hoped the government of Virginia would recognize claims he might make in Kentucky also. Boone was only one of several Long Hunters who served as guides and partners to the land speculators. While the Long Hunters were mostly interested in hunting and exploration in Kentucky, some would return there to claim land and build settlements, and several, including Boone, served as scouts and advisers to the larger entrepreneurs and land speculators. The hunters were essential to the surveyors and developers because they were familiar with the unclaimed and barely charted region.

If Boone had already been in the employ of Richard Henderson and the Hart brothers, he was now shifting his services to another entrepreneur and leader of the frontier. Whatever his plans had been earlier, Henderson was not free just yet to immigrate to Kentucky because his judgeship in North Carolina did not officially expire until 1774 or 1775.

William Russell was a man of substantial wealth, with ties to the tidewater gentry of Virginia. Educated at the College of William and Mary, he had served in the Virginia House of Burgesses and impressed the royal governor, Lord Dunmore. His second wife was the sister of Patrick Henry. Russell was restless and ambitious, and he had moved to the frontier in the 1760s, ahead of most of the settlements. His fortune had grown and would become greater still. In the meantime, Boone's family had gone back to the upper Yadkin, where his eighth child, Jesse Bryan, was born May 23, 1773. His oldest child, James, was now sixteen, a strapping youth on whom much of the farmwork fell. We don't know why Rebecca, who had refused to go to Florida in 1765, was willing to relocate to the wilderness of Kentucky. The embarrassment of debts and the possible loss of their land to creditors might have been factors. But Daniel's accounts of the glories of Kentucky may have affected Rebecca also. It would be a mistake to think that only men were drawn to the opportunities and romance of the frontier. "The wives of our western pioneers are as courageous, and as ready to enter on the line of march to plant the germ of a new settlement, as their husbands," wrote John Mason Peck, who had interviewed many such wives. Squire Boone and his wife, Jane, and their children joined the party also, as did Benjamin Cutbirth and his wife, Elizabeth, Boone's niece, and other neighbors and hunting buddies.

A warrant issued for Boone's arrest in Virginia two years later suggests that he, or someone working with him, William Cowan, bought supplies for this expedition at Draper's Meadows and had not paid. It is possible Boone was named because he was the leader of the group going to Kentucky. "We command you that you take Danl. Boone and Wm Cowan if they be found within your Bailiwick, and them safely keep." William Cowan later returned and paid the bill.

There were many farewells between family and friends who were leaving the Yadkin and those who were staying. Daniel's mother, Sarah Morgan, and a few others accompanied the emigrants for half a day before saying their final farewells. Sarah was now in her seventies, and both mother and son knew it was likely the last time they would ever see each other. It was she who had taught him tolerance and patience, a delight in the world around him, a reverence for all life. Her gift for calm acceptance was an essential part of his nature. He had inherited her tendency toward attention and joy. It has been said that both Daniel and his mother wept freely as they parted. This was one of the several occasions Daniel is reported to have wept. For all his reputation as a stoic, he was apparently not a man to hold back his tears. On February 15, 1773, Rev. George Soelle recorded in his diary a meeting with Sarah Morgan Boone. "I visited William Briant, and the old, sick, Mother Buhn. She is a Quaker by birth, but very eager for grace and the forgiveness of her sins. She was very glad that I came to her, and it was given to me to tell her of the grace through the blood of Jesus for all poor longing souls, to which she listened with many tears."

By the middle of August the party from the Yadkin had reached Russell's settlement at Castle Wood on the Clinch River. There they packed all their belongings in hickory baskets to be strapped on either side of packhorses, much like what were called panniers in England, for there was no road for wagons and carts into Kentucky. Babies as well as chickens and little pigs were carried in the baskets tied to wooden pack saddles. While some of the women and children would ride at least some of the time, men and boys drove the hogs and cattle and led the horses.

It was a large party that set out, the first attempt of whites to settle in Kentucky. White men had camped there and hunted there and fought and died there, but without women there would be no settlement, no land cleared and crops put in, no children born. The Russells had several slaves who went along, and there were a number of young adventurers such as William Bush and Michael Stoner, who would be close friends with Boone. Stoner, whose original name was Holsteiner, was born in Pennsylvania of German parents in 1748 and left his apprenticeship with a saddle maker to be a woodsman in the western lands. He would become one of Boone's favorite hunting companions, and he was already known as an expert marksman. "Stoner was an awkward Dutchman, a low chunky man," Nathan Boone told Draper. "He became a good woodsman, as he was truthful and reliable." In almost every case, frontiersmen were remembered and honored more for character and dependability than for marksmanship or scouting ability, Boone included. In the dangerous world of the West, integrity counted above all else.

The colonial governments of Virginia and North Carolina had warned settlers not to cross the mountains into Cherokee and Shawnee hunting lands. At the Treaty of Hard Labor, South Carolina, in

1768, the British government had conceded to the Cherokees the rights to the southern region of Kentucky. At the Treaty of Fort Stanwix the same year the Iroquois had agreed to give up their claim to the Great Meadow north of the Kentucky River in return for substantial payments and assurances that their homelands in upstate New York would be safe from English settlement. It was, however, all a muddle, and whatever the policies of North Carolina, Virginia, and Pennsylvania might be, they were unable to enforce them. The frontier was too wide and the gathering tide of speculators and settlers too powerful to be stopped. Lord Dunmore viewed those settling on the frontier with skepticism and despair. "Americans . . . do and will remove as their avidity and restlessness incite them," he wrote. "They acquire no attachment to Place: But wandering about seems engrafted in their Nature; and it is a weakness incident to it, that they should forever imagine the lands Further off, are Still better than those upon which they are already Settled."

And great men with official ties to the colonial governments, such as George Washington, William Russell, Patrick Henry, Richard Henderson, and a hundred others, and indeed the colonial governors themselves, could not resist the opportunities that Kentucky promised. In fact, Lord Dunmore had sent his own surveyors into the wilderness but found it wise to distance himself from their activities. Dunmore denied that he had sent Bullitt and other surveyors west of the Donelson Line (the agreed-upon limit of white settlement), but at the same time he gave official patents for much of the land that had been surveyed. One of the lawyers advising Dunmore was Patrick Henry, who had his own plans for buying land from the Cherokees. The colonial governments could no more stop the gathering rush into Kentucky than they could have curbed a flood with a sieve. It was a story that would be repeated again and again, until the great valleys of California and Oregon were settled, and the farthest plains of North Dakota.

Moving livestock and a pack train of horses through the wilderness on a scarcely visible trail was very slow work. Most livestock in the wilderness had bells on their necks, and Nathan Boone said that bells were put on horses to prevent them from getting lost. The party labored over Horton's Summit and Powell's Mountain, going about a hundred miles in two weeks. Because their progress was so slow, Boone saw they would need extra provisions, and he sent his son James back to Castle Wood, with John and Richard Mendinall, for additional supplies. William Russell, who had remained behind to finish his business and then follow with a second party, gathered the extra goods and horses and cattle and sent a guide named Crabtree and a hired man named Drake as well as his oldest son, Henry Russell, and two slaves named Adam and Charles to help the boys carry the supplies and drive livestock over the mountains.

On the night of October 9, 1773, James Boone, Henry Russell, and the rest of the party camped along the trail near where Wallen's Creek runs into Powell's River. They did not realize they were only three miles behind the main party. As the boys sat around the campfire, wolves began howling, and Crabtree laughed to see how startled his young companions were when he told them they would hear wolves howling in the treetops in Kentucky.

As they slept, a group of fifteen Delawares and two Shawnees and at least three Cherokees watched from the woods. The Indians had been to a gathering of tribes to discuss the threat to their hunting ground from white settlers. No doubt the Indians were angered by the news of a large incursion into their territories. At about dawn they fired into the sleeping group, killing the Mendinall boys immediately. They were the lucky ones. Crabtree and the hired man named Drake were wounded but fled into the forest. James Boone and Henry Russell were shot in the hips and couldn't run. The slave named Adam hid in some brush and witnessed what followed.

While the slave named Charles was frozen with fear, the Indians plundered the supplies and gathered the horses. But one or two of the braves began to slash at the wounded and crippled boys with their knives. A fever of anger and cruelty seemed to build in the Indians as

James and Henry tried to fend off the blades with their hands. Maybe it was the sight of blood on their mangled hands that incited the braves to greater cruelty. James recognized one of the torturing Indians as a Shawnee named Big Jim, whom he had met before. In fact, Big Jim had been befriended by the Boone family, Nathan Boone later told Lyman Draper. James pleaded with Big Jim to spare him, but the Shawnee's response was to begin pulling out James's fingernails.

The slave named Adam watched in horror as both James and Henry begged to be killed and not tortured further. James cried out for his mother and then screamed that he was afraid his family farther up the trail had been attacked also. The other Indians were in a hurry to get going with their plunder. Only a small number participated in the torture. Finally, the boys' skulls were beaten in with tomahawks and their bodies shot full of arrows. The arrows were not just a ritual but also a warning, a calling card, to show who had killed them and a sign of the fate of any who trespassed on Indian territory. When the Indians left they took the slave Charles with them.

Ironically the bodies were discovered that morning by a young man from Boone's party who had stolen a pack of deerskins and was riding back to the settlements. Seeing the bloody and mangled bodies, he galloped back to the camp and warned those just awaking. Fearing an imminent attack, Boone organized the men for defense, building a rude fort of brush and felled logs, and sent Squire back with a party to bury the dead. Rebecca gave Squire two linen sheets to wrap around the mutilated bodies. Before Squire and his party got to the scene, Russell and his group had already arrived there. They wrapped the Mendinalls in one sheet and James and Henry in the other and buried them in one grave, under logs, to keep the wolves from reaching them.

Adam, who had witnessed the torture scene and murders, wandered stunned in the woods for eleven days before he showed up to tell his gruesome tale. Crabtree, who had been wounded only slightly, appeared in Castle Wood about a week later. The slave Charles was found with his head split in two about forty miles farther on. Bones, thought to be those of the hired man, Drake, were found nearby twenty years later.

It took days to round up the scattered cattle while the people tried to recover from the attack. The men called a council and it was decided they were too small a party to proceed to the Cumberland Gap with the Indian threat so great. Discouraged, they returned to the Clinch River, and many went back to their homes on the Yadkin. But Boone and his family stayed on the Clinch River in a cabin lent to them by David Gass. They would remain in the area for almost two years, until Boone could organize a larger effort to settle in Kentucky.

Lord Dunmore demanded that those who had perpetrated the torture and murders be punished. The colonial Indian agent sent his deputy, Alexander Cameron, to the Cherokees at the town of Cho-tee to deliver the order. After much argument and opposition from the young braves, it was decided that a chief named No-ta-wa-gun was the guilty one and should be put to death. No-ta-wa-gun was first wounded by his appointed executioners but left alive. His relatives tried to protect him from further harm. But Alexander Cameron demanded that the sentence be carried out, and after much haranguing, No-ta-wa-gun was finally killed.

One other Cherokee who had taken part in the massacre escaped to live with the Chickasaws but was later caught and also executed. Big Jim returned north to the Shawnee towns. The chiefs warned the young Indians that this would be the fate of any who engaged in such acts of cruelty. Lord Dunmore expressed his satisfaction with the Cherokee conduct, "a remarkable instance of their good faith and strict regard to justice." The Shawnees were named by Dunmore as the main instigators of the episode. But the Shawnee Big Jim would go unpunished until he met his death in another clash with the whites thirteen years later in Ohio.

Anger against the white invaders seemed to spread among the young warriors of all the tribes, Cherokee, Mingo, Shawnee, Delaware, Wyandotte. A companion of young Simon Kenton was killed at their camp near the Kanawha. A party of hunters in Kentucky led by Gilbert and Robert Christian was attacked by a band of Cherokees led by Tom Benge. At first pretending friendship, the Indians fired on their hosts in the camp and killed four hunters. The Christian brothers escaped. Angered by the attack on Wallen's Creek, where he had been wounded, Isaac Crabtree killed three Cherokees at a social gathering at Watauga and then escaped to Kentucky, aggravating the already tense conditions on the frontier. The murder of the Boone and Russell boys seemed to set off a chain reaction of killings on both sides.

Someone who saw Boone on the Clinch River at this time described him as wearing "deer-skin coloured black and had his hair plaited and clubbed up, and was on his way to or from Powell's Valley." Apparently Boone wore his hair long but plaited all his life. Clubbed meant the braid was tied in a kind of knot behind his head. While he lived in David Gass's cabin on the Clinch, Boone spent much time hunting in the nearby mountains. In the spring of 1774 Boone went alone to hunt in Powell's Valley, and to visit the grave of his son James and Henry Russell. He pushed aside the logs over the grave when he arrived. Scratching in the ground with a stick, he decided to see if the bodies had been disturbed. Wolves had not reached the bodies, and the features of the boys were still distinguishable, blood still visible on their cut and burned heads. James Boone's hair was blond while Russell's was very dark. Boone dug the grave a little deeper and replaced the log covering. According to Lyman Draper, "There suddenly arose a severe storm, which lasted some considerable time. During its continuance, from the melancholy associations and gloominess of the place, mingled with the dismal howlings of the storm, Boone felt more dejected, as he used afterwards to relate, than he ever did in all his life."

Later, as he made camp and tried to sleep, he heard Indians prowling about. Nathan told Draper the sadness of the place made Boone feel worse than he ever had before. Whenever the death of James was mentioned he was visibly moved. In the dark he packed up and left, leaving the bell on his horse sounding so the Indians would think it was just grazing until he got some distance away. Then he rode quickly to put distance between himself and the scene.

IF BOONE had planned to attempt another settlement in Kentucky in 1774, he was frustrated by growing hostilities. The rising violence between Indians and whites on the frontier culminated in a series of events that came to be called Lord Dunmore's War. Fear and anger on both sides rose to a new pitch. Hunters in Kentucky shot Indians on sight, and Indians attacked whites without warning. As more and more surveyors poured into the Great Meadow, even the peaceable chiefs could not persuade the young warriors that the tide of settlement was not going to sweep over their hunting lands in Kentucky and reach their villages and tribal claims in Ohio. The colonies did not doubt that war was imminent. On January 25, 1774, a party of militia fired into a Shawnee encampment near Fort Pitt. In March, Lord Dunmore urged the colonies to prepare for war. A contemporary remembered, "Whoever saw an Indian in Kentucky saw an enemy — no questions were asked on either side — but from the muzzles of their rifles." Accounts of Henry Russell's murder were reiterated as evidence of the threat. Few of the published articles on the massacre mentioned James Boone by name. The Boones were not as important as the Russells. That winter and spring, parties along the Ohio River were fired on and robbed by Shawnees. One group of Shawnees claimed Colonel Croghan, commander at Fort Pitt, had told them to kill all Virginians invading their territory and merely rob those from Pennsylvania. This is an indication of extreme rivalry between the different colonies for control of the Ohio Valley.

Captain Russell, under orders from Col. William Preston, sent a party of men over the mountains to the head of Powell's River on April 15 to be on the lookout for hostile Indians coming from the north. He ordered his men to act friendly until they found out the Indians' intentions, then hurry back to warn the settlers of any invading war party. Scattered fighting between Indians and whites became more frequent all up and down the frontier. Governor Dunmore sent out a warning to all the settlements that a state of war already existed between the Indian nations and the colonies. Chiefs like Cornstalk of the Shawnees, who had been urging peace, felt betrayed by this proclamation. In retrospect it appears Dunmore may well have made things worse by exaggerating the danger. A classic way of increasing and maintaining one's power is to make people afraid. And the governor's greed for western lands may well have influenced his actions. Dunmore's alarms almost certainly heightened the tensions. It would seem that Dunmore wanted a war to further his own speculative plans for land claims in the west.

In this atmosphere of fear and apprehension, both Governor Dunmore and Colonel Preston told William Russell, in his capacity as a colonial official, that the surveyors sent into Kentucky must be warned of the danger, and that he should "employ two faithful woodsmen to repair to Kentucky to notify the surveyors of their dangers." Boone and Michael Stoner agreed to dash into Kentucky to let the surveying parties, which included Hancock Taylor, James Douglas, Isaac Hite, and John Floyd, know of the threat. Michael Stoner's only hesitation was that he didn't have a rifle. "Well, Mike, you'll have mine and I'll have another," Boone is reported to have said. "You're the man for me."

According to a deposition Boone made October 6, 1817, in St. Charles County, Missouri, he and Stoner crossed the Cumberland Mountain chain through Pound Gap, called then the Sounding Gap. Col. Andrew Lewis gave them directions. "[Lewis] directed me to cross the Cumberland mountains at what we now call the sounding Gap, at an old war-road that would convey me immediately on the waters of Big or perhaps Little Sandy." Boone added that when he received the orders from Governor Dunmore, he was told "to take the Kentucky and Meander to its Mouth" as soon as he got over the Cumberland Mountains.

The Sounding Gap is just a few miles from the headwaters of the Cumberland, Kentucky, and Big Sandy rivers. It is reported that

Boone rented a horse for sixty-two days for this journey. Apparently on horseback, Boone and Stoner crossed the mountains on an old hunter's trace, struck the Kentucky River near its source, and followed it downstream. It would be hard to imagine a more dangerous journey than the two hunters had agreed to undertake. With Indians prowling the wilderness and attacking at random, and the exact location of the surveying parties unknown, the two woodsmen had to find about two dozen men in twenty million to thirty million acres of woodland. All Boone knew was that some of the surveyors were in the Bluegrass region near the Kentucky River or maybe near the Falls of the Ohio. But in fact they could have been almost anywhere, and they could already have been killed. One of the ironies of this mission to warn the surveyors is that Floyd and his crews were claiming the best land in all of Kentucky for the officers and veterans back in Virginia. The colonial surveyors were preempting the very land that Boone and others like him yearned for. In that sense he and Stoner undertook the dangerous expedition to warn their greatest rivals for the most desirable real estate in Kentucky.

Dangerous as the mission was, and as important as its object, the foray sounds like something of a frolic too. Boone and Stoner became great friends, and Boone enjoyed telling a story of Stoner being charged by a buffalo at a salt lick while Boone collapsed with laughter. Boone liked to imitate Stoner's thick German accent when he told the story. However much laughter they may have shared on the trip, they still knew they were in great danger, and slept in thickets and canebrakes, putting their campfires out as soon as meals were cooked. And while they ate they sat back to back, on the lookout for Indians.

According to another deposition, taken April 24, 1794, at Point Pleasant, Virginia, Boone had agreed, before Lord Dunmore asked him to warn the surveyors, to survey and mark a claim in Kentucky for James Hickman. With danger gathering on all sides, Boone and his backers were still thinking of land claims and the future. "On the last of May or first [of] June 1774, Mr. James Hickman employed me to locate, enter and direct the survey of 4000 acres of land as soon as the time would admit of, and on the 26th of June the same year I was employed by Governor Dunmore to go out to that country and give the surveyors notice of the breaking out of the Indian War and I took with me Michael Stoner."

The fact that Boone and Stoner duly located and marked the four thousand acres for Hickman on what was later called Hickman Creek near future Boonesborough (on land that turned out to have already been surveyed by James Douglas) does not lessen the oddness of this hurried, dangerous trip. Considering the area they had to cross, and with the surveying parties so scattered, there has been little agreement about which surveyors Boone and Stoner actually encountered. Boone and Stoner were probably not even sure how many surveyors they were supposed to warn. Besides their rifles and supplies, they must have carried a compass, and a Gunter's chain sixty-six feet long for the surveying. Luckily Boone already knew much of Kentucky by heart. They probably carried their compass concealed except when it was actually in use. Day after day the two traveled down the Kentucky River, keeping alert for sign of Indians as well as surveyors. They made small campfires, or none, and slept in a cave when they could find one, canebrakes when they couldn't, away from buffalo traces or warrior's trails. They fired their rifles only when necessary to procure game. They stopped and listened often for the sound of voices, for the chop of a marker's axe, for the telltale bark or birdcall an Indian might make.

For much of its length the Kentucky River runs in a gorge cut through limestone. Cliffs loom high over its waters. When Boone and Stoner stepped out on the bluffs to scout the valley ahead, they did not stay there long to be spotted by those paddling on the river or hiding in thickets where a meadow opened out beside the stream. Scanning the river ahead, they quickly ducked back into cover and made their way a few more miles down the valley.

The largest surveying party was led by John Floyd, a young man only twenty-four years old working for Col. William Preston, surveyor for Fincastle County, Virginia. Educated, intelligent, mature beyond his years, Floyd, a native of Amherst County, Virginia, had true leadership ability. His dark good looks revealed his heritage — one of his grandmothers had been half Catawba. A former schoolmaster, John Floyd had been chosen by his close friend William Preston to survey the finest land in Kentucky on military warrants for veteran officers of the French and Indian War. Floating his party down the Ohio that spring, he had stopped to survey prime land in western Virginia for Col. George Washington, among others. Reaching the Bluegrass region in late spring, Floyd and his men had surveyed almost all the land around Elkhorn Creek and future Lexington by the time Boone and Stoner left for Kentucky on June 26.

One member of Floyd's crew, Thomas Hanson, kept a diary that spring and summer, and because he made detailed entries almost every day we know a good deal about Floyd's activities during those momentous weeks, when much of the finest land of Kentucky was divided up for important people back in Virginia. On Sunday, May 2, 1774, Hanson wrote, "We made a survey of this Bottom for Patrick Henry. It contains 4 or 500 acres, of very good land, including the Fort & Town. There is a Sycamore tree 33 feet in Circumference on this bottom." At no point in this journal does Hanson mention Boone and Stoner. Since Floyd split his group into three smaller parties of surveyors, it is possible Floyd encountered Boone and Stoner while Hanson was not around, but not likely. Because Floyd expressed deep gratitude to Boone later for his mission, this apparent lack of contact between Boone and Floyd remains part of the mystery hanging over the accounts of this hurried trip as the threat of war loomed ever closer.

Adding to the mystery of that summer is the later report of Robert McAfee, along with James Harrod, one of the earliest settlers in Kentucky, that Boone, "on his way to the falls to warn the surveyors of their danger from the Indians, had one lot laid off for himself" in Harrodsburg. Many historians have assumed McAfee's testimony to be true and pictured Boone claiming a lot and building a cabin on it at the Harrodsburg site, while on his way with Stoner to the Falls of the Ohio. But it is pretty clear that Harrod and his men had already left the region by the time Boone and Stoner could have arrived there. McAfee apparently was confused by a lot Squire Boone staked out and claimed with his friend Evan Hinton at Harrodsburg in late 1775 or early 1776.

On July 8 Indians attacked some of Harrod's men, and two, James Cowen and James Hamilton, were killed. Harrod and the rest packed up and headed back to the settlements, leaving more than thirty cabins deserted. They would not return until late the following winter. It took them until July 29 to reach the Clinch River.

On the Elkhorn, Floyd had split his surveying party into three groups, one led by himself, one by Hancock Taylor, and the third by James Douglas and Isaac Hite. They agreed that they would all meet on July 24 at Harrod's cabins south of the Kentucky River. But when he reached the rendezvous point on that date, Floyd found only a note that said, "Alarmed by finding some people killed, we are gone down." It was then that Floyd decided they had done enough surveying, and he and his party headed toward the Clinch River settlements also. They did not go north toward the Ohio River because that was the direction the Indians would be coming from. And poling or paddling up the Ohio to Fort Pitt was very difficult. But having reached Kentucky by the Ohio River, Floyd did not know how to find Cumberland Gap to the south. Fearing for their lives, he and his men wandered for days in the mountains of eastern Kentucky and finally found their way to Pound Gap and crossed out of the Cumberland Mountains.

It is not clear from the records where Hancock Taylor and his company were surveying between July 8 and July 27, 1774, but on July 27 Taylor, Abraham Hempinstall, and James Strother were traveling on the Kentucky River in a dugout canoe when they were attacked by Indians. Strother was killed and Taylor seriously wounded. Struggling to the bank, Taylor and Hempinstall found their companions Willis

Lee, John Willis, and John Green upstream, and the group began the long trek out of the wilderness.

For two days Taylor walked on his own, in spite of his wounds. As he weakened with fever and infection, he was carried on the third and fourth days. Late on August 1, 1774, Taylor recognized that he was dying and, helped by John Green, completed and signed his surveys to make them official. After he was dead the four other men buried him where Taylor's Fork joins Silver Creek in future Madison County; then they wrestled through thickets and mountain passes to find their way back to the settlements. It is almost certain that on the way they were found by Boone and Stoner and led back to William Russell's home, Castle Wood, on the Clinch River. James Douglas, Isaac Hite, and their small party, when they found the two men of Harrod's group killed, left the note for Floyd and located their canoes hidden on the Kentucky River. They paddled down that stream to the Ohio and descended to the Mississippi, then proceeded all the way to New Orleans, where they took a ship to the East Coast.

After leaving the region around future Frankfort, Boone and Stoner made their way down to the mouth of the Kentucky River and followed the Ohio to the Falls. Boone later reported seeing petrified buffalo dung attached to the rocks at the Falls. Floyd's party had already surveyed thirty tracts, about 40,000 choice acres, or sixty-four square miles, in that area, before they headed east to the Elkhorn, and the Bluegrass region. In all Floyd had surveyed 206,250 acres of prime land that summer, leaving more marginal land for those, like Boone, who would make later claims.

At Mann's Lick, a few miles from the Falls, Boone and Stoner happened upon another surveying party and warned them of the Indian threat. It is likely they led that group back across Kentucky by Skaggs's Trace and then on to Cumberland Gap, encountering the survivors of Hancock Taylor's company on the way.

Some historians have suggested that Boone and Stoner's expedition was mostly useless, that the surveyors had already left Kentucky before the two messengers arrived. But Boone and Stoner returned to Castle Wood the same day as the rest of Hancock Taylor's crew. "Their simultaneous arrival lends credence to Boone's claim that he 'conducted in the surveyors,' but it seems likely that when he and Stoner encountered them, they were already on their way home." Others have argued that Boone and Stoner were instrumental in leading the surveyors back to the Clinch River.

BOONE AND STONER returned to Russell's Fort on the Clinch on August 26, 1774, having traveled eight hundred miles through the wilderness in exactly two months. Boone's willingness to undertake this dangerous mission, and his successful completion of it, gave him an enhanced status among leaders such as William Russell, William Preston, and John Floyd. From this point on there seemed less doubt that he was an officer and a leader, not just a hired hand and hunter.

Meanwhile a militia had been organized under the command of Captain Russell to join the fight against the Indians to the north. Floyd recommended that Boone be added to the company. Floyd was extremely grateful to Boone for his warning mission into Kentucky and on August 28, 1774, wrote to Colonel Preston, "Captain Bledsoe says Boone has more interest [influence] than any man now disengaged; & you know what Boone has done for me by your kind directions, for which I love the man." While Boone had served in various capacities in the French and Indian War, his commission as a lieutenant in the Virginia militia in the late summer of 1774 was his first official appointment. Though he had often been looked upon as a leader and "captain" of scouting parties and hunting expeditions, his leadership had never before been formalized. The son of Quakers had become a military man. He carried the document of the commission signed by Governor Dunmore with him for most of the rest of his life.

As a new lieutenant, Boone began the march north toward the defense of the Ohio Valley. But when he had gone about a hundred miles, he was recalled by a messenger to return to the Clinch region, where he was needed to organize the defenses there. He was put in charge of Moore's Fort on the Clinch River. A Mingo chief named Logan was attacking the mountain river settlements. Logan, whose Mingo name was Tahgahjute, or Talgayeeta, is supposed to have said "the Indians is not Angry, only myself." His family had been lured into a trap and killed at Yellow Creek on the Ohio in May. Daniel Greathouse had invited some Indians to the settlement and after getting them all drunk shot every one. Included in the group were Logan's brother and his pregnant sister or sister-in-law. The baby was cut out of the woman's womb "and inpaled on a stake." Out for revenge, Logan, apparently wrongly, blamed Michael Cresap for the massacre.

Bands of Shawnees were roving through the region also, making random attacks. Most settlers abandoned their cabins and farms and gathered in forts along the river valleys. Rebecca Boone and her children sought the safety of Moore's Fort, south of Castle Wood on the Clinch. The fort was Boone's headquarters, but he and his scouts spent much of the time roving the woods on the lookout for Indians. The forts were primitive constructions with limited supplies and poor sanitation. With many settlers crowded into a small space, the conditions quickly deteriorated.

As in most wars, the greatest problem seemed to be boredom, the waiting, day after day. Appalling conditions, poor facilities for sleeping, and tedium aggravated the fear of attack. One woman at Moore's Fort reported that "the men would all go out and play at ball, and those not playing would lie down, without their guns." We assume such lax security occurred while Boone was away on patrol or organizing defense at other forts. The story is told that the men became so careless while Boone was away that one day Rebecca and her daughters Susannah and Jemima and several other women decided to scare them. Loading a half-dozen guns, they slipped out the back of the fort and fired the rifles, then ran back into the fort and locked the gates. The men dashed to the stockade but found themselves locked out and ran hither and thither in panic. "Some were in so great haste, they run right through the pond. They were all exceeding mad." While the women laughed at them, the men threatened to whip the wives and daughters who had made fools of them. In the midst of such chaos, Boone had his work cut out for him.

While most of the men in the area had joined the militia and headed north to fight the Shawnees, Boone was assigned fourteen rangers with which to patrol the Clinch. He and his men were the best defense the settlers had. "Mr. Boon is very diligent at Castle-Woods and keeps up good Orders," Col. Arthur Campbell wrote to Colonel Preston on September 29, 1774.

Chief Logan with his Mingoes and Shawnees attacked Fort Blackmore on September 23, capturing two slaves who had been sent out to feed the cattle. Logan had vowed to avenge the murder of his kinfolks on the Ohio earlier that year. He was conducting a blood feud, which is what many Indian wars amounted to, often precipitated by whites murdering Indians. Logan dared the whites to come out of the fort to recover their blacks, whom he called their "bearskins." But there was little the Indians could do against a fort. Without artillery to blow apart the gates and pickets, their only hope was starving those inside. That was not the kind of fighting that appealed to the angry Indians. Logan's party killed a number of cattle and moved on.

They appeared a week later at Moore's Fort, a few miles away, on September 29. Three men had left the fort to check a pigeon trap several hundred yards beyond the walls. Shots were fired from the timber and one of the men fell. Boone charged with others out of the stockade to the rescue and saw an Indian in war paint rip the scalp from John Duncan's head. Before they could fire a shot, the Indians faded back into the woods.

The next day a child found an Indian war club left like a calling card beside the spring. Boone thought it might be that of a southern Indian, though the Cherokees had stayed out of the trouble for the most part. Apparently he warned Col. Arthur Campbell that the neighboring Indians might now be involved, for Campbell wrote to Col. William

Preston on October 1, 1774, "Mr. Boone has sent me the War Club that was left it is different from that left at Blackmores; Mr. Boone thinks it is the Cherokees that is now annoying us." It is possible the Shawnees and Mingoes were trying to implicate their southern cousins in the conflict by planting Cherokee weapons.

In early October a guard outside Blackmore's Fort saw an Indian lurking along the bank of the river. "Murder! Murder!" he shouted, and those inside quickly closed the door of the stockade. Trapped outside, the guard was shot by the Indians. When a message reached Moore's Fort, several miles away, Capt. Daniel Smith, Boone, and about thirty others rode to the aid of Blackmore's. They arrived late in the day and camped outside the walls of the stockade. During the night several of their horses were stolen, and Boone tracked them for a distance into the hills but gave it up. It was the last incident in the region of the conflict known by the grand title Lord Dunmore's War. The war ended on October 10, 1774, at the battle of Point Pleasant far to the north, at the mouth of the Kanawha River, where Isaac Shelby, George Rogers Clark, and others, commanded by Col. Andrew Lewis, fought the Shawnees in a long, drawn-out battle. Though Point Pleasant is usually described as a victory for Lewis and the white militia, the Indians suffered only half the casualties their opponents did. Cornstalk was known as a lover of peace, and it seems he and his Native forces, though they had outperformed the whites, just got tired of fighting and agreed to a treaty. He also knew that Governor Dunmore, with another army in Ohio, was ready to march south to join the attack with Lewis's men. A surrender seemed preferable to a prolonged fight.

His actions during Lord Dunmore's War enhanced Boone's status and reputation. His leadership was recognized by a petition signed by the men who had served under him, asking that Boone be promoted to captain. Capt. Daniel Smith wrote to Col. William Preston, "Mr. Boon is an excellent woodsman. If that only would qualify him for the Office nobody would be more proper." Boone was given the promotion, and from Smith's phrasing we get a sense of how Boone was viewed at the time by some of his upper-class associates. His integrity and leadership were recognized by those with power and influence. But officers such as Preston and Russell still viewed him first as a hunter and woodsman, not quite of their class or status.

Class, the manner of a gentleman, the air of authority, were very important in the eighteenth century, even in the frontier valleys. Boone was a leader, admired by those he led, but he was *different*. It is important to keep that difference in mind when considering his later troubled career in business and politics and militia companies. Though an acknowledged and even celebrated leader, Boone never did quite fit in with the ruling class in the new territories. He was too much the woodsman and hunter, even a "white Indian."

With this promotion Boone became Capt. Daniel Boone and he would be addressed by this semimilitary, semicourtesy title until he was later promoted again. He would carry the commission with him in the years ahead in case he needed proof of his status as an officer and a gentleman. His commission was signed by Lord Dunmore himself. Boone kept the document in his "budget," or carrying pouch, until many years later it was included in an application for a land grant and lost among the bureaucratic proceedings. The commission was proof of his recognition in the world of men, as well as his achievement in the mother world of the forest.

As a captain Boone was given command of three forts on the Clinch: Fort Russell, at Castle Wood; Moore's, a few miles from Castle Wood; and Blackmore's, twenty miles farther south. But by that time the war was winding down. Soon after the Battle of Point Pleasant, Chief Cornstalk and other Shawnees signed the treaty of Camp Charlotte, agreeing to give up hunting rights in Kentucky in exchange for guarantees that English settlers would stay south of the Ohio River. But as with many treaties with the whites, not all Shawnees agreed. The Shawnees were divided and many did not concede the hunting rights in the Great Meadow. And certainly the British could not guarantee that people from the colonies would not try to settle north of the Ohio River. The treaty was more the beginning of hostilities than an end to them.

In a letter to Lord Dunmore at the close of the campaign, written down by Col. John Gibson and translated and delivered by Simon Girty, Chief Logan said:

> Colonel Cresap, the last spring, in cold blood and unprovoked, murdered all the relatives of Logan, not sparing even my women and children. There runs not a drop of my blood in the veins of any living creature. This called on me for revenge. I have sought it. I have killed many. I have fully glutted my vengeance.
>
> For my country, I rejoice at the beams of peace; but do not harbor the thought that mine is the joy of fear. Logan never felt fear. He will not turn on his own heel to save his life.
>
> Who is there to mourn for Logan? Not one.

Before he was released from his command on November 20, 1774, Boone had to sign forms for reimbursement of those who had provided supplies for the forts. "Rachel Duncin, one horse October 7, 1774 . . . one Beef Cowe prased at 3.0.0," one document read.

CHAPTER SEVEN

Where There Was No Forbidden Fruit

1775 ⤶

Once Lord Dunmore's War was over, Boone, like hundreds of others, turned his thoughts back to Kentucky. The hostilities had merely been a pause in the rush to claim the Great Meadow. And like any stream obstructed, the current swelled behind the barrier to overwhelming force once the dam was breeched. In late 1774 or early 1775 Boone reopened or began his connection with Richard Henderson in North Carolina, where Henderson had completed his term as a judge.

It is not known how Henderson made contact again with Boone. It may have been in connection with Boone's debts in the Yadkin region, or a warrant issued by his creditors. It is possible Henderson had kept in touch with Boone since the time he returned from Kentucky in 1771 or, indeed, since he first went to Kentucky in 1769. "Boone's report of the west fired these promoters with new enthusiasm." What is certain is that on August 27, 1774, the Articles of Association of the Louisa Company were drafted and signed at Hillsborough by Henderson and his partners, and sometime in the winter of 1774–75 they commissioned Boone to go among the Cherokee towns and negotiate the sale of Kentucky lands to the Louisa Company.

Boone had already given them a vivid description of Kentucky, for one of the partners, Richard Henderson's brother Nathaniel, wrote about this time, "To enter uppon a detail of the Beuty & Goodness of our Country would be a task too arduous . . . let it suffice to tell you it far exceeds any country I ever saw or herd of. I'm conscious its out of the power of any man to make you clearly sensible of the great Beuty and Richness of Kentucky."

In the late fall of 1774 Henderson and his partner Nathaniel Hart visited several Cherokee towns themselves and made a tentative agreement to purchase the Cherokee claims to Kentucky for several thousand pounds' worth of goods. Chief Attakullakulla and other leaders, including a clan matron, or "chieftess," returned with Henderson to Cross-Creek, later Fayetteville, North Carolina, to pick the goods they wanted in trade. There followed weeks of negotiations over the list of blankets and rifles, knives and trinkets. Attakullakulla, who was very old, was a legend among the Cherokees and colonial administrators. When younger he had accompanied a delegation to London and had an audience with the king. He was called the Little Carpenter. Felix Walker would later describe him: "Like as a white carpenter could make every joint and notch fit in wood, so he could bring all his views to fill and fit their places in the political machinery of his nation . . . about ninety . . . I scarcely believe he would have exceeded more in weight than a pound for each year of his life."

This bargaining with the Cherokees for the ownership of all the land between the Kentucky River and the Cumberland River's mouth on the Ohio is one of the oddest episodes in frontier history. The colonial governors of North Carolina and Virginia had forbidden anyone to try to buy or sell or settle Kentucky, claiming the land belonged to the westward extending colonies. Pennsylvania had issued a similar warning. Officially, the western lands were to be divided among officers who had served in the French and Indian War. But there was a sliver of legal logic in Henderson's plan, deriving from the 1768 Treaty of Hard Labor, when the British acknowledged that the Cherokee nation did hold rights over the Kentucky country, or at least part of it. And even Gov. Josiah Martin of North Carolina conceded that whites had a right to "lease" land from the Cherokees, as did Patrick Henry.

Richard Henderson was a brilliant, ambitious, resourceful man. He had already gone over the heads of the colonial governors and consulted the government in London. "Lord Mansfield gave Judge Henderson the 'sanction of his great authority in favor of the purchase.'" The letter of sanction was duly sent. "A true copy, made in London, April 1, 1772, was transmitted to Judge Henderson." It was all a charade, since the Indians referred to in the document were of India, not North America.

Whatever the claims and warnings of the Crown governments, surveyors and settlers, hunters and trappers, scouts and speculators, were pouring into Kentucky by the day. Most came down the Ohio from Fort Pitt, but others traveled through Cumberland Gap from the south and over the mountains from Virginia, down the Big Sandy and Red rivers. In April 1769 Pennsylvania had opened a land office at Pittsburgh and had 2,790 applications for western lands the first day. They came from all directions. Some even approached Kentucky up the Cumberland River from French Lick, headed to the cane lands and clover bottoms of the Bluegrass region. James Harrod of Pennsylvania had started building his fort at Harrodsburg in 1774 and returned to it as soon as Lord Dunmore's War was over. The whole issue of the settling of Kentucky was a confusing and exciting mess. One of the groups establishing a claim in Kentucky was the McAfee brothers, who came early in 1775. In February the McAfee brothers — James, Robert, William, and Samuel — and their associates had already gone into Kentucky to clear land and plant crops.

The Cherokee claim to much of the Kentucky country was marginal at best. Like other tribes, they had roved everywhere on the war path, and they had done some hunting on the edges of the Great Meadow. But most of their hunting was done to the south and east of the Clinch River, south and east of the Tennessee for that matter. After all, the Cherokees had the Great Smoky Mountains to hunt in and the long Blue Ridge chain and the valleys in between, extending from Virginia to Alabama. They had the valleys of the Tennessee, and the Little

Tennessee, the French Broad, the Nolichucky, the Tuckasegee, and the Holston. Or they had had those river valleys, that is, until the white settlers began invading in the 1770s.

Henderson knew the value of precedent and primary claim. Since the royal government had once acknowledged the validity of the Cherokee claim to Kentucky, all he had to do was get a document transferring that right to him and his partners. And once the deed was done, once he had attracted thousands of settlers by selling them parcels of land at bargain prices, who was to get him out of Kentucky? Who would be able to reverse the actions of the Louisa Company? And it seemed of no interest to Henderson that the Indians' ideas of "owning" land and "selling" land were very different from the whites'.

What Henderson and his partners didn't foresee was the American Revolution, which would change the very nature of claims of ownership. In retrospect it seems he should have seen what was coming. His house and property had been burned by Regulators in 1771, and he had adjourned his court in face of the protests. He was possibly depending on the turmoil of the gathering rebellion to distract the colonial governments from resisting his actions in the West.

When Henderson sent out advertisements of "Proposals for the Encouragement of settling the Lands purchased by Richard Henderson & Co." on Christmas Day 1774, Governor Dunmore referred to the Louisa Company as "Richard Henderson and other disorderly persons." Henderson was accused of placing himself above the law of Virginia. Josiah Martin, the governor of North Carolina, called Henderson's plans "contrary to Law and Justice and so pregnant with ill consequences." Both governments threatened Henderson and one official asked if Henderson had gone insane. "Archibald Neilson, deputy auditor and naval officer of the colony, inquired with quizzical anxiety: 'Pray, is Dick Henderson out of his head?'"

According to Boone's conversations with Filson eight years later, Henderson commissioned Boone to perform two main tasks. First, he was to use his acquaintance with the Cherokees to persuade them to gather at Sycamore Shoals on the Watauga River in March 1775 to ratify the agreement with Henderson's Louisa Company. Since Boone knew the Cherokee country better than almost any other white man, was respected among the Indians as a formidable scout and hunter, and was trusted, his job was to give credibility to Henderson among the scattered towns along the Little Tennessee, Oconoluftee, and Tuckasegee rivers. Henderson knew that people, both Indian and white, trusted Boone and tended to follow his advice and leadership.

It has been said that James Robertson, a leader in the Watauga settlement, suggested to Boone that the Cherokees, impressed by the example of the great wealth given to the Six Nations at Fort Stanwix by the British, might be willing, for enough money, to sell their claims to the Trans-Allegheny lands. In 1768 the British government had given the Iroquois between twenty thousand and forty thousand pounds in money, rifles, blankets, and other goods, and their assurance that the English would not settle the Iroquois region of central New York, and in return the Six Nations had renounced their claims to Kentucky and the Ohio Valley. The Cherokees hoped to reap a similar windfall for themselves from their slender claims to Kentucky lands. They had already made a profitable deal with James Robertson and the Watauga settlers, leasing land in exchange for money and trade goods, though some younger Cherokee warriors such as Dragging Canoe were not pleased by that arrangement.

The second task of Boone's assignment was to hack a trail out of the wilderness, through Cumberland Gap, into the promised land along the Kentucky River. There was neither time nor means to build a road wide enough for wagons to travel. But a path adequate for packhorses and riders, clearly marked, would serve. Rivers and creeks would still have to be forded and canebrakes threaded through, but such a road would strengthen the claims to the Kentucky land. Henderson and Boone understood that such a road was a necessary and practical thing. But it was also a psychological and symbolic effort. Whoever opened a road into the wilderness already had a superior claim on the land. Building a road, establishing access to a region, was, from Roman times, an expression of acquisition, ownership. Emperors were road builders. No one would ever again think of a region as just Indian territory once a road had been opened into it.

Nothing is more telling of the contradictions of Boone's thought and his life than his role as architect and surveyor of what some would call Boone's Trace, or later the Wilderness Road, or the Transylvania Trail, or the Road to the Old Settlements (in Virginia and North Carolina). If he valued the pristine wilderness of Kentucky, the Edenic beauty, the exhilaration of the solitary hunt, he should have been the last man willing to open a way through which settlers could spill in and ruin his paradise. Following that side of his brain, he should have been concealing the route into Kentucky and telling others it was impossible to get there. But there was the other side of Boone's mind also. Not only was he a hunter and trapper who loved solitude in the wilderness, he was a sociable man, with close ties to friends and hunting companions. And he was a family man with strong and affectionate bonds with a large extended family. His wife, his siblings, his cousins and nephews and nieces and in-laws looked up to him, depended on him, followed him, and waited for him. It was his duty to provide for them and lead them to a better future.

And Boone was a man of his era also. He was, at times, susceptible to the dream of power and wealth in the West, the unlimited opportunity, the clean slate, the beckoning future beyond the mountains, the destiny that seemed just within grasp, over the next ridge, same as other men. In Boone's time it was understood to be a man's duty to clear land and open roads, to let the light of civilization and churches into the threatening wilderness. A real man dammed water and led streams to turn gristmills and power the bellows of a blacksmith's shop, built schools, and cleared away the briars and drained swamps, killed off the wolves and panthers and rattlesnakes. Boone was, in part, a man like other men of his time. He felt the call to do what was expected of him. He could build a cabin in a day or two with nothing but an axe. He could clear land and build a fort. He could find a road and blaze the trees and clear them away, and he could inspire others to do the same. If he was not able to reconcile the two sides of himself, to think through the contradictions and conflicts implicit in his acts and ambitions, Boone was not alone.

In fairness it must be pointed out that with over two thousand miles of wilderness extending west from North Carolina to the Pacific, it may not have occurred to Boone or anyone else in 1775 that those regions could ever be so quickly settled and tamed. To Boone and his contemporaries, the wilderness must have seemed infinite, and infinitely challenging. It would be a few years before he saw how fast the forests could be chopped down and the game destroyed. No one could have believed in 1775 that the wilderness would vanish within their lifetime.

"THIS IS THE marked difference between Boone and the other Pioneers. He went out to possess; too many of them went forth to slay and destroy," his biographer W. H. Bogart wrote in 1854. In February 1775 Boone returned from his mission among the Cherokees to his family on the Clinch River. For eighteen months they had been staying in David Gass's cabin. Rebecca and the children began preparing for the second migration to Kentucky. The attempt in 1773 had not been well planned or directed. The journey of 1775 would be much larger, better organized and funded. The way would be opened and a fort built on the Kentucky River. A location near the mouth of Otter Creek had been agreed upon with Henderson and his partners. And since the land would have been bought from the Cherokees, the settlers would be safe.

Many historians, biographers, and writers have attempted to recreate the scene at Sycamore Shoals on the Watauga in March of 1775. It is one of the pivotal and archetypal images in frontier history. As many as fifteen hundred Cherokees had assembled and camped there for the negotiations, signing, and celebration. "James Robertson, also a witness, kept a day by day account, and estimated that there were 1200 Indians at the treaty." No doubt both sides thought they were getting a bargain, perhaps swindling the other. At the very least each assumed they had done well in the negotiations. It's likely that a Cherokee as wise as Attakullakulla understood Kentucky was going to be overrun by white settlers in any case and his people might as well get what they could while the getting was good. Another sucker like Henderson was not likely to show up. Attakullakulla was a diplomat, renowned for pleasing all who could be pleased. And since the transfer of Kentucky lands had already been agreed upon that winter, the whole affair at Sycamore Shoals was more a ceremonial display than an actual negotiation.

The war chief Oconostota was not so sanguine as Attakullakulla about the proceedings, and the younger chief, Attakullakulla's son Dragging Canoe, was angered by the transaction. But a consensus had been reached and there was no going back. Among the families camped along the river there was a good deal of excitement, expectation. No one was sure just how much of the loot any individual would get. The meeting grounds at Sycamore Shoals were near cabins and a fort already built by settlers who had leased some of the Cherokee hunting grounds. These new neighbors of the Watauga Association witnessed and enjoyed the proceedings and celebrations also, at the place the Cherokees called "the broken waters."

At a meeting in North Carolina the previous winter Henderson and his partners had agreed to change their name from the Louisa Company to the Transylvania Company, reminding all that the new colony was beyond the long-standing barrier of the mountains.

In *The Wilderness Road* Robert Kincaid writes, "Colonel Henderson opened the negotiations by inquiring if the Kentucky land which he sought was actually owned by the Cherokee — a needless formality to give a guise of legality to the affair. The chiefs withdrew for a solemn powwow among themselves. Next day they reported their conclusions. Without question they owned the land, they said. The claims of the

Six Nations [the Iroquois] were spurious because they never conquered the Cherokee. The Shawnee had long ago been driven out of the country."

With so many Cherokees gathered at Sycamore Shoals for the signing, it was a major effort for the Transylvania Company to feed all who had congregated day after day in growing numbers. The Cherokees called Richard Henderson "Carolina Dick." A number of interpreters were involved in the bargaining, as well as Attakullakulla, his son Dragging Canoe, Oconostota, and the chief called the Raven. The actual deed of sale gives the amount of payment as "for and in consideration of the sum of two thousand pounds of lawful money of Great Britain," but there are reports of as much as ten thousand pounds' worth of merchandise given in the bargain also. The goods offered in exchange for land were spread out in tents for the Cherokees to inspect.

Later some Cherokees would claim all the goods were shoddy, cheap blankets, cheap guns. It was reported that no liquor was permitted at the treaty signing. And the chiefs who concluded the agreement would later defend themselves by saying that the young there were tempted by the goods, whatever they were worth, and were so greedy to own them there was no stopping the sale. There was a great deal of disagreement among the Cherokees about the whole affair. Dragging Canoe in particular opposed the transaction but was overruled by the majority.

Richard Henderson was shrewd enough to know that once all the people had gathered and seen the merchandise he had brought, it was too late for any chief to stop the transaction. It would be too great an anticlimax to return to their villages and leave the guns and blankets and money.

Though the discussions among the chiefs and negotiations between Carolina Dick and the Cherokees were lengthy and serious, the element of farce in the proceedings was understood at the time by many, both buyers and sellers. Some Cherokees reminded Henderson that their nation had never claimed land beyond the Cumberland River. Henderson and his partners knew they were acting against orders from the colonial governments of North Carolina and Virginia and that the document authorizing them to negotiate with Indians was a sham. For all the heated talk and grand rhetoric, we have to suspect that individuals on both sides were grinning up their sleeves, congratulating themselves on pulling off a coup.

But Dragging Canoe was not grinning. He could not forget that this act was hastening and sanctioning the destruction of the huge hunting grounds of Kentucky, and the rush of settlers across Cherokee lands. Whatever the legal authority and promises of the agreement, there was no denying that the treaty would accelerate the settlement of land in the mountains and across the mountains. The next year Dragging Canoe would help organize an Indian confederation to vanquish the white settlements west of the mountains. On March 17, 1775, the deed of sale was inked, and Henderson bought the additional land between the Holston River and Cumberland Gap as a "path deed" to reach the lands he had already purchased.

Before Boone had left to begin chopping the road through the wilderness, the great chief Attakullakulla took him aside and said, "[W]e have given you a fine land, but I believe you will have much trouble in settling it." The legend grew that Dragging Canoe had called Kentucky "dark and bloody ground" at that time, but there is no evidence that he did so. However, he did warn that "there was a dark cloud over that Country" of Kentucky. Even so, all who witnessed the proceedings at Sycamore Shoals remembered the eloquence and authority of Attakullakulla. Though tiny in stature, he was a man of great poise and wisdom, and a master of English. Pleasant Henderson, another of Richard's brothers, later declared that the Little Carpenter was "the most fluent, graceful and eloquent orator he had ever heard."

Several days before the actual signing and subsequent celebrations, Boone had left for the fort at the Long Island of the Holston, where the road crew assembled. His pay for organizing the signing party at Sycamore Shoals and leading the road makers was to be two thousand acres of land in Henderson's new domain. The pay for those who

helped to chop the pathway to Kentucky was to be about ten pounds
for around a month of hard and dangerous work. But a greater inducement was the prospect of being among the first to reach a new colony
and claim choice parcels of land for themselves. And added to that was
the excitement of being one of Boone's advance party, just a few weeks
of chopping away from the promised land of Kentucky.

Michael Stoner signed on, as did William Bush and David Gass.
Also there was William Hays, a twenty-year-old Irish immigrant,
trained as a weaver, and well educated enough to have helped Boone
the autumn before write up his reports and accounts as a captain of the
militia. "Hays taught my father to write with an improved hand," Nathan told Draper. Hays was hard drinking and short tempered, but he
became Boone's close friend and was already courting his lively oldest
daughter, Susannah. Suzy Boone wasn't yet fifteen, but she had a reputation for being flirtatious, perhaps a little fast. Susannah was the subject of a good bit of gossip that followed her for the rest of her life and
beyond. At least one informant later claimed she was "a notorious prostitute," while others merely said she was lively and high spirited. The
early Boone scholar John Dabney Shane was told Boone had warned
Hays that if he married Susannah she might prove unfaithful. After
they were married in 1775 Hays came to his father-in-law to complain.
"Trot father, trot mother, how can you expect a pacing colt?" Boone
is supposed to have said. After her wedding Susannah accompanied
her husband and Boone's crew on their road-building journey. The
first month of her marriage would be spent cooking and keeping camp
for almost thirty rough backwoodsmen. "Mrs. Susan Hays — Boone's
daughter, was a pretty good looking woman, medium sized — rather
slim." Josiah Collins would later report to John Dabney Shane that he
had heard rumors about Susan but never knew her as other than well
behaved. "Susan when I saw her at Bnsbgh. Was a clever, pretty, well
behaved woman. These were stories that were in circulation and not
anything I saw."

In addition to William Bush, David Gass, Michael Stoner, and

William Hays, Boone's crew included his brother Squire, Benjamin Cutbirth, Samuel Tate, and William Twitty from Rutherford County, south of the Yadkin in North Carolina. Altogether the party included twenty-six people. One of the crew was Felix Walker, who would later describe Boone as "our pilot and conductor through the wilderness to the promised land." In his long career, Boone was often compared to Moses, and there was at least one parallel that his contemporaries could not have been aware of. Unlike the biblical patriarch, Boone actually reached the promised land of Canaan, but like Moses he was ultimately unable to possess and enjoy it.

To help Susannah Boone Hays feed and serve the company, a slave woman owned by Richard Callaway was sent along. Callaway had been hired to haul the tons of trade goods for the Cherokees to Sycamore Shoals. He now joined the crew of road builders. He was twelve years older than Boone, a colonel in the Virginia militia, from an affluent family, and he would figure significantly in Boone's life over the next few years. It has been said he resented having to serve under a man younger than himself who had been a mere captain in Lord Dunmore's War.

There has been a great deal of confusion over the years about what Boone's Trace actually was. The name is so well known, so familiar to all, it is often assumed to be a real road, a kind of highway cut and graded through the mountains. But with no equipment for digging and excavation, the company with Boone was prepared only to clear away trees and brush, logs and rocks, for riders and packhorses to pass through the woods. It would be years before wagons could be brought through Cumberland Gap, more than two decades. At the time, it was not called the Wilderness Road, but Boone's Trace or the Road to the Old Settlements. The term *Wilderness Road* seems to have come into use later, about 1796.

The crew's job was to make the trace clear and passable to those who would follow them. They chopped trees and saplings, brush and limbs, briars and vines, out of the way. They likely moved rocks and logs horses might stumble on, and found shallow places in streams for easy fording. They took the path around bogs and sinkholes near the creeks, and cut a way through canebrakes and curtains of grapevines. Since it was March, the woods were open and buds just beginning to break out. Felix Walker later said Boone conducted his men through the wilderness "with great propriety, intrepidity and courage." Because they had only a month to cover more than a hundred miles, the crew had to work steady and fast. It was brutal, back-breaking work. Swinging an axe fifteen minutes will tire a modern man. Swinging an axe all day leaves muscles stiff and numb. After holding an axe for hours of chopping, fingers are so stiff they hurt when they let go of the handle. The scholar Arthur K. Moore tells us, "Handiness with the axe was one criterion of fitness in the wilderness, and men accordingly acquired extraordinary skill in management of the tool. Their precision is evidenced by the notched logs of cabins surviving from the period . . . steel conquered the West."

Boone walked out in front and shot game to feed his company. No doubt he kept an eye out for panthers and bears, and Indians also. Susannah and the slave woman, whose name we don't know, dressed the game and cooked it. Bear was the preferred meat, for it was sweet and tender. But they relied more on deer, which were more plentiful in the region. It was a season of late snows and freezing rain. When they burned piles of brush, men gathered at the bonfires to warm their hands. The ground along the creeks was greasy mud that sucked on boots and moccasins.

Beyond the Cumberland Gap the trail got even rougher. A few miles farther on, Boone's crew had to follow the Cumberland River at Pine Mountain Gap, a water gap cut by the river over millions of years, then cross at a ford near Flat Lick. Although not as famous as Cumberland Gap, Pine Mountain Gap was equally important for reaching Kentucky. The Warrior's Path turned due north, but Boone guided his crew northwest toward the Louisa, as the Kentucky River was sometimes called.

Wherever possible, the axemen followed trails already beaten down by migrating herds. With few instruments, probably only a compass, Boone made no attempt at straight lines, but followed openings in the forest, the lay of the land, old fields, animal trails. Winding through mud and fast creeks, canebrakes, and overhanging limbs, the way was a road in name only. But it was a trace, meaning simply it was a route that was marked and could be followed. Leaving the Warrior's Path north of Flat Lick, Boone then guided his crew northwest along an old hunter's trail called Skaggs's Trace to Hazel Patch. From there he turned due north through several creek and river valleys toward the mouth of Otter Creek on the Kentucky River.

Richard Henderson, who followed with the main body of immigrants, found the trace Boone's men had made, "most of it hilly, stony, slippery, miry or brushy." It may have been hard to negotiate in places, going this way and that, taking advantage of openings in the wilderness; but people could follow it, at first by the dozens, then by the hundreds, and later by the thousands. Lewis Condict would later write, "Nothing can exceed the road for badness in some particular places, the mud being belly deep to our horses, & the banks of the creeks almost insurmountable, from the steepness & slippery nature." At the place called Hazel Patch, perhaps an old field or fire scald or even a kind of moor, where there was brush but few trees, they knew they were more than halfway to their destination. For Felix Walker and the other choppers, once they crossed the Rockcastle River and hacked their way through several miles of brush and thickets, there was the thrill of a new vista, "the pleasing and rapturous . . . plains of Kentucky." Also Felix Walker said that as March slid toward April and they neared their destination, "Perhaps no Adventurers Since the days of donquick sotte or before ever felt so Cheerful & Ilated in prospect, every heart abounded with Joy & excitement."

On April 1, 1775, Boone wrote to Richard Henderson one of the earliest of his letters to have been preserved. It is likely that Will Hays or someone else in the party helped him draft it. The letter, addressed to "Dear Colonel" reads in part:

> After my compliments to you, I shall acquaint you of our misfortune. On March the 25th a party of Indians fired on my company about half an hour before day, and killed Mr. Twitty and his Negro, and wounded Mr. Walker very deeply, but I hope he will recover. On March the 28th as we were hunting for provisions, we found Samuel Tate's son, who gave us an account that the Indians fired on their camp on the 27th day. My brother and I went down and found two men killed and sculped, Thomas Mcdowell and Jeremiah Mcffeeters. I have sent a man down to all the lower companies in order to gather them all to the mouth of Otter Creek.

Boone urged Henderson to come as soon as possible to swell their force, for his men were very uneasy. "Now is the time to flusterate their intentions, and keep the country whilst we are in it," he said. "If we give way to them now it will ever be the case." With Henderson was a young man from Virginia named William Calk. He kept a journal of the expedition into Kentucky. "fryday ye 7th [of April] this morning is avery hard Snowey morning & we Still continue at camp Being in number about 40 men & Some Neagroes. this Eavening Comes aletter from Capt. [Daniel] Boon at caintuck of the indians doing mischief and Some turns back."

Boone later described the attack on March 27 to John Filson, saying they were fired upon by Indians and two men were killed and two wounded. But though taken by surprise they had not been routed. Out of the dark the Indians came swinging their tomahawks. Twitty was wounded; his slave and his bulldog were killed. Felix Walker was wounded but ran with the rest of the party into the woods. As soon as it was clear the attack was over they returned to the camp, but some of the men were so shaken they packed their things and headed back to Virginia and North Carolina. They had assumed the treaty with the Cherokees would prevent such attacks. Boone and the remaining men threw together a rough structure they called Twitty's Fort. Twitty himself died after a few days suffering, but Boone helped nurse Felix Walker back to health. "He attended me as his child, cured my wounds by the use of medicines from the woods, nursed me with paternal affection until I recovered," Walker would later write in his account.

It was not certain what tribe of Indians attacked Boone's company of axemen. In the aftermath various groups accused each other. Ted Franklin Belue in *The Hunters of Kentucky* tells us, "The Chillicothes accused the Mingoes; a few blamed Dragging Canoe's Cherokees; there were rumors the Piquas to the north had dug up the hatchet. No one, he [Capt. Russell] said, was sure who had done the killings." The attackers may have been a roving band that included members of various tribes. Whoever they were, the momentum of the project broken, the men were confused and afraid. The weather continued bad, and two days after the attack it began to snow. A group had gone out hunting and was attacked and two men killed. When Samuel Tate and the other hunters returned to the main camp and told their story, there was more panic. Only Boone's calm good sense and manner of authority kept things under control. The slave woman saw someone spying on them from the woods and screamed, and there was panic again, until the intruder proved to be one of the axemen who had fled into the forest after the first attack.

While Felix Walker recovered, and the party recouped its strength and will, Boone and a few other men cut a way down to Otter Creek to the place he and Henderson's partners had chosen for a settlement on the Louisa or Kentucky River, fifteen miles away. Boone then returned to Twitty's Fort and rigged up a litter between two horses to carry Walker on to the river. The young man would never forget seeing, as they came in sight of the Great Meadow along the river, hundreds of buffalo, surprised by the appearance of the road makers, heading off from a salt lick and splashing through the stream. "Such a sight some

of us never saw before," he wrote later, "nor perhaps may never again."
Walker, and many of the other men, understood they were glimpsing a
world just before it was to disappear. And they themselves were among
the instruments of history and of its vanishing. "We felt ourselves as
passengers through a wilderness just arrived at the fields of Elysium, or
at the garden where was no forbidden fruit."

CHAPTER EIGHT

Kentucky Was the Key

1775 ↳

It is easy to forget in the twenty-first century the significance for the English-speaking eastern communities of the settling and holding of Kentucky. The Bluegrass region was valuable in itself, almost beyond description, as a place to claim and build farms and towns and future cities and great wealth. Explorers and speculators and leaders of the time understood that a foothold in Kentucky served as a buffer against the Indians, against the British to the north, and perhaps the Spanish to the west and south. But even more than that, a settled Kentucky promised to open the whole Ohio Valley to settlement. Some Indians seemed to grasp this threat implicitly and fought with tenacity, courage, and imagination the forts and stations, the farmers and surveyors, in the Great Meadow. They seemed to perceive from the first that once their buffalo hunting grounds in the Bluegrass were claimed and cleared, the land north of the Ohio would be next. Other Native leaders such as Cornstalk of the Shawnees were willing, at first, to accommodate the English settlers and did not foresee an inexorable tidal wave of westward expansion.

For the whites nothing could have been more exhilarating, more intoxicating, than the taking and keeping of land across the barrier of mountains. For once that hurdle was finally surpassed, after 150 years of hesitating and yearning in the east, the great river valleys of the central continent would be within reach. Filson described Kentucky as the "best tract of land in North-America, and probably in the world." The Ohio Valley was more beautiful and contained more land than anyone had mapped or measured. And beyond lay the Illinois country, the fertile Mississippi Valley, stretching almost to Canada in the north and to New Orleans in the south. And beyond the Mississippi, reports were heard of an even bigger river valley, the Missouri, that reached far into a mythical West and whispered rumors of mountains so high their tips sparkled with snow in July.

But whatever lay beyond, in the sunlit pastures and hills of coming years, Kentucky was the key, the first West. Kentucky was the threshold, the beachhead, to who-knew-what playlands and empires of the future, farther west.

ON THE BANKS of the Kentucky River, Boone and his men turned their efforts toward building shelters for themselves and those coming behind them at Big Lick, near the mouth of Otter Creek. Henderson's plan was to construct a substantial fortress, but first they needed cabins to protect them from the elements and animals.

When Henderson received Boone's letter of April 1, he and his larger group were deeply shaken. After the treaty ceremony at Sycamore Shoals, they had expected no trouble from Indians. They did not understand that even great chiefs such as Attakullakulla and Oconostota were powerless to control the actions of dissident individuals or roving groups of the tribe. A hunting party or group of warriors could do pretty much as it pleased. And the same was true on the side of the whites. Whatever treaties great men such as Henderson or the governor of Virginia might make, settlers and hunters in the wilderness would do virtually whatever they wanted. And the fact that Henderson had signed a treaty with the Cherokees did not mean that Shawnees or Mingoes or Delawares would not attack his expedition. Shawnees were angry because they felt their claims to the hunting grounds of the Great Meadow had been ignored by the whites and

Cherokees and Iroquois at the Treaties of Fort Stanwix and Hard Labor and Lochabar.

Even as Henderson hurried forward toward Cumberland Gap, some of the would-be settlers and hired hands abandoned the venture and turned east. And as the main party labored toward the gap, they encountered several from Boone's crew and other groups fleeing back to the old settlements. Reports of Indian attacks were sweeping through the region. Among those who had joined Henderson's party was Abraham Hanks from Virginia, but frightened by reports brought back by fleeing settlers, Hanks, as recorded by William Calk on April 13, turned back. Abraham Hanks was the uncle of Nancy Hanks, mother of the sixteenth president, Abe Lincoln.

As they inched along the trace Boone had made, Henderson was surprised to meet more and more men fleeing from Kentucky. Most were not from Boone's company of axemen but from scattered hunting and surveying parties. By then Kentucky was full of small groups of men hoping to stake a claim in the wilderness, most of them squatters. News of the Indian attacks on Boone's group sent the weak-hearted hurrying back toward North Carolina and Virginia, or up the Ohio River toward Fort Pitt. News traveled fast among the Indians also, and between the traders living among the Indians. Henderson's greatest fear was that Boone would abandon the post on the river and return with his men before Henderson's larger group arrived to reinforce the station. He knew that everything depended on Boone's leadership, character, resourcefulness. If Boone failed, the whole Transylvania Company would fail. "It was beyond a doubt," Henderson wrote later, "that our right, in effect, depended on Boone's maintaining his ground."

But the larger party was moving so slowly, and perhaps reluctantly, that Henderson decided someone should ride ahead and assure Boone that reinforcements were on the way. The only man willing to make such a journey was Capt. William Cocke, who had served in the militia during Lord Dunmore's War. Cocke said he would go if someone else would ride with him. But there were no takers, even for an inducement of ten thousand acres of Kentucky land. Henderson was desperate, and finally Cocke agreed to go alone. Provided with weapons and supplies, he set off on April 10 and arrived at Boone's camp on April 14 to find that there had been another attack on April 4 and one more man had been killed. Boone chose Michael Stoner to return to Cumberland Gap and lead Henderson and his party into Kentucky.

John Floyd and Benjamin Logan and his associates from Virginia, who came to Kentucky at almost the same time in a separate party, would take the same path but turn west at Hazel Patch and follow Skaggs's Trace to a site at Buffalo Spring where they would build St. Asaph's, later Logan's Station. Though Logan had entered Kentucky at almost exactly the same time as Henderson, he would be a strong antagonist to the Transylvania Company. John Floyd, ever the diplomat, would prove able to work with both Henderson and Col. William Preston of Fincastle County, Virginia, who held official colonial authority over the region.

The long column of men and packhorses with Henderson finally arrived on the banks of the Kentucky River on April 20 and were saluted with a volley of rifle shots. William Calk wrote in his journal that day: "Thursday 20th this morning is Clear & cool. We Start Early & git Down to Caintuck to Boons foart [Boonesborough] about 12 oclock wheare we stop. they Come out to meet us & welcom us in with a voley of guns."

Henderson's relief was considerable. He embraced Cocke and promised him yet another five thousand acres for his solitary ride across the mountains. But it was Boone to whom he felt the greatest gratitude. "It was owing to Boone's confidence in us, and the people's in him, that a stand was ever attempted in order to wait for our coming," Henderson wrote later in his account. However, he did not offer to give Boone any additional land, more than the two thousand acres he had promised at the beginning. Only his panic on the trail and his exhilaration at arriving at Boonesborough explain Henderson's generous gifts to Cocke.

Henderson was a fascinating man, of considerable means, education, ambition, vision. An English friend wrote of Henderson, "Even in the superior courts where oratory and eloquence are as brilliant and powerful as in Westminster, he soon became distinguished and eminent, and his superior genius shone forth with great splendour, and universal applause." While others might see Henderson as greedy, law-defying, a little mad, Boone viewed his employer as the good angel who had finally enabled him to settle in Kentucky. But Richard Henderson was a lawyer and businessman, dependent on men like Boone in the wilderness. In choosing Daniel Boone, in spite of his debts and credit history, Henderson proved an excellent judge of character. Without Boone, his venture would have been a disaster from the start. Its later collapse would be beyond both his and Boone's control and would have nothing to do with anyone's skill in the wilderness.

The story of Boonesborough is a wonderful combination of legend, heroism, failure, and farce. The site was originally dubbed Fort Boone by the road makers, in honor of their foreman, but Henderson wanted to give the capital of his colony a name to suggest civilization and stability, not war and danger, and he changed the name to Boonesborough. The first scattered cabins were in a hollow close to the river, but Henderson chose to place his stockade on the gently sloping meadow above the river. The hollow was filled with sycamores and contained the two springs, one fresh and bold, the other sluggish and salty. "A spring at Boonsburrow constantly emits sulphureous particles, and near the same place is a salt spring," John Filson would write later. Animals had gathered to lick the salty ground there for thousands of years, and Indians had lived there also. Historians have pointed out that the site of Sycamore Hollow resembled in many ways the treaty signing grounds at Sycamore Shoals.

Henderson's plan for a stockade included a large rectangle of log palisades, about 80 by 240 feet, with a two-story blockhouse at each corner. The second stories of the blockhouses would extend out over the palisades so defenders could shoot at those attempting to climb the walls or set the logs on fire. There would be at least eight cabins inside the walls and a front gate facing away from the river. Henderson wrote in his diary on April 21, 1775, "After some perplexity, resolved to erect a fort on the opposite side of a large lick, near the river bank, which would place us at the distance of about three hundred yards from the other fort — the only commodious place near or where we could be of any service to Boone's men, or vice versa."

The fort Henderson designed would have two gates, one in front and one in the back facing the river. There was to be about a half acre of open ground inside the fort. Boone was assigned to supervise the building of the stockade. It was clear Henderson recognized his own weakness and lack of authority in the wilderness. Boone knew how to talk to the men and he knew the woods and the manners of the woods. For much of the activity Boone was in charge. But building the stockade as planned proved more difficult than anyone expected, even for Boone. The men were not disciplined or trained as builders. They were a loose collection of hunters, adventurers, hangers-on. They wanted the best cheap land, and they wanted to claim and clear their own plots, not help in the heavy work of fort building. Instead of the cooperation expected, there was dissension. Even Henderson's partner Nathaniel Hart moved out of the settlement to his own place up the river. There seemed little interest in building common defenses against Indian attacks. The cabins at Boonesborough remained separated, not enclosed in a picket wall of upright logs. Henderson's quarters, which would form the blockhouse at one corner of the stockade, were built, but work on the fort was postponed.

In retrospect, it seems difficult to explain such lack of cooperation and sense of common purpose. It became clear to Henderson that many of his would-be settlers were rolling stones, debtors, loafers, men eager for adventure and disposed to avoid work. In a letter of June 12, 1775, Henderson wrote to a partner in North Carolina, "To give you a small specimen of the disposition of the people, it may be sufficient to assure you, that when we arrived at this place, we found Captain

Boone's men as inattentive on the score of fear, (to all appearances) as if they had been in Hillsborough. A small fort [that] only wanted two or three days' work to make it tolerably safe, was totally neglected on Mr. Cocke's arrival, and unto this day remains unfinished, notwithstanding the repeated applications of Captain Boone, and every representation of danger from ourselves." Henderson went on to explain that the men worked in their fields scattered for two miles along the river and didn't even bother to take their guns with them. About thirty men out of the original eighty had returned to the settlements over the mountains. The men who stayed seemed desperate to clear their own fields and put in crops. Without a crop they would not be able to stay the next winter and they would lose their claim on the land. No doubt that necessity of clearing a patch and planting corn was part of the explanation for the reluctance to build the fort. And many of the men may have been exhausted from the heavy work of chopping their way through the mountains, clearing land, building cabins, plowing the root-laced soil.

In our times it's hard to comprehend the settlers' rage to clear land. While we now tend to see trees as friends and forests as welcoming shade, those on the frontier more often viewed trees as enemies and forests as a refuge for Indians, panthers, wolves. It was one's duty to fell the threatening trees and tear away the brush and let the sunlight of calm and reason into the swamps and hollows. Land was there to be surveyed, brought under the axe and plow. With wilderness stretching west hundreds of miles to the Mississippi, and danger lurking in thickets and canebrakes, their only hope was to clear a space for cultivation and safety. It was the dream of settlers to have green pastures and orchards of apple and peach trees. The ground had to be divided in straight lines and the crops planted in straight lines, making sense of sprawling terrain. Sinkholes had to be filled in and springs deepened. The forest had to be driven back to acceptable boundaries. A settler went to war, not only with Indians and the British, but with briar and mighty oak tree.

And once the forest had been pushed back, the fight had only begun. On every foot of cleared space weeds sprang up like grass fire, higher than a man's head. Brambles and vines ran rampant. Seedlings took root and sumacs shot up ten feet in two months. With scythe and axe the settler did battle all summer against the army of weeds that threatened to surround and drown him. The wild growth in the hot southern sun had to be corrected and instructed. But where a forest had been cleared up and sorted out, and farmed for four or five years, the topsoil washed away if the ground was slightly tilted. Gully-washing rains and frog-strangling storms swept away the black forest mold and left clay grooved and smocked as though by giant fingers. With all the topsoil gone, the dirt no longer fit or fertile, the land was called an old field, good only for school yard and churchyard, or graveyard. The settlers had no choice but to go farther into the woods to slay more trees and rip out roots and rocks and slice open the soil for the next new field.

To build a serious fort of the size Richard Henderson planned required enormous effort. The palisades of heavy logs had to be sawed or chopped, dragged out of the woods, and set in the ground. The fence alone, as Henderson had planned it, would require close to a thousand logs. Each log had to be cut and trimmed and pulled to the building site. By June the weather was getting hot, and there were flies and mosquitoes to worry about, as well as hornets and wasps.

To set the logs upright as pickets, a ditch had to be dug, sometimes three or even four feet deep. With only picks and shovels, the ditch was made through rocks, fat roots, packed clay. The bigger roots had to be sawed or chopped, and first exposed by shoveling enough to be reached by saw or axe. Once the big logs were set, large end down, the dirt was heaped around them and tamped firm. When the logs were pegged together, the wall was even stronger. It would be difficult to imagine harder labor in the summer heat. No wonder the men preferred to be working off in their own fields, or hunting.

And once the fence and gates of the enclosure were in place, the

work was only started. To function as a fortress the structure had to
have those two-story blockhouses at each corner, the second story jutting out over the first and over the palisade. Without the raised blockhouses, those inside could not see out except through cracks between
the logs. And ideally the fort would have a walkway behind the length
of the wall where riflemen could stand or kneel and shoot at attackers. "Henderson took up his quarters in a block-house erected at this
time. It formed an angle of defense — the angle nearest the river," the
historian George Ranck tells us. To withstand attacks of more than a
few hours, the fort had to have a well and a storehouse for provisions.
There had to be a powder magazine and tools for repairing guns and
making bullets. There had to be fireplaces and pens for livestock. Any
horses or cattle left outside, the Indians would steal or kill. One visitor
to Boonesborough in 1775 wrote, "It was all anarchy and confusion, and
you could not discover what person commanded, for in fact no person
did command entirely." Henderson thought only another attack could
wake the men up to follow his commands and complete the defenses.
The Boonesborough fort would remain unfinished until 1778.

From his diary and letters we can see that Henderson was an eloquent man but uncomfortable with the conditions of frontier living.
He saw himself and his partners as the lords proprietor of a thriving
colony growing ever richer and more powerful. He had brought with
him a library of forty-eight expensive volumes. The reality of life in the
wilderness appalled him. His immigrants included men who had left
the settlements to escape authority and order, often to escape the law
itself. While Henderson reported a world that seemed to be falling
apart, Boone, who was used to frontier conditions and the men who
went there, appeared to be satisfied with their progress.

One reason the settlers were so anxious to put in crops was that
provisions were already running low. Most of what they had brought
with them was gone and they had to live on what they could shoot
until the crops came in. But game was soon scarce around the fort.

Therefore getting the new potatoes and squash, beans, and corn big enough to eat was crucial. Corn could be eaten when it first ripened, was "in the milk," about eighty days after planting. By August 1 they might have roasting ears and gritted bread made from grated, semi-hardened kernels.

While working in the woods the men had to contend with many pests. Hornets and spiders, copperheads and sting worms, lurked in the brush. Nicholas Cresswell, an English traveler in the area that summer, wrote in his journal on May 26, 1775, "Much tormented with Ticks, a small animal like a Sheeplouse, but very tough skin. They get on you by walking in the Woods . . . and if you don't take care to pick them off in time they work their heads through the skin and then you pull the body away but the head will remain in the skin, which is very disagreeable."

While many plans seemed to be going awry, and Henderson and Company were under attack from almost every front, events occurred at Boonesborough between May 23 and May 27, 1775, that seem more the stuff of myth than of history. Yet the records are explicit and detailed. Henderson called a convention of representatives from the scattered and struggling settlements in Kentucky. It was his first effort to establish government and laws in the projected colony. James Harrod of Harrodsburg and Boiling Spring, and Benjamin Logan and the settlers of St. Asaph's, were not pleased that the Transylvania Company claimed to own much of Kentucky and therefore held proprietary rights over their surveyed lands, but most saw the wisdom of gathering and organizing for a common purpose.

Henderson may not have been much of a frontiersman or construction boss, but he knew that he could buy off many who opposed him by cutting them in on a slice of his enterprise. At Martin's Fort near Powell's River he had bought off Joseph Martin by hiring him as entry taker for the company to keep a record of those migrating to Kentucky. And to bring Martin's brother Bryce into the fold he had awarded him a tract of land in the new colony. "April 3, 1775, Mr. Bryce Martin enters with me for 500 acres of land lying on the first creek after crossing Cumberland Gap northward from powels valey going toward Canetucky river. Richard Henderson."

Those chosen to represent Boonesborough at the convention were Squire Boone and Daniel Boone, William Cocke, Samuel Henderson, William Moore, and Richard Callaway. From Harrodsburg came Thomas Slaughter, John Lythe, Valentine Harmon, and James Douglas. From the new station at Boiling Spring came James Harrod, Nathan Hammond, Isaac Hite, and Azariah Davis. And from St. Asaph's, John Todd, Alexander Spotswood Dandridge, John Floyd, and Samuel Wood. Benjamin Logan, the leader at St. Asaph's, who planned to resist Henderson's claim to Kentucky land, did not attend. John Floyd, representing Col. William Preston, the official surveyor and leader of Fincastle County, Virginia, may have been there primarily to witness the proceedings, though he later proved willing to join Henderson's enterprise. It was the first attempt at organized government by the English colonists west of the mountains, and the convention got off to an auspicious start on May 24. Since there was no meetinghouse, the delegates assembled under a huge elm tree behind Henderson's camp, called the Divine Elm, later described by George W. Ranck as "that magnificent tree, the sole cathedral in a wilderness as vast and as solitary as the illimitable ocean." A platform had been built at the foot of the great tree, on which the speakers stood, and delegates sat on logs, or on the ground, or leaned on their rifles while listening. The meeting began with a prayer and perhaps a few words of exhortation by the Reverend John Lythe, an Anglican priest from Harrodsburg, possibly the only time a prayer was said for the English king on Kentucky soil. Then Henderson opened the convention with words of eloquence, of which he was a master.

"You are called and assembled at this time," Henderson said, "for a noble and honorable purpose — a purpose, however ridiculous and idle it may appear at first to superficial minds . . .

"You are placing the first cornerstone of an edifice, the height and magnificence of whose superstructure are now in the womb of futurity, and can only become great and glorious, in proportion to the excellence of its foundation . . .

"If any doubt remain against you with respect to the force and efficacy of whatever laws you now or hereafter make, be pleased to consider that all power is originally in the people; make it their interest, therefore, by impartial and beneficial laws, and you may be sure of their inclinations to see them enforced."

Henderson, as he presided over the opening of the convention under the great elm tree that spread its shade more than a hundred feet wide, outlined the kind of laws he thought should be passed for safety and to protect property. Henderson showed his training and sophistication as a lawyer and judge, stressing the importance of courts and justice, countering charges made by royal officials that his colony would be a refuge "for debtors and other persons of desperate circumstance." He outlined the necessity of organizing a militia and suggested laws against "the wanton destruction of our game." Clearly the scarcity of game around the settlement was already recognized as a serious concern only seven weeks after Boone and his men had arrived. Henderson also promised that in the new colony there would be complete religious freedom.

Because his enterprise later failed, and because of the grandiosity of his schemes, Henderson has had few defenders over the years. After his name was tainted with defeat, few could find virtue in his methods or ambitions. But his statement about power originating with the people has a surprisingly modern ring. He was speaking in a world of monarchy and colonial governments. His language is that of a lawyer of the time. He intended to impress his listeners with his authority over the English language, as he had done in court many times. But whatever his talents and accomplishments, they were doomed to be seen in the context of his later failure.

Under the elm tree, John Todd of St. Asaph's Station gave a formal response to President Henderson's address, promising that the convention would consider all the important points placed before them. The discussion began under strict parliamentary rules of procedure. There is a slightly surreal air to this scene of the delegates meeting under a tree, surrounded by wilderness, observing such courtesy and decorum. Perhaps there was a desire to counter the informality of their facilities with careful etiquette. A thousand ironies hover around the proceedings. The settlements have been established against the orders of the colonial governments and the Crown, yet they observe the best standards of English parliamentary rules. They are seated under a tree in the middle of a wilderness, vulnerable to attack at any moment. The Shawnees, who had a greater claim to the land than the Cherokees because they had hunted there more frequently, had never been consulted, and they would not forget the snub. And for all his talk about power originating with the people, Henderson planned to rule his colony as a private fiefdom.

However formally the convention began, things turned rougher as the discussion continued. As soon as Robert McAfee was appointed sergeant-at-arms, Richard Callaway, who always seemed to have a chip on his shoulder, demanded that John Gass be brought before the convention "to answer for an insult offered Col. Richard Callaway." John Gass was duly hauled in and reprimanded. In almost every detail in the history of Boonesborough, Richard Callaway comes off as illtempered, defensive, jealous, and eager to accuse and punish. At the same time he was recognized as brave and dependable. He seemed to have always had a grudge against Boone. In modern times Callaway would probably have been diagnosed as paranoid. But there was no way to get rid of him, and Boone's daughter Jemima married Callaway's nephew, Flanders Callaway.

The minutes of the convention show that Boone proposed "a bill for preserving the game, and a committee was appointed for that purpose," and also "a bill for improving the breed of horses." Most historians have noted Boone's practicality and prescience. He already saw that the very game that had drawn him to Kentucky six years before might soon be gone, and his second motion suggests that he already understood the importance of breeding fine horseflesh for the future of Kentucky.

One feature adding to the almost surreal air of this convention was the "Livery of Seizin" ceremony, which Henderson organized. It shows his feudal sense of his role and his colony, and it also reveals his love of the theatrical. To complete the transfer of Kentucky to his company he had a lawyer named John Farrar, who represented the Cherokees, hand him the deed along with a piece of turf, symbolizing the twenty million acres of the purchase. Ranck writes, "The session closed with the execution of its most important feature, the signing of the compact between the Proprietors and the People, which, crude as it is, takes historical precedence as the constitution of the first representative government ever attempted west of the Allegheny Mountains."

Henderson and the others had already decided as early as January 6, 1775, that the new colony would be called Transylvania, and Henderson and his partners would be known as the Transylvania Company. Henderson has been accused of lack of foresight, delusions of grandeur, greed, and worse, but the convention under the elm suggests there was more to the man than his detractors concede. Had circumstances been different, his company might well have prospered. As it turned out, events far from the banks of the Kentucky River were overtaking his efforts and making his struggles and eloquence irrelevant.

Since John Floyd represented Col. William Preston, who represented the government of the colony of Virginia in the western region, Henderson saw how important it was to incorporate Floyd into his enterprise. As the scholar Stephen Aron puts it, "Realizing that it was 'most advisable to secure' Floyd 'to our interests,' Henderson promised him land and gave him a lucrative job as surveyor for the Transylvania Company. Through the rest of 1775, Floyd, and by extension Preston, did not meddle with the Transylvania claims." John Floyd was not only an excellent surveyor, he was also a wise and judicious leader. Though only in his midtwenties, his intelligence and authority were generally recognized. His letters written to Col. William Preston provide much of the knowledge we have of Boonesborough and Kentucky at this period.

But there was one official Henderson had not included in his enterprise. Patrick Henry had intimated to Henderson the year before that he would like to be a part of the Louisa Company. Thomas Jefferson had also hinted he wanted to be included in the Transylvania venture. But Richard Henderson had not invited either of them, fearing they would dominate his company. Of all his mistakes this may have been the most serious. Smarting from the snub, Henry and his associates became powerful enemies of the Transylvania Company. Yet even Henry had originally conceded that the Transylvania purchase might be valid. As Neal O. Hammon tells us, "[William] Christian told Floyd that his brother-in-law, Patrick Henry, believed the purchase to be legal, and based on existing English law."

AS JUNE 1775 slid into July, Henderson's problems multiplied and compounded. When the food supply brought over the mountains was exhausted, more settlers gave up their attempts to claim land in the wilderness and headed back over Boone's Trace to the settlements. The fort was especially low on salt needed to preserve meat and cure deer hides as well as flavor food. Sweating day after day in the hot sun, men grew weak if they did not replace the salt lost through perspiration. Many of those who had come with Henderson knew nothing of hunting or farming or salt boiling. The salt springs of Kentucky would later provide an ample supply of the mineral, when the settlers had the equipment, which consisted of large iron pots, and men willing to chop the wood to keep the fires under the pots blazing for days.

After the memorable convention under the Divine Elm, nothing seemed to go right for Henderson and the Transylvania Company. He lived better than the rest because he was rich and had brought more supplies, and his servant Dan milked the cows, caught catfish from the river, raised a garden. Luckily the catfish in the Kentucky River were plentiful and large. The English traveler Nicholas Cresswell noted in his diary on May 30, "In our absence those at the Camp caught a large Catfish which measured six inches between the eyes. We supposed it would weigh 40 pounds." Filson would later report that in Kentucky there were catfish that weighed more than a hundred pounds. But the business of running Boonesborough seemed to overwhelm Henderson. He could not force the men to finish building the stockade; he could not force them to stay in Kentucky. In fact, he found he could not force them to do much of anything.

From the very beginning there were disputes about land claims. Because of haste, carelessness, and ignorance of surveying skills and methods, many boundaries were uncertain and claims overlapped. At first, because there was so much land available, these issues did not seem so important. But as time passed, the boundary conflicts became ever more serious and complicated. The problems were general all over Kentucky and the frontier, but nowhere were they worse than around Boonesborough. The rush to measure and stake new land led to a great deal of dishonesty, aggravated by incompetence. Disputes, litigation, duels, and bitterness would characterize the land business in Kentucky for decades to come. Overlapping claims were said to be "shingled," and many of the tracts registered in 1775 were already "shingled." In some instances the same ground was included in three or four over-lapping surveys. The laws of Virginia described the procedure for officially acquiring title to land: "The statutes prescribed four steps to be completed in sequence: 1) obtaining a warrant; 2) making an entry; 3) surveying the land; and 4) returning the survey and entry to the land office. Afterwards the land office issued a patent which, according to the statute, carried 'absolute verity.'" Capt. William Bailey Smith surveyed a thousand-acre tract for Boone that summer on Tate's Creek. This was, presumably, partial payment to Boone for his services to the Transylvania Company.

From the extensive diaries he kept at Boonesborough, it is obvious Henderson felt alienated and mystified by most of those he dealt with. He had brought many luxuries, including his library, with him, and reports suggest that he spent most of his time indoors. And however bad things were at Boonesborough, they were worse for the Transylvania Company back east. The governments of both North Carolina and Virginia had denounced Henderson and his partners. Josiah Martin, governor of North Carolina, called Henderson and his associates "an infamous Company of land Pyrates" and issued an official proclamation against the company on February 10, 1775. Facing only hostility from the colonial officials, Henderson and his partners turned to the new Continental Congress for support of their claim to the large tract in Kentucky, but the Transylvania Company found little support there either. Some representatives, including Thomas Jefferson, labeled Henderson's quitrent system a continuation of feudalism. Henderson's associate James Hogg wrote, "Quit rents, they say, is a mark of vassalage, and hope they shall not be established in Transylvania." Others, including John Adams, said it was a matter for the newly formed state governments to decide. Henderson knew it was unlikely either North Carolina or Virginia would recognize the purchase he had made with the Cherokees. It was all a muddle and a mess, as so much business of that time and place was.

Many already in Kentucky, including some who had come with him, doubted the validity of Henderson's claim and suspected that he would not be able to protect them against Indians. Nicholas Cresswell recorded in his diary the skepticism settlers in the region expressed about Henderson's colony: "Sunday, June 11th, 1775 . . . Found Captn. Hancock Lee camped at Elkhorn, surveying land. This is a new settlement by some Carolina Gentleman, who pretends to have purchased the Land from the Indians, but with what truth I cannot pretend to say as the Indians affirm they never sold these lands."

DANIEL BOONE left Boonesborough on June 13 to return to the Clinch River for his family, accompanied by several young settlers who were returning to Martin's Station for the badly needed salt. He also traveled with Richard Callaway, who was on his way to Virginia to recruit new settlers for Boonesborough.

That summer, while Rebecca waited for the birth of their ninth child, Boone traveled around the region persuading others to join the venture on the Kentucky River. In this he was successful, as he always seemed to be at gathering a party to follow him. Rebecca was now in her late thirties, an advanced age for childbearing in those days. It was a troubled pregnancy and difficult birth. After the baby, named William, was born in late July and died soon afterward, she was exhausted, in no condition to journey over the mountains to Boonesborough. Boone suggested to the men he had recruited that they go on ahead, but without their leader they would not budge. And since Boone would not return without his wife and family, things were at a standstill.

The history of the frontier as written has been mostly the story of men who went there. But recently scholars have been more willing to consider the role of women, and the conditions the women struggled with in settling the frontier. Kentucky had been described by Boone and others as "a good poor man's country," but as Stephen Aron says, "Rebecca Boone and her pioneer sisters . . . understood that a good poor man's country was not the same as a good poor woman's country; indeed the former was often antithetical to the latter." Others would point out that the prime Bluegrass section of Kentucky would prove inhospitable even to poor *men*.

From all the testimony we have, Rebecca Bryan Boone must have been one of the hardiest and most resilient and resourceful women in American history. But after the death of the ninth child even she was in need of rest. In a world with only the most rudimentary medicines and medical knowledge, the risk of infection after childbirth was very great. Many women died of childbed fever. Whether Rebecca had fever or not, it took her about six weeks to regain her strength enough to make the move to Kentucky. Annette Kolodny has argued that while women were sometimes as eager to go into the wilderness as men, their reasons were essentially different. Men were drawn into the new territories by visions of paradise, and promise of great wealth, women by a desire for a new home and a fertile, sustaining garden. Whatever their reasons, explicit or implicit, women began to pour into the wilderness by the hundreds and then by the thousands.

On July 18 Henderson had written in his diary, "Our salt is exhausted, and the men who went with Col. Boone for that article are not returned. We are informed that Mrs. Boone was not delivered the other day, and therefore do not know when to look for him; and, until he comes, the devil himself can't drive the others this way."

On August 10 Henderson packed up and left Boonesborough for North Carolina to plead his case with legislators. He left John Floyd in charge of the land office. Work on the fort had hardly begun, the settlement was without salt, and the land claims were in a tangle too messy to be readily sorted out. It is said that in his final weeks there, without Boone to persuade the men to cooperate, Henderson spent much of his time in his cabin with a bottle of whiskey. He would feel more at home lobbying legislators, and he would not return to Kentucky until the end of the year.

The party that left the Clinch Valley for Kentucky in mid-August 1775 with the large Boone family included seventeen single men and three families. Among them was the hot-tempered Hugh McGary from the Yadkin, Boone's former hunting companion, married to the widow Mary Ray, reported to be a strong-willed woman who alone knew how to manage McGary's tantrums. Others who had promised to go were frightened by rumors of Indian attacks and in the end stayed in the settlements. It is presumably this journey over the mountains that George Caleb Bingham later portrayed in his 1850–51 painting *Daniel Boone Escorting Settlers through the Cumberland Gap*. Deservedly one of the most famous American paintings of the nineteenth century, Bingham's picture shows a Boone of dignity and resolve. Based on the Chester Harding likeness taken from life in Boone's old age, the

portrait has Boone wearing a Quaker-style felt hat. He is leading the
horse on which Rebecca rides. Her features look very much like those
described by family and acquaintances. A long train of packhorses
and hunters follows and rugged peaks rear on either side of the path.
Flanders Callaway walks beside Boone with calm resolution. A man
stops to tie his moccasin, and a handsome dog points at a quail or
grouse somewhere in the brush. Far overhead a hawk or eagle soars
toward Kentucky. The painting is notable for its time for not showing savage Indians lurking or bears attacking. This Boone is wise and
peaceful, determined, organized. Bingham seems to catch the Quaker
spirit, the resolve and quiet authority of Boone, much as William
Carlos Williams would later portray him in words.

When Boone arrived with his family at Boonesborough on September 8, Henderson had been gone almost a month. Whatever the
conditions of the place, and there is evidence the station was something
of a shambles, Boone set to work, building a substantial cabin adjoining the fort-to-be with real glass windows and wooden floor. The care
with which he built, and the fact that he had brought his family, show
that he came for the long haul. The records of the company store attest
that he charged many items, including a hundred yards of linen cloth
for his wife and daughters.

It was time to begin preparing for the winter, and Boone made the
cabin weatherproof. Before he had left for the Clinch in June, he had
planted a field of corn and hoed and plowed it before laying it by, that
is, leaving it to grow on its own after the stalks were about knee high.
A first crop of corn on deadened acres grew explosively in soil black
as gunpowder, usually planted in hills, not rows, because of all the
roots and stumps and standing deadened tree trunks. A good crop
of corn was essential to the settlers. At Boonesborough, as now, corn
could be turned into fine whiskey by those with a knack for distilling.
Corn would become the basic ingredient of Kentucky's most popular product, bourbon. Arthur K. Moore has written, "After clearing,
the best land for a time yielded corn bountifully without exceptional

care — from forty bushels the first year to more than a hundred the third." In 1784 Filson would write that more than a hundred bushels of corn could be grown on an acre each year.

"My wife and daughter being the first white women that ever stood on the banks of Kentucke River," Boone said later. Certainly there would soon be white women at the other settlements such as Harrodsburg and St. Asaph's. It is unlikely that Boone knew of Mary Ingles, kidnapped from her home at Draper's Meadows in 1755. She was able to escape later from Big Bone Lick in Kentucky and make her way back to Draper's Meadows in forty-one days. The daughter of Boone who first lived in Kentucky was Susannah Boone Hays, who had come with the choppers of Boone's Trace. Among the folklore of her liveliness and naughtiness is a quote passed on to Rev. John Dabney Shane by Nathaniel Hart Jr. "Every Kentuckian ought to try my gait," she is reported to have said, "since I was the first white woman in Kentucky."

CHAPTER NINE

The Trace and the River

1775–1776

The Transylvania Convention had been scheduled to meet again on September 6, 1775, but Henderson and his partners had left Kentucky to petition the new state governments of Virginia and North Carolina, and the Continental Congress, for recognition of their land purchase. The proprietors of the Transylvania Company did gather in Oxford, North Carolina, and appoint Col. John Williams to take charge of Boonesborough until the next April 12. They authorized him to supervise the surveying and selling of land and the registering of deeds and to claim for the company half of any revenue from gold, silver, lead, copper, or sulfur mines. They also voted "that a present of two thousand acres of land be made to Col. Daniel Boone, with the thanks of the Proprietors, for the signal services he has rendered to the Company." But this may have been the two thousand acres Boone had been promised originally for arranging the purchase from the Cherokees and hacking out Boone's Trace and building Boonesborough.

For coordinating the meeting with the Cherokees at Sycamore Shoals, organizing the crew of axemen, marking out Boone's Trace, fighting off Indians and holding the group together until Henderson arrived with his larger party, persuading more settlers to come to Boonesborough and managing much of the business of the settlement, Boone was to be given one-fifth as much land as William Cocke was awarded for riding across the mountains to Boonesborough. They do not say an *additional* two thousand acres, only the same acreage he had been promised before. Boone had already claimed the tract of one thousand acres on Tate's Creek. But he would lose that land when the Transylvania Company purchase was declared invalid. The fact is Boone never got any acreage from the Transylvania Company. After their acquisition of twenty million acres from the Cherokees was declared null and void in November 1778, the proprietors were compensated for their losses by grants of two hundred thousand acres in each of the states of Virginia and North Carolina. They were still able to claim and sell off great chunks of prime land, but Daniel Boone never received any more than the first thousand acres from them, and he lost that.

While others such as Michael Stoner and William Cocke sued Henderson and his partners and their estates for years to win the claims they had been promised, Boone appears to have soon forgotten, or refused to trouble his mind, about his promised land. A long section of the later named Wilderness Road was called Boone's Trace and the settlement on the river was called Boonesborough. Boone's name was associated with the Transylvania Company and the settlement of Kentucky more than any other, but in the end he received little more than credit at the company store. By the time the Boonesborough land claims and overlapping surveys were being untangled in 1779–80 by the commission from the state of Virginia, which had made Kentucky its largest county, Boone had moved on to other claims and adventures.

This failure to follow through and nail down the payment for his significant services to Henderson and his partners is an important clue to Boone's personality. He had a tendency to put off unpleasant matters and turn instead to tasks he relished. He hated legal procedures and business matters and preferred to move on rather than lobby, argue, petition, sue, and wait. He lived by moving on, as his father had before him, and his grandfather George III, who had left Devonshire for Pennsylvania. Rather than doing paperwork and waiting, paying lawyers and bribing officials, he preferred to keep exploring new territory, finding fresh game and wild country. It was the farther horizon that thrilled him. He was fitted to be a woodsman, a leader of explorations, but hardly a politician, businessman, or land speculator. Boone's easy abandonment of claims near Boonesborough also shows his sense that the frontier was unlimited. There was always more land ahead, and there would always be more land. Why squabble over a few acres when the whole of Kentucky and Ohio and the regions farther west waited to be explored. Like all men, Boone was a combination of talents, accomplishments, and weaknesses. But his best talents were of a high order, and his genius recognized by virtually all who knew him.

The year 1775 was a complicated and confusing time for all, including those on the frontier, and those attempting to steer the Transylvania Company toward survival and future prosperity. At the meeting in Oxford, North Carolina, Henderson, who had left Boonesborough, and the other proprietors of the company recorded their loyalty to the Crown: "They flatter themselves that the addition of a new Colony in so fair and equitable a way, and without any expense to the Crown, will be acceptable to His Most Gracious Majesty, and that Transylvania will soon be worthy of his Royal regard and protection." But they hedged their bets also, fearing that the rebellion and Continental Congress might win in the end. They added to their proceedings this statement: "Therefore, the Memorialists hope and earnestly request, that Transylvania may be added to the number of United Colonies, and that James Hogg, Esq., be received as their delegate, and admitted to a seat in the honorable the Continental Congress." The proprietors wanted it to be known that they were willing to do business with whoever was in charge. They meant to keep their extensive holdings, no matter what government finally ruled over the region.

The records of the company store at Boonesborough show that in September 1775 Boone drew lead and powder on account for his fall hunting. It was time to lay in a supply of venison and bear meat for the winter. It was already late in the season to gather deerskins, so he would have to hurry. During the winter he would trap for beaver. Later that month Richard Callaway returned from Virginia with a number of additional families, including William Poage and his wife, and Squire Boone and his wife, Jane, arrived also. There were now enough people to maintain the settlement, and enough hunters to keep them supplied with meat. The Callaways and Poages had driven cattle and hogs, and carried ducks and chickens, over the rough trail. With the addition of Mrs. Callaway, Mrs. Poage, and Jane Boone, there were at least five women in the enclave. And more were arriving at Harrodsburg and other stations as well.

As winter began to close in on the settlers at Boonesborough, Richard Henderson returned from North Carolina with John Williams and about forty other men, including Col. Arthur Campbell from the Holston settlement. On December 21 Henderson called a meeting of the Transylvania Convention, but the weather was bad and few showed up from Harrodsburg, St. Asaph's, and Boiling Spring. John Floyd was appointed official surveyor for the colony, beating out, because of his experience in Kentucky and his connections to Col. William Preston, Colonel Campbell for the valuable post. Nathaniel Henderson was commissioned as entry taker for the land office. John Floyd immediately appointed six men as deputies and departed for a visit to Virginia.

Reading the minutes of the meeting, one can imagine Boone yawning and struggling to stay awake as the business proceeded hour after hour in good bureaucratic fashion. However, two days later events took a dramatic turn. Two boys named Sanders and McQuinney accompanied Col. Arthur Campbell across the river and then walked in separate directions. The boys were unarmed, but a short time later shots rang out. A party crossed the river to investigate and met Campbell running with only one shoe on. He had been fired on by two Indians, but they had missed. Boone led a search party across the river, but the boys could not be found. Boone saw two moccasin tracks but was unable to tell who had made them. The following Monday McQuinney was found dead and scalped in a cornfield three miles from Boonesborough. Sanders was never found, and it was assumed he had been taken by the Shawnees north to Ohio. Rumors of Campbell's cowardice spread among the settlements. Chief Cornstalk, at a meeting at Fort Pitt that fall, had expressed his fear that some unruly Shawnee braves might visit the settlements of Kentucky out of curiosity, if not belligerence. It was thought that the party that killed McQuinney and kidnapped Sanders might be those. Fear swept through the stations, and a number of settlers returned east. But when there were no more attacks, the alarm faded.

At the Treaty of Pittsburgh, signed in October 1775, many tribes in Ohio agreed to stay north of the Ohio River and to remain neutral in the Revolutionary conflict. If only it had been that simple. None who signed the treaty, Indian or American, had much control over future events.

To say the least, it was a time of uncertainty. The outcome of North Carolina and Virginia's case against the Transylvania Company was not known yet. The rebellion against the Crown was spreading and gathering momentum. The settlers were struggling to survive a long, wet, and cold winter in conditions that were hard even in clement weather. Boone was concentrating on trapping beaver and hunting for subsistence, as troubles and adversities mounted. Against all the odds, more than nine hundred claims had been entered in the land office at Boonesborough. But many of the more than half-million acres purchased had not been surveyed. Two hundred thirty acres of corn had been raised the first summer at Boonesborough. An orchard of five hundred trees had been set out. There was a substantial number of livestock and poultry.

The account books of the Transylvania Company show that lead was sold to the settlers for 16⅔ cents a pound and gunpowder cost $2.66 a pound. Hunters and laborers were paid as much as 50 cents a day. Both British pounds and Virginia dollars were in circulation in

Kentucky, and sometimes even Spanish money was used. Few of the accounts are marked paid in any currency.

BOONE HAD filed his claim for the thousand acres on Tate's Creek southwest of Boonesborough. To make the purchase valid, he had to build a cabin or shelter on the land and raise a crop of corn within a year of the claim. There is no record that he did either. But Boone had better luck helping others than helping himself. When he and Thomas Hart were hunting that winter, Hart stepped off and claimed an acreage on Jeptha Creek. To mark the site, Hart carved his initials on a beech tree. Twenty years later when the ownership of the land was in dispute, Boone led the attorneys back to the tree and showed them the carved initials, winning the case for Hart.

Having survived the long 1775–76 winter in the rough and dirty conditions of frontier cabins, the settlers who had stayed at Boonesborough emerged into the spring sun and began planting crops for a second year. Their numbers had dwindled through desertion, but those who remained had the confidence of their hard work and persistence. They had taken the risks and they had gotten through the winter. Now they could thin their blood with fresh poke greens boiled with fat, and also creesie greens, or wild mustard, that grew along the creeks. And some sought out branch clay to chew and swallow to tone their systems and replenish minerals. Clay pure as cream could be found in pockets along the banks of streams. Eating a little branch clay was a common spring ritual for many people on the frontier, both black and white. Soon it would be planting time, and the women were especially intent on making gardens. "They had brought out a stock of seeds from the old settlements and went out every bright day to plant them."

In the spring of 1776, after Daniel and Squire Boone had returned from a surveying expedition that had taken them as far as the Falls of the Ohio, heavy rains began. It was the kind of season when it seems the rain cannot stop. Day after day the Kentucky River continued to rise and the water came almost to the cabin doors at Boonesborough. For much of its length the Kentucky River runs between steep bluffs in a gorge cut through the millennia, but Boonesborough was built on a level plain that flooded easily. It looked as though the dwellings might be swamped; luckily the water stopped just at the cabin thresholds and finally began to recede. Word arrived from Harrodsburg that a Mrs. Hugh Wilson there had given birth to the first white child born in Kentucky. Of a half-dozen married women at Boonesborough, none had yet given birth.

TROUBLES continued to build and compound for the Transylvania Company. The settlers at Harrodsburg and Logan's Station and other sites, who had acted as though partly resigned to the ownership of the Transylvania Company the year before, were newly angered by news that quitrents and land prices were to be doubled. For every hundred acres the annual quitrent would be two shillings from now on. Those already in Kentucky protested that they would not pay more than they had agreed to the year before. Harrod and others had their eye on land farther west along the Ohio River, and they accused the Transylvania Company of attempting to preempt those thousands of choice acres before anyone else had a chance to survey and claim them.

Col. John Williams, the agent for the Transylvania Company, tried to placate these protesters by halting large land grants in the West for the time being. Only parcels of a thousand acres or less would be sold near the Falls, where a future town was to be laid out. The Transylvania Company opened an office at Harrodsburg as more and more settlers arrived. Benjamin Logan and his family returned to St. Asaph's, now called Logan's Station. Levi Todd returned to Kentucky with a number of the Bryan family, Rebecca's relatives, coming from the Yadkin.

At some point in the spring of 1776, in April or May, Boone apparently journeyed all the way to Williamsburg for a supply of gunpowder. On June 8 Col. William Fleming wrote to Colonel Preston, "This forenoon boon delivered 700 lbs. Powder. 100 of which is ordered for the

Point [Pleasant]. 100 is allotted for your county to the use of the committee. In consequence of an order from the Committee of Safety, I have ordered four men to escort the wagon." It is thought Boone was accompanied by some of the Callaway family to Kentucky on this same trip. To reach Kentucky the powder had to be taken out of the wagon and loaded onto packhorses.

Hundreds came into Kentucky that spring by floating or paddling down the Ohio River from Pittsburgh. Ignoring the Transylvania Company, many would stake claims in the lush meadows and luxuriant forests, build rude shelters and plant corn, nominally fulfilling the obligations of settlement, then return east to sell their claims. Greedy as these small speculators, called "cabiners," may have seemed, they were doing on a small scale essentially the same thing the larger entities such as the Transylvania Company were doing. Kentucky was a great "speck," as they liked to say, an Eden of cheap land up for the grabbing, even where previous claims had been made. "What a Buzzel is amongst People about Kantuck," a man in Virginia had commented the year before. The "buzzel" had continued to build.

"The face of the country at that time was beautiful beyond conception," Lyman Draper would write. "Nearly one half of it was covered with cane, while between the canebrakes were frequently fine open grounds, as if . . . intended by nature for cultivation. Nor was the country destitute of the finest timber — which was happily distributed for the wants of men. The soil was extremely fertile, producing in its untamed state amazing quantities of weeds of various kinds, wild grass, rye and clover. The dews were very heavy, which rendered the nights cool and refreshing. The land then appeared more level than when subsequently cleared . . . as the thickness of the growth prevented the early explorers from discovering the diversities of the surface."

Recent studies have concluded that there were more forests than meadows in the Bluegrass region previous to settlement. Many of those who saw the region at this time could not restrain themselves from extravagant praise of the soil. "When you take it between your fingers you cannot perceive any more grit than in butter," Edward Harris would write a little later, going on to say the dirt was "black as the bottom of your dung heaps." It seemed not to occur to those coming into this region that these resources could ever be exhausted. It was assumed by many that Kentucky would never be heavily populated because of the scarcity of fresh springs. This seems odd in hindsight, as if they had never thought of digging wells. Perhaps the limestone bedrock was too difficult to cut through without modern drilling and cutting equipment.

Kentucky inspired passion and awe in most who came there. The settler Nathan Reid, John Floyd's surveying assistant, would later say, "What a country it was in that day! It would be difficult for the most fertile imagination to draw an exaggerated picture of its then lovely appearance. The soil was black as ink, and light as a bank of ashes. A person passing through the woods might be tracked as easily as through snow."

"Strange as it may appear," Reid said, "it is nevertheless true, that amid all the dangers, privations and exposures of our situation, a very considerable portion of our time was spent in real enjoyment. The abundance and variety of the game — the pleasure of hunting — the novelty of the life we led — the dreams we indulged of better days to come, all combined to keep up our spirits ... We clearly foresaw that it would not be long before these lands would be justly appreciated, and sought after by thousands. Then we should be rich as we cared to be. These golden visions of the future, however, so far as I was concerned, were never realized."

As more and more of the small speculators poured into Kentucky, along with the commercial hunters and trappers, spies for the British and agents provocateurs such as the French Canadian Louis Lorimier from Montreal, worked for the British to stir up the Indians against the settlers. In the cabins and forts, talk was constant about the sightings and threats from Indians. If someone had seen a track or broken twig, or heard a strange noise, they imagined a war party was lurking in the thickets. Writing in the *North American Review* seventy years later, a writer named Perkins described Boone as sitting silent while all the talk and rumors and speculations were passed around the room. His hands never idle, he kept busy mending his leggings or molding rifle balls until it was almost dark, then he would take his rifle and slip out into the forest. "'And now,' said the loiterers by the smoldering logs, 'we shall know something sure, for old Daniel's on the track.'" Before morning Boone would return to the cabin silent as a shadow and tell them what was, or was not, in the forest around them.

In April 1776 a surveyor named Willis Lee was killed by Mingoes near the future site of Frankfort. Mingoes also captured the twin sons of Andrew McConnell of Leestown and took them back to a Shawnee town in Ohio. But the Indian agent Col. George Morgan and Chief Cornstalk were able to arrange their release. This kidnapping spread such fear throughout Kentucky that more settlers left. The life in the stations was so dangerous that when someone died of natural causes, not killed by Indians, a woman there later recalled it seemed almost an occasion for rejoicing. "When a young man was taken sick and died, after the usual manner of nature, she and the rest of the women sat up all night, gazing on him as an object of beauty."

The settlers in Kentucky were so eager for new arrivals to swell their numbers that many rode out on the trail to welcome those coming to the forts and stations. Simon Kenton aided many who came by the Ohio River, giving them directions and advice and supplies. He even built a blockhouse near the Ohio to welcome immigrants. James Estill, who lived first at Boonesborough and then moved to his own station just south of future Richmond, actually killed game and left it along the trails for those just coming into the country. He would ride out to meet those arriving and tell them where to find the meat. Those in Kentucky knew that without more settlers they could not hold out against a combined assault from Indians and the British.

On July 7, 1776, a hunter named Cooper was killed by a party of

Shawnees on the Licking River. On July 14 another man was killed on the Licking and a number of hunters and surveyors were reported missing. The threat of an Indian war hung so heavily over the region that Col. William Russell of the Clinch advised that the settlements in Kentucky be evacuated. John Floyd wrote to Col. William Preston on July 21, 1776, that many people had gone missing, and new signs of Indians were seen every day.

Even as rumors were growing of imminent Indian attacks, the angry petitioners of Harrodsburg, including James Harrod, Abraham Hite Jr., and more than eighty others, who had from the beginning resisted the Transylvania Company, were lobbying the government of Virginia to recognize their claims and complaints against Henderson. Their resentment was directed not only at the Transylvania Company but also against the surveys done at the direction of former colonial governor Dunmore. Meanwhile Henderson and his partners were lobbying the legislature in Williamsburg for title to the lands they had purchased from the Cherokees. James Hogg tried every means, including bribery, to further the interests of the Transylvania Company. As George Morgan Chinn tells it, "When Hogg offered Governor Patrick Henry a vast acreage of prime land in Transylvania in return for his support, Henry practically 'threw him out' of the office." By then Henry did not need the Transylvania Company.

One of the leaders of the Harrodsburg Revolt was George Rogers Clark, who got himself elected as a representative to the Virginia legislature. Clark understood that this quarrel among the settlements was an opportunity for the state of Virginia, for the American Revolution, and for himself. With Henderson out of the way, Clark could assume leadership of the region and further the Revolution on the western frontier.

On June 24, 1776, the Virginia Convention ruled that no private person or company could sell lands, thereby invalidating the Transylvania Company, but stated that the claims of individual settlers would be considered later by an official commission. This would prove to be the death knell for Henderson's dream of an empire across the mountains, but he would continue his petitioning and eventually be awarded four hundred thousand acres in Kentucky and Tennessee. His scout and organizer, Daniel Boone, would end up with nothing. In November 1778 the Virginia legislature officially declared the Transylvania Company's claims null and void.

ON JULY 14, 1776, one of the legendary events in Boone's long career occurred. It was a quiet Sunday afternoon at Boonesborough. There were no church services at the settlement, but earlier that day someone had read from the scriptures to an assembled group, and when "the customary Bible reading was over" Boone had lain down in his cabin to rest.

Jemima Boone, who was fourteen, had stabbed her foot on a stob of cut cane and wanted to go out on the river in a dugout canoe to soothe her sore foot in the cool water. As a young girl Jemima had enjoyed playing in the water so much she had been given the nickname "Duck." Elizabeth and Frances Callaway, daughters of Richard Callaway, sixteen and fourteen years old, respectively, agreed to accompany her. Nathan Reid had volunteered to paddle the canoe for them but had backed out. It was a beautiful afternoon and the girls glided out on the stream. Betsy and Fanny paddled by turns while Jemima hung her hurt foot in the water. They drifted several hundred yards downstream, floating and paddling carelessly. One of the Callaway girls suggested they stop on the north bank, near some cliffs, and gather flowers and young cane. But Jemima warned them they should stay away from the "Indian" shore "as it was against their fathers' orders to go on that shore at any time. The proposer observed that perhaps she was more afraid of the yellow boys than she was of disobeying her father." She was teasing, unaware that five Indians were indeed watching them from the brush on the north bank. The strong current pushed the canoe closer to that bank than they had intended to go.

Suddenly five Indians plunged out of the cane and one waded into the water to grab the line attached to the front of the dugout. As he tried to drag the craft to the shore, Fanny Callaway beat him over the head with the paddle until it broke. Betsy joined her in hitting the brave, and the other Indians waded in and threatened to overturn the canoe unless the girls got out. Once the girls were led ashore the canoe was pushed back into the stream so they couldn't use it to escape.

The three girls began screaming, hoping to be heard at Boonesborough, a quarter of a mile upstream on the other side of the river. One of the Indians grabbed Betsy Callaway by the hair and indicated he would scalp her if the girls did not shut up. The girls were pulled and pushed up the steep bank above the river, but at the top Jemima refused to go farther, pointing to her wounded foot and saying it was too painful to walk on. But the Indians waved their knives and tomahawks, threatening to kill her there if she didn't go on.

The Indians produced moccasins for Jemima, and for Fanny Callaway, who was also barefoot. Then they cut off the bottoms of the girls' dresses and petticoats so they could move faster through the brush. The girls wrapped the strips of cloth around their legs to protect them from briars and limbs. The Indians prodded them along, making their way on the tops of ridges where the ground cover was thinner. The lowlands along the streams were dense with cane and vines and thickets of cedar. Daniel Bryan would later say, "The Indians chose ground where they would make the least trail sometimes the Girls would mash down a weed the indians would straighten it up or turn it the other way."

The Indian party was made up of three Shawnees and two Cherokees. One of the Cherokees was a chief named Hanging Maw, whom Jemima had seen before, probably when the Boones were living on the Clinch. He spoke better English than the others, and Jemima told him who she was, hoping that he would remember that Boone had been friendly to him. He asked if the others were her sisters and she answered that they were all children of Daniel Boone. Hanging Maw laughed and said, "We have done pretty well for old Boone this time."

The five Indians were part of a larger group returning to Ohio from a conference at the Cherokee town of Chota. Called together in May by Dragging Canoe, the large gathering that included many Creeks and Shawnees, as well as Cherokees, angrily denounced the white settlement of Kentucky and lands over the mountains. Encouraged by British support, the young chiefs and warriors planned a concerted campaign against the American forts and stations. While his father Attakullakulla and other older chiefs remained silent in humiliation, ignored, Dragging Canoe roused those present to kill the Long Knives. The British had already given Dragging Canoe three thousand pounds of gunpowder to use against the Americans.

That afternoon the kidnappers and their prey traveled about six miles and camped near where Winchester, Kentucky, is now. The girls were tied with buffalo tugs so they could not reach each other, each bound to a tree and also to a brave. All night the girls sat with their backs to the trees they were tied to, unable to sleep. Jemima happened to have a penknife in her pocket, but her hands were bound so tightly she couldn't reach it.

The kidnapping was almost certainly not something planned by Hanging Maw and the four others. It must have been a spur-of-the-moment temptation, once they spotted the girls so far from Boonesborough. Taking prisoners or hostages lent prestige to the kidnapper, and capturing the daughters of Daniel Boone would bring even more honor. Kidnapping was understood by the Shawnees in a different way than by the whites. Their population depleted by disease and war, the villages needed additional members. Their birthrates were low. Women and children, and even men, could be adopted into the tribe, and after the correct rituals were performed and new names given to them, the adopted became members of the nations. The kidnapping of children was not unlike the program the Nazis later practiced called *Lebensborn*, where children in conquered countries were taken back to the Fatherland to become future citizens. To Hanging Maw and the others, Jemima and her supposed sisters must have looked like good candidates for adoption. At the very least they could be held for ransom, or sold to the British.

The next morning, the Indians resumed the march toward the Ohio. As they stumbled along, the girls broke twigs to guide those that might follow to rescue them. When the Indians noticed this, the captives explained they were so tired and weak they had to grab limbs to keep from falling. Some accounts claim Betsy Callaway began tearing pieces from her linen handkerchief and dropping them as clues behind her. The Indians caught her leaving signs and again threatened with their tomahawks. But the girls continued to break twigs and tear off leaves to mark the trail, and blistered their hands with the effort. Betsy Callaway had shoes with wooden heels that made deep tracks in the ground by streams and through buffalo wallows. Noticing the tracks she made, the Indians knocked the heels off her shoes, but she still took care to make discernible tracks.

Using the excuse of her sore foot, Jemima fell down again and again, delaying the progress of the party. When she fell down she would scream out, hoping that anyone following would hear. She was sure Boone and other men were on their way to rescue them. She made as much noise and trouble as she could, and the captors continued to threaten but never actually struck her. That morning they came across an old pony grazing in a meadow, and the Indians caught it as a mount for the injured Jemima. In fact, all three of the girls took turns riding the pony, but they pretended they had never ridden before and kept falling off and irritating the pony to make it unruly. The annoyed pony bit Betsy Callaway on the arm. "The horse was cross and would bite," Nathan later told Draper. The Indians laughed at the girls' clumsiness and then grew impatient. One of the Indians mounted the horse himself to demonstrate how to ride, but the lesson had little effect. The girls, who were actually experienced riders, continued to tumble off into the brush by the trail, until the Indians turned the pony loose and made their captives walk.

The Indians offered the girls buffalo tongue to eat, but the fare was tough and unsalted and pretty much inedible. The Indians sometimes referred to the prisoners as "pretty squaws" and showed they did not want to hurt them. Though they threatened the girls with tomahawks and knives, Hanging Maw and the others were surprisingly gentle with their captives. They were tolerant, even indulgent, by the standards of the wilderness. The girls were allowed to fix their hair and look for lice. Hanging Maw fondled Jemima's hair and took out the combs himself, admiring the length and brightness. In one version of the story Hanging Maw asked Jemima to dress his hair and look for lice, and she agreed. Many years later a niece told Jemima she would never have done such a thing herself. "Oh yes yes you would," said her aunt, "for the Indians were really kind to us."

By the end of the second day the Indians became talkative. They said they were on their way to the Shawnee towns north of the Ohio. They told the girls that Cherokees would attack the Watauga settlement, and a party of Cherokees were on their way to attack the Kentucky settlements. They teased the Indian whom Fanny Callaway had beaten with the paddle. That night, they camped a few miles south of the Licking River, and the girls were again tied up so tightly they couldn't sleep. Betsy Callaway, who was older, tried to cheer up the other two. The next morning the Indians seemed more confident that they had outrun any pursuers. After the party crossed Hinkston Creek, the captors felt safe enough to shoot a buffalo and cut off part of the hump for lunch. They were all hungry and the girls had had nothing to eat for two days. They stopped in a little clearing in the woods to cook the tender hump and rest.

WHEN THE girls' screams were heard at Boonesborough, Boone leapt from the bed where he had been napping and grabbed his rifle. He ran to the river without even thinking to put on his moccasins. People were dashing around sounding the alarm and grabbing weapons for pursuit. The problem was the screams were coming from the other side of the river. The dugout was gone. Boone spotted the craft far downstream, but it was out of reach. Samuel Henderson, who was engaged to Betsy Callaway, was shaving but dropped his razor and ran for his rifle. Richard Callaway, father of two of the girls, was flustered, but Boone was calm and organized. He told young John Gass to swim after the canoe, and when the dugout was brought back Boone and five others crossed to the north bank, as Callaway, Nathaniel Hart, David Hart, David Gass, Flanders Callaway, and others on horses dashed to a ford a mile down the river to cross.

Boone directed some to look upriver for the trail and some to look downriver until the tracks were found. Then he persuaded Richard Callaway and the party on horses to ride directly to the Blue Licks, where he knew the Indians would cross on their way to the Ohio, where they could intercept the kidnappers. Meanwhile, he and the others on foot could track the Indians.

It is likely that Boone used this argument to get rid of the hot-tempered and rash Callaway, leaving himself and a few others, including John Floyd, to proceed with necessary stealth. But Callaway and his party riding to the Blue Licks also provided a kind of insurance. If all else failed, they might intercept the kidnappers there. Covering about five miles before dark, Boone and several others heard a barking dog. Following the noise, they came upon a group of men building a cabin deep in the forest. There they camped for the night.

When the alarm had been given, the men of Boonesborough had been dressed in their Sunday best, which meant cloth pantaloons instead of breechclouts and deerskin leggings. Young John Gass volunteered to return to Boonesborough during the night and get ammunition, supplies, and proper clothes for the pursuers. He found his way through the dark woods, reaching the settlement, and returned to the camp before dawn with provisions, clothes, and Boone's moccasins. Clearly he was already an experienced woodsman, and a brave one.

As soon as there was light enough to follow the trail, Boone and the others set out. Three of the cabin builders joined them. After they had found where the Indians camped the night before, they lost the trail in a canebrake. The Indians had split up there and taken unlikely detours, making it difficult to decide which trail to follow. Here Boone made a critical decision: instead of following the trail, they would head in the direction they knew the party would take. That way they could move faster and perhaps be less vulnerable to an ambush. They struck out in a straight course, moving as fast as they could, crossing and recrossing the trail. They saw the bits of cloth, broken twigs, and Betsy's tracks, signs the girls were still alive. When it got dark they stopped to rest by a small stream and resumed the pursuit at daybreak. At Hinkston Creek they came on fresh tracks and Boone knew they were closing in. Since the Indians were now moving with less caution, he also knew it was time to start tracking them directly. The Indians would follow the Great Warrior's Path for a while, then slip off onto a buffalo trace, and then another trace, to confuse those pursuing. Boone followed every shift and feint. When they came upon the dead buffalo with its hump cut off, he told his companions the Indians would stop to cook their meal just ahead at the next stream. They saw a snake the Indians had killed and left flopping. They crossed a small stream that the Indians had waded for a few hundred yards to throw them off.

Using great caution, Boone and the others spread out, knowing the Indians would be stopped just ahead. If the kidnappers were not taken by surprise and killed, they would tomahawk the captives to death at the first sign of the rescuers. Within two hundred or three hundred yards they spotted the fire where the Indians were cooking the buffalo hump. One of the Indians was posted as a sentry, but he had laid down his rifle to light his pipe and pick up materials for mending his moccasins. Another Indian had lain down to rest, and one was getting wood, while another was preparing the meat. Hanging Maw had gone to the branch for some fresh water. Boone and the others crawled through the underbrush to get closer. "One in particular, big indn:, called Big Jimmy was spitting up meat on the side opposite to them. Fanny looked at him to see how he fixed his meat. She saw the blood burst out of his breast before she heard the gun." The girls were sitting on a log away from the fire when William Smith fired prematurely and missed. Then John Floyd fired, wounding the sentinel. "At the crack of the guns, the girls jumped up. Jemima shouted 'That's Daddy,' and started toward their rescuers. Father yelled to them to throw themselves flat upon the ground in case the Indians might shoot back," Nathan told Draper. The girls dropped to the ground, but in the excitement they stood again, and one rescuer, mistaking them in their ragged clothes for Indians, started to club Betsy, who wore a red bandanna on her head. Boone grabbed his arm and shouted, "For God's sake don't kill her when we have traveled so far to save her." The man, when he saw what he'd almost done, wept.

In fact, there was a good deal of weeping when it was over. Nathan Reid, one of the rescuers, later said, "The exultation of the poor girls cannot be described." They embraced and thanked their rescuers. The girls were so overcome with gratitude and the men with relief, the fleeing kidnappers were forgotten. "After the girls came to themselves enough to speak, they told us there were only five Indians . . . and could all speak good English." John Floyd also described the place as covered with thick cane, "and being so much elated on recovering the three poor little heart-broken girls, prevented our making any further search."

The girls showed the effects of the three-day ordeal. Their clothes were torn, their faces dirty and tearstained, eyes swollen from lack of sleep, legs scratched by limbs and briars. Boone wrapped blankets around them and embraced them. "Thank Almighty Providence," Boone said, "for we have the girls safe. Let's all sit down by them now and take a hearty cry." Everyone in the party wept with relief and joy. After they had calmed down, Boone remembered that he had shot an Indian and pointed to the place. A rifle was found and drops of blood led into the woods. Two bodies of Shawnees were discovered, one shot by Floyd and one, possibly, by Boone. Two years later Boone would learn that one of the Shawnees killed that day was the son of the man who would become Boone's captor and adoptive father.

The girls told Boone and the others what they had heard about the Cherokee attacks on Watauga, and the war party on its way to Kentucky. Also the girls knew that a party of Indians was camped only three miles away at the Lower Blue Licks. (Dragging Canoe and his warriors did indeed attack the Watauga settlement and were defeated on July 21, 1776. And the Cherokee invasion of Kentucky proved a failure also. After that the more peaceable chiefs among the Cherokees such as Attakullakulla began to regain their influence and authority.)

Taking as much meat from the buffalo as they could carry, the group started back toward Boonesborough. The girls had not had any sleep for two nights and were worn out from the walking and worry. But the exhilaration of being rescued enabled them to make the return journey. Samuel Henderson with his half-shaved face took a lot of teasing. But he was so pleased that Betsy, his fiancée, was safe that he probably didn't mind the rough humor. Flanders Callaway, who would later marry Jemima, was with the group of riders, and romance added to the cheer and joy of the return. When they came upon the abandoned pony again the girls took turns riding it and did not fall off a single time. By the time they got back to Boonesborough on Wednesday July 17 for a welcome and celebration, Jemima's foot was healed. Jemima later recalled that when they reached Boonesborough and were ferried across the river, her mother's joy was intense beyond description. "She laughed and cried for joy, as she always did when she was overjoyed," Jemima said.

The story of the kidnapping of Jemima Boone and the Callaway girls had already spread among the settlements of Kentucky and would soon reach across the mountains to the eastern cities and the world beyond. It became part of the legend of the frontier. Its popularity was spurred in part because Jemima was the daughter of Daniel Boone. But it was also a story that anyone could interpret in whatever way they chose. To Indian haters it was an example of the perfidy and unpredictability of the Indians. After all, Hanging Maw had pretended to be

Boone's friend. To many, the moral of the story was that Indians were never to be trusted. And the sexual overtones of the five braves grabbing the three beautiful girls from the canoe and forcing them to march in bonds added an edge of horror to the story that did not have to be explained or even commented on. To those with more liberal views of Indians, the story illustrated the code of the warriors. Though they were taking the girls into captivity, they never beat them or molested them sexually. Even though the girls impeded their progress, dropped clues for their pursuers, and made fools of the Indians with the pony, the braves showed extraordinary patience and tolerance. Hanging Maw seemed particularly gentle, even affectionate, with Jemima.

The kidnapping of Jemima and the Callaway girls also signaled the beginning of another cycle of guerilla war on the part of the Shawnees and other Ohio tribes. There would be further attacks. This was just a warning of what was to come. And those predictions seemed to be borne out in raids from the north over the next two years. To an objective observer, with the advantage of hindsight, the kidnapping shows the kind of inflammatory act a few roving Indians could commit, for which the whole nation of the Cherokees or Shawnees would be blamed. Such an act could be committed without the knowledge of the chief or tribe in general. But as far as the settlers were concerned, it was an attack by the Indian nation itself. Chief Cornstalk of the Shawnees blamed such acts by a few young braves for triggering and escalating the deadly troubles of 1777–78. Retaliation for an atrocity on either side might be made against Indians or whites unconnected with the original attack. The logic of blood and passion ruled, and the result was often tragic.

Hanging Maw's involvement in the kidnapping of the three girls has remained a mystery. He was older than his four companions and he was not known for being warlike. He returned to the Cherokee towns in the southern mountains and was considered a friend of the Americans. Hanging Maw rose to be an important chief, urging peace with Americans. He helped negotiate the Tellico Treaty of November

7, 1794. When he died in 1796 he was described by *New York Maga-zine* on May 1, 1796, as "a man distinguished for his love of peace." It is possible that Hanging Maw's traveling companions rushed to take the girls on the spur of the moment, inflamed by the angry rhetoric at the conference in Chota, and he felt he had no choice but to go along. After all, they were in territory claimed by some Shawnees, not the Cherokees, and Hanging Maw was outnumbered. Indian custom taught bowing to consensus. The kidnapping may have been so spontaneous an act it was almost an accident. But it has resonated down the halls of American history and fiction and folklore to the present day.

While Boone and his men were rescuing the girls, there had been an attack on Nathaniel Hart's homestead. His livestock and crops were destroyed, as was the orchard of five hundred apple trees. Outlying settlers gathered at Boonesborough, Harrodsburg, and Logan's Station again, and for the first time in a year work resumed on the fortification of Boonesborough. Picket walls were added between the cabins so there was a stockade, but the blockhouses at the corners were unfinished. George Morgan Chinn tells us, "Boonesborough had no water supply within the walls of the fort. When completed, twenty-six log cabins crowded the small enclosure, which measured approximately 260 by 180 feet."

In his capacity as magistrate of Transylvania, Boone officiated at the wedding of Samuel Henderson and Elizabeth Callaway on August 7, 1776. Richard Callaway, who passed up few opportunities to show his resentment of Boone, made Henderson sign a bond stating that he would later have the ceremony repeated by a higher authority when one was available. Even so, it was an occasion of celebration, merriment, and relief. According to George W. Ranck, "the guests were treated to home-grown watermelons, of which the whole station was proud."

Whatever the rumors about her begetting, Jemima was the child closest to Boone of any of his children. She later told her niece that while she was with the Indians she vowed that if she was ever rescued she would never disobey her father again, and she would stay by him. She never forgot looking into the woods and seeing Boone crawling through the brush to her rescue. When Boone was captured by the Shawnees in 1778 and taken to Chillicothe, and the rest of the family assumed he was dead and returned to the Yadkin, it was Jemima who stayed at Boonesborough waiting for his return.

AND THE AMERICAN REVOLUTION
IN KENTUCKY, 1775-1777

T HE PEOPLE OF KENTUCKY were from the first truly patriotic," Lyman Draper wrote in his unfinished *The Life of Daniel Boone*. He credited the independent spirit of the largely Scotch-Irish settlers for their support of the American cause. But Draper's claim is a gross simplification. While there was a dislike of authority and a spirit of independence among many of those who had gone to Kentucky, it was a spirit more personal than political. Many had come to Kentucky hoping to leave such issues as loyalty behind. It wasn't clear whether Kentucky was a new colony, a county in one of the older colonies, or what.

While Daniel Boone was mostly concerned with events in the wilderness far over the mountains, the war that broke out between the British government and the colonies in the East in 1775 affected much of what eventually took place in the settlement of the Middle Ground.

It is well known that many of the leaders of the American Revolution were Freemasons. Because their meetings were secret, it was easy for Freemasons to covertly organize as patriots. Franklin's high-degree membership gave him a special advantage in his negotiations for the American cause in Paris, as many of the political and intellectual leaders whose support he needed, including Voltaire and Helvetius, were Masons.

Freemasonry's ideals of fraternity, equality, freedom, reason, and high moral purpose inspired many to think about society and politics in a new way. The international nature of Freemasonry affected the American cause directly, as military leaders such as Lafayette from France and Baron von Steuben from Germany offered their services to American brothers of the apron. There were also Freemasons in the British army, and it is thought that redcoat Masons were sometimes reluctant to kill their brother Masons on the rebelling side. The first lodge in Kentucky was not established until 1788, but many Masons, including Boone, were there in 1775.

Though not a Freemason, no one was more influential in stirring America toward rebellion than Patrick Henry of Hanover County, Virginia. Born in 1736, two years after Boone, Henry tried a number of occupations before training himself for the law. He was a spellbinding public speaker. Known as a radical, he vigorously attacked the Stamp Act. As a delegate to the House of Burgesses between 1765 and 1774, and to the Continental Congress between 1774 and 1776, he made fiery speeches that were printed and quoted everywhere: "If this be treason, make the most of it" and "Give me liberty or give me death" are, of course, his best-known phrases. Elected governor of the new state of Virginia in 1776, he secretly appointed George Rogers Clark to attack British forts in the Illinois country. For the future Republic this may have been his most significant act.

George Washington, who kept the Continental Army from disintegrating in the darkest days of the Revolution, was an active Mason. Boone had met Washington in 1755 when he served with the militia and again in 1760 in Culpeper, Virginia, and it is likely that Washington inspired Boone to become a Freemason.

But the spirit of rebellion was demonstrated more explicitly in Harrodsburg than in Boonesborough. In June of 1776 the Harrodsburg community elected the Committee of Safety, whose members wrote to the new Virginia government that they were willing to aid in any way they could "the present laudable cause of American freedom." The authors of the letter hoped that Virginia's new government would recognize their claims in Kentucky and validate their deeds. George Rogers Clark and John Gabriel Jones were elected to represent the settlers.

It was in the fall of 1777 that the British decided to expand the role of their Indian allies in the west to attack the American settlements. With Indians doing most of the fighting and dying, it would cost the British relatively little to enlarge the western front in the assault on the rebelling colonies.

Lt. Gov. Henry Hamilton at Detroit (who belonged to a family that included many prominent Freemasons) was directed to use Native Americans "in making a Diversion and exciting an alarm upon the frontiers of Virginia and Pennsylvania." Hamilton offered generous bounties for scalps of settlers in the Ohio Valley. Because this policy increased the ferocity and frequency of Indian raids into Kentucky and outraged the settlers, Hamilton may have done the British more harm than good. As a result, Hamilton's offers of pardons and free land to any who crossed to the British side were later largely ignored.

Battle of the Blue Licks. George Gray. Oil on canvas on plywood. 1938. The battle on August 19, 1782, has been described as "the last battle of the American Revolution." (Courtesy Kentucky Historical Society.)

CHAPTER TEN

Light and Shadow

Describing Kentucky at this time, the historian Reuben Gold Thwaites wrote, "Hill and valley, timberland and thicket, meadow and prairie, grasslands and canebrake — these abounded on every hand, in happy distribution of light and shadow." The extraordinary beauty was matched by the extreme danger. A party of Cherokees was defeated at Island Flats on July 20, 1776, and later the settlers in Kentucky heard that the Cherokees, encouraged by the British, had attacked Watauga on the next day. As the Indian raids continued in Kentucky, more settlers returned to the East. John Floyd remarked that he had only thirty men left to defend Boonesborough. With supplies running low, and the threat of Indian attacks increasing, more and more unmarried men returned east. Floyd wrote to Preston, "I want as much to return as any person can do, but if I leave the country now, there is scarcely one single man hereabouts, but what will follow the example. When I think of the deplorable condition a few helpless families are likely to be in, I conclude to sell my life as dear as I can, in their defense rather than make an ignominious escape." The fort was low on ammunition again, and in September Col. Arthur Campbell of the Holston Valley sent a small shipment of powder and lead, which was divided among the men of the community. The supply Boone had brought from Williamsburg in June was long gone. Lead was so scarce that John Harrod and Benjamin Logan took packhorses to Long Island of the Holston to secure a supply, which they distributed among the Kentucky settlements when they returned in October.

The Kentucky communities were vulnerable at this time because only Harrodsburg had a stockade completed, or nearly completed, and none had found a supply of lead in the region or had the means of making gunpowder. And they were more than two hundred miles from the protection of the Virginia militia. In the event of a British-instigated attack by Indians, they were on their own. Too busy clearing land, raising corn, building cabins, and hunting for meat to prepare for war, most of the settlers felt helpless as the Revolutionary conflict spread over the mountains and down the Ohio Valley. It was like a continuation of Lord Dunmore's War, except now the Crown was urging the Indians to attack, rather than opposing them. "Their attempts to defend themselves constituted, in their eyes, an important military service to Virginia . . . and, as such, the settlers felt entitled to succor and supplies," Nancy O'Malley has observed.

On December 29, 1776, a Mingo chief named Captain Pluggy and his war party attacked McClelland's Station. George Rogers Clark had just arrived at McClelland's, on his way to retrieve the hidden powder the state of Virginia had given him. Captain Pluggy was killed and the Indians beaten back. Two whites, including McClelland himself, were killed. This fight with Captain Pluggy and the Mingoes was the beginning of what became known as the terrible Year of the Three Sevens, 1777, sometimes called the Terrible Sevens. It began with the death of Captain Pluggy and the esteemed McClelland, and it would not end until many more lives were lost and much blood spilled on the "dark and bloody ground." So many settlers would leave Kentucky that only Harrodsburg and Boonesborough remained occupied.

Hugh McGary, who had been elected chairman of the Kentucky Committee of Safety, sent a letter to the governor of Virginia dated February 27, 1777. "We are surrounded with enemies on every side; every day increases their numbers," the emotional McGary wrote. "Our fort is already filled with widows and orphans; their necessities call upon us daily for supplies."

Luckily there was a lull in the attacks and Benjamin Logan and his family left Harrodsburg to reoccupy Logan's Station. A message arrived from Virginia confirming Clark's commission as a major in the new state militia. Daniel Boone, James Harrod, John Todd, and Benjamin Logan were commissioned as captains. Whatever the status of the Transylvania Company, Virginia intended to recognize the Transylvania settlers as citizens of the new county and make use of their services. The militia assembled, expecting an attack.

It came March 5 when Cottawamago, or Chief Blackfish, and about seventy Shawnees attacked a party of maple syrup boilers near Harrodsburg. They killed William Ray and took as prisoner Thomas Shores. James Ray, hardly more than a boy, outran the Indians, a feat Blackfish never forgot. William Coomes hid in a tree that had fallen into a sinkhole and watched the Shawnees celebrate their victory by mutilating William Ray's body, dancing, and drinking maple syrup. Later that day James Harrod and Hugh McGary organized a party of thirty men and rode out in search of the syrup makers. When they found Ray's mangled body they thought it was the other William, Coomes, but Coomes came out of hiding and they buried Ray's body.

The attack on Harrodsburg inspired the men to continue work on the fortification of Boonesborough. Boone was able to get enough cooperation to complete most of the palisade. The blockhouses at the corners were not finished, but at least there was an enclosure, with pickets between cabins and gates that could be shut in case of attack.

Blackfish's Shawnees were still roving about. The Shawnees had every reason to attack the Kentucky settlers, who were claiming and destroying their buffalo hunting grounds. But many Shawnees were now also loyal to the British, who had once saved them from the anger of the Six Nations. Making war on the forts was a way of showing their enduring gratitude. A party appeared at Boonesborough on March 7, killed a black man working in the fields, and wounded another man.

There were more attacks on Harrodsburg and scattered settlements later in March.

On the morning of April 24, 1777, Daniel Goodman and another man left the stockade at Boonesborough to drive in some horses gathered a quarter of a mile away. They were fired on by a small party of Indians and tried to run back to the fort, but Goodman was overtaken and tomahawked and scalped. Young Simon Kenton, about to start out on a hunt, saw what was happening and shot the Indian who had taken Goodman's scalp. Then Kenton and the others chased the rest of the Indians away. Boone and about a dozen men, hearing the shots, rushed out of the stockade with their rifles. They followed Kenton out into the fields, not realizing that the small party of Indians was a decoy. More than a hundred Indians were hiding behind stumps and brush. While Boone and his men were advancing, Kenton saw an Indian about to fire on them. Kenton shot the ambusher, and while he was reloading and Boone and the others scanned the thickets, a large number of Indians rushed out to cut off their retreat to the fort.

"Boys, we are gone — let us sell our lives as dearly as we can," Boone shouted, and gave orders to charge right through the Indians. The men fired into the Shawnees and then swung their rifles as clubs. The Boonesborough men fought with fury, but Boone himself was shot in the ankle and the bone was broken. As Boone fell, an Indian rushed to tomahawk him but was shot by Kenton, who then used his rifle to club another warrior attempting to scalp Boone. The powerful Kenton picked up Boone and carried him to the fort, where Rebecca and her daughters were watching. Jemima rushed out to help carry her father inside. Three other men, John Todd, Isaac Hite, and Michael Stoner, were wounded in the melee but were helped by William Bush back to the fort. The Shawnees later admitted they lost twenty-two braves in this battle.

Back in the fort, as the wounded were being nursed, Boone said to Kenton, "Well, Simon, you have behaved like a man to-day; indeed you are a fine fellow." There is no better example of frontier under-statement. Boone and Kenton had immense respect for each other and knew they had to depend on each other. But when they spoke from the heart they used few words.

Five days later, at Harrodsburg, Francis McConnell and James Ray were practicing their marksmanship outside the fort when an Indian appeared and shot McConnell. Thinking the Indian was alone, Ray rushed at him, but just then a large number of Indians appeared and shot at Ray. Luckily he was not hit and ran the 150 yards to the fort but found the gate closed. He dropped behind a stump a few feet from the stockade wall and was pinned down there for hours while bullets kicked up dirt around him. His mother watched through a loophole in the fort. Finally Ray shouted, "For God's sake, dig a hole under the cabin wall and take me in!" The hole was made and Ray escaped through the opening. Ray would live to become a general in the War of 1812, and die on his farm in Mercer County, Kentucky, in 1835 at the age of seventy-five.

During this period of attacks, each fort sent out spies to range over the countryside to spot Indian movements. Simon Kenton and Thomas Brooks were chosen by Boone to act as spies for Boonesborough. Kenton could glide through the woods almost into the Indian camps unseen. Like George Washington, another giant of a man never wounded in battle, Kenton seemed to have a charmed life.

On May 23, 1777, Richard Callaway and John Todd left Boonesborough to represent the county of Kentucky in the Virginia legislature. With even fewer men at his disposal, Boone divided his force into two parties. While one worked the fields, plowing and planting crops, the other stood on guard, rifles loaded and primed, scanning the forest for movement. Boone often warned his men not to try to spot an Indian in the brush. He told them to look instead for the artificial straightness of a rifle barrel lying across a log or poking out of cover. Sure enough, as the men were busy in the cornfields, a guard at the fort saw the glint of the sun on a rifle and then spotted a force of about two hundred Indians approaching. He gave the alarm and the workers ran for the fort as the Indians began shooting. Two men were wounded, but they made it back into the stockade. The large body of Indians kept up a fire against the fort for the rest of the day and into the night. They continued the attack the next day also and tried to set fire to the palisades.

Michael Stoner, though he had been wounded again the day before, watched an Indian approach with a torch and shot him. Boone, crippled with the broken ankle, took part, giving directions, keeping a lookout. A number of Indians were killed, and on May 25 they withdrew.

The strategy of the Shawnees, since they had a large war party, was to attack Boonesborough, Harrodsburg, and Logan's Station by turns and sometimes simultaneously. On May 23, the same day they were raiding Boonesborough, the Indians attacked Logan's Station also. The defenders there ran so low on lead that women melted down their pewter for bullets, and two of the wives, both expert shots, Esther Whitley and Jane Menifee, took their places at the loopholes and killed Indians along with the men. Sporadic attacks continued through May and June, and neither of the stations could go to the relief of the other. One of the residents at Boonesborough, William Bailey Smith, slipped out of the fort at night during an attack, to make his way all the way back to the Yadkin for help. After a head count in the spring of 1777, Levi Todd reported that a total of 102 men and boys in Kentucky County were able to bear arms.

In one of the attacks on Harrodsburg that spring, Hugh McGary had ridden out to find the mangled body of his stepson. The next day McGary spotted a Shawnee wearing the dead boy's hunting shirt and killed him. McGary chopped the dead warrior's body into pieces and fed them to his dogs. Gossips in the area later claimed that McGary was visited by the "specter" of his stepson, who rebuked him for his bad behavior.

In July 1777 Blackfish decided to give up his campaign in Kentucky. The Shawnees had lost dozens of warriors, and none of the stockades had been taken. Laying siege to a fort was a new kind of warfare for the Shawnees, and they found that without artillery to blow apart the stockade, there was little chance of overrunning a fort. Their preference was for ambush, the hit-and-run, the harrying of smaller groups. Since they did not have cannon, there was little they could do to a well-built stockade, except kill livestock, destroy crops, and steal horses. The Indians could spread fear in the settlements, create hardship in an already hard lifestyle, and kill Kentuckians here and there, but so far they had failed to dislodge the determined settlers.

Most of the settlements in Kentucky at that time were called stations, not forts. The difference was not always of size, or even palisaded walls and blockhouses. According to Nancy O'Malley, forts were usually built by larger communities, including several families as well as single men, whereas stations were typically established by one extended family, involving relatives and friends. A fort was a public place, a station more a private community.

In August Col. John Bowman arrived under the auspices of the state of Virginia with a hundred militiamen and took over the defense of the forts. William Bailey Smith came back to Boonesborough from North Carolina with fifty extra men. Daniel Bryan, Boone's nephew, was a member of that company. Later he told Draper, "We were received with great joy. We marched into Boonesborough single [file] giving six feet between Nose and tail of our horses this made a grand show to six indians that was laying hid on a hill overlooking the fort." The Indians seem to have had Boonesborough under surveillance much of the time. It was reported that cows were sometimes hesitant to leave the fort in the morning when they sensed Indians about. In September the Kentucky County court convened again in Harrodsburg, and Boone was made a justice of the peace. These events suggested that peace and stability had returned to Kentucky.

But in the fall of 1777 something happened that guaranteed the conflict with the Indians would gather momentum, not lessen. In November, Cornstalk, a main Shawnee chief, and his son Elinipsico and several companions, while on a peaceful mission, were murdered at Fort Randolph, at Point Pleasant on the Ohio River. Cornstalk, who had come to talk peace with the Americans, was thrown into jail and then killed. He had been the most peaceable of the Shawnee leaders. At the Battle of Point Pleasant in October 1774 Cornstalk had proven himself at least the equal of the white commanders. At the Treaty of Camp Charlotte in Ohio in October 1774 his eloquence, good sense, and charisma had been noted by all who attended. Draper tells us, "When he arose, he was in nowise confused or daunted, but spoke with distinct, audible voice, without stammering or repetition and with peculiar emphasis. His look[s] while addressing Dunmore were truly grand and majestic, yet graceful and attractive." Later he had returned stolen horses to Virginians in an effort to maintain the peace. The killing of Cornstalk was a disaster for all concerned. "You may, by the Governor's proclamation, know that the crime is to us an abhorrence; that a great reward is offered, and every method fallen upon to bring those people to Justice," Col. William Fleming wrote to Blackfish and other Shawnee war chiefs. But Blackfish and Cornstalk's successor, Moluntha, were experienced in the ways of the whites, and they knew no Virginian would ever be brought to justice for killing Cornstalk.

ONCE THE Virginia state legislature ruled Henderson's claim to Kentucky null and void, Henderson and his partners closed the store at Boonesborough. Without a commissary the residents were soon short of trade goods. Stores on the Clinch and Holston rivers were more than two hundred miles away. Even if one had beaver skins, deer hides, and ginseng to trade, they had to be carried back over Boone's Trace, through woods and thickets where Indians might be lurking.

By the fall of 1777 the residents of Boonesborough, Harrodsburg, and Logan's Station, especially the women, were learning one of the basic tenets of frontier and southern Appalachian culture, "make do or do without." Those who had brought clothes to the settlements soon wore them out clearing land, farming, chopping wood, and hunting and had to rely on buckskin. It was said some left Boonesborough, not from fear of attack but because their vanity could not stand the conditions and shortage of clothes. There were so few women at the forts that the militia men, mostly young, longed for the comforts of home in Virginia.

While those in the forts had come to Kentucky looking for opportunity, adventure, land, what they found was more often danger, and even death. Of this period Sarah Graham later said, "14 persons, that I knew their faces, committed suicide." Because many were killed by Indians out in the forest, only a fraction of those who died were actually buried at Boonesborough. But when someone was killed near the fort, or died of suicide or natural causes, they had to be given a decent burial. A coffin was made of rough boards or poles, sometimes a hollowed-out log, the body wrapped in a sheet or buffalo skin, with the jaws bound by a strap. With no embalming, burials took place sooner rather than later, especially in summer.

The women were not just spinning wool and scrubbing floors. Most took an active part in the defense of the forts and stations. At Logan's Station, as we have seen, Jane Menifee and Esther Whitley were better shots than most of the men. But it was not just the women at Logan's Station who were instrumental in the defense of the settlement. At the two forts as well, Reuben Gold Thwaites tells us, the women took "turns at the port-holes, from which little puffs of white smoke would follow the sharp rifle cracks whenever a savage head revealed itself."

The more affluent families at the forts owned slaves, families such as the Callaways and Bryans. Since the records are scant we can only guess at the numbers of African Americans there before tax records were kept. The best-known slave at Boonesborough was Uncle Monk, who belonged to the Estill family. Monk was known as an outstanding hunter and marksman and was a fiddler who played for all the parties and celebrations. He also planted a large apple orchard near Boonesborough. Even more important, he knew how to make gunpowder, and some say he taught the formula to Daniel Boone: six parts saltpeter, or potassium nitrate, one part charcoal, one part sulfur by weight. The saltpeter was made by boiling down water leached through guano that had been dug out of caves, until only crystals were left. The crystals were crushed to dust to be mixed with willow charcoal and sulfur. The mixture was then boiled and stirred until the saltpeter combined with the sulfur. Ted Franklin Belue tells us the result could be doused with urine, "rendering it a black, smelly goop to be mashed flat to sun-dry; urine better oxygenated the mixture and caused the powder to 'flash' with surety." It would be hard to overestimate the importance of this knowledge and skill to an isolated community such as Boonesborough in the late 1770s. Many times the forts and scattered settlements ran desperately low and had to send riders back over the mountains for a new supply of gunpowder. As Kentuckians began to make their own gunpowder they grew increasingly self-reliant.

Besides gunpowder, perhaps the most precious commodity at the time was salt. The first problem was that most settlers had never boiled their own salt before, and they lacked the iron pots and kettles and boiling pans, in which the salty water could be steamed down to a saline residue. Another problem was that most salt springs had such a low content of salt that an enormous quantity of water had to be boiled to get a useful amount of crystals. This was true of the brine spring at Boonesborough. Only a few salt springs, like Drennon's Lick, Bullitt's Lick, and those at the Lower Blue Licks to the north, had a strong enough saline content to be practical. The blue in the springs was partly the heavy saline content that made the water throbbing out of the limestone look gray-blue. The real work of salt boiling was not carrying the buckets of water to be evaporated but chopping wood to keep the fires going day after day. Salt was so dear in the frontier settlements it quickly became a medium of exchange. "There were original notes for salt which had circulated in place of money," Robert E. McDowell tells us. Added to the other difficulties was the fact that boiling salt was a dangerous activity. Most of the salt springs were far out in the woods, closer to the Ohio, and salt boilers were especially vulnerable to Indian attack as they kept the fires blazing under the kettles day after day. There was probably no more dangerous occupation, unless it was surveying, and many salt makers were killed.

Luckily Col. John Bowman, when he arrived at Boonesborough August 1, 1777, with the Virginia militia, had brought several big iron pots. It was a very cold and snowy winter, and there were still threats of Indian raids. It was Daniel Boone who volunteered to lead thirty men to the Lower Blue Licks in the dead of winter. They left Boonesborough on January 1, 1778, with the large kettles Colonel Bowman had brought. The plan was to make enough salt, as quickly as possible, to last the settlements a year, and get back to the safety of the forts to the south. It was assumed they would be safer from Indian attack in the middle of winter. Boone would hunt each day to supply the camp with meat and keep a lookout for Indians. Packhorses would carry the salt to Boonesborough and return with supplies every few days. It is possible Boone chose the Lower Blue Licks rather than Bullitt's Lick or Drennon's Lick, which were about the same distance from Boonesborough and might have been safer from Indian attack, simply because he knew the area around the Lower Blue Licks better. He was used to hunting there, and while his crew boiled salt he could do some hunting and trapping on nearby creeks.

The springs at the Lower Blue Licks yielded about ten thousand gallons of water a day. Between five hundred and six hundred gallons had to be boiled to make a bushel, or fifty pounds, of salt. Boone's crew, working virtually around the clock through all kinds of weather, was able to make about ten bushels a day. In a month they produced several hundred bushels of salt and at least half of it had been packed back to the forts. After a month another crew would come to relieve the first.

Boone was assisted in hunting and scouting by his son-in-law Flanders Callaway and Thomas Brooks. On the cold, snowy Saturday of February 7 Boone hunted south to Hinkston Creek, while Callaway and Brooks headed upriver. Boone killed a buffalo and packed several hundred pounds of meat on his horse. "A blinding snow-storm was in progress." As he was leading the animal along the creek he looked back and saw several Shawnees pursuing him. Hoping to escape on the horse, he tried to untie the tugs holding the meat, but the strings of buffalo hide were frozen. To his horror he found his knife frozen in its sheath. He had not wiped it dry after he cut up the buffalo meat. His only hope was to run into the woods.

The four Shawnees pursuing Boone were much younger than he was. Boone was forty-three. Running in deep snow, he looked back after half a mile and found they were gaining on him. One warrior had cut the meat loose and mounted Boone's own horse. Bullets kicked up the snow around him and hit the strap of his powder horn. Boone saw escape was impossible and he leaned his rifle against a tree, a gesture of surrender. The warriors shouted with glee and laughed at him.

Though middle-of-the-winter raids were rare for the Shawnees, Blackfish had organized a party to attack the Kentucky forts in revenge for the murder of Chief Cornstalk. The young Shawnee warriors were so angry about the jail-cell execution, Blackfish had given in to their demands for a raid on Boonesborough. His party of more than a hundred warriors, on their way south, was camped on Hinkston Creek. The four scouts who caught Boone had already spotted the company of men boiling salt at the Lower Blue Licks and were on their way to inform Blackfish.

The arrival of Boone in the Shawnee camp was greeted with a great deal of celebration. Besides 120 warriors, there were two French Canadians working for the British and a black man named Pompey, who had been captured in Virginia years before and who served as a translator for Blackfish. Boone recognized among the warriors Capt. Will Emery, who had taken him prisoner eight years before on his first journey into Kentucky. When Boone introduced himself, Captain Will didn't recognize him at first, and then he said, "Howdydo, howdydo," and pointed out that Boone had not heeded his warning about the wasps and yellow jackets. Other Indians gathered round to shake hands with the famous hunter. It was an odd scene, as all displayed an exaggerated friendliness, shaking hands and greeting Boone again and again with mock enthusiasm.

Boone was taken to Cottawamago, or Blackfish, who asked Boone what the men were doing at the Lower Blue Licks. Boone hesitated to answer and was told the salt boilers had already been spied. Through the interpreter Pompey, Blackfish told Boone the Shawnees were on their way to attack Boonesborough. With the coolness and cunning he often demonstrated in emergencies, Boone studied on a plan to divert the warriors from marching south, where the stockade at Boonesborough was not complete and where there were few men to defend it. Boone accused Blackfish of working for the redcoats. The chief replied: "That is not true. When the Red Coats came to us and offered us much red paint and many guns to fight the Long Knives, we refused. Our great chief Cornstalk went to the fort of the Long Knives on Mount Pleasant on the Ohio River and talked peace with the Long Knives. But the Long Knives murdered him and his son, although they came in peace and without arms. The spirit of Chief Cornstalk calls out from his grave to us to revenge his murder. He cannot rest until we take revenge."

With friendly calm Boone said that he himself would be happy to go live with his Shawnee brothers in Ohio. He added that nearly all the men from Boonesborough were at the Lower Blue Licks and only women, children, and the sick were left at the fort. But even so, the fort was strong and would be difficult to take in such bad weather. And if the women and children *were* taken and made to march all the way to the Shawnee towns in the snow and cold, many would die.

Boone proposed that instead he would have his men at the Lower Blue Licks surrender to be prisoners, if Blackfish guaranteed they would not be tortured or forced to run the gauntlet. Then when spring came he, Boone, would accompany the Shawnees to Boonesborough with enough horses and supplies to bring the women and children to the Shawnee villages on the Little Miami River. There they would all live together in peace and brotherhood.

Blackfish and the other chiefs agreed to this arrangement. They had little enthusiasm for marching and fighting in the depths of winter, and Boone's proposal seemed to satisfy even the angry young men in the band. But they told Boone that if the salt boilers did not submit peacefully, he and they would be killed. These negotiations were conducted with politeness, even cordiality. They camped on Hinkston Creek for the night, and the next morning the large band proceeded through the deep snow to the Lower Blue Licks. It was Sunday, February 8, 1778.

The salt boilers were taking a day of rest, not because it was the Sabbath but because rising water had inundated the salt springs, making it impossible to collect brine to be boiled. They were resting by the fires. When the men saw Boone approach they assumed he was returning with the packhorses that carried salt to Boonesborough. But then Indians were spotted and the men leapt to their feet and grabbed their rifles.

"Don't fire—if you do, all will be massacred!" Boone shouted to the salt boilers. He told them they were surrounded and explained that he had been captured the day before. He told them the war party had been headed to Boonesborough, but he had made an arrangement. All would be treated well if they surrendered. Seeing they were surrounded, the men obeyed. Including Boone, they made twenty-seven prisoners. Flanders Callaway and Thomas Brooks were still out hunting and one man was away with the packhorses. "I think it was a Saturday when my father was taken," Nathan Boone told Draper, "and Sunday when he surrendered up the others."

But after the salt boilers surrendered, some of the young warriors protested that they should attack Boonesborough anyway. Cornstalk should be avenged immediately. The deal made with Boone was in no way binding. Simon Girty's brothers James and George were present, and the Frenchmen Barbee and Lorimier. Pompey translated for Boone, but in a voice so low the other prisoners could not follow. Finally Boone was allowed to address the assembly, and according to the testimony of one of the salt boilers, Joseph Jackson, many years later, this is what he said:

Brothers! What I have promised you I can much better fulfill in the spring than now. Then the weather will be warm, and the women and children can travel from Boonesborough to the Indian towns, and all live with you as one people. You have got all my young men; to kill them, as has been suggested, would displease the Great Spirit, and you could not then expect future success in hunting nor war. If you spare them, they will make you fine warriors, and excellent hunters to kill game for your squaws and children. These young men have done you no harm, they were engaged in a peaceful occupation, and unresistingly surrendered upon my assurance that such a course was the only safe one for them; and I consented to their capitulation, on the express condition that they should be made prisoners of war and treated well. I now appeal both to your honor and your humanity; spare them, and the Great Spirit will smile upon you.

All Indians, including Shawnees, respected eloquence and oratory. A chief's ability to "talk the big talk" was one of the things that gave him authority. Several times Boone demonstrated that he had this power also, and his ability with words contributed to Boone's status among Indians. It was only as the salt makers listened to these words that they realized what the discussion was all about. Many of the warriors were demanding that the prisoners be put to death. The fact that Blackfish permitted Boone to speak at length is evidence that he felt lenient toward him and the other prisoners. Many of the salt boilers later said that it is likely they would have been killed and Boonesborough taken had it not been for Boone's poise and eloquence on this occasion.

A vote was taken among the warriors, and in some accounts Boone was allowed to vote. Others say it is unlikely a prisoner was permitted to vote. As a hostage Boone was probably not entitled to a vote under tribal law. It is thought the Girty brothers voted for leniency. Fifty-nine voted to kill the prisoners and march directly to Boonesborough, and sixty-one opposed that course. Boonesborough and the prisoners were saved.

In preparation for the march north the Indians scattered dozens of bushels of salt in the snow and mud of the Blue Licks. The prisoners were loaded down with equipment and baggage. One warrior gave Boone a brass kettle to carry, but Boone shoved it back at him. An argument escalated and Boone pushed the kettle away so hard the brave fell down. The other Shawnees laughed at him, and Blackfish stepped forward and indicated that Boone was under his special protection. The huge party of warriors and prisoners marched down the Licking River a few miles and made camp for the night. When Boone noticed the Shawnees clearing a path in the snow, which he recognized as a gauntlet, he reminded Blackfish of his agreement not to torture the prisoners. Through Pompey the chief said, "O, Captain Boone, this is not intended for your men, but for you." Boone saw that he had been outwitted. He was given the choice of running the gauntlet now or waiting until they reached the Shawnee towns where the women and children could participate. Boone chose to get the ordeal over with, knowing that squaws could be more imaginative and relentless in their torture than the warriors.

After the Shawnees lined up on either side of the cleared path, armed with tomahawks and clubs, Boone braced himself at the opening and began his charge. Crouching forward, the powerfully built Boone jumped this way and that, dodging and zigzagging, feinting and sidestepping so fast it looked as though he could get through the gauntlet unscathed. But he was hit several times, and one tomahawk cut a gash on his head that bled so much the blood almost blinded him. As he neared the end of the run, a brave stepped out in front of him to deliver a deadly blow. Still dashing this way and that, Boone pretended to charge around the warrior but at the last minute butted him in the lower belly with his powerful head, as he had done to the Indian on the Juniata in 1755. The warrior went flying in the snow and the Shawnees roared with laughter as Boone finished his run at the safety post and was congratulated by his would-be torturers. They teased the fallen warrior, calling him nothing but a "damned squaw."

That evening by the campfire Barbee and Lorimier, the two French Canadians working for the British, got into an argument about whether the prisoners should have their ears slit in the Shawnee fashion. The argument turned violent and was stopped, and the salt boilers' ears were spared. The next morning James Callaway, one of the prisoners, was ordered to carry a salt kettle on his back, but he refused. Baring his head and patting the top of his head, he indicated he would rather be killed now than serve as a beast of burden. The warrior chose not to kill him, knowing a live Kentuckian was worth a hundred dollars, whereas a scalp brought only fifty dollars at the British post at Detroit. James Callaway did carry a rifle and auger for the Indians but managed to drop them both in swift-moving water during the march.

The large party crossed the Ohio River by taking turns in a "bull" boat made of buffalo hides, which would carry twenty at a time. The boat was hidden there for their use when they needed to cross the river. In the narrative he dictated to Filson five years later Boone stressed the hardships of the march into Ohio during the harsh weather of February 1778, "an uncomfortable journey, in very severe weather." It took ten days to reach the town of Chillicothe on the Little Miami River, near future Antioch College. He admitted that for the most part the Shawnees treated them well, considering the harshness of the weather and the shortage of provisions. They got so hungry the Indians killed and ate their dogs. After that all were reduced to eating elm bark, which gave them diarrhea. The diarrhea was treated by eating oak bark. Finally the Indians shot a deer and boiled its entrails to make a kind of jelly to counter the extreme effects of the oak bark. When Boone tried to swallow the jelly he threw up, and he was forced to try again and again. As he vomited, the Indians laughed at his weakness. Finally he got some of the jelly to stay down and the concoction opened his bowels. Only then was he allowed to partake of the venison. The Shawnees told him that if he had eaten meat before, "it would have killed him."

The Shawnee town they were approaching was the Chillicothe on the Little Miami River. There had been previous Shawnee villages named Chillicothe, and there would be later ones also. "The name Chillicothe means, as the aged Shawanoe chief Black Hawk related to Joseph Ficklin, *Fire that won't go out* — hence, the town of the sacred council fire." In effect, Chillicothe meant "capital town" or "central town." The "Chillicothes" were the clan from which the leaders of the Shawnee nation were often chosen. Other clans were the Piquas, the Kiskopos, and the Mequachakes. By 1778 Shawnees built their towns to look pretty much like the white stations, though bigger, with cabins and council house forming a kind of fortress. Everyone who saw the Shawnee towns in Ohio commented on how beautifully they were situated along the rivers.

As the band approached the town of Chillicothe, on February 18, the Shawnees made Ansel Goodman, one of the captives, strip off his clothes in the extreme cold and "sing as loud as he could holler. The object of that, he afterwards learnt, was to give notice of their approach." The Shawnees had not had so many white prisoners since Braddock's Defeat in 1755. They celebrated with a great war dance, and in the excitement the prisoners were made to run the gauntlet in spite of Blackfish's promise to Boone. James Callaway, with his considerable anger and strength, knocked two Indians down at the beginning of the run and surprised the rest so much he got through unscathed. William Hancock followed Boone's example and butted with his head a woman who tried to stand in his way.

It was the custom of the Shawnees to adopt prisoners they liked into their families. The practice may seem strange to us, to take a former enemy into one's family as a brother, so soon after he surrenders. Few other customs illustrate more clearly the difference between the ideas of kinship in the white and Indian cultures. In Indian wars, the tribes fighting were often closely related by blood and language, belief and tradition. Someone defeated in war, who showed courage and dignity, when given the correct instruction and initiation, and a new name, could become in effect a new brother or son. The practice illustrates a deep sense of kinship, implicit kinship, with all other people, including a noble, defeated opponent. Some prisoners were chosen to replace sons or husbands who had been killed.

When they captured women and children, and even men in battle, Indians shared their food with the captives and gave them moccasins. They taught the captives not to call out in the forest but to communicate by making noises like animals. Captured women were rarely affronted sexually, partly because of an incest taboo protecting someone who might become an adopted "sister" but more often because warriors observed a vow of celibacy until they returned from war to their villages. Among many tribes the crime of rape was punished by death. Those captured, especially adults, were often forced to run the gauntlet after they reached the village. The gauntlet, in the words of James Axtell, was "a purgative ceremony by which the bereaved Indians could exorcize their anger and anguish, and the captives could begin their cultural transformation." The next rite was the ritual bathing in a stream where the squaws scrubbed away the "whiteness" in the captive's body.

The most important stage of the process of adoption was the last, when the chief or sachem made a solemn speech describing the honor accorded to the adoptee, the duties and behavior expected from the new member of the community. Such an exhortation might last an hour or more, as would a sermon by a contemporary white preacher. Once a captive was adopted they became a full member of the tribe. Some adopted males rose to be leaders of the native community. Some became renowned chiefs, including one called Old White Chief of the Iroquois. Others who became famous leaders included Simon Girty of the Senecas and Alexander McGillivray of the Creeks. "In public office as in every sphere of Indian life, the colonial captives found that the color of their skin was unimportant; only their talent and their inclination of heart mattered," James Axtell tells us.

Boone birthplace, Oley, PA. Photograph. Ca. 1930s.
This incorporates the original building and looks surpisingly like the stone house Boone died in
in Missouri in 1820. (Courtesy Pennsylvania State Archives—Record Group 13.)

Squire and Sarah Boone tombstone, *Joppa Cemetery, Mocksville,*
North Carolina. When Boone's father, Squire, died in January 1765, this
stone, framed now in brick, was placed over his grave. *The circles with*
points in the center imply that Squire was a Freemason, as was his son
Daniel. (Photo: Benjamin R. Morgan.)

Masonic symbols. Amos
Doolittle. Engraving. From
Jeremy Cross, Masters Carpet:
The True Masonic Chart or
Hieroglyphic Monitor, *1820.*
Freemasonry was a fresh wind
sweeping through Great Britain,
Europe, and North America in
the eighteenth century, promoting
brotherhood, service, and
progressive thought. (Courtesy
National Heritage Museum,
Lexington, MA. Photography by
John M. Miller.)

Boonesborough in 1778. *Drawing. From George W. Ranck,* Boonesborough
*(Filson Club Publication No. 16), 1901. Based on a design made by Col. Richard Henderson
in 1775, this drawing shows the fort as it was finally completed in 1778.
(Courtesy Filson Historical Society, Louisville, KY.)*

"Divine Elm." Meeting of the Transylvania House of Delegates, May 1775. *Drawing.
From George W. Ranck,* Boonesborough *(Filson Club Publication No. 16), 1901.
With no building large enough for a meeting, the delegates gathered under a giant elm
outside the fort to make laws and plan the government of the future colony of Transylvania.
(Courtesy Filson Historical Society, Louisville, KY.)*

Daniel Boone's First View of Kentucky. *William T. Ranney. Oil on canvas, 36" x 56 1/2". 1849. Painters throughout the nineteenth century loved to portray Boone at the moment of his first sight of the promised land of the Kentucky Bluegrass region, often called his Pisgah vision. (Courtesy Gilcrease Museum, Tulsa, OK.)*

Cherokee Delegation Brought to London in 1730 to Enter into Articles of Friendship and Commerce with His Majesty. *Isaac Basire. Engraving. Ca. 1730. From a painting by Markham, Seven Delegates to London. The figure on the right is the future legendary chief Attakullakulla, or the Little Carpenter, so called because it was said he could join quarreling factions into a consensus. (Courtesy Smithsonian National Anthropological Archives.)*

Oval medallion with profile of Col. Richard Henderson. Designed by George H. Honig. 1929. Monument at Henderson, Kentucky, Courthouse. (Photo: Benjamin R. Morgan.)

Colonel John Floyd 1751–1783. *Artist unknown. Drawing. Ca. 1886. Floyd was said to owe his dark good looks to an Indian ancestor, but neither his charm nor his Native blood protected him from violent land disputes and being killed by Indians in 1783. (Courtesy Filson Historical Society, Louisville, KY.)*

John Filson. *Artist unknown. Painting. Ca. 1884. From Reuben T. Durrett,* John Filson: The First Historian of Kentucky *(Filson Club Publication No. 1), 1884. Though Filson (1753–88) was killed by Indians his book took on a life of its own, creating the Boone legend. (Courtesy Filson Historical Society, Louisville, KY.)*

Lyman Copeland Draper. *Daguerreotype. 1858. Draper (1815–91) devoted most of his life to collecting documents and information about the frontier history of the Ohio Valley. He planned biographies of George Rogers Clark, Boone, and many others, but published only one book,* Kings Mountain and Its Heroes, *1881, and a number of articles in newspapers. His unfinished manuscript,* The Life of Daniel Boone, *has proved to be a treasure for later scholars and writers, as is the vast collection of documents, letters, and interviews he assembled at the State Historical Society of Wisconsin. (Courtesy Wisconsin Historical Society: Image 35.)*

Daniel Boone Escorting Settlers through the Cumberland Gap. *George Caleb Bingham. Oil on canvas, 36 1/2" x 50 1/4". 1851–52. Deservedly one of the best-known portraits of Boone, this painting gets many details right, including the hat. (Mildred Lane Kemper Art Museum, Washington University in St. Louis. Gift of Nathaniel Phillips, 1890.)*

Capture of the Daughters of D. Boone and Callaway by Indians. *Karl Bodmer. Lithograph, 17 1/8" x 22 1/8". 1852. (Mildred Lane Kemper Art Museum, Washington University in St. Louis. Transfer from Special Collections, Olin Library, Washington University, 1988.)*

Monk Estill. Drawing. From Zachary F. Smith, History of Kentucky, 1895. Monk Estill played his fiddle for the dances at Boonesborough. For his actions at the Battle of Little Mountain, March 22, 1782, in which his owner James Estill was killed, Monk was given his freedom by the Estill family. (Courtesy Kentucky Historical Society.)

Col. Daniel Boone. James Otto Lewis. 1820. Stipple engraving, 8 3/16" x 13 9/16". In the years after his death Boone became an icon of popular American culture. Magazines, books, and newspapers featured his image, sometimes with some accuracy, as in this Lewis engraving. (Courtesy Saint Louis Art Museum.)

Boone cabin on Brushy Creek. Photo. Ca. 1935. When Boone and his wife, Rebecca, and youngest son, Nathan, returned to Kentucky from Virginia around 1795, he was so poor he settled in a cabin owned by his son Daniel Morgan Boone on the Brushy Fork of Hinkston Creek. (Courtesy Special Collections, University of Kentucky, Lexington.)

Nathan Boone. Anonymous painting of Boone's youngest son. Ca. 1850. Nathan Boone and his young bride, Olive Van Bibber Boone, followed the Boone migration to Missouri in 1799. Draper's interview with Nathan and Olive Boone in 1851 has provided some of our best information about Boone. (Courtesy Missouri Historical Society, St. Louis.)

Daniel Boone. Chester Harding. Oil on canvas. 1819. A young painter from Boston, Chester Harding visited Missouri in the last year of Boone's life and persuaded the old woodsman to pose for a portrait, the only known likeness done from life. (Courtesy Massachusetts Historical Society.)

Nathan Boone's stone house, Femme Osage Creek, MO. Boone's youngest son, with the help of Boone and others, built this substantial house around 1816 in the style of houses the Boones had seen in Pennsylvania. Daniel Boone died in the front room September 26, 1820. (Photo: Kevin Riebs.)

White children adopted by the Indians often chose to remain with their Indian families, even after they were rescued. Adopted women and some men made the same decision. Once they adapted to the Indian lifestyle they were reluctant to return to the settlements, when they were freed or ransomed. Many Europeans became "white Indians." On the other hand few Indians chose to live with the whites, as Crevecoeur noted.

Though all Indians, especially the young, could be cruel to prisoners when they were first brought into the village, the elders encouraged respect, sharing, mutual care. Many adoptees chose to stay with their captors, according to James Axtell, "because they found Indian life to possess a strong sense of community, abundant love, and uncommon integrity — values that the European colonists honored, if less successfully. But Indian life was attractive for other values — for social equality, mobility, adventure, and, as two adult converts acknowledged, 'the most perfect freedom, the ease of living.'" Indian lovers were sometimes called sleeping dictionaries, as a new language was learned quickly from a sexual partner. Many rescued and returned to the white community took the first opportunity to escape back to the Indians.

In white culture a sense of identity was defined more in terms of difference, deep indelible difference, of bloodline, religion, class, heritage, not to mention ethnicity and race. To the Shawnees, complete adoption was assumed to be possible because the differences between people were not perceived to be either great or indelible. A common humanity overrode mere tribal differences. To European settlers the differences seemed more essential, permanent, definitive. An analogy might be made between an animistic, metaphoric way of seeing experience. To the mind that thinks in terms of metaphor and myth, all things can seem related and be seen as likenesses, translations, parallels, and symbols of each other. To the more rational, analytical mind, it is the differences that define and make sense of experience. As Shelley puts it succinctly in "A Defense of Poetry," "Reason respects the differences, and imagination the similitudes of things." For twenty-five hundred years European culture had developed its analytical, logical way of making sense of the world of experience. At Chillicothe on the Little Miami in February 1778, that worldview would confront a more ancient, poetic, and connective way of defining identity and humanity.

CHAPTER ELEVEN

Sheltowee, Son of Blackfish

1778 ~

Daniel Boone and sixteen of his company of salt boilers were adopted by the Shawnees. Most of those adopted were selected for their bravery or strength, good looks, or congenial personality. Those who exhibited bad tempers or continued hostility were set aside to be sold to the British.

Because of his compact, powerful body, Boone was named Sheltowee, or "Big Turtle." From the very beginning, Boone seemed to have a special rapport with Blackfish. It could almost be said Boone worked a charm on the great war chief of the Shawnees. Blackfish told Boone that he had lost a son in war and Boone would replace that son. In some accounts Blackfish's son was one of the kidnappers of Jemima and the Callaway girls who had been shot.

His adoption by the Shawnees on the Little Miami is perhaps the most complicated episode in Boone's long career. Nothing illustrates the complexity of his personality and his resourcefulness more than his success as one of the tribe that was planning a massive attack on Boonesborough.

As the adopted son of the great chief, Boone was treated to an elaborate ceremony of transformation and conversion. John Mason Peck, who interviewed Boone near the end of his life, described the ritual in his biography: "The hair of the head is plucked out by a tedious and painful operation, leaving a tuft, some three or four inches in diameter, on the crown, for the scalp-lock, which is cut and dressed up with ribbons and feathers. The candidate is then taken into the river in a state of nudity, and there thoroughly washed and rubbed, 'to take all his white blood out'. The ablution is usually performed by females. He is then taken to the council-house, where the chief makes a speech, in which he expatiates upon the distinguished honors conferred on him, and the line of conduct expected from him. His head and face are painted in the most approved and fashionable style, and the ceremony is concluded with a grand feast and smoking." His hair plucked out, all except the topknot that identified him as a Shawnee brave, his whiteness washed away, Boone was given a new name and a new identity.

On March 10, 1778, the ten prisoners who were not adopted into the tribe were taken to Detroit to be traded to Henry "Hair Buyer" Hamilton for a hundred dollars each. As Blackfish's honored son, Boone got to go along. Likely Blackfish wanted to show off his prize, the great hunter and scout. An older woman of the tribe went along for the journey of several days, apparently in hopes of becoming the wife of one of the prisoners. Rejected by each of the men in turn, she at last attached herself to Nathaniel Bullock. Nathaniel was forced to carry her baggage but dropped behind the group as the woman clung to his arm. Coming to an air hole in a frozen stream, he pushed the woman into the river and she disappeared under the ice. Later he told his captors she had "stepp'd [to] one side," and they apparently thought no more about it. Boone would look back on this journey to Detroit fondly. "During our travels, the Indians entertained me well; and their affection for me was so great, that they utterly refused to leave me there with the others, though the Governor [Hamilton] offered them one hundred pounds Sterling for me."

Boone said several of the English officers at Detroit were touched by his plight and offered him aid. Knowing that Boone was a leader in Kentucky, they no doubt hoped to win him over to the British side.

Boone was so friendly they must have assumed he was not deeply committed to the American cause, and he was content to let them assume what they wanted. But when the officers offered him money, he had to refuse, knowing he could never repay their generosity. One has the impression of a great show of hospitality made toward him, no doubt in part as a gesture of friendship toward Blackfish. After all, Boone was the chief's adopted son. It is possible that Freemasons among the British officers showed a special consideration for Boone. Many members of the distinguished Hamilton family were known to be Freemasons. And Boone seemed to delight in all the attention. But it is also apparent that Hamilton and Boone had a genuine respect for each other. Three years later, when the tables were turned and Hamilton was a prisoner of the Americans at Williamsburg, it was Boone who tried to help the British officer, who was badly treated by his captors.

It was Boone's conduct at Detroit that caused forever after the question of his loyalty to the American cause. Both the Shawnees and the British governor made a great fuss over him. Hamilton gave Boone a horse and saddle and a supply of silver trinkets to use as money among the Indians. Hamilton was bribing Boone to join the Loyalist cause. In the display of entertaining Boone, it was clear the governor was also pumping him for information. Hamilton wanted to learn if the Indians knew about Burgoyne's defeat at Saratoga the fall before, and Boone informed the governor they had been told of it. Hamilton suggested that Boone tell the Shawnees the story was just a joke, that of course the British had not been defeated by the rebels.

It is said that Boone carried with him all his life the certificate of his commission in 1774 as a captain of the Virginia militia, signed by Lord Dunmore. Even while dressed as an Indian among the Shawnees, he carried the document everywhere with him. During his interview with Hamilton, Boone showed him the commission and apparently hinted that he was sympathetic to the Tory cause, and that he might persuade the settlers at Boonesborough to surrender the fort and transfer their loyalties to the British. Boone was willing to let Hamilton believe what he wanted to believe. His duplicity was certainly in his interest, and he was treated handsomely. Boone knew how to conceal himself in the wilderness, and he was also an expert at hiding his feelings when in danger. In the long run his stealth proved to be in the interest of Boonesborough, for he survived to return and warn and fortify and save the settlement.

Boone was a complex man with large sympathies, and like a good actor he could assume almost any point of view. He could reflect the manners and opinions of those he was with, whether Shawnees or British officers, Spanish officials, or rough backwoodsmen. He could charm people and persuade. As John Mack Faragher puts it, "Like the great hunter he was, Boone's greatest talent was his ability to blend in with his surroundings."

The more one studies Boone the more one suspects that he genuinely appreciated others' perspectives and values. That was why he could play his ruses so convincingly. At some level he was not faking it. He genuinely understood the position of Governor Hamilton, who stood for British law and order, custom and tradition. And he understood the position of Chief Blackfish trying to lead his tribe toward survival and a future, and he understood the grand dreams and illusions of Richard Henderson as well.

Certainly Boone charmed Governor Hamilton, and Hamilton charmed him also. Boone later said he and the other prisoners "were treated by Governor Hamilton . . . with great humanity." Boone further impressed the governor by demonstrating that he knew how to make gunpowder. While locked in his room with the necessary ingredients he made a supply of the explosive, adding yet another detail to the later reports that he gave aid to the enemy.

On April 25, 1778, Governor Hamilton wrote to his commander, General Carlton, in Canada: "By Boone's account the people of the frontier have been so incessantly harassed by parties of Indians they have not been able to sow grain and at Kentucke will not have a morsel of bread by the middle of June. Clothing is not to be had, nor do they expect relief from Congress — their dilemma will probably induce them to trust to the savages who have shown so much humanity to their prisoners & come to this place before winter." Boone had let Hamilton think just what the governor wanted to think.

Blackfish refused all the offers of the British to buy Boone. One reason was that the chief needed Boone as guide and negotiator for the planned attack on Boonesborough that spring. After all, Boone had promised to deliver Boonesborough to the Shawnees when they returned to Kentucky. A hundred pounds sterling for his adopted son was nothing compared to the honor to be won by expunging the settlements from the Great Meadow hunting grounds.

Blackfish and his party left Detroit on April 10, with Boone riding the horse Hamilton had given him. On the return journey they stopped at villages on the Huron River and the Scioto, notifying Delawares, Mingoes, and Shawnees to assemble that spring for the raid on Kentucky. Despite the hardships of the journey, Boone was delighted anew by the beauty of the Ohio country in spring. He and many others found the river valleys of Ohio unsurpassed, even by Kentucky. In Draper's words, "Such a country could not well escape his keen observation, for he loved to feast his soul upon nature in all her beautiful varieties."

WHILE BOONE and the others were away in Detroit, the salt boiler Andrew Johnson had escaped from Chillicothe. Johnson had convinced the Shawnees he was retarded and confused and afraid of guns, and they had protected him, calling him Pecula, or "Little Duck." When they found he had disappeared they expressed concern for his safety, certain that he had gotten lost and would die in the woods. Boone told them, now that Johnson had gone, that in fact he was an excellent woodsman and marksman. Johnson not only made his way back to Harrodsburg, but also led a raid into Ohio, now that he knew where the Shawnee towns were. Many of the horses in Kentucky had been stolen by the Shawnees, and Johnson and his party recovered seven mounts and returned with them across the Ohio River. When Blackfish heard of the exploit he asked Boone who could possibly have found the Shawnee towns, for no white man knew their location. "Pecula," Boone answered. "No," answered Blackfish, " . . . for he was a fool and could never have reached Kentucky." Boone explained to the incredulous chief that Little Duck was far from a fool. At that point Blackfish realized that though the Shawnees had taken many prisoners at the Blue Licks, they had also revealed the location of their towns to the Kentuckians. It was more important than ever that the forts in Kentucky be destroyed. A real weakness of the Shawnees, as it turned out, was their assumption of superiority to the whites as woodsmen and scouts. Again and again they paid for that pride. Boone later said, "Never did the Indians pursue so disastrous a policy as when they captured me and my salt-boilers, and taught us, what we did not know before, the way to their towns and the geography of their country."

Not only did Andrew Johnson tell the people back in Kentucky where the Shawnee towns were on the Little Miami River, but he told them Boone had arranged the surrender of all the salt boilers, had been adopted by Blackfish, was happy and cheerful among the Indians as a pig in mud and had promised to surrender Boonesborough to the Shawnees when they returned in the spring. It was Johnson's report that planted the rumors that Boone was a traitor.

BOONE LATER told Filson his months with the Shawnees were mostly a pleasure, and there is no reason to doubt him. "At Chelicothe I spent my time as comfortably as I could expect; was adopted, according to their custom, into a family where I became a son, and had a great share in the affection of my new parents, brothers, sisters, and friends. I was exceedingly familiar and friendly with them, always appearing as chearful and satisfied as possible, and they put great confidence in me." It was a life of hunting and trapping and fishing, in the beautiful Ohio country. As the son of the honored chief, he was treated with courtesy. Once when Boone tried to help out in the cornfields,

Blackfish told him he didn't need to work. His "mother" would grow enough corn for all of them. And when the rest of Boone's family arrived she would grow enough corn for them too. It is possible that Boone took a Shawnee wife, though we have no evidence of this. He would have been expected to take a wife at some point. The Shawnee population was being depleted, and he would have been urged to do his duty. He was a great favorite among his adoptive sisters, and they never forgot their fondness for Sheltowee, even in their old age. Boone's great-granddaughter wrote, "Grandfather Boone said he had a squaw that claimed him as her buck; said she mended and dried his leggins and patched his moccasins." We know Boone had a particular ability to adapt himself to circumstances. There are stories that he had much earlier taken a Cherokee wife. For some historians it is hard to imagine that he could have lived with the Shawnees for four months without taking a wife. Much of what we know about Indian marriages and lovemaking suggests it. Most Shawnee marriages were arranged by the parents, but sometimes young people took matters into their own hands also. "Should a maiden like the looks or the manner of a young brave she might seek a place behind him in the dance, . . . and give him her hand without a handkerchief. The giving of the naked hand always denoted a 'willingness' to be regarded as a future mate," the Shawnee Thomas Wildcat Alford later wrote. According to C. C. Trowbridge in *Shawnese Traditions*, it was not uncommon for a man to marry a widow and her daughter. "But these are cases only when a young man marries a widow, and then, finding herself in danger of being abandoned by her husband, she proposes to him a connection with her daughter & thus the connection is preserved."

When a man and woman in the tribe first married they would move into their own shelter. It was understood they needed privacy to begin their life together. Later they might live in a cabin or shelter with a large family and almost never be alone with each other again. But at the beginning it was recognized they needed private space for bonding and lovemaking. Shawnees usually married in their teens, and if a boy and girl were very young and inexperienced they were instructed in the details of lovemaking by the boy's mother. "She helped her son get an erection . . . Properly she directed his penis to the woman's vaginal orifice," the anthropologist Voegelin was told. Once the lovemaking began she left them "to follow exactly the way it was arranged for them, the way they ought to follow, the way it was intended for them." Too frequent sex was considered bad for the husband's health. Shawnee couples were not supposed to demonstrate affection in public, however passionate they were in private.

Irish men were especially popular with Indian women, who seemed to prefer red hair above all other colors. About half the Cherokee nation, for example, would eventually come to have Hibernian names. Among some nations "sex could be a way of fulfilling sacred obligations of hospitality, a way of transferring supernatural powers, a way of incorporating strangers into kinship and trade networks," Carolyn Gilman tells us. One way to acquire the medicine of a stranger was through copulation. The races mingled so quickly on meeting it appears to have been almost love at first sight.

John Lawson, who studied several of the tribes in North Carolina earlier in the eighteenth century reported, "He that is a good Hunter never misses of being a Favorite amongst the Women; the prettiest Girls being always bestowed upon the chiefest Sports-Men." Lawson observed that a man who did not sleep with the women was held in contempt by the tribe. "For when a Person that lives amongst them, is reserved from the Conversation of their Women, tis impossible for him to ever accomplish his Designs amongst the People." But in the crowded tents and bark lodges, as in the settlers' cabins, there was not always room for such preferred lovemaking. Lying among many others, couples moved as best they could under a blanket or buffalo hide, women on top at times, men at others, or side by side, loving silently and patiently. As a seminomadic people, Indians had birthrates lower than the whites. For people who hunted and gathered and moved often, nature favored smaller families. With some nations lovemaking was almost a seasonal thing, not a nightly or habitual practice.

The Shawnee supreme deity was female, called Our Grandmother, creator of people and the universe. She presided over fertility, the corn harvest, and the destiny of the people. In some stories the deity was portrayed as having two faces, one beautiful and seductive, the other ugly and vengeful. She could offer love and then turn on a miscreant with fury. One of the Shawnee legends concerns a man, who, looking for his wife, comes to a cornfield:

Perhaps he was lucky he came, for in that place corn is growing which is of curious shape. The thing which he found looked like a woman's vagina. Now he said he heard about her; the man always heard, he said. There is a saying that the Corn Person, our mother, is a woman; if it is really true that she is called this name, she will be embarrassed now when I have intercourse with her. Then he pulled out his penis; he stuck it right there where she was cracked. After he had intercourse with her, then from there he went to the house. Now the Corn Person went away along through the night. Now the old woman who stays there rose early in the morning; right now she went to the corn crib when she arose. When she arrived over there, there wasn't any corn.

The symbolic possession of the tribe, and the tribe's covenant with the female deity, was the holy bundle. Wherever the people moved, they carried the holy bundle with them. As the anthropologist Voegelin and his colleagues discovered, "The bundles provide the most sacred approach to Our Grandmother ... Conversely, the bundles provide for extremely holy, possibly esoteric communications from the Creator to the Shawnee. The bundles are a holy mystery and attract the inarticulate interest of the whole tribe." The medicine bundle might contain sacred plants, talismanic objects such a pieces of a dead snake, which "gave access to the chaotic and deadly chthonic forces," as Gregory Dowd puts it. The bundle in each town had its own appointed custodian, who consulted it as a source of wisdom and prophecy. "Daniel Boone evidently saw it among the Chillicothes in 1778 and thought it 'a kind of ark, deemed among the sacred things.'" Each village also had a ceremonial hoop, with packets of seeds and animal hair attached to it, symbolizing the male and female division of labor, and used especially in the Spring Bread Dance to "function as a prayer to Our Grandmother, the Creator, for good crops and abundant game."

Other beliefs and habits of the Shawnees are worth noting also. To the Shawnees, springs were thought to be entrances to the underworld. Passing a spring, a Shawnee warrior would stop and sprinkle tobacco around the pool and pray to the spirit of the fountain for success with his mission and a safe return to his village. After shedding human blood, a warrior had to be purified through fasting and ritual. The spirits of those he had killed must be propitiated. Any man taken in battle expected to be burned at the stake and made a death song promising his death would be avenged by his people.

As a nation the Shawnees had always been divided. There was no strong unity among the Chillicothe, Piqua, Kispoko, and Mequashake bands. The Shawnees had moved often as a way of holding on to their culture, choosing migration and its challenges rather than living near whites. By 1778 their towns included Indians from many other nations, as well as adopted whites. Politically they were divided also. The "Grenadier Squaw," Nonhelema, as well as her brother Cornstalk, warned whites of attacks. Many Americans thought Shawnees and Delawares held Ohio lands only at the discretion of the Iroquois. That assumption infuriated the Ohio Indians.

Shawnee culture at this time was particularly complex and evolving, a patchwork of traditional beliefs and practices mingling with ideas and methods acquired from the Europeans. Indians had claimed that domesticating livestock "desecrated the spirituality of animals," even as they were beginning to raise herds of their own. Travelers in the

Ohio region had noticed as early as 1760 that Indians had many cattle and demonstrated "skill in making butter and cheese." Missionaries for decades had urged Indians to give up hunting and farm and raise livestock. In some cases their message had been heeded. But many warriors felt the missionaries were trying to turn them into women, for farming had traditionally been considered women's work. Most Indians had little interest in accumulating surpluses or wealth. They cherished the principles of their ancient culture, even as it was becoming more and more difficult to distinguish between what was Indian and what was taken from the whites. By 1778 many Indians lived in wooden houses very much like those in the white settlements.

One feature of Indian society the early accounts usually failed to note was the female chief or village leader, who oversaw the lives of the women, organized the field work and harvesting, the feasts and many of the ceremonies. This woman leader had the responsibility of informing the male war chief of the view of the women when a consensus had been reached among them. One Shawnee man was heard to explain that women were allowed to speak in the council house, "because some women were wiser than some men."

There are many stories of the precautions Blackfish took to make sure that Sheltowee did not run away. Indians were assigned to shadow him when he went out riding on his horse. When he hunted he was given just enough lead and powder for one or two shots. Even so, he found ways to hoard both lead and powder, killing game with half a charge or half a bullet. Boone's expertise as a gunsmith especially impressed his Shawnee companions. He seemed able to repair and improve almost any firearm. They liked his sense of humor also. Once he extracted all the bullets from their loaded rifles and pretended to flee, and when they attempted to shoot him their guns fired empty blasts. Boone dumped the lead balls he had taken from their guns at the feet of the startled warriors. At first confused and resentful, they ended by having a good laugh with Sheltowee.

Boone did not complain about the food or the comforts in Blackfish's cabin, but he did later mention that his "mother" let her chickens roost in the same area where she cooked. In the evenings Blackfish and Sheltowee had philosophical discussions about what the Shawnees could learn from the whites and the whites from the Shawnees. Blackfish thought his people should learn agriculture from the whites, improving the soil, raising cattle, spinning and weaving wool. He was concerned about the future of his people. Under the conditions of war Shawnees did not have the leisure to improve themselves. Blackfish was prescient, for later in Missouri the Shawnees would be known for their large herds of livestock. Always a diplomat, Boone pointed out the felicities of the Indian culture and the skills he had learned from Indians about woodcraft, hunting, the beauty of life in the woods. Blackfish amused Boone by drawing maps of the region, showing him where rivers and villages were. "Blackfish would also smooth out dirt and mark out the geography of the country, apparently to amuse my father," Nathan told Draper. Like Boone, Blackfish had an extraordinary memory for detail and geography. As a sign of familiarity, "Blackfish would suck a lump of sugar a while in his mouth, take it out, and give it to Boone, whom he always addressed as 'my son.'" All his life Boone had aspired to live like an Indian, to hunt with Indians, and during the months at Chillicothe that dream was realized.

On June 1 Blackfish and a party of Shawnees left the village to boil salt at Salt Creek, near the Scioto River. On the way to the salt spring the party stopped at Paint Creek where a white man named Jimmy Rogers lived. Jimmy Rogers had been adopted by the Shawnees when young and he had continued to live with them. Boone agreed to repair Rogers's rifle and took it along with him to the lick. There Boone repaired the rifle and supplied game for the salt-making group. He later said he "found the land, for a great extent about this river, to exceed the soil of Kentucke, if possible, and remarkably well watered."

A band of Shawnees arrived at Salt Creek who had suffered a defeat from the whites at Point Pleasant, at the mouth of the Kanawha River. Blackfish persuaded them to join the expedition against Boonesborough later in the summer. Their best revenge against the humiliation on the Ohio would be to attack the Kentucky fort. Blackfish assigned Boone to repair the damaged rifles of the war party, and Boone complied, working several days on locks and stocks. As always, Boone's gunsmithing ability stood him in good stead, for he was able to hide a damaged rifle without a stock among his things and repair it, all except fitting it with a new stock.

As Blackfish talked of the approaching campaign against Boonesborough, Boone knew it was time for him to make his escape, if he was ever going to. He had hoped to escape with the other adopted prisoners, but as it turned out his chance came while he was with the party returning from the salt lick. It was June 16, and as they were returning to Chillicothe with the salt supply, a flock of turkeys was spotted in the trees in the distance. Blackfish and the other warriors grabbed their weapons and hurried to harvest some of the birds. Boone was left with the women and he saw this was the best opportunity he would have for escape. Boone quickly cut the straps that held the baggage on his horse and told his adoptive mother and the other women that he "wanted to go and see his squaw and children and dashed off." That's what the Shawnees told Joseph Jackson, still a prisoner with the new name of Fish. According to the story Boone later told his children, his Shawnee mother begged him not to go and said the warriors would overtake him and kill him. Boone later told a nephew that as he rode away "he really felt sorry."

BOONE'S ESCAPE from the Shawnees and return to Boonesborough is one of the great legends of frontier history. Riding the horse until it collapsed, Boone took off the saddle and hung it on a tree for someone else to use. He took the unstocked rifle and bag of powder and hoarded shot, a bit of jerky, and continued on foot, running down streams and along fallen logs to throw off his pursuers. He later learned the Shawnees followed him for a while but missed his trail and assumed Boone had gotten lost. It is curious that in almost every instance, the

Shawnees assumed the Kentuckians could not find their way through the wilderness. "Jimmy Rogers said that the Indians followed his trail some distance and returned, saying he would get lost. But Rogers said he knew better — that he was sure my father would go straight as a leather string home."

At the Ohio Boone found a dead poplar, which he broke into three pieces and lashed together with a grapevine. Putting his ammunition and damaged rifle on the raft, he pushed out into the stream and was carried a good ways down the river before he touched bottom on the other shore. Once he got into the woods on the south bank, Boone walked until it was dark and then stopped to sleep. During the night something grabbed his toe and woke him. He jumped up but never saw the wolf or fox or whatever it was in the dark. In the morning he rubbed the ooze from oak bark on his blistered feet and started out as soon as there was light. That day he found a sourwood sapling that appeared to be the right size and carved a section as a stock for his broken rifle. He bound the stock to the metal with strings made of hide, which had held his blanket and pack to his back. Walking on sore feet and with nothing to eat, he made it to the Blue Licks on June 19. There he shot a buffalo and cooked part of its hump for his first meal in two days. He saved the buffalo tongue for his little son Daniel Morgan, then not quite nine years old. Boone later said he was proud of the rifle he had improvised in the woods. "It had the very best lock I had ever had in my life," he said. He finally arrived at Boonesborough on Saturday, June 20, and shouted across the river for someone to come ferry him over. He had traveled 160 miles through the wilderness in under four days and had eaten only one meal.

But when he reached the fort, Boone was not greeted with the welcome he expected. Rebecca and the children, assuming he was dead, had left Boonesborough in April and returned to the Yadkin. His cabin was empty. And many of the people of Boonesborough were far from friendly. Andrew Johnson had told them that Boone had sold out his salt-boiling companions and collaborated with the Shawnees. Boone sat down exhausted in his cabin, and the family cat appeared and recognized him. Then Jemima, who had stayed at the fort waiting for her father, burst through the door. Only she had remained at Boonesborough, counting on Boone's return.

WHAT SHOULD have been a joyous homecoming and reunion was dampened by the absence of Rebecca and the other children, and the suspicions of many of his neighbors and associates at Boonesborough. Using Andrew Johnson's testimony as evidence, Richard Callaway led a faction that whispered rumors of Boone's treachery, treason, his self-serving duplicity. Many, like Simon Kenton and Nathaniel Hart, had implicit faith in Boone's integrity and understood the delicacy and difficulty of what he had done to protect Boonesborough. Others like Callaway and Benjamin Logan saw Boone's actions at the Blue Licks and Detroit in the worst light. It was true he had escaped and returned to Boonesborough at great danger and difficulty to himself, but what were his plans and motives? his detractors wondered. Had he sold out Boonesborough and the Kentucky settlements to the Tories, and was he just waiting for the Shawnees and British to arrive?

Attempting to ignore, to brush aside, the muttered rumors and sullen looks, Boone set about finishing the fortification of Boonesborough. Many of the original pickets, especially those of yellow poplar logs, had already rotted. He warned that the Shawnees under Blackfish were assembling a large army to invade Kentucky, and Boonesborough was their prime target. The palisades had to be repaired or replaced, the fourth side finished, and the blockhouses at each corner completed. A well needed to be dug inside the fort, and the magazine and supply rooms had to be restocked. Luckily Daniel's brother Squire and his family were still at Boonesborough. Squire was an excellent blacksmith and craftsman. Boone knew that the fort was under constant surveillance by Indian spies from Ohio. While a prisoner at Chillicothe he had heard many reports of activities back at Boonesborough. John Gass later told John Dabney Shane, "Boon said, the summer he was w. the indns., he could hear from Bnsbgh: every week."

It did not impress Richard Callaway that Boone set about preparing to defend the fort, rather than rushing to the Yadkin for his family. With his hair still plucked like a Shawnee, and his clothes in rags, Boone inspired rage and distrust in Callaway. The danger Boone had exposed himself to in leading the salt makers to the Blue Licks in January, and the risk of the elaborate ruse he had enacted among the Shawnees and the British, did not appease his detractors at all. But luckily many at Boonesborough did trust Boone, heeded his warning about the imminent invasion, and cooperated in rebuilding and strengthening the fort. Finally the fort was completed in the summer of 1778, more or less as it had been planned by Richard Henderson in 1775.

Even so, that summer was tense and embarrassing for Boone. He warned that the Shawnees were coming, but they did not come. The alert, the spirit of alarm that had allowed him to get so much construction and repair done on the fort, died down.

As it turned out, Boone's escape had so alarmed Blackfish that he postponed the expedition to Boonesborough. Shawnee spies were sent to watch the Kentucky settlements and they informed Blackfish of the defensive preparations at Boonesborough and Harrodsburg and Logan's Station. Because he had lost the element of surprise, and the expected cooperation of Sheltowee in the surrender of Boonesborough, the war chief decided it was prudent to wait until he had assembled an even larger force before he attacked the trespassers in Kentucky.

William Hancock escaped from the Shawnees and arrived naked and exhausted at Boonesborough on July 17. He had gotten lost in the woods and had lain down to die, only to notice his own initials carved on a nearby tree, proving he was close to the fort. Hancock informed Boone and the others that Blackfish had indeed postponed the raid but would be marching with the British and French and a larger force of at least four hundred Indians to attack Kentucky later that summer. Both Boone and Richard Callaway sent letters to Col. Arthur Campbell back on the Holston, asking for reinforcements from the Virginia militia. Boone wrote:

Boonesborough, 18th July, 1778

Dear Colonel:

Enclosed is my deposition with that of Mr. Hancock, who arrive here yesterday. He informed us of both French and Indians coming against us to the number of near four hundred, whom I expect here in twelve days from this. If men can be sent to us in five or six weeks, it would be of infinite service, as we shall lay up provisions for a siege. We are all in fine spirits, and have good crops growing, and intend to fight hard in order to secure them. I shall refer you to the bearer for particulars of this country.

I am & etc.
Daniel Boone

While he would concede that Boone had indeed saved the salt boilers by his actions in February, William Hancock was often heard to complain about the tribulations he had suffered among the Shawnees as adopted son of the chief Capt. Will Emery. What had irritated him most was Boone's apparent cheerfulness at Chillicothe. While Hancock and the other prisoners had been depressed and worried, Boone had seemed to enjoy his new position among the Indians. Boone's cheerful acceptance of his life with Blackfish's family had offended some. Hancock "used afterwards to say that he could not understand how Boone could go whistling about apparently so contented among a parcel of dirty Indians when he (Hancock) was constantly melancholy."

When the expected force still had not arrived in August, Boone proposed a scouting expedition across the Ohio to find out where the Shawnees were. Richard Callaway angrily opposed the plan, saying it would weaken the defending force at Boonesborough, just when the

Shawnees might attack. Boone argued that besides news about the Shawnees they could capture enough horses and furs at Paint Creek Town on the Scioto River to make the expedition worthwhile.

Boone won the argument and took about thirty men north to the Blue Licks. Perhaps one of his motives was just to *do* something, after waiting and waiting. Certainly he was anxious to quiet the rumors and questions about his loyalty with a demonstration of leadership and decisive action. But it is also likely Boone wanted to let Blackfish and the Shawnees know he had no intention of surrendering Boonesborough and that if they carried out the raid as planned many Indians, as well as whites, would be killed. According to John Mason Peck, "The object of Boone, in this expedition, was to alarm the Indians for the safety of their own towns and divert their attention from their premeditated attack on Boonesborough." It may have been Boone's concern for saving Indian lives as well as white lives that infuriated Callaway most.

Once the group crossed the Ohio on rafts and entered the Shawnee country, they had a skirmish with a band of warriors who were on their way to join Blackfish's gathering army. Since his group had been spotted, Boone knew it was time to return at once to Boonesborough. On this raid young Simon Kenton shot two Indians with the same bullet, killing one and wounding the other. Kenton and Alexander Montgomery remained behind in Ohio to spy on the Shawnee towns.

The large Indian force was already south of the Ohio River. Boone and his men recrossed the river and hurried day and night to reach Boonesborough, swinging wide around the Shawnee and British army to avoid detection and confrontation. They arrived back at the fort on September 6 and warned the residents that the Shawnees were camped just to the north, at the Blue Licks.

Between ten and fifteen men had arrived from Harrodsburg and Logan's Station to reinforce the defenders of Boonesborough. About sixty men were gathered at the fort the next day, September 7, 1778, when Blackfish and his army crossed the Kentucky River at a ford about a half mile downstream. No help had arrived from Col. Arthur

Campbell or the Virginia militia, but much corn had been harvested and stored in cribs inside the fort. A great many cattle and other live-stock had been brought into the enclosure. It was a clear warm day, and early in the morning women had gone to the spring for water. Boone and others patrolled the perimeter of the clearing.

Blackfish and his large party, which included the French Canadian Antoine de Quindre and a company of Detroit militia, and about four hundred Shawnees and other Indians, several chiefs, including Moluntha, as well as the Girty brothers, first appeared behind the ridge parallel to the rear of the fort. Boone spotted them in the trees there and hurried back to the stockade, yelling for his nephews Moses and Isaiah, who had been watering the stock, to run back to the fort. The boys had thought the Indians were the militia from Virginia finally coming to their rescue. They dashed back to the fort and the gate was closed.

The large body of Indians gathered in the meadow where all could see, about three hundred yards away. The Tory militia planted its flags and the Shawnees built an arbor in the peach orchard, as a headquar-ters for the chiefs, by cutting off the tops of trees and laying brush and tent cloth over poles fixed to the trunks. The people inside the fort waited, and after about half an hour, Pompey, the large black transla-tor, approached the stockade carrying a flag of truce. Four hundred and fifty feet from the wall he called out for Capt. Daniel Boone. Boone answered and Pompey yelled that Chief Blackfish had come to accept the surrender of Boonesborough, as Boone had promised last Febru-ary. Pompey said he had letters from Governor Hamilton guarantee-ing safe conduct to Detroit for all the settlers. Boone and the other leading men conferred and demanded to see the letters. But suddenly a voice was heard calling all the way from the camp in the peach orchard. "Sheltowee, Sheltowee!" Blackfish shouted. Pompey said that Blackfish wanted to talk to Boone, and Boone agreed to go outside the fort and meet the chief sixty yards from the gate. The riflemen from the walls of the stockade would cover him.

Many of those in the fort were surprised at Boone's willingness to go out and meet with the war chief. Richard Callaway in particular would remember the ease with which Boone agreed to parley as proof of his complicity with the Shawnees. All watched from the walls as Blackfish and Moluntha and several other chiefs came forward from the peach orchard to speak with Boone.

Blackfish and Boone greeted each other and shook hands as father and son. They sat on a blanket while several young Shawnees held branches over their heads for shade. John Gass, who was just a boy, watched from the walls of the fort with the others. "Everyone in the fort was then sure that Boone was gone," he said later. Others said they feared Boone was going to betray them and surrender to the Shawnees and British.

"My son, what made you leave me?" Blackfish said with tears streaming down his face. Blackfish was at least as good an actor as Boone. "I wanted to see my wife and children," Boone said. "If you had only let me know I would have let you go at any time," Blackfish answered. Boone knew nothing could be further from the truth.

Chief Moluntha broke into the friendly exchange and asked Boone why he had killed Moluntha's son on the Ohio. Boone countered that he had not been on the Ohio. "It was you," Moluntha said. "I tracked you here to this place." Boone had the embarrassment of being caught in a lie. He had certainly been in Ohio, but he hadn't known that Moluntha's son had been killed in the raid on Paint Creek Town.

Josiah Collins later told Rev. John Dabney Shane that Blackfish gave Boone an ultimatum. "Well Boone, I have come to take your fort. If you will surrender, I will take you all to Chillicothe, and you shall be treated well. If not I will put all the other prisoners to death, & reserve the young squaws for wives."

Blackfish gave Boone a letter from Hamilton and reminded him of his promise to deliver Boonesborough without a battle, made in the snow in February when he had surrendered the salt boilers at the Lower Blue Licks. Hamilton's letter offered pardon and safe conduct

for all who surrendered and came to Detroit. The British would replace lost property and give officers equivalent rank in British forces.
However, if the Americans did not surrender, they would have to face
the Shawnees and there was no more he could do for them. Blackfish
then showed Boone a wampum belt, which was the Shawnee letter to
Boonesborough. Three trails of beads connected the two ends, red for
war, black for death, white for peace. Boone had to choose which path
would be taken. Boone replied that there was much he had to think
about and talk about with the other officers at Boonesborough. Since
he had been gone so long, others had taken his place of command and
he could only consult with them about a reply.

Blackfish agreed to wait for an answer but mentioned that his people were hungry. Since the Indians could take what they wanted outside the fort anyway, Boone offered them cattle and corn in the fields,
asking that they not waste any. Blackfish presented Boone with seven
cured buffalo tongues as a delicacy for "your women." Treating each
other with friendliness and dignity, Sheltowee and Blackfish smoked a
pipe together and shook hands, and Boone returned to the fort.

Those inside the stockade suggested that the seven buffalo tongues
were poisoned, but Boone assured them that the Shawnees would not
attempt such a ploy. When the delicacies were sampled he proved to
be right.

As the men inside the fort discussed Hamilton's letter and Blackfish's
demands, Richard Callaway saw both as further evidence of Boone's
treachery. Boone explained again that his actions at Detroit and at
the Blue Licks had been a scheme to survive and return to fortify and
defend Boonesborough. Boone said that even with the overwhelming army outside, they might be able to negotiate a peace. "Boon was
blamed for this proposal; but he only meant to shake off responsibility,
and in going to make a treaty, he did it w. the intention of detaining
till the soldiers came." Samuel South, who was a boy present at the
discussion, later said about half the men wanted to surrender and half

wanted to fight. Boone asked for a show of hands or a step forward from those who wanted to surrender. "I will kill the first man who proposes surrender," Richard Callaway snapped. William Smith, who was second in command, advised that they reject the proposal and fight. Squire Boone added his voice to the discussion, saying he would fight to the death. The vote when it was taken was unanimous: they would fight. "Well, well, I'll die with the rest," Boone said.

Throughout his life Boone tried to avoid war by any means possible. But here he had no choice. The Shawnees were outside the fort and the vote had been taken. Still, it made sense to bargain for time before the killing started. Each additional day gave them time to strengthen the defenses and increased the chances that the Virginia militia might arrive with reinforcements. Boone and William Smith were chosen to parley again. Boone called to Pompey from the wall and a meeting was arranged for that afternoon.

As far as we know, Boone wore his hunting clothes to the meeting, but Smith came out dressed in a fine uniform, red tunic and plumed hat. Clothes then, as now, spoke their own language. "Dress served as a potent symbol of identity in an exotic world of strangers . . . Visibly stressing the military credentials of their own side, Boone and Smith reported that there were still more commanders within the fort." They all sat down on a panther skin in front of the fort and Blackfish asked for a reply to Hamilton's letter. Smith answered with great formality that the offer was indeed generous, but traveling all the way to Detroit would be a great hardship for women and children and old folks.

"I have brought forty horses and mares for the old people and women and children to ride," Blackfish answered. Boone thanked his Shawnee father, but said there were many leaders in the fort who had to be consulted. Blackfish agreed to another day of talks, but Boone later said he saw in the chief's eyes a hardening as he began to suspect that Sheltowee was just stalling. According to John Gass, "He saw that the indns were getting angry." Boone had promised months before to surrender the fort. So many delays did not bode well. However, Blackfish agreed to a list of ground rules for the duration of the negotiations. No Indians would come within thirty yards of the fort, and the settlers would not carry arms outside the fort. The Indians could help themselves to the cattle and crops they needed, while women would be free to go to the spring for water. But it was clear to Boone that this was the last delay they could arrange.

Blackfish's patience and willingness to negotiate and delay have seemed odd to many over the years. We don't know how much he trusted Boone to keep his word and surrender the fort as promised. What is clear is that he preferred to negotiate, hoping for a surrender, rather than to attack the fort outright. His reward would be greater if he delivered living prisoners to Hamilton in Detroit, rather than killing them in Kentucky and selling only the scalps. And though his army was much greater than the force inside the stockade, an assault on such a fort was by no means a sure thing. In fact, experience proved that without artillery it was almost impossible for an army of rifles and tomahawks and bows and arrows to take a palisaded enclosure with blockhouses at each corner. Though the roofs were not completed, the second stories of the blockhouses jutted out over the walls so riflemen could shoot at anyone attempting to climb or burn the palisades or ram the gates. Blackfish did not know how many men were inside the fort, and given such odds, his patience and willingness to negotiate show what a wise and experienced leader he was.

Since they knew their time was running out, those within the fort stepped up their defensive efforts. Riflemen stood along the walls and walkways showing weapons, and women dressed as men walked back and forth in front of the gate to make the attackers think there was a greater force inside the stockade than the sixty men. Those inside put dressed-up dummies at strategic places to look like additional defenders. Luckily Hamilton had been misinformed about the number of militia who had arrived in Kentucky that summer and had passed along this exaggerated figure to the Shawnees. There was a well in the fort, but it gave little water. Men had begun digging another well in the enclosure, and women took everything that would hold water to the spring and filled it. Indians watching called out to them, "Fine squaws, fine squaws!"

About noon on Tuesday Pompey approached the gate and shouted that Blackfish and the Shawnees wanted to look at the women in Boone's family. They had heard that Jemima was a great beauty. Boone replied that since her kidnapping Jemima and the other women were very much afraid of Indians. Pompey answered that they would only need to come to the gate where the warriors could see them. Hoping it would buy more time, Boone persuaded Jemima and several of the other women to step outside the fort. From the distance, where Blackfish and the other chiefs stood, Pompey yelled for them to let down their hair. "They took out the combs," Jemima's granddaughter later said, "and let their hair flow over their shoulders." The Indians appeared to enjoy the sight and then moved away.

Those inside the fort seem to have understood the request to see the women as a gesture on the part of Blackfish to show his appreciation and common humanity. The only resentment came from some of the men who were angry that Pompey was present. The huge black man had already irritated them with his strutting manner. As the translator, he knew he was essential, indispensable. It appeared he tried to infuriate them with his assurance and independence. They threatened to shoot him when he came within range again. Late in the day Pompey called out to the fort that it was time for an answer. Blackfish and Moluntha and the Shawnees had waited long enough. Boone and Smith and several others filed out to meet the Indians. Boone told his Shawnee father that the people inside the fort had decided to fight as long as one of them was alive. Blackfish appeared to be shocked, speechless, and then he told Boone that his answer put the Shawnees in an awkward position. Hamilton had told him to avoid a massacre. All wanted a peaceful resolution to this standoff. Blackfish suggested that they talk further, bringing chiefs from all the Shawnee towns to the meeting. Boone was surprised by the proposal and later told

Filson the added day of negotiation "sounded grateful in our ears." All along Boone had been hoping for some negotiated settlement, as had Blackfish. The two men understood each other and had a great deal in common. Boone agreed that several leaders from the fort would meet with the council of Shawnee chiefs the next day. The battle had been forestalled one more time.

On Wednesday, September 9, the women of Boonesborough prepared a large meal of venison and buffalo tongue, fresh corn and beans and squash and other vegetables, bread and milk. Tables were carried out to the meadow in front of the fort and the Shawnees were invited to the feast. The settlers hoped that with a lavish show of frontier hospitality they could demonstrate the confidence and affluence of the fort. If need be, they were prepared for a long siege.

After the feast was eaten, the Shawnee chiefs and the chosen leaders from the fort met at a spot chosen by Blackfish sixty yards from the fort, near the great elm, the Divine Elm, where the first Kentucky Convention had met three years before. The site was near the rim of the bank of the small stream that ran through Sycamore Hollow. During the previous night, Blackfish had hidden several of his best riflemen in the brush nearby. Nine of the leading men of Boonesborough were included in the delegation. Boone had instructed the riflemen in the fort to cover them from the loopholes. At the first sign of trouble they were to fire into the group without fear of hitting the settlers, "as they would be more likely, two to one, to hit an Indian than a white man."

Daniel Bryan described to Draper the seating arrangement. "They all met at the appointed place and seated in the following manner one white man and two indians one whiteman and two indians; on the back seat one indian behind every whiteman." Bryan said that each Indian who stood behind a white man carried a concealed tomahawk to prevent the whites from escaping. One chief present was named Black Hoof, another Black Bird. The Indians' faces were painted red and black for war.

After a round of formal introductions Boone pointed out that many of the Shawnees were not chiefs but young warriors. Blackfish sent some away, but Indians still outnumbered whites two to one. "Blackfish said that there was indians in that Army from twenty-four Different towns and that there must be one indian from every town." Both an American and a British militiaman kept minutes of the meeting, but the documents were later lost. Blackfish began by proposing to withdraw his army if the settlers would agree to abandon Kentucky in six weeks. This proposal was quickly rejected and Blackfish angrily demanded, "By what right did you come and settle here?" Boone replied that the region had been purchased from the Cherokees by Richard Henderson at Sycamore Shoals. Blackfish pretended he knew nothing about the Sycamore Shoals treaty and turned to a Cherokee present and asked if Boone's statement was true. The Cherokee answered that what Boone said was correct. Acting surprised, Blackfish said, "That entirely alters the case; you must keep it, and live on it in peace." Captain Smith later remembered that Blackfish proposed that both sides agree that the Ohio River was the proper boundary between them, but after a cooling-off period either side would be free to cross the river to hunt in the other's territory. Boone later told Rev. John Mason Peck that Blackfish's proposal was contingent on both sides swearing allegiance to the British Crown, "only submitting to the British authorities in Canada, and taking the oath of allegiance to the King." Blackfish had to return to Detroit with something for Hamilton.

Boone and the other men from the fort appeared to agree to the proposal. At the very least it gave them six weeks to strengthen the defenses and hope for the arrival of the militia from Virginia. It is interesting that in this instance Richard Callaway and the others seemed willing to play the same stratagem Boone had played at Chillicothe and Detroit, to pretend to be willing to submit to the Crown. It must have appeared necessary at the moment to prevent bloodshed. Who knew what would happen in the future if Blackfish withdrew his warriors across the Ohio? The Indians might never be able to assemble such a force again. "That Boone and his friends should have signed a treaty, in which the main condition was subjection to the . . . King of Great Britain, appears at first view a little more questionable," John Mason Peck commented. It is almost certain neither side had any intention of observing the terms of the treaty.

Blackfish then said he must explain to his warriors the intricate details of the agreement. He stood up and turned toward the Indians assembled at a distance. In a voice of great eloquence, sounding, some said, like a preacher, others, like a skilled orator, Blackfish addressed his army. Boone was only able to follow a few sentences of the speech, but they sounded consistent with what the chief had proposed. When he finished his address, Blackfish turned to the whites and said, "Brothers, we have made a long and lasting treaty, and now we will shake hands." Even though there were two Indians for each white, he told Boone and the others not to be alarmed, "when they were very loving, they took as near the heart as they could." He stepped up to Boone, his son, and embraced him. The other chiefs extended their arms to embrace the other Americans. The Shawnees said they would shake hands "Indian-style," with an Indian taking either arm of each white man. "This stratagem to captivate the whites had been foreseen by Boone, & according to his directions, as soon as the indns: commenced to grapple, & endeavor to secure the white men, a party in the fort, poured a full and heavy fire on them in the lump," Josiah Collins later told Draper. Boone and the others said later that they saw at that instant the whole treaty proposal had been a ploy. "But treachery took place," Nathan said, "and a scuffle ensued. My father threw Blackfish flat on the ground." The plan seemed to be to grab the men from the fort and wrestle or drag them over the nearby bank out of rifle range of the fort and hold them as hostages. When Blackfish "in that manner gave the word go the[y] all started to drag his man behind the clay Bank where they could murder them without any danger from the fort." With the leaders in custody under threat of torture and scalping and death by fire, the settlers would have to surrender the fort to the large Shawnee army. Boone had instructed his men in the fort to fire at the first sign of trouble, and they did. Blackfish had planted his marksmen nearby the night before, and as soon as the struggle began the Indians commenced firing too.

Some historians have suggested that Blackfish did not premeditate this attempt to take hostages, that he was negotiating the treaty and embracing the white leaders in good faith. Their argument is that had he planned to attack, he could have attacked earlier. It is more likely that his patience had simply worn out. Before, he had hoped Boone would surrender the fort without a fight. By the third day he knew the settlers would not surrender and that hostage taking was his only real chance to force a surrender. He knew the odds were long against him taking the fort by siege, without artillery, and he could not let his warriors return home empty handed, nor tell the British at Detroit that he had simply failed. Taking Boone and the others hostage seemed the only way to fulfill his complex obligations.

Richard Callaway was the first to throw off the Indians embracing him. As firing erupted from the fort and then from Indian rifles in the brush, the chief struggled with Boone and was thrown to the ground. A warrior nearby swung his pipe tomahawk and slashed Boone's back. All the Americans were powerful men and in the rage of the moment they overcame the warriors. Even so, it seemed a miracle that they freed themselves, since the whites were outnumbered two to one. John Mason Peck was as curious about the event as the historians following him would be: "Particular inquiries were made, by the author, of Stephen Hancock and Flanders Callaway, how it was possible for nine white men to overpower eighteen Indians. The reply was, that, expecting mischief, they were on their guard, and that Indians rarely possess physical powers equal to white men; but each declared he never could recollect how the feat was achieved. They felt assurance of success." According to Kentucky folklore, one Indian warrior was the equal of four regular soldiers, and one Kentuckian a match for two Indians. The clash in front of Boonesborough was often cited as evidence of this claim.

Boone later credited the sharpshooters from the fort for hitting enough Indians so he and his men were able to escape. "As Father used to say, it was this timely volley from the fort that saved the whites in council; and it was his opinion that when he threw Black Fish down, the other Indians thought he had fallen from a shot from the fort, and this, Father thought, probably added to their dismay and confusion." Squire Boone was hit by a rifle ball in the shoulder, but he was able to stagger back to the fort.

Boone had told the negotiators to leave their loaded rifles just inside the gate of the fort. As soon as they rushed inside they grabbed their arms and made ready for battle. The siege they had dreaded and prepared for had begun. The gate of the fort was closed and bolted.

CHAPTER TWELVE

Farthest Outpost of Rebellion

1778–1779 ⌣

After Boone and the other negotiators escaped from the treaty site and reached safety inside the fort, the firing from the fort and from the Indians in the field began in earnest. Young Ambrose Coffee lay exposed on the southeast blockhouse, watching the events unfold. Suddenly bullets began peppering around him, and when he dropped under cover and examined his clothes he found many bullet holes, though his body was untouched. "No less than fourteen bullet holes were made in his clothes, when he tumbled down into the bastion unhurt."

Suddenly the firing on both sides was deafening. The air filled with the stench of burned gunpowder. Children cried and women screamed, thinking the fort was about to be stormed. Dogs began howling in the compound and cattle bawled and horses ran to and fro, whinnying in terror. Cattle stampeded from one side of the enclosure to the other.

Squire Boone took his position at a loophole but found the pain from his wound so intense he could hardly shoulder his rifle. When things calmed down a little Daniel cut the bullet from Squire's shoulder, but the wound was so deep Squire was forced to retire to his bed. However, he kept an axe beside the bed to defend himself should the fort be taken. Luckily the tomahawk wound on Boone's back was neither deep nor serious. He took his place, directing both the fire and defensive activity. That afternoon the Indians made a charge toward the stockade, as if they planned to scale the walls, but under heavy rifle fire they retreated. The many trees, including the Divine Elm and stumps near the palisade, afforded the attackers ample cover. The banks of Lick Branch near the fort provided a blind where Indians could conceal themselves, as did an especially large sycamore log lying at the edge of the hollow.

As the firing continued, the men in the fort saw another weakness of their location. The ridges on both sides of the river were high enough to provide a view into the enclosure. An ambitious marksman from either side of the river could fire into the fort and could, of course, spy on the inhabitants. John Gass later said, "They shot into it from off both hills." The ridges were too far away for shooting with any accuracy, especially the south ridge, but the random shots killed livestock and added to the panic. It was real luck that the British had not supplied the Shawnees with swivel guns or cannon. Even one piece of artillery might have doomed the settlers.

Though primarily concerned with defending their lives and their families during the siege, the people of Boonesborough knew that a good deal depended on what happened there. With the new state government far away, engaged in a desperate war for survival and independence, the settlers were on their own. Boonesborough was the best known of the Kentucky settlements. If it fell, Harrodsburg and Logan's Station and the smaller enclaves in the wilderness would likely go also. If the forts were lost, Kentucky would be lost, and the British would control the Ohio Valley and be within striking distance of the settlements on the Holston and Clinch and Watauga rivers. Otis K. Rice says, "The determined defenders of Boonesborough did more than preserve their own station and others of central Kentucky; they enabled highly secret plans conceived earlier in 1778 by George Rogers Clark to reach fruition." Those inside the fort did not know that Clark, after taking Kaskaskia and Cohokia along the Mississippi, and the British fort at Vincennes in the Illinois country, planned an attack on Detroit, to break the British hold on the region.

In theory Richard Callaway was the ranking officer at Boonesborough, but Maj. William Bailey Smith had been commissioned commander of the fort after Boone was captured by the Shawnees. From most reports it appears that Boone was the actual leader. The firing from the outside kept up steadily through that first day and night and then the second day. The Shawnees and British had a considerable supply of powder and lead and they used it willingly. The walls of the fort crackled and thudded with the impact of bullets. Piles of harvested flax were scattered in the fields nearby, and during the night the Indians spread the flax along a fence that led to the edge of the fort. The next day they lit the flax to burn like a fuse that would set the fort on fire. Some men inside the fort risked their lives to crawl out under the kitchen wall and tear down the fence adjoining the palisades. They got back inside and the fence burned up, causing no harm.

On Friday, September 11, things were quiet in the morning. Some wondered if the Shawnees had retreated. But the gates remained closed, and later those in the fort looked out and saw the river was muddy below the fort and heard the sound of digging and roots being cut. A long cedar pole was seen moving, as though loosening the ground out of sight by the river. They guessed the Indians and British were digging a trench, or maybe a tunnel, toward the fort and under the wall, to blow up a section of the stockade, then rush into the enclosure. Or maybe they planned to tunnel under the wall and attack in the darkness. It was decided to dig a counter tunnel or trench that would intercept the tunnel from the river. At the same time, the men in the fort built a six-foot structure up over Henderson's kitchen from which to observe the enemy's mining. Intense volleys were exchanged all night while the opposing trenches were being dug. A slave named London, who was owned by Henderson and was an excellent marksman, crept out of the fort in the trench to get a better shot at the Indians nearby. In the dark, either side could aim only at the flashes or sounds of the other's weapons. London's gun refused to fire, and an Indian aimed at the snap of the hammer, or the flash in the pan, and killed him. London was a popular figure at Boonesborough and his death was a serious loss to the fort. In the heavy firing of the second night, a Dutchman named David Bundrin, an accomplished and courageous marksman, was looking through a porthole on the southwest side of the fort when a bullet struck him in the forehead. He died slowly, blood and brains leaking out of the wound as his wife, delirious with grief, thanked God "that the ball didn't hit him in the eye." Bundrin died before daybreak, just as Boone was ordering his men to cease firing and save their ammunition.

Jemima Boone was wounded slightly on one of the first days of the siege. She was constantly running back and forth carrying ammunition and drinks of water to the men. Standing in an open door she felt what might have been a slap on her backside. In fact, it was a bullet from the ridge across the river, so nearly spent it made only a shallow wound and fell out when she jerked the cloth of her dress. In the nineteenth century historians had trouble mentioning the wound because of its location. The bullet was sometimes described as hitting "the fleshy part of her back."

During the excitement of the siege, profanity was shouted between the fort and the enemy, but because of the delicacy of Victorian scholars such as Lyman Draper and the Reverend John Dabney Shane, little of the exact phrasing has come down to us. The "blackguarding," as shouted insults were called, is referred to, but not the words actually used. The most notable of the cussers was perhaps John Holder, son-in-law of the formidable Mrs. Callaway. Holder was one of those who dashed outside the fort to put out a fire the Indians had set, and as he made his sprint and quelled the blaze he hurled colorful language at the attackers. When he came back inside, safe but still swearing, Mrs. Callaway reprimanded him for his oaths, saying it would be more becoming to pray rather than to swear. "I've no time to pray, goddamnit," Holder snapped.

FROM THE beginning, the Shawnees had made attempts to set the fort on fire. Without artillery, fire was their best weapon against the log palisades. The efforts to set the enclosure ablaze intensified on the third night. John Gass would later say, "They shot arrows, with powder in a little rag, and a little punk. They set only one house on fire, the only shingled roof house there was there, Col. Henderson's." Warrior after warrior ran up to the fort and hurled torches made of hickory bark and gunpowder over the walls. Most of the torches fell harmlessly to the ground. Many Indians were killed because the torches they carried made them easy targets in the dark. Even if they carried the torches behind blankets, they had to expose themselves to throw them. When the burning arrows hit roofs, they could be swept off with poles because the roofs sloped inward, as Nathan Boone explained to Draper.

Anticipating the attempts to set the walls and roofs on fire, Squire Boone, always a resourceful tinkerer, had made squirt guns out of spare rifle barrels and bags of water that could quench blazes several feet away. Squire had even made a wooden cannon, with a gum tree log hollowed out with an auger and wrapped with iron bands, filled with powder and buckshot. While Squire was recovering from his wound, others took aim with his cannon at the Indians in the field. The results were not notable, and on the second try the whole thing exploded into splinters. From then on the Indians would taunt the fort, asking, "Why don't you fire your big wooden gun again?"

As the trench from the river got closer, men climbed on the new platform over Henderson's kitchen and hurled stones at the diggers. The rocks falling on their heads infuriated the Indian tunnelers. "Come out and fight like men," they shouted, "and not try to kill them with stones, like children." An old woman, Mrs. South, who heard the Indians cursing, asked the men not to throw any more rocks "for they might hurt [the Indians] and make them mad and then they will seek revenge." The men roared with laughter and kept repeating her warning as a joke for days.

Though he was not a digger, Pompey, the translator, seemed to participate in the tunnel building and was seen to watch the fort from a trench leading into the tunnel. His head would pop up one place, duck as men from the fort fired, then pop up at another place while they reloaded. A number of men had fired and missed him. His game was to show that he was too quick for them. The riflemen reloaded and each aimed at a different place along the rim of the trench. Finally, Pompey's head appeared just where a rifle was pointed, the trigger was squeezed, and his head appeared no more. According to Draper, it was William Collins who pulled the trigger. In other accounts it was William Hancock who killed the black interpreter.

The men in the fort began calling, "Where's Pompey?" The Indians answered in English or Shawnee, "Pompey gone hog hunting," or "Pompey ne-pan," meaning "Pompey is asleep." Before the siege was over they would admit, "Pompey nee-poo," meaning "Pompey is dead."

A rumor grew later that it was Boone who killed Pompey. But this is almost certainly not true. Boone was too busy organizing and directing the efforts to lie in wait for hours to shoot the interpreter. However, another story of the siege may have some truth in it. It seems a Shawnee brave liked to climb a tree within sight of the fort and turn, lifting his breechclout, then pat his backside, saying without need of a translator, "Kiss my ass." The tree was almost two hundred yards away, and though several men had shot at the taunting brave, they had missed.

The legend is that Boone took his finest rifle, which Draper says he called Tick-Licker because it could flick a tick off a bear's snout at a hundred yards, put in an extra load of powder, and resting the barrel on a loophole sill, took careful aim at the Shawnee mocker. When he touched the trigger the brave fell from the tree, crashing through the limbs until the body thumped on the ground. The butt patter was seen no more. Draper says, "Such a fatal shot deterred the other Indians from venturing up to remove the body . . . till after nightfall, and the hogs meanwhile rooted around the corpse." It is a colorful story, but again it is unlikely Boone was the rifleman, and the fort had many superb marksmen.

An American flag, likely an early version of the stars and stripes with the stars in a circle, called the 1777 National Flag, flew on a fifty-foot pole at the center of the fort. Firing at the pole hundreds of times, the Indians finally broke the top off. Those inside took down the pole, replaced the flag on a repaired shaft and planted it in the sky again. The flag remained there.

One of the stranger anecdotes of the siege concerns a Shawnee warrior who had a wooden false face decorated to look like an Indian wearing war paint. Hidden behind a large sycamore log about a hundred yards from the fort, he raised the false face on a stick to draw fire from the fort, then dropped the false face and fired at the exposed marksman in the loophole. He did this a number of times, until finally the men in the fort caught on. Watching the log carefully, a marksman aimed not at the false face but at the visible part of the body holding it up. When he fired, the Indian crawled away and the painted wooden face was seen no more above the log. Draper tells us, "After the siege, signs of blood were found at the spot, as well as the veritable false-face punctuated with two or three bullet holes."

The determined marksmanship from the walls took its toll on the Shawnees. One Indian had his knee shattered while hiding behind a stump close to the wall. Another was shot by three riflemen while lounging on a fence as much as three hundred yards away. The advantage of the long rifle over the British musket was proven again and again. It took longer to reload the rifle than the musket, but even that problem had been lessened. Neal O. Hammon has written, "Some unknown genius discovered that a greased patch placed over the bullet lessened the time needed to reload, and became a gas check to utilize the full force of the exploding powder . . . shot for shot, the rifle would kill more men at a greater distance using only half the powder and lead."

Finally, on Thursday night, September 17, ten days after Blackfish's army had arrived, the Shawnees made their maximum effort to burn the fort. Fire seemed their only hope, and again and again they rushed forward to fling torches onto the roofs. They had, however, learned their lesson and tried to conceal the torches with blankets until the last moment before the torch was thrown. Fire arrows were shot also, but they had little effect. The firing from both sides was so intense the sky was lit up with exploding gunpowder. Moses Boone, who was ten, later recalled that the light was so bright "any article could be plainly seen to be picked up, even to a pin."

William Patton, who had been away hunting when the siege began, hid in the woods watching the assault from a distant hill. The fires were so bright, the shouting so intense, the whoops of the Indians and screams of the women and children in the fort so loud, he was sure Boonesborough had fallen and made his way to Logan's Station to announce the sad news. In fact, the roofs of several cabins were set afire that night. Men and women rushed to tear away burning boards, throw water on burning logs. Luckily it began to rain during the night. And many Indians who had carried torches to the walls were killed. As the rain put out the last fires, all got quiet.

On Friday morning the Shawnee camp in the peach orchard appeared to be abandoned. A few shots were fired from here and there, but the firing got more and more distant. Some bands of Indians seemed to be going north toward the Ohio, others southwest toward Logan's Station and Harrodsburg, and still others south. Fearing a ploy, those in the fort waited until afternoon before opening the gate and venturing out. They saw where the tunnel from the river had caved in because of the heavy rain, and found the remains of several large torches that had been intended to set the stockade on fire. They discovered the camp in the peach orchard really was deserted. The Shawnees and the British militia had gone. They had taken with them all the bodies of Indians killed but left Pompey's body lying near the river.

Boone examined the tracks and found that about thirty Indians, probably Cherokees, had headed south. Other bands had dispersed toward the other settlements. It was later learned that Blackfish had agreed that the warriors could take some scalps and lives from the other settlements so as not to return empty handed to their Ohio towns. Blackfish knew from the beginning it was unlikely he could take Boonesborough in a siege. There is only one instance in Kentucky history of Indians, or anyone else without artillery, taking a palisaded and defended fort — Kincheloe's Station on September 2, 1782. That's why the chief had been willing to negotiate, hoping for a surrender. His attempt to seize hostages at the "treaty" ceremony was his best hope for victory. Siege had never been a Shawnee style of warfare. They were most effective at small raids, ambushes, and surprise attacks on isolated cabins and settlements. Their genius was for the decoy and ambush. After the siege was called off, the scattered warriors were more successful at taking scalps and killing whites than the big army assembled at Boonesborough had been.

Boone and the residents of Boonesborough picked up 125 pounds of lead on the ground and stuck in the logs of the fort. For eleven days Blackfish and the British had thrown everything they had at the defenders. And Boonesborough had survived. Later on that Friday the people at Logan's Station saw a group of horsemen approaching. Assuming it was Indians coming to attack, now that Boonesborough had fallen, the settlers were astonished to recognize their own men who had gone to help Boonesborough. "Why, they are our boys!" a woman shouted. The returning fighters said they could understand why William Patton had thought Boonesborough was defeated, with all the firing and screaming of the night before.

During the attack, the cattle inside the Boonesborough stockade had been given meager rations. A good many of the livestock had been killed by enemy fire and eaten by the defenders of the fort. The cows and horses, hogs and chickens, that had survived were half starved, and as soon as it was clear the Shawnees were gone, men hurried out into the gardens that were left and gathered cabbages to feed the stock. Some cattle outside had been killed by the Indians, and others were taken when the Shawnees withdrew. At least one cow that was led away got loose and returned to the fort a few days later with the strap of buffalo hide tied to her horns dragging behind her.

The people of Boonesborough stepped out of the stockade into the open carefully, blinking to see if their freedom and survival were real. A sweet wind leaned across the peach orchard where so many Shawnees had camped. They inspected the collapsed tunnel from the river that had come so close to the fort's wall. Some think that if Boonesborough had fallen, the other forts in Kentucky would likely have been taken also. The British and their Indians allies would have been free to attack the western settlements of North Carolina, Virginia, and Pennsylvania.

Boone sat down to write to Rebecca back in North Carolina to tell her of the ordeal and survival of the settlement. He told her that they had lost two men, Bundrin and London, and that four people had been wounded, including himself, Jemima, Squire, and Pemberton Rollins, who had had his arm broken by a bullet. He estimated that the Shawnees had lost thirty-seven braves. In the letter, Boone described his months of captivity with the Shawnees, his daring escape, and the intervening months while Boonesborough prepared for the attack. He told her he would return to North Carolina for his family as soon as he could, but at the moment he had to defend himself against a charge of treason from Richard Callaway and Benjamin Logan. A court-martial had been scheduled and officers of the recently arrived Virginia militia would hear the case. Boone showed his anger against the British, swearing uncharacteristically in the letter to Rebecca. "Goddamn them," he wrote, "they had set the Indians on us." Daniel Bryan, Rebecca's cousin, recalled the sentence many years later, and he remembered that Rebecca was so offended by the profanity, she had the oath cut out of the letter after it was read to her and burned it. Others present also recalled that Boone mentioned the court-martial in the letter.

When Boone talked to Filson five years afterward, he neglected to refer to the trial for treason. It was probably the greatest humiliation of his life, and he rarely talked about it later. After his extraordinary efforts to save Boonesborough from attack in February, to save the salt boilers at the Blue Licks, run the gauntlet, play his maneuver with

Blackfish and the British at Detroit, escape and walk back to Boones-borough in four days, furiously complete the fortification of Boones-borough, lead a dangerous scouting raid into Ohio, and finally organize and supervise the defense through an eleven-day siege, he was to be tried for attempting to betray the settlement.

A few days after the siege ended, Kenton and Alexander Montgomery returned from Ohio, where Boone had left them to scout and spy on the Shawnees. And a company of militia arrived from Virginia to relieve the three forts. But it is likely Boone was mostly occupied with the approaching court-martial. We know the details of the court-martial proceedings because a young trader named Daniel Trabue was present at Logan's Station when it occurred. Trabue wrote an account of his time in Kentucky, and the account was preserved and is now published. When the court-martial was held at Logan's Station, a number of settlers from the region attended. Out of loyalty to Boone, few ever mentioned it later, and apparently the records of the proceedings were destroyed. According to Trabue, the charges brought by Callaway and Logan were (in Draper's transcription):

1. That Boone had taken twenty-six men to make salt at the Blue Licks, and the Indians had caught him trapping for beaver ten miles below the Licking, and [he] voluntarily surrendered his men at the Licks to the enemy.

2. That when a prisoner, he engaged with Governor Hamilton to surrender the people of Boonesborough, to be removed to Detroit, and live under British protection and jurisdiction.

3. That returning from captivity, he encouraged a party of men to accompany him to the Paint Lick Town, weakening the garrison at a time when the arrival of an Indian army was daily expected to attack the fort.

4. That preceding the attack on Boonesborough, he was willing to take the officers of the fort, on pretense of making peace, to the Indian camp beyond the protection of guns of the garrison.

In conclusion Colonel Callaway charged that Boone favored the British cause and had used every opportunity to further the Tory effort. He urged that Boone be stripped of his commission in the Kentucky County militia.

Boone remained silent while all the charges were made. Finally, he rose to defend himself, explaining that he had surrendered the men at the Blue Licks in February to save their lives. "Capt. Daniel Boon sayed the reason he give up these men at the blue licks was that the Indeans told him they were going to Boonsbourough to take the fort. Boon said he thought he would use some stratigem." Otherwise they would have been killed and Boonesborough attacked when it was defenseless. It was true he had pretended friendship with the British at Detroit but only as a way of buying time and saving himself and the other prisoners. He had made the expedition to Paint Lick Town to find out where the Shawnees were. He had negotiated with Blackfish outside the stockade to buy time. His men had never been beyond the rifle range from the fort, as was proved in the melee after the final negotiation. His escape from the Shawnees, his rebuilding of the fort, his actions during the siege, proved his loyalty to Boonesborough and the American cause.

After Boone made his presentation, the presiding officers deliberated among themselves. The accusers, Boone, those looking on, waited in the charged air. In a short while the officers pronounced Boone innocent of all charges. To show their respect for him and his actions in the defense of Boonesborough, they recommended that he be promoted to the rank of major. Almost everyone there, except Callaway and Logan, and perhaps Andrew Johnson, who had spread the rumor of Boone's treachery in the first place, was happy with the outcome. As far as we know Boone never spoke to Callaway again. When he returned to Kentucky the next year, he moved six miles north of Boonesborough and cleared a new place in the wilderness called Boone's Station.

Trabue's final comment on the court-martial was, "Boon after that time appeared alwaise to be on the side of this government. How ever,

Col. Calleway and Capt. Ben Logan was not pleased about it." One
of the best statements of support for Boone at this time came from
Simon Kenton, who knew the complex dangers of the frontier as well
as anyone. When told of the accusations against Boone his response
was quick. "With an emphatic nod of his head he replied, 'They may
say what they please of Daniel Boone, he acted with wisdom in that
matter.'"

While the characterization of Richard Callaway that has come
down to us is of a quarrelsome, defensive man, he was also recognized
as bold and brave, instrumental in the survival of Boonesborough.
And Benjamin Logan was one of the notable men of his time, rising
to high rank in the militia, almost elected governor of Kentucky later.
It is important to consider what it was about Boone that irritated and
aroused the suspicions of these men so thoroughly. Certainly his familiarity with Indians made him suspect. But Logan and Callaway may
have sensed that in some ways Boone, like other gifted and innovative
people, played the role of double agent throughout much of his life. It
could be said that in that doubleness, seeing the world at once from
two or more points of view and acting on that multiple vision, lies the
very essence of originality and greatness. F. Scott Fitzgerald wrote in
The Crack-up, "The test of a first-rate intelligence is the ability to hold
two opposed ideas in the mind at the same time, and still retain the
ability to function." It was possibly this difference, this knack for dealing with Indians, this doubleness, that made men such as Callaway
and Logan suspect and despise Boone. Complex and original people
know that truth is rarely simple, almost never all of this or all of that,
but elusive minglings and mixtures, evolving shapes, with tinctures of
irony and paradox. Boone's actions often reveal his understanding and
even relish for the complexity and shadings of experience. He could
not have played the roles he did if at times he had not been essentially
an Indian, at other times a patient, solitary explorer, and beholder of
the wild, and at other times still a leader of settlers, a surveyor, trader,
soldier, legislator.

Though Richard Callaway would be killed by Indians within eighteen months, his body scalped and mutilated and rolled into a mud hole, the Callaway family kept stories of Boone's alleged treason alive for the next century. In all their versions of Boone's offenses, it was his ease and friendliness with the Indians that figured most prominently in their accusations. His friendship with the Shawnees was usually advanced as evidence of his disloyalty to the American cause, as if no one who got along so well with Indians was to be trusted. The fact of his friendship with Blackfish was evidence enough of treachery. "Boon never deserved anything of the country," Callaway's daughter Kezia would later say. The dream of cooperation and peace between whites and Indians that Cornstalk and Boone and many others had shared was lost forever in the rage of the Revolution, in the fires fanned by the British on the frontier, and in the greed and fear of the relentless stream of settlers into the western lands.

As soon as he was acquitted and promoted at Logan's Station, Boone made preparations to go to his family on the Yadkin. And as he traveled east he met a company of militia on their way to reinforce the settlements in Kentucky. He stopped at Watauga and encouraged his old friend James Robertson to migrate to the western region. Robertson would eventually settle at French Lick on the Cumberland River, under the auspices of the Transylvania Company, and found the settlement that would become Nashville, rising to be one of the leading men of Tennessee. Traveling with Boone to the Yadkin were Jemima and Flanders Callaway and his son-in-law William Hays.

Boone and his party reached the Yadkin by November 9, 1778, but we have few details of the reunion. He and his large family lived that winter in a cabin that belonged to Billy Bryan, husband of Boone's sister Mary. Billy was also Rebecca's uncle. That winter Boone hunted in the nearby hills and mountains, familiar to him from his youth.

There has been much speculation about trouble between Daniel and Rebecca that winter. Speaking to Filson, Boone would only say,

"The history of my going home, and returning with my family, forms a series of difficulties, an account of which would swell a volume." Nathan Boone, who was not even born until almost three years later, said the differences between Rebecca and Daniel at that time were caused by her reluctance to return to Kentucky. This explanation is certainly plausible. She had endured three years of hardship in Kentucky, lost her oldest son to Indians, survived one major attack on Boonesborough in 1777, assumed that she had returned to North Carolina a widow with a family of many children. She had already survived more than most women might in several lifetimes. Why would she want to go back to Kentucky, however enthusiastic and committed to the settlement there Daniel was? Some have implied that this was the time when Rebecca presented Boone with the "surprise" baby that could not possibly have been his. But this suggestion confuses two different periods in the Boones' marriage, his supposed return to Virginia in 1762 and his return from Boonesborough in 1778. No child was born to Rebecca between 1775 and 1781. Others have suggested that Rebecca's Tory sympathies made her reluctant to return to Kentucky. Some of her kin were committed to the Loyalist cause and a few fought for the British. After Boone's disappearance and presumed death, they might have persuaded her of the rightness of the royal cause. On the other hand, no one ever reported Rebecca making a statement of sympathy for the British side.

It is possible that rumors of Boone taking a Shawnee wife in Chillicothe had reached Rebecca's ears. When Andrew Johnson returned to Harrodsburg and Boonesborough and told everyone how happy Boone was among the Shawnees, he may have added that detail. Imagine a wife, worried about her missing husband, hearing that he is living content among the Shawnees, adopted by the chief, with an Indian bride. There is no firm evidence that this happened, but it is possible that it did, or that Rebecca thought that it did. If this was the case, she may have taken it badly, having already heard of his friendly relations with the Indians and his life of ease and privilege among the Shawnees.

What is certain is that Boone spent much of the winter, spring, and summer recruiting families to resettle in Kentucky. It was one of his special gifts. He was always able to persuade others to join his moves to new lands. His enthusiasm, confidence, and charisma were brought out by this activity. He was a storyteller who inspired others with his tales of adventure, of the wonderful land across the mountains, and the promise of a glorious future. Rebecca may have looked upon her husband, for a time, as a kind of Pied Piper, who led others to danger and their doom.

CHAPTER THIRTEEN

With Chain and Compass

1779–1782 ◡

In the years 1780–82, as Boone became in succession a land locator, or "jobber," a legislator, and a licensed surveyor, his vision of life
in the wilderness of Kentucky was complicated by conflicting land
claims, continued Indian raids, lawsuits, theft of a considerable sum
of money he carried for others. Boone's sense of purpose and calling
was challenged, diverted, and blurred, as he found himself involved in
businesses for which he was not suited, in disputes that puzzled and
embarrassed him. What had promised to be a simple life of hunting
and trapping and locating land for others became a series of aggrava-
tions, failures. The new life he sought for himself and his family proved
to be elusive. And in the background loomed the larger conflict of the
Revolution, with the British and their Indian allies determined to drive
the Americans out of Kentucky.

Among those who would join Boone in the long trek back to Kentucky in the late summer of 1779 were many sympathetic to the Tory
cause. Most just wanted to get away from the conflict and violence
and go ahead with their lives on the frontier. Some were related to
the Bryans, or were friends of the Bryans. According to William
Clinkenbeard, interviewed by John Dabney Shane in the 1840s, so
many Tories were running away from North Carolina a traveler "could
hardly get along the road for them," and most of those who went to

Kentucky at this time were Tories. Clinkenbeard was probably exaggerating, but many Tories did believe their chances of survival were better in the West where loyalties were, hopefully, less an issue.

The Virginia legislature had passed a law offering cheap land to any who would clear a few acres and build a cabin in Kentucky. "The right of preemption to four hundred acres of land was accorded to all who had settled in Kentucky before January 1, 1778. Those who had actually made improvements might claim an additional one thousand acres of adjoining land." For new settlers the price was $2.25 for a hundred acres, up to four hundred acres. An additional thousand acres could be bought for $400. First a settler obtained a warrant for a certain number of acres, then made an entry for a particular piece of ground with the land office. Next, the property had to be surveyed, and the survey registered with the land office. Only then would the land office award a patent "which according to the statute, carried 'absolute verity.'" The final step would be for the county surveyor to survey the entry with callings based on the celestial meridian rather than magnetic compass readings.

By 1779 many of the would-be settlers resented the earlier military warrants issued by the colonial governor, Dunmore. It seemed unfair that royal grants giving the finest land to officers would still be valid. But those who succeeded in settling on a tract of available land could claim a "pauper warrant," issued on credit by the county court to settlers with no money. Most business in Kentucky at that time was conducted on credit, since there was little cash to be had.

Among those who agreed to take advantage of the bargain lands were a large number of Boone's own relatives, his brothers and sisters and their spouses and children. As we know, the Boones tended to move together as a clan. Almost certainly they looked up to their famous kinsman as the leader of the extended family. Ted Franklin Belue writes, "By September 1779 Daniel had little choice: He had to return due to the insolvency of his Transylvania claims." Since Boone's mother, Sarah Morgan, had died in 1777, the terrible Year of the Three

Land-Office Treasury WARRANT, No. 1243

To the principal Surveyor of any County within the Commonwealth of Virginia.

THIS shall be your WARRANT to Survey and lay off in one or more Surveys, for *Daniel Boone* his Heirs or Assigns, the Quantity of *One Thousand* Acres of Land, due unto the said *Daniel Boone on Preemption* as by Certification the Commissioners of the Kentuchey district and in Consideration of the sum of *four hundred pounds* current Money, paid into the publick Treasury; the Payment whereof to the Treasurer hath been duly certified by the Auditors of Publick Accounts, and their Certificate received into the Land Office. GIVEN under my Hand, and the Seal of the said Office, on this *twenty Eighth* Day of *December* in the Year One Thousand Seven Hundred and *eighty*

Treasury warrant, 1775. In 1775 Kentucky was officially part of Fincastle County, Virginia. All land purchases and grants were in theory from the Crown. (Courtesy Kentucky Historial Society.)

Sevens, and was buried in Joppa Cemetery in Mocksville, North Carolina, beside her husband, Squire Sr., and their son Israel, the most important of Boone's ties with the Yadkin was gone.

Boone's large party left the Yadkin in September 1779. More than a hundred started out in a spirit of exhilaration, and were joined by others at Moccasin Gap, including the family of Abraham Lincoln, grandfather of the Great Emancipator. Many were poor people without mounts or packhorses. Some walked barefoot all the way to Kentucky, carrying children and their belongings on their backs. On the other hand, Billy Bryan had twenty-eight packhorses loaded down with his equipment and household goods. Boone had about six horses loaded with kettles and farming and blacksmith tools. He had been given two small cannon by Gen. Griffith Rutherford of the regional militia. One of the swivel guns was for the use of Boone at his new station, and the other for William Bryan at Bryan's Station. But the artillery pieces were so heavy the horses that carried them died, and after being dragged for miles behind another horse, the cannon were hidden on Yellow Creek, within six miles of Cumberland Gap, to be retrieved later. As it turned out, they never were recovered, though Boone was still concerned about them as late as 1817. Jemima, riding double across a flooded river with a small girl, was thrown into the water when the horse spooked. She and the girl were rescued and Jemima joked that the ducking was bad, "but much less so than the capture by the Indians."

Apparently Boone himself reached Logan's Station by October 14, for he is recorded as being present at the Virginia Land Commission hearing there that day. He may have ridden ahead to take care of business about his own claims. Boone and his large party of new settlers reached Boonesborough in late October 1779 and found the fort had fallen into disrepair again. In the thirteen months Boone had been away the stockade and buildings had been left unattended. One British traveler of the time compared the smell of the settlement to the sewers of European cities. Almost everything seemed to have fallen into neglect. Boone's importance as a leader is shown again and again by the chaos and negligence that reigned in his absences from Boonesborough. Other high-ranking officers were there while he was away, but none seems to have taken the trouble, or had the authority, to keep the place repaired and clean. Whatever his pretensions to leadership and authority, and his courage in war, Richard Callaway seemed to do little except look after his own interests. At the time Boone arrived, Callaway may have been away from Boonesborough, escorting prisoners, including Henry "Hair Buyer" Hamilton, to Williamsburg.

Boone stayed at Boonesborough only long enough to build a cabin six miles northwest of the fort, on land originally claimed for James Hickman in 1774, where he had cleared a cornfield before leaving Kentucky the year before. A number of family and friends followed him there and they called the new location Boone's Station. Snow had already fallen and the winter of 1779–80 proved to be the worst anyone could remember and was called the Hard Winter ever afterward. Working in a foot of snow, the settlers built a cluster of half-faces, cabins open on one side.

Meanwhile, the Virginia Land Commission that had arrived in Boonesborough awarded Boone fourteen hundred acres of land north of the Licking River, but his title to the nearby land on Boone Creek, where Boone's Station was being built, would prove to be not so clear, contested as it was by two other claimants. The Bryan relatives moved farther north to Elkhorn Creek, to establish Bryan's Station northeast of Lexington, on land that had already been surveyed by John Floyd for Col. William Preston in 1774. Later the Bryans would try to buy the land from Preston, only to find that he had already sold it to one Joseph Rogers.

On Christmas Day 1779 Boone led his family and fellow settlers to Boone's Station. Snow was deep and getting deeper. On December 19 John Floyd had written to Col. William Preston, "The day is so cold . . . and the ink freezes every moment so that I can't make the letters." It was so cold men found it hard to load their rifles or to fire them once they were loaded. Cattle froze to death in the woods. Wild turkeys, weakened by the cold until they couldn't move, smothered to death as their nose slits clogged with the ice of freezing breath. In the deep snow it was hard for animals and people to move through the woods. It was almost impossible to trap or to hunt. Daniel Trabue at Logan's Station wrote, "A number of people would be Taken sick and did actuly Die for the want of solid food."

Boone had brought a substantial supply of corn from North Carolina and he shared his hoard with his neighbors until it ran out. He also shared the game he killed in the frozen woods. It was the custom among white hunters, as among Indians, to divide their kills. No one who lived through that winter in the hastily built huts of Boone's Station ever forgot it.

Luckily there were groves of sugar maples nearby, and as the sap began to rise from the roots in February the settlers ventured out into the woods to tap the sugar trees. While the men hunted and began to clear cornfields, the women and children hurried to collect sap and boil it down into maple syrup and sugar. Starving buffalo came out of the woods to drink the sweet sap. "They could hardly drive them off they were so poor," one of Boone's relatives would later recall.

As spring came to Boone's Station, the men built more substantial cabins and fortified them with a stockade. The trees were cleared away around the palisades. The lesson of two years before had been learned. They knew they could not assume they were safe from Indian attack.

Boone and Rebecca would stay in the cabin at Boone's Station for about three years. Around 1783, when his claim to the land at Boone's Station was contested in the complex suit called *Hickman v. Boofman*, they would move on to a new and larger cabin near Marble Creek, a few miles to the southwest of Boone Creek. It is not certain when they made the move. Even though he was popular, the recognized leader among a large extended family and many friends and acquaintances, it is clear that Boone preferred his privacy. When given the option, he moved off into the woods away from neighbors. It was this tendency that gave rise to the jokes and legends about how he moved on when someone settled within miles of his cabin. In the folklore, when other settlers arrive within hearing distance or even a day's travel, the punch line was always the same: Boone says to Rebecca, "Old woman, we must move on; they're crowding us."

Most folklore and legends grow out of a grain of truth. Boone's love of solitude in the woods and privacy in his dwelling was a well-known fact. But the reality of his life, especially in the period at Boone's Station, was that Boone and Rebecca had five children still at home — Israel, in his twenties, Rebecca and Levina who were in their teens, and the younger boys Daniel Morgan and Jesse Bryan. Also with the family were six orphaned cousins of Rebecca's. Susannah and her husband, Will Hays, and their children also lived with them. As many as nineteen people lived in the big log cabins Boone built at Boone's Station and then on Marble Creek. Many of Boone's children and grandchildren, brothers and their families, lived nearby at Boone's Station.

In this period Boone continued to hunt and trap and grow corn and livestock and perhaps tobacco, but his life took a major turn during this period also. He was now forty-five, a patriarch, one of the best-known men on the frontier. He was famous for hacking Boone's Trace, for building Boonesborough, for rescuing Jemima and the Callaway girls, for living among the Shawnees and escaping, for directing the defense of Boonesborough. He very likely knew Kentucky better than any other white man, from the mountains to the Bluegrass, from the licks to the Falls of the Ohio. He knew the Green River valley and the Cumberland valley. He not only knew the land intimately but was famous for knowing it.

After the Virginia Land Commission opened its office at Boonesborough in the fall of 1779, Boone found himself in great demand by settlers, immigrants, speculators, to find land for them, to survey it, and to register the claims. Because of his fame and popularity, his recognized authority as a scout and hunter, he was drawn more and more into the whirlwind of the lucrative land business as agent and surveyor, and he also became a speculator himself.

Before and after he became a licensed surveyor, Boone worked as a land "jobber." That is, he located vacant tracts for those who had bought treasury warrants or who planned to do so. Any person desiring land in Kentucky could purchase such a warrant from the land office, entitling them to a stated number of acres that had not been entered for another claimant. Some of those who purchased warrants did not even come to Kentucky, but hired at long distance a locator such as Boone or Simon Kenton or John Floyd to choose an available tract. And most who did come to Kentucky to find land needed a guide who was familiar with the tracts already surveyed.

The big problem was there were no accurate maps of the region at that time, so even the best surveyors like Floyd had trouble knowing exactly where the boundaries of someone else's claim might be. Add to that the fact that many military warrants for veterans of the French and Indian War had been sold or traded, or in some cases never claimed, and the difficulty of locating available land was compounded. And even Floyd had undercalculated acreage of lands he surveyed by 10 or 15 percent.

To add to the confusion, the state of Virginia continued to sell land warrants long after all the best land had been claimed. Many of the later surveys done on treasury warrants were run over former claims. The latecomers hoped the original owners would forget about their claims, not pay their taxes, or decide Kentucky was too dangerous for settlement. Perhaps worst of all, Kentucky began to be overrun by "outlyers," men who arrived in small groups and traveled around building cabins in the woods, hoping to claim they had made improvements. Their "cabins" were often little more than heaps of logs. Then before they had a certain title to the piece of land, they would sell the improvement. Neal O. Hammon writes, "Some even sold the same tract to several different people."

Boone had first worked as a locator for James Hickman in 1774. He continued to work as a land jobber off and on for the rest of his years spent in Kentucky. It was one of the best ways of earning a living. He was famous for knowing the landscape of Kentucky, and he was much in demand, but he knew the land as a hunter, not as plots already registered in the land office. Many of the tracts he located or later surveyed overlapped with other claims. As the years passed, these "shingled" boundaries became a major cause of grief and ugly litigation, and a source of wealth for young lawyers such as Henry Clay. It was inevitable that those who lost their land would blame the man who had located it in the first place.

In 1783 Boone would pass an exam and be licensed as a deputy surveyor by the Commonwealth of Virginia. He was handsomely paid for finding and surveying land for others all over Kentucky, and it is said he was sometimes paid in parcels of land. "He should have part of the land claimed for his Trouble and immediately it became a custom to give one Half of the land for clearing it out of his office and this is what Boone got for Clearing out those four tracts." "Wm. Mountjoy, surveyor of Pendleton Co., surveyed it for John Grant Aug. 29, 1779 — one half of which the said Daniel [Boone] was to have for locating same." Whether Boone was given land as fees for his locating and surveying or not, he acquired parcel after parcel. He was well on his way to becoming a major landowner himself.

As one of the explorers and founders of Kentucky, Boone probably felt he was entitled as much as anyone else to share in the exploding prosperity. Nathan Boone said at one time his father may have claimed as much as a hundred thousand acres of the Great Meadow. Extant records show that Boone actually owned, at most, about 31,267 acres.

Boone was a careless businessman but not necessarily a careless surveyor. "He had no problem running simple square or oblong surveys," Nathan Boone told Lyman Draper, "and he could do the necessary calculations. I would suppose that in the woods he could run a line as straight as the next man." About the technical details of basic surveying, Boone was probably as competent as many at the time. The problem was that much of the land he surveyed overlapped with tracts claimed by others. Owners and would-be owners and lawyers were involved in boundary disputes and entangled in litigation for years to come. Officials in the land office often didn't know when claims were "shingled" since they had no way of knowing exactly where the boundaries of the claims were relative to other claims. Later the joke was that Kentucky surveyors were never accurate except by accident.

Boone's future problems were caused less by his surveying skills than by his disdain for the details of business and legal matters. Often he did not bother to register deeds properly after land was surveyed or to look up records in the county office. Or he would not follow up on a business venture to see it through, preferring to move on to another, and then another. Boone's genius in the woods and at scenes of danger seemed to desert him in the courthouse, law office, counting room. An honest man himself, he assumed everyone else was honest also and that a man's word was his bond. Again and again Boone was cheated, robbed of claims, perhaps because of faulty surveys, but more often for lack of documents, vague certificates. Boone's greatest weakness was also one of the most admirable features of his character: he trusted people. And once a claim was contested, his tendency was to abandon it and move on. He seemed unable or unwilling to adapt to the aggressive commercial and legal culture that was overwhelming the new territory. The dream of hunting and peaceful coexistence with the Indians in the garden of Kentucky was gravely threatened. He must have seen no alternative but to be a part of the new culture and over the next few years entangled himself in messes of duplicated claims, deals gone sour. He was often blamed for claims lost by others, and as a peaceable and honest man he felt obliged to pay those who accused him. He lived as a hunter, dividing what he had among others. That was the code of the woods and the frontier, share and share alike. That was the code of the Indians.

"Hospitality and kindness are among the virtues of the first settlers. Exposed to common dangers and toils, they became united by closest ties of social intercourse," John Mason Peck would write. That sense of community may have been common among the very first settlers, but it was quickly lost in the rush to develop the new territory. The hunger to acquire land seemed insatiable and reckless. Around this time John Todd, who lived at Lexington, wrote to a friend, "I am afraid to lose sight of my house lest some invader should take possession."

Nowhere else in North America was the change from frontier to a culture with pretensions to polite society, gentility, and commercial prosperity more rapid than in Kentucky. Between 1775, when Boone built Boonesborough, and 1792, when Kentucky was admitted into the union as a state, the Bluegrass region was transformed from a wilderness of buffalo, Indians, and hunters to a district of plantations, towns, horse farms, courthouses, ballrooms and racetracks, law offices and schools. The first Latin school in Kentucky was established in Lexington in the early 1780s. Small holdings were replaced by large plantations producing hemp worked by slaves. The transformation must have been disconcerting for many, especially those as fond of privacy as

Boone. As Otis K. Rice writes, "In the spring of 1780 three hundred boatloads of settlers arrived at the Falls of the Ohio alone."

The irony was probably not entirely lost on Boone at this time that his exploration, his organizing, his opening of Boone's Trace, had helped bring on this flood of greed and contention and pretension. As the Indians retreated farther north of the Ohio River, because of attacks on their villages, so did the game. Heavy hunting and trapping, and wanton killing of buffalo, took their toll. Soon no buffalo at all were to be seen at the licks or in the meadows. Bears could be found in the mountains to the east, but you had to go farther and farther to hunt them. The beavers thinned out quickly along the streams and soon disappeared. The canebrakes were cut down as the land was cleared, and soon the whispering cane where panthers and bears and Shawnees and turkeys hid was just a memory.

It is painful to watch Boone at this period move out of his chosen calling of hunter, scout, leader, and settler, into realms for which he was so ill suited. There are hundreds of documents, letters, in Boone's handwriting, pertaining to his land surveys and speculations. The business grew so rapidly he may have lost count of some of the parcels and acres and titles. "The 2000 acres of Land you ar to make me a titel to out of your 5000 acres," Boone wrote to one client, "I have sold to Mr. James Parbery and Desire you would Make him a Deed."

Boone located and surveyed claims for former Transylvania Company associates such as Thomas and Nathaniel Hart. He was getting into the big time and becoming one of the big men of the frontier, like the Harts, like Henderson and Logan. In February of 1780 Boone agreed to collect money and land certificates from a number of friends, including the Harts and his son-in-law Will Hays, and to ride to the capital in Williamsburg to purchase treasury warrants for more land. With each treasury warrant, he and his friends and acquaintances could claim a specified number of acres wherever they could find land not already surveyed and registered. The Harts gave him twenty-four hundred pounds, and his son-in-law Will Hays four hundred pounds for a land claim on the Licking River. It was said that Boone carried with him more than twenty thousand dollars in Virginia money devalued by inflation and that all that money was stolen from him at an inn in Virginia.

Recent scholarship has thrown new light on the incident, though many aspects of the episode remain a mystery. It is not known who Boone's traveling companion was on that journey to Williamsburg. Examining Fayette County, Kentucky, land records and court documents, and reports of the robbery in the July 26, 1780, issue of the *Virginia Gazette*, the scholar Neal O. Hammon discovered that Boone was robbed of 6,061 pounds' worth of land certificates at the home of one "James Byrd of James City County" on the night of March 20, 1780. James City County is the county where Williamsburg is located. The certificates, signed by the clerk of the Commissioners Court, stated that the citizen named was eligible to buy vacant land in Kentucky at a designated price.

The distance from Boone's Station to Williamsburg was over six hundred miles, and much of that distance was over very rough trails. The winter of 1779–80 was the coldest on record, and no doubt Boone and his companion had to travel much of the way through ice and snow. Until the travelers passed beyond Cumberland Gap going east, there was still a danger of being attacked by small bands of Indians. Experienced travelers usually slept in thickets or canebrakes, with no fires, so as not to be spotted by brigands or Indians. But with weather so bitter cold they probably had no choice but to keep a fire burning all night.

John May, who traveled this route in the other direction a little later in the year, recorded these details: "[It is] uninhabited Country the most rugged and dismal I ever passed through, there being thousands of dead Horses Cattle on the Road Side which occasioned a continual Stench; and one Half the way there were no Springs, which compelled us to make use of water from the Streams in which many of these dead animals lay."

The route Boone and his companion would have taken, after they crossed through Moccasin Gap and then the Holston at about the site of later Kingsport, Tennessee, would take them east to Wolf Hills (later Abingdon) and on toward Draper's Meadows, on the New River. From there they proceeded to Roanoke, and then down the James River valley to the tidewater region. It shows the extraordinary trust placed in Boone that so many would ask him to carry their savings and purchase certificates over this dangerous route to Williamsburg.

Taverns in those days were often just private dwellings beside the road where guests were served in the dining area and some travelers unrolled their blankets or bearskins by the parlor fire. Those paying more for lodging would sleep in an upstairs bedroom. It seems almost certain that the food or drink Boone and his associate were served at James Byrd's house was drugged, for as soon as they retired to their room and locked the door, they fell into a deep sleep and never woke until daylight. When they did rise they found the door open, the saddlebags rifled, and Boone's papers scattered on the floor. Some money that Boone had been carrying was found in bottles in the basement, but most of the money, and the certificates for land, were gone, all except Boone's own warrants, which he must have kept in a separate place, probably his personal wallet or budget. The landlord, of course, declared his innocence and claimed he had no idea what they were talking about. The house was searched, and the yard and stables were searched. Only the small amount of money in the bottles in the cellar was ever found.

History and folklore are filled with stories of travelers robbed and even murdered at inns. Certainly the American frontier was familiar with many such stories. But James City County was far from the Virginia frontier, in the oldest and most settled part of the Old Dominion. We cannot know if Boone failed to take necessary precautions or was acquainted with those who managed the tavern. The best-known account of the robbery, told by Nathan Boone to Draper, describes an old woman hiding in a chest or wardrobe until the men were asleep and then fleeing with the notes. Nathan Boone said, "The door was found open next morning." But the court records of Fayette County make it clear Boone was robbed of a sheaf of land certificates. This is an odd theft because the certificates were numbered and could be traced after they were used. A good guess is that the thief thought he or she was stealing paper money in the dark and was disappointed to find that many sheets were certificates for land that had to be purchased, located, surveyed, then registered in the land office, and probably threw them away or burned them.

The price of land was inflating rapidly in Kentucky. By 1780 the land in the Bluegrass region had been claimed, some tracts by two or three parties at once, and the old military warrants for veterans had been taken up, many sold to speculators. Boone had gone to Williamsburg with his friends' money and certificates to buy preemption warrants at the old low price of forty pounds per one hundred acres, or four hundred pounds per thousand acres, which was "dirt" cheap compared to the selling prices in Louisville and Lexington. (British currency still seemed to be the medium of exchange in land transactions, even as Americans were fighting the Crown for independence.)

After the robbery Boone had no choice but to ride back to Kentucky empty handed and face the investors who had lost their cash and their land warrants. Some spread rumors that Boone had stolen the money and certificates and made up the story of the robbery. It was a painful and humiliating episode, second perhaps only to the court-martial of eighteen months before. Luckily the Harts and Hayses and some of the others trusted Boone implicitly and never asked him to cover their losses. He was sorry especially because others had lost so much. It would seem that many of Boone's friends recovered at least some of their losses, for "Receipts from Public Auditors," June 23, 1781, in the Land Office of Fayette County, records a list of figures: "We the Public Auditors of the Commonwealth of Virginia do hereby certify that William Hays hath delivered us the Treasurers receipt for four hundred pounds . . . and that the said William Hays is entitled to one thousand acres . . . on preemption of waste or unappropriated Lands within this commonwealth . . . given under my hands this 23rd June 1781 T. C. Randolph."

Thomas Hart wrote a strong statement of trust in Boone to his brother Nathaniel on August 3, 1780:

> I feel for the poor people who perhaps are to loose even their preemptions by it, but I must Say I feel more for poor Boone whose Character I am told Suffers by it, much degenerated, must the people of this Age be, when Amoungst them are to be found men to Censure and Blast the Character and Reputation of a person So Just and upright and in whose Breast is a Seat of Virtue too pure to admit of a thought so Base and dishonorable I have known Boone in times of Old, when Poverty and distress had him fast by the hand, And in these Wretched Sircumstances I ever found him of a Noble and generous Soul despising every thing mean.

HART'S GENEROUS testimonial to Boone's character rings with conviction. It squares with everything we know about Boone's actions, then and later. He had known the Harts since his days on the Yadkin. The integrity and goodwill he seemed to bring to his business make even sadder the defeats he suffered again and again in his ventures. A similar pattern can be seen in the lives of other frontiersmen. The famous scout Simon Kenton ended his life of daring exploits and notable successes with little wealth to show for all his deeds. Likewise with the most famous man on the Kentucky frontier after Daniel Boone, George Rogers Clark.

It is likely that Boone visited Lt. Gov. Henry Hamilton in prison on this trip to Williamsburg. Hamilton had been escorted to the capital by Richard Callaway along with other prisoners taken by George Rogers Clark at Vincennes the year before. Hamilton was brutally treated, kept in a cold, filthy dungeon because of the perhaps exaggerated reports of him buying Kentucky scalps from Indians. After he was released Hamilton wrote an account of the incarceration, and the visit by Boone: "A Major [Boone] and thirty-seven Americans with their arms fell into the hands of a party of Indians, not one of whom was put to death, and the very officer having escaped from them, had the generosity to go to Williamsburg at the time I was confined in the dungeon there to remonstrate against the injustice and inhumanity of the Governor [Jefferson] and Council of Virginia."

THE WORLD that Boone had found in Kentucky in 1769 was beginning to fade away. In May of 1779 Col. John Bowman of the Virginia militia had led a force of three hundred men across the Ohio to attack Shawnee towns. In a dawn raid on Chillicothe, Blackfish was wounded. But a number of Shawnees had already moved farther north and west. On that raid Bowman lost nine of his men and killed only two Shawnees. But Blackfish, or Cottawamago, died of his wounds a short time later. The great leader, Boone's adopted father, was gone. In his account of the expedition Daniel Trabue wrote that Bowman "made a broken trip of it, got some of our best men killed, and killed very few Indians."

Conditions in Kentucky worsened in 1780. Hunters and settlers continued to be killed. Many simply disappeared. "Hardly a week passes without someone being scalped between this and the Falls," John Floyd wrote to Col. William Preston on May 31, 1780, "and I have almost got too cowardly to travel about the woods without company." Not only was Kentucky changing quickly, but the Shawnee world that Boone had gotten to know in 1778 was rapidly ceasing to exist. Along with the buffalo, the Indian survivors were moving westward in front of the relentless wave of settlers. They still made raids into Kentucky, but their beautiful towns, so gracefully situated and constructed on the Scioto and Little Miami rivers, were becoming ghost towns, soon to be plowed under by the first generation of white farmers.

A number of Shawnees, encouraged by the British, were still determined to resist the settlements in Kentucky. On June 24 and 25,

1780, respectively, a force of Indians, with British soldiers who did have artillery, captured both Ruddle's and Martin's stations and took many prisoners. After the forts fell, Henry Bird, the British commander, was unable to prevent his Indian allies from abusing, torturing, and murdering prisoners. On the march to Ohio many of the prisoners, in George Morgan Chinn's words, "fell by the wayside and were summarily relieved of their suffering by the tomahawk." Captain Bird claimed later to be appalled by the cruelty of his Indian allies and, unable to prevent the prolonged torture, cut short the campaign. Had Bird continued the expedition with his artillery he might have taken most of the forts in Kentucky.

To answer successful raids by the British and Indians on Ruddle's Station and Martin's Station in Kentucky, and devastating attacks on travelers on the Ohio River, George Rogers Clark organized an army of eleven hundred in the summer of 1780 to return to Ohio. Boone, eighteen years older than Clark, agreed to serve as a scout. On August 1 the Americans crossed the Ohio and headed north. They found Chillicothe deserted and burned to the ground. The remaining Shawnees had retreated north to the town of Piqua. As the Americans approached, the Shawnees at Piqua killed many of the prisoners they had taken at Ruddle's and Martin's stations. Both sides fought with a fury many present had never seen. The Americans killed and took scalps and even ripped scalps from bodies in graves. One witness reported seeing a woman's belly ripped open and her body "otherwise" mangled. After an intense and sustained battle, the Shawnees pulled back from Piqua and the Americans looted and burned the town and surrounding cornfields. Clark and his men returned to Kentucky feeling they had avenged the raids on Ruddle's and Martin's stations. The Shawnees moved farther north and built new towns.

It was a time of increased violence along the Ohio River. "Once a keelboat came floating down the Ohio River 'with every person on it dead,' Benjamin Allen remembered. 'Found an Indian's fingers in it that had been chopped off.'"

THE RAIDS into Kentucky by scattered bands of Indians continued. In March 1780 Col. Richard Callaway, Boone's old nemesis, had
been killed as he attempted to build a ferry with his slaves for use
on the Kentucky River near Boonesborough. He had escorted Henry
"Hair Buyer" Hamilton as a prisoner to Williamsburg and while in the
capital had secured the valuable ferry contract from the government
of Virginia. "In the town of Boonesborough, in the county of Kentucky, across the Kentucky River to the land on the opposite shore, the
price for a man three shillings and for a horse the same, the keeping
of which last mentioned ferry and emoluments arising therefrom, are
hereby given to Richard Callaway." His body was scalped and disfigured, thrown into a sinkhole. Hunters at this time were attacked in the
woods almost daily.

Much of the lore about Boone's resourcefulness has its origins in
this period. In one of the best-known tales, Boone is growing tobacco
at his new claim at Boone's Station. As Peck tells the story, "At a short
distance from his cabin, he had raised a small patch of tobacco to supply his neighbors, (for Boone never used the 'filthy weed' himself) the
amount perhaps of one hundred and fifty hills." Some have said that
Rebecca smoked tobacco in a pipe. It is late summer and he is hanging
racks of tobacco leaves high in his barn to cure when four Shawnee
warriors appear below. "Yes, Boone, we have got you again," they say.
"We carry you off to Chillicothe this time." Boone greets them warmly
and tells them how glad he is to see his Shawnee brothers again. High
on the racks above them he grabs a great armful of dusty, drying tobacco and hurls it down into their faces below. Stunned and blinded,
the Shawnees cough and stumble, wiping the stinging dust from their
eyes as Boone jumps down and runs to his cabin for his rifle. "The old
man, in telling the story, imitated their gestures and tones of voice with
great glee." Nathan Boone, talking with Lyman Draper years later,
discounted the story, saying that neither his father nor his mother ever
used tobacco in any form.

That summer of 1780 Boone and a large party of men hunted deer south of the Kentucky River. So many settlers had poured into Kentucky that cloth was very scarce. They needed the deer hides to make buckskin clothes. One evening by the campfire Boone warned that he heard or sensed Indians nearby. He quietly directed his men to roll up some of the hides they had taken in blankets and arrange them around the campfire, then hide in the trees with their rifles. All night they waited and near dawn shots were fired, thudding into the blankets. Then the Shawnees rushed into the camp with their tomahawks and were killed or routed by the hidden hunters.

While hunting by himself on Slate Creek, Boone was fired upon and he jumped into the nearest thicket and worked his way downstream into a canebrake. Holding his rifle aimed at an opening where he was sure the Indian would appear, he was taken aback to see two warriors emerge from the woods. If he shot one, he could be killed by the other before he could reload. Pondering what he might do, he waited until the Indians were in line, one behind the other. Taking careful aim, he killed one and wounded the other, who dropped his gun and fled. Boone took the better Indian rifle and threw the other away. Since Boone later claimed he was sure he had killed only one Indian in his life, this story is probably not true.

The stories about Boone continued to multiply. Boone himself told anecdotes and created anecdotes that became the stuff of legend. But stories about some figures spread and grow, are repeated and multiplied, as naturally as honeysuckle covers a road bank. It is a phenomenon well known in all cultures and times. The things most of us do are forgotten, however novel or exceptional they may seem at the time. But for some, their every act seems to generate a legend that thrives like a seed in rich soil. At some point whether the story is true or not doesn't much matter. It's the color, the novelty, the twist, that counts. The hero is mostly a name to which the deeds and exploits, qualities of character, can be attached. The figure becomes a springboard for the folk imagination, for collective memory and record of a culture. In early American frontier history the two figures who seemed to catch the folk imagination most intensely were Daniel Boone and John Chapman, or Johnny Appleseed. In both cases the subjects were real historical figures who did many unusual things. But in the folk imagination, they quickly became symbolic, exemplars of deeds and characteristics a culture aspired to and wanted to be remembered for. The stories of figures like Boone and Chapman help keep a culture alive and help people remember who they are, or at least who they would like to be.

One of the stories about Boone rooted all too much in fact occurred in October 1780. Returning from Clark's raid into Ohio, Daniel and his younger brother Ned stopped to rest their horses, loaded with game killed on the way home. While they paused in a meadow, Ned suggested they crack some walnuts or hickory nuts ripening in a grove nearby. Boone warned that this was a place where they were likely to see Indians. Ned teased Daniel for his fear and began to crack nuts on a rock. While Ned was occupied, Boone saw a bear in the woods, followed and shot it. "Edward [Ned] sat down to crack some hickory nuts — a bear came Near by them[.] Danl. Took his Rifle ran & shot the bear." Suddenly shots rang out in the woods and Boone realized they had walked into such an ambush as he had feared. Looking back, he saw Shawnees gathered around Ned's body. "We have killed Daniel Boone," he heard one of the braves exclaim. The legend was that even Rebecca said Ned looked very much like Daniel.

Boone had no choice but to run and hide in a canebrake. The Shawnees sent their dog into the cane for Boone and he had to kill the dog and fade farther into the brake. Lying flat, he watched as the Shawnees found their dead dog, cursed the thicket, and turned away. After all, why risk hunting through the cane when they had just killed the great Daniel Boone. Running all night, Daniel reached Boone's Station by morning and without pause organized a party to return to the scene of Ned's death. As they approached the nut trees, they saw a wildcat eating Ned's flesh. Daniel Bryan later said that Ned's head had been cut off by the Shawnees as evidence that they had really killed Daniel

Boone, but it is more likely they just took his scalp. Boone and his men followed the trail of the Shawnees all the way to the Ohio River. But it was too late; the warriors had already crossed. On the way back to Boone's Station, Daniel and his son Israel and a nephew-in-law named Peter Scholl stopped near the Blue Licks to kill game for Ned's widow, Martha, sister of Rebecca, and mother of five children.

With the death of Ned, Boone assumed an even larger responsibility as head of the extended family. His many obligations as provider and protector no doubt made it seem even more necessary to add the profits of locating and surveying land to his income as hunter and trapper and farmer. And to his already multiple tasks he soon added another: legislator. He was elected to represent Kentucky in the Virginia legislature when the session was convened the next spring.

By then, the Virginia legislature met in Richmond, not colonial Williamsburg. The session opened May 7, 1781, but soon had to be adjourned, as Cornwallis and the British army were approaching the city on the James. The feared cavalry commander Lt. Col. Banastre Tarleton, "Bloody Tarleton," was directed to capture the lawmakers. Tarleton had made his reputation in the Carolinas, where he never took prisoners. "Tarleton's Quarter," the Overmountain Men had shouted at Kings Mountain October 7, 1780, meaning, "We won't take prisoners either."

As Tarleton and his dragoons approached Charlottesville, the legislators slipped away to the west. Boone and a friend from Kentucky, John Jouett, stayed behind to save some of the horses. Horses were much sought after by the invading army. As Boone and his friend rode away from Charlottesville on June 4, 1781, they were overtaken by a unit of dragoons. Dressed in his hunting clothes, Boone was not suspected of being a lawmaker, and chatted several minutes with the commander, possibly Tarleton himself. When they came to a fork in the road, John Jouett, hoping to get away from the British, thoughtlessly said, "Wait a minute, Captain Boone, and I'll go with you." They were arrested and put in prison.

Boone was kept under arrest for a while with other local officials and then given a parole. One story is that he was locked in a coal house and passed the time by singing, as he had often done alone in the wilderness. Col. William Preston wrote to John Floyd on June 17, 1781, from Fort Chiswell, Virginia, that Boone had been taken prisoner. In any case, Boone was let go in a few days, and there has been a good deal of speculation ever since about why he was released so quickly. His descendants said Boone had to swear an oath to never take up arms against the Crown again. Detractors have pointed to the oath as yet another example of Boone's willingness to cooperate with the British when it suited him, evidence of his opportunistic, wishy-washy character. Others have suggested it was Rebecca's Loyalist relatives who got Boone released so quickly. Nathan Boone, our best source for many aspects of Boone's life, merely said, "My father was conveyed to the British camp and put into a coal house . . . He very probably explained his title of captain by referring to his old Dunmore commission. My father also may have pretended contentment and sung songs while confined." Someone hearing the story in the nineteenth century would have thought of Paul and Silas, described in Acts 16:25 as jailed for preaching and singing hymns in chains until an earthquake shook down the jail and freed them. "Boone was reimbursed for his trouble and attendance of the Legislature 2900 pounds of tobacco."

By June of 1781 Lord Cornwallis's campaign was beginning to fall apart. Morale was low in the British corps and he was running out of men and supplies. The British were in no condition to take more prisoners. The oath was probably understood as a mere formality on both sides. As soon as he was released, Boone rejoined the legislature where it had reconvened at Staunton. There is no evidence that Boone was a very active or effective legislator at this time. He was out of his element in committees and long meetings conducted according to parliamentary procedure. He was awkward at the deal making and exchanges of favors, which are the very essence of political success. He would never become an effective politician as some contemporaries such as Isaac

Shelby and James Robertson would, and he was anything but a backroom man or lobbyist. He returned to Kentucky for the summer and continued with his farming and surveying.

Whatever his contribution to the legislative process, Boone must have been aware of the impression he made on the other legislators. While others wore fine coats and silks, in the company of Thomas Jefferson, Boone wore his hunting clothes, appearing to some more Indian than white. "I recollect very well when I saw Col. Boone," John Redd told Draper. "He was dressed in real backwoods stile, he had a common jeans [rough twill] suit, with buckskin leggings neatily beaded. His leggings were manufactured by the Indians."

Returning to the assembly in the fall, Boone came by way of Pennsylvania and stopped in Oley to visit relatives he had not seen in decades. He was probably in no hurry to join the lawmakers, and when he did arrive in Richmond he stayed away from meetings so often, J. P. Hale tells us, the speaker gave an order "that the Sergeant-at-Arms attending the House take in his custody Daniel Boone." It seems likely he was out hunting instead of sitting in the chamber.

DANIEL AND REBECCA'S last child, Nathan, had been born March 2, 1781. It was Nathan who would live far into the next century and spend three weeks talking with Lyman Draper about his father. Nathan's wife, Olive Van Bibber, would also add valuable information to the interviews. The story is that Nathan was born when Boone was away, and several other babies were also born in the Boone family. Asked if he could identify his own baby, he picked out Nathan.

By the time the Virginia legislature began its session that fall, Cornwallis was trapped on the peninsula at Yorktown as Washington and Lafayette and Rochambeau closed in and began a siege, and the French navy blockaded the Chesapeake, preventing the British navy from coming to his rescue. Cornwallis surrendered his forces on October 17, 1781. The main campaign of the Revolution was over, but there would be continued action in the South and New England, and bloody fighting in the West, especially in Kentucky, before the treaty was signed in 1783.

Apparently defeated in the former colonies on the Atlantic, the British had no intention of giving up their claims to the interior, the Ohio Valley and forts such as Detroit. They still controlled Canada and could send their forces south across the Great Lakes any time they chose. And they still had powerful Indian allies in the Shawnees and Mingoes and Delawares and Wyandottes in the region. The war in the West was far from over. In fact, 1782 proved to be Kentucky's "Year of Blood," one of the deadliest in frontier history. The violence in the Ohio Valley escalated early in the year and never let up. In March a party of Pennsylvania militia crossed the Ohio in retaliation for Indian raids and attacked the Moravian Indian settlements of Gnaddenhutten, Salem, and Shoenbrunn, killing ninety to a hundred unarmed men, women, and children. Those Indians had been converted by the Moravians and were pacifists. Col. David Williamson led the raid, and one explanation for the brutality was that he and his men saw an Indian woman wearing a dress that had belonged to a white woman killed in an earlier Indian attack. As Neal O. Hammon describes the event: "On March 5, 1782 Williamson and volunteers [from Pennsylvania] rounded up most of the missionary Indians in the area and confined them in some outbuildings . . . The next day the mission Indians were taken out, three-at-a-time and executed with mallets or clubs. Twenty-nine men, twenty-seven women, and thirty-four children were killed." After those at Gnaddenhutten, which means huts of mercy, were killed, more Indians were brought from the village of Salem and executed. The massacre at Gnaddenhutten was one of the worst atrocities of the Revolutionary era and set off a new round of retaliatory raids from the Ohio tribes. Within days an army of Wyandottes attacked Estill's Station in Kentucky and captured a girl and the slave named Monk Estill. They killed the girl in front of the stockade and took Monk prisoner.

Monk Estill is a well-known figure in early Kentucky history. When the Estill family first came to Kentucky they lived at Boonesborough, and Boone knew James Estill and his family and Monk there. James Estill, Monk's owner, was away when the kidnapping occurred, but as soon as he returned he organized a party of eighteen men to pursue the Wyandottes. The posse caught up with the Indians at Little Mountain on March 22, 1782, and fought an intense battle that lasted for two hours.

Monk shouted to his owner that twenty-five Indians opposed the whites. Estill split his force into three groups to complicate the attack. He and six others were killed and seven wounded. Approximately seventeen Wyandottes were killed. Monk escaped during the battle and carried a wounded man all the way back to Estill's Station, twenty-five miles away. For his valor he was freed by the Estill family and lived a long life, noted for his orchards, and later his son became a well-known Baptist preacher. Monk Estill was very likely the first free black man in Kentucky, one of four thousand African Americans estimated by Filson to reside in the region in 1784.

In June of 1782 another American militia returned to Ohio to avenge the many Indian attacks across the Ohio River. Led by Col. William Crawford, who had worked as a scout and surveyor for George Washington, the force of five hundred was lured deeper into the interior and defeated by the Indians on the upper Sandusky River. Crawford was taken prisoner and tortured, along with a surgeon named Dr. Knight. Crawford, Dr. Knight, and eight other prisoners were taken to Half King's Town on the upper Sandusky on June 10, 1782. Simon Girty was among the party of Indians and promised to help the prisoners. As it turned out, Girty was unable or unwilling to aid them. On June 11 all the captives were painted black, sign of a death sentence, and four were tomahawked and scalped. The rest were then taken to a Delaware town nearby, where all but Dr. Knight and Colonel Crawford were killed by women and boys.

At four o'clock in the afternoon a fire was made and Dr. Knight and Colonel Crawford were beaten by all present and bound to separate posts. Speeches were made, reminding those present of the Gnadden-hutten massacre, and Crawford's ears were cut off. Then the Indians took turns prodding Crawford over his naked body with burning poles. Women threw live coals on the ground and made Crawford walk on them. Crawford begged Girty to shoot him, but the "white" Indian laughed at him.

After two hours Crawford was pushed face down into embers and scalped. An old woman threw coals on his mutilated head, and he was made to walk around the post as the Indians jabbed him with burning sticks. Dr. Knight was taken away, but later reports said that after Crawford was unconscious and could not be revived for more torture, he was roasted over the fire.

The British Loyalist officer Capt. William Caldwell, who was present at the torture, wrote to his commanding officer at Detroit two days later, "Crawford died like a hero; never changed his countenance, tho' they scalped him alive, then laid hot ashes upon his head; after which they roasted him by a slow fire." Accounts of the torture of Crawford inspired even greater rage and fear among the residents of Kentucky.

THE FURY OF the Indian attacks increased, and with experience the raids were conducted with added cunning. In August 1782 a small party of Indians attacked Hoy's Station and captured two boys. It was a diversionary raid, to draw the militia away while the main force of Indians made their attack elsewhere. Captain Holder and a company followed the party with the kidnapped boys and were defeated on August 14, losing four men. Meanwhile Boone was organizing a force from Fayette County. Holder's group returned and reported their losses, and Boone realized things had taken a very serious turn.

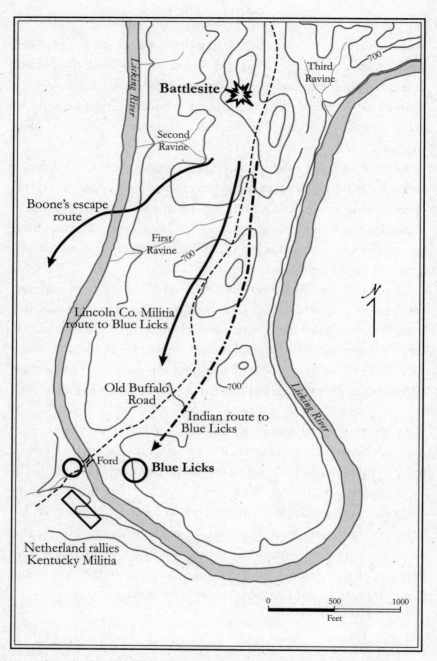

Map of the Battle of the Blue Licks. On the morning of August 19, 1782, the Kentucky militia pursued the Indians and British forces, which had attacked Bryan's Station, to the Licking River. Boone warned that an ambush was likely in the woods across the river. (Courtesy Neal O. Hammon, 2005.)

CHAPTER FOURTEEN

Father, I Won't Leave You

1782 ↳

At least three hundred warriors were gathering in Ohio in August 1782 to attack the Kentucky settlements. Led by British officers and Wyandottes, the army included Delawares, Mingoes, Miamis, as well as some Shawnees and Cherokees. Perhaps there were more than five hundred or six hundred. Before they left Ohio, Simon Girty, the white man raised by Indians, who had joined the British and Indian forces in 1778, roused them with a passionate speech. He concluded his oratory with this paragraph:

> Brothers, the intruders on your lands exult in the success that has crowned their flagitious acts. . . . They are planting fruit trees and ploughing the lands where not long since were the cane break and the clover field. Was there a voice in the trees of the forest, or articulate sounds in the gurgling waters, every part of this country would call on you to chase away these ruthless invaders, who are laying it waste. Unless you rise in the majesty of your might, and exterminate their whole race, you may bid adieu to the hunting ground of your fathers, to the delicious flesh of the animals with which they once abounded, and to the skins with which you were once enabled to purchase your clothing and your rum.

It is impossible to read Girty's words without hearing the truth in them. By 1782 the Shawnees and the Mingoes and Delawares and

Wyandottes knew it was now or never. Either they drove the white settlers out of the Great Meadow or they would lose forever their finest
hunting ground and therefore their relatively luxurious lifestyle on the
rivers in Ohio. What had once been Indian backyards had become Indian graveyards instead. The Iroquois had been driven from their lands
in New York and forced to surrender to General Sullivan in 1779. George
Rogers Clark had already taken forts farther west along the Mississippi.
The buffalo were rapidly vanishing from the Middle Ground. As the
British war back east wound down after Yorktown in October 1781,
the Ohio Indians felt more desperate about their future than ever. As
Colin C. Calloway says, "Burned villages and crops, murdered chiefs,
divided councils, and civil wars, migrations, towns and forts choked with
refugees, economic disruptions, breaking of ancient traditions, losses in
battle and to disease and hunger, betrayal to their enemies, all made the
American Revolution one of the darkest periods in American Indian
history." The war had promoted unity among the Indian nations and
then destroyed that unity. The desperation in Girty's speech was real
and justified. They had to act immediately, and they had to win.

Simon Girty was one of the most controversial figures on the American frontier. Captured by Indians as a teenager in 1756 along with his
three brothers, raised by Senecas in the western region of New York,
he served as a scout and interpreter for the Americans at the beginning of the Revolution but switched to the British side in 1778 when he
was not paid the two dollars a day he had been promised. Living primarily with Wyandottes, he was fluent in all the Indian tongues. He
befriended both Boone and Simon Kenton when they were captives of
the Shawnees, but because of his leadership in raids on Kentucky and
his presence at the torture of Colonel Crawford, he became a hated
man on the frontier, viewed as a devil, a fiend of demonic cruelty. Following his exhortations, he and his brother George helped lead the raid
on Bryan's Station a few miles northeast of Lexington on August 16,
1782, along with three British officers, William Caldwell, Alexander
McKee, and Matthew Elliott.

The attack on Bryan's Station began with eerie silence. The Indians osmosed through the woods in the night and early morning and took positions under cover around the fort. The Indians were not certain how many men were in the fort or how many had been drawn away by the diversionary raid on Hoy's Station a few days earlier. With the Indians were prisoners taken two years before at Ruddle's and Martin's stations. No one is sure why the prisoners were brought along to observe the attack.

Bryan's Station is always referred to as a station and not a fort because it was founded as a private settlement by the Bryan family. It had, however, grown quickly, attracting many residents. With a palisade wall, and fortified with blockhouses at the corners, the enclosure would fit most definitions of a fort. According to Neal O. Hammon, "The fort [Bryan's Station] in 1782 was said to be one of the largest in the West, at 150 feet wide by 600 feet long."

The forty-four men inside the fort kept watch at the loopholes and shot one Indian who ventured into the open. The settlers had not had time to bring the cattle inside the stockade or to fill their water buckets at the spring. One of the springs outside the walls had been covered and could be reached by a trench, but apparently the trench was unfinished, or the covered spring had gone dry in the hot August weather. Most accounts describe the necessity of going outside the gate to get a supply of water. A hundred acres of corn and other vegetables spread out in front of the fort.

Two men — Thomas Ball and Nicholas Thompson — were sent out before dawn as messengers to Lexington. They gambled that the Indians would stay hidden and let them through rather than reveal their presence, and they won that gamble. It is possible that the whole Indian force had not arrived that early in the morning and that Indians kept arriving and taking their positions throughout the morning. It is also possible that the full force of Indians that had crossed the Ohio never arrived at Bryan's Station, some staying near the Licking River in hopes of staging an ambush later.

The settlers inside the fort were desperately in need of water, and it was decided to let the women and children and some slaves go out to the spring, as if no Indians were suspected. Again, they gambled that the Indians would not want to give away their positions and numbers. Later accounts claimed that only white women went out to the spring, but it is likely children and slaves joined them. The survivor Grandmother Tomlinson would say, "It was decided to act for a while as if we did not suspect the ambushcade by the spring . . . We were not all to go in a crowd, but stringing along two or three together." Before the women and children and slaves ventured outside, a prayer service was held inside the fort. Grandmother Tomlinson later told the *Madison Democrat* that "from that awful hour I date my hope of heaven." The water carriers took off their moccasins and filed out through the gate, carrying every noggin and piggin available.

Led by Jemima Suggett Johnson, the procession strolled to the spring. They saw moccasins in the brush and a hand holding a tomahawk but pretended not to notice. "They were not twenty steps from me, and I trembled so I could hardly stand." The white women and children and servants chatted as if unconcerned. They were covered by rifles from the fort but were still exposed to rifle fire from the surrounding woods. Because the spring was shallow in the August drought, they had to tediously dip water with gourds to fill their vessels.

The Indians and British watched, perhaps astonished by the boldness of the women and children and slaves. And then they were thrilled to think their presence was unsuspected. They imagined they still controlled the element of surprise and those inside the fort must think the Indian who had been shot earlier was a lone scout. As the sun rose and birds sang in the trees, the Indians let the party return to the gate with splashing buckets and kettles. The men welcomed them at the gate and closed the big doors. There were tears of relief and hugs all around.

This episode in the siege of Bryan's Station, often retold over the years, has a resounding significance in the story of the frontier. Though overshadowed by the men in most histories of heroic action in the set-

tlements, it can't be repeated enough that the women made it possible
to claim and hold land in Kentucky and elsewhere.

IN THE AUGUST heat it is unlikely Bryan's Station could have held
out for long without the supply of fresh water brought in so boldly by
white women, children, and slaves at dawn. As the sun got higher and
the day hotter, the Indians in the woods, assuming they had not been
spotted, waited for the men to open the gates and go out to tend the
stock and work in the fields. But the gates remained shut and all was
quiet except for a crow here, a squirrel chattering there. It has been assumed by most historians that a large force of Indians and British militia surrounded Bryan's Station that day but remained hidden in the
woods. The British officer Caldwell later said three hundred Indians
took part in the raid. But most accounts mention the eerie silence and
the spooky sense of a vast number lurking out of sight. Apparently the
large force was never actually observed by those inside the fort.

Both sides knew it was almost impossible to take a twelve-foot-high
stockade without artillery. Girty and Caldwell had no artillery, but
those inside the fort had no way of knowing that.

Girty sent a band out into the open on the far side of the fort beyond
the spring, as a bait to draw men out of the fort. Deciding to play along
with the game, thirteen men went out the cabins' back doors and fired
at the Indians, making as much noise as possible, hoping to give the
impression of a larger force leaving the fort, then ran back inside the
stockade. Trusting the garrison had been emptied, Girty ordered his
forces to begin the attack. The clearing beside the cornfield was narrow
and Indians had to run out into the open to fire within range of the
walls. Riflemen inside picked them off as they dashed into the open.
A few Indians reached the fort and set the outside cabins on fire. As
the Indians withdrew from the first attack, the cabins blazed in the
wind, sending showers of sparks onto buildings in the enclosure. The
dry shingles and poles caught easily, but luckily the wind shifted and
turned the showers of sparks away from the fort.

After the first assault, those in the stockade were relieved that no sign of artillery had been revealed. If the Indians and British had artillery, they would have already used it. The firing began again and continued for hours. As Indians came out into the open to fire, a few at a time, the riflemen from the fort continued to pick them off. The settlers in Kentucky had learned a great deal about defending themselves since the siege of Boonesborough four years before and there were no trees close to the fort for the Indians to hide behind. After hours of fire on the fort, only two inside the stockade had been killed.

Because they could not get close enough to use torches, the Indians shot fire arrows into the stockade. If an arrow stuck in a roof and caught the shingles, a child was sent to knock the burning shingles loose. One fire arrow was reputed to have landed near a cradle. "A lighted arrow from an Indian bow fell upon the sugar-trough cradle in which the infant, Richard M. Johnson, was lying. His little sister Betsy promptly extinguished the flame." Johnson would later become a hero of the Battle of the Thames and vice president of the United States.

Meanwhile the two messengers who had ridden out before daybreak had reached Lexington and found that the main force of the militia had gone after the band of Indians who had attacked Hoy's Station. The messengers rode on to Boone's Station, where Capt. William Ellis and a company of men had gathered. Boone was apparently away recruiting more men. At two o'clock that afternoon the relief force reached Bryan's Station. The Indians had faded back into the cover of the woods. All looked peaceful when the militia arrived. It was decided that the horsemen would ride as fast as they could to the fort's gate, and Levi Todd's thirty men on foot would ease through the cornfield under cover until they were near the stockade's walls. Captain Ellis was a pious man, a frontier preacher, and whether it was prayer or sheer bravado that saved them, he and his men charged through a hail of Indian fire to the gate of the fort, which swung open for them. The considerable dust cloud kicked up by the horses' feet is also credited with protecting them, and the force of Indians firing at them may have been smaller than was assumed at the time.

Levi Todd and his men on foot had come through the wide cornfield almost to the fort, but when they heard the cries of Ellis's galloping troops and the firing, they turned back into the corn, only to confront a line of angry Indians. Had they continued as planned to the stockade they might have run through the gate with the horsemen. But having turned back, they had to fight their way through the Indians. Luckily the Indians had already fired their weapons at the dashing horsemen, and as they struggled to reload, the militiamen aimed their rifles at them and retreated into the leafy rows. Those watching from the fort waited for the riflemen to advance again, but Todd and his militia withdrew into the forest and returned to Lexington, having lost two men.

Conceding that the fort could not be taken now that its defense had been increased, Girty came forward and stood on a stump near the wall to offer a proposal. With an air of friendliness and courtesy, reminding those inside that he knew many personally, he offered protection and safety if they surrendered. He told them artillery was on the way and the fort would be blown down.

Among the settlers at Bryan's Station was a young man named Aaron Reynolds, like John Holder of Boonesborough, notorious for his profanity. With Girty threatening on his stump outside the wall, Reynolds's talents as a swearer were called upon. He climbed up inside a chimney near the wall, and with only his head exposed above the rim answered Girty. Victorian scholars who passed on the anecdote only give us a laundered paraphrase. Standing on stacked barrels inside the fireplace, Reynolds began by shouting to Girty that he (Reynolds) had two lowdown dogs named Simon and Girty. Girty answered that this was too serious an occasion for malicious joking.

Reynolds claimed that the Kentucky militia was on its way to Bryan's Station. In one version of his remarks he began by shouting,

"Know you! Know you! Yes, we know you well. Know Simon Girty! Yes: he is the renegado, cowardly villain, who loves to murder women and children, especially those of his own people. Know Simon Girty! Yes: his father must have been a panther and his mother a wolf. I have a worthless dog that kills lambs: instead of shooting him I have named him Simon Girty." But Reynolds was just warming up. "If you and your gang of murderers stay here another day, we will have your scalps drying in the sun on the roofs of these cabins," Reynolds yelled, and swung into higher gear and said they had plenty of ammunition to beat "such a son of a bitch as Girty" and all they needed was hickories to whip the "yellow hides" of his Indian allies. It was said Girty "took great offense at the levity and want of politeness of his adversary."

Capt. John Craig, commander of the station, then shouted from the wall that the fort would never surrender. Girty threatened that the next day would prove otherwise. Aaron Reynolds turned his dog loose to attack Girty, and Girty retreated. There was sporadic firing from both sides during the night, but the following morning the Indians were found to be gone. The woods and broken cornfields were silent. Hundreds of hogs and cattle had been killed, outbuildings burned, including a tanning shed, and a ropewalk, and cornfields laid waste, but Girty and Caldwell and the other British and Indians were gone.

IN RESPONSE to the raid on Bryan's Station, men from Lexington, Harrodsburg, Boonesborough, and Boone's Station assembled at Boone's Station and headed north in pursuit of the retreating Indians. Boone had been appointed lieutenant colonel of the new Fayette County militia and he commanded forty-four men from his district. Col. John Todd of Lexington was the nominal commander of the 182 men who set out on August 17, 1782. Lt. Col. Stephen Trigg of Lincoln County, Maj. Hugh McGary of Harrodsburg, Maj. Silas Harlin, Maj. Edward Bulger, and Maj. Levi Todd were also leading. As was often the case with frontier militias, there seemed almost as many officers as private soldiers, and none of them had much authority over the hastily mustered and untrained ranks. The actual numbers were twenty-five officers and 157 enlisted men. While John Todd was an experienced soldier, Trigg had never fought Indians before. This lack of authority, experience, and recognized chain of command could prove disastrous when decisions had to be made quickly and carried out decisively.

The little army arrived at Bryan's Station to find the Indians had gone. In conference with the officers there, Major McGary suggested they wait for a larger militia force commanded by Col. Ben Logan to arrive. Logan was gathering upward of five hundred men, and with a force that size a decisive victory could be achieved over Girty and the British and their Indian allies. Colonel Todd accused McGary of timidity and said if they did not follow now the Indians would reach the Ohio River and cross, and it would be too late to attack them. Todd's argument was persuasive and the officers agreed to leave in the morning. It is possible that Boone preferred not to wait for Logan but to serve under Todd, since Logan had been one of the accusers at the court-martial four years before. McGary, known for his bad temper, brooded on Todd's suggestion that he was timid. On the frontier, no suggestion could hurt a man's pride more than the hint that he was a coward. In a world where the willingness and ability to defend oneself with gun or knife or fists could be a daily necessity, it was dangerous to be thought timid. The adage was that cowards did not even start out and the weak died on the way to the Middle Ground.

After they left Bryan's Station on August 17, Girty and the Indians followed an old hunter's trail down Elkhorn Creek, then turned north, arriving at the ruins of Ruddle's Station near the end of the day. Crossing the Licking River they camped for the night near the ghostly ruins, twenty-two miles from Bryan's Station.

On August 18 the militia rode north, following the Indian trail to within a few miles of the Lower Blue Licks. As they traveled, Boone noticed a peculiar paradox. From the number of campfires at the Indians' campsites, where they had feasted on cattle from Bryan's Station, he estimated there were nearly five hundred in Girty's party. The Indians left many signs, broken twigs, as if hoping to be followed. According to John Mason Peck, "Their camp fires were left burning; their trail was plainly marked; and every indication showed that they desired a pursuit, for they even marked the trees with their tomahawks along their path." Boone thought they might have walked in each other's tracks, as though trying to conceal their large number.

Boone knew an ambush was one of the Indians' favorite tactics, and all the signs pointed to an ambush. The militia arrived at the Licking River, near the Blue Licks, early on Monday morning, August 19. One version of events is that Todd and Trigg called a meeting of the officers and Boone warned them that an ambush was likely. He pointed to the terrain across the river, where the stream made a long, looping bend, roughly in the shape of a sock. Much of the rising ground inside the loop had been licked and trampled bare over the centuries. But farther up the hill, on the higher ground, three ravines dropped off the height going down to the river. On the right a razor-backed ridge ran above the trail, giving a commanding view of the approach uphill. The ravines and ridge were perfect hiding places for the Indians as they watched the Kentuckians advance over the bare, sloping ground. When the Kentucky militia arrived, they saw some Indians hurrying across the river, the spies who had been monitoring their approach.

Some accounts say the officers held a conference, while several Indians strolled out in plain view far up the hill, smoking their pipes. Boone pointed out that they were decoys, hoping to suggest that there were just a few unsuspecting Indians in the woods across the hill, and that the large force was already far away, near the Ohio River. Boone had hunted and camped at the Blue Licks many times. It was here he had surrendered the salt boilers to Blackfish and the Shawnees. It was near here that he had rescued his daughter Jemima and the two Callaway girls. "They wish to seduce a pursuing enemy into an ambush," Boone argued. Boone's experience and his argument and the evidence he presented seemed to persuade Colonels Todd and Trigg to wait for Logan's larger force. "I caution you against crossing the river at any rate, before spies have reconnoitered the ground," Boone added. It was at this point that McGary, still smarting from Todd's humiliating suggestion at Bryan's Station, asserted there was no reason for delay.

For the sake of argument the officers began to discuss the choice of tactics, if they did decide to attack immediately. Boone suggested that if they made a move now they should divide their men and let half cross the river at a ford upstream. Then the two groups could attack the Indians from different sides, weakening the effects of an ambush. Boone's plan might have been adopted and executed by a better organized and better trained force. Neal O. Hammon writes, "Another account by Boone's grandson was that Boone suggested that they only reconnoiter in the rear of [British officer] Caldwell." This would have been excellent advice, to gather intelligence about the size and position of the enemy before rushing ahead. But militias rarely used complex strategies or even flanking movements. They either fired from the cover of trees or rushed straight ahead into a battle. Two men volunteered to ride along the river looking for Indians, but they came back after a few minutes reporting they had seen none.

"By Godly," McGary shouted, "why not fight them then?" And then he turned to Boone and said he had never known Daniel to be a coward before. "No man has ever dared to call me a coward," Boone shot back. Tears came into Boone's eyes he was so surprised and hurt by the accusation. His integrity and long experience with Indians seemed to count for little in the face of such anger. Boone, the man of caution, who tried to avoid bloodshed, calm in emergencies, was swept aside in an instant of fury. In Nathan Boone's account, "'I can go as far [in an Indian fight] as any man,'" Boone shouted back, "and took his place in front of the advancing soldiers, as did the other officers." Nathan's wife, Olive, told Draper that Boone felt McGary was angry because it was Boone who had suggested they wait for Logan's larger force.

As tempers flared, McGary, still mounted on his horse, yelled, "Them that ain't cowards follow me, and I'll show where the yellow dogs are." The men that McGary had brought from Harrodsburg followed him, and then others followed also. An evil chemistry seemed to be at work. None of the men wanted to be seen by their fellow soldiers as cowards. Once a few went, the others had to go. The colonels watching them follow the excited major were helpless to stop the process set in motion. As most of the men rode their horses into the river, Todd and Trigg and Boone rode with them. It was the worst mistake of Boone's life. Some who knew him in later years said he never forgave himself for losing his temper at the Blue Licks that morning. Had he kept calm, as was his habit, he might have prevented the debacle. That he let himself be provoked by the unstable McGary showed a weakness in his leadership and in his character.

Other historians have argued that the conference of officers by the river never occurred. It was never mentioned in available records by any officers who were there but was first described by Humphrey Marshall in his 1824 *History of Kentucky*. According to Neal O. Hammon, the small Kentucky army may have paused only to cross the river single file at a narrow ford. Colonel Todd's first mistake was to place his men in a position where retreat would be so difficult. His second was to advance his men across a wide, open space toward an enemy concealed by trees and brush on higher ground.

All accounts agree that once across the river the militia was divided into three companies: Trigg led to the right, Harlin and McGary commanded the Lincoln County men in the middle, and Boone led his men from Fayette County on the left. The company included a number of his relatives, cousins, and nephews, as well as his son Israel. According to Levi Todd's letter to his brother Robert, written August 26, 1782, one week after the battle, all the men in the militia rode their horses across the river. Still mounted they crossed almost three-quarters of a mile of open ground sloping upward inside the loop of the river. "We rode up within 60 yards, dismounted, gave and sustained a heavy and general Fire." Apparently the Kentuckians did not get off their horses until they were within shooting range of the Indians hidden in the ravines and timber on the ridge.

Once on foot the three companies stretched out across the terrain in a long line, holding their rifles ready and advancing toward the brush and scattered trees. About two dozen men, led by Major Harlin, did not dismount but rushed forward ahead of the middle company, perhaps to probe the enemy's positions. Those riders took the first fire, and all but two were killed.

It is a peculiar fact that in most battles each participant remembers events in a different way. The reason is that in the heat of action each sees his part of the field and never has the leisure to survey the whole. Frightened, excited, disoriented, a soldier may have a particular impression that is often a distortion. The Battle of the Blue Licks was no exception. Every man who was there and survived told a somewhat different version of events. The battle, once it began, unfolded quick as the flash and crash of lightning followed by thunder and was over so soon many were not sure exactly what had happened.

Almost all versions agree that Boone's company advanced farthest up the hill into the woods along the first ravine, firing as they moved forward. According to Levi Todd they covered nearly a hundred yards of ground after dismounting. Later, when Boone studied the battle, he decided that the Indians had pulled back in front of him and his men to draw them into the trap of a ravine. It is possible Girty or Caldwell and the Indians had targeted Boone in particular, perhaps hoping to take him prisoner. As Boone led his men on foot up the flank of the hill, an Indian rose from behind a stump and Boone raised his gun. Boone was carrying a special fowling piece that he had loaded with extra powder and several bullets as well as buckshot, appropriate for fighting at close range. Before he pulled the trigger he said to the gun, "You be there!" as though giving an order, and after the blast the Indian fell dead. He later told his son Nathan that "he was only positive of having killed this one" Indian in his long life. Boone and his company pushed ahead, firing and reloading, and the Indians retreated in front of them. It appeared to Boone's men from Fayette County that they were winning the battle.

The advantage the Kentucky settlers usually had over the Indians was their long rifles. Indians were more often armed with British muskets, which were far from accurate. Under the right conditions Kentuckians could kill Indians while out of range of all but the luckiest musket fire. But at the Blue Licks the militia advanced so close to the enemy in the brush and trees, they lost that superiority. A musket could be reloaded quicker than a rifle, and the Indians had tomahawks and war clubs, while the Kentuckians lacked bayonets and swords that could have been effective in close, hand-to-hand fighting. It appears almost certain the Indian forces fell back before Boone's company, hoping to draw them farther into the woods and cut off their retreat.

Riding his horse near the middle of the line, Col. John Todd was hit in the left chest and fell soon after the battle started. The early loss of their leader likely shook the confidence of the advancing men. The fire from the brush was so intense and the scream of bullets so sickening, McGary's line began to crumble. Men fired at the Indians and tried to reload in the smoke and confusion. Powder horns and bullet pouches dropped in the weeds and were lost. Bullets seemed to come from every direction, and so many fell that the rest panicked and started to back away, trying to recall where they had left their horses. Indians suddenly rushed at them swinging tomahawks, painted in the colors of war, red and black, their faces black as fiends from a nightmare. Indians sprang from every bush and bank of weeds, every briar patch and tangle of honeysuckle vines, and came tearing down the slope screaming at the limit of their breath and slashing with tomahawks and war clubs. For once the Long Knives did not have their long knives. The men from Lincoln County had nothing to swing but their empty rifles, and many had their heads bashed in with tomahawks as they turned to dash for their horses. Warriors advanced, shooting from rocks and stumps, ditches and buffalo wallows.

Those in the center of the field who looked to the right would have seen that things had gone even worse on that flank. Leading his men up the slope toward the woods at the top of the hill, Colonel Trigg had ignored the steep ridge on his right, jutting between his company and the river. Assuming the Indians were hiding straight ahead, Trigg and his company were astounded when a thundering fire broke out from the sumac bushes and shrubs on the razor-backed ridge. It is possible more than half the Indian forces were concealed on that ridge, for the firing was so heavy from that direction that most of Trigg's men, and Trigg himself, were killed in minutes. No other company took such extreme losses so quickly.

No sooner had the Indians, hidden in the brush along the ridge, delivered their deadly fire than they sprang out swinging tomahawks and clubs, killing survivors of the first fire, taking scalps and prisoners for later torture. But it was not just scalps and prisoners the Indians were after, for just down the slope stood as many as 180 horses, already saddled and bridled. Blankets and provisions, extra lead and powder, as well as booty such as knives and pistols, were tied to the saddles or hidden in the saddlebags.

Many of the horses brought into Kentucky by settlers were small breeds from Virginia and North Carolina, ancestors of the quarter horse. They were tough and quick and dependable. Few trophies of war were more valuable than captured horses. Luckily for the panicked and stumbling Kentuckians, many braves were more intent on seizing horses than taking scalps. Scores of Indians poured out of the thickets to grab the mounts. Swinging their rifles as clubs, some of the militia tried to resist, but they were outnumbered and overwhelmed. Those who were able began to run toward the river.

In the confusion of the firing, the screams and war whoops, smoke and smell of blood, the horses panicked too and ran back and forth and down the long slope toward the river. Indians pursued in a general stampede of horses, militia, and wounded toward the ford across the river.

Seeing they were cut off on the right and behind them, the men with McGary in the middle ran to the left to get behind Boone's company. Boone, with his son Israel, nephews Samuel, Squire, and Thomas

Boone, Abraham, Peter, and Joseph Scholl, and other family members and friends, was still moving forward, firing and reloading, as Indians withdrew before them toward the hilltop and the second ravine. Boone's calm authority kept his men organized and concentrating on the advance. They were not even aware of what had happened on their right and behind them. Boone's authority as a leader was never demonstrated more clearly.

Boone and his men were astonished when McGary rode up behind them and yelled, "Boone, why are you not retreating?" It was only then that Boone looked across the slope and saw that Trigg and Todd and the two other companies had been swept away. The field behind them was a pandemonium of men scrambling to catch and mount horses, Indians clubbing and scalping, wounded men trying to reach the river, others attempting to wade or swim across. Indians on horses rode around tomahawking and trampling men, cutting them off at the water's edge. Indians and white men wrestled in the river, thrashing and screaming. It appeared that most of the senior officers except Boone and McGary and Levi Todd had been killed.

Realizing that he had no choice, and that his company had been drawn dangerously forward, far beyond any safe retreat, Boone shouted to his men to run to the left into the trees. Farther down the ridge the Licking River entered a gorge. If they could reach the river in that direction they might be able to swim across to the safety of the woods on the south bank. Some would later say the battle lasted only five minutes, but other accounts would describe the action as occurring in about fifteen minutes. In any case, it all happened very quickly. Men who could catch a horse, any horse, mounted and rode for their lives. Those who could not find a horse ran toward the river, dodging Indians, hoping to dodge bullets, tomahawks, scalping knives. "We . . . were obliged to retreat," was Boone's cool understatement to Filson a year later.

When McGary reached them, Boone and his men were about three-quarters of a mile from the river. Luckily many of the Indians were

intent on grabbing horses, taking scalps and booty, and few noticed
Boone's men fleeing to the left. As he backed away, facing the chaos
of the battlefield, guarding his men as they retreated, Boone saw his
son Israel nearby. Seizing a horse that belonged to his brother Ned's
widow, he ordered Israel to mount and get away.

"Father, I won't leave you," Israel answered.

Looking around for another mount for himself, Boone heard a thud
behind him and wheeled to see Israel knocked to the ground by a bullet in his heart, bleeding from the mouth and already dying. Boone's
instinct was to pick up his son and carry him toward the river. But it
was too late to do anything but leave the body and mount the horse
himself and get away.

Later accounts that blamed McGary for the plunge into battle
may have been intended to divert attention from the mistakes made
by Todd and Trigg. The decision to advance over a half mile of open
ground, uphill, below a sharp parallel ridge on the right, toward a concealed enemy at least twice the size of the Kentucky force, ensured
disaster. Todd failed by not scouting and probing the enemy to find
out its location and numbers. Trigg, a recent arrival in Kentucky with
the Land Commission, had almost no fighting experience. No one,
including Boone, later wanted to blame the dead colonels. There is no
recorded instance of Boone's blaming McGary. According to his family, Boone blamed himself and George Rogers Clark, commander of
the Kentucky militia, who maintained his garrison in Louisville, too
far away to protect the Bluegrass region.

Around seventy-seven Kentuckians were killed. Fifteen of the
twenty-five officers were killed, including Col. John Todd and Col.
Stephen Trigg and Maj. Silas Harlin and Maj. Edward Bulger. Boone
later said that of all the terrible things he had witnessed in his life, the
death of Israel was the worst. Tears came to his eyes whenever he mentioned the battle. He felt responsible for the disaster at the Blue Licks,
and he blamed himself for bringing Israel along when he was not yet
completely recovered from a fever. "Father used to be deeply affected,

even to tears, when he spoke of the Blue Licks defeat and the death of his son," Nathan told Draper.

Boone and his company, those that were left, reassembled downstream on the south bank of the river. Upstream, where the main body of the militia was, men already across the river turned to cover those still struggling to cross. Some Indians kept up the attack, right to the edge of the river and into it. Boone later decided it was the early loss of their leaders that made the men panic, Nathan Boone explained to Draper.

Benjamin Netherland, one of the mounted militiamen, had already gotten across the river. Though he had fought in a number of battles in the Revolution, including Guilford Courthouse, Netherland was rumored to be something of a coward. At the Blue Licks, however, instead of riding away to safety, he turned his horse and ordered the fleeing men to stop and cover those struggling to cross behind them. "Let's halt, boys, and give them a fire," Netherland shouted. As many as twenty fleeing militiamen stopped to fire at the pursuing Indians and thereby saved many of their comrades. A half century later Capt. Robert Patterson would commend Netherland, saying, "I cannot ever forget the part you acted in the Battle of the Blue Licks."

Aaron Reynolds, who had been scolded by Patterson earlier for cursing, and then given a quart of whiskey for desisting, saved Patterson that day by seizing a horse and putting the wounded Patterson in the saddle and sending him across the river to safety. Reynolds planned to swim the river himself, but his buckskin pants were soaked and heavy and he sat down to take them off. While he was seated, Indians grabbed him, made him a prisoner, then left him under a single guard while the fight continued. Noticing that the guarding Indian's rifle was not primed to fire, Reynolds knocked him out with his fists and escaped. Wearing only his shirt, Reynolds swam the river and ran all the way to Bryan's Station to tell what had happened. Captain Patterson soon arrived on horseback and confirmed his story.

In gratitude the captain awarded him two hundred acres of land, and the once foul-mouthed Reynolds settled down to become a Baptist and a farmer. It was said the story illustrated the good a well-placed gift of whiskey can do.

That afternoon and evening the Indians had an orgy of amusement and torture with the wounded and prisoners taken at the Blue Licks. The bodies were later found with their hands tied, the skin cut and burned in the long hours of torture. One prisoner who later escaped, Jesse Yocum, said he "did not know how many they burned but the smell of a human was the awfullest smell he ever [smelled] in his life." The British officers later claimed they discouraged the torture but were unable to do much about it. Men fleeing from the disaster at the Blue Licks met Logan's larger army advancing from Bryan's Station. Logan deployed his men to fight, expecting the Indians to pursue the retreating militia. But the Indians did not appear. They were busy scalping and torturing the prisoners and wounded back at the Lower Blue Licks.

The Blue Licks was the last major battle of the American Revolution, and it was a horrifying defeat for the Americans. In the aftermath of the battle the people of Kentucky were stunned. Many packed up their belongings to head back east. One man offered his whole farm for a horse on which to carry his family away. "Lawrence offered my father the whole 1400 acres of his preemption, where Lawrence's station then was, for one little black horse to carry his family back to Virginia," Sarah Graham told John Dabney Shane. George Rogers Clark blamed the officers who were in charge there. "The Conduct of those unfortunate Gents was Extremely reprehensible," he wrote. As overall commander of forces in Kentucky, Clark said he had primarily intended for officers such as Todd and Trigg to patrol along the Ohio River on the lookout for invading Indians. Instead, they had let a large army reach Bryan's Station with no warning, and then played into an obvious ambush at the Lower Blue Licks.

Col. Arthur Campbell on the Holston River blamed the militia's weapons and style of fighting for the defeat, as well as the bad judgment of the officers. Without bayonets and swords, the men at the Blue Licks were helpless once they fired their rifles and the Indians rushed at them with tomahawks and clubs. Campbell wrote on October 3, 1782, to Col. William Davies, "All our late defeats have been occasion[ed] thro' neglect of these [weapons], and a want of proper authority and capacity in the Commanding Officers. Never was the lives of so many valuable men lost more shamefully than in the late action of the 19th of August, and that not a little thro' the vain and seditious expressions of a Major McGeary [*sic*]."

McGary himself defended his actions at the Blue Licks, writing to Benjamin Logan that though his "bad conduct" was blamed for the defeat, the charge was being made by officers who rushed to confront the Indians without waiting for Logan's larger force. McGary said, "Colonels Todd and Trigg were for immediate pursuit, alleging, that, if they waited for Colonel Logan, he would bear off the laurels of victory." His behavior at the Blue Licks would not be the last actions for which McGary was censured. Hugh McGary was disliked by many who knew him. John Mason Peck described McGary to Mann Butler: "He was a fractious, ill tempered man, hated by the people & constantly engaged in fights and affrays — He followed the current of migration towards the Green River country, but the people would not associate with him." But in 1782 Hugh McGary defended himself vigorously, arguing, perhaps correctly, that Todd and Trigg were responsible for the massacre.

After such a disaster there is a lot of blame to go around, and though Boone's name is rarely mentioned in any of the recriminations, Boone did not let himself off so easily. He knew that losing his temper when snarled at by McGary was a serious failure of leadership at a critical moment. That his outburst was so uncharacteristic of him made the episode all the stranger and more painful. All his life he had shown calm good sense in moments of danger. Boone's relative Abraham

Scholl, who was with the company from Boone's Station at the battle, said Boone "rather blamed himself in some degree for the Blue Licks battle." For the rest of his life, Boone broke down and wept when he mentioned the battle. It was the greatest failure of his life. It was the occasion when his capacity for clearheadedness deserted him. His son Israel and seventy-six others had been killed as a result of his lapse. He may never have completely trusted himself again. The battle marked the end of the most important period of his life.

In the years after the battle, stories circulated that Israel had been urged to get up from his sickbed to join the pursuit of the Indians. Boone bore the weight of guilt because he had let his son go when he was not well. In some versions of the story Boone had shamed his son into going, saying, "I am sorry to think I raised a timid son." Many years later Boone's granddaughter Delinda Boone Craig said it was Boone's insistence that made him so ashamed the rest of his life. "Israel ought not to have gone, and would not but for his chiding," she said. But Olive Van Bibber Boone maintained just the opposite. She told Draper that Boone had tried to dissuade Israel from joining the militia that pursued the Indians to the Blue Licks. "Israel had long been sick previously and had recovered or nearly so, leaving him with a stiff neck, and his father and family tried all they could to persuade him not to go, but he would go."

There are conflicting stories about where Boone buried his son Israel. Some biographers say he returned to the Blue Licks, found the body, which was so badly eaten by animals and birds and bloated by the heat as to be unrecognizable except for a piece of clothing, or by its location in a thicket. Nathan said that Boone returned to the Blue Licks a few days later with a burial party and dug a separate grave for Israel there. Still others report that Israel's body was thrown into the mass grave with the other bodies that were found mutilated and decaying.

All accounts agree that Boone returned to the scene of the battle with the burial party. As they approached the site they saw buzzards circling over the river and hillside. Animals were gnawing the scattered bodies and all who were there never forgot the overwhelming stench. Bodies caught on rocks and snags in the river had been partly eaten by fish. Like Israel's, bodies lying in the sun were so bloated and partly torn by scalping Indians and animals almost none could be identified. In John Bradford's words: "A solemn silence pervaded the whole party as they approached the field of battle. No sound was uttered but the cry of the gorged vulture hovering over their heads . . . The remains of the mangled bodies were so distended by the excessive heat of the weather, or so disfigured by the tomahawk, vultures and wild beasts, that it was impossible to distinguish one individual from another."

The bodies were laid in a sinkhole across the hilltop, near the scene of the fighting, and covered with as much dirt and rocks as they could scrape together without picks and shovels.

The Battle of the Blue Licks has always been rightly described as a terrible defeat for the Kentuckians and the American cause. Few seem to have realized that it was also something of a failure for Girty and the British and their Indian allies also. If the plan had been to draw *all* the Kentucky militias, including Logan's four hundred men, into the ambush and kill them in one complete victory that would drive the settlers out of Kentucky forever, then it was at best a partial victory. Because Todd, and perhaps McGary, plunged directly into battle, Logan's larger force was saved, and the forts and stations in Kentucky were saved. Had Todd waited until Logan arrived, many more would have been killed and the Kentucky militia might still have lost the battle. The hundreds of Indians firing from the thickets could well have changed the course of American history in the Ohio Valley.

As he lived with his bereavement and disappointment with himself, Boone did not neglect his duties as colonel of the Fayette County militia. With John Todd dead he was now in command, a full colonel and county lieutenant. Boone wrote letters to officials back in Virginia, describing the recent battle and explaining the desperate needs of the frontier communities. The defeat at the Blue Licks was the lowest point in his life and also the lowest point in the unfolding story of the western settlements. To many it looked as though Kentucky would have to be abandoned. It was simply too dangerous a place to raise a family. The dreams of prosperity and plenty were apparently coming to an end. "I know Sir, that your Situation at present is something critical," Boone wrote to the governor on August 30, 1782, "but are we to be totally forgotten?" Boone asked the governor for a force of five hundred men. If something was not done quickly, Kentucky would soon be depopulated, Boone wrote. "But I can no longer Encourage my neighbors, nor myself to risque our Lives here at such Extraordinary hazzards."

On September 2, 1782, a force of Indians attacked Kincheloe's Station in Jefferson County and killed or captured thirty-seven people. The party of 150 Indians paused with their prisoners near Jeptha's Knob, as if waiting for the county militia to attack them. But with the example of the Blue Licks ambush fresh in mind and only fifty-four men at his disposal, Col. John Floyd wisely refused to attack. The Indians and their prisoners retreated across the Ohio River.

Boone believed that much of the problem was that the defense of the Kentucky settlements was under the leadership of George Rogers Clark, far away in Louisville. In his letter to the governor Boone urged that the men of the Bluegrass region be organized for their own defense under the county lieutenants. "But if you put them under the Direction of Genl: Clarke, they will be Little or no Service to our Settlement, as he lies 100 miles West of us, and the Indians north East, and our men are often called to the Falls to guard them."

In October 1782 Boone and other officers of the county militia began to assemble a large expeditionary force to be led by General George Rogers Clark in a campaign against the Shawnee towns in Ohio. More than eleven hundred men were mustered and they crossed the Ohio River on November 1, two days before the British signed the preliminary peace agreement with the Americans. The Indians may not have known for certain yet that they were losing their British allies at Detroit. Colin C. Calloway tells us that when they did learn the peace terms they would feel betrayed. "Indian speakers in council after council expressed their anger and disbelief that their British allies had betrayed them and handed their lands over to their American and Spanish enemies." Not sure about the policies of the new republic, the Indians were confronted with uncertainty on all sides.

There had been more Wyandottes than any other nation in the Indian force at the Blue Licks, but the Kentucky militia did not attempt to march north to the Wyandotte villages between the Sandusky and Cuyahoga rivers. Instead Clark and his large force again burned Chillicothe and Piqua and other Shawnee towns, destroyed crops and storehouses. But they encountered little resistance and killed only twenty Indians before returning to Kentucky. The invasion was largely symbolic, except that as a result more Indians moved farther north and west.

Another of Clark's projects was to build a gunboat to patrol the Ohio River and prevent Indian raids into Kentucky. The craft was seventy-three feet long, with forty-six oars and a complement of 110 men. Called the *Miami*, it was designed to carry eight cannons, averaging about three pounds in size. The long clumsy galley proved to have little effect in preventing Indian incursions across the river. The invaders simply hid in the forest until the gunboat was out of sight and then crossed the river quickly in their skin boats. The gunboat could only have been useful attacking forts along the river, but neither the British nor the Indians had such forts.

It would be twelve more years before the Shawnees and Miamis would finally be defeated by "Mad" Anthony Wayne at Fallen Timbers near Toledo, August 20, 1794, after the humiliating defeats the Indians delivered to Colonel Harmar in 1790 and General St. Clair in 1791. Twelve years and one day after the defeat at the Blue Licks,

Wayne, having studied Indian tactics at the Blue Licks and elsewhere, told his men to approach the Indians hidden in the brush and fallen trees of a hurricane-leveled forest, let the Shawnees and Miamis fire at them, then rush them with bayonets and swords while the Indians were trying to reload among the tangled limbs and trunks and the cavalry prevented them from fleeing. This time the Long Knives used their long knives. The tactic worked and the Shawnees and Miamis were soundly defeated.

AFTER THE RETURN from Ohio, Boone and a group of men from Boone's Station, including Will Hays and Flanders Callaway, camped for several days at the mouth of Limestone Creek on the Ohio River. It was already a popular landing place for immigrants and travelers coming down the Ohio and was the logical entrance to the settlements in the Great Meadow. Filson described, "The mouth of Limestone Creek, where is a fine harbor for boats coming down the Ohio . . . now a common landing." As always, Boone had an eye out for new land, new places to settle. After the humiliating defeat at the Blue Licks and the death of Israel, he may have felt it was time to move on. Everything at Boone's Station reminded him of Israel and his own failure and guilt. Also his land at Boone's Station was being claimed by another party. The land he had surveyed there overlapped with two earlier claims, including that of James Hickman. He had sold one tract of land, surveyed by Floyd, to Alex Cleveland, which was also claimed by Hickman and his heirs. Around 1783 Boone moved his family a few miles west to Marble Creek. But he may have already had a move north to the Ohio River in mind. Peter Harget would later give a deposition, saying that in October or November of 1782, when he was camping on Limestone Creek with Boone, Flanders Callaway, Will Hays, and others, "Boone wanted to examine the land abt. The mouth of limestone, and then talked of settling there, and did settle there in 1785."

Instead of brooding on loss and his mistakes, it was better to plan to move on to new opportunities. It was Boone's habit, and his destiny, to keep moving toward a future of risk and unlimited potential. Simon Kenton already had a station near Limestone Creek, and the business of land surveying and trading was booming, especially now that the Shawnees had moved farther to the north. At the temporary home on Marble Creek, Boone would later choose Limestone as the place where he would establish himself and his extended family.

CHAPTER FIFTEEN

Filson, Fame, and Failure

1783 – 1785 ↶

With the move to Marble Creek around 1783, Boone's life entered a new phase, almost another dispensation. He was almost fifty and the events for which he would be remembered were mostly behind him: his long 1769 – 71 hunt into Kentucky, his negotiations with the Cherokees for the Transylvania Company, hacking Boone's Trace and building Boonesborough in 1775, the rescue of Jemima in 1776, his adoption by the Shawnees in 1778, and his heroic escape and defense of Boonesborough. The debacle at the Blue Licks marked an end to his era of exploits, heroism, genius. And to really put a period to that phase of his life, he was about to become famous. He may have been a legend on the frontier for a dozen years already, but he was about to become even more of a legend back east, in Britain, and on the Continent. It is hard for anyone, even a man of Daniel Boone's modesty, cheer, courtesy, and resourcefulness, to survive his own legend.

"Two darling sons, and a brother, have I lost by savage hands, which have also taken from me forty valuable horses, and abundance of cattle," he told John Filson in 1783. John Filson had come west to make his fortune also. His idea was to write a book about Kentucky and make a map of the region that would sell well and bring even more investors and settlers to the West. And part of his plan was to include the life story of Kentucky's most famous citizen, Daniel Boone.

Filson's biographer, John Walton, writes: "The earliest references to Filson have him surveying and teaching school: the first, one of the most practical and respected vocations on the frontier; and the second, not without at least some respectability . . . Filson, however, immediately set about a third and most extraordinary activity — he began writing a book."

Many have commented on the stilted style of the narration in Filson's "Adventures of Col. Daniel Boon," included as a chapter in *The Discovery, Settlement and Present State of Kentucke.* The former schoolmaster Filson cast Boone's narrative in the proper and decorative language of the time. From the many documents in his own handwriting we know Boone was an uncertain speller, and among backwoodsmen Boone probably talked their language. But there is reason to suspect that Boone could speak more proper English in the right company, when the occasion demanded it. He had grown up among educated Quakers, and he knew how to match his speech and behavior to his audience, whether Shawnees who loved eloquence, or rough hunters, or learned lawyers such as Richard Henderson, or British officers such as Hamilton.

Almost everyone has assumed it is only Filson's construction of Boone's voice that comes through in the narrative of the "autobiography." But it may be that Filson's text is not so entirely unlike Boone's actual telling of his story in the 1783 or 1784 interviews. Filson says in his introduction that the story is "from his own mouth." Boone was talking to an educated easterner, and he was about to move into town to establish himself as a leading citizen and businessman. He was leaving the woods for the greater world. It is just possible that Filson's narrative reflects with some accuracy the way Boone actually spoke to him, doctored up and corrected here and there. It certainly reflects the way Boone saw himself or wanted to view himself. In fact Boone certified the story true in every detail.

John Filson was about thirty years old when he came to Kentucky in 1783. A native of Chester County, Pennsylvania, he had taught school

(49)

APPENDIX.

The ADVENTURES of Col. DA-NIEL BOON; containing a NARRA-TIVE of the WARS of Kentucke.

CURIOSITY is natural to the soul of man, and interesting objects have a power-ful influence on our affections. Let these influ-encing powers actuate, by the permission or dis-posal of Providence, from selfish or social views, yet in time the mysterious will of Heaven is un-folded , and we behold our conduct, from what-soever motives excited, operating to answer the important designs of heaven. Thus we behold Kentucke, lately an howling wilderness, the habi-tation of savages and wild beasts, become a fruitful field; this region, so favourably distinguished by nature, now become the habitation of civilization, at a period unparalleled in history, in the midst of a raging war, and under all the disadvantages

Adventures of Col. Daniel Boon by John Filson. Published as an appendix to John Filson's The Discovery, Settlement and Present State of Kentucke, 1784, this supposed autobiography made Boone famous in America, Europe, and Britain. Late in his life Boone declared that every word of the account was true. (Photo: Benjamin R. Morgan.)

near Wilmington, Delaware, during the Revolution. With the war over he decided to strike out for the West and seek his destiny, as so many others were doing. He invested a small inheritance in Kentucky land and set out to inspect his property. Going by way of Pittsburgh, he took a barge down the Ohio River, landing very likely at Limestone, where Boone would later become the best-known citizen.

Unlike most of those arriving in Kentucky to make their fortunes, Filson planned on writing a book and making a map of "Kentucke" to attract investors. He had put his inheritance in twelve thousand acres of land and he hoped to advertise his holdings with a little book. Let others kill a buck to make a buck; he would write a book to make a buck. Filson himself became something of a legend in American history. He is always portrayed as awkward, inept, stumbling around the rough frontier towns and settlements, pencil and notebook in hand, interviewing hunters and Indian fighters. However clumsy he appeared, he was so insistent he usually got the story he wanted. Walton tells us, "He acquired a reputation for annoying persistence." Kentuckians found that the only way to get rid of the nagging schoolmaster was to tell him what he wanted to know. He was fortunate to meet Boone, and his timing was perfect. As he was planning to set himself up for a career in business, surveying, and possibly politics, Boone was willing, even enthusiastic, to advise the newcomer and tell his story. Flattered that the eastern schoolmaster wanted to publish an account of his life, Boone rose to the occasion and gave Filson what he sought. "Curiosity is natural to the soul of man, and interesting objects have a powerful influence on our affections," the memoir begins. The first note Boone struck was about his hunger for exploration and discovery, his capacity for wonder. He began to reminisce about his struggle to reach the paradise of Kentucky, the risks he had taken, the tragic losses of two sons and a brother, the kidnapping of Jemima, the captivity with the Shawnees, the heroic escape to warn and fortify Boonesborough, the extended siege of Boonesborough. It was as though Boone had been waiting all his life to tell this story. He didn't mention the court-martial for treason at Logan's Station, but he did stress the devastating losses at the Blue Licks the summer before.

It is quite possible Boone did look back on his quest for Kentucky as heroic, almost a knightly quest for the Holy Grail. In all the Arthurian stories the Grail is never pursued with more determination and hope than that with which Boone and others had sought the meadows and hunting paradise of Kentucky. Boone was later described as "naturally romantic." Boone himself could not have written the account as Filson did, but Filson could not have written as he did either without a great deal of the tone and aphoristic asides coming from the subject himself. The voice of the Boone narrative is in many ways different from the rest of Filson's book about "Kentucke." "Certainly the most florid writing in Filson's book on Kentucky occurs in some of the descriptive passages and in his prophecy," John Walton says. Filson portrayed Boone pretty much as Boone saw himself in 1783, and as he wanted to be seen. The air of the quest, which some have said was inspired by familiarity with medieval literature, is more likely taken from *The Pilgrim's Progress*, which Boone and everyone else on the frontier knew. The Boone-Filson collaboration produced a text that has been a classic of frontier literature ever since. Walton observes, "He [Boone] has been the inspiration for a substantial portion of American literature."

"It was the first of May, in the year 1769, that I resigned my domestic happiness for a time, and left my family and peaceable habitation on the Yadkin River, in North-Carolina, to wander through the wilderness of America, in quest of the country of Kentucke." The style is that of a quest narrative, of a knight errant in search of a paradise. But it fits the adventure narrative also, as popularized by Defoe in *Robinson Crusoe*. After the Bible and *The Pilgrim's Progress*, *Robinson Crusoe* was perhaps the mostly widely read book in North America in the eighteenth century. Published in 1719 by the fifty-nine-year-old dissenter, journalist, spy, and sometimes double agent, Daniel Defoe, the book, often called the first novel in English, went through printing after printing and edition after edition. Thought by the public to be a factual memoir, not a work of fiction, *Robinson Crusoe* was modeled on the true account of the adventures of the Scottish sailor Alexander Selkirk as published by Richard Steele in 1713. Though largely unnoticed by scholars and historians writing about Boone, Defoe's novel deeply influenced the way Boone told his story and the way Filson wrote down the narrative. Crusoe's story is told in the first person and not only describes one man's heroic struggle for survival in the wilderness but is interspersed with moral meditations on the growth of character, humility, and wisdom.

After he finds himself alone on the desert island, Crusoe says, "[A]s my reason began to master my despondency, I began to comfort myself as well as I could, and to set the good against the evil, that I might have something to distinguish my case from worse." Describing the period when he was alone in Kentucky after the departure of his brother Squire for North Carolina in May 1770, Boone tells us, "[I was] by myself, without bread, salt, or sugar, without company of my fellow creatures or even a horse or dog. I never before was under greater necessity of exercising philosophy and fortitude."

Much of Crusoe's story is taken up with details of his survival, how he built a shelter, enlarged his cave, planted grain, hunted. But alternating with the descriptions and narrative are passages of philosophical comment. "And let this stand as a direction from the experience of the most miserable of all conditions in this world, that we always find in it something to comfort ourselves from, and to set in the description of good and evil, on the credit side of the account." Boone also describes in some detail the way he and his brother Squire struggled in the wilderness, threatened by Indians, loneliness, the unknown. And then, like Crusoe, he will turn from narrative to philosophical observation. "Thus situated, many hundred miles from our families in the howling wilderness, I believe few would have equally enjoyed the happiness we experienced. I often observed to my brother, You see now how little nature requires to be satisfied."

Filson and Boone understood, as did Defoe, that even an adventure story had to make a moral point. Besides many parallels in technical details about survival, landscape, solitude, there are similarities in the passages of meditation. But there are also many echoes of Crusoe's story in the accounts of his life Boone gave to others besides Filson. One example is the motif of the father figure who comes in dreams to warn the son of imminent danger. Crusoe again and again reminds the reader of warnings his father gave him before he left to go to sea. Sick with ague, he writes in his journal June 27 of a vision or dream in which he saw a man descend from the sky amid flames and say in a terrible voice, "[S]eeing all these things have not brought thee to repentance, now thou shalt die." Boone later said that after he and Stewart were released by the Indians in December 1769, he dreamed he was attacked by hornets and yellow jackets, as the chief Will Emery had warned he would be if he ever returned to Kentucky. The creek they were camped on, a tributary of Otter Creek, just east of Richmond, Kentucky, was named Dreaming Creek, and is still called that to this day. The inference in Crusoe's story of the dream is that the man with the terrible voice who comes to warn him is his father or is like his father. Throughout his later life Boone claimed that his father, Squire, appeared to him in dreams, often to warn him of approaching danger. John Bakeless says, "Each time when captured, robbed or defeated he . . . dreamed unfavorably about his father." Crusoe mentions again and again his daily Bible reading. Near the end of his life Boone would write to his sister-in-law that he read the scriptures daily. And Nathan would tell Draper that the Bible was Boone's favorite reading.

In no place does the Filson account echo Crusoe more closely than in the summing up and rounding off at the end. "Many dark and sleepless nights have I been a companion for owls, separated from the chearful society of men, scorched by the Summer's sun, and pinched by Winter's cold, an instrument ordained to settle the wilderness. But now the scene is changed: peace crowns the sylvan shade . . . I now live in peace and safety, enjoying the sweets of liberty, and the bounties of Providence." This conclusion was no doubt added by Filson after he had interviewed Boone and returned east. But the similarities in tone and gesture to Defoe are unmistakable. "How strange a chequer-work of Providence is the life of man; and by what secret differing springs are the affections hurried about as different circumstances present."

One of the most memorable passages in the Boone-Filson narrative is the description of the Cumberland Mountains as Boone approaches the Cumberland Gap for the first time in 1769. Filson had never seen those mountains in 1784, so the images and associations and details have to be Boone's own. "The aspect of these cliffs is so wild and horrid, that it is impossible to behold them without terror. The spectator is apt to imagine that nature had formerly suffered some violent convulsion; and that these are the dismembered remains of the dreadful shock; the ruins, not of Persepolis or Palmyra, but of the world!"

Anyone who has seen the cliff-rimmed mountains near Cumberland Gap knows how forbidding they appear, how they would inspire dread in one on foot or horseback searching for a pass through the awesome barrier. The description foreshadows the other strain of romanticism, not of Wordsworth or Emerson, but of Poe, who would later write, "The scenery which presented itself on all sides, although scarcely entitled to be called grand, had about it an indescribable, and to me, a delicious aspect of dreary desolation."

One of the best-known passages in Filson's "The Adventures of Col. Daniel Boon" tells of Boone's time alone in the woods after Squire has returned to the settlements for supplies. He describes climbing a mountain to look over the land ahead, and his epiphany of Pisgah vision. "I surveyed the famous river Ohio that rolled in silent dignity, marking the western boundary of Kentucke with inconceivable grandeur. At a distance I beheld the mountains lift their venerable brows and penetrate the clouds."

THE TIMING OF Filson's visit to Kentucky and the timing of the publication of his book with its detailed map of "Kentucke" could not have been better. With the Revolution over, settlers were streaming over the mountains, floating and rowing down the Ohio, riding and walking over Boone's Trace. *The Discovery, Settlement and Present State of Kentucke*, which contains "The Adventures of Col. Daniel Boon," was printed in Wilmington, Delaware, in 1784 and sold out its first printing. It was carried to England and to Europe and translated into French and German. Jean-Jacques Rousseau had died in 1778, but his vision of the "natural man" had taken hold in advanced circles in Europe and helped prepare the way for the romantic legend of Daniel Boone and the image of the wilderness of America as the new Eden.

Thomas Jefferson in Paris read the narrative, as did the naturalist and author Buffon. In 1790 William Bartram's *Travels* would be published in England and further stimulate the romantic image of the American wilderness, inspiring both Wordsworth and Coleridge. Bartram was inspired in part by Filson's little book. Byron would later celebrate the hero "General Boone" in a famous passage of *Don Juan*. Very quickly Boone became a celebrity and symbol of the American West, the natural man, the frontier hero. And Filson's book became a landmark in American culture. Walton tells us, "Interest in his subject was high, and he contemplated a second edition; but when General Washington failed to send on an endorsement, the idea was abandoned." Washington hesitated to endorse Filson's effort because the map he had made, while a very good sketch, was not geometrically exact.

The Boone legend began with Filson's little narrative in 1784 and continues to this day, despite a number of attempts to debunk it. Boone's story and character stand up remarkably well under critical scrutiny. Boone's character has some of the resilience shown in history by his contemporaries Washington, Franklin, Jefferson, Adams, and Hamilton. They seem to be figures that we need in our history and in our image of ourselves, and no amount of quibbling and skepticism diminishes their stature very much. In the words of the scholar Arthur K. Moore, "Boone the frontiersman, as an acknowledged agent of progress, sanctioned the civilizing process, whatever the cost to the Indians and to his own kind, and thereby put a happy face on a matter which somewhat troubled the American conscience."

One argument for the high fictive content of Filson's narrative has always been the literary and historical allusions scattered throughout the text. No slightly educated backwoodsman such as Boone could possibly have made reference to "the ruins, not of Persepolis or Palmyra, but of the world!" when describing the rugged cliffs leading to the Cumberland Gap. Very likely that comparison was added by Filson. But, on the other hand, supposedly uneducated people will sometimes surprise you with odd bits of information accumulated by hearsay or random reading. Boone's son Nathan said his father loved to read history books and likely took them with him on his hunting trips. George Rogers Clark, for example, was a man of considerable scholarship, though he lived on the frontier. There is no reason Boone could not have heard of the ancient ruins from friends such as Richard Henderson. The allusion to Persepolis and Palmyra would not have come out in conversation with fellow hunters, but when talking to an educated easterner writing down his story, Boone just might have drawn on his capacious memory and made the comparison. Anyone who has served in the army, or worked on a construction crew, or sailed on a ship, knows that unlikely people can demonstrate surprising bits of erudition.

When *The Discovery, Settlement and Present State of Kentucke* appeared it included an endorsement signed by "Daniel Boon, Levi Todd, James Harrod." They were willing to say they had examined the text and map and could "recommend them to the public, as exceeding good performances, containing as accurate a description of our country as we think can possibly be given; much preferable to any in our knowledge extant, and think it will be of great utility to the publick." In effect, Boone was providing a blurb for his own autobiography.

Filson's book was published on Boone's fiftieth birthday, and throughout the remaining thirty-six years of his life he never offered anything but praise for the volume. Visitors read passages from "The Adventures" to him and he reiterated his faith in their truthfulness. "All true: Every word truth!" the old hunter was heard to say more than once. Filson's narrative is our best window into the way Boone viewed himself and wanted others to view him, in 1783 and later.

Filson elevated Boone to a celebrity from which, in J. Winston Coleman's words, "neither the love of friends nor the hatred of enemies has . . . been able to remove him." Filson portrayed a Boone who, according to Richard Slotkin, was "a model of the republican citizen . . . when the newly independent nation was looking for some self-image appropriate to its stature and ideology."

Four years after publishing his book and map, Filson was killed by Indians on land he was inspecting near future Cincinnati. In a eulogy to Filson, written a century later, Col. Reuben Durrett, founder of the Filson History Club of Louisville, observed, "No little mound attracts to his last resting-place, and no inscription tells of his deeds; but he will live, in his map of Kentucky and in his narrative of Boone, when others, laid beneath marble columns surmounted by brazen epitaphs, are remembered no more." However unlikely a figure he cut among his contemporaries, Filson's writing has had a sustained influence on American history, folklore, and literature. "A man does not have to be great to be important," Filson's biographer says. "As an entrepreneur Filson was a failure. As a person he was uncongenial. As an intellectual he was undistinguished. But because he undertook some tedious and petty tasks, he made a substantial contribution to American history and letters: book and map sped the settlement of the West; in his tale of the adventures of Daniel Boone he created the prototype of our national hero."

However much pleasure Boone took in Filson's account and his new fame, neither seemed to do him much good in the years that followed. With his exceptional gifts and achievements Boone won renown, and the new recognition seemed to undermine the gifts, the faculties that had made him known. Leaving the woods to become a trader and public official, surveyor and land agent, Boone turned in directions where his talents were weakest. His new fame brought him ever more business, surveying jobs for which he may not have been fully qualified, speculation he was unwilling to pursue to a satisfactory or profitable conclusion, transactions with con men and even government contracts to supply militias and prisoners. He would have gotten in trouble in any case. He spread himself too thin, and his enhanced reputation accelerated the process. Reviewing the years 1785–95 one cannot help but feel that Boone lost his focus, that he was out of his element and out of his depth in some significant ways. It is possible that he never quite recovered from the grief and guilt over the defeat at the Blue Licks and the loss of Israel. Boone kept going, and to outward appearances prospered, doing even better than before. He had position and apparent wealth, and he made a substantial amount of money as a surveyor. But in fact he was getting deeper in debt because of his carelessness with business and legal details and documents.

At Limestone Boone built a large house for his family, which served also as a tavern, Boone's Tavern. The lumber for the building came from dismantled flat boats brought down the Ohio from Pittsburgh. He built a store and warehouse also and set himself up to sell goods to travelers arriving on the Ohio, to trade in furs and deerskins, ginseng, herbs, all the commodities of the frontier economy. In the tavern he sold meals and spirits and lodging. He traded in guns and gun repair. He lent money on little more security than a man's word. He bought and sold horses and no doubt served as a kind of pawnbroker for the region. And of course he got more and more deeply into the land business, continuing to survey land for himself and for dozens of clients.

He was now a licensed surveyor, an official surveyor, first in Fayette County, then in Lincoln County. "Thomas Allin and Samuel Grant the persons appointed to examine Daniel Boone having reported that he is able and qualified to execute the Office of a Deputy Surveyor of this county the said Boone had the Oath of Office administered to him." Once Boone was certified as a surveyor in one county, it was a mere formality to be certified in others. In 1783 Boone made around forty surveys, in spite of persistent attacks by Indians in the area.

Because of his reputation as a hunter and guide, a man of integrity and an officer of the militia, the builder of Boone's Trace, over which more settlers were streaming every day, Boone was in a position of power and wealth and influence. For some men, such as Isaac Shelby, the tavern, warehouse, and surveying business would have been stepping stones to even greater wealth, a governorship, a general's commission, a seat in the United States Senate when Kentucky became a state in 1792, a great mansion in Louisville when the settlement at the Falls became a city, or a plantation in the region around Lexington. For a woodsman like Boone, no such security and prosperity awaited.

Boone's world was the wilderness, and the families at the edge of the wilderness. Almost all his best work was done in the woods. The forest was the meeting place between white and Indian culture, where the two worlds challenged each other and mingled, mirrored, and merged. Boone's genius was at its best in that complex, evolving zone, part Indian, part white, mostly natural. While he claimed to have never been lost in the woods, he was often lost when he came out of the woods, into politics, law courts, commercial enterprise. He was at home with trees around him, and animals and stars, and Indians. He lost his way where the trace became a turnpike, the trail became a street. The town was a foreign country.

By settling at Limestone Boone positioned himself at the meeting place of river traffic and overland travel. Limestone was the spot where those who had floated down the river from Pittsburgh or Redstone needed to trade boats and eastern goods and cash for horses, tools, and supplies for the journey into the interior. They also needed information about settlements and land, about routes and the danger from Indians. No one knew more about Kentucky than Boone, and no one was more famous for knowing Kentucky. Going to see Colonel Boone was a good place to start if you wanted to settle or invest in Kentucky. There was no reason he should not make a fortune, while so many with half his achievements were getting rich in the world he had helped explore and open. The fortune was lying in plain sight to be made. In his new enterprises Boone left the woods, returning to the forests and cane lands only with his surveying crews to mark boundaries, point out old haunts. He passed the jug around among his men and recounted his exploits in the early days, and they admired him. He acquired more land than he knew what to do with. He sometimes did not bother to properly register the titles to some of the land he surveyed. Mere paperwork could always be taken care of later. That was work for lawyers and clerks. He was Daniel Boone, and he did the things that attracted him and excited him.

He was the leading citizen of Limestone, maybe the leading citizen of Kentucky, if it came to that. He had earned the right to affluence and ease. He wanted to give presents of land to his many children and foster children when they married, following the example of his father before him. He still hunted for sport from time to time, but he had moved into town. He had come out of the mother wilderness to take his place in the larger father world.

At the tavern where Boone lived and worked, Rebecca ran the kitchen, probably with the help of her daughter Rebecca Boone Goe. The son-in-law Philip Goe already had a reputation as a drunk, but even so, Boone put much of his business in Goe's hands. That fact alone suggests Boone's lack of care with business. Family unity was more important than practicality and profit.

The new prosperity and status of the Boones is shown by the tax rolls of 1787, where the family is listed as owning seven slaves. The slaves very likely served in the tavern, as well as in the store and warehouse, and perhaps on the surveying crew. Though some writers have tried to argue that Boone disapproved of slavery, there is little evidence for the argument. In the prosperous years in Limestone, slaves were very much a part of his household and his business. In this period of his life Boone got far indeed from his Quaker upbringing.

Beautifully placed on the river though it was, the town of Limestone was probably not much to brag about. As late as 1792 James Taylor from Virginia described it as "a muddy hole of a place with two or three log houses and a tavern." Another traveler described the riverfront: "In this harbour are seen a few Kentucky boats, generally laying near the mouth [of the creek], many of which have been broken up to form those straggling houses which are perceived on the bank." He referred to Limestone as "the fag [worn out] end of Kentuckey." In the boom economy of Kentucky around 1786 there was an intoxication and expansiveness. Fortunes were made quickly, and lost quickly. It was like a gold rush, except the gold was the land itself. Everyone was buying. Investors from the east and Europe bought up great tracts of land and sold them off in parcels through agents such as Boone and never laid eyes or foot on the property themselves. Everyone needed their claims located and surveyed. Boone kept a crew of rodmen and chainmen busy surveying for his clients. Tradition says that he kept them well supplied with "Old Monongahela." He was a popular man. An official surveyor, he was also a colonel in the militia, sheriff, and county coroner. With these duties added to all his tavern keeping, store keeping, horse trading, horse breeding, warehousing duties, one has the impression of someone seriously overextended. He had too many irons in the fire to keep a close eye on any one. According to Neal O. Hammon, "[In 1783] he made 24 surveys and covered 17,305 acres."

The enterprise with the largest legal and commercial ramifications was land. In the beginning, exact boundary lines probably didn't seem to matter. There was so much land a few acres here or a few there didn't make a lot of difference. Certainly a few hundred feet in either direction didn't seem all that significant. But as more and more land was bought and cleared, surveyed and sold, and sold again, boundary lines and accurate plats became important. It has been said that Boone's competence as a surveyor was about average for his time. But the standards of the time were fairly low. As deputy surveyor Boone had the authority to lay out tracts and make plats and register them in the county deed office. With few instruments except a chain and a compass, a surveyor like Boone, with little knowledge of trigonometry or geometry, depended largely on landmarks, a stream, a hill, a boulder, a big tree. In the style of surveying called metes and bounds, a surveyor ran a line from a landmark in the direction of a compass reading. One obvious weakness of the method was that the stream might shift, the tree die or be confused with another tree, the boulder be lost. Another was that the compass reading might shift over time as the magnetic pole moved. Less important for a short line, such a shift or mistaken reading could make a significant difference with a boundary miles in length. Boone lacked the equipment and training to set his callings by the North Star.

Hammon tells us, "A surveying party would need a compass and Boone's assistants may have used a chain for measurements, but some frontier chainmen reported using a buffalo tug or grapevine (supposedly cut to the proper distance)." If a surveyor such as Boone was lucky, he was surveying on level ground. Things got more complicated in rough terrain with thickets, ravines, the rise and fall of ridges, or if he had to calculate acreage along an uneven boundary such as a stream or bluff. A deed might say that a property ran "to the top of the hill." Deciding later where the top of the hill was would be an act of interpretation, within a range of several yards, especially if the hill was long or heavily wooded. Boone probably had neither the equipment nor training to practice the technique of leveling, to calculate the rise and fall of land.

It was easier if a surveyor had an adjoining property line and a deed, or best of all a map, to survey from. This method was called butts and bounds. The accuracy of a survey is greatly enhanced if the surveyor has an established "corner" to start from, a location that is already known in a deed as the boundary of adjoining property. With a certain corner and careful compass readings a competent surveyor has a chance of making a fairly accurate survey. And if a surveyor was really skilled and careful he might even take a reading from the North Star, establishing a permanent angle of direction from the corner. One of the most competent surveyors in Kentucky at the time was considered to be John Floyd. Yet later studies of his surveys found that his acreage counts were often off by as much as 15 percent.

In the heady times of early Kentucky settlement, it may never have occurred to Boone that more cautious methods should be followed. After all, surveyors elsewhere seemed to be doing as he did. Some surveyors couldn't read, much less calculate acreage accurately. And even those who could read jotted down callings such as "from the big sycamore to bend in Stinking Creek." The worst were what were called chimney corner surveyors, those who wrote up plats without ever going into the field or compiled maps from sketchy or fictitious notes. It was a time when even honest men operated by methods that would later be considered fraudulent. "All Boone's entries were mighty vague," William Risk later recalled. Yet there is little evidence that Boone's surveys were any more vague than those of his contemporaries.

By the time Kentucky became a state in 1792, many of the land claims were still overlapped. The Virginia land office far back in Richmond, without accurate maps of the region, had granted warrants for more land than actually existed in the Bluegrass. The greed and carelessness of the first decade created work for ambitious lawyers for decades to come. Over that period the Great Meadow would cease to be a land of buffalo and hunters and become a land of lawyers, politicians and accountants, slave owners and hemp planters. However much he might come to hate that change, Boone was as much to blame as any other single human being.

Yet in the mid-1780s Boone seemed to prosper. In spite of his imaginative spelling, he kept up an enormous correspondence with clients and would-be clients. His holdings multiplied and compounded. That he knew the land best as a hunting ground, rather than as real estate, never seemed to occur to anyone, maybe not even him. Boone relied on his son-in-law Will Hays in much of his land business. He used his profits from surveying to buy more land. But as his holdings increased it became more and more essential to survey and register deeds properly, to defend titles with documents and by legal process, even going to court. In these years of boom and prosperity he accumulated a pyramid of shingled holdings and uncertain claims that were more liabilities than assets. And rather than see his claims secured by due process, he preferred to keep moving on to others, selling what he had cheap and buying dear. He was carried along by the momentum of the new economy and frenzy that swept the region after the Revolution ended, and like someone caught up in a flood, he could neither go back nor step aside to safer ground.

CHAPTER SIXTEEN

A Deale of Sine Is Seen

1786 – 1788 ↳

While Boone grew more and more deeply entangled in his surveying and business ventures, the problems with Indians had not disappeared. The Shawnees and other tribes had moved some of their towns farther north and west, but they still crossed the river into Kentucky and raided settlements. As a leading citizen of the territory, Boone worked to keep things calm along the river. He wrote to the governor of Virginia asking for more reinforcements for the militia. "A Deale of Sine is Seen in Different places, in purtikular Limeston," he warned Patrick Henry. "An Inden Warr is Expcted." George Rogers Clark, commander of the Kentucky militia, was still far away in Louisville, and the forts to protect the Bluegrass region had not been built.

One chief of the Shawnees was Moluntha, whom Boone had known since his days of captivity at Chillicothe. Several tribes signed a peace agreement with the American government at Fort MacIntosh just down the river from Limestone in January of 1785. A year later Moluntha and the Shawnees made their own treaty with the Americans. But even as the treaty was being signed, parties from Kentucky were crossing the river to steal Indian horses. When Boone tried to persuade them to return the horses, he met so much opposition he gave it up. No doubt he was suspected of disloyalty, because of his old ties with the Shawnees. As an official and popular authority figure, Boone had to act with diplomacy and caution.

Many Shawnees and members of other tribes were angry at Moluntha for ceding lands in southern Ohio to the Americans, and they continued raids into Kentucky. In April 1786 Moluntha and the chief named the Shade asked the British for help, stating that the American treaty makers had deceived them about their real intentions. Both Boone and Levi Todd asked the government of Virginia for aid in repelling the attacks and securing the lands along the Ohio River. Angry residents of Kentucky were demanding separation from Virginia and the creation of a new state that could defend itself.

Finally, Gen. George Rogers Clark, on his own initiative, planned another offensive against the Indians in Ohio. He called for Col. Benjamin Logan to attack the Shawnee towns at the head of the Mad River, a tributary of the Miami, while Clark himself led a larger force against the villages on the Wabash. Hearing of the planned campaign, the Shawnees sent four hundred warriors to the defense of the Wabash villages, leaving their own towns relatively undefended.

On September 29, 1786, Logan led eight hundred Kentuckians across the Ohio, with Boone heading one of the battalions. Boone must have swallowed some pride to serve under one of the men who had brought charges of treason against him at the court-martial in 1778. He demonstrated again and again in his long life that he did not hold grudges. It took the large force a week to reach the Shawnee towns, now farther to the north and west of Old Chillicothe and Piqua. Simon Girty, who was with the Shawnees, later reported that when the Kentucky militia arrived, the Indians raised an American flag to show they had changed their loyalties with the end of the Revolution. In fact, the militia had trouble finding the villages at all. Marching farther and farther north into the very flat country of central western Ohio, they searched for days for signs of the Indians. Finally a pack of dogs was spotted, and Boone said to follow the dogs and the dogs would lead them to the villages, which they did. After seven days of marching the Kentuckians were angry and hungry. Whether the Shawnees raised the American flag or not, the militia plunged in for the attack and most of the Indians fled.

Col. Thomas Kennedy attacked a group of running women with his sword, including a captive white girl. The other men began to tease him, yelling, "Who hacked the squaws? Who hacked the squaws?" And then one would answer, "Tom Kennedy." The Kentuckians grabbed pots of mush and stew cooking over fires and devoured them. In one pot they found a turtle boiled whole, and some men who had already eaten from the pot lost their stomachs. As Boone and Simon Kenton and their company rode into the village, Boone spied a familiar warrior. "Mind that fellow," Boone shouted. "I know him — it's Big Jim, who killed my son in Powell's Valley." In the past thirteen years Big Jim's reputation as a murderer and torturer had grown. Hearing his name called, Big Jim wheeled around and shot one of Boone's party just as he himself was hit with a bullet. As the Kentuckians, perhaps thinking Big Jim was dead, went to the aid of their wounded comrade, Big Jim rose from the grass, reloaded his rifle, and shot another Kentuckian. While Big Jim was reloading yet again, Simon Kenton charged through the grass and drove his hunting knife into the Shawnee's heart. The Kentuckians scalped Big Jim and slashed his body while Boone stood by in a daze.

The raid was not a particular success. More Kentuckians were killed than Indians, and most of the Shawnees had fled. Ironically, among those killed were several chiefs who had tried to make peace with the Americans. A number of prisoners were rounded up, mostly women and children. The plan had been to take hostages who could later be traded for American prisoners the Indians held. Among those captured was Moluntha who, instead of running, held up the American flag and a copy of the treaty he had signed earlier that year. Thinking he was protected by the document, his cocked hat, and his white official robe, he surrendered himself and his extended family, including a leading woman of the tribe named Nonhelema, sister of the late chief, Cornstalk. Because of her imposing manner and tall figure — some accounts say she was six and a half feet tall — Americans had labeled her the Grenadier Squaw. Such prisoners were very valuable in the economy of prisoner exchange and peace negotiations.

Later that day, in the aftermath of the attack, Boone and other Kentuckians were chatting with the prisoners, probably in a combination of Shawnee, English, and sign language. A pipe was passed around and no doubt Boone and Moluntha mentioned the old days at Chillicothe when Boone was Sheltowee, Blackfish's son. Boone had a knack for this kind of wilderness courtesy, an example of his respect for Indians, and indeed for all people, that endeared him to the Indians.

Suddenly Hugh McGary, who was commanding the militia from Lincoln County, appeared, and Moluntha extended his hand in greeting. "Was you in the Battle of Blue Licks?" McGary asked. His rash and deadly behavior at the Blue Licks hung over McGary as a shame he could not erase. Moluntha's English was not very good, and he had not been at the Battle of the Blue Licks, but he nodded, probably just being friendly, having no idea what McGary had asked. "Then God damn you," McGary yelled, and took his hatchet from his belt. "I will show you Blue Licks play," McGary added, and with a mighty swing split the old chief's head like a ripe gourd. The women and children ran screaming, thinking another massacre was beginning. McGary then turned to attack Nonhelema and injured her hand or arm before he was restrained. Some Kentuckians, including Simon Kenton, later said they considered killing McGary on the spot. As it turned out McGary was court-martialed for killing Moluntha and stripped of his commission for a year. But he suffered no other punishment.

Later the same day the "squaw hacker" Thomas Kennedy attacked and scalped an Indian sitting peacefully in his tent. According to some accounts he set fire to the tent and burned the Indian alive. Kennedy was rebuked but not punished. Boone's disgust with his fellow Kentuckians had been growing for some time, and this raid may well have caused him to vow to be a protector of Indians, never a killer, ever again. As far as we know it was a vow he kept.

In all the sad history of the Indian conflicts along the frontier, there is example after example of the kind of atrocities McGary and Kennedy perpetrated. Leaders on both sides might try to restrain their men, honor treaties, protect women, but individuals such as Big Jim and Hugh McGary made their own rules and enacted their murderous passions, dragging all the rest into the inferno of paranoia and hate. Men who were there, and some who were not, said later that McGary should have been shot when he defied the colonels and yelled all were cowards who did not follow him across the Licking River August 19, 1782. Such a timely shot might have saved hundreds of lives and smoothed the history of the frontier as the settlements grew toward statehood. And McGary deserved to be shot again when he murdered Moluntha and fueled another round of conflict with the Shawnees.

After the attack in 1786 the Shawnees moved their towns still farther north, to the head of the Miami River. Later they would move again and settle on the Maumee and Auglaize rivers.

ONE OF THE businesses Boone had added to his many other enterprises at Limestone was the housing of prisoners taken in the Indian battles. Because he had lived with the Shawnees, Boone was often asked to negotiate the exchange of prisoners. He built a kind of jail and charged the state of Virginia in several bills that have been preserved. In fact "Daniel Boone's Indan Book," the ledger in which he kept these accounts, still exists. Apparently he liked his prisoners to be happy, for one of the first entries made after he returned from the raid with Logan reads, "State of Virginia Dr. 19 galons of whiskey Delivered to indins priserer on there first arrival at Limestone, _3/0/0/." Happy prisoners were safe prisoners, and safe prisoners were good business.

But by 1786 some of Boone's business ventures were beginning to get out of control, especially the land and surveying businesses. As early as 1785 he had been involved in the complicated lawsuit of

Boofman v. Hickman. This dispute had its origins in Boone's 1774 journey into Kentucky with Michael Stoner to warn the surveyors of the
coming Indian attacks. On that trip Boone had taken on the assignment of locating a four-thousand-acre parcel of land for James Hickman
on a stream that became known as Hickman Creek. When Boone
returned to Kentucky the next year to build Boonesborough, he had
been warned by another surveyor, James Douglas, that the land he
had marked for Hickman had already been claimed. "He told me he
had surveyed the same land in 1774 and that I had better move the
entry," Boone deposed in 1794. To avoid trouble, Boone had two tracts
of two thousand acres each surveyed on Boone's Creek for Hickman,
to replace the original claim. This time the surveying was done by
John Floyd. A few months later Floyd told Boone that the land he had
surveyed for Hickman was overlapped with an earlier survey done for
a client named Jacob Boofman. Floyd offered to survey another parcel
for Hickman, but Boone refused, since Hickman had already lost one
surveyed parcel. Jacob Boofman was a chainman on Floyd's surveying crew. Because of intervening conflicts with the Indians the issue
was left hanging for a while. Floyd returned to Virginia for a visit and
Boone assumed Hickman retained the title to the two tracts that had
been designated for him in 1775.

Three years later Hickman decided to come to Kentucky to claim
his land and was told by Col. William Preston that he had title to
only one of the two-thousand-acre properties. Surprised and angry,
Hickman confronted Boone and Floyd at the Virginia land office in
Harrodsburg in May 1780. Boone explained what had happened and
Floyd and Hickman got into a heated argument. "Hickman, Floyd
and myself was face to face where I rehearsed over the circumstances
from first to last, and Hickman demanded a platt or field notes from
Floyd." Hickman demanded his second two thousand acres and Floyd
refused. Floyd handed over his survey notes, but he was a close friend
of Colonel Preston's and assumed the district official would side with
him in the dispute.

Thinking the issue settled, Boone asked Floyd that summer of 1780 to survey land for his son Israel on Boone's Creek. Floyd told Boone that Hickman had never registered his claim on the west side of the creek; therefore, he was surveying that land for Boofman, and he would map out four hundred acres in addition for Israel Boone. Apparently Boone assumed Hickman had given up his attempt to claim that tract, and therefore some of it might as well go to Israel. But unknown to either Boone or Floyd, Hickman had pursued the matter over Floyd's head with Preston and won title to the second two thousand acres on the west side of Boone's Creek. Before he learned of Hickman's official patent, Boone had entered claims for twelve other pieces of property on the creek and sold some of them off to raise money for still other purchases. One of the tracts he sold was within the boundaries Hickman had won title to.

For a long time Boone did not seem aware of the conflicting claims, but around 1783 he informed Floyd. On March 27, 1783, Floyd wrote to Preston, "Boone built his station on part of the land I surveyed for Boofman and is now aware of it. behold, it takes in his settlement [which] is the reason this is brought to his memory." It is likely that this tangle of disputed claims added to the incentive to move, first to Marble Creek, then north to Limestone.

In 1785 Hickman came to Marble Creek or Limestone and showed Boone his deed to the land on Boone's Creek. He accused Boone of conspiring with Floyd to cheat him. Boone argued that they had both been imposed on by Floyd. But Floyd had been killed in a fight with Indians in 1783 and could not help sort out the dispute. It was the kind of legal mess Boone hated most. Boone argued that everything he had done was done in good faith, and he offered to replace Hickman's claim with double the number of acres on the Licking River, but Hickman refused. "Said Boone also told deponent that he had sold part of the defendant's land while he thought it was his son's right, but that he would give the defendant two acres for one on waters of Licking in lieu of what he had sold." After all, Boone's Creek was in the preferred Bluegrass region. Boone finally agreed to restore Hickman's land or give him equal acreage on Boone's Creek.

Jacob Boofman, the chainman, was already dead also, but he had taken possession of the property Floyd had surveyed for him, and his family had inherited the land. Hickman had to sue them, and the case dragged on for years before Hickman finally won. In 1794 when his title was established, Boone gave Hickman almost a square mile of land on Boone's Creek for ten pounds. Twenty years after the first survey, he was trying to do the right thing for his former client. But as in so many other cases, he was giving away what most businessmen would have fought for or sold for a profit. As the scholar Stephen Aron has said, "Boone was ill-equipped for the cut-throat practices of notable speculators. He was out of place in the courthouses and legislative halls where successful engrossers won their most important victories."

"Little by little his wealth melted away," his son Nathan later said. Some of the setbacks Boone suffered in the 1780s were simply the result of bad luck. For example, some of the documents for Boone's land deals, purchases, surveys, maps, titles, were in the hands of Col. John Floyd. When Floyd was killed by Indians in 1783 some of these papers were lost, along with Floyd's corroborating testimony, and Boone was deprived of evidence for claims where boundaries were disputed or titles contested. When it came to business, Boone seemed to have more than his share of bad breaks. From the loss of more than twenty thousand dollars at the inn in James City County, Virginia, in 1780, to the partial loss of a huge shipment of ginseng in a boating accident in 1788, to the loss of ten thousand acres in Fayette County to the swindler Gilbert Imlay, he encountered misfortunes with his investments and enterprises on a grand scale.

Among his multiple ventures in the 1780s was lending money to friends and acquaintances. At his warehouse in Limestone he ran a kind of frontier bank, where trappers and hunters could deposit furs and hides, ginseng and other products of the forest, as well as tobacco, and draw on their account from Boone's store. Friends would borrow money and simply forget to pay it back. A passage in his account book for 1784 reads:

Aprl 14 lent money to several persons
Nov. 12 lent Wm Hays & Jim Jones money
Dec. 20 lent James Harrod & Danville 3-0-6d
Dec. 20 lent Owen Owens & Daniel -12-shillings

According to Nathan, Boone stood security for a five-hundred-pound debt for a man named Ebenezer Plat in February 1786 and sold him a horse, saddle, bridle, and male slave on credit, and Ebenezer Plat was never seen again. It was Boone who ended up paying off the five-hundred-pound note. "Captain Plat was in New Orleans, so my father never got his property or its worth again, and this was the only Negro boy my father then possessed." Even worse was the case of Gilbert Imlay, an elegant and charming crook who had served as an officer in the Revolution in New Jersey. On August 15, 1785, Boone gave ten thousand acres between Hinkston Creek and the Licking River to Imlay on a promise to pay in installments, without even a down payment. Imlay never paid Boone a cent, sold the huge tract to somebody else, pocketed the money, and vanished from Kentucky. Imlay wrote to Boone from Virginia in 1786, apologizing for never paying for the purchase and suggesting Boone sell the tract to someone else. But Imlay had already sold the land to the notorious soldier and double agent James Wilkinson. Wilkinson was an officer in the American army but also an agent of the Spanish government, a slanderer of his betters such as Anthony Wayne, and a crook. He promoted the tract of land swindled from Boone as a property "located and surveyed by Col. Daniel Boone."

Creditors and victims of Imlay's intrigues from all over the country pursued him with warrants and duns and denunciations in newspapers, but he had already escaped to England. Imlay's talents proved as useful in the literary world as they had in America. In London he published *A Topographical Description of the Territory of North America* and included a version of Filson's narrative of Boone's life. Imlay formed a connection with the renowned feminist Mary Wollstonecraft, mother of Shelley's future wife, the author of *Frankenstein*. Imlay fathered her first child, Fannie, and ended up cheating her also. It was Imlay, through his connections with Wollstonecraft and William Godwin, who made Boone known to the English Romantics.

Throughout the 1780s Boone got deeper and deeper in debt, as he had to sell off land at dirt cheap prices just to pay his taxes, and he became embroiled in ever more lawsuits, mostly brought against him. He rarely went to court himself. Between 1786 and 1789 he was involved in at least ten lawsuits. He was sued for his contested surveys, lost titles, signatures on others' debts. Boone sometimes found it difficult to collect his fees for surveying. On July 17, 1785, he wrote a client, Nathaniel Rochester, "Sir, I must be plain with you. I am entirely out of cash and the chain men and Markers must be paid on the spot and I want 2 or 3 guineas for my own use. Sir, if you will send me six guineas by my little son it shall be settled on our first meeting, by Sir, your humble servant. Daniel Boone."

Historians, including Arthur K. Moore, have pointed out that heroes such as Boone were essential to the settlement of the frontier, but once the wilderness and Indians were gone the society had little use for the men themselves. It was the legend that was important.

It is painful to consider a man of Boone's talents and predilections enmeshed in such a labyrinth of debt, litigation, recrimination. Boone the hunter and explorer, the scout and visionary, was now bogged down in chicanery and greed, debt and con men. In spite of his fame and earlier successes, he had sunk to the level of horse trader and, apparently, even slave trader. The woodsman who had sought and loved the paradise of the wilderness, the Eden of Kentucky, had been swept along into the land boom with the worst of society. "It is apparent that without wealth, breeding, and education, the backwoodsmen fitted little better than the Indians and varmints into such a setting," Arthur K. Moore observed. Boone went along with the new times, but he did not change with the new age. He was still willing to divide what he had among his friends and associates, as he had back in his hunting days. Boone had failed himself and by doing so had failed many others also. His debts were beginning to outrun his assets and income.

Because of his Quaker upbringing, his respect for Indians, his peaceable nature, it is surprising that Boone accepted slavery so easily, owned slaves when he could afford them, and even traded in slaves. One would have thought that his experience as a captive of the Shawnees might have made him more sensitive to the issue of bondage, that his sense of fairness and honor would have led him to oppose slavery. It is a disturbing truth that even the best people tend to accept what they are familiar with, what they see practiced day after day around them.

Daniel Drake, who was brought to Kentucky as a boy around this time, was a lifelong opponent of slavery, in his career as a doctor. In his memoirs he left an account of a neighbor in Kentucky that reminds us of the reality of slavery on the frontier:

This man had a wife older and proportionably larger than himself, with two or three little children. He was very poor, and yet owned a negro man in middle life, and a woman rather old, at least twice the age of himself. His treatment of both was cruel in the extreme. A single pair of the flimsiest negro shoes was all the man got in the year, and the old woman was quite as miserably clothed. They were fed on stinted diet. Both worked in the field, and were pushed under the whip to the extremest degree. Its use on the man did not excite our feelings so much as that on the old woman. She had been his nurse in infancy, and yet he would tie her up, strip her back naked, and whip her with a cowhide till the blood would flow to her feet, and her screams would reach our ears at the distance of more than three hundred yards. Of course, we were greatly delighted when he left us.

Because he was Col. Daniel Boone, and because he knew the land better than anyone else, and because he was an official of Fayette

County, Boone was called on to testify again and again in hearings and trials. Since someone lost in every suit, Boone came to be hated by many. After being the greatest hero of Kentucky in 1784, by the late 1780s Boone was despised by scores of settlers for their losses and embarrassments. Rumors of the earlier accusations of his disloyalty still circulated. The descendants of Richard Callaway never tired of accusing Boone of treason in 1778. A number of times his life was threatened. His son Nathan later told Draper, "In addition to premeditated personal injury, he felt he was a target for assassination." Nothing hurt his feelings as much as accusations of dishonesty. Boone was especially sensitive to slights upon his character, in a place and time where such sensitivity was a liability.

Any business that took his mind away from the controversies and lawsuits of the land business would have been welcome. As a county official experienced in Indian affairs, Boone was called upon to negotiate with the Shawnees for the release of the prisoners he had been boarding on his property. In effect, Boone was the Indian agent in the area for the state of Virginia. In February 1787 he supplied two prisoners, a French Canadian and his Indian wife, with horses and provisions and sent them to the Shawnee towns to the north with an offer to exchange prisoners. In March, Captain Johnny, the new main chief after the death of Moluntha, brought three captive white children to Limestone to show his good faith. Chief Noamohouoh, who came with the delegation, declared that the Shawnees wanted nothing but peace, but he demanded that Queen Nonhelema be released from the keep in Danville, Kentucky, and Boone agreed to the request.

But Col. Benjamin Logan was not pleased with Boone's promise, and Col. Robert Patterson, who had Nonhelema in his charge, would not give her up. An angry exchange of letters passed between Boone and Patterson. Patterson had served as captain under Boone's command in the Fayette County militia at the Battle of the Blue Licks. Boone offered to take responsibility for the transaction. He had given his word to the Shawnee chief. "I flater myself [that you will] Send the Indian woman with the bearer," Boone wrote to Patterson. Finally Patterson did give up the Queen, but Boone's friendliness and ease in dealing with Indians always made him suspect among his fellow officers. In this case, Logan and Patterson may have been reluctant to hand over their most valuable prisoner without anything in return except the three white children and Noamohouoh's promise of peace. However, Logan clearly respected Boone's honesty, and each of Boone's expense accounts for boarding Indian prisoners was duly signed by Logan and forwarded on to the capital in Richmond.

In April 1787 a Shawnee chief named Captain Wolf arrived with nine American captives to be traded for Shawnees. In late August, Captain Johnny came to the north bank of the Ohio River with seventy-five warriors and a number of white prisoners and sent word across the river to Limestone where, Ted Franklin Belue tells us, "the Shawnees often ferried across to visit their beloved white brother, Sheltowee, and buy whiskey and supplies." Boone crossed the river to negotiate with him. The Shawnee chief explained that it had taken him two months to round up the prisoners from the scattered Shawnee towns. Boone was accompanied by Col. Benjamin Logan, and when Captain Johnny insisted that the Shawnees only wanted peace, though they did not concede any Ohio territory to the whites, Logan told Captain Johnny that if the Shawnees did not live in peace the Americans would take their Ohio lands from them. If they kept their word the Ohio River would remain the boundary between the whites and the Indians. "Go home and live at peace, and I will assure you, no army shall march against you from Kentucke."

Boone was at his best as liaison and diplomat, arranging the exchange of prisoners. Most of the Shawnees trusted him and he spoke their language in more senses than one. At this exchange in August 1787, wives who had been kidnapped were reunited with husbands, and children returned to parents. A girl named Chloe Flinn, who had lost her parents and had been captured by Shawnees, was taken in by Daniel and Rebecca and looked after until her kin were located in Virginia. She never forgot Boone's kindness and later named a son, Boone Ballard, in his honor.

The evening after the exchange, Boone invited the Shawnees across the river for a great feast, offering them barbecue from two steers and kegs of whiskey. There was music and dancing, and Indians and whites seemed to get along well, until one Kentuckian spotted a stolen mare in the possession of a Shawnee. Far gone in his cups, the man bragged he would take the mare back for the widow, its owner, even if he had to scalp every Indian present. Boone, ever the peacemaker, with the help of Simon Kenton, arranged to trade the mare for a keg of whiskey and returned the horse to the widow. Present at the exchange and barbecue was a young Shawnee named Blue Jacket. It has been said that Blue Jacket was a white American who had been captured as a teenager and had chosen to live with those who had captured and adopted him. Recent scholarship suggests that Blue Jacket was in fact born a Shawnee. Blue Jacket became particularly good friends with Boone's son Daniel Morgan and the two hunted together in the fall of 1787. Blue Jacket established a friendship with the whole Boone family and promised to protect Limestone residents from attacks and capture.

The next year, Blue Jacket was captured by raiders from Kentucky intent on stealing Shawnee horses. As they beat him into submission, Blue Jacket yelled, "Boone! Boone!" and explained he was a friend of Daniel Boone. The raiders took their prisoner to Limestone, where Boone agreed to lock him up in the cabin that served as a kind of jail. Then he invited the horse thieves to have a drink on him at the tavern. The men all got drunk, and during the night Blue Jacket found a knife stuck in the cabin wall, used it to cut the ropes that bound him, and escaped.

Blue Jacket rose to be a mighty chief of the Shawnees and, with Little Turtle of the Miamis, helped defeat the American armies of Harmar and St. Clair. He survived the Battle of Fallen Timbers in 1794 and lived to be an associate of Tecumseh in the next century. He always considered Daniel Boone his friend. Whatever his experience with other white men, he never forgot Boone's kindness and perhaps Boone's sense of humor.

However complicated Boone's land dealing had become, his life as a public official was not over. In the fall of 1787 he was again elected to represent his county in the Virginia legislature. Traveling to Richmond with Rebecca and Nathan, he was probably relieved to hand over his businesses to sons-in-law Will Hays and Philip Goe. In Richmond he introduced bills to create ferries on the Kentucky River and supported a resolution demanding that Britain give up its forts in the western territories. In this stint as a legislator Boone seems to have been more attentive than he had been six years earlier. Perhaps the presence of Rebecca in Richmond encouraged him to be more active in his office. Perhaps with age he saw his responsibilities in a new way.

ONE OF THE legends about Boone is that in 1788 he and his sons dug "fifteen tons" of ginseng to carry up the Ohio to the eastern market. Boone had dug ginseng for the China market and traded in the root for years. Ginseng was one of the treasures of the woods, along with beaver pelts and deerskins. "By the next spring we had some twelve or fifteen tons, which we loaded into a keelboat, and Father started up the river with his family with him," Nathan told Draper in 1851. Over the years, biographers and historians have repeated this story of Boone and his sons Daniel Morgan and Jesse, along with Rebecca and Nathan, poling a keelboat loaded with fifteen tons of ginseng up the Ohio and running aground on an island near Point Pleasant. Hit by a drifting log, the boat took on water. Poling the ruined cargo and damaged boat to shore, they were taken in by the Van Bibber family, whom years before Boone had rescued in a snowstorm.

It is a wonderful story, but no one ever seems to have tried to visualize how much ginseng fifteen tons would be. Ginseng, after it is dug, is dried and very light. Fifteen tons, or thirty thousand pounds, would fill a warehouse or a ship. What Boone and his sons were actually transporting was fifteen *tuns*, or barrels. And much of it had been dug by others and sold to Boone. "Father was busily employed in digging ginseng. He employed several hands for this work and also bought up what he could." In fact, a great deal of the ginseng was bought from others. In "Daniel Boone's Account Book" we find this entry: "Oct. 9th 1788, recd. 15 caggs of ginseng of Capt. Fagan for Hart." Tobacco and many other products were transported in barrels, and coopers were much in demand in frontier towns. A tun was a cask and could be different sizes, though a ton was also a measure of volume in a ship, not weight. Fifteen barrels of ginseng might well fit into a keelboat to be poled up a river. And the kegs had to be small enough to load onto packhorses at the end of the river journey for transporting to Maryland. When Nathan Boone told Draper the story, Draper simply mistook the term, and historians through the years have passed on his mistake. Also it is likely the trip up the river was made in the fall of 1788, not the spring. Nathan was recalling events that happened sixty-three years earlier, when he was only seven years old.

(Scholars have found Nathan's testimony especially reliable, but he is not always correct. "In the fall of 1784 we moved out of Boone's Station and settled his farm, a new place on Marble Creek, about five miles west of Boone's Station," Nathan told Draper. Nathan, who was only three years old in 1784, was almost certainly mistaken. In 1784 Filson published his map of "Kentucke" and located Boone near Marble Creek, not Boone's Station. And Boone's land was apparently not on Marble Creek itself, but only in the area.)

The story of the ginseng does, however, have a somewhat happy ending. Enjoying a renewed friendship with the Van Bibbers, the Boones repaired the keelboat and dried out as much of the cargo as they could. The Van Bibbers would befriend the Boones when they later moved to Point Pleasant, and young Nathan would marry Olive Van Bibber, a relative, eleven years later. Continuing their journey up the Ohio to Pittsburgh, and then up the Monongahela to Redstone, they loaded the kegs on packhorses and carried them over the Cumberland Road to Hagerstown, Maryland, where Boone sold the damaged ginseng to an old acquaintance from Transylvania Company days, Thomas Hart, who had a store there. He got only half what he had hoped for.

AFTER DISPOSING of the fifteen barrels of "sang," while Daniel Morgan and Jesse returned to Kentucky, Boone and Rebecca and Nathan rode north to visit relatives near Oley, Pennsylvania, where Boone had grown up. Residents in Pennsylvania recalled years later that Boone stayed for several months, and while Rebecca was talkative and cheerful, Boone was quiet and dour. His son Nathan later said it was while they were visiting in Pennsylvania that his father resolved to leave Kentucky. "Then he also decided to take up residence at Point Pleasant and not return to Maysville [Limestone] as he had originally intended." The accusations and lawsuits had become too much for Boone. While he was away a few months he realized just how much stress he had been living with. Rachael Lightfoot, who recalled the Boones from this visit, described him as "dark complexioned & stern looking — very taciturn and gloomy." But she described Rebecca as "very pleasant and sociable and spoke very freely of their affairs and bereavement."

This visit to the place of his birth and childhood appears to be another turning point in Boone's life. Seeing his Quaker relations again, he may have thought how far he had strayed from the teachings of peace and tolerance. Seeing the places where he had hunted and herded cattle as a boy, he may have recalled his mother and felt the call of the woods again, and been reminded how essential a life in the wilderness was for him. It was the sensuous body of the land he loved, not the head full of numbers and laws and vexations of authority. His fame and success and the whisper of wealth and the culture of land grabbing had distracted and led him astray from what mattered to him. Back in Pennsylvania he must have seen his recent life in a hard, sober light.

From Nathan's comments to Draper, we gather that Boone thought long and hard while resting in Pennsylvania. He was fifty-four years old, and he didn't want to spend the rest of his life fighting lawsuits, appearing in court, answering angry clients of his land surveys and sales. Kentucky had gotten away from him. The beavers and buffalo and Indians had been replaced by lawyers and politicians and crooks. Even the small farms were being replaced by plantations. "In place of cane, the cabin sites were now overgrown by hemp, the slave-produced cash crop which brought central Kentucky planters great prosperity in the antebellum era."

BY 1788 THE irony could not have been lost on Boone that he, as much as any other single human being, had helped create the world that was now repugnant to him, so raging and relentless in growth and greed. And he must have seen, perhaps for the first time, the contradiction and conflict at the heart of so much of his effort: to lead white people into the wilderness and make it safe for them was to destroy the very object of his quest. The paradox had been present in almost everything he had done, and yet he had ignored or misunderstood it. Whenever the recognition came to him, it must have been sobering, for he had to see that his genius and his talents virtually canceled each other out. Wherever he went, many others would follow. He wanted to enjoy and keep the object of his desire at the same time. For all his achievements and fame, his kindness and compassion, cunning and knowledge, Boone had made a fool of himself, too. He had acted the fool, and he must have come to that hard view of his life.

It was a recognition most of us come to, whatever our accomplishments and worldly success or failure. The foolishness is inherent in our nature, and few of us escape it, even if we recognize our kinks and smallnesses for what they are. As he sat in Pennsylvania and thought and thought and said little, Boone became a wiser man, and by the time he and Rebecca and Nathan returned to Kentucky he was perhaps a somewhat different man.

Once back in Kentucky, Boone began a process of selling off much of the property he had acquired and closing down a number of the businesses he had started. There were many outstanding disputes and lawsuits to deal with, but he curbed his speculation in land. He continued to do some surveying, but on a smaller scale. He turned over his land business to son-in-law Will Hays, and his store and tavern were to be managed by Philip Goe. He was scaling back, giving up the expansive, entrepreneurial ambition and intoxication that had ruined him.

It was Point Pleasant at the mouth of the Kanawha River that attracted. The Van Bibbers lived there, and he needed friendly faces. The rivers appealed to him, both the Kanawha and the Ohio, and the mountains of that part of western Virginia were less settled than much of Kentucky.

While he prepared for the move to Point Pleasant during the fall and winter and into the spring of 1789, Boone and his sons spent much time hunting and gathering ginseng. They probably looked for the herb while hunting deer in summer and early fall. Once dug, the roots had to be dried and packed in barrels. Boone also bought a number of horses, which Jesse and Daniel Morgan drove over the mountains to sell in Hagerstown. Besides European breeds of draft and saddle horses, some of these mounts may have been Indian ponies. Choctaw ponies were one of the special breeds of frontier Kentucky. Some of the horses in the region were of Spanish origin, brought up from the nations in the south and west, and some were brought from Canada.

In 1789 Boone loaded another keelboat with kegs of ginseng and he and Rebecca and Nathan poled up the river again. But when they met Jesse and Daniel Morgan at Redstone, Boone was told the bottom had dropped out of the ginseng market. He would hardly cover his costs on that trip, and he also found out a number of the horses he had sent to Maryland had been lost in the rough mountain country of Virginia.

Boone could not be blamed if he decided there was a jinx on his business ventures. Almost every business he attempted failed. He could not seem to transfer his skill and cleverness in the woods and his charisma with people into a profitable line of work. Perhaps he gave up too quickly on some ventures or gave in too easily to adversity. Perhaps his heart was not really in a lot of his enterprises in this period.

But the harder he worked the less his efforts seemed to succeed. He spent much of 1789 hauling freight and passengers in his keelboat on the Ohio. Every day one could see flatboats and keelboats, rafts and canoes, on *la belle rivière*. Around 1788 to 1789 Boone and his family were a part of this river traffic, poling, rowing, sometimes sailing on the big water artery that brought more immigrants by the day if not the hour.

The story of Boone's failure in Kentucky was the story of many first explorers and settlers. By 1789 he knew his health and happiness lay in the wilderness, and he determined to return there. He was fifty-five years old, and he had suffered from fifteen tons of bad luck. But he was ready to make another move, a new beginning. And so in the fall of 1789 he moved to Point Pleasant.

THOUGH BOONE WAS MOST famous for hacking out the trace that later became known as the Wilderness Road, he, like most frontiersmen of his day, was also a navigator of rivers. Having acquired his own keelboat around 1788, he plied the Ohio between Limestone and Point Pleasant in Virginia, and as far upstream as Pittsburgh and beyond, to Redstone on the Monongahela.

The smallest crafts used in the wilderness were the canoe and bull boat, both of which originated with the Indians. A bull boat was constructed from "bull" buffalo hides stitched together and sealed with resin, then stretched over a wooden frame. Shawnees used them mostly to ferry across rivers such as the Ohio. They carried the boat hides with them, and could build a frame quickly from saplings and withes.

For longer journeys a canoe was preferable. Most of the canoes in Kentucky were dugouts. Boone used canoes to travel on rivers and creeks to hunt. On April 9, 1797, the Englishman Francis Baily encountered Boone paddling a canoe on the Ohio near the mouth of the Big Sandy, on his way to hunt north of the river. Said Baily, "I . . . found that he was one of that class of men who, from nature and habit, was nearly allied in disposition and manners to an Indian."

Many if not most of those coming down the Ohio to Kentucky in the 1780s and 1790s traveled on flatboats. Constructed in boatyards at Pittsburgh or at sites on the Monongahela, flatboats had evolved from rafts of logs. They were guided by a long oar in the back and one shorter oar on either side.

Because a flatboat was propelled by the current, it was especially vulnerable to Indian raids. Many who traveled by flatboat down the Ohio were killed by Indians or died from diseases caused by the foul conditions on board or from drinking contaminated river water. A flatboat could travel only downstream, and when its destination was reached the wood was sold for building or firewood. Flatboats not only brought people down the river but carried produce, pork, ginseng, maple syrup, bear grease, and whiskey down the Mississippi to New Orleans.

The most important craft on the river was the keelboat. Sleek and rounded, the wooden keelboat was pointed at both ends. Its name came from the large keel that ran from bow to stern to protect the hull. Keelboats were usually about forty feet long, seven to nine feet wide. The deck was enclosed in a cabin that protected passengers, crew, cargo. The keelboat could go both downstream and upstream. On either side of the cabin, along the gunwales, lay a track called a running board. Three to nine men on each side drove their iron-tipped twenty-foot poles into the riverbed and pushed. Going upstream in a fast current, the men with poles stepped to the front of the runway and, driving the poles into the mud, walked backward, shoving the boat ahead with their feet on the cleated runway.

In drought there was hardly enough water to float a keelboat along the edge of the river. The crew sometimes had to take a towline and pull the boat up the worst stretches. This was called cordelling. A crew was lucky to travel six miles a day upstream by cordelling. Even harder was the "warping" technique, whereby a rope was fixed to a tree or boulder far upstream and the boat was hauled forward by reeling in the rope with a windlass or pulling it hand over hand.

In flood time, when the river was spread out among the trees along the banks, the keelboatmen could push the craft upstream by grabbing limbs and saplings and pulling, threading a way through the half-sunken forest, on water smooth as the floor of a ballroom. This method was called bushwhacking. Where a powerful river emptied into a larger stream, there were sometimes "boils" that shot a boat sideways and could capsize it. One of the most common dangers was wind. A sudden gust could catch a keelboat and send it crashing into the bank or other boats, or onto a sandbar. And on rare occasions when a crevasse—caused by rain or flooding—opened in a levee, a keelboat was sucked into the spill and wrecked.

Hard as it was to pole or row, or sometimes tow a keelboat upstream, it was still easier and cheaper than carrying cargo overland on pack animals. Roads fit for wagons would not reach Kentucky until near the end of the eighteenth century.

Keelboat. Edwin Tunis. Drawing. *Frontier Living,* 1961. While the flatboat, or broadhorn, was the most common craft for bringing settlers and cargo down the Ohio River to Kentucky, it was the keelboat that came to dominate river traffic in the era before the introduction of the steamboat. (Photo: Benjamin R. Morgan.)

CHAPTER SEVENTEEN

Going East to Go West

1789 – 1797 ↜

The move to Point Pleasant at the mouth of the Kanawha River in 1789 was a step forward for Boone and also a step back. It was a step forward in the sense that he was returning to the woods, to a cabin in the more thinly settled Virginia frontier along the Ohio where he could hunt and dig ginseng and trap mink and beaver. The move was a step backward in the long pilgrimage of his life because he was going to a place he already knew, a step back because it was to the northeast and Boone's progress had been essentially westward, a step backward in the sense that he was retreating from the vexed land and surveying business in Kentucky.

He had turned the land business over to Will Hays and others to untangle and conduct as best they could, and he sold his store and tavern and warehouse in Limestone. He was stepping back from his many official duties at Limestone also, where he had been lieutenant colonel of the militia, coroner, representative to the legislature. In 1788 he had also been made a trustee of the nearby town of Washington, Kentucky. He was returning to the woods to simplify his life. He was tired of the warehouse, the tavern, the jail, and the land office. In the east the representatives of the thirteen new states were thrashing out the document that would become the United States Constitution. Boone was more focused on his own constitution.

But the new life in Point Pleasant turned out not to be as different as Boone must have hoped. At the new location, where the rivers met, Boone opened a little store and continued to trade in furs and hides, bear meat and ginseng. He may have brought goods to trade from the store he had sold in Limestone. It would have been the natural thing to do. He was backing away from business but only a few steps at a time. Everyone knew of Boone and everyone stopped at his store. There was swelling traffic on the Ohio, and many hunters and trappers and "sang" diggers in the Kanawha Valley brought their harvest down that river to trade for supplies, traps, guns, staples, whiskey. One visitor recalled sleeping in the store overnight and being awakened by grease from bear bacon dripping on his face.

Boone shipped most of the furs and hides and ginseng he accumulated to a merchant in Maryland named Vanlear. "1790 Apl. 27 Van Lears, merchtr., write from Williamsport, Md. 'Every prospect of deerskins and fur commanding a good price' . . . '2 Barrells Ginseng.'" The hunting was done by his sons Daniel Morgan and Jesse, and records show that though Boone sent many barrels of ginseng and bales of beaver skins, he never got out of debt to Vanlear, because the merchant sent him trade goods in return. No matter where he lived, or the volume of business he conducted, Boone was hounded by debt. It was the story of his Yadkin years, and the Kentucky years, and it continued to be the story of his Point Pleasant years. Boone was a gambler, always betting that his luck would change. He lived with his passions and enthusiasms, hopeful that debts would take care of themselves as he moved on to each new enterprise.

"The year 1790 marks the end of an era — the heroic age of the pioneers of the Old Southwest," wrote Archibald Henderson in 1920. If Boone's most heroic actions were in the past, there were still considerable challenges to face, as Indians attacked the settlements along the Ohio again and again. And Boone's reputation for heroic action continued to grow. In October 1790 the *European Magazine*, published in London, featured an article titled "Adventures of Colonel Daniel

Boone, one of the original Settlers of Kentucky; containing the Wars with the Indians on the Ohio, from 1769 to the Year 1784, &c. written by Himself." It was yet another reprinting of a version of Filson's "Adventures."

At Point Pleasant Boone even worked from time to time at his old profession of surveying. But gone were the heady days when he had his own teams with assistants whom he kept supplied with "Old Monongahela." And no sooner had Boone arrived at Point Pleasant in 1789 than he was commissioned lieutenant colonel of the county militia. There were still Indian raids across the Ohio, and Boone organized the defense when settlers gathered at a local fort. The Shawnees attacked Tackett's Fort in 1789 and Fort Lee in 1790. But the greatest danger was from small raiding parties that crossed the river and killed settlers in their fields or along woodland trails.

While Boone's friend John Van Bibber was making maple syrup in a grove on the north bank of the Ohio, his daughter Rachel and son Joseph crossed the river in a canoe intending to join him. A party of Shawnees captured them and killed and scalped the daughter and took his son prisoner. A number of other members of Van Bibber's extended family were killed in Indian raids. More than once Daniel and his son Daniel Morgan encountered Indians in the woods and had to flee or hide. Several times it was reported that Boone had been killed by Indians, but these stories turned out to be "greatly exaggerated," as Mark Twain later said of his own reported death.

In 1791 Boone was once more elected a county representative to the Virginia legislature. It was his third stint as a lawmaker, and his election shows the high regard his new neighbors had for him. He took Rebecca and ten-year-old Nathan to Richmond with him for the sessions and served quietly and faithfully with the lawmaking body. Boone was, in fact, in Richmond when Kentucky separated from Virginia and became a state itself in 1792. Later Nathan recalled his visits to Richmond as a boy, and the travel back and forth, as an idyllic time.

Far from the land disputes and debts in Kentucky, Boone had made a new start. He seemed to relish his work with the legislature. Nathan would remember picnics by the James River, and his mother roasting oysters over an open fire. The route to and from Kanawha was over the Midland Trail, and once they stopped in the Shenandoah Valley to visit Boone's old friend Henry Miller, now a prosperous owner of an ironworks. "There my father saw among Miller's cattle an animal of unusually large horns; he expressed a wish that he had one of them, as it would make a splendid powder horn." Miller killed the steer and gave a horn to Boone to carve into a powder horn for Nathan. Scraping and carving horns was a favorite pastime for Boone, carving buttons and spoons and powder horns. As he sat by the fire and talked or listened, Boone preferred to keep his hands busy, making something useful. (This visit to Henry Miller's farm likely occurred during Boone's 1787 term in the legislature, since Miller apparently died in 1790.)

In 1791 Boone seemed ready to make himself useful in other ways. He proposed to the governor of Virginia that he, Boone, act as commissary to the militia forces in the western part of the state. It was the kind of appointment where a crook might make a killing, but an honest man such as Boone could realize at best a modest profit from a huge amount of hardship and effort. Agreeing to supply militias in the backwoods, with Indians lurking along the trails and with floods and snowstorms threatening, and sources of supply hundreds of miles away over mountain paths, was no small undertaking. Likely Boone expected to supply most of the forts along the Ohio and Monongahela with the game he shot himself.

Boone wrote to the governor, "Sum purson Must Carry out the armantstion to Red Stone. I would undertake it, on condition I have the a pintment to vitel the company at Kanhowway." That is, if given the contract to supply the garrison at Kanawha with meat and provisions, he would undertake the dangerous task of carrying powder and lead across the mountains to Red Stone and other forts. He was given the job. It is possible that no one else applied for the honor.

When the legislative session closed just before Christmas, Boone was issued from the state armory four hundred pounds of gunpowder, sixteen hundred pounds of lead, and a keg of rifle flints to be distributed to the forts in the western part of the state. Roads in much of the mountains were little more than trails, so Boone had to distribute more than a ton of supplies by packhorse. With ice storms and snows, floods and Indian threats, it took him until April to reach all the widely separated forts. It is likely the respective officers were not pleased with the months of delay in getting their supplies and ammunition.

Boone discovered he had taken on more than he could manage. Because of his many debts he was unable to purchase on credit sufficient quantities of bacon and flour to supply the militia in his district, and he ran short of provisions. What had seemed an obvious way to make a little money and serve the state and local security turned quickly into a headache if not a nightmare.

Col. George Clendinen of the local militia assumed Boone was bringing lead and powder for the county garrison also, but that had not been Boone's understanding. Capt. Hugh Caperton of the Point Pleasant militia, who had been a friend of Boone's, proved impatient and ill tempered. He accused Boone of incompetence and riled Boone into a shouting match. Boone stormed off and would have nothing further to do with Caperton. When Colonel Clendinen came to investigate Captain Caperton's accusations of Boone's failure to supply the militia, Boone was not to be found. He had disappeared into the forest, and when he was finally tracked down he would only say, "Captain Caperton did not do to my likes." He would have no more to do with the matter.

For failure to fulfill his contract with the state, Boone could have been court-martialed. But Colonel Clendinen chose to appoint another supplier and not embarrass the old frontiersman further. Caperton must have been a difficult man to work with, for he was soon afterward relieved of his command by court-martial. Once again an attempt to establish a business had blown up in Boone's face. Boone must have had nightmares about his lifelong losses. He had lost fortune after fortune in furs to the Indians. He had lost thousands of acres of Kentucky land to contested surveys, incomplete deeds, dishonest speculators, bad management. He had lost fields and houses, sugar groves, forts, and meadows. He had lost two sons and a favorite brother to Indians. He had lost dozens of friends and acquaintances in Indian wars. Now he lost interest in business completely. His failure with the provisioning contract shows he was getting old. At fifty-seven he was beginning to feel the effects of years of exposure and hardship. Even his extraordinary constitution was subject to arthritis and fatigue. His celebrated patience had worn thin.

Within months of the confrontation with Caperton, Boone would close his store at Point Pleasant and move to a cabin sixty miles away on a hill with a commanding view of the Kanawha valley, near the future Charleston. Once again he was a squatter, and he assigned his nephew John Grant his power of attorney to look after his property and affairs in Kentucky. He told Grant and his children to not even bother to contest claims. Lawsuits cost more money and trouble than they were worth. "Though he had fought as hard and long for Kentucky as any other person, he would rather be poor than retain an acre of land or a farthing of money so long as claims and debts hung over him," Nathan later said. Boone was finished with business and legal affairs, and he spent his days the way he liked best, hunting and trapping, wandering the woods on the beautiful hills along the Kanawha.

Luckily there were still beaver in the region. They had mostly been trapped out in Kentucky. But in the mountains of Virginia, in what became West Virginia, there were still dams and colonies along the creeks. Setting traps was easier than hunting. Skins were lighter to carry out of the woods than deer hides or heavy bearskins and hams. And beaver fur was still one of the most valuable products in the woods. Skins and a few traps could be carried by a man approaching sixty with arthritis. Annette Kolodny tells us, "As Boone grew older and increasingly enfeebled by rheumatism, moreover, it became common knowledge that Rebecca accompanied him into the woods, helping her husband to bring down the game, aiming and firing when his knotted fingers could not, and generally proving as valuable a companion as any son or Indian might be."

At times his rheumatism got so bad he could hardly walk. It was reported that a hunting companion named Worth had to carry the old hunter across streams. It must have been humiliating for the famous long hunter to be so helpless in the woods. The arthritis would come and go, depending on the weather and his exertions, but at its worst he was almost crippled. Even afflicted, it was said, Boone killed more deer than any of his neighbors because he knew their habits so thoroughly. He especially enjoyed hunting deer in Teaze's Valley, a few miles south of Point Pleasant, where there were so many deer tracks it was impossible to follow one particular deer unless it was bleeding.

A description of Boone given to Draper by one who knew him in this period provides yet another impression of him in late middle age. "His large head, full chest, square shoulders, and stout form are still impressed upon my mind. He was (I think) about five feet ten inches in height, and his weight say 175. He was solid in mind as well as in body, never frivolous . . . but was always quiet, meditative, and impressive, unpretentious, kind, and friendly in his manner." This is an appealing portrait of Boone at the time he had suffered such losses. It diverges in some points from the testimony of his son Nathan, who put his father's height at five eight, adding that his "hair was moderately black, eyes blue, and he had fair skin."

Boone's generosity to friends and fellow hunters is attested by those who knew him on the Kanawha. It was said that in 1792 he trapped with one Robert Safford and caught over a hundred beavers. At the end of the season he presented Safford with his best tomahawk and his favorite trap called Old Isaac. Fame, tragedy, and loss had not taken away his thoughtfulness and kindness. Even the arthritis had not changed his disposition or shaken his poise.

IT IS NOT clear exactly when or why Daniel and Rebecca and Nathan left the cabin on the Kanawha and returned to Kentucky. Perhaps they wanted to be closer to their other children and grandchildren living in northern Kentucky. Or maybe Boone was just restless again. It is also possible that the continued Indian raids into Kanawha country encouraged the Boones to move farther away from both the Ohio and the Kanawha rivers.

In 1793 Nathan had been sent to Kentucky to attend a Baptist school near Lexington. Later he told Draper it was he who encouraged his parents to return to Kentucky, in part because the interior of Kentucky was safer from Indian attack than the mountains of Virginia. Nathan had many memories of hunting with his father and avoiding encounters with the Shawnees. Once, they were camped in a heavy fog and Boone heard Indians across the river chopping wood. He knew they were making a raft to cross the river. Boone loaded the canoe with the meat they had killed and pushed off, floating downstream in the fog. "On the way Father put his head over the canoe and close to the water and said he thought he could catch a glimpse of the Indians. He had looked between the surface of the water and the fog . . . Soon we were beyond harm." That same night horses were stolen from Daniel Morgan Boone and Matthias Van Bibber.

Though Boone himself was no longer engaged in Indian fighting, hostilities between whites and Indians had by no means ceased in the Ohio country. American forces had suffered two major defeats at the hands of the Shawnees, Miamis, and other tribes while the Boones lived at Point Pleasant and on the Kanawha. Col. Josiah Harmar, who commanded an army of about fifteen hundred, lost many men in a confrontation with a force led by Little Turtle, of the Miamis, and Blue Jacket, of the Shawnees, in the Maumee Valley in 1790. His successor, Gen. Arthur St. Clair, lost almost nine hundred men in a battle with Little Turtle and Blue Jacket on the Wabash, about twenty miles north of later Greenville, Ohio, November 4, 1791. St. Clair's was the greatest loss of any battle between American forces and Indians on the western frontier, more than triple that of Custer at the Little Big Horn in 1876. In 1793 "Mad" Anthony Wayne was appointed commander of the western forces.

Wayne assembled a group of volunteers in Pittsburgh and moved them down the Ohio River. Then in the Cincinnati area he recruited more men and for a year trained them in Indian fighting at forts along the Miami River. Wayne and his little army marched north in 1794 to confront the Shawnees and Miamis in the Maumee region and defeat them at the Battle of Fallen Timbers. The next year the Shawnees and Miamis signed the treaty of Greenville with the United States, giving up their claims to much of the region north of the Ohio, ending the worst of the Indian raids across the Ohio. The Shawnees chose to move west, many going all the way to the Missouri.

Whether Boone left the Kanawha area to get farther from Indian raids or not, he and Rebecca and Nathan returned to Kentucky in 1794 or 1795. He left a very good impression of himself among his neighbors in the Kanawha region. Writing a century later, a resident and descendant of pioneers in the area, J. P. Hale, said that Boone was not remembered sufficiently "for his qualities and experience as a counselor, commander, and legislator, in which fields, notwithstanding his rare modesty and lack of self-asserting, he was appreciated and put forward by his contemporaries." Hale went on to write, in his short biography of Boone, that the old frontiersman hardly seemed aware of the heroic deeds he had done "but seemed to be driven on, irresistibly, by that deep seated instinct for adventure which nature had implanted in him, and whose only gratification could be found among the wilds of the frontier."

One thing that may have brought Boone back to Kentucky was the bear hunting on the Levisa Fork of the Big Sandy. Each winter Daniel and Rebecca and one or two of their sons returned there to kill bears, collect bearskins, smoke bear bacon, and render bear flesh into oil. A man named William Champ later said he encountered Boone and his wife and two daughters with their husbands on the Big Sandy living in half-face camps, where they "ate their meals from a common rough tray, very much like a Sap trough, placed on a bench instead of a table, each using as needed a butcher knife to cut meat, & using forks made of cane, with tines or prongs, & and having only bread to eat with the meat." Bears were so abundant that Boone killed 155 in one season, and he killed one monster bear that weighed between five hundred and six hundred pounds. A bearskin was worth about two dollars, but the meat of each animal was worth more than twice that. Boone's arthritis was so bad at times that Rebecca had to carry his rifle for him, but he killed record numbers of bears all the same. And since she was known as an excellent shot, Rebecca very likely killed her share of the bruins also.

One of the creeks where they camped was named Greasy Creek because they rendered bear fat there, enough to fill several barrels. Bear grease could be sold for a dollar a gallon. One bear might yield twenty gallons of oil. Boone bragged that he had once killed eleven bears before breakfast. With his commercial hunting conducted on such a scale, it is hard to imagine how Boone thought the game population could be sustained. The last buffalo in the Bluegrass had been killed around 1790. This is still one of the paradoxes of Boone's life and his character. Because he had been a professional hunter most of his life, the paradox was probably not as clear to Boone as it is to us in hindsight. After all, he did not know in 1795 that the buffalo would disappear from the prairie even farther west, that the beaver would retreat to the most remote valleys of the western mountains, and that passenger pigeons, ivory-billed woodpeckers, and Carolina parakeets would become apparently extinct. Whatever may have passed through his mind, he needed to recoup his fortunes a little, and the bears were still there, in the Big Sandy country, by the hundreds if not the thousands. And besides, if he didn't kill them, somebody else would.

It seems that by the summer of 1795 the Boones had moved back to Kentucky, settling in a cabin on property owned by Daniel

Morgan Boone on Brushy Fork of Hinkston Creek near the Blue Licks, near where Boone was captured by the Shawnees in 1778. Boone and Nathan cleared land and planted several acres of crops. The place on Brushy Creek was safer from Indian raids than the towns along the Ohio, but the game had been depleted in the region, the deer almost entirely gone. In winter the Boones still hunted bears over the mountains on the Big Sandy, but around their cabin there was little game, not even turkeys. The legend is that Daniel Boone was reduced to eating mutton! Of course someone really poor would have had to eat mush or live on grits and beans. But for a great hunter, eating mutton was a sign of reduced circumstances.

The three or four years spent on Brushy Creek were hard by any standards. Boone's land was mostly gone, contested, or under litigation. Because of his contested surveys, he was being sued for fraud, even by the families of his old friends from the Transylvania Company, Thomas and Nathaniel Hart. It seemed he would never hear the last of the land business. The opinion of many angry landowners in Kentucky was that Boone had cheated them. Some, including young Henry Clay, who had married into the Hart family, sued him.

According to Stephen Aron, "In 1797, the surveyor general of Kentucky reported to the legislature that while grants for approximately twenty-four million acres had been issued, the state contained only half that much acreage." The mess of land disputes extended far beyond Boone, of course. He was only the most famous of those enmeshed in the litigation. Prominent men such as William Fleming, who had served as a Virginia land commissioner in 1779–80, lost even more than Boone in the Kentucky land confusion.

Searching for a new livelihood, Boone heard that Kentucky was going to rebuild the Wilderness Road as a road for wagons and carriages. It was still called Boone's Trace by many. It occurred to him that maybe he could get the contract for widening and improving Boone's Trace. With no other prospects in sight, Boone took pen in weathered hand February 11, 1796, and wrote to his former associate Isaac Shelby, now governor of the new state of Kentucky.

> Sir – After my best Respts to your Excelancy and family I wish
> to inform you that I have sum intention of undertaking this New
> Rode that is to be cut through the Wilderness and I think my Self
> intitled to the ofer of the Bisness as I first Marked out that Rode in
> March 1775 and Never rec'd anything for my trubel and Sepose I am
> no Statesman I am a Woodsman and think My Self as Capable of
> Marking and Cutting that Rode, as any other man Sir if you think
> with Me I would thank you to wright me a Line by the post the first
> oportuneaty and he will lodge it at Mr. John Milers on Hinkston
> fork as I wish to know Wheer and when it is to be Latt So I may at-
> tend at the time I am Deer Sir
>
> *Your very omble servent Daniel Boone*

It must have cost Daniel Boone a lot to write that letter to his young former associate. Boone never was one to put on airs, but it was almost certainly painful to ask for the contract and remind the governor that he had hacked out the first Wilderness Road. Implicit in the letter is his admission of need, never an easy thing for someone of Boone's independence and pride. He must have thought a long time before finally sending the letter. But the request did him no good. As far as we can tell, Governor Shelby did not even bother to answer his former friend, the old frontiersman down on his luck. The letter was preserved with his other papers but never given a response. The silence, and the award of the contract to someone else, did nothing to make Boone feel at home in Kentucky.

Isaac Shelby was one of the outstanding officers of the American Revolution in the South and West. When only thirty, he had led his militia to victories at Thicketty Fort, Musgrove's Mill, and Kings Mountain in South Carolina. More than anyone, he was the architect of the victory over Patrick Ferguson in the latter battle. He had surveyed land in Kentucky in 1775 and was an outstanding leader and politician. He would later be instrumental in the victory over the British at the battle of the Thames in Canada in 1813. As the first governor of Kentucky, he was no doubt overwhelmed by requests for favors, petitions. Political pressures were probably brought to bear for some petitioners. Besides, Boone's probity had been questioned, and his reputation as a surveyor was under a cloud. He had failed and was living in a borrowed cabin. He was old, and Shelby had likely heard of Boone's failure as a commissary for the Virginia militia. And the old scout had no experience at building roads other than chopping out rough trails for packhorses. True, he had built forts and bridges, cabins, boats, rafts, gunstocks, and every kind of backwoods furniture. And he had surveyed a road from the Yadkin to Salisbury in the 1750s. But that was long ago. Shelby acted as almost any executive would have under the circumstances. James Knox and Joseph Crockett were commissioned to rebuild Boone's Trace. But even the route rebuilt by Knox and Crockett in the 1790s was little more than a trail for pack animals "until 1818, when definite legislative steps were taken to widen the roadway and to improve the fords."

When the Wilderness Road was rebuilt for wagons, it followed a different route from the one Boone and later Crabtree had followed. History was already replacing and bypassing his most notable work. The old scout and hunter might be celebrated as a hero in literature, because the country needed a hero in its march toward progress and culture and wealth, but the woodsman himself was no longer wanted.

WHILE LIVING on Brushy Creek, Boone again returned to surveying. It was a skill in demand, and in spite of all the lawsuits and disputed claims, Boone must have been recognized as a competent surveyor. Neal O. Hammon tells us, "In 1796 he began surveying again, and made at least ten more surveys in Madison and Mason Counties."

One enterprise Daniel and Rebecca pursued with vigor on Brushy Creek was sugar making. When they returned from the bear hunt on the Big Sandy in late winter, the sap was rising in the maple groves. As snow melted on the south slopes, and ice along the creeks began to drip and run, and arbutus bloomed in sheltered spots, they scattered through the woods tapping trees and hanging cups to catch the sweet tears drawn from the roots and trunk and branches. The drops filled cups and the cups filled noggins and buckets. Over a furnace in the woods they boiled the juice until it was syrup, and then until the syrup was sugar. Husband and wife worked day after day extracting and concentrating the sweetness from the trees on the hillsides in late winter, as they had done so many times over the past forty years.

From time to time Boone was summoned to appear at court about an unpaid debt or faulty land claim. For all his fame, that was his main contact with the world at this time: summonses and indictments, threats and duns. The quiet work of sap gathering must have seemed a sweet refuge indeed.

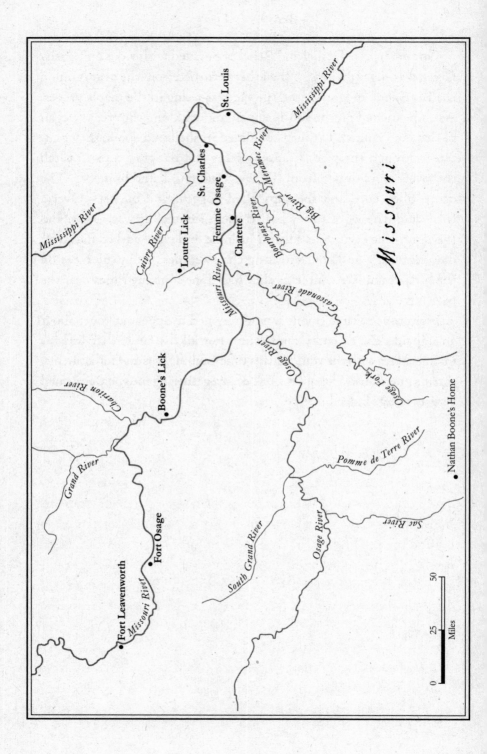

CHAPTER EIGHTEEN

To the Farther West

1798 – 1808 ↳

In the late 1790s Boone and his family began to plan a move to the Missouri territory, far to the west. The continuing summonses to court in land disputes, angry clients or former clients, accusations of fraud, certainly encouraged such a move. A sheriff tried to serve a warrant for his arrest but found he had already left Brushy Creek. But there were other factors in the Boones' decision to go west as well. The game was depleted in Kentucky; the buffalo were gone, the beaver and deer were scarce, and elk had disappeared. Even with arthritis and the weakness of age, he still preferred hunting to any other occupation. He needed wilderness and wild animals. It might even be said that he needed Indians. What was a hunt or a wilderness without Indians? What was a forest without the challenge of Native Americans lurking and spying? He was happiest in the Middle Ground with Indians nearby. By 1798 Boone knew quite well that when the Indians left, the game would soon follow. There was no way to have one without the other. A wilderness without Indians was a contradiction in terms. But after the treaty of Greenville in 1795, the Indians were virtually gone from Kentucky and much of Ohio.

"Nowhere in America has the almost instantaneous change from uncultivated waste to the elegances of civilization, been so striking," said a guidebook for immigrants to the west in 1818. The hunters had been replaced by small farmers who had been replaced by the slave-owning planters. The main crop in the Bluegrass region was hemp, and soon there were many establishments producing rope and sacks and canvas from the hemp. With the prosperity came pretensions to culture. Among other things, it was that pretension to gentility that Boone wanted to escape. "A hunter's life is one of constant excitement," James B. Finley later wrote. "His wants are but few, and . . . His employment does not lead him to covetousness, and he is always characterized by a genuine hospitality. His hut or cabin is always a sure asylum for the hungry and destitute." Boone needed a community that believed, as he did, in sharing both abundance and hardship.

The natural pull to the west, always to the west, to the unknown, to the future, was enhanced by the political considerations of the times. The Spanish controlled the territory of Louisiana, that is, the land west of the Mississippi. After the Treaty of San Lorenzo between the United States and Spain in 1795, the Spanish government embarked on a policy to encourage Americans to settle in the Missouri region to establish a presence, a kind of buffer, against British incursions down the Mississippi from Canada and, ironically, American incursions from the east.

After Spain went to war with Britain in 1796, the Spanish governor of Missouri sent handbills into the American states advertising cheap land and liberal conditions in their new territory. Lt. Gov. Zenon Trudeau welcomed all settlers and let it be known that, although the Spanish government required settlers to be Roman Catholics, he would not enforce the regulation with much strictness. The actual wording of the document was, "[T]heir children must absolutely be Catholics, and he who will not conform to these considerations shall not be admitted, and shall be obliged to retire immediately, although he be a man of great property." But Spanish officials made it clear that however strict the letter of the official policy, it would be applied in a most flexible fashion. As Kentucky and Tennessee and western Virginia were becoming thickly settled, the poorest people, the most recent immigrants, and the more adventurous and restless began looking for land farther west. Some looked north and west of the Ohio River, at former Shawnee lands and the Illinois country. More looked farther west, across the Father of Waters.

Boone's son Daniel Morgan, a hunter and wanderer like his father, was the first in the family to explore Missouri. As early as 1795 he had gone into the region of Mississippi to hunt and explore. In 1797 he entered Missouri, scouting for land he and his family might claim. As many have pointed out, Daniel Morgan was following the family tradition of a son's going to investigate new land, as his grandfather Squire Boone had gone to Pennsylvania almost a hundred years before. "He [Boone] wanted to know the quantity of land granted to new settlers, heads of families and children, and servants. He also wanted to know if settlers were required to embrace the Catholic religion," Nathan told Draper.

Daniel Morgan found a particularly attractive spot on the banks of Femme Osage Creek where game was plentiful and the soil rich, with easy access to the Missouri River. Then Daniel Morgan went to see Lt. Gov. Zenon Trudeau to introduce himself and ask what conditions the regional government might set if Daniel Boone came to Missouri as a settler.

Trudeau was delighted at the prospect, for he knew that wherever the famous Daniel Boone went, others would follow. He told Daniel Morgan that though the law limited the amount of land that could be granted to any one immigrant to about a square mile or eight hundred "arpents," in Daniel Boone's case each member of his family would also be granted six hundred "arpents." And he let Daniel Morgan know that the religious restriction would not be enforced.

Daniel Morgan filed his claim for the tract on Femme Osage Creek and with four slaves built a cabin and cleared land for crops. Lieutenant Governor Trudeau waived all the rules for the son of Daniel Boone and granted him the land outright, without the usual stipulation of a one-year wait. The grant noted that besides slaves Daniel Morgan had a number of cattle.

In 1798 Daniel and Rebecca and Nathan had made the move from Brushy Creek to near the mouth of the Little Sandy on the Ohio. This appears to have been an intermediate step as they planned their relocation westward. Daniel's brother Squire and his family had joined them, after failed attempts to settle in Mississippi, New Orleans, Florida, and Pennsylvania. As restless as his more famous brother, Squire was ready to try his luck again in the new territory of Missouri.

Daniel Morgan left his land on Femme Osage Creek in the charge of his slaves in the fall of 1798 and returned to Kentucky, bringing with him a letter from Lt. Gov. Zenon Trudeau to Daniel Boone. The letter inviting the old pioneer to Missouri must have been especially welcome at a time when former clients were trying to have Boone arrested, swearing out warrants for his debts, and summoning him to court as a defendant and witness.

On September 19, 1798, the *Kentucky Gazette* in Lexington listed lands to be auctioned. "WILL BE SOLD: On Thursday of the 4th of October next, at the court-house in Lexington, the following tracts of land, or for as much of each tract as will pay the tax and interest due thereon . . . Lands returned by the sheriffs of the different counties, as lying in Fayette County . . . Daniel Boon, 500.do 160, Jessamine; 300, Little Hickman." Property on which Boone had not paid taxes was being auctioned off. As one acquaintance put it, "Boone was soured against Kentucky." Boone told Francis Baily, an English traveler who met him in 1797, that people in Kentucky "were got too proud," and that he was "unwilling to live among men who were shackled in their habits."

The rumors spread about Boone's business practices and surveying gave him an added incentive to leave Kentucky. Some of the accusations were remembered and embellished and passed on to John Dabney Shane. "When Boone went out to the site to find the tree he had marked as the corner of the property 'twas said he couldn't find the entry, and leaving his company, made one and dirtied (rubbed) over the fresh marks so as to conceal the fraud.' Boone's trick was discovered, however, which disallowed the entry. Risk speculated that it was embarrassment over this matter that prompted Boone to move to Missouri." But another version of these events was given to Draper by Boone's nephew Daniel Bryan: "Boone's honor compelled him to pay up his bond as long as he owned an acre of land of Kentucky. And not able to satisfy all he was harrast and pestered so much that he bade farewell to Kentucky."

Right up to the end of his time in Kentucky, Boone was involved one way or another with land and surveying. As late as July 13, 1798, he had accompanied the deputy surveyor, John Ballenger, to Stinking Creek to survey one of his old campsites on the Warrior's Path.

IN THE SPRING of 1799 Boone and his family began to prepare for the removal to Spanish territory. It was a large family undertaking, like the move to Pennsylvania from Devonshire, and to the Yadkin from Pennsylvania, and to Boonesborough from the Yadkin. Boone's daughters Susannah and Jemima and their families were going, plus Squire and his extended family, all except his wife, Jane, who was not well and was worn out by travel and childbearing. Squire would go on ahead and build a house, hoping that Jane would follow later.

Boone selected an enormous tulip poplar not far from their cabin on the Little Sandy River. Nathan told Draper, "We found an unusually large poplar tree half a mile up the Little Sandy just below the falls and used it to make a large pirogue. This boat was five feet in diameter and between fifty and sixty feet long. It would hold five tons of our goods." Boone and his sons cut down the tree and spent weeks hollowing out the trunk into a huge dugout to carry Rebecca and their belongings to Missouri. Squire and his sons made another dugout for their use and it is likely there were other boats to add to the small flotilla on the Ohio.

Besides family, a hired man, and several slaves, a number of Daniel

Morgan's bachelor friends joined the party to seek their fortunes in Missouri. It must have thrilled Boone to once again be forming a convoy of family and friends to go in quest of new land, and a new life. Among the hugs and farewells, last-minute preparations, there was the exhilaration of emptying out yet another cabin, leaving behind what was not wanted or too heavy to carry, leaving the familiar and routine, selling a few things, giving away more, breaking away from the failed and soiled, facing the next minute, the next year. "He said that when he left Kentucky, he did it with the intention of never stepping his feet upon Kentucky soil again; and if he was compelled to lose his head on the block or revisit Kentucky, he would not hesitate to choose the former," Nathan reported.

Boone divided his migrating party into two groups, those who would travel by boat down the Ohio and those who would go by land driving cattle and hogs and horses. Those going overland, including Boone himself, would follow the forest trails and fords and take ferries across the large rivers. The livestock drovers included Will Hays and his son, Will Hays Jr., and they chose a route that took them through Lexington, Louisville, and Vincennes.

As the party started out, young Nathan, then eighteen, grew increasingly agitated. He was crushed to be leaving behind Olive Van Bibber, who lived nearby on the Ohio and was known as the prettiest girl in the region. Every step took him down the river away from his sweetheart. Olive was even younger than Nathan, a mere sixteen. He wasn't sure she would marry him, and he wasn't sure, even if she did agree to marry him, that she would be willing to accompany him to Missouri. By the time the group reached their old hometown of Limestone, Nathan knew he had no choice but to go back up the river and propose to Olive. There were already two marriages between the Boone and Van Bibber families. Boones had known Van Bibbers as far back as Oley, in Pennsylvania. Maybe Olive would consent to another joining of the clans.

Daniel and Rebecca agreed to let their youngest son break away from the party and go back up the river. Nathan bought a marriage license and turned back. He must have found his sweetheart willing, for on September 26, 1799, he married Olive Van Bibber on the Little Sandy and the two set out to follow the Boone company to Missouri. It was a match that would last more than fifty-five years, until Nathan's death in 1856, and produce fourteen children. In the extended conversations Lyman Draper recorded with Nathan and Olive in 1851, Olive would show her liveliness and good sense and excellent memory. Traveling by horseback and sleeping on the ground, living on game Nathan killed, the newlyweds spent the month of their honeymoon reaching Missouri. Held up in Vincennes a week with a crippled horse, they still reached their destination not long after the small flotilla and herd of hogs and cattle arrived in St. Louis.

It was supposedly at a stop in Cincinnati that Boone was heard to say he was on his way west because Kentucky was "too crowded — I want more elbow room." The phrase would attach itself to his legend and never be forgotten.

Lt. Gov. Zenon Trudeau had been replaced by Don Charles Dehault Delassus, but Trudeau had stayed on to welcome Daniel Boone and his company. John M. Krum remembered Boone's riding into St. Louis in a hunting shirt and with his rifle on his shoulder, two knives in his belt, "accompanied by three or four hunting dogs." Boone showed his knack for ceremony and the theatrical, appropriate to the occasion. He was received with full military honors, drums, flags, drawn sabers, salutes. Boone must certainly have relished the honor and respect shown him. He gave the new governor a list of those with him who would need additional land. Delassus informed Boone that the land would be granted and that he, Daniel Boone, would be made "syndic" of the tract, that is, administrator and leader of his own district. The appointment as syndic would become official on June 11, 1800. The Spanish government was extending to Boone a kind of feudal authority in the area he and his people were settling. Boone would have the power to grant parcels of land to whomever he chose. Clearly

Trudeau and Delassus were willing to do almost anything in their power to make Boone welcome and to encourage others to join him.

Later Boone said he only went to Missouri because he was certain it would become part of the United States. Since he could see the force of westward expansion in Kentucky and Tennessee and beyond, this may well have been true. But at the time, he gave no sign that he thought the territory would later be transferred to the United States. He very likely understood that Trudeau and Delassus wanted more American settlers as a buffer against the British to the north and Americans to the east. It now seems odd that the Spanish assumed American immigrants to Louisiana would become loyal Spanish subjects and not further the American expansion westward. But in 1799 Boone seemed quite happy to be escaping from United States territory.

AFTER THE ceremonies in St. Louis, Boone and his large entourage made their way west from St. Louis along the bank of the Missouri River. After they reached the land Daniel Morgan and his slaves had cleared, Daniel and Rebecca settled in one side of the large dogtrot cabin Daniel Morgan had built the year before. Boone assigned tracts to his children and relatives and friends, and they began marking boundaries, cutting trees, and building cabins. Once again Boone was living on the frontier, between white civilization and Indian ways, where he felt most at home.

Daniel Morgan's double log cabin stood on a height overlooking the wide river meadows and bottomlands. Boone chose as his own plot of land the acreage between Daniel Morgan's tract and the river. It was rich fertile soil, but most of the tract would be eaten away in the two hundred years afterward as the Big Muddy shifted its course again and again.

Nathan Boone, arriving with his sixteen-year-old bride, traded a packhorse for a claim nearby. "I purchased the home grant of Robert Hall, for which I gave my only horse, saddle, and bridle, so subsequently got his concession at Loutre Lick." On their way to Loutre Creek,

Nathan and Olive crossed the Missouri at St. Charles in a skiff, with
Nathan rowing the boat and Olive steering and holding the reins of
the horse to be traded, which swam behind them. When Nathan and
Olive arrived in Missouri they had a guinea of English money, but after
purchasing twenty-five pounds of flour they had only a half-dollar left
as they settled on their new acreage. Jemima and Flanders Callaway
settled with their children farther down the creek. Sadly, Susannah
Boone Hays, the once lively older daughter, died of fever soon after
arriving in Missouri. The mother of ten, she was the first of the clan to
be planted in the burial ground in Missouri.

Boone had escaped once more from the stifling routines of society
to a world where the beaver were plentiful, Indians not far away, where
no one questioned his authority or character and his freedom to hunt
and trap and wander as he chose. There were no land taxes in Missouri in 1800. Reuben Gold Thwaites would write, "[T]hrough several
years to come he was wont to declare that, next to his first long hunt in
Kentucky, this was the happiest period of his life." At sixty-five Boone
was as avid a woodsman as ever, when the arthritis relented.

On May 2, 1800, Daniel Morgan married Sara Lewis, daughter of a
neighbor, in St. Charles. Daniel Morgan was thirty years old, but Sara
was only fourteen, though already statuesque and mature, described
by those who remembered her as "Amazonian." The newlyweds lived
in the other end of the double cabin.

Boone had crossed many rivers in his long life, and he had paddled
on the Kentucky and piloted a keelboat up and down the Ohio. But
the Missouri River was something new. When he and his party first
crossed to the north bank several miles west of St. Louis, they likely
saw the Big Muddy at a period of low water. Unlike the Kentucky
River, which ran in a deep limestone canyon throughout much of its
course, the Missouri was a new river that swung restlessly between alluvial bottomlands, changing its course, eating away fields, altering its
channels. The bluffs along the Missouri were often a mile back from
the stream itself.

Early explorers had named it the Big Muddy because of its heavy burden of silt. The French explorer Marquette, who had first recorded the Algonquian Fox tribe name "Missouri" in 1673, noted how the brown waters of the Missouri did not readily mix with the gray water from the Mississippi for about a hundred miles downstream. The Indians told Marquette the river was named Pekitanoui, meaning "muddy water." But Europeans named the river after the Indian tribe who lived on its banks, the Missouris, "people of the canoes." Where the rivers joined, the Missouri crashed into the Mississippi with such violence spray shot into the air and the Mississippi ran rougher. In *Life on the Mississippi* Mark Twain describes the mouth of the "savage" Missouri: "a torrent of yellow mud rushed furiously athwart the calm blue current of the Mississippi, boiling and surging and sweeping in its course logs, branches, and uprooted trees." At 2,565 miles from the snowcapped Rockies in Montana to its mouth at the Mississippi 17 miles north of St. Louis, the Missouri was the longest river in North America, draining an area of 589,000 square miles. Its major tributaries were the Yellowstone and the Platte, and it could be navigated, with difficulty, all the way to the Great Falls in Montana.

Because the headwater streams in the high plains and Rockies froze in winter, the Missouri shrank drastically from December through March. In cold spells it froze as far south as St. Charles. When the ice broke in spring, the river was especially dangerous because of stampeding, crushing ice floes. At low water it was almost impossible to keep a boat from running aground on sandbars or hitting snags. In flood the raging current was too powerful to pole or row against. The poet T. S. Eliot, who was born in St. Louis in 1888, referred to the river in the poem "The Dry Salvages" as a "strong brown god — sullen, untamed, and intractable."

WHAT BOONE saw when he crossed the Missouri that October was a river so muddy it looked at times fecal, sometimes bloody. The wild Missouri must have thrilled Boone as it had thrilled Indians and explorers and would thrill Lewis and Clark, and the mountain men, and immigrants coming after them. However dark and menacing its currents, the river's waters had been snow on brilliant peaks, dripped from spruce trees, had been touched by western Indians and grizzly bears.

There was never any doubt that the Missouri was a man's river, brawny, brawling. French boatmen who had plied its waters for years trading whiskey, blankets, rifles for furs with the Indians along its banks, bragged that they drank the water of the river, cherishing the minerals in its silt. If newcomers sprinkled cornmeal in a cup of river water to precipitate out the mud, they were said to be losing the "pith" of the water. "It is a thoroughly masculine river, a burly, husky, bulldozer of a stream, which has taken on the biggest job of moving dirt in North America," Stanley Vestal wrote in his history of the Missouri.

The river Boone found in Missouri, the one he would settle beside, paddle on, trap on, voyage on to the hunting grounds upstream, was crooked and ornery every mile of its length, and the channels and currents within each mile were crooked also. Even so there is every reason to believe that Boone fell in love with the Missouri. The river was as untamed as the west he sought. The Missouri was no river for birch bark canoes. Only a wooden dugout could resist the snags and gravel bars. One way to navigate the Big Muddy was to lash two dugouts together with a kind of platform in between for carrying furs or supplies.

East of the river stretched woodlands and tall-grass prairie, with enough rainfall for corn and vegetable crops. West of the Missouri the high plains and short-grass prairie began, fit only for wheat and small grain, and farther upstream the Rocky Mountains rose out of the plains without warning. East of the river Woodland Indians eased through the forests on foot, but west of the river the Plains Indians rode horses as if they were centaurs and followed the herds of buffalo. Missouri was not only the place where western waters mingled with waters from the east, but it was also the territory where Indian and white immigrants from the east encroached on land claimed by

Osages and other western Indians. It was the place where North met South, and English speakers met Spanish and French. Missouri would become the battle line, the site where conflicting visions of America's future would collide and contend far into the nineteenth century.

From the time he was a boy, Boone had yearned for the West. He had followed the stars to the Cherokee country and the Tennessee country, and he had gone farther into the Shawnee country of Kentucky and Ohio. But in Missouri he was about to touch the true West, the far West. The waters of the Missouri passed through Osage Indian country, Kansa country, Crow and Cheyenne, Sioux and Arikara, Blackfeet country. At the age of sixty-five Boone must have felt he had reached a new and dramatic threshold.

It would be said that mules in Missouri got their cussedness from drinking water from the Big Muddy, the most cussed of all rivers. And some of that stubbornness rubbed off on the people too. Boone would discover that boatmen coming down the river might sing beautifully at times, but they also liked to yell at each other, and at those they passed on the banks, not just greetings but ribald jokes, insults, obscenities, challenges, brags, all in the spirit of frontier humor, camaraderie. The profanity would have reminded Boone of the gifted Aaron Reynolds of Bryan's Station, and the insults hurled over the stockade walls at the siege of Boonesborough. It would remind him of the roughness and relish of the old days, when he was young and the threat in Kentucky was from Indians, not lawyers.

With the glowing phrases and welcome of Delassus and Trudeau ringing in his ears and plumping up his vanity, after the defeats and humiliations in Kentucky, Boone accepted the honors and lived on Daniel Morgan's already cleared property on Femme Osage Creek, about thirty miles up the Missouri, not bothering to clear even an acre of the arpents granted in his name. He would never bother to follow through with registering his own grant or getting the governor's guarantee in writing that he would not have to clear land or plant crops on his claims. It was the old story. Paperwork was a bother, a nuisance. A deed could always be written out by some menial clerk and registered later. In the meantime there was new land to explore, a river to paddle on, a wilderness filled with buffalo and beaver and Osage Indians. It was like old times.

Because he was to be the honored "syndic," Boone was assured by the Spanish governor that he could do, or not do, virtually whatever he chose. Delassus promised Boone that if a substantial number of additional immigrants could be attracted to Missouri, Boone's personal grant would be expanded tenfold. It was all so easy and thrilling, and Boone did not get the necessary documents to guarantee the promise. According to some accounts he needed to get official deeds registered in the capital in New Orleans, and he never bothered with that either. When Louisiana was bought by the United States four years later, Boone did not have one properly registered deed to show to the new American land commission charged with verifying and transferring claims. And he still had not cleared up an acre of land or built a cabin of his own on the land. A "cabin" could be little more than a pile of sticks, but Boone did not even make that token effort.

Boone hunted and trapped in the nearby woods and along the great river, familiarizing himself with the new country. Besides beaver, the river and creeks had otter, mink, muskrat. Foxes and wolves roamed the hills. The lowlands did not have as many bears as the mountains of Kentucky, but there were deer aplenty. As he had done in North Carolina and his first years in Kentucky, Boone depended on his hunting and trapping for his income. Hides and furs could be taken to market in St. Louis, where they brought higher prices than they had in the backwoods of North Carolina and Kentucky. Nathan told Draper: "In the latter part of the summer of 1801 or 1802, my father joined us on a deer hunt for a while. He then visited a hunting camp of the Shawnee and met Jimmy Rogers and Jackson whose Indian name was 'Fish.' They along with an old squaw, were survivors of his old acquaintances when a prisoner in 1778." This was the same Joseph Jackson who had been taken prisoner at the Blue Licks in 1778. He had chosen to spend much of the rest of his life with the Shawnees. Jackson would later be interviewed by Lyman Draper in Bourbon County, Kentucky, in April 1844 shortly before his death.

BOONE'S FIRST encounters with the Osage Indians were much like his initial contacts with Cherokees and Shawnees. Out hunting with Nathan and Daniel Morgan, he met a party of forty or fifty Osages. As was his habit, Boone smiled and shook hands and said "Howdy." One of the warriors admired Daniel Morgan's fine rifle and offered to trade his own cheap gun for the excellent Kentucky weapon. The Osages called a gun a *wa-ho-ton-the*, "thing that causes things to cry out," and most of their weapons were muskets procured from the French. Daniel Morgan was furious and refused, but Boone persuaded him to relent. Later Boone pointed out that they were lucky to lose only the fine rifle, not their furs or even their scalps.

By the second winter in Missouri, even though he had collected many pelts and deer hides for trading, Boone was already in debt to the merchant in St. Louis who provided his supplies. The old woodsman seemed constitutionally unable to stay out of debt.

In succeeding years, even as he assumed the role of syndic, he roamed farther afield in his hunting. His arthritis must have abated, for he took to poling or paddling far upriver to the tributaries of the Missouri such as the Grand and Osage and Gasconade. His companion on these trips was sometimes Nathan or Daniel Morgan, but often it was Daniel Morgan's slave named Derry Coburn. Derry had a family of his own, and he was an enthusiastic woodsman. He and Boone hunted together for years and became close friends.

According to Nathan Boone, "[Derry Coburn] was a good Negro. He would relate with much gusto stories about his two hunting trips with Father, especially the difficulties they had with the Indians, always giving himself the precedent in the narrative." One neighbor later recalled that from the time he was about twenty-two, Derry Coburn had accompanied Boone on hunting and trapping expeditions.

It was said that Boone and Coburn became so accustomed to each other's company, familiar with the other's habits, that they could hunt all day without saying a word. In the woods it is better to keep quiet, to attract no notice from animals or Indians, and the two understood each other without speaking. Many times during his long career Boone's hunting companions were African Americans. The scout who first led him across the Blue Ridge was the herdsman Burrell. It was Pompey who interpreted for him and guided him in the ways of the Shawnees at Chillicothe, enabling him to survive and eventually escape. There is a rumor it was Monk Estill who had taught him how to make gunpowder when nothing was more precious or essential in the Kentucky settlements. But it is important that we not forget that Derry Coburn was a slave and that Boone was the father of Derry's white owner. However congenial the two men were, the reality was that Derry was not a fellow hunter but a servant who cooked and cleaned up around the camp, dressed the game, and carried the supplies and baggage. We should guard against the tradition of sentimentalizing such relationships.

Boone and Derry Coburn went on longer and longer hunts and journeys of exploration. They paddled up the Grand River and later reached the Rocky Mountains, going as far as the Yellowstone with a larger hunting party. Boone was very much aware of the wilderness to the west, the great plains and higher mountains, and though he was seventy years old, he wanted to go there and apparently did. Hunters later reported encountering Boone at the Great Salt Lake, but that claim is less certain. What is certain is that he would have traveled there had he been able. The West was in his thoughts. In a few short years the Rockies and the Great Basin, the High Sierras and the Cascades, would be swarming with hunters and trappers and explorers called mountain men, such as Jim Bridger and Jedediah Smith, Hugh Glass and the Bent brothers, trapping beaver and killing grizzlies on an astronomical scale. These men would model themselves after Boone and follow in his footsteps, going ever farther west. If he had been younger he would have gone there himself. But unlike Boone, the mountain men did not take their families into the wilderness, did not, for the most part, have his charisma or rapport with the Indians, and would not have a Filson to make their stories classics.

Derry Coburn lived until 1851, and Nathan talked to Lyman Draper about him. Among the stories told about Boone and Coburn was one of a hunt around 1803 when, after spotting Indian sign, the two men lay low for many days, not daring to fire their rifles. Finally, when he thought it safe, Boone shot a deer and "hoppused" it into camp. Just as they were cooking the venison and it was ready to devour, a party of Osages appeared firing guns in the air and yelling. They took all Boone's and Coburn's furs. Even worse, they took the venison, just as the two starved men were ready to relish it. Losing a fortune in furs was one thing. Losing tender venison when you are hungry was another. "He never was so mad in his life," Derry later said of Boone.

Hunting on the Grand River, Boone and Derry stayed in a cave and accumulated a supply of meat and furs. One morning they rose to discover a large party of Osages had camped close by but hadn't spotted them. It snowed that day, hiding Boone's traps and tracks. There was nothing for Boone and Coburn to do but huddle in the cave, building only tiny fires behind cover to cook bits of meat. Finally, after twenty days, the Indians moved on and Boone and Derry were free to go outside. Boone described the ordeal later to John Mason Peck. "He stated to the writer, that he had never felt so much anxiety in his life for so long a period, lest they should discover his traps and search out his camp. He was not discovered by the Indians, and when the snow melted away they departed." But on the same day a trap sprang on Boone's hand. Unable to open the trap with his other hand he had to stumble back to camp. Before Derry got the trap open, Boone's bloody hand was partly frostbitten.

As syndic of the Femme Osage region, Boone was expected to act as local magistrate or justice of the peace. Among his duties was the trial of small crimes. Larger cases were sent on to the courts in St. Charles or St. Louis. Under the Spanish system a syndic was a kind of *patrón* and when Louisiana was passed to the French in 1800 nothing much changed. Delassus remained in charge of Missouri as lieutenant governor.

Boone held his court under an elm near Daniel Morgan's cabin called the Judgement Tree or the Justice Tree. The court under the elm echoes the Divine Elm of Boonesborough, where Richard Henderson held the first convention of Kentucky in May of 1775. As syndic, Boone was sheriff, judge, and jury all wrapped up in one. Nathan Boone later said his father ruled "more by *equity* than by law." Most of the petty criminal cases Boone heard were like that of the man who had stolen a hog. Given the choice of being sent for trial in St. Charles or whipped and sent home, most offenders chose the lash. When he returned home the hog thief was asked how his hearing went. "Whipped *and cleared*," was his proud answer. Sometimes Boone laid on the whip himself, as when an offender cursed him and said if Boone were not an old man he would beat him up. "Let not my gray hairs stand in the way," Boone shouted and wielded the lash with his own hand. In one case one neighbor had bitten off the ear of another in a fight. "A Certain James Meek & the bearer hereof Bery Vaigrant had some difference which Came to blows and in the scuffle the said James Meek bit a piece of Bery Vaigrants left Ear." In frontier fighting, eyes were gouged out and noses or ears bitten off or pulled out by the roots.

Neighbors who witnessed Boone holding court under the Justice Tree said they had never seen him act with more relish and sense of purpose. After a lifetime of being summoned to court for unpaid debts and disputed boundaries, it was gratifying to sit or stand behind the bench rather than in front of it. People who knew Boone at this time said they had never known him to take as much satisfaction in any appointment as he did in the office of syndic. It was a role he rehearsed and performed with particular appreciation.

A story that shows Boone had not lost his generosity and compassion, whatever capacity he served in, concerns a cow taken from a widow in lieu of an unpaid debt. Since the unpaid debt was a fact, Boone had no choice but to let the aggressive lender keep the cow. "Take it and go," Boone said, "but never look an honest man in the face again." And then Boone told the widow he would give her a better cow, and he proved as good as his word.

When Louisiana passed to American control in 1804, Delassus recommended Boone to his successor. "Mr. Boone, a respectable old man, just and impartial, he has already since I appointed him offered his resignation owing to his infirmities — Believing I know his probity I have induced him to remain, in view of my confidence in him for the public good," the governor wrote.

Certainly the most difficult case Boone had to deal with concerned the killing of his son-in-law Will Hays by Hays's son-in-law James Davis. Hays was a man of short temper who got in fights and beat his wife, Susannah, now dead, repeatedly when he was drinking. The once lively Susannah had often carried bruises from his abuse. "Hays used to whip aunt fearfully," Evira L. Coshow told Draper. On more than one occasion Boone had beaten Hays to punish him for his domestic violence. Once Boone's sons had tied Hays to a tree for Boone to whip, after he had yet again beaten Susannah. After Susannah's death in 1800, Hays's behavior grew even worse. He drank more and quarreled and fought and threatened. "Hays was a brave man and always foremost, but he was bad tempered and drank to excess," Nathan told Draper.

In his cups Hays got into a quarrel with James Davis, who was married to Hays's daughter Jemima. Hays told Davis that if he ever came to his house again he would kill him. But Davis, assuming that when Hays sobered up he would forget the threat, stopped by Hays's house a short time later in December 1804 while looking for his horse. Hays ordered him inside, but Davis said no, he had to find his horse and ride into town where he was serving on the grand jury. But Hays had not forgotten his anger or his threat. "Hays said if he would not come in he would make him and went to get his rifle," Abner Bryan told Draper. Cursing Davis, Hays ran into his cabin and Davis dashed to the safety of a tree. With his rifle cocked Hays pursued Davis, yelling that all the trees in the woods could not protect him. As Hays got closer, Davis, with his own rifle cocked, stepped out from behind the tree and shot Hays in the chest. Hays died a few hours later.

As syndic, Boone was required to arrest James Davis and escort him to the jail in St. Charles. There he arranged a three-thousand-dollar bond for Davis and later, during the trial, served as a character witness for the defendant. Eventually Davis was acquitted. Hays's son Daniel Boone Hays had witnessed the shooting and told Boone that Davis fired in self-defense.

The administrators of Louisiana, under Spanish and French rule, treated Boone and the other American settlers with flexibility and tolerance. Though every immigrant was required by law to profess the Roman Catholic faith, this restriction was usually satisfied with a general question such as, "Do you believe in God?" which Baptists and Methodists could easily answer in the affirmative. "An affirmative answer being given to these and sundry other questions of a general nature, the declaration, 'Un bon Catholique,' would close the ceremony, and confirm the privilege of an adopted citizen." Lieutenant Governor Delassus even permitted evangelists to enter the territory and conduct revivals, and when he knew they were ready to leave he would threaten them and order them out of the territory. Then they were free to return and evangelize again, and again when they were ready to leave he would expel them. One preacher who returned repeatedly was Rev. John Clark, who at the end of each tour was threatened with jail and a fine. "This was repeated so often, as to furnish a pleasant joke with the preacher and his friends." It was a liberal arrangement, similar to the one he made with Boone about his land grant.

BOONE'S FIRST years in Missouri were especially satisfying. Rebecca and Daniel lived as they had for most of their lives. While staying in Daniel Morgan's cabin, they went out to a sugar camp in their first year in Missouri in the early spring. Nathan told Draper, "At sugar-making time in February my father and mother went to my place and built a half-faced camp (cabins with three sides and the front open) where they made three or four hundred pounds of sugar. It took them several weeks."

All his life Boone's troubles appeared to come in waves. The good periods seemed to happen when he started out in the wilderness and experienced an idyll of hunting and trapping and exploration of new territory, digging ginseng, making maple syrup, boiling salt, clearing some land. But then misfortune caught up with him and his troubles accumulated and compounded.

In the spring of 1803 Boone heard that his daughter Levina had died back in Kentucky at the age of thirty-six, leaving eight children. Her husband, Joseph Scholl, who had been with Boone at the Battle of the Blue Licks, brought the children to Missouri and settled there. Boone's daughter Rebecca took consumption and died in 1805 in the cabin on Brushy Creek, and soon after that her husband, Philip Goe, known as a heavy drinker, also died. Daniel Morgan Boone returned to Kentucky and brought five of Rebecca's seven children to Missouri.

That life in the Missouri wilderness was much harder on women than on men goes almost without saying. Besides the cold, the heat, the wet, the dirt, the diet of cornmeal and meat, they lacked medicine and medical attention. Most women had child after child. Daniel Morgan's young wife, Sara, bore twelve children. Nathan Boone's wife, Olive Van Bibber Boone, the beauty of the Little Sandy, married at the age of sixteen and taken west, once with a slave companion built a chimney and added a floor to their cabin while Nathan was away on a hunt. She was pregnant at the time. Nathan himself would later brag, "With stones for the fireplace, sticks for the chimney, and mud for mortar these lone women erected a chimney, the draft of which proved decidedly the best of any on the farm." Olive went on to have fourteen children. Besides the bearing and rearing of children, the cooking and housework, these women did the outdoor work also. When the men were away hunting, the women, along with the children, did all the work.

After injuring his hand in the beaver trap, Boone was not able to go on extended hunts for a while. He and Rebecca moved to a cabin farther up Femme Osage Creek, leaving Daniel Morgan's cabin to his rapidly growing family. At the new location Boone could help with sugar making and shoot turkeys and other game from the yard. Each February Rebecca and Daniel joined Jemima and Flanders Callaway twenty miles farther up the Missouri to make maple sugar near the Callaway property at the mouth of Charette Creek. It is likely that near the age of seventy Boone lacked the strength for clearing land and building a cabin, and since neither was required immediately, he put off the effort and nursed his arthritis and hunted when he could.

When Spain gave the Louisiana territory back to France in 1800, many Americans were alarmed. All the land from New Orleans to Canada, from the Mississippi to the Rocky Mountains, was now in the hands of the aggressive, ambitious Napoleon. The port of New Orleans and the Mississippi were essential to the American settlements in the West. By 1802 it seemed crucial to American interests to purchase New Orleans and at least part of Louisiana.

President Jefferson instructed the American minister to France, Robert R. Livingston, to make an offer to the French, and he appointed James Monroe to travel to Paris to lead the negotiations. A revolt in Haiti had dimmed Napoleon's hopes for an empire in the New World, and with war with Britain looming, France needed money and feared it could not hold Louisiana in any case against a British invasion. The timing was good for the Americans. On April 29, 1803, Monroe and the American delegation agreed to pay France fifteen million dollars for the whole territory. Almost all Americans approved the acquisition except some Federalists, mostly in New England. The Americans took possession of New Orleans, the capital, on December 20, 1803.

The purchase doubled the area of the United States, and the tide of immigrants to the West began to surge.

As far back as his days as secretary of state under Washington, Jefferson had planned an exploration of the West for scientific, commercial, and political purposes. As soon as the purchase became a fact he chose Meriwether Lewis, his secretary, to lead such an expedition. Lewis selected William Clark, younger brother of George Rogers Clark, as co-commander. Their brief was to explore westward to the Rockies and find a route to the Pacific. They were charged with making maps, keeping journals, gathering specimens of wildlife, making diplomatic contact with the Indians, looking out for America's future interests. They set out up the Missouri in May 1804, passing near Boone's residence. It is not clear whether they visited Boone on their way or not.

WHEN MISSOURI became a territory of the United States in late 1803, the American government reassured the settlers in the region that their legitimate claims would be recognized and the transition would be smooth to the new political and administrative system.

As more white settlers, as well as displaced eastern Indians such as the Shawnees, moved into Missouri and hunters ranged farther west into the hunting ground of the Osages and other regional tribes, the Missouri Indians grew angrier and more aggressive. It was the old story. At first a few new hunters appear and they seem no real threat to the Natives. The white and immigrant Indian hunters are friendly; there is even a friendly rivalry. Warriors rough up a few and take their traps and furs, but the hunters keep coming. They multiply and multiply again. The buffalo and elk, bear and beaver, begin to thin out. The rights to a region, a whole way of life, become threatened.

On a long hunt to the Kansa River in December 1804, Nathan Boone and Matthias Van Bibber encountered a band of Osages, were ordered to get out of their country and were stripped of their horses and furs. No sooner had the Osages left than a band of Kansa Indians appeared. Angry that the Osages had beaten them to the furs and horses, they stripped Nathan and Matthias, known as Tice, of their clothes and supplies but left them one cheap gun and a meager supply of powder and lead. It was the middle of a bitter winter and they had no coats.

In an epic journey that became part of the folklore of the region, Nathan and Tice walked down the Missouri Valley through snow and extreme cold. Only their urging of each other on kept them going, as frostbite and starvation weakened and slowed them. They were saved when Nathan shot a panther and they feasted on the raw flesh and wrapped themselves in the skin. "We fastened our fur vests with strings, and though our arms were still exposed, they added vastly to our comfort," Nathan told Draper. A hundred miles from home they finally met a hunting party that included one of Jemima Callaway's sons, and the two men were carried home on litters, reaching there on Christmas Eve. Tice Van Bibber later died of the effects of this exposure. Nathan spent months recovering. Whatever the horror Olive felt seeing her young husband brought home on a litter, she later joked about the incident, saying it was the first Christmas Nathan had spent at home since their marriage, "and I had to thank the Indians for that."

In the fall of 1805, after James Davis's acquittal of the murder of Will Hays, after Boone's hand had recovered from the injury in the steel trap, and after Nathan had recovered from the terrible journey down the Missouri in the cold, Boone's sons took him on a hunt up the Gasconade River, south of the Missouri, where there were fewer Osage Indians. It was a successful hunt, and old Boone was thrilled to be back in the woods. But just as they were about to return home at Christmas the weather turned deadly cold and ice began to form on the river. Fearing they could not cross with ice chunks floating in the stream, Boone and his sons camped overnight on the bank. Next morning the Missouri River was frozen and they decided to walk across. The sons made it to the northern shore, but Boone stepped on thin ice within yards of the bank and fell through. He yelled to his sons not to come to him and risk falling in themselves. Nathan started a bonfire on the bank while his father stumbled and scrambled his way through broken ice and mud to the shore. His sons stripped Boone of his wet clothes and warmed him by the blazing fire. They carried Boone home in time for Christmas dinner, but the exposure in the cold water further weakened him and aggravated his rheumatism.

One of the happy events of 1805–6, according to Nathan Boone, was a surprise visit from the old friend of Boonesborough days, Simon Kenton. Like Boone, Kenton had endured the hardships and dangers of early exploration and settlement of Kentucky, only to lose his land claims in the Bluegrass. He had fought in several battles and been captured and tortured by Shawnees, and made a daring escape back to Kentucky. He had been befriended by Simon Girty and remained forever loyal to him. Kenton had been loyal to Boone also and had defended him when others accused Boone of treason and duplicity. Nathan told Draper, "My father had great confidence in Kenton as a spy and woodsman. Kenton visited Missouri in the spring or summer of 1805 or 1806 and spent about a week at our house."

Losing his holdings in Kentucky, Kenton had moved north into Ohio and helped settle and develop that territory. He raised a family and when his business ventures failed was forced to depend on his children. After his first wife died, he married her younger first cousin and suggested they take a trip to Missouri. Their visit to the West had occurred just before the Boones moved there in 1799. When Kenton arrived at the Boone cabin in 1805, he did not introduce himself but asked Rebecca for lodging. According to Kenton's children, she answered that they had no room. "You would if you knew who I am," Kenton said. When he stepped closer Rebecca recognized him, threw aside her clay pipe, and rushed to hug him. Boone was out back chopping firewood, and when she called to him that he had a visitor, Boone assumed it was just a neighbor and continued chopping. When he finally came to the house and saw his old friend Kenton he burst into tears. "The venison supper was almost ready when he appeared. There followed a week of reunion," Edna Kenton would write.

Kenton and Boone recounted their many struggles and adventures and failures. Kenton had even spent time in a debtor's prison. "The old pioneers seemed to enjoy themselves finely in recounting their old Kentucky troubles and hardships," Nathan told Draper. In spite of their bitter experiences in Kentucky, both Boone and Kenton recalled their days there with special affection. In this they were like most other pioneers. Arthur K. Moore tell us, "Timothy Flint perceived an almost mystical fervor in the oldest settlers as they recalled the surpassing beauty of Kentucky in their youth, when they set about destroying the scene which was ever to be their fondest recollection."

Boone had many visitors in Missouri, including a Shawnee "sister" who had moved west with the remnants of the tribe. But none was more welcome than Kenton. At the time of Kenton's visit, Boone was recovering from his fall through the ice and was threatened with loss of all his land in the transition to American rule. No doubt it was a comfort to remember and lament the passing of the frontier with another veteran of those vivid times, who was also a legend, and who had also lost everything to lawyers and the changing culture. Kenton had been made a brigadier general of the Ohio militia and he was a hero of the frontier, but like Boone he never seemed able to hold on to the property he acquired. The French botanist François André Michaux, who visited Kentucky in 1802, commented, "incertitude of property is an inexhaustible source of tedious and expensive lawsuits which serve to enrich the professional gentlemen of the country."

On the terrible walk back in the cold from the encounter with the Osage and Kansa warriors, Nathan Boone and Tice Van Bibber had discovered a number of salt springs about a hundred and twenty miles up the Missouri from the Femme Osage. After he had recovered from the ordeal, Nathan and his brother Daniel Morgan returned to the salt springs and decided to begin a salt-boiling operation. The place became known as Boone's Lick and throughout 1805 the brothers kept a half-dozen men working there, chopping wood and firing kettles. Salt was selling for $2.50 a bushel and Nathan carried hundreds of bushels to market in St. Louis on rafts and keelboats.

Contrary to the popular impression, Boone himself was not involved in this salt operation. He was old and in no condition to go off into the wilderness to boil salt, as he had done many times before in Kentucky and Ohio. According to the family, he was "opposed to the scheme from the beginning." He had too many bad associations with salt works at the Blue Licks. Boone knew it was hard labor for dubious profit, and far up the Missouri the salt works were vulnerable to Indian attacks. Only surveying was more dangerous than salt boiling. In December 1805 the salt boilers were attacked and the works destroyed. Though reopened the next year, the operation, true to Boone's prediction, never returned the profits Nathan and Daniel Morgan had hoped for.

However, the name Boone's Lick drew many settlers to that region. Assuming Daniel Boone himself worked there or lived there, or owned the works, immigrants poured into the area. The Boone name acted as a mysterious magnet, as it had at Boonesbrough, Boone's Station, Limestone, and the Femme Osage. Wherever Boone went others wanted to follow. It was a name that suggested safety and new opportunity. To follow Boone, to be connected to Boone, was to connect with a part of history, with the romance of a legend and new territory.

At the very time the Boone name and legend were attracting more and more settlers to Missouri, the man himself was informed that none of his claims to land in Missouri had proved valid. According to American law, he had not fulfilled his commitment, whatever the assurances Lieutenant Governor Delassus had given him. Syndic of the district he might have been under the old regime, but such a position and title did not exist under the American administration. Boone appeared before the land commission on February 13, 1806, with his original letter from Don Zenon Trudeau, his certificates of survey, his commission as syndic. What he could not produce was evidence that he had ever improved or lived on any of his land claims. And he had never registered his deeds with the proper officials in New Orleans. The governor had told Boone the requirements would be waived, but Don Charles had never said so in writing.

So many speculators were altering documents and surveys, taking advantage of the confused conditions by changing dates and deeds, that the commission decided to be strict with Boone. It is possible they wanted to show they were not influenced by his fame. Likely they also knew of the accusations against him in Kentucky, of fraud and questionable surveys and titles. Perhaps some were jealous of his reputation, the preferential treatment he had been given by the Spanish, the legend and the hero. They declared all his claims invalid. General James Wilkinson had become governor of Louisiana in 1805 and he held the office for a year until forced to resign. It is possible that scoundrel and traitor set the commissioners in Missouri against Boone. After all, it was Wilkinson who had helped Imlay swindle the ten thousand acres from Boone in Kentucky in 1785.

Even under the cloud of his disputed claims, Boone was still willing to serve his community in 1807, as he had in almost all the places he had lived. "Meriwether Lewis, [new] governor of Louisiana Territory, appoints Boone justice of the Femme Osage township."

The commission kept Boone waiting for three years before delivering their devastating verdict. By the time they handed down their ruling in 1809, Boone's health had further deteriorated. But he still insisted on taking another hunting trip with his friend Derry Coburn. The whole family protested, but Boone argued that trapping was the only way he had of making a little money. "My wife is getting old and needs some little coffee and other refreshments, and I have no other way of paying for them but by trapping," Boone told his nephew Daniel Bryan.

But once he and Coburn were out in the woods, Boone was stricken by an attack that convinced him he could not go on. The weather was stormy and he decided that his time was up. As soon as the storm passed he had Derry help him to the top of a hill where he marked out a spot for his grave. Expecting the worst, and preparing himself and Derry for his approaching death, Boone was surprised when the attack began to wane. He and his companion slowly made their way back home and Boone agreed to consult a doctor.

Done All the Good That I Can

1809–1820 ↪

With the help of his friend Judge John Coburn, Boone, at the age of seventy-five, prepared a petition to Congress for restoration of his lost land in Missouri. Describing himself as "an aged, infirm, worn-out man," Boone dictated an account of his life to his grandson, to augment the petition Judge Coburn was preparing. Boone was not in the habit of speaking at length about his life. He had been the kind of man who preferred to look forward rather than backward. But spurred by his recent brush with death, and inspired by the promise of the petition to Congress, he also spoke about his long life with a neighbor named Stephen Hempstead. Hempstead passed on much of the information Boone told him to his brother Edward Hempstead, a lawyer in St. Louis helping to complete the petition to Congress. Many years later Stephen Hempstead wrote down his memories for Lyman Draper.

For all his physical weakness and disappointments, the gathering of information for the petition and the help of prominent lawyers seemed to inspire Boone with a new hope. As he looked back over his long career he saw the range and scale of his achievements. Despite all the failures and humiliations, the accusations of treason and fraud, his skills and leadership, his endurance and discoveries were recognized by many. However poor and feeble he had become, he had done great things, and his deeds were remembered, and would be remembered. Our opinion of ourselves is, to a large degree, a reflection of the opinion of others. In his poverty and sickness, it meant a lot to Boone that others recognized his extraordinary accomplishments.

When the rejection of his appeal came in December 1809, Boone did not seem surprised, or as disturbed as he might have been. It was as if he had come to a kind of peace with himself. If one or two others believed in him, saw him as he saw himself, that was enough.

Elizabeth Corbin, sister of Sara Lewis, wife of Daniel Morgan Boone, later recalled her brother-in-law and his famous father. Her comments confirm the descriptions by others of Boone as calm and quiet. "My brother-in-law, Col. Boone, was very kind to me, and I was therefore much attached to him . . . Like his father, the old pioneer (whom at a later date I saw much) he had a soft, almost effeminate voice, and extremely mild and pleasant manners. In fact, most, if not all of the old hunters, who spent most of their time in the deep solitude of the then unbroken woods, spoke in low soft tones. I do not, among my acquaintances, recall an exception."

Two friends from the Kentucky days who showed up in Missouri in 1810 were James Bridges and Michael Stoner, both of whom had served as axemen in 1775, chopping out Boone's Trace. Bridges had been hunting with James Harrod in 1792 when Harrod disappeared. There were rumors that Bridges might have killed Harrod, but no one ever found any proof. Bridges and Stoner were on their way to explore and hunt in the upper Missouri and Boone could not resist their invitation to join them. Perhaps his arthritis was better. More likely his enthusiasm for seeing the Great Plains and Rocky Mountains was so intense he brushed aside any pains and ailments. He formed a party with Flanders Callaway and Will Hays Jr. and Callaway's slave Mose, as well as Stoner and Bridges. It is said that Derry Coburn accompanied Boone also.

According to Hays, the party reached the Yellowstone and was away for six months. It was a long hunt, on the scale of Boone's original forays into Kentucky, except the distances were now greater, the mountains higher, the bears more dangerous. It must have been a special satisfaction to explore the new regions with Michael Stoner, who had accompanied Boone into Kentucky in 1774 on the mission to warn the surveyors of Indian hostility. Such events give Boone's life a pleasing symmetry and show the long-term loyalty he inspired in his friends. It goes without saying that the old hunter relished the wonders of the Rockies, snowcapped and shining, buffalo herds stretching to the horizon, streams swollen with beaver dams, geysers and fumaroles belching steam like vents from Hades, grizzlies, elk, moose, mountain sheep. The forests were of lodgepole pine, piñon pine, Douglas fir. The hunt was so successful that the party returned to Missouri with several skin boats filled with furs. Stephen Hempstead claimed to have witnessed the return of the band early in 1811. One boat was rowed by a black man with Boone steering in the rear. The party carried their cargo to St. Louis to get the best prices for their furs. "The canoe was covered with Bear skins and she landed first the stern and the steersman got out and then the bowmen rowed her around and they landed. This was done to enable to land, and not disturb the cargo, the whole middle being full and covered. Mr. Callaway and the Negro rowed in front and Colo. Boone steared . . . the value of their furs and skins I cannot state but it was considerable." The expedition to the Yellowstone was a triumph. But as with most victories, the success of the hunt probably made Boone feel all the more keenly that he was not able to go again, farther and higher up the Missouri, across the Rockies, into the Columbia valley and the Cascades. Lewis and Clark had been there. Scouts for the Astor fur company were going there. Had he been twenty years younger he would have pushed on to the Pacific, the final West.

As with other periods of Boone's life, there are many rumors and legends about his later years in Missouri. According to Nathan, Daniel and Rebecca took a room in St. Charles around 1809 to be near Nathan's son James, who was in school there and homesick. "When my father heard of it, he and Mother went down, took a room in St. Charles, and kept house there for some time and made a home for little son James." Living in town may have been more convenient for Boone, as he was treated by a doctor there. It was during this stay in St. Charles that he talked with Stephen Hempstead every night for a month. "He rented a house nearly opposite to mine for a while." When sugar-making time came in February, they likely returned to Jemima and Flanders Callaway's maple grove for the annual ritual of sap boiling.

Some have claimed that Boone returned to Kentucky around 1810 to visit his brother Squire, who lived on the Indiana side of the Ohio. It would have been on this supposed visit to Kentucky that Boone encountered the bird painter and naturalist John James Audubon, who was co-owner of a store at Henderson, Kentucky. According to Audubon, who later painted a portrait of Boone from memory, the two went hunting together and the frontiersman demonstrated how to "bark" a squirrel, killing the animal with the force of a bullet hitting bark but not touching the animal. "I perceived that the ball had hit the piece of bark immediately beneath the squirrel, and shivered it into splinters, the concussion produced by which had killed the animal and sent it whirling."

In Audubon's account, Boone also related a tale about escaping from Indians by getting them drunk, and one about marking a spot by blazing a tree and then locating the exact tree years later after the blaze had grown over, thereby proving a boundary claim. Like Filson, Audubon makes Boone sound eloquent and educated, formal in his speech. Audubon never let mere facts stand in the way of good storytelling, and no doubt he enhanced the account with some of his own phrasing, but it is quite possible Boone spoke more formally to some listeners, as he had apparently with Filson. It is possible that Audubon's story includes many actual phrases from Boone's speech, along with a good deal of fiction and fine phrasing, smoothed out for a genteel public. "There were then thousands of buffaloes on the hills in Kentucky; the land looked as if it never would become poor; and to hunt in those days was a pleasure indeed. But when I was left to myself on the banks of the Green River, I dare say for the last time in my life, a few *signs* only of deer were to be seen."

Audubon's story has so much detail, it is likely he did meet Boone and talk with him. But the encounter probably occurred in Missouri instead of Kentucky. Boone had left Kentucky before Audubon ever arrived in North America in 1803. Audubon traveled widely to find and paint birds. But writing up his account years later in England for his *Ornithological Biography*, the painter may have decided it would sound more convincing if he placed the meeting in Kentucky. After all, Boone was famous for exploring and settling Kentucky, not Missouri. Whether the meeting occurred or not, the image of an encounter between the two giants of the American wilderness caught the attention of readers in the 1830s when Audubon published his *Ornithological Biography* and has lodged in the memory and imagination ever since. It is a meeting that should have occurred: Boone the explorer, the scout and ultimate man of the wilderness, meeting the greatest of the naturalist-artists in modern history. Audubon would do as much as anyone else except Filson to bring the legend of Boone to the future. His portraits in words and oils are indelible in our history. His account amplifies the transition of Boone from actual, historical human being with all his faults and failures, into the realm of heroic art and myth. In that sense the meeting between the two occurred, whether on the banks of the Ohio or the Missouri or on the shores of Audubon's vision. In any case it was a significant encounter.

Many years later, in 1890, Abner Bryan, son of Jonathan Bryan, wrote to Draper, "It is quite certain Dl. Boone did return to Ky after he settled in Missouri. He sold his land, took the proceeds & went to Kentucky, & paid up his old debts — & returned home with four bits in his pocket & said now he had paid his debts — and could die happy — no one would say he was dishonest." But Bryan's account sounds so much like that in Peck's biography of 1847 it may be discounted as testimony. He may have been simply repeating what he had read.

We know that Boone was in Missouri in 1811 when John Jacob Astor's party of fur traders ascended the river on their way to the Pacific, for they recorded that they visited him. In *Astoria*, which Washington Irving published in 1835, Boone is described as just back from a hunt where he had taken sixty beavers. "The old man was still erect in form, strong in limb and unflinching in spirit." He watched the expedition depart, wishing he could join them.

During the War of 1812 the British encouraged Indian attacks on settlers in Missouri. It was a kind of replay of the attacks in the Revolutionary period on Kentucky. Osages attacked outlying farms and towns again and again. Boone attempted to join the militia, but he was refused. At seventy-eight, he was allowed to serve as a nurse and to assist at the forts. No doubt he advised the younger men on tactics and encouraged them at moments of danger and low morale. Several times Boone and Rebecca had to seek shelter at a nearby fort.

While Boone and Rebecca were living near Jemima and Flanders Callaway during the sugar-making season of 1813, Rebecca suddenly became sick. Nathan told Draper, "She remained there about a month. When she was not feeling well, she rode to Callaway's house, and after a few weeks of sickness, she died there, on March 18, 1813." After a marriage of fifty-six years, Boone was devastated by the loss. Though he had spent much of their married life away from Rebecca, hunting and trapping, serving in militias and legislatures, held captive by Indians, Boone had depended completely on her. For him, she had moved to Virginia, back to the Yadkin, to the Clinch and to Kentucky, back to the Yadkin again, then to Boone's Station, to Marble Creek, to Limestone, to Point Pleasant, up the Kanawha, to Brushy Creek, to the Little Sandy, and then to Missouri. Boone's life cannot be imagined without Rebecca. It is unlikely he could imagine a future without her. Rebecca had spent most of her life in crowded, smoke-filled cabins, surrounded by her children and grandchildren, nephews and nieces. She had given birth to ten, and she had eighteen grandchildren. It is quite possible she saw nothing remarkable about her life; after all, many others had lived in much the same way.

She was buried on a hill near the Callaway house, overlooking the Tuque Creek valley. Boone's granddaughter Susannah Callaway later said Rebecca's death was "the Saddest affliction of his life." But there was hardly time for mourning. The threat of Indian attacks caused the Callaways to move to Daniel Morgan's fort, several miles away. Included in the baggage they carried to the Femme Osage was the manuscript of the autobiography Boone had dictated to his grandson John Callaway. The canoe that carried the manuscript along with household goods hit a log and capsized. The account of Boone's life in his own "voice" was lost to posterity. Boone was probably too old and grieved by Rebecca's death to attempt the autobiography again. The bad luck that had found Boone so many times, and in so many places, had not forgotten him.

Certainly the jinx that had followed Boone so faithfully did not desert him early the following year. Judge Coburn had assembled another petition to put before Congress, arguing that Boone, who had led so many to settle and develop the West, owned not a foot of land. As the painstakingly assembled petition moved toward a successful decision, the lawyer Edward Hempstead told the committee that Boone did not want the ten-thousand-acre tract stated in the petition, only the original thousand arpents he had been given by Lieutenant Governor Delassus in 1799. Boone was awarded the smaller parcel of land.

Boone was furious that Congress and President Madison had given him such a minimal tract for all his services. He threatened to refuse the grant. In any case he had to sell most of the land the following year to pay off creditors in Kentucky still suing him for debts and land deals made decades before. As soon as they heard Boone had been awarded land, creditors descended on him. "For this reason my father, Colonel Daniel Boone, disposed of every acre of his old Spanish grant, which had been confirmed by Congress, to liquidate these demands," Nathan said.

In this unhappy period, a man whose late wife had been given a parcel of land by Boone years before when she was an orphan rescued from Indians, traveled all the way to Missouri to confront Boone. The property had been lost to another claimant, and the husband badgered Boone to pay for the lost gift. The normally courteous and soft-spoken Boone was so annoyed by the man's persistence he told him "he had come a great distance to suck a bull, and he reckoned he would have to go home dry."

As the War of 1812 wound down, more settlers poured into Missouri. Thousands were attracted to the region by the name Boone's Lick. Though Boone had nothing to do with the salt works there, the name caught the popular imagination and seemed to promise a rich and abundant life in the new territory. The trace Nathan and Daniel Morgan made to reach the salt works became known as Boone's Lick Road, and thousands of settlers followed it west in the years to come, connecting with the Santa Fe Trail or the Oregon Trail. The wilderness of Missouri began to disappear under the arriving axes and plows.

The Reverend John Mason Peck, who interviewed Boone and wrote one of the early biographies, described the flood of immigrants to the Boone's Lick region after the War of 1812 ended. "The 'new-comers' like a mountain torrent, poured into the country faster than it was possible to provide corn for breadstuff. Some families came in the spring of 1815; but in the winter, spring, summer, and autumn of 1816, they came like an avalanche. It seemed as though Kentucky and Tennessee were breaking up and moving to the 'Far West.' Caravan after caravan passed over the prairies of Illinois, crossing the 'great river' at St. Louis, all bound to the Boone's Lick."

Another minister and author who interviewed Boone in his last years, Rev. Timothy Flint, wrote the first book-length biography, published in 1833. Though he cannot always be relied on for facts, Flint provides some colorful details about Boone's last years. "After the peace, he occupied himself in hunting, trapping, and exploring the country — being absent sometimes for two or three months at a time — solacing his aged ear with the music of his young days — the howl of

the nocturnal wolf — and the war song of the prowling savages . . .
When the writer lived in St. Charles, in 1816, Colonel Boone, with the
return of peace, had resumed his Kentucky habits."

Even in his old age, as Missouri began to be cleared and settled,
thanks in part to the lure of his name, Boone was thinking of the farther west. With Derry Coburn and others he explored Kansas and
perhaps reached as far north as the Dakotas. His descendant Wade
Hays later said that Boone and Will Hays Jr. made a second trip to the
Yellowstone, though most historians think this unlikely. And though
he knew he would never see it, the Pacific Coast was much on Boone's
mind. Several who spoke with him in his final decade remembered his
enthusiasm for the West Coast, called Alta California by the Spanish.
Wade Hays wrote, "Daniel Boone had a vary great idea of the Pacific
Co[a]st[.] [H]e described it vary accurate for some reason, I supose
from talking with Indians." Even as an old man Boone did not lose his
fascination with exploration. His failing eyes followed the sunset over
the wide bottomlands and hurrying waters of the Missouri.

After he was besieged by creditors trying to collect for old debts in
Kentucky, when his grant came through in 1814, Boone was still planning hunting expeditions. Officers at Fort Osage, near future Kansas
City, reported that Boone spent two weeks with them in 1816 on his
way to the Platt River. According to Nathan, his father traveled as far
as Iowa in April 1816 with a hunter named Indian Phillips but had to
stay at Fort Leavenworth for several days because of sickness. "While
at the fort he became acquainted with Captain Bennett Riley of the
army, who was then in command. He recovered sufficiently to return
home, and Phillips returned with him." In Missouri Boone associated
with Indians often. They were all part of the same larger community.

In 1816 Boone began dictating yet another narrative of his life to the
husband of one of his granddaughters, Dr. John Jones. While Boone
stayed with the Joneses and was treated for his various ailments, the
old hunter told Jones the story of his eighty-two years, and the young
doctor wrote it down. "He went there for the double purpose of placing
himself under the doctor's medical care and advice for the scrofulous

affection that sometimes bothered him and also to dictate to the doctor a narrative of his life and adventures," Nathan told Draper. But Boone soon tired of the project and the manuscript was later lost.

The loss of all the certain accounts of his life from Boone's own lips and in his own words has added to the mystery of his life and character. It is as though there is something about Boone just beyond reach, something unknown and unknowable. He cannot be known "in his own words" because he belongs as much to myth and the collective imagination as to history. We have hundreds of documents in his handwriting, yet we feel he is best "known" in the words of others such as Filson, Audubon, and Peck. There are a number of figures in history who seem to recede the more we study them, always larger than life, hovering between biography and legend. George Washington is one. No matter how much we study his life we never feel we "know" the Father of his Country. Perhaps Robert E. Lee, the so-called marble man, is another. There can be no biography of Shakespeare because the Bard is the voice of his characters, the very voice of nature and history. How could one write a true portrait of Leonardo da Vinci, the ideal model of originality and genius? Such figures become their deeds and the public imagination of those deeds. And something of the same is true for Boone. No matter how many details and documents we have about Boone, he somehow slides back into the amber twilight of legend, projected in the folk imagination and the words of others. As Emily Dickinson said of nature:

> But nature is a stranger yet;
> The ones that cite her most
> Have never passed her haunted house,
> Nor simplified her ghost.
>
> To pity those that know her not
> Is helped by the regret
> That those who know her, know her less
> The nearer her they get.

However elusive his character might be, Boone's relish of the wild and freedom, his sense of being at home for long expanses of time with only animals and hills and clouds for companions, put him at the head of a class of woodsmen of the eighteenth and nineteenth centuries, including William Bartram — who explored the wilds of Florida and Georgia, as well as the Carolinas, delighting in both the wildlife and the Natives — and Audubon, Thoreau, John Muir. These men, and hundreds like them less famous, were at home in the pristine wilderness that lay at their feet and just beyond the next hill. They were sometimes men of ambition, but their ambitions were directed toward wonder and curiosity. They were willing to take enormous risks to see new places, and find new places within themselves, to feel like Adam stepping into an endless garden of canebrakes and meadows, mountains and rivers sparkling in the distance, waiting to be explored and named. They learned from the Indians, and some associated closely with Indians. Later poets, such as Bryant, Emerson, Whitman, and Dickinson, would return again and again to the essential solitary glimpse of paradise, putting into words and into sounds a strain of experience already deeply rooted in American culture, an ideal and a longing.

In the fall of 1817 Boone went hunting again, this time with his grandson James. He had hunted every fall since he was big enough to throw a spear or swing a club. He and James wandered up the Missouri, and the old man was exhilarated to be in the woods again. A duck landed by their campfire, as though offering itself for their breakfast. But the cold began to tell on the old man's joints, and they turned back after a few days. Yet his urge to hunt was as great as it had ever been. Nathan told Draper, "My father said he was as naturally inclined each fall to go hunting and trapping as the farmer is in spring to set about putting in his crops."

In the years after Rebecca's death, Boone never kept house himself but moved from Nathan's house to Jemima's to Daniel Morgan's and then Jesse's. Jesse had arrived from Kentucky in 1816. But primarily Boone lived with Jemima and Flanders Callaway, near Rebecca's grave.

Many visitors searched him out, to hear stories of the old days in Kentucky, of the Indians and the Revolution. The Reverend John Mason Peck, who would later publish his biography in 1847, interviewed Boone in December 1818, not long after newspapers had mistakenly reported his death. Expecting to meet a rough, intimidating frontiersman, Peck found instead a "countenance . . . ruddy and fair, and [he] exhibited the simplicity of a child. His voice was soft and melodious. A smile frequently played over his features in conversation."

Peck noticed how solicitous Boone's family was of the old man's comfort, showing great affection for the patriarch. "Every member of his family appeared to delight in administering to his comforts," Peck later wrote. As he recounted his life, Boone stressed that though he had experienced hardships and dangers, others had also. "He was sociable, communicative in replying to questions, but not in introducing incidents of his own history. He was intelligent, for he had treasured up the experience and observation of more than fourscore years."

The portrait that emerges from Peck's account is of a wise and resigned old man. He recounted the loss of his lands in Kentucky and Missouri and said that tracts of land had always "proved an injury rather than a benefit." The lessons he had been taught had made him "indifferent to the affairs of the world." It appears that in his last years Boone recognized the difference between his life in the woods as a trapper and hunter, his life with his family on the frontier, and his ventures in the world of business and politics. Most who met Boone in these last years gave pretty much the same account of the old scout. Boone liked to stress that over the years his best and most reliable friends had been Indians. In his final years he seemed to wax more romantic and affectionate than ever toward Native Americans, remembering them as a people of honor and compassion. He had always identified with Indian culture, since his youth in Pennsylvania, and in his old age, safe in Jemima's home, he recalled mostly the good things from his many encounters, transactions, and captivities with Native Americans.

Once Boone said that "while I could never with safety repose confidence in a Yankee, [I] have never been deceived by an Indian." Much has been made of the comment over the years, and though the sentiment was probably real, he was forgetting or ignoring the many times his furs had been taken by Indians, many of his family and friends who had been killed by Indians, the torture and death of his son James by Big Jim, the killing of his brother Ned and his son Israel, the kidnapping of Jemima and the Callaway girls, the attempt by Blackfish to take him and eight other treaty signers hostage at Boonesborough. But Boone's affection for Indians, especially the Shawnee family that had adopted him, many of whom now came to visit him in Missouri, revealed the part of himself that truly was more in sympathy with the Indian ways than with the white culture. It showed the doubleness in his nature, which had been part of his special character, his *difference*, from the beginning.

Many believe that Boone in his final years saw clearly the contradictions of his life, how his "love of Nature" had led not to a future of peaceful hunting with Indians but to the destruction of the hunting grounds the Indians had preserved so long. Boone blamed the lawyers and speculators and politicians, calling them "Yankees," meaning Americans; most of the Yankees Boone knew came from Virginia and North Carolina. And yet he saw that some of the blame must rest with him also. If he had been an instrument ordained to settle the wilderness, as Filson said he was, for the Indians he was an "*instrument* by which they lost their hunting grounds." The contradictions of his life were all too obvious at times to the elderly explorer.

The story of Boone is the story of America. From the Blue Ridge to the Bluegrass, from the Yadkin to the Yellowstone, no man sought and loved the wilderness with more passion and dedication. Yet none did more to lead settlers and developers to destroy that wilderness in a few short decades. Richard Slotkin says, "He destroys the wilderness and the game by the very acts which reveal his love for them." Few white men of his time came close to understanding and appreciating the Native Americans as well as Boone did, yet few did as much, ultimately, to displace the Indians and destroy their habitat and culture. A man of peacefulness and goodwill, Boone spent much of his life involved with or witness to border wars, with the French, the Cherokees, the British, Shawnees, Loyalists, Wyandottes, Osages, Kansas.

THERE ARE several mysteries and paradoxes about Boone's last years. A few who talked with him then reported he was bitter, sardonic, that he shunned society and civilization. Though he had always preferred the isolation of the woods, apparently he was even more repelled in his final decade by the corruptions and indignities of the world. His family noted that seeing a visitor approaching the house, the old man would sometimes take his cane and hobble out the back door to avoid questions and gawking strangers. "Many heroic actions and chivalrous adventures are related of me which exist only in the region of fancy. With me the world has taken liberties," Boone said. "And yet I have been but a common man."

One of the abiding mysteries about Boone's last years is the question of whether he ever returned to Kentucky after leaving in 1799. There are many stories of his return to the Bluegrass to pay his debts. He seems to have been sighted almost as often as Elvis. Once his land grant came through in 1814 he had enough funds to settle his accounts in Kentucky. Rev. John Mason Peck wrote that Boone had kept no record books or documents "and knew not how much he owed, nor to whom he was indebted, but in the honest simplicity of his nature, he went to all with whom he had had dealings and paid whatever was demanded." Since Peck is not always the most accurate of biographers, his story might be discounted. But Peck had interviewed Boone at length, unlike all the other biographers except Flint and Filson.

And yet the members of Boone's immediate family claimed that he never returned to Kentucky after 1799. The daughter of Jacob Boone later said that Daniel never visited her family in Limestone. Just a few weeks before his death, Boone told a neighbor he had kept his promise never to return to Kentucky. Nathan Boone, one of the most reliable sources about Boone's last years, told Draper that his father never set foot in Kentucky again. The weight of evidence seems to be on the side of the family denials, yet the stories of Boone's return to Kentucky are convincing also. It is a question no one seems able to resolve, another example of apparent but conflicting truths that refuse to be reconciled.

Since Boone moved between his children's homes in his later years, it is possible he visited Kentucky while each thought he was staying with one of the others, or was off on an extended hunting trip. He may have wanted to return and pay his debts quietly, without any fuss. The old sometimes relish such acts of covert independence.

Over the past 175 years biographers have discussed Boone's religious beliefs in a number of ways. Early biographers sometimes portrayed the frontiersman as a devout Christian, almost a missionary bringing the gospel and Protestant culture to the savage wilderness. Some, for instance, asserted Boone never touched liquor, imposing Victorian abstinence on a man not only of the frontier but of the eighteenth century. The many accounts of him passing the bottle to companions, as well as the records of his frequent purchases of spirits, give the lie to that pious claim.

According to a letter by James Robertson, Boone and all his family were converted by an Episcopalian missionary while living with the Robertsons on the Watauga River around 1772. That claim is almost certainly not true. For one thing, there were no Episcopalians until after the American Revolution, when American Anglicans formed their own organization. Still others would claim that Boone was essentially a Baptist. James Bradley would tell Draper, "Col. Daniel Boone was a Baptist in sentiment, was not a church member, but was religiously inclined."

In fact, we have no record of Boone ever joining a church. It is possible that the disputes and contentions between the Quakers and his father, Squire, made him reluctant to join any congregation. Boone was a cheerful, peaceable man who avoided quarrels and arguments. He possibly associated church membership with feuds and petty self-righteousness. It was how one lived, not the outward displays of piety, that proved one's character and spirituality. "Colo. Boone was a firm believer in a divine overrule of providence and related many instances in his eventful life where he thought it had been particularly exercised towards him," Stephen Hempstead told Draper.

Boone's granddaughter Delinda married a Baptist preacher named James Craig, and a number of other Boone relations and friends answered the call to the pulpit. There were sometimes Bible readings and devotions on Sundays at Boonesborough. And of course, we know Boone took the Bible as well as other books to read by the campfire on his hunting trips. In 1816 he wrote a remarkable letter to his widowed sister-in-law:

october the 19th 1816

Deer Sister

    With pleasure I Red a Later from your sun Samuel Boone who infrms me that you are yett Liveing and in good health Considering your age I wright to you to Latt you know I have Not forgot you and to inform you of my own Situation Sence the Death of you Sister Rabacah I leve with flanders Calaway But am at present at my sun Nathans and in tolarabel halth you can gass at my feilings by your own as we are So Near one age I Need Not write you of our satuation as Samuel Bradley or James grimes Can inform you of Every Surcomstance Relating to our famaly and how we Leve in this World and what Chance we Shall have in the next we know Not for my part I am as ignerant as a Child all the Relegan I have to Love and fear god beleve in Jeses Christ Don all the good to my Nighbour and my self that I Can and Do as Little harm as I Can helpe and trust on gods marcy for the Rest and I beleve god neve made a man of my prisepel to be Lost and I flater my Self Deer sister that you are well on your way in Cristianaty gave my Love to all your Childran and all my frends fearwell my Deer sister.

Daniel Boone

Mrs. Sarah Boone

    NB   I Red a Later yesterday from sister Hanah peninton by hir grand sun Dal Ringe She and all hir Childran are Well at present

This letter is of particular interest for several reasons. Though its spelling is wild and inconsistent, the voice of the man comes through vividly. One has the sense of an old man who spoke much better than he wrote. What is evident is Boone's humility and simplicity, his affection for his family and his goodwill toward his fellow man. He admits his ignorance, but his claims for himself, though modest, are significant. He concedes he is childlike but has tried to do good, or at least little harm. He believes in a God of mercy, who honors integrity. It is the letter of a man at peace with himself. There is no hint of bitterness. The many failures and disappointments have left him humble, accepting.

Boone often attended services held by Baptists when he was visiting Jemima. He was present at a service preached by Rev. John Mason Peck. It was a time when revivals were sweeping the Missouri region, following the period that historians call the Second Great Awakening. But there is an independence and wit in Boone, of the kind we associate with Thoreau. As Thoreau was dying the abolitionist Parker Pillsbury asked him "how the opposite shore might appear to him." "One world at a time," the author of *Civil Disobedience* snapped. When the sage of Walden was asked on his deathbed by his aunt Louisa if he had made peace with God, Thoreau replied, "I did not know we had ever quarreled." When a Baptist preacher named James E. Welch asked Boone if he had "experienced a change in your feelings toward the Saviour" Boone fired back, "No sir, I always loved God ever since I could recollect."

"His [Boone's] worship was in secret, and he placed his hopes in the Savior," his son Nathan told Draper. "In his latter years my father was a great student of the Bible. He was seldom seen reading any other book and fully believed in the great truths of Christianity."

Boone had never lost the influence of the Quakers in Pennsylvania. His peaceableness and reticence, his tolerance and ease with other races, his love of fairness, seemed derived in part from early contact with the Friends. But some thought he was deeply influenced by Indian beliefs also. Timothy Flint said outright, "He worshipped, as he often said, the Great Spirit — for the woods were his books and his temple, and the creed of the red men naturally became his."

While the Indians had been absorbing many of the teachings of the Moravians and Methodists and other denominations, men like Boone were assimilating an Indian sense of a sacred, animistic wilderness and meshing it all into a single creed of goodwill and respect for others and all life. As mentioned earlier, the ideas and poetry that would be expressed a few decades later by Emerson, Thoreau, and Whitman were already at work in the minds and hearts and pulse of men such as Boone and William Bartram, who had also been brought up as a Quaker. Probably Boone would have agreed with Emerson when he said, "I like the silent church before the service begins, better than any preaching." If the genius of American thought and literature was created from the fusion of New England spiritual zeal and the naturalism of the Enlightenment, it was also deeply informed by the American experience of the wilderness, the great forests and vistas of the West, the spirit of the frontier men and women and the Native hunters and holy men they encountered, fought with, imitated, learned from.

If in his old age Boone viewed his relations with Indians through amber-tinted binoculars and renewed affection, the affection and respect were returned by those who had known him as Sheltowee at Chillicothe. The younger daughters of Blackfish were now old women, but they remembered Boone's kindness to them. Boone visited Indian friends at their homes also.

The attempts by some to debunk the myth of Boone as frontier hero and Indian fighter have actually enhanced the legend of Boone as a man of peace and goodwill. As the historian Arthur K. Moore phrased it, "Many a Kentuckian engaged in much more heroic actions with the Shawnee than Boone . . . There is slight evidence that Boone ever knowingly killed an Indian and no record of a violent hand-to-hand combat . . . Boone seems to have dealt with the Indians by . . . placating them." Even his would-be detractors concede Boone was a man of humanity and peace.

IN HIS FINAL years Boone's moods could change with the weather. To some visitors he spoke of his disappointment with civilization and especially Kentucky. To others he could appear cheerful and at peace with his life and his lot. At times he was angry about the legends and fictions that had been written and circulated and repeated about him. To the end of his life he was aware of his effect and his fame. Commenting on reports that he still went hunting in his last years, Boone told Peck, "I would not believe that tale if I told it myself. I have not watched the deer's lick for ten years. My eyesight is too far gone to hunt."

In 1816 Boone and Nathan began to build a stone house near Nathan and Olive's cabin on Femme Osage Creek. Since Boone himself was eighty-two years old and arthritic, it is assumed that most of the heavy work was done by Nathan, and his father served as a helper and adviser. But local tradition in Missouri has it that Boone did at least some of the carpentry, including the pegged wooden doors. It is quite possible that the idea of the large stone house, and the design of the house, were as much Boone's as Nathan's. The house was meant to look like those the Boones had seen years before in Pennsylvania. Squire had begun work on a smaller stone house near Cuivre River before he had to return to Kentucky around 1801. Building something permanent of stone seemed to be on the Boones' minds, after their many moves from log cabin to cave to half-face camp to log cabin.

Nathan cut the blue limestone from a nearby quarry and dragged the blocks on a sled pulled by oxen to the site. Most of the stones were about three feet wide and weighed several hundred pounds. To cut such rocks from the hillside required hundreds of holes drilled by hammer and hand-turned bit. After the block was broken loose by an explosion of black powder in the holes, the piece had to be dressed to size with hammer and chisel. To prepare one stone could take hours, sparks flying from the chisel point, stench of burned metal, limestone chips, and dust.

The trick of dressing stone is to cut each piece within acceptable limits of exactness. Since every stone cuts differently, has a different feel to the touch and eye—what masons sometimes refer to as flavor—it is a matter of approximation, chipping and measuring and chipping again, to find an acceptable tolerance of straightness, plumbness. Part of the beauty of stonework is the roughness, within the overall exactness. Since it took Nathan and his father three years to build the house, with time out for farming and hunting, we can guess they extracted each stone from the quarry, dressed it, and dragged it to the building site one day at a time. Boone's skill as a blacksmith must have been put to use sharpening the tools and replacing broken drills and hammers and chisels.

Once all the stones were cut and hauled to the site on the gentle hillside near a spring, the work had only begun. The plans for the house called for a structure twenty-six by forty-six feet with three-foot-thick walls and two main stories, a full basement where the cooking was done, and a large attic. It was a kind of American castle, with gun ports in the first story. Nathan had lived in log cabins all his life. He had been born at Boone's Station, had lived on Marble Creek, at Limestone and Point Pleasant. He and Olive began their marriage camping under the stars on the way to Missouri and then settling in a small cabin on Loutre Creek before they obtained the claim on Femme Osage.

The stone house was built as a monument to the Boones' long struggle and trek from Pennsylvania to North Carolina, to Kentucky and Virginia, and on to Missouri. It was a manor house, a family seat. But the house was also a fortress, against Indian attacks, against the uncertain future, and against the many failures and embarrassments of

Boone's career, his debts and losses, his constant moves. With the great stone house, Nathan was reaching toward stability as well as prominence. He wanted to build a dwelling that would last for centuries.

It cannot have been easy for Nathan and the other sons to live in the shadow of their famous father. Boone had been away from home much of the time when they were young. He might be famous elsewhere, but at home he was most often in debt, and most of the work of farming and procuring a subsistence was left to Rebecca and the children. The family had been forced to keep moving, under a cloud of lawsuits, accusations, rumors of treason. As the youngest and favored son, with more education than the rest, Nathan must have felt more than his brothers and sisters the necessity of proving himself against the rumors of inherited instability and fecklessness.

Nathan, with the help and advice of his father, cut walnut logs three feet in diameter and hewed beams nearly a foot thick and two to two and a half feet tall. The joists and sills and beams of the house looked like something out of a cathedral in the Old World. The frame of the house was pegged together, mortised and tenoned, from heavy timbers. Father and son sawed and planed thick oak boards for the floors, and pegged them into place. The planks were made one at a time with a whipsaw, as one sawyer stood in a pit beneath the log and the second held the other end of the saw above the log. Anyone who has ever tried to saw or drill oak lumber knows how it resists even the sharpest tools. As the stone walls were made, each stone was swung into place by block and tackle. But first a bed of mortar had to be spread on the stone the next block was to rest on. The mortar itself was made from lime and sand and water, sometimes with a little clay thrown in: one part lime, three parts sand, and enough water to make a paste that could be spread and shaped with a trowel.

After Boone's death Nathan would say his father had been entitled to Masonic honors, though he had none at his funeral since there were no Masonic lodges in the district. Though Boone had been initiated into Freemasonry years earlier, in this one period near the end of his

life Boone worked literally as a mason, helping where he could, sometimes wielding the trowel, perhaps mixing the mortar and keeping it
wet until used. Often the oldest member of a masonry crew was responsible for keeping the "mud" soft and ready to be spread.

Boone had given Nathan a fine silver watch for his twenty-seventh
birthday on March 2, 1808. The timepiece survived Nathan's cam-
paigns as an officer in the Missouri militia and the U.S. Army. Nathan
would be commissioned a major and then a lieutenant colonel in the
army and serve at posts in Kansas, Wisconsin, and Oklahoma. Made
by William Hopetown in London in 1783, the watch is still owned by a
descendant in Pasadena, California. A fine watch was a traditional gift
from a father to a son, a sign of continuity, dignity, maturity. Boone,
who had always told time by the sun and stars, when he had cared to
tell it at all, wanted Nathan to have this symbol and gadget of the new
era that was coming into being.

It is said the attic of Nathan's palatial house was used for dances
in the years after it was built. With furniture cleared away from the
thick oak floor, the neighbors and boys and girls of the region, those
who did not disapprove of dancing for religious reasons, would gather
on Saturday evenings with a fiddler or sometimes even a small band
called an orcestry for dance reels and jigs. Every community seemed
to have its fiddler, who was often also a good storyteller, with a knack
for quips and jokes. Nathan and Olive had fourteen children, and it is
pleasing to think of the family gathering in the large attic with their
friends and stepping to the fiddle music and banjo picking, listening to
ballads and slightly smutty tales, and singing the ballads and love songs
of the day. The rolling Missouri countryside must have been sweetened
by the music and glow of their frolics as fireflies winked their amorous
codes in the meadows and orchards.

As it turned out, Nathan was more like his father than either of
them may have realized. Nathan would later serve in the Missouri
Constitutional Convention, as well as in the militia and U.S. Army.
But like his father he accumulated debts. In spite of his prominence,

his recognized ability as a leader, his skill as an artisan like his father
and uncle Squire, Nathan's finances grew more and more precarious
as his debts mounted, until in 1837 he had to sell his stone mansion on
Femme Osage Creek and move his family far to the west, to Greene
County, Missouri, build a log house on the prairie, and start all over
again. Like his father before him, Nathan must have discovered that
the only thing permanent was alternating growth and loss, and the
legends that seemed to attach themselves to the Boone name wherever
they went.

EVEN IN THE sad years after the death of Rebecca, and throughout
his long decline, Boone kept something of his dry wit and relish of
irony. After he fell ill while hunting with his grandson James Boone
in November of 1817 and was taken to the home of Isaac Van Bibber,
Nathan was summoned. Assuming that his father had already died,
Nathan ordered a coffin to be made while he went to get the body of
the old pioneer. "I gave directions before leaving home for a coffin to
be made so the funeral might take place immediately on my return,"
Nathan said.

But Boone had not died. In fact he had rallied and was able to return with Nathan. And when he saw the coffin Nathan had ordered,
Boone was not at all pleased. Made of plain boards it was "too rough
and uncouth." For all his modesty and good manners, Boone had a
sense of style and dignity. The plain coffin was used for a relative and
Boone ordered a fine coffin made for himself to match the one he had
commissioned for Rebecca in 1813.

"Soon after this event, he gave directions to a cabinet-maker in the
settlement to prepare a coffin of black walnut for himself, which was
done accordingly, and it was kept in his dwelling for several years," Peck
would write. But according to Peck, Boone later decided the walnut
coffin was not good enough either. He gave that coffin for someone
else's burial and ordered an even better one for himself. "Another of
cherry was prepared, and placed under his bed, where it continued

until it received his mortal remains." The cherry coffin was a handsome piece of work, and the old man took pleasure in showing it off. Elizabeth Corbin, sister of Daniel Morgan Boone's wife, Sara, later told Draper, "[T]he coffin appeared marvelously beautiful! The fame of it spread among the simple minded settlers, and it had exceedingly numerous visitors." Later the coffin was stored at Nathan's new stone house, but from time to time Boone would take it out to admire and study. His granddaughter Delinda later remembered that he would "rub and polish it up, and cooly whistle while doing it." Others said he would lie down in the coffin to show how well it fit him, and sometimes he would take a nap in it, scaring the children.

Even as a feeble old man Boone was still the performer, larger than life. If he had to be an old man in his second childhood, waiting for death to claim him, then he would play the role in a way nobody would ever forget. He continued to improvise and expand the role of Daniel Boone created many years before. He had always been able to make himself memorable. His coffin was the finest that could be had, and he was going to enjoy it and be *seen* enjoying it.

No doubt Boone took comfort in making death so familiar. The box he would later rest in was right here now, and he could dust it and rub it with oil. His hands had never been idle, whether scraping a steer horn to make a powder horn, oiling his traps, or repairing his rifle. The Reverend Nathan Kouns, who visited Boone in 1818, reported, "[H]e commenced scraping a horn with a piece of glass, and said he was going to make a powder horn as he intended to go out and hunt in the fall. He soon laid it aside and I learned from Capt. Lamme that he had been five years at work on the same horn in view of a fall hunt still in the future." Boone had always admired fine workmanship. He carved fine powder horns for his grandchildren and neighbors, and he repaired rifles friends and neighbors brought to him. His craftsman brother Squire had died in 1815, but Daniel Boone was a craftsman too. He would make his last days a work of art.

Like almost all men and women who have the opportunity, Boone enjoyed his grandchildren. He could tell them stories and rhymes, wise sayings, and anecdotes from his own childhood and his long adventurous life. And his curiosity never left him. He questioned visitors and family members about current events and news of the day, of the frontier advancing ever farther west.

Sometimes he took a bearskin or deerskin out under a tree and would lie on it whistling or singing to himself. It is an image that reminds us of Caspar Mansker's story of finding Boone alone in the wilderness of Kentucky lying on his back and singing, and of his singing when locked in the coal house in Charlottesville in 1781. Boone never lost his relish for solitude and forest, for singing and keeping company with his favorite friend, himself. And he liked to be *seen* enjoying his solitude. His eyes were not good enough to hunt and his legs too feeble to carry him into the forest, but it still pleased him to be among trees, in the freedom of the open air. The Reverend James E. Welch described his person as he saw him in 1818. "He was rather low of stature, broad shoulders, high cheek bones, very mild countenance, fair complexion, soft and quiet in his manner, but little to say unless spoken to, amiable and kind in his feelings, very fond of quiet retirement, of cool self-possession, and indomitable perseverance."

Among Boone's last noted visitors was a young painter from Massachusetts named Chester Harding. Harding came to Charette to paint Boone's portrait at the very end of his life. Finding the old hunter roasting venison on a ramrod in a small cabin behind Jemima's house, the painter asked if he could do a portrait. Boone was hard of hearing and may not have understood the request. He had little experience with portrait painters. But Jemima understood the importance of the opportunity and persuaded her father to overcome his timidity or modesty and sit. The result was the only portrait from life that exists.

Though he was old and frail in the Harding painting, the powerful presence of Boone comes through in the portrait. No longer the muscular "Big Turtle" of his prime, Boone still shows his character and will. It is the picture of a man who means to do what he sets out to do. We are all in Harding's debt for his last-minute likeness of Boone. According to the family, Boone was surprised to see himself captured so convincingly on canvas. Harding's portrait was later revised by others to make Boone look younger and healthier. Harding captured the dignity and strength of the elusive Boone. As he sketched, the young painter questioned Boone about his career, which now stretched into its ninth decade. Had he ever been lost in his wandering? Harding asked. "No," Boone said, "I can't say I was ever lost, but I was *bewildered* once for three days."

In August of 1820 Boone grew weaker and became subject to a fever that waxed and waned but always seemed to return. "He began to complain of an acute burning sensation, such as he never before felt . . . which continually grew worse." He was treated again by his granddaughter's husband Dr. John Jones, but nothing seemed able to dispel the fever for good. Possibly it was an infection of the heart tissue. Before, he had always been able to throw off his afflictions, but this time the fever lingered. He seemed to sense that this infection was something different and asked to be taken to Nathan's house for one last visit.

Dr. Jones warned that he was much too sick to travel, but after a number of delays Nathan came for him in a carriage and drove him to the stone house. They arrived at the new house on September 21, 1820, and Olive fixed a special dinner for her father-in-law, including his favorite dish, sweet potatoes. Tradition says he overindulged and also ate cookies and candy the doting children pressed on him. The excess sweets made him worse. Neighbors and relatives gathered to greet the old man, guessing that it would be his last visit.

The next day, Boone said he still felt stuffed and would take only a bowl of milk. His fever returned, and he decided to lie down in a bed fixed for him in the front room of the house. In the days that followed, Boone stayed in bed and it was clear that things had taken a new turn. Even when sick before, he had gotten up and stirred about. Jemima and

her family arrived on September 25 and Dr. Jones offered Boone medicine, probably laudanum. Boone said that this was his last sickness and
refused anything. He wanted to keep his mind clear. He had always
been lucid and alert, and he wanted to end his life with his perceptions
as acute as possible.

In the nineteenth century people talked about a "beautiful death." It
was as though one's death was a work of art, something to be crafted,
an achievement. Deaths were described and critiqued, commented on,
compared to others', admired. A beautiful death was one's final accomplishment. In modern times most people, except for those who
are killed in accidents or by sudden heart attacks, die in hospitals or
hospices, often far from family and home. Usually the old have been
isolated for years in nursing homes and hospitals, in an air-conditioned
and sterilized world of care by professionals. Death is hidden away in
its own proper sphere. Too often, the last place modern people see is
an equipped room in a large institution of care and dying.

Before the age of retirement homes and hospitals and nursing homes,
the old died at home. If they were lucky to have a large caring family,
children and grandchildren, friends and cousins, gathered around in
a death vigil. In a world without modern medicine, the old felt death
coming on, recognized it. People gathered in the bedroom and said
their farewells, and the one dying had his or her final say. There were
kisses and hugs and sharing of memories. Quarrels and grudges were
resolved, grievances aired, forgiveness offered and received. Final requests were made. There were prayers and hymn singing, visits by the
minister as well as the local doctor. The subject might describe the
sensations of dying, the gathering of stillness and ease, the feeling of
weightlessness and coolness. Sometimes the dying heard music or saw
a pleasing light that might take the shape of an angel. Sometimes family members saw a dove or other bird light at a window, or heard the
scrape of wood being planed, as if a coffin were being made.

If the dying person was very lucky, he just closed his eyes and stopped breathing, as the soothing rest closed in or opened out into an infinite stillness. But for some there was a long death struggle as lungs tried to keep breathing and heart failed and struggled to restart, kicking in again and again, always getting weaker. Breath rasped in the throat and got shorter, until instead of breath there was only a rattle of air.

On his last day, Boone, who knew he was dying, said, "I am about worn out." The acute burning around his heart was worse than he had felt before. He asked for his coffin to be brought down from the attic, and he touched the polished wood with his cane to reassure himself of its strength. He described the kind of funeral he wanted and reminded them to bury him beside Rebecca on the hill overlooking the bottomlands to the river. A servant shaved the old man and Jemima cut his hair to suit him. Granddaughter Delinda even brushed his teeth. Boone asked his daughter-in-law Olive to sing some of his favorite songs. He expressed pleasure in his long life and health, his attempts to do good and not harm others, his faith in the mercy of God.

As morning approached, Boone asked for a bowl of warm milk, which he drank with relish. Then all the family members, including the slaves, filed in to say a final good-bye and receive his farewell. He told each one not to be sad, for he had lived a long and fruitful life. As Nathan and Jemima held a hand on either side, he said, "I am going; don't grieve for me, my time has come." He died just after the sun had risen, September 26, 1820.

Boone's body was carried in his fine coffin to Jemima's house and a large crowd assembled for the funeral there two days later. James Craig preached the funeral in the barn, which was the only building large enough to hold the number who had gathered. In the sermon Nathan's son-in-law saluted Boone for his explorations and development of the West, and for his defense of the settlements. It is not mentioned whether or not any Shawnees attended the funeral. Boone's nephew Daniel Bryan later told Draper, "Daniel Boone died . . . in the state of Missouri not owning as Much land as would make his grave."

The crowd then followed the coffin and an American flag to the hilltop a mile away where Boone was placed in the earth beside Rebecca.
The long hunt and pilgrimage to the west that had started almost
eighty-six years earlier in Pennsylvania were over. Now there were only
memories, stories, and legends.

CHAPTER TWENTY

Across the River into Legend

1820–1856 ↳

The story of Daniel Boone is a story of rivers. He had crossed the Schuylkill and the Susquehanna and the Potomac, the Shenandoah and the Yadkin. He had crossed the Holston and the Watauga, the Clinch and Powell's River. Beyond the Cumberland Gap he had crossed the Cumberland and the Kentucky and the Big Sandy, the Licking and the Ohio, the Kanawha and the Scioto, the Miami and the Little Miami. He had crossed the Mississippi and followed the Missouri, the Gasconade, the Grand, and the Yellowstone. When Boone crossed that final river, the Styx or the Jordan, his larger life as mythic figure, legend and icon of the West, was just beginning. Even Boone could not have imagined the scale and speed with which his story would grow and spread and influence the culture and imagination of the developing nation. Within a few decades of his death his image and his character would be portrayed and transformed in a hundred different ways and under different names to become a quintessence of America's ideal of itself, its origins and aspirations, its destiny. He would inspire thinkers and artists and writers from Thomas Cole to James Fenimore Cooper, to Ralph Waldo Emerson and Henry David Thoreau and Lord Byron, and through them and others he would inspire a nation to some of its finest achievements, and to some of its worst. The young nation needed a hero and a symbol, and along with George Washington and perhaps Franklin, no man fit the bill as well as Daniel Boone. According to Richard Slotkin, "[I]t was the figure of Daniel Boone, the solitary, Indian-like hunter of the deep woods, that became the most significant, most emotionally compelling myth-hero of the early republic. The other myth-figures are reflections or variations of this basic type."

The young republic needed Boone, the icon of curiosity, courage, character, and wonder. Cultures find in a few individuals the symbols of their ideals. Thanks to Filson and then many other biographers, Boone's story was repeated and embellished, magnified and extended to illustrate everything from temperance to Manifest Destiny. A cousin of Rebecca's, Daniel Bryan, published an epic in verse in 1816 called *The Mountain Muse*. Portraying Boone as a heroic, almost saintly woodsman, the poem ran to 250 pages and contained far more fiction than history. When the poem was read to him, Boone is supposed to have declared it "too highly colored and exaggerated" and to have observed that such projects should be delayed until the subject "was put in the ground."

It is well known that Cooper used Boone and the legend of Boone as the model for Leatherstocking, Hawkeye of *The Last of the Mohicans*, Natty Bumppo in *Deerslayer*, and the hero in three other novels of the frontier. Cooper was the first internationally popular American fiction writer, and he spread the image of the frontier hero to millions of readers. Called Pathfinder, in *Pathfinder*, the noble scout figures as Leatherstocking or Natty Bumppo in the mythic story of *The Pioneers* and as the Trapper in *Prairie*, the personification of strength, courage, responsibility, in a violent and threatening wilderness. As Annette Kolodny says, "The figure who most enduringly embodies the myth of America's westward expansion is Daniel Boone, passed down to us in later incarnations as Cooper's Leatherstocking, Faulkner's Boon Hogganbeck, and A. B. Guthrie's Boon in *The Big Sky*."

Lord Byron added to Boone's reputation by portraying him as

General Boone in *Don Juan* in 1822, two years after the frontiersman's death. Byron's Boone is an ancient woodsman, still active in his ninetieth year, a hunter, but a man of peace who kills no humans. Byron's poem contributed to the image of Boone as the noble patriarch of the natural world, untainted by the bloody cruelty of civilization and its wars. His portrait extended the Romantic vision of Boone as ideal hero living in harmony with the wilderness and simple virtues, who "Enjoyed the lonely vigorous, harmless days / Of his old age in wilds of deepest maze."

Though almost all Boone biographers have belittled Byron's rendering of Boone as poetic fantasy, the poet captured something of an essential feature of Boone's personality, the qualities that made him thrill to the solitude in the Kentucky wilds of 1770, the love of reaching out ever farther toward the opening in the forest that ended at the horizon, and Byron recognized Boone's love of peace.

The pleasure and exuberance Boone experienced in the wilderness would later find their place in the paintings of the Hudson River school, in such artists as Thomas Cole, Asher B. Durand, and Frederick Church and in the work of George Caleb Bingham. Boone's relish of the wilderness and the West would inform and help define the culture and consciousness of the new republic, even as his pioneering had helped destroy that wilderness.

An organization for boys, called the Sons of Daniel Boone, founded in 1905 by Dan Beard, was the precursor to the Boy Scouts of America. By then Boone had long been established as an iconic figure presiding over America's ideal of itself. He occupies "a kind of no-man's land between the wilderness that is and the settlement that will be, neither a builder nor farmer, but a hunter, a Nimrod providentially equipped to explore the vast cipher of the continent and mark a trail for others." To the environmentally sensitive, Boone is a reminder of missed opportunities, of a paradise lost, a primary symbol of our conflicted desires, confused destiny, our ideals and ambitions inspiring and undercutting each other.

Boone's greatest influence on our culture and literature and self-image is shown in more implicit, subtle, and indirect instances. While Boone is explicitly invoked, named or unnamed, in many novels and poems and in painting after painting, including George Caleb Bingham's *Daniel Boone Escorting Settlers through the Cumberland Gap* (1851–52) and Thomas Cole's *Daniel Boone at His Cabin at Great Osage Lake* (1826), Boone's presence is influential in places where he is not named but is immanent as a model so familiar he is already implicit in the very fabric of American culture and mythology. According to Richard Slotkin, "The figure and the myth-narrative that emerged from the early Boone literature became archetypal for the American literature which followed: an American hero is the lover of the spirit of the wilderness, and his acts of love and sacred affirmation are acts of violence against that spirit and her avatars."

As the myth building continued, the crushing failures Boone had suffered were forgotten or ignored. As with Washington, his accumulated failures did not seem to diminish his legend but actually enhanced it. "Boone's stature, paradoxically, was largely unaffected by painful, repeated failure. His fortunes began to decline simultaneously with the end of the Revolutionary War and the publication of Filson's biography."

When Emerson began to formulate and define the aspirations of the young nation in *Nature* in 1836 and "Self-Reliance" in 1839, he appealed again and again to the independent, versatile, resourceful man who is undaunted by adversity. The image of Boone had become so embedded in the collective memory and imagination by then that he does not need to be named. He has become an ideal, transformed beyond the mere woodsman and hunter. "But if a man would be alone, let him look at the stars . . . Nature never became a toy to a wise spirit. The flowers, the animals, the mountains, reflected the wisdom of his best hour, as much as they had delighted the simplicity of his childhood." In his celebration of resourcefulness and independence, Emerson describes the country boy who is not tied down to a profession but who "*teams it, farms it, peddles it*, keeps a school, preaches, edits a newspaper, goes to Congress, buys a township, and so forth, in successive years, and always, like a cat, falls on his feet, is worth a hundred of these city dolls." This self-reliant man walks ahead with his days and feels no shame "in not studying a profession, for he does not postpone his life, but lives already."

And a little later in the same address Emerson catches much of the spirit of Boone's solitude and reverence. "Prayer is a contemplation of the facts of life from the highest point of view. It is the soliloquy of a beholding and jubilant soul. It is the spirit of God pronouncing his works good." Emerson can write it down in 1839, but the legendary Boone had lived this perception and passion decades before, along rivers and in forests and among dangers that likely surpassed Emerson's imagination. Or at least that is the way the culture remembered Boone and the way we like to remember Boone. Essays such as "Circles" and "Fate" resonate with the wisdom and assurance of a Boone, cheerful in the face of defeat and failure, pushing on to the end of the horizon, beyond the next mountain range where another vista opens. The image of Boone helped inspire and inform this quest of the essential and transforming self, and the vibrant future. In "Circles" Emerson says, "Nothing great was ever achieved without enthusiasm. The way of life is wonderful; it is by abandonment."

Again and again in his essays and journals we see Emerson defining the often contradictory experiences and aspirations Boone had enacted and illustrated. In *Nature* Emerson says, "The health of the eye seems to demand a horizon. We are never tired so long as we can see far enough." And later he celebrates the world as it is. "[A] fact is true poetry, and the most beautiful of fables." "In the tranquil landscape, and especially in the distant line of the horizon, man beholds somewhat as beautiful as his own nature."

As Richard Slotkin explains it, "In each case, the image of Boone was made to serve as the embodiment of local values or cultural assumptions and as the vicarious resolver of the dilemmas that preoccupied that culture. In the development of these variant images of Boone we can trace the emergence of American national consciousness, the process of cultural differentiation that finally divided the Euro-Americans from the Europeans."

If the legend inspired by Boone inspired Emerson, it is not surprising that it also influenced Emerson's handyman and neighbor, Henry David Thoreau. Since Thoreau's subject is often a celebration of "wildness" and the relish of wildness and solitude, it is likely that the Boone figure was even more important to the resident of the cabin in the Walden woods. Thoreau did most of his traveling in word and spirit near Concord, but his metaphors often imply and draw on the kind of extended voyages Boone and other frontiersmen actually made into the unexplored, unmapped wilderness. Thoreau celebrated the American Indian, and the subtitle of his most famous book is *Life in the Woods*. "I love to be alone. I never found the companion that was so companionable as solitude."

Thoreau begins his essay "Walking" by saying, "I wish to speak a word for Nature, for absolute freedom and wildness, as contrasted with a freedom and culture merely civil." The spirit of Boone hovers over every page of the essay, published in 1862 after Thoreau's death. With exuberance, and often with tongue in cheek, Thoreau's essay is a celebration of freedom and adventure. "I believe that there is a subtile magnetism in Nature, which, if we unconsciously yield to it, will direct us aright."

Thoreau finds his walking is directed toward the west. Like his forerunner in the Kentucky woods, the West draws him inexorably. "The future lies that way to me, and the earth seems more unexhausted and richer on that side . . . I must walk toward Oregon, and not toward Europe." Referring to Columbus and Michaux and other explorers, Thoreau says, "I should be ashamed to think that Adam in paradise was more favorably situated on the whole than the backwoodsman in this country." Thoreau describes turning away from the antiquities of Europe and even Massachusetts and facing the West. "The West of which I speak is but another name for the Wild; and what I have been preparing to say is, that in Wildness is the preservation of the World."

Implicit in Thoreau's anthem to wildness is a contradiction similar to that of Boone's career. Boone's love of wilderness leads him to bring others to destroy it. Thoreau's love of wilderness is stated in the context of the high civilization of Concord at the moment of its greatest cultural achievement. "I believe in the forest, and in the meadow, and in the night in which the corn grows," Thoreau says, echoing the Apostle's Creed, and he celebrates the darker skins of those who live in the woods and is ashamed of his own paleness. Like Boone, he would become an Indian, seeking the wildest part of the wilderness. "When I would recreate myself, I seek the darkest wood, the thickest and most interminable, and, to the citizen, most dismal swamp. I enter a swamp as a sacred place — a *sanctum sanctorum*. There is the strength, the marrow of Nature."

And then Thoreau turns to the political consideration of wildness and freedom, and the emotional and psychological dimensions. The wildness is in us more than it is in the forest. He celebrates the Indian custom of naming and renaming individuals after their actions and attributes. He relishes the wonder of a child as opposed to the habits and tameness of grown men. Thoreau salutes instinct and spontaneity over habit and instruction. Darkness and ignorance can inspire more than the merely familiar. Like Boone, and also young Abe Lincoln, Thoreau made his living as a surveyor, translating the surface of the earth into angles and numbers, but it was simple wonder that appealed to him most. "I found my account in climbing a tree once. It was a tall white pine, on top of a hill; and though I got well pitched, I was well paid for it, for I discovered new mountains in the horizon which I had never seen before, — so much more of the earth and the heavens."

By Thoreau's time, Boone's forward-pressing Pisgah vision had become the type and archetype to which American poets and philosophers and even politicians appealed. Thoreau published *Walden* in 1854, and the next year an equally remarkable book of verse was published in New York, *Leaves of Grass* by Walt Whitman. Just as expansive and wild as Thoreau's work, Whitman's poems spilled in long, flowing lines that seemed at times to imitate bird calls and ocean waves, and at other times the bel canto opera of which Whitman was so fond. A former journalist and editor turned real estate agent and carpenter, Whitman celebrated himself and his body as the measure of all nature and society.

No poet of the Romantic era extolled the wonder of childhood more effectively than Whitman. When we read his "There Was a Child Went Forth" we may think of the young Daniel Boone discovering the woods around him north of Oley.

> There was a child went forth every day,
> And the first object he look'd upon, that object he became,
> And that object became part of him for the day or a certain part of the
>   day,
> Or for many years or stretching cycles of years.
>
> The early lilacs became part of this child,
> And grass and white and red morning-glories, and white and red
>   clover, and the song of the phoebe-bird,
> And the Third-month lambs and the sow's pink-faint litter, and the
>   mare's foal and the cow's calf . . .

Wonder and wildness are the bedrock on which Whitman's persona and vision are grounded.

> Alone far in the wilds and mountains I hunt,
> Wandering amazed at my lightness and glee,
> In the late afternoon choosing a safe spot to pass the night,
> Kindling a fire and broiling the fresh-kill'd game,
> Falling asleep on the gathered leaves with my dog and gun by my side.

By the time Whitman wrote these lines in the 1850s the image and legend of Boone had pervaded the American consciousness and been repeated so often he did not need to be named to be invoked. Boone had become a figure of America's ideal self, a touchstone of poetry and history and national identity. By the 1850s the legend of Boone had been extended and adjusted with the legends of other western frontiersmen: Davy Crockett, Jim Bridger, Jedediah Smith, and Kit Carson, Boone's distant kinsman. The lore of the mountain men of the Rockies, from Hugh Glass to John Colter and the Bent brothers, was an echo of the original story of Boone, first created by Filson in 1784, but much simplified. Henry Nash Smith tells us, "The fur trapper, or Mountain Man, was much more clearly uncivilized than Daniel Boone had been."

In his visionary zeal Whitman seems completely unaware that the Open Road he invites the reader to follow may lead ultimately to the shopping mall, the choked and smelly expressway, the polluted landscape. As the poet Louis Simpson would write in 1959, "The Open Road goes to the used-car lot." Whitman shares with Boone a romantic innocence about the consequences of their quest and the vexed destiny that in a few decades would be all too manifest.

William Bartram's *Travels* had been published in 1790, creating a detailed portrait of the untamed wilderness of North America as a paradise, a new Eden. While Boone was hacking Boone's Trace and building Boonesborough, Bartram was studying the splendor of the Great Smoky Mountains and northern Georgia. Richard Slotkin tells us, "[Bartram's] record bears the distinctive markings of the mind of Filson's Boone. There are frequent echoes of Filson's phraseology, but more significant is his sharing of Boone's expectation of receiving wisdom from the wilderness and his consequent willingness to submit himself to experience in it."

Recent scholars have argued that Bartram and the figure of Boone created by Filson influenced British romanticism as well as American. Both Wordsworth and Coleridge read Bartram's *Travels* as young poets, and because of Gilbert Imlay's connection with Mary Wollstonecraft and William Godwin they knew of Filson's "The Adventures of Col. Daniel Boon" also. It is ironic that some of the ideals of English Romantic poetry would be imported from the American wilderness by a scoundrel such as Imlay. As Maurice Manning states it, "Boone was a living example of the synthesis of the mental and physical experience, which is both natural and humane, and which became Wordsworth's primary aesthetic." The intense emotions and perceptions of an ideal and natural nobility that would be created in English Romantic poetry had already been lived in "an uncouth place like Kentucky, by rough-hewn rustics like Boone."

The legend of Boone complemented but transcended the account of Bartram because of the added dimension of heroism given to Boone, the questing knight, the Moses leading his people to the Promised Land, the lover who consummates his passion for the body of the beautiful untamed land. And other dimensions of the Boone story had entered the popular imagination by the 1850s also, among them the picture of Boone the patriarch in Missouri, surrounded by his extended, affectionate family, honored by all who knew him. In "I Sing the Body Electric" Whitman portrays just such a noble figure.

> I knew a man, a common farmer, the father of five sons,
> And in them the fathers of sons, and in them the fathers of sons.
> This man was of wonderful vigor, calmness, beauty of person,
> The shape of his head, the pale yellow and white of his hair and
>   beard, the immeasurable meaning of his black eyes, the richness and
>   breadth of his manners,
> These I used to go and visit him to see, he was wise also,
> He was six feet tall, he was over eighty years old, his sons were massive,
>   clean, bearded, tan-faced, handsome,
> They and his daughters loved him, all who saw him loved him,
> They did not love him by allowance, they loved him with personal love,
> He drank water only, the blood show'd like scarlet through the clear-
>   brown skin of his face,
> He was a frequent gunner and fisher, he sail'd his boat himself, he had
>   a fine one presented to him by a shipjoiner, he had fowling-pieces
>   presented to him by men that loved him

When he went with his five sons and many grand-sons to hunt or fish,
you would pick him out as the most beautiful and vigorous of the
gang.
You would wish long and long to be with him, you would wish to sit by
him in the boat that you might touch each other.

Whitman had absorbed, either directly or indirectly, the portrait of Boone as an old man presented by Peck in 1847 in *Life of Daniel Boone*, surrounded by his admiring and affectionate family, hunting with his sons and grandsons and friends, still hunting and taking excursions in his boat.

The metaphor in Whitman's poetry that resonates most colorfully with the Boone legend is that of the open road. In "Song of the Open Road," published in the 1856 second edition of *Leaves of Grass*, Whitman evokes an image of freedom and wandering as a way of life as thrilling as Thoreau's metaphor of walking. The open road is the way of beauty and freedom, a life of discovery and wonder, a path to the shining future, the Edenic west of brotherhood.

From this hour I ordain myself loos'd of limits and imaginary lines,
Going where I list, my own master total and absolute,
Listening to others, considering well what they say,
Pausing, searching, receiving, contemplating,
Gently, but with undeniable will, divesting myself of the holds that
would hold me.

I inhale great draughts of space.
The east and the west are mine, and the north and the south are mine.

I am larger, better than I thought,
I did not know I held so much goodness.

It is interesting that Boone and Bartram and Whitman came from Quaker families. The spirit of patience and peacefulness of the Friends seems to have informed the lives and vision of all three. An essential part of Whitman's message is patience.

The earth never tires,
The earth is rude, silent, incomprehensible at first, Nature is rude and
*   incomprehensible at first,*
Be not discouraged, keep on, there are divine things well envelop'd,
I swear to you there are divine things more beautiful than words can tell.

Later critics would point out the dangers of romantic illusions about self and country. Critics in the twentieth century would blame many failures and compromises in American culture on the extravagant visions of triumph and destiny that writers such as Whitman, and the heroic legends such as that of Daniel Boone, had inspired. The exuberance of Emerson and Whitman would do nothing to deflect the cataclysm of the Civil War. The cherished solitude of Boone and Thoreau in the natural world could not prevent the ruin of rivers and erosion of land, however glorious the aspirations and the individual insights and integrity.

In the Whitman of the 1850s we hear someone putting into words and lines the awe and reckless freedom Boone must have felt alone in the strange expanse of Kentucky in 1770. The awe and wonder have spread into the collective memory of the culture and been distilled as art decades later by Walt Whitman.

Allons! the road is before us!
It is safe — I have tried it — my own feet have tried it well — be not
*   detained!*

As poet and prophet, Whitman appeals to the reader in the role of guide or scout. He will lead us on the open road through the wilderness to the West, the land of wonder. He is the poet of that assurance, the American ideal, a Daniel Boone, blazing a path to the sunset, over gaps and through swamps and meadows and canebrakes, to the possibilities of our future. He is the definitive American poet of the nineteenth century because he expresses that essence of America's myth of itself, the epitome of its aspirations, embodied almost a century before in the life and legend of Daniel Boone.

Acknowledgments

FIRST I MUST express my indebtedness to my friends in Kentucky. Neal O. Hammon served as guide at many sites, including Boonesborough, Bryan's Station, Boone's Station, and Big Bone Lick. From the beginning he shared both his erudition and his considerable collection of documents about Boone and the history of Kentucky. Richard Taylor lent me books from his personal library, gave me a tour of historic Frankfort, and provided me with hours of informative conversation. It was Richard who started me thinking of writing about Boone on a tour of the Kentucky River almost thirty years ago. Nancy O'Malley also gave me the benefit of her expertise in conversations at such sites as Boone's Station, Marble Creek, Brushy Creek, and Maysville. Julian Campbell helped fill in some of the gaps in my knowledge of the historical ecology of the Bluegrass region. George Brosi offered advice and encouragement at a crucial time. Jonathan Greene and Dobree Adams always welcomed me to Frankfort and Riverbend Farm and provided introductions to Kentucky history and historians.

My friend Loyal Jones of Berea introduced me to several themes in Kentucky history and pointed me in the direction I would need to go. Jay Buckner and Tim Jordan of Berea College Public Relations Office provided me with a copy of the Boone portrait in the Boone Tavern. Bill Cooke of the Kentucky Horse Park informed me of the prevalence of the quarter horse in early Kentucky history, and Dr. Phil

Sponenburg explained the importance of Spanish and Indian horses in the period of settlement.

Kathryn Weiss shared her passion and scholarship about the Bryan family history with me and prevented me from making a number of mistakes about Rebecca Boone's ancestors. Ken Kamper of the Boone Society guided me through Nathan's house on Femme Osage Creek and gave me a wealth of information about Boone's life in Missouri.

I have been especially fortunate in the help I have received from archivists and librarians. Robert Anthony and his staff at the North Carolina Collection of the Wilson Library at the University of North Carolina at Chapel Hill from the beginning of this project found relevant documents, opened the Henderson Papers for my inspection, and provided copies whenever I needed them. William Marshall of the University of Kentucky library archives came to my rescue when I was looking for a particular letter, as did Vaughn Stanley and Lisa McCown of the Leyburn Library at Washington and Lee University. James J. Holmberg and his staff at the Filson Historical Society welcomed me to their collection and found the files I needed to consult. Mary Winters, Lynn Hollingsworth, Bill Morris, and Jim Kastner of the Kentucky Historical Society in Frankfort again and again offered me their help in locating documents in the Boone Family biographical files. The staff of the Kentucky State Archives in Frankfort found files of the *Kentucky Gazette* for me to explore. Mrs. Jane Brown of the Montgomery County Museum in Christiansburg, Virginia, provided a copy of the original arrest warrant for Daniel Boone issued there. The staff of the Wilderness Road Museum in Newbern, Virginia, gave me a tour of their historic buildings and provided much information about that section of the Great Wagon Road.

At Cornell University Peter Hirtle of Olin Library ordered a copy of the Spraker Boone Family Genealogy for my use. Robin Messing and the staff of the microfilm library again and again came to my rescue as I inched my way through films of the Draper Manuscripts. The staff of the Kroch Rare Books Room found volume after volume I needed to consult. The Olin Interlibrary Loan staff borrowed books and microfilms many times for my use. I would like to especially thank Sarah Thomas, former Cornell University librarian, for helping to make so many materials available to me, and Nicole Margirier for locating an elusive illustration.

I also owe a debt of gratitude to the staff of the Missouri Historical Society in St. Louis and to my daughter Laurel and her husband, Kevin Riebs, for showing me around the Boone sites in St. Charles County, Missouri. Daniel Meyer, Julia Gardner, and the staff of Special Collections of the Regenstein Library at the University of Chicago were unstintingly gracious and helpful in guiding me through the Durrett Collection there. I have also greatly benefited from the services of the Furman University library, the Duke University library, and the East Carolina University library. I would also like to thank Larry Odzack and the staff of the North Carolina State Archives in Raleigh for helping me locate court records from colonial Rowan County.

Many individuals have been of special help in providing information and encouragement throughout this project: Joseph Flora, my first professor of English at UNC–Chapel Hill; Cece Conway of Appalachian State University; John and Suzanne Canfield of Winnetka, Illinois; Park Lochlair; Pat and Resa Bizarro; Josh Beckworth at Appalachian State University; former chancellor Frank Borkowski of Appalachian State University; Sandra Ballard of Appalachian State University; and Tense Banks of Linville Falls. Randell Jones, author of *In the Footsteps of Daniel Boone*, provided much crucial information and enthusiasm for this biography. Ted Franklin Belue gave me the benefit of his considerable scholarship concerning Kentucky and Native American cultures.

At Cornell University my colleagues Jonathan Culler, Molly Hite, Marianne Marsh, and Laura Brown provided travel funds that enabled me to visit a number of archives and historical sites. Robin Doxtater helped sort out those accounts as well as my eccentric recordkeeping.

The staff at the Boone Birthplace in Oley, Pennsylvania, shared their expertise on a cold rainy day in October. I would also like to thank those who have generously read portions or all of the manuscript and helped me correct many mistakes: Neal O. Hammon, Nancy O'Malley, Ted Franklin Belue, and Stephen Aron. Any mistakes remaining are, of course, my own responsibility. Ted Arnold of the Cornell Store again and again located and acquired the books I needed, both old and new.

I owe a great debt to my agent, Liz Darhansoff, for encouraging and making this project possible, to my outstanding editor Shannon Ravenel for guiding me through the long process of writing and editing, and Elisabeth Scharlatt and her staff at Algonquin Books of Chapel Hill for ensuring that this study of Boone would reach the reading public. I would like to thank Anne Winslow for her memorable work as a designer, and Brunson Hoole, managing editor of Algonquin Books of Chapel Hill, for an exemplary job of coordinating all the editorial efforts involved in the project. I am fortunate indeed to have been led through the editorial maze by Jude Grant.

My son, Benjamin, generously provided digital copies of several illustrations and photographed the Squire and Sarah Boone tombstone in Mocksville, North Carolina. I owe much gratitude to my wife, Nancy, for her sharp editorial eye, advice, and patience throughout a long and challenging project.

Notes

Throughout the notes, DM refers to the Draper Manuscripts, State Historical Society of Wisconsin, Madison.

Introduction

xi   *"He never delighted in shedding human blood"* John Mason Peck, *Life of Daniel Boone*, 189.

xi   *"All history resolves itself very easily"* Ralph Waldo Emerson, "Self-Reliance," in *Emerson's Prose and Poetry*, 126.

xii   *"For me, the most striking"* Nelson L. Dawson, "Introduction," 6.

xiii   *Only recently have we* Maurice Manning, *A Companion for Owls*, 127–28.

xiii   *"Such productions ought to be left"* Lyman Copeland Draper interview with Joseph Scholl, 1868, DM24S218.

xiii   *"My eyesight is too far gone"* Peck, 4.

xiv   *Flint is supposed to have answered* John Mack Faragher, *Daniel Boone*, 323.

xiv   *"more elbow room"* Timothy Flint, *Biographical Memoir of Daniel Boone*, 178.

xiv   *"No one will say, when I am gone"* Peck, 174.

xv   *"I am a small bit of a fellow"* Draper to William Martin c. 1842, quoted in William B. Hesseltine, *Pioneer Mission*, 41.

xix   *"I am no Statesman"* John Bakeless, *Daniel Boone*, 349.

xx   *"They may say what they please"* Lyman Copeland Draper, *The Life of Daniel Boone*, 524.

One: The Mother World of the Forest

3   *"I am constrained to make mention"* John James Van Noppen and Ina Woestemeyer Van Noppen, *Daniel Boone Backwoodsman*, 36.

5   *"the roughest and rudest of all"* Quoted in Wynford Vaughn-Thomas, *A History of Wales*, 22.

5   *Morgan, had called himself Pelagius* Margaret Drabble, ed., *The Oxford Companion to English Literature*, 750.

6   *certificate "of his orderly and good conversation"* Hazel Atterbury Spraker, *The Boone Family*, 590.

6   *"forwardship in giving his consent"* Spraker, 591.

6   *Squire Boone has been described as a rather small man* Reuben Gold Thwaites, *Daniel Boone*, 5.

7   *"At a solemn assembly of the said people"* Spraker, 32; Gwyneth Minutes, DM1C19.

7   *"Our condition at present"* Van Noppen and Van Noppen, 63.

7   *campaign against the "Flatfeet"* Van Noppen and Van Noppen, 63.

8   *George IV and his wife, Deborah, deeded land* Spraker, 589.

8   *"Boones and Lincolns several times"* Andrew Shaaber, Librarian, Historical Society of Berks County, PA, to Archibald Henderson, September 1, 1913, Henderson Papers.

9   *One early biographer described the infant* H. Addington Bruce, *Daniel Boone and the Wilderness Road*, 6.

9   *"keeping him and petting him"* Lyman Copeland Draper, *The Life of Daniel Boone*, 109.

10   *"He learned lessons of the snow"* W. H. Bogart, *Daniel Boone and the Hunters of Kentucky*, 24.

10   *milking and butter making were considered* Daniel Drake, *Pioneer Life in Kentucky*, 92.

10   *Indians still lived in the neighborhood* Andrew Shaaber to Archibald Henderson, September 1, 1913, Henderson Papers.

11   *"If thee has not brought up"* Draper, 113.

11   *"but a common man"* "A Traveler," *Cincinnati National Republican*, August 19, 1823, DM16C67.

12   *Neversink mountain range northwest* Thwaites, 10.

12   *When asked if he was lost* Lawrence Elliott, *The Long Hunter*, 15.

13   *there was a part of Boone that never grew up* Richard Taylor in conversation with the author, August 4, 2005.

13   *"I want thee to tell thy mother the whole truth"* Draper, 110.

13   *"Canst thou not beg?"* John Mack Faragher, *Daniel Boone*, 13.

15   *"it was a pretty dear shot"* Draper, 114.

15   *Squire never solved the mystery* Draper, 115.

15   *One of the pranks credited to Boone* Randell Jones, *In the Footsteps of Daniel Boone*, 4.

16   *"Hunt the Indian"* William Boone Douglass, "The Ancestry and Boyhood of Daniel Boone," 18.

16   *Just as the creature was about to leap* Abner Bryan to Lyman Copeland

Draper, February 12–14, 1890, DM4C60; William S. Bryan and Robert Rose, *Pioneer Families of Missouri*, 4.

16   *Sarah Boone rebuked her son for violence* Timothy Flint, *Biographical Memoir of Daniel Boone*, 32–34.

17   *Boone was actually taught to read and write* Draper, 112.

17   *"He could at first do little more"* Draper, 112.

17   *"Let the girls do the spelling"* Douglass, 14.

17   *"They took the powder horn and left the ink horn"* Bogart, 14.

17   *"in the mighty solitudes"* Bogart, 22.

18   *"Your company is desired greatly"* Draper, 339.

18   *As John Mack Faragher has pointed out* Faragher, 20.

19   *"King of the Schuylkill Delawares"* Faragher, 19.

People of the Forest

22   *What Europeans saw as virgin land* Francis Jennings, *The Invasion of America*, 15.

22   *Nor did they raise livestock* William Cronon, *Changes in the Land*, 37.

22   *To them, all living things had spirits* Virginia DeJohn Anderson, *Creatures of Empire*, 30.

22   *Owning land in the white way* Cronon, 65.

23   *Indians were rich by "desiring little"* Cronon, 80.

23   *In 1709 an English colonist* James H. Merrell, *The Catawbas*, 35.

23   *concluded the invaders were stupid* James Axtell, *The Invasion Within*, 12.

Two: The Hills beyond the Yadkin

25   *"fiddle-footed"* Frederic G. Cassidy and Joan Houston Hall, *Dictionary of American English*, 2:400.

25   *"itching foot"* John Bakeless, *Daniel Boone*, 5.

25   *More and more young women* John Mack Faragher, *Daniel Boone*, 24.

26   *"led to more souls being made"* Stephen Aron, *How the West Was Lost*, 180.

26   *"Becca Bell 'is with child to one Brown'"* Aron, 179.

26   *"94 percent of the brides"* Charles Woodmason, *The Carolina Backcountry on the Eve of the Revolution*, 7, 100.

26   *"to speak with Squire Boone about his son's"* Henderson Papers.

26   *"giving Room to a reflecting Spirit"* Minutes of the Exeter Monthly Meeting of Friends, Book A, DM1C55.

26   *"his coming to a Godly Sorrow"* DM1C56.

27   *he had never known anything good* Peter Houston, *A Sketch of the Life and Character of Daniel Boone*, 30; DM20C84[46–47]. There is some doubt about the authenticity of the Peter Houston account. See Neal

O. Hammon and Wilson Zaring, "What Is Wrong with the Peter Houston Story?"

28   *The call of the West was in the blood* Arthur K. Moore, *The Frontier Mind*, 4.

29   *Farmers at river crossings made extra money* Parke Rouse Jr., *The Great Wagon Road*, 69, 99, 101.

29   *According to a report made to* John Preston Arthur, *A History of Watauga County*, 3.

29   *"William L. Boone told me they tarried"* Neal O. Hammon, ed., *My Father, Daniel Boone*, 12.

30   *"The Soil is exceedingly rich"* William Byrd, *William Byrd's Histories of the Dividing Line Betwixt Virginia and North Carolina*, 300.

30   *Some historians think that the name Yadkin* Mary C. Dalton to Lyman Copeland Draper, June 22, 1885, DM8C83[1].

31   *Sakona* James H. Merrell, *The Catawabas*, 22.

31   *The buffalo were mostly gone* Byrd, 286, 288.

31   *"a general jamboree or frolic"* John James Van Noppen and Ina Woestemeyer Van Noppen, *Daniel Boon Backwoodsman*, 77.

31   *"Boone was very profligate"* H. H. McDowell to Draper, August 10, 1887, DM20C39[3].

32   *Records show that Squire served* Entry for October 4, 1750. Secretary of State, Granville Proprietary Land Office, Entries, Warrants, and Surveys, 1748–1763 (Microfilm S. 108.270). North Carolina State Archives, Raleigh. Courtesy of Kathryn Weiss.

34   *"The Land was very good and free"* John Lawson, *Lawson's History of North Carolina*, 43.

36   *"Woodmason was only one of many"* David Hackett Fischer, *Albion's Seed*, 680; Woodmason, 30, 61.

36   *Squire served on local juries* Rowan County, North Carolina, *Minutes Court of Pleas and Quarter Sessions* for 1755 to 1767, Vol. 1.

36   *"He never took any delight in farming"* Daniel Bryan to Draper, February 27, 1843, DM22C5.

37   *Beaver were usually speared with a barbed gig* Ted Franklin Belue, letter to the author, August 9, 2006.

39   *"The boldest supposedly outdid William Tell"* Aron, 24.

40   *"Well, if it has come to this"* Lyman Copeland Draper, *The Life of Daniel Boone*, 128.

40   *"I often went hunting with them"* John Filson, *The Discovery, Settlement and Present State of Kentucke*, 65.

42   *If hunters such as James Patton had tried* Ted Franklin Belue, *The Hunters of Kentucky*, 22.

42   *"From 1754 to 1759, Washington spent"* Joseph J. Ellis, *His Excellency*, 12.

43   *"smil'd at my Ignorance, and reply'd"* Belue, 60.

43 *According to Daniel Boone's son Nathan* Hammon, ed., 10.

44 *Washington would encourage the establishment* Bernard Faÿ, *Revolution and Freemasonry, 1680–1800*, 245.

45 *"No savage shall inherit the land"* Francis Jennings, *Empire of Fortune*, 154–55.

45 *"Entire companies were wiped out"* Ellis, 22.

45 *blamed Braddock for not using spies* Hammon, ed., 13.

Three: The Yadkin Was the Wild West

46 *The Indian fell on the rocks below* Ralph Clayton, *St. Louis Christian Democrat*, May 10, 1877, DM7C43[2–3].

46 *the only Indian he was sure he ever killed* Neal O. Hammon, ed., *My Father, Daniel Boone*, 78.

48 *"Morgan Bryan came to Pa about 1700"* J. D. Bryan to Archibald Henderson, October 15, 1897, Henderson Papers.

49 *"the same heroic . . . nature"* Annette Kolodny, *The Land before Her*, 82.

49 *"It is said by some that she was a fair shot"* Kolodny, 83.

49 *"one of the handsomest persons"* G. Hedrick to Lyman Copeland Draper, June 26, 1866, DM28C67.

49 *larger than the average woman* Daniel Bryan to Draper, October 24, 1843, DM22C9[1]. Though many historians have referred to Daniel Bryan as Daniel *Boone* Bryan, possibly to distinguish him from the author of *The Mountain Muse*, he seems not to have used the middle name himself. See Weiss, "An Introduction to Daniel Bryan," 9.

49 *her pleasant manner and speech* Daniel Bryan to Draper, October 24, 1853, DM22C9[1].

49 *"One of the neatest and best of house keepers"* L. W. Boggs to Draper, January 18, 1857, DM23C27[2].

49 *"my little girl"* Rebecca Boone Lamond to Draper, August 23, 1845, DM22C35[1].

50 *"And if there was any 'shining of the eyes'"* Hammon, ed., 19; DM6S40–41.

50 *The sexual resonance of the story* Discussed in John Mack Faragher, *Daniel Boone*, 44.

50 *an example of the way Rebecca was marginalized* Kolodny, 88.

50 *"to try her temper"* Hammon, ed., 19.

51 *Rebecca saw what Daniel was about* Michael Lofaro, *Daniel Boone*, 16.

51 *"You, like my hunting shirt"* R. G. Prunty to Draper, January 26, 1883, DM16C57[3].

51 *"Flint effectively annihilated any"* Kolodny, 89.

55 *"deerskin in the red before the frosts"* Ted Franklin Belue, *The Hunters of Kentucky*, 71.

56   "*There is a period in the history*" Henry David Thoreau, *Walden*, 212.

56   "*hoppusing*" John Bakeless, *Daniel Boone*, 364.

57   "*Later Boone met with him and gave him*" Hammon, ed., 37.

58   "*I believe I could whip you*" Draper interview with Isaiah Boone, 1846, DM19C113.

58   "*Fort Dobbs was an oblong*" Reuben Gold Thwaites, *Daniel Boone*, 37.

59   "*The people about here are wild*" *Records of the Moravian Church*, 1:40–41.

59   *A group of Cherokees* Archibald Henderson, *The Conquest of the Old Southwest*, 74; Lyman Copeland Draper, *The Life of Daniel Boone*, 145–46.

60   *Boone later told his son Nathan* Hammon, ed., 14.

Domestic Arts

63   *William Clinkenbeard . . . told John Dabney Shane* John Dabney Shane interview with William Clinkenbeard, 1840s DM11CC55.

63   "*Noggins hollowed out of knots*" George Morgan Chinn, *Kentucky Settlement and Statehood, 1750–1800*, 337.

Four: In Search of the Real West

65   "*A Deed of Gift from Squire Boone*" Rowan County, North Carolina, *Minutes, Court of Pleas and Quarter Sessions*, 2:277.

66   *he had been turned into a ghost* Pat Alderman, *The Overmountain Men*, 11.

66   "*I have often heard Father speak*" Neal O. Hammon, ed., *My Father, Daniel Boone*, 15.

67   *A beaver skin was a unit* John Sanders to Archibald Henderson ca. 1913, Henderson Papers.

67   "*the isolate woodland son*" Annette Kolodny, *The Land before Her*, 5.

67   *built earlier for herders* John Preston Arthur, *A History of Watauga County*, 19; John Preston Arthur, *Western North Carolina*, 82.

68   "*he never crossed a route*" W. W. Lenon to Lyman Copeland Draper, October 20, 1882, DM9C216[2].

68   *They named the place Wolf Hills* Lewis Preston Summers, *Annals of Southwestern Virginia History, 1769–1800*, 76; Archibald Henderson, *The Conquest of the Old Southwest*, 134.

69   *referred to as a "Boone"* John Mack Faragher, *Daniel Boone*, 54.

69   *to be called an excellent hunter* Stephen Aron, *How the West Was Lost*, 27.

69   *the gentry resented their* Aron, 15.

69   "*strait to them all with unerring accuracy*" John C. Barkley to Draper, January 22, 1887. DM9C230[2].

69   *"I wouldn't give a tinker's damn"* and the other quotes in this paragraph
      James Van Noppen and Ina Woestemeyer Van Noppen, *Daniel Boone
      Backwoodsman*, 191–92.

70   *"the habit of contemplation"* John Mason Peck, *Life of Daniel Boone*, 18.

70   *"If a man would be alone"* Ralph Waldo Emerson, "Nature," in
      Emerson's Prose and Poetry, 28.

71   *Boone learned to watch the direction* Hammon, ed., 17.

71   *"In middle life, he read"* Hammon, ed., 139.

71   *"His worship was in secret"* Hammon, ed., 139.

71   *"Ah, Wide Mouth"* Draper interview with George Smith 1844,
      DM32S481. See also DM31C31 and DM2B157–158.

73   *"Tawbers no make so"* Wellborn Coffey to Draper, September 28, 1884,
      DM19C240.

73   *"Daniel Boone / come on boys"* Joe Nickell and John F. Fischer, "Daniel
      Boone Fakelore," 464–65.

74   *"When Boone returned home"* Elizabeth A. Perkins, *Border Life*, 26.

74   *Ned "looked so much like Daniel"* Silas W. Parris, writing for Thomas
      Norman to Draper, October 15 and November 3, 1884, DM2C53.

74   *In almost all versions* Faragher, 59–60.

75   *witnesses such as James Norman have so many facts wrong* Ken Kamper
      letter to the author, March 2005.

75   *"he brought his family back to the Yadkin"* H. Addington Bruce, *Daniel
      Boone and the Wilderness Road*, 43.

75   *The genealogist Spraker,* Hazel Atterbury Spraker, *The Boone Family*, 119.

76   *"She had supposed him dead"* Stephen Hempstead to Draper, February
      15, 1863, DM16C76[2].

77   *frontier culture in the eighteenth century was* Faragher, 60–61.

77   *"You had better have staid at home"* Stephen Cooper interview with
      Draper, 1889, DM11C101.

79   *essentially a poet* Timothy Flint, *Biographical Memoir of Daniel Boone*, 63.

79   *"slow pay"* and as *"not thrifty"* J. Rumple to Draper, August 30, 1883,
      DM8C190[2].

80   *"geography and locography of these woods"* Henderson, 109.

80   *"I am richer than the man"* Bruce, 47.

80   *Nathan Boone would later say* Hammon, ed., 17.

81   to *"God and man by . . . the circumference"* and *"the Divine Spirit
      indwelling"* Arthur Edward Waite, *The New Encyclopedia of Freema-
      sonry*, 2:111–12.

81   *a symbol of the creation of the world* Robert Macoy, *A Dictionary of
      Freemasonry*, 311.

82   *One document from the trip records* "Daniel Boone's Account Book,"
      ca. 1765, DM4C75[2].

82   *"Slaughter was fond of gambling"* Hammon, ed., 15–16.

82   *muddy trails and swamps, with little game* Ruben Gold Thwaites, *Daniel Boone*, 65.

84   *"The place is getting entirely too"* J. Rumple to Draper ca. 1885, DM8C182[5].

84   *They had many narrow escapes* Thwaites, 67.

85   *"leading to the Mesopotamia of Kentucky"* Henderson, *The Conquest of the Old Southwest*, 140.

85   *His plan was to reach* Bruce, 48.

86   *He entertained the folks* Moses Boone to Draper, fall 1846, DM19C3.

Five: Visions of Eden

88   *Considering the Six Nations the slaves of* Gregory Evans Dowd, *A Spirited Resistance*, 43.

89   *"Kentucky was, first and perhaps foremost"* Daniel Blake Smith, "This Idea in Heaven," 77.

90   *"the dark and bloody ground"* John Filson, *The Discovery, Settlement, and Present State of Kentucke*, 8.

90   *"the meadow-land"* George R. Stewart, *American Place Names*, 237.

90   *"Bloody River"* George Morgan Chinn, *Kentucky Settlement and Statehood, 1750–1800*, 9.

90   *It has even been suggested* Arthur K. Moore, *The Frontier Mind*, 13.

90   *"the land of tomorrow"* Chinn, 7.

90   *"Kain-tuck-ee is a Shawanese word"* John Mason Peck, *Life of Daniel Boone*, 26n.

90   *an invention of the whites* Neal O. Hammon, "Separating Facts from Myth," 6.

90   *it was favored by the Cherokees* Thomas P. Field, "The Indian Place Names of Kentucky," 18.

91   *Whatever they called it* Moore, 4.

91   *we find this record of the* Salisbury District Superior Court, *Trial, App., & Reference Dock*, 1770, North Carolina State Archives, Raleigh, NC. Courtesy of Kathryn Weiss.

92   *"He wasn't just bird counting"* Thomas D. Clark, *Frankfort State Journal*.

92   *"He was considered the Patrick Henry of North Carolina"* Lyman Copeland Draper, *The Life of Daniel Boone*, 331.

92   *"As confidential agent of the land company"* Archibald Henderson, *The Conquest of the Old Southwest*, 149.

93   *his father was not employed* Neal O. Hammon, ed., *My Father, Daniel Boone*, 17.

93   *"[Boone] had the honor"* Jethro Rumple to Lyman Copeland Draper, August 3, 1883, DM8C190[1].

93   *Archibald Henderson wrote that Boone* Archibald Henderson, *The Significance of the Transylvania Company*, 11.

94   A descendant of Nathaniel Hart later said JDS interview with
        Nathaniel Hart Jr., DM17CC204.
95   "My father even said he never" Hammon, ed., 29.
95   Ouasiota, according to some Chinn, 18.
95   sciota means "deer" Field, "The Indian Place Names of Kentucky," 18.
95   "Path of the Armed Ones" David M. Burns, Gateway, 16.
95   "some parts of [the trails] had become worn down" William E. Myer,
        Indian Trails of the Southeast, 743–44.
96   "Stand at Cumberland Gap" Frederick Jackson Turner, The Frontier in
        American History, 35.
97   "this important difference" Draper, 211.
97   "What Daniel Boone saw from Pilot Knob" Moore, 3.
98   "On the seventh day of June following" Filson, 51.
98   Some say bluegrass came from England Gerald R. Alvey, Kentucky Blue-
        grass Country, 15.
99   According to the historian George W. Ranck George W. Ranck, Boones-
        borough, 18n3.
99   Christopher Gist had noted Chinn, 15.
99   the Iroquois had cleared the region Stephen Aron, How the West Was
        Lost, 7.
99   "The realized niche" Nancy O'Malley, Stockading Up, 310.
99   Recently ecologists studying the records Julian J. N. Campbell, The Land
        of Cane and Clover, 9.
99   The botanist Short in 1828 C. W. Short, "Prodomos Florula Lexingto-
        niensis, Secundum Florens Di Oestatum Digeste," 1:252.
99   Some said there were no leaves American Museum 11 (1792): 12, quoted in
        Moore, 12.
100   George Croghan, a trader who A. Gwyn Henderson, "The Lower
        Shawnee Town on Ohio," 30.
100   "[T]he skin was thoroughly rubbed across" Draper, 212.
100   "He was on a mission" William Gilmore Simms, "Daniel Boone — The
        First Hunter in Kentucky," 157.
101   "Here the mother that he had worshiped" Charles Wilkins Webber, The
        Hunter Naturalist, 168.
101   "[Boone] only felt yearnings" Webber, 162.
102   Elk hides were cut up Thwaites, 75.
102   "In the decline of the day" Filson, 52.
103   quickly hide the accumulated pelts Hammon, ed., 24.
103   "for this is Indian's hunting ground" Draper, 216.
103   "[t]he Shawness . . . were a scattered people" Stephen Aron, "Pigs and
        Hunters," 186n22.
104   Different groups of Indians lived Colin G. Calloway, The American
        Revolution in Indian Country, 16, 161.

104   *At Chillicothe at least three languages*   Aron, "Pigs and Hunters," 186.

104   *Indians had fought among themselves*   Aron, "Pigs and Hunters," 187.

104   *The Reverend David McClure recorded*   Aron, "Pigs and Hunters," 188.

105   *"Steal horse, ha?"*   Hammon, ed., 25.

105   *Boone later said he was pretty sure*   Filson, 52.

106   *"Our meeting so fortunately"*   Filson, 53.

106   *According to some reports*   Thwaites, 79.

106   *Archibald Henderson would state positively*   Henderson, *The Conquest of the Old Southwest*, 153.

107   *Boone never saw John Findley again*   Draper, 224n24.

107   *"Saith that in the year 1770"*   Deposition to Commission, September 15, 1796 in Clark County Kentucky, before George Smith, DM4C93.

108   *"My father always thought that Stewart"*   Hammon, ed., 29.

108   *"We were then in a dangerous, helpless"*   Filson, 53.

110   *"He now proceeded to make"*   Henderson, *The Conquest of the Old Southwest*, 155–56.

111   *"Boone deliberately chose the peace"*   William Carlos Williams, *In the American Grain*, 131.

111   *"The idea of a beloved wife"*   Filson, 54.

112   *"naturally romantic and fond of the chase"*   "A Traveler," Cincinnati National Republican, August 19, 1823, DM16C67.

112   *"seven elephants"*   Draper, 248n17.

112   *"giant sloths and giant beaver bones"*   Thomas Ashe, *Travels in America*, 40–49.

112   *cure "the itch by once bathing"*   Filson, 33.

113   *Other formations were called*   J. C. Currens, "Caves," 174–76.

114   *"While I was looking at him"*   Hammon, ed., 32.

114   *"It was understood*   Hammon, ed., 32.

115   *"and it may have been the means"*   Draper, 245.

115   *"D.B. — 1770" carved on it*   Draper, 245.

115   *Boone was surprised by Indians*   Draper, 245.

115   *took a leap*   DM3B37 Draper interview with "Mr. Wolf," n.d., DM31C1[41].

115   *"To many it would have been the means"*   W. H. Bogart, *Daniel Boone and the Hunters of Kentucky*, 77.

116   *"For three months he was alone"*   Williams, 136.

116   *"seen deep truths about himself"*   Bruce Selcraig, "The Real Robinson Crusoe," 89.

116   *They killed the mother wolf*   Draper, 247.

117   *"But if a man would be alone"*   Ralph Waldo Emerson, "Nature," in *Emerson's Prose and Poetry*, 28.

118   *"Prayer is the contemplation of"*   Ralph Waldo Emerson, "Self-Reliance," in *Emerson's Prose and Poetry*, 132.

119   *George Washington, who owned tracts*   O'Malley, 13.

119 *"[Washington] looked west to the land"* Joseph J. Ellis, *His Excellency*, 39.

119 *When Washington renovated* Ellis, 53.

120 *"Upon a large, spreading beech tree"* Draper, 263.

120 *It was Daniel Boone, alone in the forest* Draper, 264.

121 *"'Bledsoe told me,' says General Hall"* Draper, 264; Henderson, *The Conquest of the Old Southwest*, 128–29.

122 *It is likely Squire and Daniel* Draper, 265–66; DM3B65.

123 *A party was formed in the settlements* Draper, 267–68.

Regulators

124 Information in "Regulators" is summarized from William S. Powell, *North Carolina through Four Centuries*, 146–59.

Six: Return to the Bluegrass Island

126 *"Bluegrass island"* Ted Franklin Belue, *The Hunters of Kentucky*, 82.

126 *"The reports of his extended explorations"* Archibald Henderson, *The Conquest of the Old Southwest*, 158–59.

127 *Boone's description of the land* Shaw Livermore, *Early American Land Companies*, 91.

128 *"She is by nature a quiet soul"* Rev. George Soelle's diary, Moravian Archives, Henderson Papers, translated by Adelaide Fries.

129 *"You need not refuse me for you"* John B. Roark to Draper, March 30, 1885, DM16C81[1].

129 *"We therefore command you that you attach"* Rowan County Records, in Boone Family Biographical File, Kentucky Historical Society.

130 *Nathan told Draper* Neal O. Hammon, ed., *My Father, Daniel Boone*, 45.

130 *"[Watauga] sets a dangerous example"* Henderson, 199.

130 *the Watauga experiment set a precedent* Henderson, 200.

130 *"D.B. 1773"* Deposition of David Hill, September 1, 1800, DM4C128.

130 *in the Green River country* Samuel Duncan to Draper, February 21, 1852, DM4C131.

131 *"heaven is a Kentucky of a place"* The Christian Traveler (New York, 1828), 47–48, quoted in Arthur K. Moore, *The Frontier Mind*, 24.

131 *According to some accounts* George Morgan Chinn, *Kentucky Settlement and Statehood, 1750–1800*, 45.

131 *Capt. Thomas Bullitt surveyed tracts* Nancy O'Malley, *Stockading Up*, 14.

132 *"under the guize of hunting game"* Stephen Aron, *How the West Was Lost*, 61.

133 *"The wives of our western pioneers"* John Mason Peck, *Life of Daniel Boone*, 37–38.

133 *"We command you that you take"* The original arrest warrant in the

Christiansburg, Virginia, courthouse has been lost, but Mrs. Jane Brown of the Montgomery County Museum owns a photocopy.

134 *"I visited William Briant"* Rev. George Soelle's diary, Moravian Archives, Henderson Papers.

134 *"Stoner was an awkward Dutchman"* Hammon, ed., 42.

135 *"Americans . . . do and will remove"* Louis Phelps Kellogg and Reuben Gold Thwaites, *Documentary History of Dunmore's War, 1774,* 371.

135 *Dunmore denied that he had sent* Otis K. Rice, *Frontier Kentucky,* 52.

135 *who had his own plans for* Henderson, 207; see also James Hall, *The Romance of Western History,* 155–56.

136 *Nathan Boone said that bells* Hammon, ed., 24.

136 *told them they would hear wolves* Lyman Copeland Draper, *The Life of Daniel Boone,* 287.

137 *Big Jim had been befriended by* Hammon, ed., 39.

137 *The slave Charles was found with his head* Rice, 60.

138 *"a remarkable instance of their good faith"* Draper, 290.

139 *The Christian brothers escaped* Draper, 291–92.

139 *"deer-skin coloured black"* Draper, 292.

139 *"There suddenly arose a severe"* Draper, 304.

139 *Whenever the death of James was mentioned* Hammon, ed., 42.

140 *"Whosoever saw an Indian in Kentucky"* Draper, 299, quoted from John Jeremiah Jacob, *Biographical Sketch of the Life of the Late Capt. Michael Cresap,* 53–54.

140 *One group of Shawnees claimed* Draper, 302.

141 *It would seem that Dunmore wanted a war* Henderson, 209.

141 *"employ two faithful woodsmen"* Draper, 305.

141 *"Well, Mike, you'll have mine"* George W. Stoner, son of Michael, interview with Draper, November 28, 1868, DM24C55.

141 *"[Lewis] directed me to cross"* Boone deposition, October 6, 1817. St. Charles County, MO; DM6C105.

142 *Boone liked to imitate* Draper, 307–8.

142 *"On the last of May or first [of] June 1774"* Neal O. Hammon, "John Filson's Error," 462–63.

144 *"We made a survey of this"* DM4J58–84; Kellogg and Thwaites, 118.

144 *"on his way to the falls"* Neal O. Hammon, "Separating Facts from Myths," 3.

145 *"Alarmed by finding some people killed"* Draper, 309.

147 *"Their simultaneous arrival lends credence"* Rice, 56.

147 *Others have argued* O'Malley, 15.

147 *"Captain Bledsoe says Boone has"* Kellogg and Thwaites, 168; DM33S254–256.

148 *"the Indians is not Angry"* Kellogg and Thwaites, 246–47.

148   *Daniel Greathouse had invited* Michael Lofaro, *Daniel Boone*, 45.

148   *"the men would all go out and play at ball"* John Dabney Shane interview with Mrs. Samuel Scott, 1840s, DM11CC225.

148   *"Some were in so great haste"* Shane interview with Mrs. Samuel Scott, 1840s, DM11CC226.

149   *"Mr. Boon is very diligent at Castle-Woods"* Col. Arthur Campbell to Col. Wlliam Preston, September 29, 1774; Kellogg and Thwaites, 218.

149   *"bearskins"* John Mack Faragher, *Daniel Boone*, 103.

150   *"Mr. Boone has sent me the War Club"* Kellogg and Thwaites, 220; DM3QQ109.

150   *It is possible the Shawnees* Kellogg and Thwaites, 220 – 21.

150   *"Murder! Murder!" he shouted* Kellogg and Thwaites, 244.

150   *Though Point Pleasant is usually* Reuben Gold Thwaites, *Daniel Boone*, 111.

150   *"Mr. Boon is an excellent woodsman"* Kellogg and Thwaites, 249.

152   *In a letter to Lord Dunmore* Richard Taylor, *Girty*, 62.

152   *"Colonel Cresap, the last spring"* Draper, 328n8.

152   *"Rachel Duncin, one house"* DM4C75[1].

Seven: Where There Was No Forbidden Fruit

153   *"Boone's report of the west"* Thomas D. Clark, *A History of Kentucky*, 60.

153   *"To enter upon a detail of the Beuty"* Archibald Henderson, *The Conquest of the Old Southwest*, 233.

154   *"Like as a white carpenter could"* Felix Walker's narrative, quoted in George W. Ranck, *Boonesborough*, 162, reprinted from *DeBow's Review*, February 1854.

154   *And even Gov. Josiah Martin of North Carolina* James Hall, *The Romance of Western History*, 155 – 56.

155   *"Lord Mansfield gave Judge Henderson"* and *"A true copy"* Henderson, *The Conquest of the Old Southwest*, 201; DM2CC34[9].

155   *It was all a charade* John Bakeless, *Daniel Boone*, 83. The source of this legal ruse may have been a document called the Camden-Yorke opinion of 1757, which James Hogg, a partner in the Transylvania Company, discovered in the fall of 1775 and used retroactively as authorization for the Transylvania purchase. Though many promoters in North America invoked the Camden-Yorke opinion for their own purposes, the document refers explicitly to the East India Company. See W. S. Lester, *The Transylvania Colony*, 27.

155   *In April 1769 Pennsylvania* Otis K. Rice, *Frontier Kentucky*, 38.

155   *In February the McAfee brothers* George Morgan Chinn, *Kentucky Settlement and Statehood, 1750 – 1800*, 81.

156 *"Proposals for the Encouragement"* Ranck, 182.

156 *"contrary to Law and Justice"* Ranck, 150.

156 *"Archibald Neilson, deputy auditor"* Henderson, *The Conquest of the Old Southwest,* 219.

157 *It has been said that James Robertson* Archibald Henderson, *The Transylvania Company and the Founding of Henderson, Kentucky,* 7.

158 *"the Road to the Old Settlements"* Neal O. Hammon, conversation with the author, March 17, 2005.

159 *"This is the marked difference"* W. H. Bogart, *Daniel Boone and the Hunters of Kentucky,* 117.

159 *A location near the mouth of Otter Creek* Nancy O'Malley, *Searching for Boonesborough,* 15.

159 *"James Robertson, also a witness"* Neal O. Hammon, "No Stranger to Difficulty," 53.

160 *"Colonel Henderson opened the negotiations"* Robert Lee Kincaid, *The Wilderness Road,* 96.

161 *" for and in consideration of the sum"* Ranck, 151.

161 *It was reported that no liquor* Henderson, *The Conquest of the Old Southwest,* 225.

162 *On March 17, 1775, the deed of sale was inked* Lyman Copeland Draper, *The Life of Daniel Boone,* 333.

162 *"[W]e have given you a fine land"* Draper, 333.

162 *"there was a dark cloud over that Country"* John Haywood, *The Civil and Political History of the State of Tennessee,* 58–59.

162 *"the most fluent, graceful"* Draper's notes from Pleasant Henderson, DM30S74.

163 *trained as a weaver* Hazel Atterbury Spraker, *The Boone Family,* 115.

163 *"Hays taught my father to write"* Neal O. Hammon, ed., *My Father, Daniel Boone,* 45.

163 *"a notorious prostitute"* John Dabney Shane interview with Nathaniel Hart, 1843–44, DM17CC195.

163 *"Trot father, trot mother"* Josiah Collins to Shane, 1840, DM12CC97.

163 *"Mrs. Susan Hays — Boone's daughter"* Abner Bryan to Draper, February 12–14, 1890, DM4C51.

163 *"Susan when I saw her"* Josiah Collins to Shane, 1840s, DM12CC97.

164 *"our pilot and conductor"* Ranck, 163.

165 *"with great propriety, intrepidity"* Ranck, 167.

165 *"Handiness with the axe"* Arthur K. Moore, *The Frontier Mind,* 56.

165 *Although not as famous* Ellen Eslinger, ed., *Running Mad for Kentucky,* 11.

166 *From there he turned due north* Nancy O'Malley, *Stockading Up,* 19.

166 *"most of it hilly, stony"* Draper, 345.

166 *"Nothing can exceed the road"* Eslinger, ed., 28.

166 *"the pleasing and rapturous . . . plains"* and *"Perhaps no Adventurers"*
Ranck, 163.

167 *"Dear Colonel"* Draper, 339.

167 *"fryday ye 7th"* Eslinger, ed., 72.

167 *Boone later described the attack* John Filson, *The Discovery, Settlement and Present State of Kentucke*, 59.

168 *"He attended me as his child"* Ranck, 167.

168 *"The Chillicothes accused the Mingoes"* Ted Franklin Belue, *The Hunters of Kentucky*, 99.

168 *"Such a sight some of us never"* Ranck, 166.

169 *"We felt ourselves as passengers"* Ranck, 164.

Eight: Kentucky Was the Key

171 *"best tract of land in North-American"* John Filson, *The Discovery, Settlement, and Present State of Kentucke*, 7.

172 *Hanks, as recorded by William Calk* Ellen Eslinger, ed., *Running Mad for Kentucky*, 73, 263n1.

172 *News traveled fast* Neal O. Hammon, e-mail to the author, October 19, 2005.

172 *"It was beyond a doubt"* Lyman Copeland Draper, *The Life of Daniel Boone*, 342.

173 *"Thursday 20th this morning is Clear"* Eslinger, ed., 73.

173 *"It was owing to Boone's confidence"* Draper, 342.

174 *"Even in the superior courts"* Archibald Henderson, *The Conquest of the Old Southwest*, 104–5.

174 *"A spring at Boonsburrow constantly"* Filson, 31.

174 *Historians have pointed out* George W. Ranck, *Boonesborough*, 20.

175 *"After some perplexity, resolved"* Draper, 346.

175 *The fort Henderson designed* Ranck, 36.

175 *"To give you a small specimen"* Draper, 372.

178 *"Henderson took up his quarters"* Ranck, 26.

178 *"It was all anarchy and confusion"* J. F. D. Smyth, *A Tour of the United States of America*, 1:217, quoted in W. S. Lester, *The Transylvania Company*, 111.

179 *"Much tormented with Ticks"* Nicholas Cresswell, *The Journal of Nicholas Cresswell*, 79.

180 *"April 3, 1775, Mr. Bryce Martin enters"* Richard Henderson journal, quoted in Robert Lee Kincaid, *The Wilderness Road*, 106.

180 *"that magnificent tree, the sole cathedral"* Ranck, 31.

180 *A platform had been built* H. Addington Bruce, *Daniel Boone and the Wilderness Road*, 122.

180 *possibly the only time a prayer* Ruby Addison Henry, *The First West*, 51.

180   *"You are called and assembled"* Draper, 365–66.

181   *"for debtors and other persons"* Robert Cain, ed., *Colonial Records of North Carolina,* 9:1175–76.

182   *"to answer for an insult offered"* Draper, 367.

182   *"a bill for preserving the game"* Ranck, 204–6.

183   *"The session closed with"* Ranck, 30.

183   *Henderson and the others had already decided* Lester, 22–23.

183   *"Realizing that it was 'most advisable'"* Stephen Aron, *How the West Was Lost,* 67.

184   *Smarting from the snub, Henry* Aron, 63.

184   *"Christian told Floyd that"* Neal O. Hammon, "No Stranger to Difficulty," 55.

185   *"In our absence those at the camp"* Cresswell, 80.

185   *catfish that weighed more than a hundred* Filson, 25.

185   *"The statutes prescribed four steps"* Mary K. Bonsteel Tachau, "Land Claims, Early," 535.

186   *"an infamous Company of land Pyrates"* Henderson, 238.

186   *"Quit rents, they say, is a mark"* Ranck, 43.

186   *Many already in Kentucky* Otis K. Rice, *Frontier Kentucky,* 117.

186   *"Sunday, June 11th, 1775"* Cresswell, 84.

187   *"Rebecca Boone and her pioneer sisters"* Aron, 3.

187   *would prove inhospitable even to poor men* Arthur K. Moore, *The Frontier Mind,* 4–5.

188   *Men were drawn into the new* Annette Kolodny, *The Land before Her,* 8.

188   *"Our salt is exhausted"* Draper, 382.

189   *"After clearing, the best land for a time yielded"* Moore, 13.

190   *In 1784 Filson would write* Filson, 24.

190   *"My wife and daughter being the first"* Filson, 60.

190   *"Every Kentuckian ought to try my gait"* Shane interview with Nathaniel Hart Jr., 1843–44, DM17CC195.

Nine: The Trace and the River

191   *"that a present of two thousand acres"* George W. Ranck, *Boonesborough,* 214.

192   *While others such as Michael Stoner* Stephen Aron, *How the West Was Lost,* 77.

193   *"They flatter themselves that the addition"* Ranck, 215–16.

193   *"Therefore, the Memorialists hope"* Ranck, 216.

195   *many tribes in Ohio* Otis K. Rice, *Frontier Kentucky,* 87.

195   *The account books of the Transylvania Company* Lyman Copeland Draper, *The Life of Daniel Boone,* 393.

196   *Twenty years later when the ownership* Daniel Boone, deposition, July 27, 1795, Shelby County Deed Book, B1, 272–73.

196 *"They had brought out a stock of seeds"* Elizabeth Fries Ellet, *Pioneer Women of the West*, 49.

197 *"This forenoon boon delivered 700 lbs."* DM4QQ47.

198 *"What a Buzzel is amongst"* John Brown to Col. William Preston, May 5, 1775, DM4QQ15.

198 *"The face of the country at that time"* Draper, 406.

198 *there were more forests than meadows* Julian J. N. Campbell, *The Land of Cane and Clover*, 2.

198 *"When you take it between your fingers"* Craig Thompson Friend, *Along the Maysville Road*, 48.

199 *"What a country it was"* Draper, 406–7.

200 *"'And now'"* Draper, 408.

200 *"When a young man was taken sick"* Told by Dr. Orlando Brown in W. H. Bogart, *Daniel Boone and the Hunters of Kentucky*, 125.

200 *He would ride out to meet* Thomas Speed, *The Wilderness Road*, 45.

201 *Col. William Russell of the Clinch* Michael Lofaro, *Daniel Boone*, 68.

201 *new signs of Indians were seen every day* John Floyd to Col. William Preston, July 21, 1776, DM33S300-305.

201 *Their resentment was directed* Neal O. Hammon, "No Stranger to Difficulty," 68.

201 *"When Hogg offered Governor Patrick Henry"* George Morgan Chinn, *Kentucky Settlement and Statehood, 1750–1800*, 114.

201 *On June 24, 1776, the Virginia Convention* Draper, 410.

202 *In November 1778 the Virginia legislature* Reuben Gold Thwaites, *Daniel Boone*, 134n.

202 *"the customary Bible reading"* Ranck, 49.

202 *the nickname "Duck"* Daniel Bryan to Draper, DM22C14[11]; Ella Hazel Atterbury Spraker, *The Boone Family*, 119.

202 *"as it was against their fathers' orders"* Stephen Hempstead to Lyman Copeland Draper, February 15, 1863, DM16C76.

203 *"The Indians chose ground"* Daniel Bryan to Draper, February 27, 1843, DM22C5[9].

203 *"We have done pretty well for old Boone"* Draper, 413.

204 *the young chiefs and warriors planned* Gregory Evans Dowd, *A Spirited Resistance*, 48.

204 *The British had already given Dragging Canoe* Dowd, 49.

205 *"The horse was cross and would bite"* Neal O. Hammon, ed., *My Father, Daniel Boone*, 49.

206 *"pretty squaws"* Draper, 415.

206 *"Oh yes yes you would"* Draper interview with Delinda Boone Craig, 1866, DM30C48.

208 *"One in particular, big indn:, called Big Jimmy"* John Dabney Shane interview with Josiah Collins, 1840s, DM12CC75.

209 *"At the crack of the guns"* Hammon, ed., 50.

209 *"For God's sake don't kill her"* Draper, 420.

209 *"The exultation of the poor girls"* Draper, 420.

209 *"After the girls came to themselves"* John Floyd to Col. William Preston, July 21, 1776, DM33S300-305.

209 *"Thank Almighty Providence"* Evira L. Coshow to Draper, March 31, 1885, DM21C29.

210 *Dragging Canoe and his warriors did* Dowd, 53.

210 *"She laughed and cried for joy"* Evira L. Coshow to Draper, May 2, 1885, DM21C37[2].

211 *Hanging Maw rose to be* Pat Alderman, *The Overmountain Men*, 276.

212 *"a man distinguished for his love"* New York Magazine, May 1, 1796, 280, DM6S337.

212 *"Boonesborough had no water supply"* Chinn, 93.

212 *Boone officiated* Draper, 423.

212 *"the guests were treated"* Ranck, 53.

212 *She later told her niece* Evira L. Coshow to Draper, June 12, 1885, DM21C48[1].

Freemasonry

214 *"The people of Kentucky were from the first"* Lyman Copeland Draper, *The Life of Daniel Boone*, 393.

214 *The first lodge in Kentucky* J. Winston Coleman Jr. *Masonry in the Bluegrass*, 9–44.

215 *The Harrodsburg community* Nancy O'Malley, *Stockading Up*, 16.

215 *"the present laudable cause"* George W. Ranck, *Boonesborough*, 245.

215 *"in making a Diversion and exciting"* Randolph C. Downes, *Council Fires on the Upper Ohio*, 195; John Mack Faragher, *Daniel Boone*, 151.

Ten: Light and Shadow

216 *"Hill and valley, timberland and thicket"* Reuben Gold Thwaites, *Daniel Boone*, 131.

216 *"I want as much to return"* John Floyd to Col. William Preston, July 21, 1776, DM33S300-305.

217 *"Their attempts to defend themselves"* Nancy O'Malley, *Stockading Up*, 16.

217 *"We are surrounded with enemies"* Lyman Copeland Draper, *The Life of Daniel Boone*, 435.

218 *When they found Ray's mangled body* Draper, 438.

219 *"Boys we are gone — let us sell"* Draper, 440.

219 *"Well, Simon, you behaved like a man"* Draper, 441.

220 *"For God's sake, dig a hole under"* Draper, 442.

221 *two of the wives, both expert shots* George Morgan Chinn, *Kentucky Settlement and Statehood, 1750–1800*, 159.

221 *Levi Todd reported that a total* Neal O. Hammon and Richard Taylor, *Virginia's Western War, 1775–1786*, 53.

221 *visited by the "specter" of his stepson* JDS interview with Mrs. Sarah Graham, ca. 1840, DM12CC45.

222 *According to Nancy O'Malley* Nancy O'Malley, "Frontier Defenses and Pioneer Strategies in the Historic Settlement Era," 64.

222 *"We were received with great joy"* Daniel Bryan to Lyman Copeland Draper, February 27, 1843, DM22C5[11].

222 *cows were sometimes hesitant* John Dabney Shane interview with John Gass, 1840s, DM11CC12.

222 *In November, Cornstalk* Otis K. Rice, *Frontier Kentucky*, 93.

223 *"When he arose, he was in nowise confused"* Louise Phelps Kellogg and Reuben Gold Thwaites, *Documentary History of Dunmore's War, 1774*, 433, DM3Dxviii.

223 *"You may, by the Governor's"* Col. William Fleming to the Shawnee chiefs. William Fleming Papers, Washington and Lee University, File PP4, Leyburn Library, Lexington, VA.

224 *what they found was more often danger* Daniel Blake Smith, "This Idea in Heaven," 95.

224 *"14 persons, that I knew"* Lucien Beckner, "Interview with Sarah Graham," 244, quoted in Smith, 93.

224 *took "turns at the port-holes, from which"* Thwaites, 142.

225 *"rendering it a black smelly goop"* Ted Franklin Belue, *The Hunters of Kentucky*, 165.

225 *"There were original notes for salt"* Robert E. McDowell, "Bullitt's Lick," 27.

226 *"A blinding snow-storm was in progress"* Thwaites, 147.

227 *It was an odd scene* Neal O. Hammon, ed., *My Father, Daniel Boone*, 54–55.

228 *"That is not true"* John James Van Noppen and Ina Woestemeyer Van Noppen, *Daniel Boone Backwoodsman*, 139.

229 *"Don't fire — if you do, all will be massacred"* Draper, 464.

229 *"I think it was a Saturday"* Hammon, ed., 53.

230 *"Brothers! What I have promised you"* Draper, 465.

230 *As a hostage Boone was probably not* Draper, 490nm.

231 *"O, Captain Boone, this is not intended"* Draper, 466.

231 *nothing but a "damned squaw"* Draper, 467.

232 *a scalp brought only fifty dollars* Draper interview with Joseph Jackson, 1844, DM11C62[10].

232 *"an uncomfortable journey, in very severe weather"* John Filson, *The Discovery, Settlement, and Present State of Kentucke*, 63.

232 *"it would have killed him"* Draper, 469.

233 *"The name Chillicothe means"* Draper, 487n11.

233 *"Chillicothes" were the clan from which* Belue, 13.

233   *"sing as loud as he could holler"* Ansel Goodman petition for Revolutionary War pension, October 29, 1832, DM11C28[2].

234   *Captured women were rarely affronted* Axtell, 310–11.

234   *"a purgative ceremony by which"* Axtell, 313–14.

234   *Such an exhortation might last* Axtell, 314.

234   *"In public office as in every"* Axtell, 321.

235   *On the other hand few Indians chose* James Axtell, *The Invasion Within*, 303; J. Hector St. John de Crevecoeur, *Letters from an American Farmer*, 215.

235   *"because they found Indian life to possess"* Axtell, 327.

235   *Many rescued and returned* Axtell, 309.

235   *"Reason respects the differences"* Percy Bysshe Shelley, "A Defense of Poetry," 783.

Eleven: Sheltowee, Son of Blackfish

237   *"The hair of the head is plucked"* Peck, 73.

238   *"stepp'd [to] one side"* Lyman Copeland Draper, *The Life of Daniel Boone*, 470–71.

238   *"During our travels, the Indians"* John Filson, *The Discovery, Settlement, and Present State of Kentucke*, 64.

239   *Hamilton suggested that Boone tell* Draper, 471.

240   *"Like the great hunter he was"* John Mack Faragher, *Daniel Boone*, 170.

240   *"were treated by Governor Hamilton"* Filson, 64.

240   *"By Boone's account the people of the frontier"* Governor Hamilton to General Carlton, April 25, 1778, Haldimand Papers, *Michigan Historical Collections*, 9:435.

241   *"Such a country could not well escape"* Draper, 473.

242   *"No answered Blackfish,"* Draper, 474.

242   *"Never did the Indians pursue"* Reuben Gold Thwaites, *Daniel Boone*, 165.

242   *"At Chelicothe I spent my time"* Filson, 64–65.

243   *"Grandfather Boone said he had a squaw"* Evira L. Coshow to Lyman Copeland Draper, March 14 and April 23, 1885, DM31C24[12–13].

243   *"Should a maiden like the looks"* Thomas Wildcat Alford, *Civilization*, 67.

243   *"But these are cases only"* Trowbridge, 32–33.

244   *"She helped her son get an erection,"* C. F. Voegelin, John F. Yegerlehner, and Florence M. Robinett, *Shawnee Law*, 37.

244   *Too frequent sex was considered bad* Voegelin, Yegerlehner, and Robinett, *Shawnee Law*, 39.

244   *Shawnee couples were not supposed to demonstrate* C. C. Trowbridge, *Shawnese Traditions*, 34.

244   *"sex could be a way of fulfilling"* Carolyn Gilman, "A World of Women," 46.

244   *"He that is a good Hunter never"* John Lawson, *Lawson's History of North Carolina*, 30, 195.

244   *"For when a Person"* Lawson, 195.

245   *"Perhaps he was lucky he came"* Voegelin, C. F., and E. W. Voegelin, "The Shawnee Female Deity in Historical Perspective," 7.

245   *"The bundles provide"* Voegelin, Yegerlehner, and Robinett, 18.

246   *"gave access to the chaotic and deadly"* Gregory Evans Dowd, *A Spirited Resistance*, 10.

246   *"Daniel Boone evidently saw it"* John Sugden, *Blue Jacket*, 15.

246   *"function as a prayer"* James H. Howard, *Shawnee!*, 397.

246   *To the Shawnees springs were thought to be* Dowd, 11.

246   *Any man taken in battle expected* Dowd, 14.

246   *The Shawnees had moved often* Colin G. Calloway, *The American Revolution in Indian Country*, 163.

246   *"desecrated the spirituality of animals"* Stephen Aron, "Pigs and Hunters," 189.

247   *"skill in making butter and cheese"* Aron, 190.

247   *But many warriors felt the missionaries* Aron, 193.

247   *This woman leader had the responsibility* Aron, 195.

247   *"because some women were wiser than some men"* Calloway, 64.

248   *let her chickens roost* Draper interview with Isaiah Boone, 1846, DM19C76.

248   *"Blackfish would also smooth out dirt"* Neal O. Hammon, ed., *My Father, Daniel Boone*, 60.

248   *"Blackfish would suck a lump"* Hammon, ed., 59.

248   *"found the land, for a great extent"* Filson, 66.

249   *"wanted to go and see his squaw and children"* Draper interview with Joseph Jackson, 1844, DM11C62[11].

249   *"he really felt sorry"* Eligah Bryan to Draper, May 12, 1885, DM4C33[3–4].

250   *"Jimmy Rogers said that the Indians"* Hammon, ed., 61.

250   *He bound the stock to the metal* Draper, 480.

250   *"It had the very best lock"* Draper, 480.

252   *"Boon said, the summer he was"* John Dabney Shane interview with John Gass, 1840s, DM11CC14.

253   *"Dear Colonel:"* Draper, 497.

253   *"used afterwards to say"* Draper, 481.

254   *"The object of Boone, in this expedition"* Peck, 78.

256   *"Everyone in the fort was then sure"* JDS interview with John Gass, 1840, DM11CC12.

256   *"If you had only let me know I would have let you"* Draper, 500–501.

256   *"It was you," Moluntha said* Draper, 502; John Bradford, *The Voice of the Frontier*, 19.

256   *"Well Boone, I have come to take"* Shane interview with Josiah Collins, 1840s, DM12CC74.

257   *"Boon was blamed for this proposal"* Shane interview with John Gass, 1840s, DM11CC13.

258   *Boone asked for a show of hands* Shane interview with Jesse Daniel, ca. 1843, DM11CC94.

258   *"I will kill the first man who"* Shane interview with Nathaniel Hart, Jr., ca. 1843–44, DM17CC198.

258   *Squire Boone added his voice* John Gass to Draper, December 1844, DM24C73[2].

258   *"Well, well, I'll die"* Draper, 501.

258   *"Dress served as a potent symbol"* Elizabeth A. Perkins, *Border Life*, 88.

258   *"I have brought forty horses"* Bradford, 19.

258   *"He saw that the indns were getting angry"* Shane interview with John Gass, 1840s, DM11CC13.

260   *"Fine squaws, fine squaws!"* Draper interview with Moses Boone, 1846, DM19C11.

260   *"They took out the combs"* Evira L. Coshow to Draper, March 14, 1885, DM21C27.

261   *"sounded grateful in our ears"* Filson, 69.

261   *"as they would be more likely, two to one"* Draper, 505.

261   *"They all met at the appointed place"* Daniel Bryan to Draper, February 27, 1843, DM22C5[15].

262   *"Blackfish said that there was indians"* Daniel Bryan to Draper, February 27, 1843, DM22C5[15].

262   *"By what right did you come and"* Draper, 506.

262   *"That entirely alters the case"* Draper, 506.

262   *"only submitting to the British authorities"* Peck, 82–83.

262   *"That Boone and his friends should have"* Peck, 89.

263   *"Brothers, we have made a long"* and *"when they were very loving"* Shane interview with John Gass, 1840s, DM11CC13.

263   *"This stratagem to captivate the whites"* Shane interview with Josiah Collins, 1840s, DM12CC75.

263   *"But treachery took place"* Hammon, ed., 67.

263   *"in that manner gave the word go"* Daniel Bryan to Draper, February 27, 1843, DM22C5[16].

264   *"Particular inquiries were made, by"* Peck, 84.

265   *"As Father used to say, it was"* Hammon, ed., 68.

Twelve: Farthest Outpost of Rebellion

266   *"No less than fourteen bullet"* Lyman Copeland Draper, *The Life of Daniel Boone*, 508.

267   *"They shot into it from off both hills"* John Dabney Shane interview with John Gass, 1840s, DM11CC14.

267   *"The determined defenders of Boonesborough"*   Otis K. Rice, *Frontier Kentucky*, 96.

268   *Some wondered if the Shawnees had retreated*   George W. Ranck, *Boonesborough*, 91.

268   *London's gun refused to fire*   Draper, 512.

269   *Bundrin died before daybreak*   Draper, 512, 524n8.

269   *"the fleshy part of her back"*   Draper interview with Nathan and Olive Boone, 1851, DM6S142.

269   *"I've no time to pray, goddamnit"*   Shane interview with John Gass, 1840s, DM11CC13.

270   *"They shot arrows, with powder"*   Shane interview with John Gass, 1840s, DM11CC13.

270   *When the burning arrows hit roofs*   Neal O. Hammon, ed., *My Father, Daniel Boone*, 68.

270   *"Why don't you fire your big wooden gun"*   Draper, 515.

270   *"Come out and fight like men"*   Draper, 513.

270   *"for they might hurt [the Indians]"*   Draper, 513.

271   *According to Draper, it was William Collins*   Draper, 512. In other accounts it was William Hancock. Draper interview with Ephraim McLean, May 17, 1884, DM16C7[3–4].

271   *"Pompey is dead"*   Draper, 512.

271   *"Such a fatal shot deterred"*   Draper, 516–17.

272   *"After the siege, signs of blood"*   Draper, 517.

272   *"Some unknown genius discovered"*   Neal O. Hammon, *Daniel Boone and the Defeat at the Blue Licks*, 32–33.

273   *"any article could be plainly seen"*   Draper interview with Moses Boone, 1846, DM19oD21-22.

274   *picked up 125 pounds of lead*   Draper, 519.

274   *"Why, they are our boys!"*   Draper, 519.

274   *At least one cow that was led away*   Draper, 518.

275   *if Boonesborough had fallen*   Archibald Henderson, *The Conquest of the Old Southwest*, 276–77.

275   *"Goddamn them," he wrote*   Daniel Bryan to Draper, ca. 1843, DM22C14[12].

276   *According to Trabue, the charges brought*   Daniel Trabue, *Westward into Kentucky*, 63; Draper, 520.

277   *"Capt. Daniel Boon sayed the reason he"*   Trabue, 63.

277   *"Boon after that time appeared alwaise to be"*   Trabue, 64.

278   *"With an emphatic nod of his head"*   Draper, 524, DM11C76. Draper interview with John and Sarah Kenton McCord, 1851, DM5S80.

278   *"The test of a first-rate intelligence"*   F. Scott Fitzgerald, *The Crack-up*, 69.

279   *"Boon never deserved anything of the country"*   Shane interview with Jesse Daniel, ca. 1843, DM11CC94; Trabue, 172n47.

280   *"The history of my going home"*   Filson, 73.

Thirteen: With Chain and Compass

282   *"could hardly get along the road for them"* John Dabney Shane interview with William Clinkenbeard, 1840s, DM11CC55.

283   *Tories did believe their chances of survival were* Ted Franklin Belue, *The Hunters of Kentucky*, 130.

283   *"The right of preemption to four hundred acres"* Otis K. Rice, *Frontier Kentucky*, 119.

283   *"which according to the statute,"* Mary K. Bonsteel Tachau, "Land Claims, Early," 535.

283   *a "pauper warrant"* Neal O. Hammon, "Settlers, Land Jobbers, and Outlyers," 254.

283   *"By September 1779 Daniel had little choice"* Belue, 130.

285   *As it turned out, they never were recovered* John Bakeless, *Daniel Boone*, 241; Kathryn Weiss, "Two Swivel Guns," 11–15.

285   *"but much less so than the capture by"* Peter Houston notes, May 2, 1842, DM20C84[15].

285   *Apparently Boone himself reached Logan's Station"* Neal O. Hammon and Wilson Zaring, "What Is Wrong with the Peter Houston Story?" 3.

285   *One British traveler of the time* Durrett Collection, University of Chicago, Codex 67.

286   *"The day is so cold . . . and the ink"* John Floyd to Col. William Preston, December 19, 1779, DM17CC123.

286   *"A number of people would be Taken sick"* Daniel Trabue, *Westward into Kentucky*, 75.

287   *"They could hardly drive them off"* Elizabeth Boone Scholl to Draper, January 5, 1856, DM23C104[2].

287   *"Old woman, we must move"* Christopher Mann to Draper, October 15, 1885, DM15C26[2].

289   *"Some even sold the same tract"* Neal O. Hammon, "Settlers, Land Jobbers, and Outlyers," 241.

289   *"He should have part of the land claimed"* James Bridges Deposition, January 21, 1816, DM27C84.

290   *"Wm. Mountjoy, surveyor of Pendleton Co."* Durrett Collection, R. H. Collins Papers, Box 1, Folder 4.

290   *Nathan Boone said at one time his father* Neal O. Hammon, ed., *My Father, Daniel Boone*, 110.

290   *"He had no problem running simple square"* Hammon, ed., 111.

291   *"Hospitality and kindness are among the virtues"* John Mason Peck, *Life of Daniel Boone*, 148.

291   *"I am afraid to lose sight of my house"* Reuben Gold Thwaites, *Daniel Boone*, 131.

292   *"In the spring of 1780 three hundred boatloads"* Rice, 102.

292   *"The 2000 acres of Land you ar to make me a titel"* Bakeless, 343.

293   *Recent scholarship has thrown new light* Neal O. Hammon, "The Boone Robbery," 3.

293   *"[It is] uninhabited Country the most rugged"* Hammon, "The Boone Robbery," 2.

294   *Only the small amount of money* Draper interview with Nathan and Olive Boone, 1851, DM6S146.

295   *"The door was found open next morning"* Hammon, ed., 71.

295   *"Receipts from Public Auditors"* Hammon, "The Boone Robbery," 1.

296   *"I feel for the poor people"* Bakeless, 245–46; DM33S324–325; *Presbyterian Historical Society Journal* 14 (1930–31): 343.

296   *Likewise with the most famous* Draper, 400–401n1.

297   *"A Major [Boone] and thirty-seven Americans"* Barnhart, *Henry Hamilton and George Rogers Clark in the American Revolution*, 36.

297   *"made a broken trip of it"* Trabue, 68.

297   *"Hardly a week passes without someone"* John Floyd to Col. William Preston, May 31, 1780, DM17CC127–128.

298   *"fell by the wayside and were"* George Morgan Chinn, *Kentucky Settlement and Statehood, 1750–1800*, 235.

298   *One witness reported seeing a woman's belly* John Mack Faragher, *Daniel Boone*, 210; William Holman to Henry Bird, August 15, 1780. Canadian Archives, Haldimand Papers 10 (1888): 418–19.

298   *"Found an Indian's fingers in it"* Lucien Beckner, "Interview with Benjamin Allen," *Filson Club Historical Quarterly* 5 (1931): 89, quoted in Daniel Blake Smith, "This Idea in Heaven," 88. From Shane's interview with Benjamin Allen, 1840s, DM11CC67–79.

299   *"In the town of Boonesborough"* House of Burgesses 1779, Henderson Papers.

299   *"At a short distance from his cabin"* Peck, 142.

299   *"Yes, Boone, we have got you again"* Evira L. Coshow to Draper, March 11, 1883, DM21C24[7].

299   *"The old man, in telling the story"* Peck, 144.

299   *ever used tobacco in any form* Hammon, ed., 140.

300   *Then the Shawnees rushed into the camp* Lawrence Elliott, *The Long Hunter*, 158.

300   *While hunting by himself* Peter Houston narrative, May 2, 1842, DM20C84[22].

301   *"Edward [Ned] sat down to crack"* Daniel Bryan to Draper, April 14, 1843; DM22C7.

301   *"We have killed Daniel Boone"* Thomas S. Bouchelle to Draper, July 28, 1884, DM9C68[5].

302   *but it is more likely they just took his scalp* Nancy O'Malley, in conversation with the author, March 17, 2005.

302   *"Wait a minute, Captain Boone, and I'll go"* Hammon, ed., 73.

303   *Col. William Preston wrote to John Floyd* Col. William Preston to John Floyd, June 17, 1781, DM13C21[3–17]; John Cook Wyllie, "Daniel Boone's Adventure in Charlottesville," 11–12.

303   *"My father was conveyed to the British"* Hammon, ed., 73.

303   *"Boone was reimbursed for his trouble"* Wyllie, 16.

304   *"I recollect very well when I saw Col. Boone"* John Redd to Draper, ca. 1848, DM10NN101; Draper, 181nb.

304   *"that the Sergeant-at-Arms attending the House"* Faragher, 214.

305   *"On March 5, 1782 Williamson and volunteers"* Neal O. Hammon, *Daniel Boone and the Defeat at Blue Licks*, 11.

306   *one of four thousand African Anericans* Michael Lofaro, *Daniel Boone*, 120.

307   *"Crawford died like a hero"* Mark M. Boatner III, *Encyclopedia of the American Revolution*, 306.

307   *Boone realized things had taken a very serious turn* Filson, 74.

Fourteen: Father, I Won't Leave You

309   *"Brothers, the intruders on your lands"* John Bradford, *The Voice of the Frontier*, 49–50.

310   *What had once been Indian backyards* Colin G. Calloway, *The American Revolution in Indian Country*, 26.

310   *"Burned villages and crops, murdered chiefs"* Calloway, 290.

311   *No one is sure why the prisoners* John Bakeless, *Daniel Boone*, 274.

311   *"The fort [Bryan's Station] in 1782 was said to be"* Neal O. Hammon, *Daniel Boone and the Defeat at Blue Licks*, 22.

311   *One of the springs outside the walls* Rebecca Grant Lamond to Lyman Copeland Draper, March 22, 1853, DM22C41[2].

311   *the covered spring had gone dry* Grandmother Tomlinson, *Madison Democrat*, June 11, 1876, DM13C64.

312   *"It was decided to act for a while"* Grandmother Tomlinson, *Madison Democrat*, June 11, 1876, DM13C64.

312   *"from that awful hour"* Grandmother Tomlinson, *Madison Democrat*, June 11, 1876, DM13C64.

312   *"They were not twenty steps"* Grandmother Tomlinson, *Madison Democrat*, June 11, 1876, DM13C64.

312   *Because the spring was shallow in the August* Durrett, *Bryant's Station*, 53.

313   *The British officer Caldwell later said three hundred* Bennett H. Young, *The Battle of the Blue Licks*, 208.

314   *"A lighted arrow from an Indian bow"* Durrett, 42.

316   *"Know you! Know you! Yes we know"* Lambert Lilly, *The Adventures of Daniel Boone, Kentucky Rifleman*, 107.

316   *"If you and your gang of murderers"* Bradford, 53; Bakeless, 286–87.

317   *Trigg had never fought Indians* Hammon, 34.

317   *It is possible that Boone preferred not to wait* Hammon, 38–39.

317   *The adage was that cowards did not* Young, 137.

318   *"Their camp fires were left burning"* John Mason Peck, *Life of Daniel Boone*, 118.

318   *they might have walked in each other's tracks* Robert Wickliffe, "The Life of Col. John Todd," ms. ca. 1840s, DM5C51[8].

318   *they saw some Indians hurrying* Hammon, 50.

318   *"They wish to seduce a pursuing enemy"* Robert Wickliffe, "The Life of Col. John Todd," ms. ca. 1840s, DM5C51[8].

318   *"I caution you against crossing the river"* Bradford, 56.

319   *"Another account by Boone's grandson was"* Hammon, 52.

319   *Two men volunteered to ride* Young, 167.

319   *"By Godly," McGary shouted* John Dabney Shane interview with Jacob Stevens ca. 1840s, DM12CC134.

319   *"I can go as far [in an Indian fight] as any man"* Hammon, ed., *My Father, Daniel Boone*, 76.

319   *Nathan's wife, Olive, told Draper* Hammon, ed., 79.

319   *"Them that ain't cowards follow me"* Shane interview with Jacob Stevens, ca. 1840s, DM12CC134.

320   *may have paused only to cross* Hammon, 51.

320   *"We rode up within 60 yards, dismounted"* Young, 219.

321   *"You be there!"* Hammon, ed., 78.

321   *"he was only positive"* Hammon, ed., 78.

324   *"We . . . were obliged to retreat"* John Filson, *The Discovery, Settlement and Present State of Kentucke*, 76.

325   *"Father, I won't leave you"* Hammon, ed., 79.

325   *"Father used to be deeply affected"* Hammon, ed., 78.

326   *Boone later decided* Hammon, ed., 77–78.

326   *"Let's halt, boys"* Bakeless, 301; Abner Bryan to Draper, February 12–13, 1890, DM13C34–35 and DM4C50.

326   *"I cannot ever forget the part"* Young, 183; Bakeless, 302; John W. Van Cleve, "Colonel Robert Patterson," 344–47.

327   *"did not know how many they burned"* Shane interview with Sarah Graham, ca. 1840s, DM12CC50.

327   *"Lawrence offered my father the whole"* Shane interview with Sarah Graham, ca. 1840s, DM12CC50.

327   *"The Conduct of those unfortunate Gents"* Young, 201; *Calendar of Virginia State Papers* 3:345.

328   *"All our late defeats have been occasion[ed]"* Young, 221–22; *Calendar of Virginia State Papers* 3:337.

328   *"Colonels Todd and Trigg were for immediate"* Peck, 129.

328   *"He was a fractious, ill tempered"* Peck to Mann Butler, January 12,

1855, Henderson Papers; Durrett Collection, Butler Papers, Box 1, Folder 1.

329   *"rather blamed himself in some degree"* Joseph Scholl to Draper, 1868, DM24S213.

329   *"Israel ought not to have gone"* Draper interview with Delinda Boone Craig, 1866, DM30C63.

329   *"Israel had long been sick"* Hammon, ed., 79–80.

329   *dug a separate grave for Israel there* Faragher, 222.

330   *"A solemn silence pervaded the whole"* Bradford, 58.

330   *covered with as much dirt and rocks* Bradford, 58.

331   *"I know Sir, that your Situation"* Young, 216; Calendar of Virginia State Papers 3:275.

331   *The Indians and their prisoners retreated* Neal O. Hammon and Richard Taylor, *Virginia's Western War, 1775–1786*, 167.

331   *"But if you put them under the Direction"* Young, 216; Calendar of Virginia State Papers 3:275.

332   *"Indian speakers in council after council"* Calloway, 273.

333   *"The mouth of Limestone Creek"* Filson, 17.

333   *"Boone wanted to examine the land"* Peter Harget Deposition, April 30, 1814, Durrett Collection, R. H. Collins Papers, Box 1, Folder 4, 107.

Fifteen: Filson, Fame, and Failure

335   *"Two darling sons, and a brother, have I lost"* John Filson, *The Discovery, Settlement and Present State of Kentucke*, 80.

336   *"The earliest references to Filson"* John Walton, *John Filson of Kentucke*, 27.

336   *"from his own mouth"* Filson, 6.

336   *Boone certified the story true* Filson, 3.

338   *"He acquired a reputation for annoying"* Walton, 28.

338   *"Curiosity is natural to the soul of man"* Filson, 49.

339   *"Certainly the most florid writing"* Walton, 47; Filson, 107–9.

339   *"He [Boone] has been the inspiration"* Walton, 50.

339   *"It was the first of May, in the year 1769"* Filson, 50.

340   *"[A]s my reason began to master my despondency"* Daniel Defoe, *The Life and Strange and Surprising Adventures of Robinson Crusoe*, 76.

340   *"[I was] by myself, without bread"* Filson, 54.

340   *"And let this stand as a direction"* Defoe, 77.

340   *"Thus situated, many hundred miles from"* Filson, 53.

341   *"[S]eeing all these things have not brought thee"* Defoe, 101.

341   *was named Dreaming Creek* John Bakeless, *Daniel Boone*, 51–52; Thomas Speed, *The Wilderness Road*, 69; Draper interview with Nathan and Olive Boone, 1851, DM6S282.

341 *"Each time when captured, robbed"* Bakeless, 244; Draper interview with Nathan and Olive Boone, 1851, DM6S282.

341 *"Many dark and sleepless nights have I been"* Filson, 80–81.

341 *"How strange a chequer-work of Providence"* Defoe, 182.

341 *"The aspect of these cliffs is so wild"* Filson, 57–58.

342 *"The scenery which presented itself on all sides"* Edgar Allan Poe, "A Tale of the Ragged Mountains," 3:942.

342 *"I surveyed the famous river Ohio"* Filson, 55.

343 *"Interest in his subject was high"* Walton, 73.

343 *"Boone the frontiersman, as an acknowledged"* Arthur K. Moore, *The Frontier Mind*, 147–48.

344 *"All true: Every word truth!"* John A. McClung, *Sketches of Western Adventure*, 79–80.

344 *"neither the love of friends nor the hatred of enemies"* J. Winston Coleman, *Six Sketches of Kentucky*, 71.

344 *"a model of the republican citizen"* Richard Slotkin, *The Fatal Environment*, 67.

345 *"No little mound attracts to his last resting-place"* Reuben T. Durrett, *John Filson, the First Historian of Kentucky*, 93.

345 *"A man does not have to be great"* Walton, 126.

346 *"Thomas Allin and Samuel Grant the persons appointed"* Lincoln County Court Order Book One, 79, August Court, 1783.

346 *In 1783 Boone made around forty surveys* Willard Rouse Jillson, "Daniel Boone as Surveyor," *Kentucky School Journal*, 32.

348 *"a muddy hole of a place"* Ellen Eslinger, *Running Mad for Kentucky*, 19.

348 *"In this harbour are seen"* Eslinger, 18–19.

348 *"the fag [worn out] end of Kentucky"* Eslinger, 19.

349 *"[In 1783] he made 24 surveys"* Neal O. Hammon, "Daniel Boone the Surveyor," 3.

350 *"A surveying party would need a compass"* Hammon, 3.

350 *Yet later studies of his surveys* Neal O. Hammon and Richard Taylor, *Virginia's Western War 1775–1786*, xxiv.

351 *"All Boone's entries were mighty vague"* John Dabney Shane interview with William Risk, ca. 1840s, DM11CC87.

Sixteen: A Deale of Sine Is Seen

352 *"A Deale of Sine is Seen in Different places"* Daniel Boone to Gov. Patrick Henry, August 16, 1785, DM32C81A.

353 *In April 1786 Moluntha and the chief named the Shade* Colin G. Calloway, *The American Revolution in Indian Country*, 176.

353 *Simon Girty, who was with the Shawnees* Michigan Historical Collection 24 (1895): 35.

353   *the dogs would lead them to the villages* Neal O. Hammon, ed., *My Father, Daniel Boone*, 81.

354   *"Who hacked the squaws?"* Abner Bryan to Lyman Copeland Draper, 1890, DM4C50.

354   *"Mind that fellow," Boone shouted* Hammon, ed., 81.

355   *"Was you in the Battle of Blue Licks?"* and *"Then God damn you . . . I will show you"* John Dabney Shane interview with Isaac Clinkenbeard, 1840s, DM11CC3.

355   *Moluntha's English was not very good* Draper interview with Joseph Jackson, 1844, DM11C63[34].

356   *Later they would move again* Calloway, 178.

356   *"State of Virginia Dr. 19 galons of whiskey"* David I. Bushnell Jr., "Daniel Boone at Limestone 1781–1787," 3.

357   *"He told me he had surveyed the same land"* Deposition of Daniel Boone, Point Pleasant, Virginia, April 24, 1794; Neal O. Hammon, "John Filson's Error," 463.

357   *"Hickman, Floyd and myself was face to face"* Deposition of Daniel Boone, Point Pleasant, Virginia, April 24, 1794; Hammon, 463.

358   *"Boone built his station on part of the land"* John Floyd to Col. William Preston, March 27, 1783, DM33S320.

358   *"Said Boone also told deponent"* Deposition of Richard Hickman, May 26, 1790, Fayette County, taken before Charles Morgan and James McMillan, *Fayette County Records*, 1:170–85.

359   *"Boone was ill-equipped for the cut-throat"* Stephen Aron, *How the West Was Lost*, 82.

359   *"Little by little his wealth melted away"* Hammon, ed., 110.

360   *"Aprl 14 lent money to several persons"* "Daniel Boone's Account Book," DM14C92.

360   *"Captain Plat was in New Orleans"* Hammon, ed., 109.

360   *"located and surveyed by Col. Daniel Boone"* *Lexington Herald*, February 13, 1927, Kentucky Historical Society.

361   *It was Imlay . . . who made Boone known* Maurice Manning, *A Companion for Owls*, 118.

361   *"Sir, I must be plain with you"* Daniel Boone to Nathaniel Rochester, July 17, 1785, DM14C7.

361   *Historians, including Arthur K. Moore* Arthur K. Moore, *The Frontier Mind*, 158.

361   *"It is apparent that without wealth"* Moore, 144.

362   *"This man had a wife older"* Daniel Drake, *Pioneer Life in Kentucky*, 205–6.

363   *"In addition to premeditated personal injury"* Hammon, ed., 110.

363   *"I flater myself [that you will] Send"* Daniel Boone to Col. Robert Patterson, March 16, 1787, DM26C176[1].

364 *"the Shawnees often ferried across to visit"* Ted Franklin Belue, *The Hunters of Kentucky*, 242.

364 *"Go home and live at peace, and I will assure"* Benjamin Logan, *Kentucky Gazette*, August 18, 1787, DM33S17-25.

365 *She never forgot Boone's kindness* Boone Ballard to Draper, December 6, 1882, DM14C50[4].

365 *Boone . . . arranged to trade the mare* Draper interview with George Edmonds, 1863, DM19S83.

365 *Recent scholarship suggests that Blue Jacket* John Sugden, *Blue Jacket*, 1–4; Belue, 296n4.

365 *"Boone! Boone!"* Shane interview with Thomas Jones, ca. 1840s, DM12CC233.

365 *The men all got drunk* JSD interview with Thomas Jones, ca. 1840s, DM12CC233.

366 *"By the next spring we had some twelve or fifteen tons"* Hammon, ed., 82.

367 *"Father was busily employed in digging"* Hammon, ed., 81–82.

367 *"Oct. 9th 1788, recd. 15 caggs of ginseng of Capt. Fagan"* John Bakeless, *Daniel Boone*, 331; "Daniel Boone's Account Book," 330, DM14C92, DM6S330.

367 *"In the fall of 1784 we moved out of Boone's Station"* Hammon, ed., 80.

368 *"Then he also decided to take up residence"* Hammon, ed., 84.

368 *"dark complexioned & stern looking"* John F. Watson to Draper, March 4, 1853, DM1C19[2].

369 *"In place of cane, the cabin sites were now"* Elizabeth A. Perkins, *Border Life*, 147.

370 *Some of the horses in the region* Dr. Phil Sponenburg, Letter to the author, August 15, 2005.

Boating in the West

372 *"I . . . found that he was one of that class of men"* Francis Baily, *Journal of a Tour in the Unsettled Parts of North America in 1796–1797*, 115–117.

Seventeen: Going East to Go West

375 *One visitor recalled sleeping in the store* John Dabney Shane interview with James Lane, ca. 1840s, DM12CC57.

375 *"1790 Apl. 27 Van Lears, merchtr., write"* DM27C6.

375 *he never got out of debt to Vanlear* DM27C30.

375 *"The year 1790 marks the end of an era"* Archibald Henderson, *The Conquest of the Old Southwest*, 348.

375 *"Adventures of Colonel Daniel Boone"* European Magazine, October 1790, Kentucky State Archives.

376 *even worked from time to time at his old profession* John P. Hale, *Trans-Allegheny Pioneers*, 170–71.

377 *"There my father saw among Miller's cattle"* Neal O. Hammon, ed., *My Father, Daniel Boone*, 90.

377 *(This visit to Henry Miller's farm)* Daniel Bryan to Draper, 1844, DM22C14.

377 *"Sum purson Must Carry out"* DM14C105.

378 *"Captain Caperton did not do to my likes"* W. S. Laidley, "Daniel Boone in the Kanawha Valley," 2 (1913): 11.

379 *"Though he had fought as hard"* Hammon, ed., 110; DM6S219.

379 *"As Boone grew older and increasingly enfeebled"* Annette Kolodny, *The Land before Her*, 83; John Bakeless, *Daniel Boone*, 347.

380 *It was reported that a hunting companion* J. P. Hale, "Daniel Boone, Some Facts and Incidents Not Hitherto Published," 10.

380 *killed more deer than any of his neighbors* Lyman Copeland Draper note from Edward Bryan, October 20, 1863, DM19S170.

380 *He especially enjoyed hunting deer in Teaze's Valley* Ralph Clayton to Draper, April 10, 1883, DM16C45.

380 *"His large head, full chest, square shoulders"* Reuben Gold Thwaites, *Daniel Boone*, 212–13.

380 *"hair was moderately black, eyes blue"* Hammon, ed., 140.

380 *It was said that in 1792* Hale, 9.

381 *Later he told Draper* Hammon, ed., 101.

381 *"On the way Father put his head over"* Hammon, ed., 99.

382 *"for his qualities and experience as a counselor"* Hale, 5.

382 *"but seemed to be driven"* Hale, 5.

383 *"ate their meals from a common rough tray"* Draper interview with William Champ, 1863, DM15C31.

383 *One bear might yield twenty gallons* Hammon, ed., 102.

384 *The legend is that Daniel Boone* John Mack Faragher, *Daniel Boone*, 272.

384 *"In 1797, the surveyor general of Kentucky"* Stephen Aron, *How the West Was Lost*, 84.

385 *"Sir–After my best Respts to your Excelancy"* Bakeless, 349; Samuel M. Wilson, "Daniel Boone, 1734–1934," 44.

386 *"until 1818, when definite legislative steps were taken"* Thomas D. Clark, *A History of Kentucky*, 258.

386 *When the Wilderness Road was rebuilt* Ellen Eslinger, ed., *Running Mad for Kentucky*, 66.

386 *"In 1796 he began surveying again"* Neal O. Hammon, "Daniel Boone, the Surveyor," 6.

Eighteen: To the Farther West

389 *A sheriff tried to serve a warrant* Stephen Aron, *How the West Was Lost*, 85.

389 *"Nowhere in America has the almost instantaneous"* Aron, *How the West Was Lost*, 2; William Darby, *The Emigrant's Guide to the Western and Southwestern States and Territories*, 206.

390 *"A hunter's life is one of constant excitement"* James B. Finley, *Autobiography of the Rev. James B. Finley*, 96.

390 *the Spanish government embarked on a policy to encourage* John Mason Peck, *Life of Daniel Boone*, 168.

390 *"[T]heir children must absolutely be Catholics"* "Terms of Settlement in Missouri," *Carolina Gazette*, November 14, 1799.

391 *"He [Boone] wanted to know the quantity of land"* Neal O. Hammon, ed., *My Father, Daniel Boone*, 107.

392 *The grant noted that besides slaves* Boone Family Papers, Missouri Historical Society.

392 *"WILL BE SOLD: On Thursday of the 4th"* *Kentucky Gazette*, September 19, 1798, Kentucky State Archives.

392 *"Boone was soured against Kentucky"* Edward Coles to Lyman Copeland Draper, 1848, DM6S310–311.

392 *"unwilling to live among men who were"* Francis Baily, *Journal of a Tour in the Unsettled Parts of North America, 1796–1797*, 116.

392 *"When Boone went out to the site"* Elizabeth A. Perkins, *Border Life*, 134–35; JDS interview with William Risk, 1840s, DM11CC87.

393 *"Boone's honor compelled him"* Daniel Bryan to Draper, April 14, 1843, DM22C7.

393 *As late as July 13, 1798, he had* Neal O. Hammon, "Daniel Boone the Surveyor," 6.

393 *"We found an unusually large poplar tree"* Hammon, ed., 108.

394 *"He said that when he left Kentucky"* Hammon, ed., 111.

394 *they chose a route that took them* Hazel Atterbury Spraker, *The Boone Family*, 117.

394 *known as the prettiest girl* DM65332[3]. Quoted from *History of the Lower Scioto Valley*, 102.

395 *"too crowded—I want more elbow room"* Timothy Flint, *Biographical Memoir of Daniel Boone*, 178.

395 *"accompanied by three or four hunting dogs"* John M. Krum to Draper, January 17, 1883, DM16C54[1–2].

396 *Later Boone said he only went* Peck, 167.

396 *"I purchased the home grant of Robert Hall"* Hammon, ed., 113.

397 *"[T]hrough several years to come"* Reuben Gold Thwaites, *Daniel Boone*, 224.

397   On May 2, 1800, Daniel Morgan Boone Family Papers, Missouri Historical Society.

398   the river was named Pekitanoui Stephen Aron, *American Confluence*, 21.

398   Where the rivers joined, the Missouri Aron, *American Confluence*, xvii–xviii.

398   "a torrent of yellow mud rushed" Mark Twain, *Life on the Mississippi, Mississippi Writings*, 235.

398   "strong brown god — sullen, untamed, and intractable" T. S. Eliot, "The Dry Salvages," in *Complete Poems and Plays, 1909–1950*, 130.

399   "It is a thoroughly masculine river" Stanley Vestal, *The Missouri*, 5.

400   It was the place where North met South Aron, *American Confluence*, xxi.

401   "In the latter part of the summer of 1801" Hammon, ed., 119.

402   The Osages called a gun a wa-ho-ton-the Aron, *American Confluence*, 37.

402   Later Boone pointed out that they were lucky Samuel Boone to Draper, July 5, 1854, DM22C73[3].

402   "[Derry Coburn] was a good Negro" Hammon, ed., 128.

404   "He never was so mad in his life" S. H. Jones to Draper, August 23, 1889, DM21C14[1–2].

404   "He stated to the writer" Peck, 176.

404   Before Derry got the trap open John Mack Faragher, *Daniel Boone*, 285.

405   "more by equity than by law" Draper interview with Nathan Boone, 1851, DM6S225.

405   "Whipped and cleared" William Bryan and Robert Rose, *Pioneer Families of Missouri*, 89.

405   "Let not my gray hairs" Millard Fillmore Stipes, *Gleanings in Missouri History*, 196.

405   "A Certain James Meek & the bearer" Daniel Boone Papers, June 30, 1804, DM15C65.

405   People who knew Boone at this time Thwaites, 226.

406   "Take it and go," Boone said Stipes, 196.

406   "Mr. Boone, a respectable old man" Delassus to his successor Stoddard, 1804. Quoted by Frederick L. Billon to Draper, April 17, 1885, DM15C64.

406   "Hays used to whip aunt fearfully" Evira L. Coshow to Draper, May 3, 1887, DM21C63[3].

406   "Hays was a brave man and always foremost" Hammon, ed., 75.

407   "Hays said if he would not come in" Abner Bryan to Draper, 1890, DM4C58.

407   "An affirmative answer being given" Peck, 170.

407   "This was repeated so often" Bryan and Rose, 45.

408   "At sugar-making time in February" Hammon, ed., 113.

408   "With stones for the fireplace, sticks for the" Hammon, ed., 125.

411   "We fastened our fur vests with strings" Hammon, ed., 124.

411   "and I had to thank the Indians for that" Hammon, ed., 124.

412   "My father had great confidence in Kenton" Hammon, ed., 47.

413   "The venison supper was almost ready" Edna Kenton, Simon Kenton, 262.

413   "The old pioneers seemed to enjoy themselves" Hammon, ed., 47.

413   "Timothy Flint perceived an almost mystical" Arthur K. Moore, The Frontier Mind, 43; Timothy Flint, Recollections of the Last Ten Years, 66–67.

413   "incertitude of property is an inexhaustible source" Thomas D. Clark, The History of Kentucky, 90.

414   "opposed to the scheme from the beginning" Joseph McCormick to Draper, November 12, 1871, DM30C111.

415   And he had never registered his deeds Bryan and Rose, 41.

415   "Meriwether Lewis, [new] governor of Louisiana" Lyman Copeland Draper, The Life of Daniel Boone, xxi.

415   "My wife is getting old and needs" Daniel Bryan to Draper, ca. 1844, DM22C14[14].

Nineteen: Done All the Good That I Can

418   "My brother-in-law, Col. Boone" Elizabeth Corbin to M. D. Lewis, Daily Dispatch (St. Louis), April 2, 1868, DM16C97.

419   The hunt was so successful George Stoner to Lyman Copeland Draper, 1868, DM24C55[10–11].

419   "The canoe was covered with Bear skins" Stephen Hempstead to Draper, March 6, 1863, DM16C78[2].

419   "When my father heard of it" Neal O. Hammon, ed., My Father, Daniel Boone, 115.

420   "He rented a house nearly opposite" Stephen Hempstead to Draper, March 5, 1863, DM16C75.

420   "I perceived that the ball had hit the piece of bark" John James Audubon, Delineations of American Scenery and Character, 60–61.

420   "There were then thousands of buffaloes" John James Audubon, Ornithological Biography, 1:506.

421   "It is quite certain Dl. Boone did return to Ky" Abner Bryan to Draper, 1890, DM4C56.

422   "The old man was still erect in form" Washington Irving, Astoria, 298.

422   "She remained there about a month" Hammon, ed., 135.

423   It is quite possible she saw nothing remarkable Carolyn Lott, Rebecca Boone, 24–25.

423   "the Saddest affliction of his life" Evira L. Coshow to Draper, May 25, 1885, DM21C45[2].

423   *"For this reason my father, Colonel Daniel Boone"* Hammon, ed., 116.

424   *"he had come a great distance to suck a bull"* Hammon, ed., 117.

424   *"The 'new-comers' like a mountain torrent"* John Mason Peck, *Forty Years of Pioneer Life,* 146.

424   *"After the peace, he occupied himself in hunting"* Timothy Flint, *Biographical Memoir of Daniel Boone,* 185.

425   *"Daniel Boone had a vary great idea of the Pacific"* Michael Lofaro, *Daniel Boone,* 171; *"Daniel Boone &"* Manuscript 130, Wade Hays Family History, Seaver Center for Western History Research, Natural History Museum of Los Angeles County, CA.

425   *"While at the fort he became acquainted"* Hammon, ed., 136.

425   *"He went there for the double purpose of"* Hammon, ed., 136.

426   *"But nature is a stranger yet"* Emily Dickinson, No. 1400, in *The Complete Poems of Emily Dickinson,* 599–600.

427   *"My father said he was as naturally inclined"* Hammon, ed., 137.

428   *"a countenance . . . ruddy and fair"* Peck, 187.

428   *"Every member of his family appeared to delight"* Peck, 187.

428   *"He was sociable, communicative"* Peck, 187.

428   *"proved an injury rather than a benefit"* and *"indifferent to the affairs of the world"* David Todd, quoted in Louise Phelps Kellogg, "The Fame of Daniel Boone," 49.

428   *"while I could never with safety repose"* C. Wilder, *Life and Adventures of Colonel Daniel Boone, the First White Settler of Kentucky,* 33.

429   *"instrument by which they lost their hunting grounds"* "A Traveler," *Cincinnati National Republican,* August 19, 1823, DM16C67.

429   *"He destroys the wilderness and the game"* Richard Slotkin, *Regeneration through Violence,* 425.

430   *take his cane and hobble out* Draper interview with Nathan and Olive Boone, 1851, DM6S277.

430   *"Many heroic actions and chivalrous adventures"* "A Traveler," DM16C67.

430   *"and knew not how much he owed"* Peck, 174.

431   *According to a letter by James Robertson* Harriette Arnow, *Seedtime on the Cumberland,* 200; Felix Robertson to Draper, April 6, 1855, DM6XX651.

431   *"Col. Daniel Boone was a Baptist in sentiment"* James Bradley to Draper, August 1890, DM29C77[C].

432   *"Colo. Boone was a firm believer"* Stephen Hempstead to Draper, February 15, 1863, DM16C76[4].

432   *There were sometimes Bible readings* George W. Ranck, *Boonesborough,* 49.

432   *"Deer Sister"* Daniel Boone Papers, DM27C88-89[1].

433   *"One world at a time"* and *"I did not know"* Robert D. Richardson Jr., *Henry David Thoreau,* 389.

433 "No sir, I always loved God ever since" James E. Welch in *Christian Repository* (Louisville), March 1860, DM16C47.

433 "His [Boone's] worship was in secret" Hammon, ed., 139.

434 "He worshipped, as he often said" Flint, 186.

434 "I like the silent church before the service" Ralph Waldo Emerson, "Self-Reliance," in *Emerson's Prose and Poetry*, 130.

435 "Many a Kentuckian engaged in much more heroic" Arthur K. Moore, *The Frontier Mind*, 97.

435 "I would not believe that tale" Peck, 4.

437 *After Boone's death Nathan would say* Hammon, ed., 139.

438 *Boone had given Nathan a fine silver watch* Lucile Morris Upton and John K. Hulston, *Nathan Boone, the Neglected Hero*, 73.

439 "I gave directions before leaving home" Hammon, ed., 137.

439 "too rough and uncouth" Hammon, ed., 138.

439 "Soon after this event" Peck, 184.

439 "Another of cherry was prepared" Peck, 184.

440 "[T]he coffin appeared marvelously beautiful!" Elizabeth Corbin to M. D. Lewis, *Daily Dispatch* (St. Louis), April 2, 1868, DM16C97.

440 "rub and polish it up, and cooly whistle" Delinda Boone Craig interview with Draper, 1866, DM30C78.

440 *he would lie down in the coffin to show* William S. Bryan and Robert Rose, *Pioneer Families of Missouri*, 49; DM21C45[3].

440 "[H]e commenced scraping a horn" Nathan Kouns to Draper, January 16, 1863, DM16C36.

440 *he repaired rifles friends and neighbors* Bryan and Rose, 50; Peck, 185.

441 "He was rather low of stature" James E. Welch in the *Christian Repository* (Louisville), March 1860, DM16C47.

442 "No . . . I can't say I was ever lost" Chester Harding, *My Egotistigraphy*, 35–36.

442 "He began to complain of an acute burning" Hammon, ed., 139.

444 "I am going; don't grieve for me" and the account of Boone's death Draper interview with Delinda Boone Craig, 1866, DM30C83.

444 "Daniel Boone died" Daniel Bryan to Draper, April 14, 1843, DM22C7.

Twenty: Across the River into Legend

447 "[I]t was the figure of Daniel Boone" Richard Slotkin, *Regeneration through Violence*, 21.

447 "too highly colored" Lyman Copeland Draper interview with Joseph Scholl, 1868, DM24S218.

447 "The figure who most enduringly embodies" Annette Kolodny, *The Land before Her*, 28.

448 "Enjoyed the lonely vigorous, harmless days" George Gordon, Lord Byron, *Byron's Don Juan*, Eighth canto, stanza 5, lines 64–65.

448 *An organization for boys* and *"a kind of no-man's land"* Richard Taylor, "Daniel Boone as American Icon," 518, 522.

449 *"The figure and the myth-narrative"* Slotkin, 22.

449 *"Boone's stature, paradoxically, was largely unaffected"* Nelson L. Dawson, "Introduction," 1.

449 *"But if a man would be alone"* Ralph Waldo Emerson, "Nature," in *Emerson's Prose and Poetry*, 28.

449 *"teams it, farms it, peddles it"* Ralph Waldo Emerson, "Self-Reliance," in *Emerson's Prose and Poetry*, 132.

450 *"Prayer is contemplation of the facts"* Emerson, "Self-Reliance," 132.

450 *"Nothing great was ever achieved without enthusiasm"* Ralph Waldo Emerson, "Circles," in *Emerson's Prose and Poetry*, 181.

450 *"The health of the eye seems to demand a horizon"* Emerson, "Nature," 31.

450 *"[A] fact is true poetry"* Emerson, "Nature," 54.

450 *"In the tranquil landscape"* Emerson, "Nature," 29.

450 *"In each case, the image of Boone"* Slotkin, 313.

451 *"I love to be alone"* Henry David Thoreau, *Walden*, 135.

451 *"I wish to speak a word for Nature"* Henry David Thoreau, "Walking," in *Excursions*, 161.

451 *"I believe that there is a subtile magnetism"* Thoreau, "Walking," 175.

451 *"The future lies that way to me"* Thoreau, "Walking," 176–77.

451 *"I should be ashamed to think"* Thoreau, "Walking," 183.

451 *"The West of which I speak is but"* Thoreau, "Walking," 185.

452 *"I believe in the forest, and in the meadow"* Thoreau, "Walking," 185.

452 *"When I would recreate myself"* Thoreau, "Walking," 190.

452 *"I found my account in climbing a tree"* Thoreau, "Walking," 210.

453 *"There was a child went forth"* Walt Whitman, "There Was a Child Went Forth," in *Whitman*, 491.

453 *"Alone far in the wilds and mountains I hunt"* Walt Whitman, "Song of Myself," in *Whitman*, 196.

454 *"The fur trapper, or Mountain Man"* Henry Nash Smith, *The Virgin Land*, 88.

454 *"The Open Road goes to the used-car lot"* Lewis Simpson, "Walt Whitman at Bear Mountain," in *Selected Poems*, 119–20.

454 *"[Bartram's] record bears the distinctive markings"* Slotkin, 325.

455 *"Boone was a living example"* Maurice Manning, *A Companion for Owls*, 125.

455 *"an uncouth place like Kentucky"* Manning, 128.

455 *"I knew a man, a common farmer, the father"* Walt Whitman, "I Sing the Body Electric," in *Whitman*, 252–53.

456 *"From this hour I ordain myself loos'd"* Walt Whitman, "Song of the Open Road," in *Whitman*, 299–300.

457 *"The earth never tires"* Whitman, "Song of the Open Road," 302.

457 *"Allons! the road is before us"* Whitman, "Song of the Open Road," 307.

Bibliography

Abbott, John S. C. *Daniel Boone, Pioneer of Kentucky*. New York: Dodd & Mead, 1872.

Alderman, Pat. *The Overmountain Men*. Johnson City, TN: The Overmountain Press, 1986.

Alford, Thomas Wildcat. *Civilization*. Norman: University of Oklahoma Press, 1936.

———. "Shawnee Domestic and Tribal Life." In *Old Chillecothe*, edited by W. A. Galloway, 170–206. Xenia, OH: The Buckeye Press, 1936.

Alvey, R. Gerald. *Kentucky Bluegrass Country*. Jackson: University Press of Mississippi, 1992.

Alvord, Clarence Walworth "Daniel Boone." *American Mercury*, June 8, 1926, 226–70.

———. "The Daniel Boone Myth." *Journal of the Illinois State Historical Society* 19 (April–July 1926): 16–30.

Anderson, Virginia DeJohn. *Creatures of Empire: How Domestic Animals Transformed Early America*. New York: Oxford University Press, 2004.

Andrae, Rolla P. *The True Brief History of Daniel Boone*. Old Monroe, MO: Daniel Boone Home, 1985.

Arnow, Harriette Simpson. *Seedtime on the Cumberland*. New York: Macmillan, 1960.

Aron, Stephen. *American Confluence*. Bloomington and Indianapolis: Indiana University Press, 2006.

———. *How the West Was Lost: The Transformation of Kentucky from Daniel Boone to Henry Clay*. Baltimore, MD: Johns Hopkins University Press, 1996.

———. "Pigs and Hunters: 'Rights in the Woods' on the Trans-

Appalachian Frontier." In *Contact Points: American Frontiers from the Mohawk Valley to the Mississippi 1750–1830*, edited by Andrew R. L. Cayton and Fredrika J. Teute, 175–204. Chapel Hill: University of North Carolina Press, 1998.

Arthur, John Preston. *A History of Watauga County*. Reprint of the 1915 edition, Johnson City, TN: The Overmountain Press, 1992.

———. *Western North Carolina: A History*. Raleigh, NC: Edwards & Broughton, 1914.

Ashe, Thomas. *Travels in America Performed in 1806, for the Purpose of Exploring the Rivers Allegheny, Monongahela, Ohio, and Mississippi, and Ascertaining the Produce and Condition of Their Banks and Vicinity*. Newburyport, MA: W. Sawyer, 1808.

Audubon, John James. *Delineations of American Scenery and Character*. 1926. Reprint, New York: Arno, 1970.

———. *Ornithological Biography*. 5 vols. Edinburgh: A. Black, 1831–39.

Axtell, James. *The Invasion Within: The Contest of Cultures in Colonial North America*. New York: Oxford University Press, 1985.

Baily, Francis. *Journal of a Tour in the Unsettled Parts of North America, 1796 and 1797*. Reprint of the 1856 edition, Carbondale: University of Southern Illinois Press, 1969.

Bailyn, Bernard, et al. *The Great Republic: A History of the American People*. Boston: Little, Brown, 1977.

Bakeless, John. *Daniel Boone: Master of the Wilderness*. New York: William Morrow, 1939.

Baldwin, Leland D. *The Keelboat Age on Western Waters*. Pittsburgh, PA: University of Pittsburgh Press, 1941.

Barnhart, John D. *Henry Hamilton and George Rogers Clark in the American Revolution*. Crawfordsville, IN: R. E. Banta, 1951.

Bartram, William. *Travels of William Bartram*. 1791. Reprint of 1928 edition, edited by Mark Van Doren, New York: Dover, 1955.

Beckner, Lucien. "Eskippakithiki: The Last Indian Town in Kentucky." *Filson Club History Quarterly* 6 (1932): 355–82.

———. "Interview with Sarah Graham." *Filson Club History Quarterly* 9 (1935): 222–41.

Belue, Ted Franklin. *The Hunters of Kentucky*. Mechanicsburg, PA: Stackpole Books, 2003.

———. *The Long Hunt: Death of the Buffalo East of the Mississippi*. Mechanicsburg, PA: Stackpole Books, 1996.

Biggers, Jeff. *The United States of Appalachia*. Emeryville, CA: Shoemaker & Hoard, 2006.

Boatner, Mark M., III. *Encyclopedia of the American Revolution*. Mechanicsburg, PA: Stackpole Books, 1994.

Bogart, W. H. *Daniel Boone and the Hunters of Kentucky*. Auburn, NY: Miller, Orton & Mulligan, 1854.

Brackenridge, Henry Marie. *Recollections of Persons and Places in the West*. Philadelphia: J. B. Lippincott, 1868.

Bradford, John. *The Voice of the Frontier: John Bradford's Notes on Kentucky*. Edited by Thomas D. Clark. Lexington: University Press of Kentucky, 1993.

Brown, Douglas Summers. *The Catawba Indians: The People of the River*. Columbia: University of South Carolina Press, 1966.

Bruce, H. Addington. *Daniel Boone and the Wilderness Road*. New York: Macmillan, 1910.

Bryan, Daniel. *The Mountain Muse: Comprising the Adventures of Daniel Boone; and the Powers of Virtuous and Refined Beauty*. Harrisonburg, VA: Davidson & Bourne, 1813.

Bryan, William S. "Daniel Boone's Western Palatinate." *Missouri Historical Review* 3 (1906–9): 198–99.

Bryan, William S., and Robert Rose. *Pioneer Families of Missouri*. St. Louis, MO: Brand, 1876.

Burnett, Peter H. *Recollections and Opinions of an Old Pioneer*. New York: D. Appleton, 1880.

Burns, David M. *Gateway: Dr. Thomas Walker and the Opening of Kentucky*. Middleboro, KY: Bell County Historical Society, 2000.

Bushnell, David L., Jr. "Daniel Boone at Limestone, 1786–1787." *Virginia Magazine of History and Biography* 25 (January 1917): 1–11.

Butler, Mann. *A History of the Commonwealth of Kentucky*. Louisville, KY: Wilcox, Dickerman, 1834.

Byrd, William. *William Byrd's Histories of the Dividing Line Betwixt Virginia and North Carolina*, edited by William Boyd, 1929. Reprint, New York: Dover, 1967.

Byron, George Gordon, Lord. *Byron's Don Juan: A Variorum Edition*. Edited by Truman Guy Steffan and Willis W. Pratt. Austin: University of Texas Press, 1957.

Cain, Robert J., ed. *Colonial Records of North Carolina: Records of the Executive Council, 1755–1775*. Vol. 9. Raleigh, NC: Division of Archives and History, North Carolina Department of Cultural Resources, 1994.

Calendar of Virginia State Papers. Vols. 3 and 5. Richmond, VA: R. F. Walker, 1875–93.

Calloway, Colin G. *The American Revolution in Indian Country*. New York: Cambridge University Press, 1995.

Campbell, Julian J. N. *The Land of Cane and Clover: Resettlement Vegetation in the So-Called Bluegrass Region of Kentucky.* Lexington: University Press of Kentucky, 1985.

Cassidy, Frederic G., and Joan Houston Hall. *Dictionary of American Regional English.* Vol. 2. Cambridge, MA: The Belknap Press of Harvard University Press, 1991.

Cayton, Andrew R. L. and Fredrika J. Teute, eds. *Contact Points: American Frontiers from the Mohawk Valley to the Mississippi, 1750–1830.* Chapel Hill: University of North Carolina Press, 1998.

Chernow, Ron. *Alexander Hamilton.* New York: Penguin Press, 2004.

Chinn, George Morgan. *Kentucky Settlement and Statehood, 1750–1800.* Frankfort: Kentucky Historical Society, 1975.

Clark, Thomas D. *Frankfort State Journal.* January 11, 1970.

———. *A History of Kentucky.* New York: Prentice-Hall, 1937.

Coleman, J. Winston, Jr. *Masonry in the Bluegrass.* Lexington, KY: Transylvania Press, 1933.

———. *Six Sketches of Kentucky.* Edited by Edward T. Houlihan. Lexington, KY: Henry Clay Press, 1996.

Collins, Lewis. *Historical Sketches of Kentucky.* Cincinnati, OH: Collins & James, 1847.

Collins, R. H. *History of Kentucky.* Louisville, KY: Richard H. Collins, 1877.

Conway, W. Fred. *The Incredible Adventures of Daniel Boone's Kid Brother.* New Albany, IN: 1992.

Cresswell, Nicholas. *The Journal of Nicholas Cresswell.* New York: Dial Press, 1924.

Crevecoeur, J. Hector St. John de. *Letters from an American Farmer.* New York: Dutton, 1957.

Cronon, William. *Changes in the Land: Indians, Colonists and the Ecology of New England.* New York: Hill & Wang, 1983.

Currens, J. C. "Caves." In *The Kentucky Encyclopedia,* edited by John E. Kleber, 174–76. Lexington: University Press of Kentucky, 1992.

Darby, William. *The Emigrant's Guide to the Western and Southwestern States and Territories.* New York: Kirk & Mercein, 1818.

Darlington, William M. *Christopher Gist's Journals.* New York: Argonaut Press, 1966.

Dawson, Nelson L. "Introduction." In *My Father, Daniel Boone: The Draper Interviews with Daniel Boone,* edited by Neal O. Hammon, 1–7. Lexington, KY: University Press of Kentucky, 1999.

Defoe, Daniel. *The Life and Strange and Surprising Adventures of Robinson Crusoe,* illustrated by Frederick Rhead. New York: Harper & Brothers, 1900.

De Hoyos, Arturo, and S. Brent Morris, eds. *Freemasonry in Context: History, Ritual, Controversy.* Oxford: Lexington Books, 2004.

Demott, Bobby J. *Freemasonry in American Culture.* Lanham, MD: University Press of America, 1986.

Dicken Garcia, Hazel. *To Western Woods.* Rutherford, NJ: Fairleigh Dickinson University Press, 1991.

Dickinson, Emily. *The Complete Poems of Emily Dickinson.* Edited by Thomas H. Johnson. Boston: Little, Brown, 1960.

Dixon, Max. *The Wataugans.* Tennessee in the Eighteenth Century: A Bicentennial Series, 1976. Nashville: Tennessee American Revolution Bicentennial Commission, 1976.

Doddridge, Joseph. *Notes on the Settlement and Indian Wars of the Western Parts of Virginia and Pennsylvania from 1763 to 1783.* Albany, NY: Joel Munsell, 1876.

Douglass, William Boone. "The Ancestry and Boyhood of Daniel Boone." *Kentucky School Journal* 13 (September 1934): 13–19.

Dowd, Gregory Evans. *A Spirited Resistance: The North American Indian Struggle for Unity 1745–1815.* Baltimore, MD: Johns Hopkins University Press, 1992.

Downes, Randolph C. *Council Fires on the Upper Ohio: A Narrative of Indian Affairs in the Upper Ohio Valley until 1795.* Pittsburgh, PA: University of Pittsburgh Press, 1940.

———. *Frontier Ohio, 1788–1803.* Columbus: Ohio State Archaeological and Historical Society, 1935.

Drabble, Margaret, ed. *The Oxford Companion to English Literature.* Oxford, England: Oxford University Press, 1985.

Drake, Daniel. *Pioneer Life in Kentucky.* Cincinnati: Robert Clarke, 1870.

Draper, Lyman Copeland. *The Life of Daniel Boone.* Edited by Ted Franklin Belue. Mechanicsburg, PA: Stackpole Books, 1998.

Draper Manuscripts. State Historical Society of Wisconsin, Madison.

Durrett, Reuben T. *Bryant's Station.* Filson Club Publications No. 12. Louisville, KY: J. P. Morton, 1897.

———. *John Filson, the First Historian of Kentucky.* Louisville, KY: Filson Club Publications, 1884.

Ehle, John. *Trail of Tears: The Rise and Fall of the Cherokee Nation.* New York: Anchor Books, 1988.

Eliot, T. S. *Complete Poems and Plays, 1909–1950.* New York: Harcourt, Brace & World, 1962.

Ellet, Elizabeth Fries. *Pioneer Women of the West.* 1852. Reprint, Freeport, NY: Books for Libraries Press, 1973.

Elliott, Lawrence. *The Long Hunter: A New Life of Daniel Boone.* New York: Reader's Digest Press, 1976.

Ellis, Joseph J. *His Excellency*. New York: Alfred A. Knopf, 2004.

Ellis, William E. *The Kentucky River*. Lexington: University Press of Kentucky, 2000.

Emerson, Ralph Waldo. *Emerson's Prose and Poetry*. Edited by Joel Porte and Saundra Morris. New York: W. W. Norton, 2001.

Eslinger, Ellen, ed. *Running Mad for Kentucky: Frontier Travel Accounts*. Lexington: University Press of Kentucky, 2004.

European Magazine. 1790. Kentucky State Archives. Frankfort, KY.

Faragher, John Mack. *Daniel Boone: The Life and Legend of an American Pioneer*. New York: Holt, 1992.

———. *The Encyclopedia of Colonial and Revolutionary America*. New York: Facts on File, 1990.

Faÿ, Bernard. *Revolution and Freemasonry, 1680–1800*. Boston: Little, Brown, 1935.

Ferguson, Thomas W. *Daniel Boone*. N.p., 1977.

Field, Thomas P. "The Indian Place Names of Kentucky." In *The Kentucky Sampler*, edited by Harrison Lowell and Nelson L. Dawson, 11–23. Lexington: University Press of Kentucky, 1977.

Filson, John. *The Discovery, Settlement and Present State of Kentucke*. 1784. Reprint, New York: Corinth Books, 1962.

Finley, James B. *Autobiography of the Rev. James B. Finley, or, Pioneer Life in the West*. Edited by W. P. Strickland. Cincinnati, 1854.

Fischer, David Hackett. *Albion's Seed*. New York: Oxford University Press, 1989.

Fitzgerald, F. Scott. *The Crack-up*. New York: New Directions, 1945.

Flint, Timothy. *Biographical Memoir of Daniel Boone*. 1833. Reprint, New Haven, CT: NCUP, 1967.

———. *Recollections of the Last Ten Years, Passed in Occasional Residences and Journeyings in the Valley of the Mississippi*. 1826. Reprint, New York: Da Capo Press, 1968.

Friend, Craig Thompson. *Along the Maysville Road*. Knoxville: University of Tennessee Press, 2005.

———, ed. *The Buzzel about Kentuck: Settling the Promised Land*. Lexington: University Press of Kentucky, 1999.

Fries, Adelaide L. *Records of the Moravians of North Carolina*. Vol. 2, *1752–1775*. Raleigh: North Carolina Historical Commission, 1925.

Galloway, William A. *Old Chillicothe*. Xenia, OH: The Buckeye Press, 1934.

Gilman, Carolyn. "A World of Women." *Gateway Heritage* 24 (fall 2003–winter 2004): 44–47.

Haldimand Papers. Pioneer and Historical Society of the State of Michigan. *Michigan Historical Collections*. Vol. 9. 1886.

Hale, John P. *Daniel Boone*. N.p., n.d.

———. *Trans-Allegheny Pioneers*. 1886. 3rd ed. Edited by Harold J. Dudley. Radford, VA: Roberta Ingles Steele, 1971.

Hall, James. *The Romance of Western History*. Cincinnati, OH: Applegate, 1857.

———. *Sketches of History, Life, and Manners in the West*. Volumes 1–2. Philadelphia, 1835.

Hammon, Neal O. "The Boone Robbery." Unpublished manuscript in author's possession.

———. *Daniel Boone and the Defeat at Blue Licks*. Minneapolis, MN: The Boone Society, 2005.

———. "Daniel Boone, the Surveyor." Unpublished manuscript in author's possession.

———. *Early Kentucky Land Records, 1773–1780*. Filson Club Publications, 2nd ser., no. 5. Louisville, KY: Filson Club Publications, 1992.

———. "John Filson's Error." *Filson Club History Quarterly* 59 (1985): 462–63.

———. ed. *My Father, Daniel Boone: The Draper Interviews with Nathan Boone*. Lexington: University Press of Kentucky, 1999.

———. "No Stranger to Difficulty," Unpublished manuscript, in author's possession.

———. "Separating Facts from Myths." Unpublished manuscript, in author's possession.

———. "Settlers, Land Jobbers, and Outlyers: A Quantitative Analysis of Land Acquisition on the Kentucky Frontier." *Register of the Kentucky Historical Society* 84, no. 3 (Summer 1986): 241–62.

Hammon, Neal O., and Richard Taylor. *Virginia's Western War, 1775–1786*. Mechanicsburg, PA: Stackpole Books, 2002.

Hammon, Neal O., and Wilson Zaring. "What Is Wrong with the Peter Houston Story?" Unpublished essay, in author's possession.

Harding, Chester. *My Egotistigraphy*. Cambridge, MA: John Wilson Press, 1866.

Harper, Josephine L. *Guide to the Draper Manuscripts*. Madison: State Historical Society of Wisconsin, 1983.

Hartley, Cecil B. *Life of Daniel Boone*. Philadelphia: Porter & Coates, 1865.

Haywood, John. *The Civil and Political History of the State of Tennessee*. Knoxville: Heiskell & Brown, 1823.

Heath, Craig. L. *George M. Bedinger Papers in the Draper Manuscript Collection*. Bowie, MD: Heritage Books, 2002.

Henderson, A. Gwyn. "The Lower Shawnee Town on Ohio." In *The Buzzel about Kentuck*, edited by Craig Thompson Friend, 25 – 55. Lexington: University Press of Kentucky, 1999.

Henderson, Archibald. *The Conquest of the Old Southwest*. New York: The Century Company, 1920.

———. *The Significance of the Transylvania Company*. N.p, n.d.

———. *The Transylvania Company and the Founding of Henderson, Kentucky*. Henderson, KY, 1929.

Henderson Papers. Wilson Library, University of North Carolina, Chapel Hill.

Henry, Ruby Addison. *The First West*. Nashville, TN: Aurora Publishing, 1982.

Hesseltine, William B. *Pioneer's Mission: The Story of Lyman Copeland Draper*. Madison: State Historical Society of Wisconsin, 1954.

Hill, Leonard U. *John Johnston and the Indians*. Piqua, OH: privately printed, 1957.

Houston, Peter. *A Sketch of the Life and Character of Daniel Boone*. Edited by Ted Franklin Belue. Mechanicsburg, PA: Stackpole Books, 1997.

Howard, James H. *Shawnee!* Athens: Ohio University Press, 1981.

Hurt, R. Douglas. *Nathan Boone and the American Frontier*. Columbia and London: University of Missouri Press, 1998.

Imlay, Gilbert. *A Topographical Description of the Western Territory of North America*. London, 1793. Reprint, New York: Johnson Reprint Corporation, 1968.

Irving, Washington. *Astoria*. In *Three Western Narratives*, edited by James P. Ronda. New York: Library of America, 2004.

Jacob, John Jeremiah. *Biographical Sketch of the Life of the Late Capt. Michael Cresap*. Cumberland, MD: J. M. Buchanan, 1826.

Jennings, Francis. *Empire of Fortune: Crowns, Colonies, and Tribes in the Seven Years War in America*. New York: W. W. Norton, 1988.

———. *The Invasion of America: Indians, Colonialism, and the Cant of Conquest*. New York: W. W. Norton, 1976.

Jillson, Willard Rouse. *The Boone Narrative*. Louisville: The Standard Printing Company, 1932.

———. "Daniel Boone as Surveyor." *Kentucky School Journal* (spring 1934): 32 – 36.

———. *Pioneer Kentucky*. Frankfort, KY: State Journal, 1934.

———. *With Compass and Chain: A Brief Narrative of the Activities of Col. Daniel Boone as a Land Surveyor in Kentucky*. Frankfort, KY: Roberts Printing Co., 1954.

Johnson, Patricia Givens. *William Preston and the Allegheny Patriots*. Blacksburg, VA: Walpa Publishing, 1976. Reprint 1992.

Jones, Randell. *In the Footsteps of Daniel Boone.* Winston-Salem, NC: John F. Blair, 2005.

Kellogg, Louise Phelps. "The Fame of Daniel Boone." *Report of the Daniel Boone Bicentennial Commission.* N.p., n.d.

Kellogg, Louise Phelps, and Reuben Gold Thwaites. *Documentary History of Dunmore's War, 1774.* Madison: State Historical Society of Wisconsin, 1905.

Kenton, Edna. *Simon Kenton: His Life and Period, 1755–1836.* Garden City, NY: Doubleday, Doran, 1930.

Kentucky Gazette. Kentucky State Archives. Frankfort, KY.

Kincaid, Robert Lee. *The Wilderness Road.* Indianapolis, IN: Bobbs, Merrill, 1947.

Kleber, John E., ed. *The Kentucky Encyclopedia.* Lexington: University Press of Kentucky, 1992.

Kolodny, Annette. *The Land Before Her.* Chapel Hill: University of North Carolina Press, 1984.

Laidley, W. S. "Daniel Boone in the Kanawha Valley." *Register of the Kentucky Historical Society* 2 (1913): 9–12.

Lawson, John. *Lawson's History of North Carolina.* Edited by F. L. Harris. Richmond: Garrett & Massie, 1952.

Lennhoff, Eugen. *The Freemasons: The History, Nature, Development and Secret of the Royal Art.* Translated by Einar Frame. New York: Oxford University Press. 1934.

Lester, W. S. *The Transylvania Company.* Spencer, IN: Samuel R. Guard, 1935.

Lilly, Lambert. *The Adventures of Daniel Boone, Kentucky Rifleman.* 1854.

Livermore, Shaw. *Early American Land Companies.* 1939. Reprint, New York: Octagon Books, 1968.

Lofaro, Michael A. *Daniel Boone: An American Life.* Lexington: University Press of Kentucky, 2003.

Lossing, Benson J. "Daniel Boone." *Harper's New Monthly Magazine* 19 (October, 1859): 577–601.

Lott, Carolyn. *Rebecca Boone: The Life of a Woman on the American Frontier.* Privately printed, 2005.

Lowell, Harrison, and Nelson L. Dawson, eds. *A Kentucky Sampler.* Lexington: University Press of Kentucky, 1977.

Macoy, Robert. *A Dictionary of Freemasonry.* 1873. Reprint, New York: Gramercy Books, 2000.

Manning, Maurice. *A Companion for Owls.* Orlando, FL: Harcourt, 2004.

Marshall, Everett G. *Rich Man: Daniel Boone: An Historical Report on the*

Boone Trail Highway and Memorial Association. Dugspur, VA: Sugartree Enterprises, 2003.

Marshall, Humphrey. *The History of Kentucky.* Frankfort, KY, 1812.

Maurice, George H. *Daniel Boone in North Carolina.* Eagle Springs, NC, 1959.

McClung, John A. *Sketches of Western Adventure.* Maysville, KY: L. Collins, 1832.

McCullough, David. *1776.* New York: Simon & Schuster, 2005.

McDowell, Robert E. "Bullitt's Lick, the Related Saltworks and Settlements." In *A Kentucky Sampler,* edited by Harrison Lowell and Nelson L. Dawson, 23–53. Lexington: University Press of Kentucky, 1977.

Merrell, James H. *The Catawbas.* New York: Chelsea House, 1989.

Michigan Historical Collection. Vol. 24. University of Michigan, Ann Arbor.

Moore, Arthur K. *The Frontier Mind: A Cultural Analysis of the Kentucky Frontiersman.* Lexington: University Press of Kentucky, 1957.

Myer, William Edward. *Indian Trails of the Southeast.* Forty-second Annual Report of the Bureau of American Ethnology, 1924–25. Washington, DC, 1928.

Nickell, Joe, and John F. Fischer, "Daniel Boone Fakelore." *Filson Club History Quarterly* 62 (1988): 442–66.

Nobles, Gregory H., and James A. Henretta. *Evolution and Revolution: American Society, 1600–1820.* Lexington, MA: D. C. Heath, 1987.

O'Malley, Nancy. "Frontier Defenses and Pioneer Strategies in the Historic Settlement Era." In *The Buzzel about Kentuck,* edited by Craig Thompson Friend, 57–75. Lexington: University Press of Kentucky, 1999.

———. *Searching for Boonesborough.* Kentucky Heritage Council. University of Kentucky Archaeological Report No. 193. 1989. Revised 1990.

———. *Stockading Up.* University of Kentucky Archaeological Report No. 127. Lexington: Kentucky Heritage Council, 1987.

Peck, John Mason. *Forty Years of Pioneer Life.* 1854. Reprint, Carbondale: Southern Illinois University Press, 1965.

———. *Life of Daniel Boone.* 1847. Makers of American History Series. Reprint, New York: The University Society, 1904.

Perkins, Elizabeth A. *Border Life: Experience and Memory in the Revolutionary Ohio Valley.* Chapel Hill: University of North Carolina Press, 1998.

Poe, Edgar Allan. *Collected Works of Edgar Allan Poe.* 3 vols. Edited by Thomas Ollive Mabbott. Cambridge, MA: Belknap Press of Harvard University Press, 1978.

Powell, William S. *North Carolina through Four Centuries.* Chapel Hill: University of North Carolina Press, 1989.

Ramsey, Robert W. *Carolina Cradle*. Chapel Hill: University of North Carolina Press, 1964.

Ranck, George W. *Boonesborough*. Filson Club Publication No. 16. Louisville, KY: Filson Club Publications, 1901.

Rice, Otis K. *Frontier Kentucky*. Lexington: University Press of Kentucky, 1975.

Richardson, Robert D., Jr. *Henry Thoreau: A Life of the Mind*. Berkeley: University of California Press, 1986.

Ridley, Jasper. *The Freemasons: A History of the World's Most Powerful Secret Society*. New York: Arcade Publishing, 2001.

Robertson, James Rood. *The First American Frontier*. New York: Arno Press and The New York Times, 1971.

———, ed. *Petitions of the Early Inhabitants of Kentucky to the General Assembly of Virginia 1769–1792*. Filson Club Publications No. 27. Louisville, KY: J. P. Morton, 1914.

Rouse, Parke, Jr. *The Great Wagon Road*. Richmond, VA: The Dietz Press, 1995.

Rowan County, North Carolina. *Minutes, Court of Pleas and Quarter Sessions*. Vols. 1 (1753–67) and 2 (1768–72). Raleigh: North Carolina Department of Archives and History.

Rumple, Jethro. *A History of Rowan County*. Reprint of 1881 edition, Salisbury, NC: Elizabeth Maxwell Steele Chapter of D.A.R., 1929.

Sanderlin, John B. "Ethnic Origins of Early Kentucky Land Grantees." *Register of the Kentucky Historical Society* 85, no. 2 (spring 1987): 103–10.

Schiff, Stacy. *The Great Improvisation: Franklin, France, and the Birth of America*. New York: Henry Holt, 2005.

Selcraig, Bruce. "The Real Robinson Crusoe." *The Smithsonian*, July 2005, 82–90.

Shelley, Percy Bysshe, "A Defense of Poetry." In *The Norton Anthology of English Literature*, edited by M. H. Abrams, Robert M. Adams, David Daiches, E. Talbot Donaldson, George H. Ford, Lawrence Lipking, Samuel Holt Monk, and Hallett Smith, 2:782–94. New York: W. W. Norton, 1979.

Short, Charles W. "Prodomus Florula Lexingtoniensis, Secundum Florens Di Oestatum Digeste." Pts. 1–4. *Transylvania Journal of Medicine* 1 (1828): 250–65, 407–22, 560–75; 2 (1829): 438–53.

Simms, William Gilmore. "Daniel Boone — The First Hunter in Kentucky." In *Views and Reviews in American Literature, History, and Fiction*, edited by C. Hugh Holman, 148–77. Cambridge, MA: Belknap Press of Harvard University Press, 1962.

Simpson, Louis. *Selected Poems.* New York: Harcourt, Brace, & World, 1965.

Slotkin, Richard. *The Fatal Environment.* New York: Atheneum, 1985.

———. *Regeneration through Violence: The Mythology of the American Frontier, 1600–1860.* 1973. Reprint, Norman: University of Oklahoma Press, 2000.

Smith, Daniel Blake. "This Idea in Heaven." In *The Buzzel about Kentuck,* edited by Craig Thompson Friend, 77–98. Lexington: University Press of Kentucky, 1999.

Smith, Henry Nash. *Virgin Land: The American West as Symbol and Myth.* New York: Vintage Books, 1957.

Smyth, J. F. D. *A Tour of the United States of America.* Vol,. 1. London: G. Robinson, 1784.

Speed, Thomas. *The Wilderness Road.* Louisville, KY: J. P. Morton, 1886.

Spraker, Hazel Atterbury. *The Boone Family.* 1922. Reprint, Salem, MA: Higginson, 2005.

Stewart, George R. *American Place Names.* New York: Oxford University Press, 1970.

Stipes, Millard Fillmore. *Gleanings in Missouri History.* Jamesport, MO, 1904.

Sugden, John. *Blue Jacket: Warrior of the Shawnees.* Lincoln: University of Nebraska Press, 2000.

Summers, Lewis Preston. *Annals of Southwest Virginia, 1769–1800.* Kingsport, TN: Kingsport Press, 1929.

———. *History of Southwest Virginia, 1746–1786.* Richmond, VA: J. L. Printing Co., 1903.

Sweeney, J. Gray. *The Columbus of the Woods: Daniel Boone and the Typology of Manifest Destiny.* St. Louis, MO: Washington University Gallery of Art, 1992.

Tabbert, Mark A. *American Freemasons: Three Centuries of Building Communities.* Lexington, MA: National Heritage Museum; New York: New York University Press, 2005.

Tachau, Mary K. Bonsteel. "Land Claims, Early." In *The Kentucky Encyclopedia,* edited by John E. Kleber, 535. Lexington: University Press of Kentucky, 1992.

Taylor, Richard. "Daniel Boone as American Icon." *Register of the Kentucky Historical Society* 102, no. 4 (autumn 2004): 513–34.

———. *Girty.* 3rd ed. Lexington, KY: Wind Publications, 2006.

———. *The Great Crossing.* Frankfort, KY: Buffalo Crossing Distillery, 1996.

Thompson, Lawrence S. *Kentucky Tradition.* Hamden, CT: The Shoe String Press, 1956.

Thoreau, Henry David. *Excursions.* Edited by Leo Marx. 1863. Reprint, New York: Corinth Books, 1962.

———. *Walden*. 1854. Reprint, Princeton, NJ: Princeton University Press, 1971.

Thwaites, Reuben Gold. *Daniel Boone*. 1902. Reprint, Williamstown, MA: Corner House Publishers, 1977.

Toulmin, Harry. *The Western Country in 1793*. San Marino, CA: Huntington Library, 1948.

Trabue, Daniel. *Westward into Kentucky: The Narrative of Daniel Trabue*. Edited by Chester Raymond Young. Lexington: University Press of Kentucky, 1981.

Trowbridge, C. C. *Shawnese Traditions*. Edited by Vernon Kinietz and E. W. Voegelin. Occasional Contributions from the Museum of Anthropology. University of Michigan, no. 9. Ann Arbor: University of Michigan Press, 1939.

Trumbull, John. *The Adventures of Colonel Daniel Boon*. Norwich, CT, 1786.

Tunis, Edwin. *Colonial Living*. Cleveland: World Publishing, 1957.

———. *Frontier Living*. Cleveland: World Publishing, 1961.

Turner, Frederick Jackson. *The Frontier in American History*. 1920. Reprint, New York: Holt, 1962.

Twain, Mark. *Mississippi Writings*. Edited by Guy Cardwell. New York: Library of America, 1982.

Upton, Lucile Morris, and John K. Hulston. *Nathan Boone the Neglected Hero*. Edited by Carole Bills. Republic, MO: Western Printing, 1984.

Van Cleve, John W. "Colonel Robert Patterson." *American Pioneer* 2 (1843): 344–47.

Van Noppen, John James, and Ina Woestemeyer Van Noppen. *Daniel Boone Backwoodsman: The Green Woods Were His Portion*. Boone, NC: The Appalachian Press, 1966.

Vaughn-Thomas, Wynford. *Wales: A History*. London: Michael Joseph, 1985.

Vestal, Stanley. *The Missouri*. 1945. Reprint, Lincoln: University of Nebraska Press, 1964.

Voegelin, C. F., and E. W. Voegelin. "The Shawnee Female Deity in Historical Perspective." *American Anthropologist* 46, no. 3 (July–September 1944): 370–75.

Voegelin, C. F., John F. Yegerlehner, and Florence M. Robinett. *Shawnee Laws: Perceptual Statements for the Language and for the Content*. American Anthropological Association Memoirs, no. 79. Chicago: University of Chicago Press, 1954.

Waite, Arthur Edward. *A New Encyclopedia of Freemasonry*. New York: Wings Books, 1996.

Walker, Felix. "Narrative of an Adventure in Kentucky in the Year 1775." *De Bow's Review* 16 (February 1854): 150–56. Reprinted in Ranck, *Boonesborough*.

Walton, John. *John Filson of Kentucke*. Lexington: University of Kentucky Press, 1956.

Webber, Charles Wilkins. *The Hunter Naturalist: Romance of Sporting or Wild Scenes and Wild Hunters*. Philadelphia: Lippincott, Grambo, 1854.

Weiss, Kathryn. "Daniel Boone and the Bryans from a Different Perspective." *Compass* (April 2005): 4–7; 9, no. 3 (July 2005): 5–8. (Published by the Boone Society, Inc., Hot Springs National Park, AR.).

———. "An Introduction to Daniel Bryan." *Compass* 10, no. 4 (October 2006): 9–11. (Published by the Boone Society, Inc., Hot Springs National Park, AR.)

———. "Two Swivel Guns." *Compass* 10, no. 1 (January 2006): 11–15. (Published by the Boone Society, Inc., Hot Springs National Park, AR.).

Welch, James E. *Christian Repository*. Louisville, 1860.

Weslager, C. A. *The Log Cabin in America*. New Brunswick: Rutgers University Press, 1969.

White, Clare. *William Fleming, Patriot*. Baltimore: Gateway Press, Inc., 2001.

White, Richard. *The Middle Ground: Indians, Empires, and Republics in the Great Lakes Region, 1650–1815*. Cambridge: Cambridge University Press, 1991.

Whitman, Walt. *Whitman: Poetry and Prose*. Edited by Justin Kaplan. New York: Library of America, 1982.

Wilder, C. *The Life and Adventures of Daniel Boon, the First White Settler in Kentucky*. 1823. Reprint, New York: Heartman's Historical Series, 1916.

Williams, William Carlos. *In the American Grain*. 1925. Reprint, New York: New Directions, 1956.

Wilson, Samuel M. "Daniel Boone, 1734–1934." *The Daniel Boone Bicentennial* (Kentucky Historical Society Doc. No. SC98176). N.p.: [1936?].

Woodmason, Charles. *The Carolina Backcountry on the Eve of the Revolution*. Chapel Hill: University of North Carolina Press, 1953.

Wyllie, John Cook. "Daniel Boone's Adventures in Charlottesville in 1781: Some Incidents Connected with Tarlton's Raid." *Magazine of Albemarle County History* 19 (1960–61): 5–18.

Young, Bennett H. *The Battle of the Blue Licks*. Filson Club Publications No. 12. Louisville: J. P. Morton, 1897.

Index

RANDI ANGLIN

ROBERT MORGAN was raised on his family's farm in the North Carolina mountains. He is the author of eleven books of poetry and eight books of fiction, including the bestselling novel *Gap Creek*. Winner of a 2007 Academy of Arts and Letters Award for Literature and the Thomas Wolfe Memorial Literary Award, he lives in Ithaca, New York, where he teaches at Cornell University.